WARD CANTRELL. Rugged, handsome, and charismatic, he ran from the law and hid his fear even from himself....

LESLIE POWERS. A beautiful, proper Bostonian, she is not prepared for the savagery of the Wild West....

MARK POWERS. Villainous and cruel, his life was ruled by greed. But even he had better watch his step....

ISABEL MENDOZA. A poor Mexican girl living on the edge of Powers's ranch, she is powerless to stop his treachery....

"Mixes Western atmosphere with Eastern sophistication...the story has everything...train robberies, cattle rustling, kidnapping, and romance."

Jane Steinbach,
Rendezvous

Also by Joyce Brandon
Published by Ballantine Books:

THE LADY AND THE LAWMAN

THE
LADY
AND
THE
OUTLAW

Joyce Brandon

BALLANTINE BOOKS • NEW YORK

Library of Congress Catalog Card Number: 85-90707

ISBN 0-345-34814-1

Manufactured in the United States of America

First Edition: August 1985
Second Printing: October 1987

I would like to dedicate this book to Cheryl Woodruff, my editor, and to John, my husband, lover, and soul mate.

CHAPTER
ONE

August 3, 1888

"Why are we slowing down here?" Leslie Powers demanded of the conductor who paused, frowning, beside their seat. He was a tall man, paunchy, black-garbed, with the inevitable mustache and serviceable watch on a long gold chain hanging across his vest. He peered out the half-open window of the passenger coach, mopping his perspiring brow with a dingy handkerchief, and squinted at the endless expanse of desert that baked under the midday sun.

"Don't rightly know, ma'am," he mumbled, scratching his balding head. "Never stopped here before."

Brakes screeched as they were applied with a heavy hand. Annette muttered something in French and clutched frantically at the yarn ball that tumbled off her lap. A woman at the front of the long passenger car stood up and threw off the *rebozo* that had covered her long black hair and dark, smoldering features. She whirled, brandishing the gun she held. A man in the back of the car, who had risen slowly, leveled his gun and shouted over the noise of the brakes.

"Keep looking straight ahead! Hands on your heads! Keep it slow and easy, and nobody gets hurt. Do it!" His tone demanded compliance. Leslie could feel her arms going up of their own volition.

"Well, I'll be dang blasted!" the man in front of Leslie muttered as he slowly complied with the order. "A holdup." There was a volley of darkly uttered oaths as other men followed his example. Women gasped at the language.

The bandit started up the aisle, and Leslie turned to look in spite of the warning. The bottom half of his face was hidden beneath a red bandana, and his eyes were shaded by a dark hat pulled low on his forehead. Tawny wheat-colored hair curled crisply along the nape of his sun-bronzed neck. His lean, straight form was clad in dusty brown trousers and shirt, half covered by a vest that had long ago faded. Like her mother, Leslie usually saw colors first, because they were the tools of her trade, but in this bandit she saw

1

motion and resolute masculine aggressiveness. His body telegraphed a clear message that no disobedience would be tolerated.

Spurs jingled when the bandit moved. "Howdy, Ben, Sam,
Three Fingers," he said amiably, nodding as if he were meeting
them on the street, his voice low and richly masculine. He took
each weapon, ignoring the looks of chagrin and disgust. He
dropped them into a sack he had pulled out of his back pants pocket
and started to move on, but the one he had called Ben spoke in a
voice loud enough for all to hear.

"You overstepped yourself this time, mister. We were expecting you."

The gunman chuckled softly. "I see you were," he said dryly.
Now his eyes, a clear cornflower blue so intense in color that they
reminded Leslie of mother-of-pearl, fairly danced with mischief.

"I can't imagine Kincaid's making much money in the train
business when half the passengers are hired guns, riding the train
free. Me and my men had a helluva time finding hotel rooms in
Tucson with all the special agents around. Had a hard time getting
a good night's rest with you fellows stomping in and out all the
time."

Ben shrugged, ignoring the gunman's contempt for their inepti-
tude as railroad detectives. He was listening for gunfire that would
announce to this cocky bandit that the posse hidden in the closed
boxcar had made its move. He grimaced. What was taking them so
long?

"Kincaid has authorized me to make you a proposition," he
said tersely, "if you'll listen for a minute."

The bandit's blue eyes narrowed into wicked slits. "Like
what?" he demanded, obviously skeptical.

"There's a job waiting for you if you want to come work with us
instead of against us."

The bandit laughed, a rich husky baritone that sounded completely relaxed, unhurried. "Stretching a rope?" he demanded, his
smooth, low-pitched words taunting the suddenly uncomfortable
detective. "Tell Mr. Kincaid I'm satisfied with our present arrangement," he said firmly, starting to move forward again.

"Wait!" Ben made a move to reach out but thought better of it
as the gunman pointed the heavy revolver point blank at his forehead. Leslie could feel herself tensing, as if that would somehow
help the man called Ben withstand the force of a bullet slamming
into his forehead.

"Wait!" Ben said again, nervously. "The offer is serious. Kincaid can arrange a pardon."

"Now why would Kincaid want to do that?"

Ben, thankful to still be alive, dragged his arm across his perspiring brow. "Maybe he thinks that if you're working for the railroad, he'll get more silver to the bank."

The gunman shook his head, chuckling softly, but when he spoke there was no doubt that he meant every word. "Tell your Mr. Kincaid I'm *particular* about who I work for. There are some things he can't buy."

Leslie was watching his eyes. The dancing lights she had seen before were gone, replaced by something almost tangible in its intensity. Was it bitterness? Hate? Irony? There was no way to tell from his coolly drawled words. Before she could decide, Ben called after the gunman. "You better think it over! This may be your last chance. . . ."

The outlaw didn't look like he considered it very seriously. He had turned his attention back to the other occupants, moving up the aisle toward Leslie, gathering guns from the unprotesting men. Neither of the bandits had done anything threatening to the passengers, but Leslie could feel her heart beating a wild staccato of fear against her throat and temples.

"Don't move, *señor*!"

Leslie's attention was drawn back to the woman at the front of the coach. Now she was pointing her pistol menacingly at one of the men seated across from Leslie. Caught in the act of pulling his own revolver, he cursed and raised his hands slowly, and the woman, who looked no more than a slip of a girl, relaxed the snarl of defiance that had come over her pretty face. She looked too young to be robbing trains, almost childlike, with a soft golden complexion, brown eyes, and full red lips. Very Spanish-looking, with mother-of-pearl combs holding back her abundant hair. She was like one of those highly romanticized creatures from the pulp magazines Leslie had read because her father lived in what everyone called the Wild West.

"Nice and easy," the gunman said smoothly as he came even with her seat. Annette's cold fingers bit into Leslie's wrist as the poor woman sucked in a ragged breath. In self-defense, to keep her circulation from being cut off, she took Annette's hand in her own.

"Everybody does what they're told and nobody gets hurt. Just relax. This won't take long," the bandit said, starting to move past her seat.

"How very thoughtful of you!" Leslie said caustically.

The bandit looked at her for the first time, catching her reproachful glance and holding it. His eyes, close up, were the pale blue of the noonday sky and filled with the same diffuse intensity. Now they flicked over her appraisingly, taking in the slender curves beneath her very proper traveling gown. The bandana flattened slightly, as if he were smiling, and he winked, his eyes filled with appreciation or amusement. Caught off guard, she flushed with heat. His eyes darted from her eyes to her mouth. She wanted to reject his bold scrutiny with a haughty shrug of indifference, but her hand moved up to fidget with the very proper traveling bonnet that temporarily contained the heavy black mass of her hair, keeping it chastely away from the creamy white oval of her face.

The sudden heat in his eyes brought the realization to her that she was practically flirting with him—flirting with an outlaw in the midst of a holdup. Angry sparks kindled and flared in her longlashed green eyes. She lifted her skirts and pulled them back as if she feared contamination. Now the gunman's eyes fairly danced. Tiny pinpricks of light shimmered in their depths before he touched the brim of his hat and moved past her to continue his trip to the front of the coach.

At some point in that almost wordless exchange Leslie had stood up. She didn't know she had shrugged off Annette's hand and was following the bandit's lithe form with her eyes, feeling somehow bested or rejected, until the Mexican girl's voice suddenly jarred her.

"Keep your eyes to yourself, you *gringa puta*!" she snapped, her dark eyes filled with feral heat. The female trainrobber looked like a tawny gold puma set to attack; but Leslie, who had been hot, tired, and frustrated on this train for five days, felt no instinct to withdraw from the challenge in the other woman's eyes, even if she did have a gun.

"Don't tell me what to do, you female cretin! You're not exactly a magnolia blossom!" Leslie snapped, her eyes exchanging sudden hatred with the young woman. That slur would have withered any female at Wellesley College, but it was hardly devastating enough for a young savage who consorted with train robbers. It did earn Leslie a startled look from the gunman, though, before he moved forward again, tossing the sack of guns over his shoulder. He grabbed his girlfriend around the waist with one arm to keep her from leaping on top of Leslie.

The girl squirmed wildly in his embrace. "We aren't here so

you can cat-fight with the passengers,'' he reminded her, his voice firm. Chastised by the grimness of his husky voice, she became still, and the outlaw lowered her onto her feet so she could stand.

"That *gringa puta* . . .'' she snarled, switching to rapid-fire Spanish, her dark eyes spitting fury at Leslie.

"Enough.'' The gunman cut her off with the increasing pressure of his arm around her rib cage and the suddenly cold finality of that one quietly uttered word. If that hadn't stopped her, Leslie felt sure that the look in his suddenly cold eyes, which had taken on the flat, unyielding quality of new steel, would have, had the girl turned to look.

Going limp suddenly, the *bandita* said something submissive and conciliatory in Spanish, and Leslie saw him relax his grip on her. The girl stepped slightly away from him, rearranging her garments and casting a haughty, scornful look at Leslie.

"What did that milk-faced daughter of a brood sow call me?'' she asked sullenly, switching to English.

The twinkle was back in his blue eyes. "Relax. She just returned your compliment in kind,'' he said. His eyes found Leslie's, and he winked at her again, sending that furious heat back into her cheeks.

The Mexican girl straightened her blouse where the bandit's hands had rumpled it and began to unbutton the waistband of her skirt. Her bold eyes swept the room, and she let the skirt drop to reveal a pair of boy's pants. She smiled with pride and defiance, clearly enjoying the chagrin of the women, whose eyes plainly showed their outrage. She gave Leslie, whose face had remained coldly impassive, a deliberately sultry look, and smoothed her left hand over her slender hip, straightening some imaginary wrinkle in the tight fabric. Without waiting for a response, she stooped gracefully, lithe and catlike, retrieved the skirt, and tossed it carelessly over her shoulder, flashing a contemptuous smile at Leslie.

Three gunshots rent the sudden stillness, and the outlaw became all business again. "Let's go,'' he said, swinging the sackful of guns over his broad shoulder. His brown hand closed over the girl's, and they turned to leap down the steps.

Leslie leaned across Annette, whose usually ruddy face had turned quite pale. She saw masked bandits leaving the other coaches, the locomotive, and the mail car. They ran purposefully, converging on a man who was leading a string of horses. Leslie saw the bandit boost the girl up onto a small red mustang, then leap gracefully into the saddle of a big black horse. The animal stretched out its long powerful neck, with the man leaning forward on its back, and she could see horse and rider, like one, stretching into the long, easy strides that would carry them away from pursuit. She watched until he was only a cloud of gray dust in the distance, blending into the monotony of the Arizona desert.

"Well, it's over," she said, more to herself than to Annette. Still dazed, she glanced around at the other occupants of the passenger car and noticed that she and Annette were practically alone. The men had all rushed outside and were milling around like lost children.

"Ohhh!" With that, Annette, who was usually entirely unflappable, swooned.

CHAPTER
Two

"Oh, no!" Leslie said under her breath as she moved quickly to catch Annette before she slid off the hard wooden seat and onto the soot-covered floor.

"Here, miss. Allow me, please." The young man who had rushed forward to help fished a tiny bottle of smelling salts out of his pants pocket and held it under Annette's nose.

She revived almost instantly and pushed his hand away. "*Non!* I can't breathe!"

"Sorry, ma'am, but you fainted."

"Oh, *non, mademoiselle!* How could I? How ashamed I am!" she moaned, covering her pale cheeks with shaking hands.

Now that the danger was past, Leslie could feel tremors in her own midriff and rushed to reassure her lady's maid. "Nonsense, Annette. There is nothing to be ashamed of. If I'd thought of it first, I would have swooned too! It was very exciting, wasn't it?"

"*Oui!* Terrifying! Exciting!"

"What's happening now? Why are all those men running around out there?" she asked.

But the young man was gazing shyly into Annette's eyes and seemed oblivious to everything else. "Excuse me," Leslie said, waving her dainty hand in front of him.

Caught, he blushed and pretended to peer out the window past

Annette, as if searching for the answer to her question while he composed himself. "They're looking for our guns," he said, his gray eyes narrowed against the glare of the sun.

"Our guns?" she asked, frowning at the men outside who looked like they were participants in a wild and hurried Easter egg hunt.

"They wouldn't leave us out here without our guns. Too much danger from marauding bandits or escaped Indians."

"I didn't realize that outlaws care what happens to their victims," she said, lifting an expressive black brow.

"Some don't, I suppose. But that was the Devil's Canyon Gang. Their style is easy to recognize. They take control of the whole train—every boxcar, Pullman coach, mail car, locomotive, everything—disarm the passengers, clean out the safe, and dump the guns in the bushes, then disappear into the mountains. I've read about them, but I never thought I would actually get to see them in action," he said, his voice filled with awe.

"The Devil's Canyon Gang?" she asked, frowning out the window. "How did they get that name?"

"Because the one and only time they were seriously pursued, they disappeared into Devil's Canyon, and no one could find them."

Leslie noticed the interest in Annette's eyes for the young man and decided to draw him out. "My, you sound very knowledgeable about this Devil's Canyon Gang." He had nice eyes, and she could see him beginning to color. He looked young, probably only a few years older than her nineteen years, but he appeared to be the sort of gentleman that two women on a train could talk to without getting into trouble. She relaxed a little, smiling at the way his eyes kept slipping back to Annette's flushed face.

"I've followed their activities," he admitted. "The newspapers print stories about the Devil's Canyon Gang. Seems people love to read about them." He colored suddenly, his chipmunk cheeks turning pink. "Oh, excuse me, ma'am. I entreat you to forgive my lack of manners. Would—would I be too forward if I introduced myself?"

"Please do," Leslie said, smiling.

"John Loving, at your service." The warm glow from their smiles made him bold, but not bold enough to speak directly to the young Frenchwoman. "You were magnificent against those bandits, miss. I had the feeling that if you were one of the detectives we would have seen an entirely different show," he ended gallantly.

Leslie laughed, a golden tinkle of notes climbing a scale. "Leslie Powers. And this is Annette Guillet. Thank you for your concern. And for being there with the smelling salts. Are you the official swoon control officer aboard this train?"

"He ees very good at it, no?" Annette asked, beaming at him. John Loving blushed from neck to hairline, and Leslie decided that she liked him. He looked very stern and proper, until he smiled, and then he looked mischievous in a sort of quiet way.

He shrugged. "I work in the Texas and Pacific's main office—or I will—as soon as we get to Phoenix. I'm going to be Mr. Summers's assistant. He's right under Mr. Kincaid."

"Sounds like a very important position, *monsieur*."

The pink in his fat, muscular cheeks darkened again, and Leslie decided it was time to change the subject before John Loving, who looked very earnest, crawled under one of those hard wooden seats in embarrassment. "Tell me about this gang," she said quickly. "Why are you so sure they left the guns?"

"See those men using crowbars on the boxcar?"

She leaned across Annette to peer out the window. "Yes." She couldn't actually see what they were doing, but assumed Loving was correct.

"The bandits nailed the boxcar shut sometime before they stopped the train. There's a posse inside. The gang always seems to know the important things ahead of time—as if they have inside information. . . ."

"Over here!" a masculine voice yelled from outside. By the stampede that followed, Leslie could tell they had found the guns.

"What are they going to do now?" she asked, watching armed men on horseback jumping from the boxcar onto the ground.

"Follow them, but they won't catch them."

"How do you know that?" she asked, noting that John Loving had considerable admiration for the bandits.

He shrugged. "The gang has too many friends. They don't rob ordinary people, seldom hurt anyone, not even posses. They're sort of looked up to—like modern-day Robin Hoods—especially by the Mexicans."

"Does the Texas and Pacific know you speak so highly of the bandits who rob their trains?" she asked, teasing him.

Loving sneaked another look at Annette and nodded, his young face solemn. "Mr. Kincaid talks the same way, and he *is* the Texas and Pacific."

"Is he the one they were talking about? The one who offered that bandit a pardon and a job?"

"Yes. The same."

"But why would he do that?"

"Kincaid's probably one of the richest men in the United States. I guess he considers it good business. He knows that some people resent the railroads for taking all the best land and that most ordinary folks admire men who can take some small part of it back."

"Do railroads really take land away from people?"

"No, not really. Congress grants the railroad one square mile of land for every mile of track the company lays if they complete a stretch of track tying two towns together.

"Kincaid built a line all the way from San Diego to El Paso. The company owns millions of acres of land now. And sometimes the land is occupied by a homesteader or a squatter who doesn't want to move when the railroad takes possession. The railroad usually does what it can to help the people relocate, but sometimes nothing helps, and it ends badly. Some say the leader of the gang may have been one of the squatters who used to ranch around here."

"You sound like quite an admirer of Mr. Kincaid's railroad."

"It's hard not to admire such a visionary. I'm learning everything I can from him."

"I thought for a moment that you wanted to be just like that outlaw." She laughed, completely recovered now from her earlier fright. "Who do you think is the gang's leader?"

"Some folks think it's Clay Allison, a big, sandy-haired fellow with a loud, booming voice. This chap was more like Sam Bass, the Texas outlaw, soft-spoken with smooth manners. Allison is sort of a blowhard, and if it had been him, half the men on the train would probably have been shot or killed. Personally, I think it's Ward Cantrell."

They were interrupted by the men climbing back into the coach, stamping their feet, cursing, and breathing hard from the exertion of running around searching for their guns. Smiling at Leslie, the one named Ben stopped beside Loving and put his arm around the young man's shoulders.

"Our boy giving you all the lowdown, miss?" he asked in a jocular manner.

"Why, yes, he was telling me all about the Devil's Canyon Gang. . . ."

"Don't nobody know much about that gang. Leastways no one outside the gang. Myself—I reckon that yaller-haired fellow with the little chili pepper wench that we saw is the leader. I always usedta think it was Clay Allison till I got a look at him today. Reckon now that there was Ward Cantrell."

A third man stopped and joined the conversation. He was tall, lanky, with a face that looked like tanned leather.

"Cantrell ain't no train robber," he said emphatically. "Cantrell is a gunfighter. I seen him once in Taos. Greased lightning. Killed three men 'cause they beat and robbed a friend of his—an old cripple man Cantrell took a likin' to. The old man had a little money. Guess to them it was like smellin' whiskey through the jailhouse window—couldn't resist it! Killed 'em 'fore the last one cleared leather."

"Cantrell went up against Dodge Merril in Holbrook five years ago," another man interjected. "Didn't see it, but Cantrell walked away from that fight without a scratch. Cut the article out and saved it. You know how those damned reporters are always swarming around. They's three of 'em in the lead Pullman coach right this minute, writing up a storm. Them slick eastern rags pay big money for stories about western bad men. I heard tell the *New York Times* has a half-dozen reporters don't do nothing 'cept roam from town to town writing fast as they can."

Ben grunted in disgust. "I happen to know there's a lot of men sidle up to them greenhorns that call themselves writers and fill them so full of bull . . . excuse me, ma'am, I mean hogwash."

"Well, yeah, they's a lot of exaggeratin' goes on, ain't denying that, but when it comes to letting Judge Colt settle a dispute, I put my money on Cantrell any day. He don't need to rob trains. Hell— 'scuse me, ma'am—I heard they's a man up in Wyoming paying a cool five hundred dollars a head for every blasted one of his enemies turns up dead, no questions asked. Cantrell could spend a couple weeks up there and ride away a right rich man."

"Like shootin' fish in a tank for a man like him," another man agreed, nodding his shaggy head.

Breathing hard from exertion, a fourth man stopped beside Ben. "Hey, Ben," he panted, "Allison died last year! A loaded wagon ran over his neck—broke it clean as a whistle. Died in Cimarron last summer."

Ben grimaced. "Coulda been Cantrell. 'Bout the same build. This feller was a towhead—so's Cantrell."

"Naw! Didn't you fellers get a look at 'em? Rigged like a

puncher, he was, for comfort, not for looks. The top cover was a good Stetson; bandana was silk for ridin' drag. I seen his saddle—it was low horn, rimfire, and there was a good rope hanging on it. I know a cowpuncher when I see his rig. Cain't fool me! A good-looking, long-backed cowpuncher sittin' on a high-forked, full-stamped Texas saddle with a live hoss between his legs is something I cain't be wrong about. If he ain't from Texas, he buys his rig there anyway," he ended flatly.

"Could be he just rigs himself real careful like so's he don't stand out in a crowd," Ben said thoughtfully. "I seen a man once, California fancy man, he was. Custom-made boots with them extra long heels, silver spurs, packing a silver-plated forty-five Colt with a pearl handle. When the sun hit that feller he blazed up like a big piece of jewelry. Could see him for miles on a sunny day. Barrin' Mexicans, he was the fanciest cow-dogger I ever did see. But he spent all his time admiring what a fine shadow he cast."

The train started to move, and the men headed toward their seats, still talking. "Yeah," one of them said, "I seen Cantrell less than a month ago in Silver City, New Mexico, with one of the purtiest little chili pepper wenches I ever did see. Course, this little tamale he had with him today weren't no slouch. If it was Cantrell, and I'd swear it was, I heard he got himself a hankering after the little *chileñas*, won't even give the white girls a tumble."

A woman up front turned horrified eyes on the speaker, her thin face looking permanently shocked, then stared at Leslie as if she had somehow caused the offending conversation, before she gathered her young daughter into her arms, covering the girl's ears with her hands. Leslie suppressed her own smile and spent the rest of the trip listening, most of the time to Annette, who was appalled by so many tales of murder and by how impressed they all sounded with an outlaw who was good at it.

They weren't yet off the train, and it was already apparent that this Wild West was all that the nickel novels and pulp magazines claimed it was—maybe more.

For days Leslie had stared out the window, watching the West unroll before her disbelieving eyes. In the settlements they had passed through, she had seen tall, gaunt scarecrows of women wearing their dingy dark-colored frocks and their slat bonnets, and she could only imagine the deprivations that had brought them to look the way they did. On the farms laid out beside the railroad tracks she had seen women walking behind teams of horses, plowing long, slightly crooked furrows, staggering over clods of dirt.

When the train passed, invariably the woman would straighten her back and lean on the plow, watching the train until it was out of sight, her face impassive. Each time, Leslie felt a lump in her throat, imagining herself in the woman's place.

She glanced out the window now and saw a small, square log cabin sitting like a blemish on the desert, surrounded by cactuses. There was a woman standing beside a large, round pot that hung over a small fire. Smoke curled up in a pale wisp around her, swirling her skirts. She was stirring her laundry with a long stick, and Leslie could see her look up at the train.

Her own life in comparison had been almost leisurely. Thanks to her father's generosity, she and her mother had been able to afford domestic help, leaving them free of daily drudgery so they could pursue their interests in art. Leslie had been born in 1869 while a wounded nation muddled through its reconstruction. She was nineteen now, and not much had changed. Black males were enfranchised in name only. Women were still holding conventions trying to secure the right to vote, and politicians were still plundering the nation's resources while greedy investors made and lost fortunes.

Leslie sat easily on the hard wooden seat, her slender back straight and proud. Annette stifled a groan and picked up her fan to wave it impatiently, wishing she had as easy a disposition as her mistress. Leslie Powers, lovely and talented, from a comfortable home, seemed to her to have lived a charmed existence, until recently. She had been the only child of affectionate, indulgent parents who were both dead now. Her father had gone west fifteen years before and had been killed four months ago in an accident on the ranch he owned with his brother. Leslie's mother, an artist, well known for her vibrant landscapes, had died only three weeks before him when an abscess burst, flooding her system with poison. All this only two months before the end of the school year and her nineteenth birthday. Only Leslie's boundless energy and fortitude had enabled her to struggle through those last weeks and to endure both losses with amazing strength for one so young. She had been quite close to her mother. They had shared an intimacy more common to sisters than to mother and daughter. While it had been obvious to Annette that Leslie was shattered inside, she had functioned with admirable competence.

Just as she did now. Annette, who was an odd mixture of flat-footed common sense and hysteria, marveled at the younger woman's even temperament and wondered what thoughts flitted through her mistress's orderly mind as she gazed out the dust-coated window.

Leslie swayed with the monotonous, undulating motion of the rail car. Her slender white hand left the smoothly polished mahogany armrest to pat impatiently with her limp handkerchief at her perspiring brow. For the hundredth time since she had left Wellesley, Massachusettes, for Phoenix, Arizona, she was questioning her sanity. When she had been safely at home, amid the customary refinement and ease of civilization as it was practiced in Wellesley, she had been bored by it. Now that she had experienced a taste of the Wild West, she was miserable from the oppressive heat and fully aware of the numerous opportunities for disaster.

So far only the scenery had made this trip bearable and only then because she lived and breathed art. She saw the world not as a moving panorama but as a landscape. Riding a train through Kansas had been like floating across an ocean of tall, pale grass that stretched out endlessly.

New Mexico, with its strange, vast, contorted rock formations, had thrilled and amazed her. Expanses of sterile, unblemished sand with enormous, fantastic crags jutting up into a cloudless blue sky—her mind groped for words to describe adequately the rock imagery of New Mexico, where massive monoliths dotted the arid tracts, rising up like decaying, abandoned castles.

I must have been insane to come west, she thought. After all, she reminded herself, I didn't come when my father was alive. Why did I come now? Because Uncle Mark had written that last letter, making it sound like he wanted and needed her? Was it his insistence or her mother's memory that had started this journey?

. Leslie stared out the soot-coated window at the Arizona desert. If she had had a sketch pad, she would have been tempted to try to capture the fierceness and mystery of this wild, bandit-haunted landscape that spilled away from either side of the train. . . . She would start with the clouds that hovered at the horizon, so white they looked like colossal cotton balls hanging over the sparse mountains. Then she would . . .

As always happened when she was experiencing something that could be captured artistically, she wanted desperately to share the experience with her mother. But her mother, who had always seemed too fragile, was dead. In the last hour of her life, while Leslie had still denied that death could claim anyone she loved, her mother had insisted on talking instead of resting as Dr. Klein had advised.

Now, over the monotonous clank-a-tee-clunk of the wheels against the tracks, Leslie could again see her mother's dear, wan face, hear her mother's voice edged with pain: "Leslie, I've never been a proper mother to you. My selfishness and fear kept you from knowing your own father. No, don't stop me. I need to say these things. You need to hear them." Her pale hand, so translucent that Leslie could see the blueness of the veins beneath the skin, waved her daughter's protestations aside. "I was never good at self-sacrifice. I was an impatient mother. I wanted you to hurry and grow up so I would be free to paint." She sighed as if words were an effort for her, but she stopped Leslie's attempt to silence her. "I cheated you of your father's presence; I cheated him of knowing you—all because of my painting. . . . You paid a dear price for my selfishness. . . ."

"Mama, please, you're perfect, Mama. No one could be a better mother than you," she had whispered, meaning it. In her guilt, her mother had forgotten how much they had shared. Now Leslie rushed to remind her, only to be shushed into silence.

"Hush, child. Listen," she said urgently. "Don't spend your life alone as I did. Don't be so filled with fear that you cannot live life. You have wonderful, warm instincts. Use them. And forgive me if you can. . . ."

"Mama, please," she said, the vacantness of her mother's expression scaring her, filling her pounding heart with pain and helplessness. "I know you love me, Mama."

"It's not enough. And now I'm dying before you even finish school," she said, her eyes closing with the effort. "Now I am abandoning you."

"No, Mama, you'll get well. I know you will."

"Leslie, go to him. Go to your father. You're like him in so many ways. He was so bursting with life and energy, as you are. I should have sent you long ago. But I was selfish." She patted her daughter's head. "Promise me you will go."

"I promise, Mama. We'll go together."

But her mother had died within the hour. Her father had answered immediately in response to her telegram, sending her money for necessary expenses and her transportation to Arizona. Part of her had wanted to go flying into his arms, but another part of her was too wrenched by her mother's death. She had moved like a sleepwalker, unable to make any definite decision. Ten days later word came to her that her father had been killed in an accident. Then he seemed little more than an image conjured from photographs, pieced together by words and phrases uttered by her mother. Now that the woman who had created him for her was gone, so was he. At times she wondered if he had ever existed at all.

Wellesley College had graduated Leslie with honors, but she had barely noticed. It had taken four months for her to come to terms with her parents' deaths. She and her mother had been unusually close, and in the end it was this closeness that had saved her. Margaret Powers' love now rested inside her without that earlier sense of abandonment and rage. At last she had made peace with her mother's legacy—she trusted life enough to risk again.

Now, glancing out the window of the train with eyes dimmed by a mist of tears, she knew that Phoenix was only miles away. Annette, who had been crocheting, sighed beside her, and Leslie reached over and absently patted the woman's hand. Annette had been her family's cook, maid, and housekeeper for three years and a source of much comfort these past months. Her simple French-peasant mentality had been a godsend. While in the throes of depression, Leslie had agonized over every decision; Annette merely decided, typified by the look on her plump, cheerful face when Leslie had asked her if she would accompany her to Arizona. *"Oui, mademoiselle,* your *maman* would wish it."

Leslie sighed. Boston, New York, Wellesley were another world entirely, in no way similar to the barren sweeps of land that stretched away forever into dreamy ghostliness on either side of this wretched train.

She picked up her reticule and used it to stir the tepid air. If the windows were open, soot and sparks flew in, filling her head with visions of burning passengers, but if the windows were closed, she could barely breathe. She cursed herself for packing her fan in one of her trunks, where it was completely useless to her. Then, irritated with herself for whimpering, she settled back and closed her eyes, determined that since she had initiated this "adventure," she would endure it as stoically as possible.

She would see her uncle, come to an agreement about the value of her father's share of their joint holdings, get her money, and leave. She would go back to Boston to continue her studies—in a civilized city where people appreciated the finer things in life and didn't glorify the questionable virtues of train robbers and murderers.

CHAPTER
THREE

"Hey, Ward!" Doug Paggett said, nudging Ward in the ribs. "Whooee! Would you look at that little beauty. That is some high-tone fluff if I ever seen it!"

Ward heard his good friend but chose to ignore him. Instead he smiled down upon the petite Mexican girl clinging so worshipfully to his arm. Little Maria. Her skin was a soft golden brown that looked ripe to bursting. She wore a loose *camisa,* gathered at the sleeves and around the neck, and nothing, not even a shift, under it. Her dark brown nipples pressed like tiny buds against the soft cotton. She snuggled close against him, looking as eager as he to leave this fiesta crowd and find a quiet place where they could get to know each other better.

"Tell me you wouldn't like to get next to that little beauty." Doug persisted, jabbing him again with his sharp elbow. "I bet she smells like lilacs and rosewater, all powdery and perfumy. Makes my body ache just thinking about it." he whispered.

"Well, go get her." Ward chuckled, not taking his eyes off Maria, whose firm flesh was practically simmering against his hand.

"You're going to be so sorry . . ." Doug warned, shaking his head.

Ward laughed, but there was something in Doug's voice akin to awe that finally motivated him to look up and search out the "little beauty" Doug was raving about.

"There!" Doug hissed, pointing.

Ward followed his friend's finger. A woman in a white gown and hat was stepping out of a carriage about half a block away. In profile all he could see was that she was beautifully gowned, no doubt the height of fashion, with her skirt pulled tight over her hips, outlining a flawlessly slender figure. A bustle of ruffles and flounces cascaded behind her as she was lifted down by the man helping her disembark from the fancy phaeton. It was no wonder that Doug had noticed her. She was as out of place in the fiesta crowd as a pile of gold coins in a pigsty.

He'd always thought bustles ridiculous, but on this woman, offset by a tantalizing glimpse of a dainty ankle, it made for a very charming picture. Instead of standing her in the dusty street her escort changed his mind in mid-swing, gathered her into his arms, and carried her to the rough plank sidewalk, where he gallantly deposited her.

"Isn't that romantic?" a woman beside Ward whispered to her companion.

"Pure de ole foolish, if you ask me," the man grumped. "No one but a fool would tote a perfectly healthy woman around in this heat."

"Well, I think it's romantic," she said, irritated.

"A woman who cain't walk to the sidewalk by herself shouldn't be allowed to come to town," the man persisted.

"I don't know why I bother to talk to you," she said, dismissing her husband and turning to a female companion. "Aren't they a handsome couple?"

"I purely love the way he dotes on her," the friend whispered. "D'you s'pose he could still love her as much as he seems to? Don't rightly seem possible, does it?"

"I wouldn't give a flip one way or the other. He treats her like he worships the ground she walks on. . . . That would be good enough for me."

Obviously disgusted, their male companion turned away and spat a stream of tobacco into the dust at their feet.

Ward was typically unimpressed by fancy gowns, but there was something about this woman that held his interest even though Maria was squirming impatiently against him, pressing her warm breast to his arm, demanding his attention. Absently, he found her hand and caressed it while he squinted at the other woman, trying to see beneath the rakishly angled Rembrandt-style hat that covered part of her face and most of her hair.

She lifted her skirts and started to walk toward where Ward, Maria, and Doug were standing in the shade in front of the saloon. And while she was completely circumspect, there was no way she could hide the vibrant energy that radiated from her movements. Ward smiled to himself. Only a dancer could look so graceful and so leashed at the same time, as if she were only momentarily contained—as though any second she would throw off her restraint and leap into dance.

Now he urgently wanted to pierce the anonymity of her fancy gear, but something deep inside resisted. And as if he had no control over it, he felt his attention shift. He turned away and scanned the holiday crowd.

Phoenix had changed in the six years since he had first visited the town. There had been no Paris bonnets then. In 1882 it had been a pleasant little farming town, surrounded by cotton plantations, acres of wild alfalfa, peaches, beans, and corn, all because an enterprising man by the name of Swilling had seen the ancient irrigation canals abandoned by the Indians who used to farm the Salt River Valley and had formed his own irrigation company. Swilling had cleaned out the silt and sand and made the canals functional again. His friend who had the forage contract with the army joined him, and they began raising alfalfa instead of just hacking down what they could find along the river banks. Their farms supplied hay to Fort McDowell and fruit brandies to neighboring towns. There had been cattle then too, but for the most part the ranchers respected the farmers. The cattle roamed the brakes where farming was impossible or where the irrigation canals did not reach. Few cowboys bothered the residents. Phoenix had been a sleepy little town of two thousand, half white, half Mexican, with the Mexicans living south of town in adobe huts, tents, and squalid shacks.

Now Kincaid's railroad had changed all that. Phoenix had become a magnet for cattle drovers from the north who wanted to ship their cattle back east for the big prices the Texans had been getting for years by driving up the trail to Dodge City.

The population had doubled since the arrival of the steel tracks and the soot-spewing locomotives. Now there was a fancy hotel—the Bricewood West. Thinking of the name brought a rush of bitterness. Kincaid's Bricewood West—an expensive and authentic copy of a French Second Empire palazzo set in the middle of the Arizona desert. Leave it to a bastard like Kincaid to pull a stunt like that, Ward thought bitterly.

Doug nudged him again, and he forced his angry thoughts back to the female he was supposed to be admiring—probably one of Kincaid's imported females. Kincaid was notorious for hiring any local who wanted a job and was still attracting easterners by the thousands to swell the towns along the path of the railroad—sort of like building a railroad to nowhere and bringing in the people to use it. But Ward had to admit that, as much as he hated the man, Kincaid did have a few good ideas. Women had a civilizing influence. They insisted upon all the trappings of civilization—no matter where they had to live. Put a woman down in the middle of the

Sahara or the Arizona desert and pretty soon a French dress shop would spring up across the street from her. Without turning his head he could see La Roche Fashions only two doors from where the elegantly groomed couple had paused. A banner over the door announced the latest in Paris originals.

The woman in white turned toward Ward, not seeing him, searching the fiesta crowd, and he saw her face for the first time. A pale, perfect oval of creamy skin, wide dark eyes, a lush curve of wide lips. . . . Ward felt an involuntary pang of recognition—like a fist in the stomach—and wondered why he hadn't recognized her escort. . . .

Jenn!

Jenn . . .

A pulse began to pound in his temples. The part of him that had loved her was jumping up and down inside, wanting to cry out to her, ''Jenn, Jenn, I'm here! I'm here!'' He could imagine her joy at seeing him, but the part that remembered the way she had abandoned him in favor of Kincaid throttled his momentary joy, and he stood there with his breath turning to pain in his lungs and throat, like a solid column of ice, all the way down to his belly, a long, slow ache he could not control. . . .

His emotions in a turmoil of confusion, he continued to watch her walking with that brisk, leashed elegance through the festive, noisy crowd. The man at her side, Chantry Kincaid III, was as solid and sturdy as Jenn was luminous and ethereal. Eight years had changed him very little—still lean, still as smooth and handsome as he had been when they'd met him. ''He reminds me of a barbarian,'' Jenn had remarked after she saw him for the first time. ''Attila the Hun in a green velvet Prince Albert coat—wicked good looks and all the assurance in the world.'' They had laughed about it then, until Jenn had succumbed to those wicked good looks and the challenge promised in Kincaid's deceptively warm green eyes.

No doubt Kincaid still moved in the hard, realistic world of business where he took what he wanted with diabolic ease, whether it be a railroad, a string of warehouses that just happened to belong to someone else, or a woman. Jenn had been quite a feather in Kincaid's cap. At twenty-three, when they had first met, she was already a legend—the daughter of one of New York's most respectable old families and a sensation on the stage—unheard of in polite society, but Jenn had carried it off with her customary verve and elan.

Time and the reality of Phoenix suddenly vanished in a flood of
memory. Eight years of Ward's life peeled back as though it had
never existed.

He was back in the house on Fifty-seventh Street, in New York
City, across from the park. The moon glistened on the icy trees and
streets. From his upstairs bedroom window, the pond in the middle
of the park looked like a large oblong silver serving platter left outside by accident. His name was Peter then. Peter Van Vleet. If he
looked north out that window, up the wide expanse of Fifth Avenue, he could see a row of houses like the one he and his sister
lived in. Fifty-seventh Street was an avenue of millionaires'
mansions—a long tree-shaded avenue lined by looming chateaus,
cavernous castles, villas, neo-Renaissance palazzos, and in the
middle of all that opulence, the Van Vleet townhouse, bought at a
time when the Van Vleets had more wealth than those social up-
starts, the Astors.

A woman named Bettina had shared his bed and snuggled
warmly against him. He didn't know what had brought her there
that night. He hadn't asked. He hadn't seen anyone associated
with Kincaid since the night Kincaid's men had beaten him sense-
less. He hadn't wanted to see anyone. Except Bettina had come to
him, after he thought Simone had betrayed him to Kincaid's men,
and he couldn't think of any reason to send her away. Except that
Jennie had never liked her. He was just beginning to feel like he
might live, and the first thing that came back was his need for a
woman. So Bettina had stayed. He reached over and slapped her
smooth, white, thrusting buttocks.

"Go get us some food."

"What do you want?"

"Bring everything. I can't keep this up without food."

Bettina scampered cheerfully off the bed, grabbed his robe off
the floor, and did as she was told. They ate in the center of the bed,
and then in the middle of a sentence, with her mouth full of apple,
she started talking about Jenn.

"Did you know your sister came back today?"

Peter refused to let Bettina know he had been agonizing in a
sickbed, wondering why his sister hadn't even bothered to see if he
had lived or died.

"From where?"

"Don't you know? Her honeymoon! What kind of brother are
you anyway?" She giggled mischievously, took another bite of the

apple, and continued. "Mr. Kincaid came back ages ago—she just showed up this morning. What a row that was!"

He could feel the blood draining out of his head to be replaced by a giant heartbeat. *Married to Kincaid? His sister?* The last time he had seen Jenn was the night he had been beaten so brutally that he could barely breathe through the mess they had made of his nose and mouth. That night, three weeks ago, Jenn had been horrified and repulsed at what Kincaid's hired thugs had done to him. How could she now have married the man responsible for his beating and left on her honeymoon? He had the sudden urge to throttle Bettina, to choke the truth out of her.

Rage burned in him like a fever. Jenn couldn't have married Kincaid. She knew Kincaid had tricked their mother out of her proxies, then had used them to bankrupt the Van Vleet warehouses. She knew Kincaid's interference had driven their father to kill their mother and then himself. Jenn knew! That's why she had finally agreed to help him expose Kincaid for what he was. He felt like throwing back his head and howling in his pain and disbelief.

"Peter, you're not listening to me," Bettina protested.

So he arranged his face into a listening mask, trying to ignore the hard ache in his chest. He felt as if part of his insides had been ripped out. Any second his remaining blood and organs would stop working.

Bettina squirmed her round little bottom into the bed. She loved to gossip, so Peter knew he would hear every detail no matter what he did. Bettina worked for Kincaid as a chorus girl in the same theater where Jenn was the headliner—the New York Bricewood's Grand Salon. The Bricewood East was the *ne plus ultra* of the hotel and gambling circuit and Kincaid's pet project. It was the headquarters for all Kincaid's other enterprises as well.

"Your sister came back like one of the furies," Bettina said. "She fired Edgar, that tight-assed little know-it-all who used to run the lift, and . . ." She paused, eyeing him to see the impact of her words. "And Simone."

That jarred him only slightly. "Why?"

"That's not all she did. She threw Latitia Laurey's clothes and all her things out of Mr. Kincaid's suite. And Latitia! I didn't see it, but I would have given anything to have been there. Your sister may look like such a lady that butter wouldn't melt in her mouth, but she can sure fight for what she wants. Can you imagine that? She came home from her honeymoon, and he had already moved another woman into what was supposed to be their love-nest!''

Bettina wiggled in anticipation, watching him with her enormous baby-doll eyes as if he would be able to explain his sister's actions. He shrugged and plumped the pillow at his back, pretending that his sister was no concern of his. To distract her, he reached over and caressed the firm underswell of her breast and saw the nipple blossom and harden.

"Peter, stop that. I won't be able to concentrate.'' She settled herself like a chicken making a nest. "Your sister came back again in the evening, in the middle of a big, ritzy dinner party that Kincaid and Latitia were giving. This part is absolutely delicious! One of the serving girls told me about it. Well—not exactly—she heard it from one of the girls who was there, though. Anyway, your sister threw Latitia Laurey, Miss High-and-Mighty herself, out of that party bodily. Can you imagine? In front of all Latitia's hoity-toity friends! She even had enough spunk to dump a bowl of some gooey salad down the front of Latitia's dress. She ran out of there screaming like a banshee. I bet that was a real cat fight,'' she said with satisfaction.

Peter closed his eyes, trying not to see it. The thought of his sister lowering herself to the level of a street-fighting, hair-pulling harridan for a man like Kincaid nauseated him.

The next morning Peter rang the Bricewood East and asked for Mrs. Kincaid. When he heard his sister's voice on the line, he quietly broke the connection forever. . . . That afternoon he joined the cavalry and gave notice at the brokerage firm where he had worked since leaving Harvard.

Three nights later, when Simone came, he was packing to leave for the Dakota badlands. He had gotten the assignment he had asked for. And the promise of a commission in six months.

Simone. She reminded him of a wounded doe, a wary forest creature, with her brown eyes full of stars. A strange mixture of goodness, need, and weakness.

When he closed the doors to the study, she rose from where she had been huddled beside the fire, looking very small and vulnerable. Was this the same woman who had spent two loving hours in his bed so he would be sure to be home when Kincaid's men came for him?

She moved toward him, but something stopped her—perhaps the look in his eyes. "Oh, Peter, *chèri*,'' she whispered, biting her lush bottom lip. "I didn't know you had been hurt until to-night. . . . I came as soon as I found out. Are you all right?"

"Yes."

"I waited for you. I hoped you would come to see me. . . ."

She looked so defenseless that he couldn't bring himself to hurt her. Maybe she had been taken in and used by Kincaid, too. Why should he expect Simone to be any smarter than he or his sister?

"I've been busy. I'm leaving tomorrow."

"Oh! Oh, I'm sorry," she said brokenly. "You're going away for good!"

"I joined the cavalry."

"Oh, Peter, chèri. . . ." She started to cry. Tears came up in her brown eyes, turning them into oceans of pain. She'd never gotten anything she wanted, she'd confided. Sometimes she got close, but someone or something always snatched it away.

Still crying, she reached up gently and touched his face where the greenish tinge of a bruise still showed. His aristocratic nose looked broader, with a hump that probably wouldn't ever go away.

"Oh, your poor face, your poor broken face. . . . It was so beautiful," she said mournfully.

Peter grimaced. Beautiful? Maybe Kincaid had done him a favor. He liked this one better. It looked lived in.

Her lips started to tremble and tears streamed down her pale cheeks in a solid sheet. "Those men who did this came after I left, didn't they? Oh, Peter, I swear to you that I didn't know. . . ."

He shrugged. "It's all right. It doesn't matter. . . ."

Simone turned away, sobbing brokenly, and he moved to hold her almost by instinct.

"Oh, Peter, chèri, I didn't know. I didn't know. . . ."

He stroked her slender back, sighing. "It's all right."

"No, it isn't. It never will be. I love you. More than anything. More than life . . . I will die if you leave me."

"Hush. People don't die of love," he said gently.

No, they died of much worse things—especially Simone. Things that left a man's gut twisted with hate. But he hadn't known that when he had decided to bring Simone with him.

An urgent whisper at his side jarred him back to the present. Maria was tugging on his arm. He glanced down at her face, at the dusty Phoenix street, the fiesta crowd that was milling and pushing and shouting, and then glanced back at his sister. Once he had gotten over his hurt and rage, he had tried to be fair to Jenn, but there was no way he could justify what she had done. Was it any wonder that the railroad that he and Doug and the rest of the gang lived off of, like it was their own private little money tree, was owned by Kincaid?

His head buzzed with a dull, puzzled anger. . . .

Jennifer Van Vleet Kincaid. My sister the whore, he thought. Part of him rose up in anger at his blasphemous words, but the embittered part of him swelled up and silenced the protest. How he had loved her, worshipped her. The way only a little brother can love and worship an older sister.

"Hey, Ward," Doug whispered. "What'd I tell you? Ain't she somethin'?"

CHAPTER
FOUR

Ward's head snapped around, and Doug recoiled at the look of fury on his friend's face.

"All right, all right. Sorry I brought it up," Doug mumbled, stepping back to disappear into the crowd.

Ward dragged in a deep breath, willing himself to relax. He was as surprised as Doug had been at that blind and heedless instinct to defend his sister's honor, that is, if a woman who married the man who had stripped her of family and fortune could still have honor.

Or perhaps, he thought bitterly, the act of marriage cancels out all the rest. Was that the way it worked? Did a man have a right to feel betrayed when another person, even a sister, chose to live life on her own terms? Even when he didn't understand or approve?

Ward's lips twisted into a wry smile. When had Jenn ever sought approval? His or anyone else's? She might look like a wisp of silver, without substance, as innocent and pure as a vestal virgin, in her fashionable white brocade, but she was as spirited as any female he had ever known. She had spent her life in training to be a ballerina. And when she wasn't dancing she was singing, because she could not decide which was her first love. Physically, she was as strong as spring steel. Mentally she was as determined as any woman on earth to have her own way. Her wide purple eyes could flash with imperious scorn, melt icebergs with their poignant appeal, or tantalize, seduce, bewitch. Now he thoroughly understood why Kincaid had carried her from the carriage to the sidewalk. The man was no doubt besotted with her.

Maria nudged him again, and he felt like a fool standing in the hot sun, eulogizing his treacherous, beautiful sister. . . .But self-righteousness also sickened him. Wasn't it possible that Jenn's only error had been one of judgment? What gave him the right to stand aside and judge her, then to inflict his childish punishment by running away? Jenn had once loved him completely.

He was remembering a time when their nanny had jerked him up by the arm and begun to whip him across his bare thighs with a belt. He could not remember the reason for his punishment or how old he had been. He only remembered that Jenn, her face tight with rage and determination, had thrown herself between him and the stinging blows of that belt, screaming invectives at the woman. In anger, the nanny had turned on Jenn and punished her soundly. Their combined screams had attracted head cook's attention, and the nanny was fired, but Jenn had carried welts for days.

Maria stamped her foot, demanding his attention. He looked down at her, but his voice failed him.

"Ward, *mio*." Maria pouted, a note of demand in her voice.

"Come on," he said, his own voice harsh, strained. Part of him was being pulled toward his sister, irresistibly, but another part, even stubborner than the other, took Maria's arm and guided her through the crowd. If Jenn had loved him, she would have at least checked to see if he had survived the beating of Kincaid's thugs; she would have tried to find him long before now. Kincaid's finely wrought network of hired talent could find anything it set out to locate.

"Let's go find us a nice quiet place," he said abruptly, burning with the sudden desire to forget Jenn and all the memories that went with her. Forgiving those who trespassed against you was for saints and the dying; if Jenn had seen him and recognized him, he might not have been able to turn away. But she hadn't.

"But where?" Maria demanded, smiling.

That was a good point. They were in the middle of the fiesta crowd in the hottest part of the day. It wasn't going to be easy to find some privacy. He had a room at the Rancher's Hotel, but women weren't allowed in the rooms.

Maria's family had a covered wagon tied up next to the livery stable. The whole family shared it at night, but now, at midday, it was deserted. Her parents were avid Catholics and were probably attending one of the many masses at the old Spanish mission, celebrating Mexican independence, the purpose of the fiesta days.

"Come," she said, scampering up into the deep well of the wagon. Ward stepped on the small platform and leaped easily inside. He knelt on the pallet that covered the floor of the wagon, cleared it of strewn garments, and Maria slipped eagerly into his arms, lifting her lips to be kissed.

Maria was seventeen, and she didn't know how old this *caballero* Ward was. She only knew that he was so *rubio* and so handsome that she had been unable to resist him. Now his warm mouth was on her face, burning into her lips, her cheeks, her eyes. She was breathless and weak with the unexpected trembling he had started in her helpless body. Never had she felt anything like this when the young men of her acquaintance had managed to steal a kiss. Never had her body trembled and collapsed the way it did now.

His tongue teased her lips and darted into her mouth, causing ripples the length of her body. One warm hand slipped from her back, where his fingers were pressing against her spine, leaving a burning trail to her breast. His fingers caressed the sensitive engorged nipples, and she moaned in her throat at the heat that surged into her belly. His kiss deepened, and his hand slipped down to stroke her smooth inner thigh. Heat flooded Maria, but a small voice, the voice of her dear mama, interrupted her. An internal argument ensued, and the part of her that liked the way Ward's lips and his hands made her feel argued with much eloquence against her mother's imagined voice, which was loud and insistent, even though it was losing the argument on every point.

She struggled against him. "No, Ward, *mio*, please . . ."

He laughed softly and forced her down onto the pallet. "Hush. You want half of Phoenix looking in this wagon, seeing us like this?"

"No, Ward, no, I can't," she panted, beginning to struggle against him.

Ward lifted his head and looked into the girl's eyes. "For Christ's sake," he grumbled. "Why not?"

"Please," she begged him. "Don't do that!"

Ward's hand was on her thigh, beneath the thin cotton skirt. Her skin was soft and pliant beneath his touch. Her eyes pleaded with him even while they told him yes. Only moments ago she had led him in here. Moments before that she had pressed her hungry little body against him as if she were as eager as any female he had ever bedded. Now she was saying no.

Ward sat up abruptly, a thought forming in his mind. "Are you . . . Have you done this before?"

"N-no," Maria whispered, tears beginning to slip down her cheeks.

"Damn! Have you seen my hat?" he demanded, cursing the luck that would cause him to pick a virgin out of all the available women in Phoenix.

Heartbroken, Maria threw her arms around his neck, clinging tightly to him. She was trembling all over, and the tears were wetting his neck. He held her for a moment, stroking her dark hair. "Wipe your face," he said, brushing the tears off her cheeks. "Why didn't you tell me?"

"I didn't know. . . . I thought I could do it," she said, breaking into new sobs. He pulled her close and soothed her until her broken sobs subsided.

"You can hit me if you want to," she said, sniffing.

He laughed in spite of the warring emotions that still seethed within him. Between this little vixen and the Kincaids, he was having one helluva day. Hitting her would serve no purpose and was not something he would even consider. If he was angry at anyone, it was at himself, not the girl. While Doug Paggett and his men might think him an irrepressible cocksman, he alone knew he had thrown back more fish than he had kept, though he wasn't above letting the false attributes circulate, since they added to his image. Now he pulled away, gently but firmly.

"I'm so ashamed," she said.

He noticed a pair of trousers that had been flung almost out of the wagon in their original haste to make a place on the pallet. He tossed them back into the pile of clothes beside the pallet, then took her hands and pulled her to her feet. He wiped her tears again and teased her until she was smiling, then laughing in his arms.

"Next year at fiesta time, you be here," he said, threatening her playfully. "Then, if you don't behave yourself . . ." He put his fist to her jaw pretending to hit her. "Next year," he warned.

She laughed, nodding her pleasure.

"And if I don't find you, I will come looking for you, *comprende*?"

Maria nodded and hugged him as tightly as if he had just saved her life.

CHAPTER
FIVE

"*Magnifique, mademoiselle,* you will be zee most elegant young lady in zee fiesta parade," Annette breathed, stepping back after she had buttoned the last of the long row of tiny gold buttons.

"I have carefully weighed my uncle's request, and while I agree that every impulse of feeling should be guided by reason, I cannot indulge his whim in the matter of this parade," Leslie said, turning to admire the gown in the full-length mirror. They were in an elegant suite of rooms at the Bricewood West, which was a paragon of grandeur compared to the dusty squalor of Phoenix.

Annette sighed, dazzled by her mistress's delicate language as well as the striking picture she made in the golden gown. Leslie was taller than average, elegantly slender, with a face that reflected the sweetness of a sunny disposition combined with a charming vagueness that came from preoccupation with her own thoughts. After three years in the same house with her, Annette realized that Leslie Powers lived almost entirely in her imagination. Her wide-apart lime-green eyes reflected both the innocence of her genteel upbringing and intelligence honed by fourteen years of intensive schooling. Thanks to Margaret Powers, Leslie had received a fine education from serious and demanding instructors who did not subscribe to the common view that a woman's primary responsibility was to marry, raise children, and be charming at table. Leslie had graduated from Wellesley College at the top of her class, proficient in algebra, biology, chemistry, Latin, history, French, English composition, and geography. She had also excelled in a variety of art classes where she'd mastered everything from color and light to neo-classical traditions.

Most young women her age exchanged endless visits with other young women, received young men into chaperoned parlors, and contemplated marriage. Their dainty fingers were curled around china cups at tea with friends, who whispered, giggled, and gossiped among themselves. Leslie rarely walked out with a young man more than once. She had been introduced to handsome young stockbrokers, barristers just out of law school, and even a dapper young physician. And while Leslie was polite in her responses, her manner always revealed that although she was not bored, she was certainly not eager. Few young men possessed the composure to cope with such indifference.

And like most people dedicated to their work, Leslie was never happier than when her surroundings managed to take care of themselves without her help. She had known a moment of ecstasy when she entered the Bricewood suite and saw a small sign beside the light key which said, "This room is equipped with electric light. Do not attempt to light with match. Simply turn key on wall by this sign. The use of electricity for lighting is in no way harmful to your health, nor does it affect the soundness of your sleep."

She and Annette, both accustomed to electricity in large eastern hotels, had smiled with superior glee at the time. Now she turned, surveying her slender figure in the mirror, dabbing with a slender, graceful hand at the glow of perspiration on her smooth brow. While she was too well cultivated and gently reared to speak all her thoughts, even to her maid, she personally believed there was something sinister about her uncle's request.

"*Oui*, breathtaking, *mademoiselle*," Annette exclaimed, clasping her tiny hands under her chin in admiration. She was only three years older than Leslie, and her guileless blue eyes were filled with rapture at the elegant vision of her mistress before her. "And," she said, knitting her straight tawny brows in a frown, "your uncle eez a very determined man."

Leslie Marlowe Powers lifted her firm chin and turned to look over her shoulder to see herself at another angle. The gown her uncle had practically ordered her to wear was beautiful—there was no question of that. It was the most extravagant creation Leslie had ever seen, obviously an antique, probably from the romantic era of Madame de Pompadour's court, when female fashions were distinguished by full sleeves and skirts, square, low-cut necklines, and narrow waists. The inlay in the bodice was intricately and lavishly embroidered and piped in thick gold thread; truly a dress fit for a queen. Even the gold slippers were perfect, including the way their soft, costly leather molded itself to her feet like a caress.

"That is true," she sighed. "He is singular in his desire to control my activities. Unfortunately I am equally determined not to ride in the parade.''

But there was a note of regret in her voice, and looking into the mirror, she could see that her cheeks were flushed with color. The lime-greenness of her eyes fairly leaped out at her from the mirror. She *was* excited by the opportunity to wear such a magnificent gown. Weeks of being deprived of suitable companionship must have undone her, else she wouldn't be considering it. She wasn't usually obstinate, but her uncle's plan to display her in this fashion had repelled her. He had made elaborate plans and preparations: outfitting his riders with fancy charo suits, silver-studded saddles, and blooded horses. The horse he had chosen for her was a pure white Arabian—so she could ''gleam like a little jewel,'' he had said. Her reason warned her that, to her uncle and Dallas Younger, this was not just a casual, frolicsome event. . . .

Usually she would not have had even a passing interest in wearing this gown, but she had been on the ranch for three weeks, and frankly, she missed the opportunities to wear fine gowns and be appreciated by young men she admired. There was some tension as well over Dallas Younger and his unwanted attentions. When he wasn't working away from the ranch house, he dogged her steps, making sly, insinuating remarks.

The plump Frenchwoman was about to reply when they heard a loud knock on the door. Annette whirled as if she had been caught in some mischief and rushed to the door. ''Who is zere?'' she demanded.

''It's us.''

''It eez your uncle, *mademoiselle*.''

''Let him in.''

Mark Powers and Dallas Younger shuffled into the room and stopped in the middle of the oriental rug in front of the horsehair sofa. Leslie was instantly aware of Younger's eyes on her body and felt herself flushing with a renewal of the irritation she felt when he was near her. The man had made life miserable for her since her arrival. He had apparently decided that she was going to be his woman, and he seemed perfectly capable of ignoring her feelings in the matter.

He was a rough-hewn giant, well liked and obviously respected by other rough men. He was built like a lumberjack, with slightly more refinement of feature, so that to the casual eye he appeared quite handsome, but there was such an air of careless arrogance about him that Leslie mentally recoiled. He was a man perfectly capable of ignoring her wishes, and she was too accustomed to having her opinions considered to find such thoughtlessness attractive.

Now he was devouring her with his dark eyes. Frowning, she glanced from Younger's ruddy face to her uncle, her expression demanding that he reprimand his foreman, but Uncle Mark did not appear to take notice.

Powers cleared his throat. "Well, now," he said, taking in the sight of her, "you do me proud—real proud!"

Leslie's eyes widened in surprise and frustration. She needed his protection, and all he gave her was his approval of how she looked in the gown he had provided.

Mark Powers was a stocky man with an open, usually friendly face and an infectious smile that he used to his advantage. He had a wide, short neck to match his stocky build, and a face with small features—nose, mouth—even his eyes were small. And while he might look like pictures she had seen of her father, she knew from her mother that the resemblance ended there. Her father had been an honorable man. She had only known Mark Powers for a few short weeks, but she felt no sense of security from his guardianship.

For although she had not been mistreated, Powers routinely made decisions for her that he fully expected her to abide by. She had decided that he was conservative, quiet, a little sneaky in his relations with people, not particularly intelligent, but a man who had done well because he didn't let his affairs become too complicated. He could be easily embarrassed—he was not a man who relaxed with people until he knew them quite well. He presented such a neutral image to the world that he affronted no one, except her.

In dealing with her, he had been both generous and as tight as the bark on a tree, which suggested to her that he was subject to moods. His moods seemed dictated by how her desires might conflict with the welfare of what he considered "his ranch." If spending money enhanced his or the ranch's image, he was generous; if it did not, he was deaf to her needs. He was a hard worker, rising before dawn and tending to the business of the ranch until late in the evening. He was liked by his contemporaries, but known intimately by no one. She knew he thought himself a good uncle.

"Thank you, Uncle Mark," she said, temporarily thrown off guard by the look of pride in his eyes. She would deal with Younger's rudeness later, with her uncle in private.

She had more important matters that demanded her attention now. She took a deep breath and faced him. "Uncle Mark, I know this parade is important to you, but . . ." The deceptively merry look in his eyes faded, but she plunged ahead; ". . . but I feel strongly advised against it."

"Nonsense!" he said, anger turning his small eyes the color of bright jade. "Of course you will!" His face had turned red with rising anger, and Annette's warning look cautioned her not to enrage him further, but she was loath to back down.

"I fail to see what difference my riding in a parade will make," she said reasonably.

Her uncle, who was a scant three inches taller than her five feet five inches, puffed up like an angry adder, and Leslie braced herself, but before either of them could reply, Younger stepped between them.

"Hey! Enough of this here yellin' and carryin' on." He took Leslie's hand in his and spun her around, ignoring her cry of surprise and protest. "It's about time you wore something that shows off that pretty little shape of yours, sweet thing," he said, pulling her into his arms. "This sure beats those high-necked, high-falutin schoolteacher duds you been wearin'."

"Let me go!" she hissed, struggling with all her strength against Younger's steely hands, which were around her waist. She felt his fingers groping her spine and the flare of her hips. Enraged, she kicked him. "Get your hands off me!"

"Owww!" Dallas yelped.

"Heah!" Powers scolded. "Ain't no call to get rough."

Leslie glared first at Younger, who had loosed his hold on her, and then at her uncle. "Aren't you going to do anything?" she demanded of her uncle.

"Dallas don't mean no harm," he said, "do you, boy?"

"None atall," Dallas agreed, grimacing. "I like my women feisty." His ruddy, sun-darkened face glistened above her. A lock of his crisp black hair had fallen forward, and he looked like some evil, smiling wolf, waiting for the right moment to continue the attack.

Leslie checked her temper with an effort. "You presume far too much, Mr. Younger," she said, controlling her voice as best she could.

"City women!" Younger said, winking at her uncle and feigning injury, spreading his hands as if appealing to Mark Powers for vindication.

"He . . . mauled me!" she protested. "He mauled me and you just watched him!"

"Now, simmer down, Leslie. Nobody mauled you. Dallas is a fine young man who just happens to like you, and you should be grateful that he does."

"Likes me!" Leslie gasped. She was too much a lady to mention aloud that Dallas Younger had panted after her like a dog in heat since the day she arrived.

"Don't reckon you understand our ways here, Leslie. Dallas means no harm. I only want what's best for you. . . ."

"Then buy me out and send me home," she said, taking the chance that had presented itself.

A scowl knit his brows, reminding her how irritable he could become when she tried to force him into negotiating with her. "At the right time, we'll talk about that, but in the meantime, as long as you're living under my roof, you'll do as I say. And I say you *are* going to ride in that parade," he growled, his small mouth pursed into a look of such angry impatience that Leslie had to force herself not to flinch visibly.

"Or what?" she asked quietly, her heart pounding.

"Don't get uppity with me, young lady. You will do as I say. Dammit, you're just a woman! You don't know or care how hard I've worked to get this ranch to the point it's at now. You don't understand anything I try to tell you! What the hell do you know about building a ranch? You're here to tear it apart. I've worked and sweated half my life for this ranch, and by God I'm not going to sell it just so some snot-nosed city filly can trot back to her ritzy friends with a pocket full of money she didn't earn."

Leslie paled. The import of his words frightened her. Did he mean that there was absolutely no chance of his ever buying her out? Her money was almost gone. How would she get back home? And how would she live after she got there? Trying to ignore her fear, she spoke firmly. "I respect your love for what you consider to be your ranch, but my father worked just as hard as you did. He earned it for me. As his rightful heir, part of it belongs to me. . . ."

Her uncle's salt-and-pepper brows pulled down into a heavy ledge of disapproval. Thrown off guard by the correctness of her logic, he cleared his throat. "I said we'll talk about it. In the meantime, you'll do as I say, and I say you are going to ride in that parade!"

"Do I also have to put up with Dallas Younger?" she

demanded, flashing a look of scorn at the man who was grinning his enjoyment of the ruckus.

"You could do worse. He knows how to take care of a woman—not like those panty-waist do-nothings you're used to."

"I've never needed the questionable protection of a gun-fighter," she said quietly, allowing her eyes to reflect a measure of her disgust as they swept down Younger's tall, sturdy form. Dallas threw back his dark head and laughed, supremely unaffected by what he considered her prissy fastidiousness. Leslie could see Annette's plump form behind him, her face pinched with concern for her mistress.

"You may be glad to have him around someday," Powers said vehemently.

"I find that difficult to imagine."

"You gonna ride in that parade?" he asked, his tone both final and threatening.

"Are we going to seriously discuss settling my father's estate?" she shot back at him.

"All right! You ride in that parade," he said more calmly, "and we'll talk about your share of the ranch when we get home tonight. Fair enough?"

Leslie nodded. "I'll ride if you promise."

"Out here a man's word is his bond," he said gruffly.

CHAPTER
SIX

"Oh!" Leslie gasped when the door had closed behind her uncle and Dallas Younger. "They sorely try my patience!"

"Oui, mademoiselle," Annette breathed, stepping forward to smooth the skirt of the voluminous gown where Leslie's fingers had crumpled the shiny gold cloth.

"Sorry," Leslie muttered. She covered her face with her hands for a moment and then straightened. "I will not let them turn me into a whimpering wreck," she said to herself, turning. She walked to the window, lifted it, and leaned out as far as she could. Heat enveloped her, making her realize her mistake at once, but she had felt so stifled by the exchange with her uncle and Younger that she didn't care.

The hotel faced south, and from the third floor she had a view of every rooftop in Phoenix except those lying behind the hotel. She shrugged off her anger and irritation and breathed deeply of the hot, dusty air that was rising from the street below. The sidewalks were crowded with holiday revelers. Sounds of music, tinny and exuberant, floated above the raucous laughter and the babble of voices. Horses standing in the streets occasionally whinnied and stamped. The sharp smell of their urine caused her to wrinkle her nose, but it was not enough to drive her back inside.

A cowboy and a young girl left the crowd and turned down the alley across the street from where she watched. The man was dressed in the rough garb of a seasoned cowpuncher. Leslie could see very little of his face, which was sheltered from view by a tan-colored Stetson, but somehow his overall appearance seemed familiar. He was taller than average, with narrow hips and broad shoulders, and he moved with lithe purposefulness. The young woman was small and voluptuous and wore the casual dress of the *peones* in the settlements they had passed through on the train. The girl was giggling, but the young man's actions were more urgent than frolicsome. They stopped beside a covered wagon that was tied up against the outside wall of the livery stable. The man took off his hat and wiped his forehead with his sleeve. He was strikingly handsome—darkly sun-tanned with blond hair that had no red—like pale wheat against the warm teak of his face.

They paused there only a moment and then he lifted her up into the wagon and followed her inside. Leslie smiled. She watched as they embraced and then crawled on hands and knees to the center of the wagon out of her range of vision.

"Annette, come here," she whispered excitedly.

"What?" she asked softly, responding to the urgency in her mistress's tone.

"Look at that wagon. A cowboy and a young woman crawled inside. I think they are going to . . . you know."

A mischievous light dawned in Annette's eyes. *"Oui?"*

"Yes," Leslie said, giggling in response to Annette's obvious delight.

Annette leaned out the window to get a better look, almost lost her balance, and squealed. Leslie grabbed her and pulled her back in. "Not so far!" Leslie gasped, breathless.

"Pardon, mademoiselle," she whispered, giggling. She righted

herself, and they watched in silence for a few moments. Leslie
Powers frequently surprised Annette. This time because she was
not a simpering ninny the way so many of her gently reared contemporaries were. Thanks to her mother's excellent common sense
and careful preparations, Leslie knew far more than most young
ladies her age about what went on between grown men and their
women, and far more about all of life's experiences than her sheltered peers.

According to her grandmother Eliza, Leslie's mother's liberal
approach in raising Leslie constituted laxness. Letting Leslie run
wild among museums and theaters and other worldly places
showed "an unprecedented lack of parental vigilance." In spite of
grandmother Eliza's howls of outrage, Leslie had grown into an
inscrutable combination of audacity, intelligence, and innocence.
Even Eliza had to admit that she appeared to be a well-conducted
young lady for all her notions about 'painting' and artistic expression.

In reality, Leslie was dedicated to becoming an outstanding
landscape painter. She had not chosen this goal lightly. She knew
it would mean working long hours and studying for years to perfect
her technique and learn the craft.

Leslie's attention drifted back to the street beneath the window.
Nothing was moving in the wagon in the alley. From the window
she could see the round, platelike turntable where they turned the
locomotives. Down on the railroad tracks, a boxcar with its doors
gaping open waited to be filled with milling, noisy cargo. The
shiny black locomotive breathed heavily, sending up wads of
smoke so dense that they looked like puffs of blue-gray cotton
above the stack.

Immediately below she could see the parade officials working at
clearing the wagons, buggies, horses, and people off the dusty
boulevard so that the parade could begin. Men shouted remarks—
some good-natured, some lewd—but no one seemed to take offense. She decided that the women who lived here had given up
trying to civilize the ruffians who came into town. There were
parts of Boston that were rough and undisciplined like this—every
big city had its slum and its slum dwellers. Unfortunately, it appeared that in Phoenix there was no separation between the ruffians and the more genteel citizens or between the saloons and the
churches.

To the east she could see where fences cut the land into neat
squares. To the south the streets of the town fell into a scattering of

rude hovels. Beyond the last sparse cluster of square boxlike shacks was the inevitable desert, reaching away into infinity, it seemed, gray and brown and covered with what her uncle called chaparral or greasewood or mesquite. Phoenix was not really a city, merely a cluster of already dilapidated frame buildings surrounding a row of stores and saloons and one real building—the hotel she was in.

Annette giggled, and Leslie's attention was drawn back to the wagon. "What did I miss?"

"See?" Annette whispered. "His *pantalon*!"

"His pants?" Leslie repeated, covering her mouth. This was the most excitement she had experienced since the train robbery. She felt like she was back in school participating in some delicious naughtiness. "He took off his pants?"

"See, zay are zere," she said, pointing to one pant leg that was carelessly thrown over the tailgate of the wagon.

Leslie searched the crowd below, but no one seemed to be paying any attention to the wagon. She peered into it, but she could see nothing. Beyond the Bricewood West and the dirty rooftops of the town's buildings there was nothing to look at that brought a sense of joy or exuberance to the eye. It was just a dirty little town in the middle of a hard, hot, flat desert with unbearably hot days and cold nights, but inside the hotel was another matter entirely. The Bricewood West was a small version of the Plaza in New York City. Its Garden Courtyard with vaulted ceiling of translucent glass was the equal of anything she had seen anywhere. Even in the short time she had been here, Leslie could tell that the hotel's Garden Courtyard had become a cultural and social center for the town's residents. People congregated beneath the large overhead fans to relax amid towering potted palms and graceful ferns. It was an oasis of civilization in the midst of filth and squalor.

There was still nothing to see in the wagon. She thought she detected a slight swaying motion and blushed to think what that might mean. Annette still leaned out the window. Sighing, Leslie straightened and scanned the horizon where she knew the river curved around Phoenix to the northeast. Younger had called it the Verde River. "Those red devils used to be thick as thieves along this stretch," he had said as they had ridden past a thick stand of alfalfa that grew along the banks. She could imagine half-naked Indians reaping the wild grasses that grew in the rich loam along the river bottoms.

If she squinted and blocked out the encroaching cluster of

houses, the desert was almost pretty. It had a sort of sparse elegance about it, an immenseness of its own that was awesome, almost grand, but it could never equal for her the cool green beauty
of precise landscaping and sparkling white houses, so perfect with
their pitched roofs and their cavernous front porches. She loved
big Gothic houses with turrets, gables, cornices, and flying but-
tresses. There were mysteries in houses like that, sometimes a secret cellar off the back porch with its two wooden doors opening
onto damp, dark, blackness that could go down and down indefinitely.

Annette squealed, and Leslie's attention was drawn instantly
back to Phoenix, only to find that Annette's excited squeak was
occasioned by her almost losing her footing again.

So much for adventure, Leslie thought ruefully. The only hint of
that had been the train robbery she'd witnessed. The only man in
Phoenix who even looked interesting so far was in that wagon
making love to someone else. She scolded herself for even thinking about such things, but with men like Dallas Younger around,
who would blame her for looking? There was little opportunity for
romance in a town that looked like it could have been built in three
days by an inexperienced box maker. Unless, of course, you were
a peasant girl who would cavort in broad daylight with strangers.
Leslie smiled at herself. Was she jealous?

Annette nudged her and giggled. "Zey are coming out," she
whispered, her voice breathless.

Leslie leaned out the window to see. The young man helped the
girl down. She was clinging to him, her face dewy and adoring.
She snuggled close against him; he kissed her on the forehead
briefly, placed his hat on his head, and they walked toward the
crowded street.

Leslie didn't stop to think about decorum. She leaned out the
window and yelled. The man looked up, and they waved at him,
then burst into giggles. The girl on the street turned bright red. The
man grinned and waved back at them.

Gasping and giggling, Annette and Leslie collapsed across the
bed. "Do you think he will recognize us if he sees us again?" Leslie asked when their laughter had subsided.

Annette clapped her hands over her mouth, her eyes round and
mischievously questioning. She shrugged.

"Did you ever see that young man you were so interested in?
What was his name, John?"

Annette sighed. *"Non."*

Leslie grinned. "Still hoping?"

Annette shrugged and wiggled her body in an unconsciously provocative way. "*Oui* . . . but of course."

"Well, why don't you walk down to the railroad offices and see if you can stumble onto him?"

Annette looked horrified. "*Mademoiselle!* I am a lady!"

Leslie snorted. "Ladies don't almost fall out of windows to watch things they shouldn't even be aware of. Besides, if you don't ever take matters into your own hands, you may be an old maid. He looked too shy to ever approach you. . . ."

There was faint horror in Annette's eyes as she contemplated becoming the aggressor. "Then I shall be. But I don't think so. . . . He will come to me. . . ."

Leslie sighed. "I hope you're right."

CHAPTER
SEVEN

The Bull Whiskey Saloon was crowded to overflowing with the gay holiday crowd. "Parade's coming!" someone yelled.

"Yahoo! Let's see them purty girls!"

The boisterous crowd surged out the double swinging doors. Ward and Doug were hanging back, taking their time. When they finally took their places at the edge of the wide street the first participants were at the north end of town.

Raucous yells greeted two pretty Mexican *señoritas* who rode in all their finery, supporting a red and white banner twelve feet in length that announced the *Fiesta Days Parade*. They were followed by a dozen colorfully dressed *señoritas*: walking, swinging their wide skirts, smiling gaily. The girls on the outside, near the crowd, were throwing flowers that must have been imported from eastern nurseries.

Next came an open carriage with four local politicians waving their hats, smiling widely; then three ornately dressed *vaqueros* looking like Spanish *conquistadores*, their heavy, silver-studded chaps and saddle skirts shimmering in the late afternoon sun.

The *vaqueros* were followed by a choir of young girls and boys dressed in long white robes, singing a song that *gringos* wouldn't

recognize. Their angelic faces were lifted heavenward in shining
piety, which wrenched a chuckle and a ribald comment from Doug
Paggett.

"Hey, Ward, how would you like to have those three chinchil-
las in the front row—all at once? Wouldn't that be something?"

Ward only smiled and lifted an eyebrow. He liked the young
ones but not that young. Doug Paggett, with his unruly shock of
black hair and his mustache, looked older than Ward, but he was
actually several years younger. He seemed a lot younger sometimes, when they were with females. He seemed to go out of control, no longer resembling the cool-headed second lieutenant who
(without destroying the contents) could set a charge of dynamite to
blow any safe the Texas and Pacific could devise.

The choir was followed by a procession of papier-mâché statuary, elaborately shaped and painted to resemble the busts of famous revolutionary Mexican leaders. The colorful busts bobbed
along on thin brown legs and were followed by a long red-and-
yellow paper dragon that weaved from one side of the street to the
other, exactly like a sidewinder, propelled by at least a hundred
legs, the humps on its colorful back undulating like waves on the
ocean. Doug laughed delightedly—probably, Ward decided, having the time of his life trying to decide which of those young brown
dragon legs belonged to girls.

The dragon was followed by a Mexican band playing loud, pa-
triotic music, and then by a contingent of dark-garbed riders that
brought a hush over the crowd. At least fifteen men, resplendent in
silver-edged black charro suits, riding sleek-looking blooded stal-
lions and armed to the teeth, with two guns at every waist and
a rifle sheath on every saddle, rode behind a girl dressed like a
Spanish queen, her beautiful gold dress gleaming in the afternoon
sunlight, her carriage as proud on the stately white horse as any
queen. Ward recognized her as one of the females who had
laughed at him when he was leaving Maria's wagon.

One of the men beside Ward cursed. "Powers got himself a new
woman?"

Another man laughed softly. "Naw! She ain't Powers's woman.
B'longs to Dallas Younger. That must be the little filly from back
east I heard him braggin' about last night."

Someone else spoke up, also softly, since it wouldn't be healthy
to be openly contemptuous. "They got a lotta guts marching in the
parade. Anyone who's done the folks around here the way they
have should be in jail!"

Ward, who hadn't been in Phoenix for at least two years and wasn't aware of any changes that might have been taking place, felt an instinctive tightening of muscles in his broad back, which he made a conscious effort to relax. Politics didn't interest him— not even politics like the Powers Ranch played so openly. Ward vowed not to get involved in other people's business, but habits were strong, especially survival habits. His eyes narrowed, and he studied each face in that slow-moving group of misfits. They were the roughest he had seen since riding with the Jackson Hole Gang. They made the Clantons look like choirboys. Three of them he recognized; the rest he would remember next time he saw them.

The girl on the white horse was riding from side to side in the wide street, tossing flowers at the smiling faces in the crowd. When she zigzagged across to Ward's side of the street, she looked at the crowd and their eyes met. She recognized him as the man she'd seen climbing into and out of the wagon with the pretty Mexican girl, and he remembered her as the one Belen had almost torn into when they had robbed the Texas and Pacific. He had watched her without her knowledge on the train because she was one of those rare women who seem comfortable within themselves. She probably hadn't seen him because she didn't have searching eyes.

When he had boarded the train in Tucson, he had seen her talking in her quiet way with her lady's maid, and he had appreciated her friendliness and openness. It struck him then that she was one of those singular women without guile. She looked relaxed and composed—like a beautiful swan who would ride a choppy lake as serenely as a placid one. During the train robbery, he had been impressed again, because it had been obvious that while she might be amused by the excitement of a lifestyle wilder than her own, she was not in the least tempted by it. She could be mischievous when the mood struck her, he thought, remembering the way she had leaned out that window to taunt him. . . .

She was prettier than he remembered. She had exquisite coloring, but it didn't take a connoisseur to appreciate coal-black hair and creamy white skin, especially when the gown she wore made it apparent that she was as graceful and comely of limb as she was of face.

"Which one is Younger?" he asked of the lantern-jawed, mustached man who had said she was Younger's woman.

"The one on that dun. Thinks he's a real ladies' man!" he snorted. "Dallas Younger is Powers' foreman. Want my opinion—it's not 'cause he's hell on cows!"

Younger had no doubt earned his reputation. There was a healthy arrogance in his lithe frame that was easy to identify. The man wasn't afraid of man or beast, and it was apparent from the look on his handsome face that he wasn't often required to prove it. One look from those steel gray eyes would discourage anyone but the most suicidal.

Ward couldn't tell, when the lady's eyes caught and held his, whether the stirring he felt was his innate competitiveness or a response to the look in her eyes: a look that fluctuated between chagrin at her own position, recognition of him, and mild interest.

He didn't have time to dwell on it beyond that one instant because a feisty little red dog pushed past them, ignoring his owner's shout, "No, Pepito! No!" and ran into the dusty street, straight at the front legs of the silky white Arabian.

The playful mutt, an alley mixture of terrier and anonymous parentage, nipped at the sleek white fetlocks, barking ferociously. The big white horse, naturally nervous and high-strung, reared, almost unseating the startled girl. Leslie, caught off guard, with her hands more occupied by the basket of flowers than the reins, screamed and dropped everything in her scramble to keep from being thrown.

Without thinking, Ward leaped forward and grabbed the reins she had dropped before they hit the ground. He dragged the horse's head down before he could bolt and then looked up, expecting to see relief on the girl's face. But Leslie was mortified and angry. Not at the man who had saved her, but at herself for agreeing to ride in this stupid parade and to throw stupid flowers at people who looked like they resented her. She had been painfully conscious of the open hostility rippling through the crowd as they passed by. Since she had gotten herself into this mess and couldn't think of any way to get out of it, she had forced herself to concentrate on the faces of the guilelessly adoring children. But when she had almost been thrown, the adults had made themselves felt, cautiously. She had seen, all in a flash, smiles of triumph and open snickers, and her anger now caused her to jerk the reins out of Ward's hands and turn the horse sharply, accidentally knocking him down. Leslie watched in mounting horror as one atrocity seemed to follow another.

Her scream had brought Dallas Younger and her uncle to her side. Before she could react, her uncle shouted an order, cursing savagely while she watched, speechless with fear and anger, as

Younger pulled his rifle from its sheath and used it like a club on the man who was just coming to his feet.

"No! No!" she screamed frantically, but if they heard her outraged cries over the mounting roar of the crowd, they ignored them. Ward slumped limply into the powdery gray dust. Powers's men formed a threatening phalanx behind Younger, and the crowd that had started to surge forward stopped, quieted.

"No harm done here!" Younger yelled at the row upon row of resentful faces. "Get that bastard out of the way! This is a parade! Not a damned side show!"

Doug Paggett, who had been on the verge of drawing his gun, thought better of it in the face of the determined and concerted opposition and rushed forward to drag his friend's limp form out of the street.

The Powers contingent moved slowly forward, but Leslie felt like a statue, stiff and pale, her flowers forgotten in the dirt. She could not believe what her eyes had seen! Dallas Younger, who had seemed perfectly normal, at least for Arizona, had practically killed that man just for trying to save her from an embarrassing spill!

Dazed, she rode stiffly, until her senses began to return. With a conscious effort to still the wild pounding of her heart, she stopped her horse and started to turn it. That man might be crude and churlish, making love to Mexican girls in broad daylight, but he had tried to help her!

"Heah! What the hell you doing?"

"I'm going back there!"

"Like hell you are! You're a Powers. Sit up straight!"

Leslie's mouth dropped open. She couldn't believe her ears. Her uncle was talking to her exactly like he talked to the Mexican servants in his kitchen.

Powers grabbed the reins from her nerveless fingers and the parade moved forward again. Leslie was a captive wedged in between her uncle and Dallas Younger, whose flat gray eyes shot her a warning look.

Doug Paggett and the man who had been most vocal about the Powers outfit half carried, half dragged, Ward Cantrell into the deserted saloon.

"He hurt bad?"

"Cain't tell for sure. He's breathin' though," Doug said,

frowning down at his friend. Uncharacteristically, his hands trembled at the thought that Cantrell might be badly injured.

The stranger parted the tawny hair on Ward's head and peered knowingly at his scalp. He repeated this until he satisfied himself he had uncovered the entire area.

"'Pears to be all right. Got a concussion sure, though."

"Those bastards!" Doug swore. "I saw who did it. I'm gonna kill him!"

"Better leave well enough alone," the man said kindly. "They've killed men for a lot less than accosting one of their womenfolk! They don't ride alone."

"Jesus!" Doug picked up an unfinished drink off the table above Ward and held it to Ward's lips. He spilled some of the liquid into Ward's slack mouth and was rewarded with a groan. Ward's eyes opened tentatively, focused on the worried face of his friend, then closed. The light behind Doug was a blinding ache to Ward's tortured skull. He could feel his brain throbbing with each heartbeat.

"You all right?"

Ward squinted at Doug. "What happened?" he groaned.

"You ain't hung over, that's for sure! You got hit on the head!"

Ward reached up and touched his head, wincing.

"That bitch hit me?" he asked, his memory slowly returning.

"'Twarn't her," the stranger volunteered. "She just knocked you down so's he could hit you—Younger!"

"The hell you say? Who the hell is Younger?" he asked, not remembering they had already gone over this earlier.

"Powers's strawboss. Texan. Right dangerous with a gun, from what I hear."

Ward struggled into a sitting position. He tried to stand, but his legs didn't respond. It took him two tries before he made it.

"Hey! What the hell do you think you're gonna do?" Doug demanded, not liking the look on his friend's face.

"I'm going to kill that bastard Younger," Ward said grimly.

The stranger, a long-faced New England type, shook his head. "Wouldn't try that if'n I was you, mister. Younger ain't about to meet you alone, 'cause he don't have to. Powers has fifty men in town right now, and half of them are gunfighters."

"Fifty men?" Ward asked, squinting at the man.

"At least fifty." He nodded.

"Whatcha gonna do, Ward?" Doug asked.

Ward rubbed his neck, turning it from side to side to see if it still worked. "I'm going to finish my drink and then see about dinner."

"What about Younger?"

"Someday we'll meet when I don't have a headache and he doesn't have fifty men with him," he said quietly.

CHAPTER
EIGHT

Leslie rode sidesaddle beside Annette, keeping the subdued Frenchwoman between her and the others like a buffer, avoiding Younger and his attempts to placate her with cheerful conversation.

The sun set, and the desert, ever responsive, cooled. Chill night air fanned her flushed cheeks, and her agitation slowly diminished with the exertion of the ride. It was dark when they reached the ranch. A silver wedge was rising over the mountains to the east. The ranch house sat like a fortress on the hill, glistening under the stars.

They climbed the gentle slope quickly, the horses as eager as Leslie to end this ride. Once inside the protective walls, she dismounted and relinquished her reins to the young Mexican boys who ran out to greet the horsemen. Uncle Mark, apparently anticipating her, stepped up onto the wooden porch where he towered over her. "Go to my office, young lady," he said, his manner brusque.

Determined not to be cowed by him, Leslie swept past Younger, ignoring the hand he extended to help her up the stairs. She preceded her uncle into the room he used as an office and watched in silence as he settled himself into the big leather chair behind the desk. He had arranged his features into a conciliatory mask, but he fairly reeked with the self-confidence of a man who could not lose.

"Now, Leslie," he said. "You wanted to talk to me?"

Her hands tightened on the edge of the chair and she leaned forward. "I want you to buy me out so I can go back home," she said quickly.

"Uh-huh," he said. "And what do you think of the ranch?" he asked.

"What do you mean?"

"Well, you are your father's heir. It is, roughly speaking, half yours."

"I don't understand," she said softly.

"Well," he said. "You will appreciate that a half-interest in a steer cannot be divided until the steer is either slaughtered or sold to a third party for money."

"Yes, sir, I understand that," Leslie said, feeling uncomfortable, "but the ranch isn't a steer."

"Your father owned an undivided half-interest in this ranch. And frankly, Leslie, I don't think you could manage your half of the ranch," he said, smiling at the ridiculousness of her struggling with the myriad details involved.

Irritated at his obvious pleasure in what he saw as her incompetence, she leaned forward. "There is no need. If you would only purchase my half from me . . ."

"I have no intentions of selling or dividing any part of the ranch," he said gruffly. "This is my home! And while you may have an interest in the ranch, there is no way for you to turn that interest into money without my cooperation. Your signature on any document attempting that would be as worthless as a pile of grama grass in wheat country," he declared, slamming his fist onto his desk.

"I understand your desire to keep the ranch together, Uncle Mark," she said, controlling herself with an effort. "But I was hoping we could reach an agreement where you would purchase my interest for an amount that would be less than its actual value."

"Cash is not something we keep in great quantities. Cash is for buying cows. I can turn my money over many times by putting it into cows. And without my signature, your interest is totally without value. However," he said, holding up his hand to forestall her heated words, "you are my brother's daughter, and I have no intention of keeping you from enjoying your inheritance. You are welcome here as long as you live, Leslie."

"What? What do you mean?" she asked, incredulous.

"Your father and I spent our life's blood to build this ranch. It was always his wish that you should live here with him. I see no other way to resolve this impasse." He shrugged. "My only wish is to take care of you. I can't do that if you're gallivanting around in some city where a body can't see the sky for the haze." He leaned back in his chair, his face darkened by a look of righteous indignation. He crossed his arms over his chest, determined to get through what he saw as an unpleasant duty to an ungrateful and bothersome relative.

Recognizing that stubborn look for what it was, Leslie nearly despaired. She was not accustomed to having her wishes entirely disregarded. But time and again since arriving in Phoenix she had discussed matters with her uncle only to find either instantly or later that he hadn't taken her seriously at all, as if he were listening to a child.

Now, grim with parental purpose and righteousness, Mark Powers sat like a block of granite—impervious to reason—determined to "take care of her."

"I am not a child," Leslie said grimly.

"I never had any children of my own, Leslie, but I do know that children need guidance. I don't hold with that newfangled horse baloney your mother put such store in. You might want to read the law of the land. It'll be clear to you that I'm the one who'll be held responsible for you," he said, leaning forward. "I happen to be your legal guardian."

"I'm nineteen years old!" she protested.

"An unmarried woman needs a guardian until she reaches majority. As your only surviving relative in this territory, I am your guardian. My dear, it behooves me to care for you until you marry a fine young man who will father children my brother would be proud of."

Leslie leaned back in the chair, feeling the room closing in on her. Face pale and glowing, she sat forward. "And I suppose your being my guardian also entitles you to pick my husband for me?"

Something unrecognizable glittered in his jade green eyes, and Leslie paled. Her uncle, though his veneer of earnest regard had not worn through, frightened her suddenly. Was it possible she had skipped blithely off the train and into a trap? Had this man purposely lured her here, knowing all the time that he fully intended to toss her like a bone to his lusty foreman?

His eyes were guarded again. "I would respect your wishes insofar as that is reasonable, but I could not allow you to marry someone who would be a detriment to you."

Leslie could barely speak around the knot that had formed in her throat. "You mean you want me to marry an asset like Dallas Younger," she said bitterly.

Her uncle's brows crowded his eyes in a scowl. "Well, Dallas would make you a fine husband, no doubt about that."

"And if I refuse?"

He shrugged. "You may marry or not, as you wish. Obviously I do not expect you to manage your own financial interests. A woman needs a man to do those things for her."

A dozen angry responses trembled on her lips, but now there was triumph glittering undisguised in Powers's small green eyes. Leslie stood up and turned to leave the room, but her uncle's sanctimonious words stopped her.

"Leslie, few things are asked of you. You live a remarkably carefree existence, but keep in mind that obedience is an important virtue in a young lady."

"Have I been disobedient?" Leslie asked, her voice little more than a whisper.

He paused, and his lips tightened. "It's not safe for you to venture out alone," he said, ignoring her question. "When you want to leave the ranch you're to ask permission. Am I understood?" A sly look crept into his eyes.

"Or what?" she demanded.

"Don't get uppity with me, Leslie. You just do as you're told. When you go out I want two of Younger's men with you to protect you."

"Protect me?" she gasped. "From what?"

"From danger! From Indians! How the hell should I know from what? From whatever threatens you!" he said furiously, his face turning beet red.

Back in her room, as Leslie dressed for bed, she realized that her uncle planned to gain her half-interest in the ranch by either keeping her prisoner or forcing her to marry Dallas Younger. She feared that there was almost nothing she could do about it, unless she was willing to sign everything over to him. He would have no need of her then.

Leslie toyed with the idea, but something stubborn and intractable in her rejected that choice. She might have to fall back on that, and she would before she would allow herself to be forced into a marriage pact with that barbarian Dallas Younger.

CHAPTER
NINE

Ward had been riding for three hours, and it was mid-morning with the sun already beating down when he got his first glimpse of the Mendoza farm. It was exactly as he remembered it—like a pencil drawing in a magazine he'd seen when Arizona was still a place to be read about. The small adobe house looked like a pueblo with small windows, squatting at the base of the mountain. He could see a horse in the corral, two shaggy cows in a pen, and multicolored chickens pecking at the hard ground. The house was on the east side of the mountain and would be shaded from the afternoon sun.

There was a new barbed-wire fence enclosing both the *casa* and the garden where the Mendozas grew the vegetables for their table. Food was plentiful because Mama had built her house next to a natural artesian well and taught young Pedro to dig shallow ditches to irrigate the small plot. Even the ancient one, Grandpapa, helped with the garden.

Ward stopped on a rise in the desert, amid the yellowed sand and the dark tumbleweed, in the shade of a saguaro. It had been a long time since he had been there—too long probably. It felt like homecoming in his chest. It was a good feeling.

He smiled. Mama was probably still fighting off the young *vaqueros* from her pretty daughter. If he remembered right, Isabel must be almost nineteen by now. She had been fifteen when Mama had found him delirious in the desert and packed him home to tend his bullet wound. He would have died without her help. He had taken a bullet in the back when he and the gang were fleeing from a posse. He had bled heavily and could not keep up the pace necessary to get to safety before the posse overtook them. He had veered off in another direction, lost the pursuers, who hadn't noticed his breaking away, and collapsed sometime during the night. By morning, he was watching the buzzards circling overhead. By high noon they had formed a ring around him, and occasionally one of the brave ones would waddle clumsily toward him and he would shoot it. Mama had arrived in the afternoon, when he was so weak he could barely move. She hadn't asked any questions. She had

simply shoved him up onto her horse, tied him on, and hurried
back to her home, where she spent many weeks nursing him back
to health.

Isabel, her daughter, was young and skittish and eager to test her
charms on Ward. He had been younger then, and, if possible, even
more responsive to the enticing jiggle of a willing female. Isabel
had followed him everywhere when he was strong enough to begin
moving around. If he shoed a horse, she was underfoot. If he tried
to take a nap, she would accidentally drop something to wake him.
When he spoke, she hung on every word. And being male, he had
known that he could have her. He had contemplated it in his mind
and rejected it. Once his strength returned, and with it his desire
for a woman, she brought him more than one sleepless night.

One afternoon, while Mama was in town and Pedro and his
grandfather were away from the *casa*, Isabel fixed his lunch and
the two of them sat at the table talking.

Isabel giggled too much and flirted in the breathless, excited
way young, inexperienced girls did, and Ward was flattered, but
he knew enough about girls to know that while Isabel might enjoy
the thought of his making love to her, she would not be prepared
for the actuality of it. She was just testing her equipment on him to
see if it worked. He flirted with her and enjoyed her attention, but
he did not take her seriously, even though it would have relieved
him greatly if he could have ignored his own sense of responsibility to her and the woman who had saved his life.

The thought of Mama always brought a smile to his lips. She
was fierce and devout, and she would not tolerate having her
daughter taken lightly. The second time he had visited with them,
long after the gunshot wound had healed, Mama had seen the way his
blue eyes watched her Isabel, and she had sent the girl outside to
work in the garden with her brother.

"Señor Ward, you are my guest. I have taken you in when you
would have died. I treated your wound, fed you, prayed for you,
bathed your head when you raved with the fever, but I will not let
you sleep with my Isabel. She is a good girl but foolish where men
are concerned. She would be easy for one as handsome as you.
You have the ways and the looks to tempt young girls."

Ward started to protest his innocence, but Mama stopped him
with a raised hand.

"I know what you are going to say, and it is not necessary. You
see, I am not blind, and I know that you have respected my daughter in spite of her clumsy attempts to have you do otherwise."

Ward was suddenly grateful that he had nothing serious to hide from this woman. Her eyes were too direct and he would never be able to lie to her convincingly. He returned her steady look with one of his own. "It pleases me that you have seen this," he said, meaning it.

She snorted. "I am not so old or so foolish that I cannot remember the fever in young blood! You want my Isabel, and you are very fair. She is much affected. I see it in the sway of her skinny hips when you watch her. She prances like a young doe. I have also seen that while you found her attractive and available, you chose to put my interests and the girl's above your own. For that, Señor Ward, I am grateful. You are a man of honor. It would grieve me sorely if it were otherwise."

Ward flushed. He felt suddenly as if she could read his mind. "*Señora* Mendoza, I'm a hunted outlaw," he reminded her, his voice unaccountably husky. "I didn't shoot myself. . . ."

Now her round face with the knowing eyes came alive with its intensity. "Honor is a thing of the soul, not of circumstance," she said flatly. From that day forward she called him thee and thou, and he called her Mama.

Originally, the interior of the Mendoza house had consisted of one big room used as three rooms: a kitchen and two bedrooms, separated by sheets for privacy. The kitchen was as big as both other rooms, and it was in there that Mama Mendoza had spread a pallet on the floor for him. Two years ago he and Pedro had built a wooden lean-to at the back of the house so that Pedro and Grandpapa could share a room, while Isabel and Mama shared another, returning the orginal house to its function as kitchen and cultural center.

They didn't speak of Isabel again, but Ward continued to protect the lovely young creature, even though she severely tested his resolve from time to time. In the last four years the Mendozas had become like family, until now they were all he wanted or needed. And they suited his lifestyle. He could drop in whenever he felt the need and always be assured of a welcome.

Although he still had family in New York City—aunts, uncles, cousins—there was no one he cared to communicate with, no one who had claim to his heart the way Jenn had. He hadn't written to or heard from anyone, not even his sister, since he had joined the cavalry. It had been, as he thought back on it, melodramatic and immature, but at the time it had seemed entirely right.

Now he could smile about such foolishness, but at the time he joined the cavalry, he had been deadly serious. He didn't get serious about things anymore. He didn't take on fifty men to prove he was a man, and he didn't fight over women who meant nothing to him. He was an outlaw and a killer of men, not a crusader.

Ward's mental wandering jolted to an end when Isabel saw him riding over the rise . She dropped the vegetables she had been gathering and ran excitedly into the house yelling to her *madre*. "Mama! Mama! Ward is coming!"

Mama Mendoza glanced up from the sock she was mending. Isabel's pretty face was flushed with excitement. Mama knew Isabel probably loved Ward Cantrell more than she loved Pedro, because to Isabel, Ward was gossip, excitement, gifts, tender interest, and an attractive man to tease and torment but who was safe and admiring. Mama sighed. What could be more perfect than that? Mama Mendoza got heavily to her feet, relief washing over her features for just a moment before she allowed her pleasure to show. "Run meet him, silly chicken. See if I care!" she said, smiling. The girl would do so anyway—no matter what. She was like a three-year-old when Ward came.

Isabel ran from the small adobe house, wiping her hands and poking at her hair, trying frantically to arrange the long straight hair into something less childish. In her haste to greet Ward it bounced and flew around her face, and she gave up.

Ward spurred his horse into a run and met her under the cottonwood trees. He dismounted, gave her a friendly bearhug, and swung her around, telling her how pretty she was while she, overcome with happiness, smothered him with kisses.

"Guess what, Ward! Guess!" she demanded, leaning back in the circle of his arms.

He grinned. "I know. You are married and you have six children and one of them, a boy, looks like me. You ran out here to warn me because your husband is going to shoot me."

"No, *idiota*! Foolish talk is not what I want to hear. Guess, really!" she said vehemently, stamping her pretty foot.

"I can't imagine what could bring such a flush to your pretty cheeks unless there is a new man in your life," he said, laughing.

"Guess, really!" she begged, pinching his arm.

Mama walked toward their nonsense, shaking her head. They were like playful bear cubs together: Ward refusing to guess to torment her and Isabel pinching and hitting him while he laughed and fended her off.

Mama came into the middle of this, and Ward set the playful Isabel aside to give Mama a hug.

"It's good to be home," Ward said, meaning it. Mama hugged him tightly and stepped back, smiling at him. She was trying to be cheerful, but it was apparent to Ward that she was troubled. He made a note to ask her later about the changes he had already sensed. But for now, he did not want to spoil Isabel's fun.

Grinning, with Isabel bouncing excitedly at his side, Ward turned to the bulging saddlebags he had on the rump of his horse. The big black stamped and pawed the ground. He had smelled the cool clear water and was eager to get to it.

"Pedro!" Mama yelled.

"*Sí*, Mama?" The answer came from the small lean-to behind the house that served as a barn for the animals and the horse that Pedro rode to town for supplies. At night it was a roost also for the chickens.

"Come at once, Pedro!" Isabel yelled. "*Señor* Ward has come!"

The young man who joined them was a surprise for Ward. Pedro had grown into a young man. Last summer he had been seventeen and a beanpole. Now he had filled out and was a handsome lad with the same friendly brown eyes that Isabel had. Mama was squat and plain, with nothing of beauty in her face, but her children were comely.

"He is almost a man, no?" Isabel asked proudly.

"Welcome, *Señor* Ward." Pedro grinned. "Mama and Isabel speak often of you. We prayed for your safe return."

"Thank you, Pedro. It is good to be back." Ward held out his hand solemnly, and the young man took it, pleased to be treated like an equal by this man he admired, loved, and worried about. Pedro had heard the stories about Ward Cantrell, and he had asked Mama about them, because he had seen outlaws who had been hanged by the neck. Their bodies had been laid out on the sidewalk in Phoenix for all to take warning. *Señor* Ward was the only adult male who had ever taken an interest in him. Ward had spent much time showing him how to care for the horse he had bought for him, how to mend the fine leather saddle that had been his last gift, even how to clean and care for himself properly. The thought of this man, with his smiling eyes and his ready humor stilled forever, lying on some sidewalk, cold and stiff, with arms folded across his chest, displayed in death as a warning to others, had filled him with anger and despair. When he had asked Mama about his fears, he had been puzzled and then pleased with her explanation: "God does not have accidents. He assigns each man to his task, and it is only important that he do it well."

And from the stories Pedro heard when he went into town, it was apparent to him that *Señor* Ward did his task very well indeed. Pedro took Ward's horse to water and care for him, and Ward followed Mama inside, with Isabel still imploring him to guess her secret.

"Tell me your secret, or I will keep all my gifts," Ward teased her.

"Give me my gift, or I will not tell you ever!" she countered happily. There was too much loneliness in her heart not to squeeze every ounce of affection and attention from this handsome *gringo* she loved.

Ward relented and dropped to his knees to beg her to share her secret. "I have a *novio*," she rushed to tell him. "A young man from what Mama calls 'a good family,' " she said, dimpling. "And we have received permission from our parents to be married in the church at Christmas."

"Isabel, how could you?" Ward demanded, feigning injury. He clutched his heart and looked stricken, and Isabel burst into peals of wicked laughter. When she stopped laughing he took her aside, and she sobered.

"This young man, do you love him?"

Her eyes widened. "*Sí*, I love him so much I would die for him."

Ward frowned. "Does he love you?"

A smile lighted her face, and it was like the sun breaking through dense clouds unexpectedly. "*Sí.*"

"Is he good to you?"

She nodded and he could tell by the smile that she was not lying. "Does he have a job? Some way to take care of you?"

"*Sí*, his papa is a landowner. He works very hard. That is why I do not see him so very often. . . ."

"Does he treat you with respect?"

"Unfortunately he does. . . ." She smiled, nodding, her face flushed with pleasure at the opportunity to talk about her *novio*, and Ward relaxed, content that all was well.

Everyone loved Ward's gifts: a pretty gown with dress-up shoes for Isabel, a rifle for Pedro, wine and tobacco for Grandpapa, and a new shawl for Mama Manuela with two hundred dollars in five-dollar bills tucked inside. To her that was a year's worth of security.

After dinner Isabel proudly brought out a large basket piled high with white satin. Her eyes wide with wonder at the fine lustrous fabric, she explained to Ward that it was to be her wedding gown. It had taken her and Mama a week to cut the numerous pieces from the bolt of fabric Ward's last generous gift of money had bought for them. "We will never finish it," she wailed. "Never!"

Ward looked at Mama with alarm and fished into his pants. He dragged out a handful of bills and gave them all to Isabel. "Hire some seamstresses," he said, scowling. "I don't want you walking down the aisle in a half-finished gown."

Mama slapped his hand. "Put thy money away. That is her way of telling thee she wants thee to help with the sewing." She laughed. Pedro snorted at the thought of Ward Cantrell, a famous gunfighter, sewing with women.

"You need my help, little one?"

Isabel shrugged, appalled at what she had started.

Ward looked from Pedro's contorted face to Isabel's. "Well," he said, "don't just stand there. Get me a needle."

Isabel squealed with delight and rushed to comply. Pedro scowled his disbelief, but Ward cuffed him lightly and followed Isabel, watching intently as she threaded a needle for him. Pedro, seeing Ward's example, sighed and took the next needle from his sister's hands. Delighted, Mama got both of them started, and then settled down at the table across from Ward. She sewed and watched Ward, his big, deft hands working so carefully in the delicate fabric, and it gave her much pleasure that he set such a good example for her son. Pedro was too prone to take his sister lightly.

Laughing, giggling, saying outrageous things to one another, they sewed at the table, huddled around the brightest lamp until their backs were cramped. Mama laid her sewing aside, sighed, then patted the worn wood of the table with her chubby brown hand, causing Ward to look up from his stitching. "Is there a woman whose face thou carryest in thy heart?"

Startled, Ward scowled. The face that flashed into memory at her question was Jenn's. "No," he said grimly, knowing that she was hoping for a sweetheart, not a sister.

Mama sighed, disappointed. "That is most tragic—thou wouldst make a fine husband and father." Isabel nodded in agreement, but Pedro looked pleased that Ward had not become anything as boring as that. He wanted adventure and excitement for himself and his friend.

Ward shook his head. "I'm an outlaw, remember?"

Mama ignored his words. "What dost thou want for thyself? More than just being a fugitive . . ."

Ward stopped sewing and fingered the white satin. "I want a home," he said softly, meeting Mama's gaze.

At first, after Simone's death, he had rejected all symbols of commitment, but after six years his wounds had healed. He was tired of running, hungry for a piece of land . . . a house . . . a woman to meet him at the door, shading her face against the setting sun, welcoming him with quiet eyes, maybe even a child to run down the steps to fling his small body at him crying, "Daddy, Daddy . . ."

A hollow ache started inside him. He had surprised himself. Mama saw it and was the one to break up the group, sending Pedro and Isabel to bed. "Go, shoo, the sun comes up at the same time, no matter when you go to bed, and you are both hard to wake."

Grumbling, they kissed Ward good-night and went to their separate pallets. Mama carefully folded the sewn fabric and put the basket away. Ward poured himself a cup of coffee and sat down at the table beside her. He had noticed a new set of frown lines around Mama's mouth and that her eyes darted to the window repeatedly, even when she was pretending to be relaxed. "You look tense, Mama."

"Thou didst see the fence?"

"Problems?"

"*Sí. Señor* Powers wants my water for his cattle." Her face took on a stubborn fierceness.

Ward frowned. There was that name again. It was turning up with alarming regularity and always in a way to cause the hair on the back of his neck to bristle. "Powers? His ranch is miles from here," Ward said.

"*Sí*. That is the way it was, but he has been growing. Now there is no longer anyone left between his rangeland and ours. He has offered to buy our land, but where would we go? This is our home," she said, spreading her hands.

"What happened to your neighbors? The Randolph family?"

"Killed, along with other homesteaders."

"Powers?"

"It was made to look like Indians, but the tracks were of horses with shoes.'' Ward didn't like the sound of what Mama was telling him. If it was true, Powers and his riders were as dangerous as they looked. But even Powers could not run roughshod over his neighbors without someone taking exception to it. There was still law in the Arizona Territory. Maybe not as well organized as in parts east, but there was a sheriff and the United States marshal and the military up north who would serve as a deterrent, even to a man like Powers.

Ward patted Mama's hand. ''Before I leave,'' he promised, ''I will see Powers and explain to him you do not want to move. His men will not bother you again.''

''He will not listen.'' Mama shook her head sadly. For the first time since he had known her he saw fear in Mama's eyes. Deep wrinkles creased her forehead, and the stern lines on either side of her mouth had deepened. She was showing her age. He had always assumed she was indestructible.

''He will listen, Mama,'' Ward said grimly, determined to take some of the burden off her already stooped shoulders. ''You just have to know how to talk to a man like that.''

CHAPTER
TEN

Ward had been home a week. It was September tenth and the weather was growing cooler in the evenings. The nights were marked by first frost, and the leaves had begun to turn so that the evening sun, seen through a grove of aspen trees in the mountains near the Mendozas' small home, was a blazing white ball that turned sparse, dangling leaves into luminous gold. The white slender tree trunks with their black markings looked like a speckled toothpick forest. The leaves, all fiery and splendorous, seemed detached from the spindly trunks, more like golden clouds that clustered around to protect the pale rootlike trunks. The grass, wherever the sun touched it, was the color of straw.

Ward's horse, a big black one, stopped at his urging. The air was still and pungent with smells of the forest: pine, spruce, fir, rotting wood, and the smell of blood from the deer tied over the flanks of his horse. Mama Manuela would turn the buck into steaks for dinner after she had cured the meat. He kicked the black into a gallop. It would be sundown when he got back, as it was. No time to dawdle, but he did. He gathered strength from solitude. It was necessary to him.

He hadn't realized it until he joined the cavalry and discovered that military life was lived in a state of togetherness that a civilian would find incredible—there was no place inside the fort where a man could be alone. The need for privacy had been compounded by a burly drill sergeant who didn't allow any sign of emotion on a man's face, night or day. Once, shortly after he had enlisted, the pressure became so great on him that he had searched until he'd found a small corner between buildings where he could stand and be out of the sight of all eyes for ten whole minutes. The cavalry had become more bearable after he was commissioned.

The sun was slipping beneath the jagged rim of the mountain ridge that surrounded the rolling hills of the desert when he finally saw the Mendoza house, small and squat beneath the escarpment. He stopped his horse. Nothing was moving, not even the chickens who usually pecked incessantly at the earth. Unaccustomed stillness set off an alarm inside him. He held the horse firmly. He'd been a fugitive too long to ignore the warning in ominous silence. Maybe Doug had been captured and told them where to find him. He squinted his keen eyes, scanning the scene ahead of him until he saw a dark shape against the dim red earth. Kicking his horse forward, he refused to think.

The fence was down. The small garden had been trampled into dust. Not even the chickens remained. The goat lay tangled in barbed wire that had been pulled loose from its posts and lay curled into a snarl beside the lean-to barn.

He had approached from the rear, and when he rounded the corner to the front of the house, he saw what he feared most. Mama Manuela was a crumpled shape in the dust. Pedro, his hands still clutching the new rifle, was sprawled like a ragdoll only a few feet from her. Both dead. No need to kneel beside them, but he did, partly from shock and partly from the need to know that he had not overlooked helping them if anything could help. Pedro's skull had been crushed. Mama's stout form was riddled with bleeding bullet holes.

Sickened and filled with dread, he walked inside the house. Grandpapa was sprawled in a corner, sitting like a doll that had been jammed there by an angry hand. His open eyes were staring at the wall opposite, like some grim watchman. Ward turned and saw the horror that must have been his last.

Isabel lay on the pallet Mama had put there for him. Naked, her shapely legs splayed and bloody, her warm brown skin marked by bruises, her pretty face swollen and blackened where ruthless fists had smashed into it. Hands that had worked so carefully in white satin were clenched into fists, her nails red with blood. He found a blanket and covered her, then stumbled outside, away from the house, and sagged against one of the cottonwoods, gasping for breath. Without realizing it, he must have been holding his breath, not willing to breathe that smell of death, already heavy and sweet in the small cabin.

Drenched with sweat, sick to his soul, he forced himself to walk a widening circle around the cabin until he found clear prints of departing horses.

Then he knew that Mama had been right. These were not Indian ponies. They were shod, and several of the prints would be easy to recognize again. Grimly, he filed the information in memory and then took a shovel from the barn. He dug a grave—one big one. He carried each of his family in turn and laid them gently to rest, then knelt and bowed his head, but no words came to him, no tears, no comfort. Finally he stood and vowed to Mama that he would send a priest to bless the grave for her. Then he shoveled dirt onto the canvas he had covered them with.

Exhausted, Ward sat under the tree and carved their names onto a shingle, then strapped it to a stake and drove it into the soft earth at the head of the grave. Then he hacked off a portion of the deer's hind quarter and went inside to take some of Mama's salt to pack it in. As he left the small house he saw the white wedding gown lying on the floor, discarded. He remembered the way Mama, Isabel, and Pedro had looked, teasing one another and giggling over each perfect stitch. He could see Isabel's face as she told him how much she loved her *novio* and how happy they would be. He stopped and knelt beside Isabel's gown. He picked it up and walked to the table. His brown sturdy hands, sore with unaccustomed blisters from digging the first grave he had ever dug, carefully smoothed the lustrous fabric. He had meant only to put it on the table, but the feel of it under his hands released a full set of memories. He could see Isabel's pretty face, beaming with joy at the thought of the happiest day in her life, Pedro's youthful manliness as he struggled with the tiny needle and the slippery white fabric, and Mama Manuela, beaming with pride at the closeness of her family and their love for one another. The feelings he'd been numb to before, as he'd knelt at the grave, rose up in him now and his hands tightened in the soiled, torn fabric. His teeth clamped together in rage, and his blue eyes hardened, then closed, and he gathered up the white satin and began tearing it into a dozen pieces.

The next morning when the sun slipped over the eastern horizon, Ward was on a hill overlooking the Powers spread. The house and barns were inside seven-foot walls, and armed men were everywhere. Ward watched all day until he spotted his prey on the road from the enclosure. After they had moved out of sight he rode down and inspected their tracks. Markings from several of these hooves matched the unique prints he had seen in the Mendoza yard.

He straightened, not at all surprised that Powers' elite corps, the same men who had ridden in the parade, had been the ones who murdered the Mendozas. That Younger was the leader of the group only hardened his purpose. Ward knew, in that moment, looking at the fresh prints, that he was going to kill them, and he knew almost in the same breath how he was going to do it. He couldn't ride in there and take on the whole bunch single-handedly—not if he wanted to be effective. He would wait until Younger's woman came out, and he'd take her. Younger and all his men would come after them. Fifteen to one he could handle, especially since he got to lead. North into the mountains—a man could take his time, hide and strike at will. He would save Younger for last.

Ward waited the two days until she left the enclosure. He saw the big door swing open, then the woman, her hair streaming back like a black cloud, followed by two heavily armed escorts.

To get back to the ranch house, the trio had to ride through a grove of aspen trees. When they came out he was behind a boulder with a rifle trained on them. He had chosen his spot carefully and was far enough away from the fortress so that shots fired wouldn't be heard.

"Halt! Don't move!" he yelled.

"What the hell!" The man on her left clawed at the gun in his holster, and Leslie heard an explosion and saw him jerk. His horse screamed and then bolted, dropping its limp burden to the ground. Her own horse reared up, and she jerked on the reins, barely comprehending what was happening. The bullets came too close together, like a rolling explosion. Her horse reared again and lunged wildly. She clawed at the horse's mane, trying to retain her seat, but the horse moved one direction and she the other. Screaming, she tried to regain her balance as the horse caught the bit in its teeth and bolted. The man fired again; her horse ran erratically trying to change direction, and she could feel herself leave the saddle to sail through the air, right at the man who was shooting at them.

It all happened too fast for her. She saw the ground coming up at her, but nothing else.

CHAPTER
ELEVEN

Younger,
I buried the Mendoza family two days ago. I have your woman. I'm going to sell her to the Indians after I'm done with her.

Cantrell

Dallas Younger read the note that had been taken off the body of one of his men and crumpled it with a curse and a snarl that contorted his usually handsome face.

"That bastard!" Younger bellowed for the Indian tracker, Warmfoot. When the Indian appeared before him, he explained in pidgin Apache that he wanted him to find Cantrell. "I'll follow soon as I can. You leave a clear trail, hear?"

Powers took the note, smoothed it against his chest, read it with his lips pursed into anger and surprise. "Who the hell is Cantrell?" he demanded.

"He's the gunfighter that met Dodge Merril in Holbrook a few years back. Faced the Merril gang down single-handed after that— sent 'em crawlin', or so the story goes."

"You seen him?"

"No, but I reckon I will."

"You ain't going after him, are you?"

"Hell, yes! He's got Leslie. That's your niece."

"She ain't nothing but trouble to me," Powers said flatly.

Younger glared at him, disgust pulling the corners of his lips down. Powers ignored him. He understood Younger and his kind. They had some fancy code about killing that was supposed to make everything all right, but a man was just as dead whether you shot him in a fair fight or in his sleep. With his code, all he had to do was wait. Cantrell would take care of his problem for him. Then the ranch would be all his.

They were standing on the long porch of the main house. The porch overhang shaded them from the hot sun of late afternoon. Powers mopped his forehead and gazed out across the gentle slope that fell away from the house. The yellowed grass was stiff and dry, reminding him how remorseless the desert sun was. Leslie was a rank tenderfoot; she wouldn't last long in the Arizona desert. He didn't speak. He was waiting for Younger to let the reality of his words sink in.

The house was only four years old, built after the railroad came to Phoenix, bringing with it prosperity for many. That was when rustling cattle, or burning brands on mavericks, started paying so well. This had been his home. His brother Charlie, Leslie's father, had been planning to build his a ways off, down by the cottonwoods, so he and that good-for-nothing wife he planned to bring out would have some privacy, except he hadn't lived long enough to build it. He'd found out about the rustling activities carried out by Younger and his men and had threatened to make trouble.

And while he would never condone killing his own brother, he had been secretly relieved when Charlie had died. No one knew exactly what Charlie Powers had been doing, afoot in a gully, when someone ran a large herd of steers down it, trampling him, but Mark Powers was not about to look a gift horse in the mouth. He might suspect Younger, but he'd never confront the man with it. Just as Younger should now accept what had happened to Leslie.

Younger finally expelled a heavy breath. "That would look like hell! Some bastard kidnaps your niece and you just write her off," he growled. "How the hell is that going to look to the folks in town? Like we ain't got guts enough to take back what belongs to us, that's how."

Powers frowned. "Reckon you're right about that, but you'd be doing us both a favor if you brought her back dead. Maybe you can hang that bastard Cantrell for killing her. Be damn sure he ain't alive when you bring him back."

Younger turned away in disgust. He went to the bunkhouse. The only one there of the men he fully trusted was Sam Farmer. Sam was a lanky, raw-boned, red-haired Arkansan.

"Who the hell led the raid on the Mendozas?" he demanded of

the man who was stretched out on his bunk, counting flies as they buzzed overhead.

"The boss did."

"Did Powers know about it?"

"Don't know. Didn't never come up. Why you asking?"

"'Cause it was the stupidest piece of work I seen in my whole damned life!" Younger exploded. "You assholes rode in there and killed the women and kids, and now Ward Cantrell is after my ass."

"Cantrell! Jesus!" Sam came upright off the bunk.

"How the hell did Cantrell get mixed up in this?"

"How the hell should I know? Maybe he's slept with so many of them little *chileñas* he thinks he's one of 'em."

Farmer pushed the red hair off his suddenly pale face. Freckles stood out against the pasty whiteness. "How'd you find out he's after you?"

"'Cause the bastard wrote me a note," he growled. "He killed Spike and that drunk he rides with, and he took Powers's niece. Damn!" Younger's face was hard with fury. "Round up the boys and tell them to toss their bedrolls over hosses. We're riding out in ten minutes, and we won't be back until we find that bastard and the girl."

Leslie woke up slowly, painfully. After a second of frowning into inky darkness she realized she was on a horse, riding in front of someone, cradled like a babe in strong arms. Her aching head was on his shoulder, and she could smell a warm, musky man smell mingled with leather, tobacco, and sweat—a salty smell that was not altogether unpleasant. She stirred to relieve her cramped muscles and heard a husky masculine chuckle, followed by a voice that seemed vaguely familiar.

"So, you've decided to live after all."

"What happened?"

"Hit your head when you fell."

His voice did not sound like any of the men on her uncle's ranch. "Who are you?" she asked in growing alarm.

"It doesn't matter," he said grimly.

"Where are you taking me?"

Ward felt involuntary anger rising up inside him, rough and heated, and made a conscious effort to control it. She sounded as if she had just stepped out of the sacred halls of Radcliffe—the haughty insolence that only Daddy's money and Mother's hand-picked tutors could buy. A lifetime of privilege followed by an Ivy League college and carefully chaperoned dates with Harvard undergraduates. What the hell was a woman like this doing with Dallas Younger? "Save your strength," he said grimly. "You're going to need it."

"You . . . you . . . kidnapped me? But why? I haven't any money. No one would pay to get me back."

"Too bad for you, then."

CHAPTER
TWELVE

Leslie twisted around to look at her abductor and was aware of her breasts brushing against his arm. In the darkness all she could make out was a silhouette, a grim, dark profile against the lighter sky.

"They'll come after me, you know—Dallas Younger will follow me. He'll kill you when he finds us. . . ." she warned him nervously.

He laughed softly, a strangely undaunted sound. "I'm counting on it."

Leslie lapsed into silence. Her head ached with a determined throb; pain laced through her temples as the flying hooves hit the ground. They were riding fast, over what looked like level ground. She had wanted to escape, but not this way. Where was he taking her? Into the desert?

Now, huddled tensely in his arms, shivering from the chill bite of cold autumn winds, memory, like an unwelcome visitor, was slowly returning. She recalled the two men who had been with her before, the strident shout, "Halt! Don't move!" the men grasping for their guns, the volley of gunshots rolling one on another, the screaming horses. She felt revulsion, nausea, and then anger and turned on him abruptly, almost unseating herself.

"You killed those two men!" she hissed.

"Somebody had to," he replied harshly.

Rage, fed by her terror, spewed up from the depths of her and blinded Leslie to everything except the urge to strike out. "Let me down!'' Her fists pummeled his face and chest. "Let me go! You killer! Dirty animal killer!''

Her furious twisting and flailing almost unseated them both before Ward could get her under control. He jerked the horse to a halt and dismounted, dragging her off unceremoniously. "You damned little bitch!'' He slapped her once to get her attention, then pinned her on the hard ground while she screamed in terror as the horse's hooves stamped just inches from her head. She struggled frantically against him, expecting anything, but his rough hand only held her still while he slipped a noose over her neck and adjusted the knot.

"What are you doing to me? You beast! I hate you! Do you hear me? Kill me! Go ahead! Filthy killer!'' But there was a tremor of fear in her voice.

"You want to ride alone, you can ride alone,'' he said softly, his voice as calm and unaffected as if he were telling her it was dinnertime. "The other end of this rope is going to be tied to my saddle. You either keep up or you break your pretty little neck, you hear?'' He lifted her onto the horse, astride a western saddle, handling her easily in spite of her struggles. Then he mounted a horse she didn't recall seeing or hearing before.

She learned that night what terror was. He was traveling fast, and she lived in constant fear that he would deliberately jerk her off just so she would break her neck, or that her horse or his would stumble. She had visions of dying slowly of a broken neck while those clumsy black birds Younger had called buzzards circled overhead. Or falling off her mount to be dragged to death.

She prayed that Dallas Younger would follow, and remembered her uncle's words: "You could do a lot worse than a man like Younger.'' And as furious as she was, she realized that Younger, with his slow Texas drawl and masculine arrogance, would come after her. . . .

"Look out!'' Cantrell yelled. "Duck!''

Leslie heard the urgent warning just in time. She ducked and her horse barely skimmed under the branch of a dead tree that had loomed up out of the blackness. Her heart leaped into her throat, pounding wildly, but the danger was past. She slowly settled back down, and, trembling, she hung on to that damned torturing horse, cursing the pain in her side and the crashing agony inside her skull. She continued to hang on until the savage pain was permanently lodged in her side, fear became commonplace, and hope had turned to resignation.

For lack of anything better to do she watched the moon rise, arc overhead, and set. Still that maniac kept up the same killing pace. If obstinance hadn't been a family trait handed down from mother to daughter for generations, she would have thrown herself to the ground and broken her own neck. Death couldn't possibly be this bad.

She had been on the very brink of death when she was fifteen, and it had been nothing compared to this! She had contracted a mysterious fever and had lain with her arms crossed over her chest, her body swaddled in warm blankets, sipping only water for days, and the only thought she had ever had was that she wouldn't mind dying—she just wanted it over with! She had no patience for whimpering, not even her own. She had been able to hear people talking about her. She had known what they said and how concerned they were, but it was as if she had watched from some lofty vantage point, not as a participant but as a not-too-concerned spectator, grateful for the distance she had managed to put between herself and that feeble alien shell.

Now she hurt all over, and there was no escape. She had never been so truly afraid before, and she resented this fact almost as much as she hated the cause of her misery.

They rode all night. When the sun was just beginning to spread warm light in the eastern sky, he finally "whoaed" his horse and raised his hand in a signal for her to stop.

They were in a canyon with sheer, soaring walls that looked gray in the first pink flush of dawn. The canyon, rough, immense, almost as broad as a valley, looked like a continuation of the high desert. The floor and halfway up the walls were covered by creosote, sage, and rocks that looked like they had been shoved up through the hard granite floor.

No one would ever find her. She was at the mercy of a madman, and she was so tired that she barely cared. He would probably kill her and leave her for the buzzards, but she didn't feel upset—she was numb.

He dismounted and came to her side to help her down. She had no strength to resist, but when he reached for her, she kicked him in the side. "Don't touch me!"

He grimaced and stepped back, his eyes cold.

"Those men didn't do anything to you! You killed them in cold blood! For nothing!"

"Not exactly for nothing," he said calmly, moving away to

loosen his saddle cinch. "I needed a body to tack a note on so Younger would know where to come looking for you."

Her eyes opened wider in horror and disbelief. "You needed something to pin a note on, so you killed two men? Animal!" That one word was filled with such revulsion and hatred that Ward almost flinched under the searing contempt in her narrowed green eyes.

"Get down," he ordered curtly. There was a veiled threat in his controlled husky-quiet voice that scared her more than violence would have. She could feel her face draining of color. There was something infinitely terrifying in his cold blue eyes, as if he didn't care which way it went. He could kill her as easily as he had those men. Younger would still follow him, whether she was dead or alive.

"All right! Just don't touch me!" she said fiercely. She practically threw herself out of the saddle. She was in pain, and her anger, which was always formidable, was in full bloom. Unfortunately, her legs, which had been cramped and chilled for hours —she wasn't dressed for riding in the cold of an Arizona night— collapsed, and she fell headlong into the dirt.

"You're doing real fine," he drawled. "The cave is that direction." He started off with the other end of her rope in his hands, leading her and the horses, and she had to scramble to her feet and follow him before he dragged her or the horses stepped on her. She fell and hurt her knee and would have cried if he hadn't been there; as it was, she just glared with hatred at his damned back and stumbled ahead.

The sheer walls of the canyon were smooth, flesh-colored granite that looked like they had been carved by a glacier's passage. The cave, once she came to it, was much bigger inside than it looked from the outside. Leslie could imagine spiders, bats, and hairy black animals from the smells, but she was too weary to move, much less run. She leaned against the wall of the cave, dusty and panting from the exertion of climbing the hill from the canyon floor, her mouth dry and aching with thirst, but she wouldn't ask this madman for anything, even if she died right there.

He led them deep inside the mountain, paused, looked back, and then began to unsaddle their mounts. He spread the blankets on the floor of the cave, ignoring her, and she bored her hatred into his broad back, torn between refusing to lie on his blankets and refusing to let him intimidate her.

His tasks done for the moment, Ward poured water into a tin pan for each horse, then took a long drink out of the canteen and passed it to the girl. She looked like she might fling it back in his face, but common sense and thirst prevailed. She drank painfully and gave it back, watching him warily the whole time.

"What are you going to do with me?" she finally asked, her eyes staring stubbornly at the ground, refusing to meet his.

Ward stopped what he was doing long enough to really look at her. She was dressed in a formal riding habit that was probably all the rage in Boston for trotting sedately around the quad at the height of the social season. Now it hung in filthy tatters around her ankles where cactus and mesquite had torn the skirt in passing. Her face was coated with dust, but even dirty and disheveled, she retained a quality of ladylike refinement and beauty that both impressed and unnerved him.

He recalled what he had told Younger, but he realized that he was no longer capable of either violating her himself or allowing anyone else to do it. He didn't want to take his revenge on her personally, but he would not be turned from his purpose. He needed her as bait for Younger and those bastards who had slaughtered Mama Mendoza, Isabel, Pedro, and Grandpapa.

He couldn't name them without recalling the horror they must have endured before they died, and it was this memory that hardened his purpose and made his words harsher than they might have been.

"Nothing you can't handle," he said gruffly. He regretted his words as soon as they left his lips. It was suddenly very easy to see what was on her mind. He glanced from her terrified face to the blankets he had spread out on the floor of the cave. The thought of having to cope with a hysterical, screaming woman chilled his blood. He was too exhausted to be thinking very lucidly himself. He hadn't slept more than an hour at a time in days. He decided to ignore everything except the basics. He rummaged in his saddle-bags until he found some beef jerky. "Here," he said, putting the coarse stick into her hand to distract her. "Eat this."

She took it tentatively and touched her tongue and lips to it. The smell seemed pleasant. She tried to bite into it. "Ow!" she grumped.

"Suck it. It'll last longer that way. So will your teeth."

Once she grew accustomed to it, the flavor melted into her mouth and was incredibly delicious, but the saltiness only re-

minded her how thirsty she was. She knelt on the hard earth to relieve her shaking legs. "Can I have some water?"

He passed her the canteen again and then lay down on the blankets, leaving a place beside him, which jarred her frazzled nerves.
She watched with mounting uneasiness as her kidnapper arranged
another blanket into a roll to serve as his pillow. "You'd better
take advantage of this opportunity to sleep," he said, lying back.

Leslie refused to move from where she was even though she felt
like an animal kneeling in the dirt with a rope around her neck.
Sunlight was spreading into the cave, widening the wedge of
brightness, so she knew that even though they were far back in the
cave, they would be able to see clearly until after sunset. She shivered. The cave was chilled now and would probably stay cool
enough throughout the day so that sleep would be possible. She
desperately wanted to sleep, but she was not able to willingly lie
down next to any man on a blanket with no chaperone within a
hundred miles.

Ward sighed and stood up. He took her by the shoulders. She
started to struggle against him, but he was far too strong for her.
She heard herself moan in fear, and it was such a pitiful, wounded-
creature sound that she clamped her teeth together.

"I don't have time for your foolishness. Now lie down. I don't
give a damn whether you sleep or not, but if you know what's good
for you, you'll lie real still so I can sleep." He measured out
enough rope so she could lie down and then he tied the other end of
the rope around his lean waist. His eyes closed and Leslie could
see the tension slowly relaxing. In moments he was asleep. He
had prudently placed his guns off to one side of the blankets so she
couldn't reach them without waking him.

The cave was lit by reflected sunlight, so that its mouth, far
above where they were, was bright and glaring. Down here the
light was soft and muted. Too dim for painting, but she could
study her captor at will. His broad chest rose and fell with his deep
breathing.

She recognized him with a start. This was the cowboy who had
tried to save her from falling during the parade, the same cowboy
she had taunted from the hotel window. Knowing that, she was not
so terrified by him, unless he was one of those mad-dog killers she
had read about; but looking at him, at the lean, square-jawed hand-
someness of his face and the tawny wheat-colored hair that had attracted her to him in that crowd, she could not believe he was a

mad-dog killer. But why had he kidnapped her? Why had he killed those men?

He turned over onto his side, away from her, and Leslie sighed and lay down beside him. She was too exhausted to worry about all that now. She closed her eyes and huddled tiredly on her sliver of the blanket, careful not to touch him, until she slipped into a dreamless sleep that was like floating on the surface of a warm lake.

It seemed like only seconds had passed when she felt rough hands shake her awake. The cave, when she opened her eyes, was dark as a potful of black paint. She could see nothing, not even a dim outline, and she couldn't remember where she was or whom she was with.

CHAPTER
THIRTEEN

"No, please, leave me alone," she groaned. "Let me sleep. . . ."

"You'd better eat something. Last chance you'll have."

"Oh, no, please."

"Sit up. It's almost dawn. We're moving out." She struggled fitfully against his hard hands, turning to face the sound of his voice. Now he was a dark shape against the lightening cave. His strong hands lifted her into a sitting position, not unkindly, but any movement at all wrenched a groan from her. Every muscle felt torn. "All those hours in the saddle took a little of the starch out of you anyway," he said, and she thought she could hear amusement in his voice.

In the end, she ate the biscuits and jerky and sipped the water and was grateful for what she was able to choke down, because when they finished eating, they rode until the sun came up and then all that day with only a few stops to rest the horses. She felt like a squaw or a dog with the rope around her neck and a dead man's hat on her head. She was in pain, all over, and had given up hope of rescue. She had ridden the paths surrounding Wellesley. All the young ladies in her set rode, and she had imagined herself a good rider, but no more. Trying to keep up with a man who rode like an extension of his horse, effortlessly, hour after hour, never tiring, who didn't seem to need food or water, and barely noticed her, except when she slowed him down, was a nightmare. . . .

Riding over dunes covered with blue sage, beneath sandstone cliffs that dwarfed the occasional gnarled trees, Leslie stole furtive glances at her captor when she could do so without being obvious. He was tall, with a lean, muscular form that explained why he was able to handle her so effortlessly. He had broad, tapering shoulders, narrow hips, and long legs that he used to control his horse. Awake, his lean, square jaw looked manly and resolute. He was clean-shaven in a land where every man wore either a beard or a handlebar mustache. He hadn't shaved today, but his beard stubble was so fair that it didn't darken his cheeks. He had eyes the same shade of blue as the noonday sky, a light azure that picked up the light and reflected it. He rarely spoke to her, but his eyes, which were by some miracle of birth highly expressive, telegraphed his moods. When she provoked him, his brows crowded his eyes, narrowing them into slits and cooling the vibrant color. When he was amused, she could see the merriment shimmering in the blue depths. When he lifted his hat to wipe his perspiring brow, his hair was the color of pale straw with steaks of silver that glinted in the sunlight. Its fairness contrasted handsomely with the burnt teak of his skin. Leslie gnashed her teeth, despising him all the more. If he were maimed and gnarled, his actions might have been excusable on the grounds that a lonely outcast deserved to avenge himself on a heartless, disregarding world, but this man had no such excuse for behaving as he did.

They rode interminably. Several times he dismounted to chip at the granite with a small axe. What was he doing? Certainly not marking a trail? She finally decided that whatever he was doing must have a meaning beyond her experience.

Anger and curiosity slowly turned to apathy under the relentless glare of the sun. It wasn't until they stopped for the night beside a wide shallow stream that wound its silent way through a rugged rock-strewn canyon that she found strength to speak. "I know you," she said, her voice hardly more than a hoarse whisper.

He merely glanced at her, lifting an expressive eyebrow as he tied her rope to the trunk of a slender tree. Leslie went on, "You're the one who caught my horse—during the parade."

Ward's hand instinctively moved up to rub the back of his head. "I won't do that again," he promised.

"Younger hit you," Leslie said hastily. "I tried to stop him. Is that why you're doing this?"

"No." Ward shook his head. "I have another matter to settle with Younger."

"What are you going to do with me?" she asked.

"Sell you to the Indians if you don't behave," he growled. Ignoring her gasp of outrage, he turned to his saddlebags. He took out a jar and tied the big stallion securely, then gentled him by rubbing his cheek against the horse's flank to distract the animal while his hands gently worked a gooey salve into a wound on the horse's flank. It occurred to Leslie, who knew a little about horses, that her captor was practically tying himself into a knot to accommodate his horse and spare the animal pain.

"I saw you climb in that wagon with that Mexican girl, too," she said, guardedly.

Ward turned to face her, smiling suddenly, as if the memory of that particular event pleased him. "Oh, yes, Maria," he said. "We have a date to meet each other next year."

"To do the same thing, no doubt," Leslie ventured, with her voice reflecting more than she meant it to.

"I hope not," Ward replied ruefully. Leslie lapsed into puzzled silence then, but she continued to watch her captor as he moved around their campsite. "What's your name?"

He turned and his eyes were amused and questioning, as if he were wondering at her motives. "Cantrell."

"Ward Cantrell!" she breathed.

"How did you know that?" he asked, frowning.

She smiled, enjoying his surprise. "You rob trains too, don't you?" she asked. Somehow, realizing he was the train robber brought an involuntary flush to her cheeks.

Ward turned to her again, amused. "Why is it I can't do anything without you being there?"

"I would just as soon have passed on this one," she said, shrugging a slender shoulder. Ward laughed but didn't reply. He knelt and rubbed his hands in the sand, using it like a rag to wipe off the smelly salve.

"On the train," Leslie couldn't help saying, "you had another Mexican girl at your side."

"Oh, yes." Ward nodded. "Belen."

Leslie lapsed into silence for a moment. She was remembering what someone on the train had said about his having a taste for only Mexican girls and not giving white girls a tumble. "Is it true?" she asked.

"Is what true?" Cantrell countered.

"That you love only Mexican girls?"

Ward was surprised into silence while he thought about it. "Where did you hear that?"

"Someone on the train said it," Leslie answered, waving her hand around. "Is it true?"

Ward was slow to answer. "Maybe," he said. "I never thought about it." He fed the horse and then took some cans out of his saddlebags.

By the time he handed her a tin plate with beans, bacon, and a dry biscuit on it, she took it without response, making him slant a suspicious look at her. She knelt in the dirt, eating absently, and he shook his head, marveling at what a good appetite she had for such a slender little thing. Maybe it takes a lot of energy to feed that temper of hers, he thought. He finished eating, rinsed the utensils in the creek, packed them away, and started unbuckling his gunbelts. He laid them down, out of her reach by several feet, and then began to unbutton his shirt.

"What are you going to do?" she asked, fear clamping icy fingers around her throat in spite of the stifling heat from the setting sun. She had never been given to hysterics and despised girls who were, but her heart began to pound frightfully, and her stomach lurched in terror.

Ward didn't respond to her nervous question, suspecting coyness. He was going to take a bath, and he couldn't undress near the water, because he would be leaving his guns and clothes within her easy reach. And, he rationalized, it wasn't like Younger's woman would be seeing anything new.

He undressed as if he were alone, efficiently, matter-of-factly, unselfconsciously, until he was down to his thin cotton drawers, and even through her fear, or perhaps because of it, she was struck by the arrogant, smooth-muscled strength and masculinity in that sun-gold frame.

She had never seen a naked man, except on canvas, and only the Greeks had ever caught the lean, straight-limbed grace of line she now saw. The artist in her watched unashamed, as she would have viewed any new art form. In the light of a sinking sun, his skin was golden and rife with rippling power—more Herculean than Adonian with those muscular shoulders tapering into long, narrow sinews that were flat and smooth at his waist, lean and powerful in his long legs. Part of her rejoiced in the subjective pleasure of critical analysis, but the female in her was remembering, crazily, the face of the young Mexican girl who had come out of the wagon in Phoenix with him—that young, plaintive face, all dewy and adoring. But fear, that hard knot of heavy pain, filling her throat and chest, stifled even that wicked thought when he started to approach her.

She had been so dazed, watching him, that she was taken by surprise. He glanced at her, his eyes narrowed, and he froze for a second. Frowning, she watched him move slowly toward his gun. He scooped the revolver into his hand, crouching, and said, "Don't move."

"What?"

He pointed the gun at her, fired, and missed, but Leslie was on her feet, running, before he could aim again, completely forgetting the rope that was around her neck. She heard him yell, but she did not heed his cry. She raced away from him. At almost the same instant that the rope snapped taut he caught her arm, else she might have broken her neck.

"No!" she gasped, her voice barely more than a hoarse whisper. Her heart was pounding so hard she thought she would surely die. He turned her and shoved her back toward where she had been sitting. Leslie screamed and began to fight like a wild thing, but he forced her back to the blanket she had been kneeling on. "See that," he growled.

"Ohhh!" she gasped, recoiling from the sight of a broad, clumsy-looking lizard that was moving quickly away from the spot she had been sitting on. Its fat, stumpy tail was wagging from side to side as it hurried out of sight.

"I wasn't shooting at you," he said unnecessarily.

"Echhh!" she squealed. "What is that thing?"

"A Gila monster . . ."

She turned on him, furious. "Well, you could have told me! You almost scared me to death!"

"If I had politely engaged you in conversation first, he might have bitten you! Would you rather I scared hell out of you or he filled you with deadly venom?"

She jerked her arm out of his steely grip. "You're hurting me!"

"Well, dammit," he growled, "make up your mind what you want to fight about."

"Leave me alone," she whimpered.

He dragged in a furious breath, but the fury was only partly at her. He was blaming himself for almost getting her killed. When he had seen the giant lizard waddling toward her, he had realized the full extent of how he had interfered in her life. If she had died, her blood would have been on his hands. But the danger was past, and he was in no mood to let her out of his sight again. He picked her up and carried her to the water.

"What are you doing? Put me down!"

"I'm giving you a chance to cool off before you bust something." He put her on her feet in the knee-deep water.

"Ohhh!" she gasped, preparing to strike out at him or bolt again. To forestall the eventuality, he pushed her down and straddled her body. To silence her, he pushed her head under the water and brought it up. "Shut up or I'll drown you." She sputtered and he prepared to dunk her again.

"You understand?" he asked. She coughed and sputtered and slowly stopped struggling. "I'm here to take a bath," he said grimly. "Get your clothes off. They're all wet anyway. You might as well have a real bath too." Her eyes filled with terror. "You going to behave yourself?" he asked, shaking her.

His knees were on either side of her breasts, and she could feel his manhood against her belly with only the cotton drawers to contain it. She would have agreed to anything to get out of that position. She nodded and his hand left her face. "Get your clothes off," he growled.

"I . . . I . . . won't," she stammered, looking like she was going to cry. She might be a little doxie, he thought, but she looked like a frightened sea nymph with her hair still dripping around her face and shoulders. He wondered what the hell she thought he could do to her that Younger hadn't already done.

He shrugged. "Suit yourself. I can cut them off, but then you won't have anything to ride in, will you?"

Leslie bit back a groan. He left her to go back for soap, and she staggered to her feet, her skirt hanging like lead around her. She stood there uncertainly, not knowing what to do, but she felt the cold silky water on her legs, and suddenly she didn't care what he did. She wanted a real bath. Besides, he would do what he wanted anyway. She might as well resign herself to her fate. If it wasn't him, it would be Dallas Younger. She realized she was no longer in control of her life. Her control had been an illusion only. Either Younger or Cantrell would take her before the week was out. She had become some sort of prize, to be fought over and won. She shivered and was unable to tell whether it was from her thoughts or from feeling the cold water against her calves. She decided that she might as well do what she wanted.

Ward saw her begin to comply and couldn't believe it. Only a second ago she had looked like a cornered bobcat—ready to take his eyes out—now she was undressing as if she were there alone. He would never understand the female mind.

She took off the cumbersome riding habit and left it to soak in the shallow water. Now, wearing only a lacy, ruffled chemise and slip that was of fine textured material, she removed her shoes and poured the water out of them before she tossed them onto the bank with a look of disgust that told him he had probably ruined the fine leather. She refused to remove the chemise and slip, but when she turned back and began to wash herself, the water soaked through the thin fabric and it became so transparent that it conveniently disappeared. Her firm young body took his breath away—hard pink nipples darkened the tips of crazily tilted, cone-shaped breasts, pointing straight up as if begging to be kissed. The provocative underswell fairly called out to his hands to cup the tender whiteness. Her waist was firm and slim, flaring gently into sweetly curved buttocks and graceful legs. The skin he could see was like creamy white carnation petals. She was a brunette with skin like a blond—no visible body hair.

She washed herself, oblivious to his admiring appraisal. She seemed satisfied that she had maintained her modesty, and he smiled, knowing she would be mortified if she knew how useless her protective garment had become. He sighed, appreciating her rich female gracefulness while she basked in girlish self-absorption. Completely unnerved, he held out the soap.

She took it and lathered herself all over with it, reaching under her chemise and slip, glaring at him until he turned his back. The water was cold, but it felt better than anything she had ever felt. Her spirits were immediately lifted. She hated being dirty and hot; she hated having a rope around her neck; she hated him, but since she had no choice, she decided to make the best of it. Why not? She'd never been given to brooding or depression. She despised girls who cried all the time.

"What are you up to now?" Ward asked, scowling at the way she seemed to have adjusted. Leslie turned wide green eyes on him, looking over her slender white shoulder; the sweet curve of her back and buttocks tempting him.

"Whatever do you mean?"

"Why are you cooperating?"

"Because I wanted a bath. It was a good idea, even if it comes from a rotten animal like you."

He grinned then, his straight white teeth like a flash of summer lightning. He had the most soulful eyes she had ever seen. She could read volumes in them, but now she just wanted to put them in her pocket, after she had ripped them out.

"Do you just change like that?" he asked, snapping his fingers. "If it pleases you?"

"Of course. I do exactly what pleases me. Why shouldn't I?" she asked, tossing the long black mass of tangled wet curls.

Jesus! he thought. In that second, with her pretty chin up and green sparks shooting out of her eyes, she looked like a brunette version of Jenn. He could almost hear his sister's sultry, haughty voice as she explained to him eight years ago that she didn't fall in love with all her lovers. Very modern. Very independent. Just like this little white-skinned, sweet-curving female who had probably survived a lot more than most women twice her age. Younger was rough stuff. Ward could hardly recognize his own voice when he finally spoke.

CHAPTER
FOURTEEN

"You're pretty cocky for such a slender little thing."

The tone of his husky voice set off a small pulse in her throat, and her voice was strangely whispery. "Look who's talking."

He grinned in spite of himself. "I'm not cocky."

"You do exactly as you please," she corrected, feeling a jolt of strange energy and visualizing herself at the front of a passenger coach, holding a gun on the startled passengers while he moved up the aisles relieving them of their guns. Her cheeks flushed with heat, and she said the meanest thing she could think of. "I'm sure all men rob trains and kidnap women."

He lifted an eyebrow in a gesture that told her she had won that round, and they both fell silent. Almost in unison they turned their backs and began to wash seriously.

She finished as quickly as she could and then began to scrub the soggy garment she had worn for two days, trying to wash the grime off it. It was torn in dozens of places.

"Think I could use the soap?" he asked.

She glanced up and was instantly sorry that she had. He was facing her, standing over her, and his wet drawers concealed nothing from her startled gaze. She turned her head away and held out her hand with the soap in it. She felt his warm hand close around the soap, brushing her skin. Without looking up again, she wrung the water out of her garment, then waded out of the stream and spread her clothes on the mesquite bushes.

By the time Cantrell came out of the creek and pulled his trousers on, she was settled in the middle of their bedroll in her wet chemise and slip, admiring the colorful sunset. Red, gold, and purple clouds swaggered like flamboyant galleons sailing above the western horizon. Off in the distance, beyond the trees that grew along the slender creek, she could see a black tableland rising up to the horizon, its outline spikey with slender, pointed trees that she guessed were either pine or spruce. The setting sun bathed the foreground in heavy gold glamour, intensifying the contrast. She longed for the tools to capture that marvelous natural display.

One of the horses snorted and stamped, and she sighed, remembering that she wasn't there to marvel at natural phenomena. She was concerned now with survival, and suddenly it pleased her that it wasn't the same dreary type of survival her friends at school had talked about. This was real life-and-death, trial-by-fire survival. "I suppose you intend to sell me to the Indians," she said, remembering his earlier remark.

His eyes widened momentarily. Then a smile flickered in the blue depths. "They aren't as uninformed as you might think. Besides, there are laws about taking advantage of them."

"What *are* you going to do with me? Why am I here?"

"Don't ask so damned many questions," he said, his forehead puckered with his displeasure. Angered, she stood up, and he noticed she had taken the rope off. It lay beside the blanket. "You little hellcat. How did you get that off?"

She shrugged. "It wasn't so hard," she said defiantly.

"Where do you think you're going?" he said to her back as she turned and strolled away. There was no urgency in his question, because he was too distracted by the sight of her firm rounded buttocks beneath the wet, clinging fabric. He was already hard from the ordeal of bathing next to her. It might not be such a bad idea to bed Younger's woman after all. Anyone who could put up with Younger would not be injured too badly by anything he could do to her.

"I'm going to the powder room," she said, the lift of her chin haughty.

"Stay close by," he growled.

"I will not!" she said, horrified by the thought of his hearing or seeing her while she was so intimately engaged.

"Might want to look where you're going," he said dryly.

She turned, and her look of defiance turned into fear. The animal in front of her, a small ground squirrel, stood up in alarm on its hind legs, and she stopped, her heart pounding frightfully. Then, before she could move, a large bird, its wings spread wide in flight, swooped down and caught the squirrel in its talons. Leslie was looking into its eyes at the instant it realized its doom, and she felt the hopelessness and dread of the small animal transmitted to her. But worse than that, the look in the bird's eyes, so matter-of-fact and efficient that it stunned her, reminded her of Cantrell. Before she could react, the bird flew away with its kill, and Leslie turned her back and began, quite unexpectedly, to cry.

She sat down in the dirt, sobbing, and she did not know whether it was from the frightening ordeal she had managed to endure or for the poor little squirrel.

Ward watched her for several moments; then he walked over and lifted her to her feet. Leslie allowed herself to be pulled up into his arms. He held her close, stroking her head while she cried, and it was strangely comforting to her. Partly because she knew it would be harder for him to mistreat her in the future if she could soften his heart toward her now, however momentarily.

Leslie pressed against Ward shamelessly, feigning complete unawareness of their intimacy. Unfortunately, he was using her collapse to his advantage as well. His warm hand caressed her spine and moved down her waist to press her hips against his. She felt the bulge of his manhood through his trousers. Remembering the way it had looked through that transparent cloth—she felt strangely unable to assert herself against him. She was suddenly recalling what one of the girls at school told her—that a man's member had a bone in it. But it hadn't looked that way at all. It had looked soft, almost touchable, she thought, flushing at the wickedness of her thoughts. But now, strangely, it felt bony against her belly. His warm hand came up to touch her face, brush her lips.

"What are you doing?" she asked nervously.

"I think I'm going to kiss you."

Startled, she searched his handsome face for some sign. She knew that she could not allow him to take even a small liberty—her position was too vulnerable—but she was incapable of resisting. Her heart leaped into a hard, fast rhythm that made her feel breathless. Before she could think of a reply, his warm fingers lifted her chin, and he lowered his head. The pulse under her chin leaped. She felt flooded with weakness. His soft lips brushed hers, and her legs went rubbery. She wanted to protest, but nothing about her seemed to be working.

After that first tentative kiss, his embrace tightened.

"Open your mouth," he whispered.

For some reason that she could not imagine, her lips parted in response. This time when his lips covered hers, his tongue darted into her mouth, causing a warm ache in her belly.

"Put your arms around my neck," he murmured against her cheek. She moaned, but her arms obeyed him. This time when he kissed her his tongue explored her mouth, and his warm hand slid again to her cheek, then down to her breast.

"No, please," she whispered, feeling new fear.

His hand moved to her back and burned into the trembling flesh there as it caressed her again, moving from the curve of her spine to her shoulder and then around to her breast. His fingers teased the hard little nipple, and she cried out, but he only pulled her closer against him and deepened his probing kiss. Now, much to her amazement, her knees buckled.

"Here, lie down," she heard him say, lifting her to carry her back to the blanket.

"No . . . please," she whispered.

"Hush. You don't know what you want."

Now she was lying on the blanket with the scratchy wool against her back and him welded to her front. His lips abandoned hers to explore the sweep of her neck and the rosy tips of her firm little cone-shaped breasts. His wet tongue traced imaginary circles around the swollen nipples until she shuddered and cried out. His warm hand nudged her legs open and brushed softly against the sensitive inner thigh. He pulled the cloth of her pantalets aside, and his fingers tried to slip inside. "No, please . . ." she moaned.

His lips stopped her protests. One hand squeezed and kneaded her breasts while the other hand strayed back between her legs. She shuddered again, but this time, her treacherous body arched against him, seeking his hands.

He sighed against her cheek. "That's right, love, hold me tight." His hand deftly undid the buttons on his trousers. Leslie knew what he was doing, but part of her seemed aloof from that knowledge. His fingers slipped inside her pantalets and brushed through the tight curls between her legs; one probing finger insinuated itself inside her, and his warm, smooth shocking member was nudging at her, ready to follow it.

Out of curiosity she had lain still under his ministrations, but now she knew she could no longer convince herself that all was well. Her kidnapper was about to do the unthinkable.

"No!" she cried, beginning to struggle in earnest. She pressed her thighs tightly closed, barring his entry.

"Easy, hellcat! Settle down," he whispered, reclaiming her mouth. He kissed her long and hard, ignoring her struggles to stop him, until they were both breathless. When he had reduced her to quivering helplessness, his head moved lower to tease the sensitive inner thighs. Even in the state she was in, burning with unaccustomed desire, she felt alarm bells ringing in her head. But part of her wanted to know. Part of her wanted to experience everything that a man like this could or would do to a woman. Part of her was sick of wondering what it was men did to women that they wouldn't talk about. But her terror was too great. Gasping with fear and the effort it took to make herself stop him, she caught him by the hair and dragged his head up.

"Ow!" he yelped. "Dammit."

"Well, don't do that!"

"Little hypocrite," he growled, taking in the glazed look of desire that she couldn't hide. "You know you want it."

Her cheeks flushed scarlet. His piercing blue eyes seared into her, confirming his words; then slowly his mouth reclaimed her own, and she felt herself relaxing. His tongue claimed her mouth while his deft hands relieved her of the wet garments.

"No! Please, no!" she moaned, feeling like a hypocrite but unable to stop the instinctive plea.

"Hush, relax," he urged, gentling her.

"No, please," she whimpered.

"You would never forgive me if I believed you, you little liar," he growled against her throat. His mouth closed around her dark rose nipple, torturing it while his hand stripped the soggy chemise and pantalets away from her body. "You're beautiful, little one," he whispered. "It's no wonder Younger is so eager to have you back."

She groaned, but even as she did her body arched into his, betraying her with its neediness. She decided in that instant that perhaps he was right. She was on fire. Why should she deprive herself of the delicious promise that shimmered in his touch? Her fate was sealed in any case. Either this man would take her and have his way with her, or Dallas Younger would. And Younger's touch truly filled her with revulsion.

Ward leaned away from her, his hands caressing her. He would have liked to spend hours caressing her soft skin, but her artless movements had stirred his own passions to the breaking point. He opened her legs and guided himself into the narrow sheath there. She cried out and her eyes flew open, and they were as startled as a doe confronted by a grizzly. He thrust into her, and a scalding pain wrenched a gasping cry from her lips.

Shocked, he closed her eyes with his lips and concentrated on kissing her lips and then her breasts until she began to relax. Then, slowly, gradually, he began to move again, his male weapon creating friction against her most intimate surfaces. Her hands clutched at his broad back, wanting him closer. She was filled with tautness and an indescribable need that was becoming intolerable, until his body, sturdy and lean against her own, stiffened suddenly, and she hung suspended for a moment on a wave of aching breathlessness. Unexpectedly, he withdrew.

She cried out and threw her head back, her body arching frantically to find him again. Groaning, he shoved three fingers into her, and the terrible tension inside her exploded into gasping heat and bonelessness.

He rolled over and pulled her on top of him, breathing as if he had run for miles. Her own breathing was as labored as his. Limp and exhausted, she closed her eyes and just floated in the warm aftermath. She had no idea how long they lay like that. When she opened her eyes it was dark overhead, bright at the horizon. The moon shimmered on the water, streaking it with brightness. A coyote howled in the distance.

CHAPTER
FIFTEEN

"I thought you were Younger's woman."

"I'm nobody's woman. I belong to me."

"You're damned cynical for a girl."

"Maybe I just sound cynical because I've never been . . . been . . ."

He chuckled softly. "You'll get used to it."

How could he sound so cruel? Only moments ago he had been warmth and ecstasy; now he was turning her roughly to tie her hands behind her back. She struggled against him, but it was useless. "What are you doing?" she hissed.

"Just making sure you'll be here when I get back."

Real terror darkened her lime-green eyes, and Ward leaned down and took her face between his hands. "You'll be safe here. Just keep quiet and be still and you won't attract anything you can't handle."

Her skin under his hands was soft as silk and sheened with a fine mist of perspiration from their lovemaking. Her lips were soft and full, and he couldn't resist tasting them again. She moaned a soft protest and clamped her lips shut, to cheat him of any pleasure.

He continued kissing her, and she continued stubbornly to resist, until suddenly, without warning, his thumb moved into her mouth, forcing her lips apart. She squirmed and cried out, realizing too late that she had made a mistake. With one thumb jammed between her jaws, his hot lips reclaimed her own. Now his tongue jabbed into her mouth, dueling with hers until her anger and outrage diminished, overcome by her body's unmistakable response. A wave of heat washed into her, and she felt her mouth go slack beneath his searching lips. She wanted to keep fighting him, but there was something dizzying about being so completely helpless and open to him. So aware of his rough thumb in her mouth, so aware of his tongue and lips ravaging her mouth. Tremors shook her body. His warm hand moved down to cup her breast. His fingers played with the taut, swollen nipple and a heartbeat started in that secret place between her legs. She moaned in the back of her throat, and her body went limp.

"Oh, Jesus," he groaned. He sat up abruptly and ran his fingers through his hair. "If Younger had planned this, he couldn't have done a better job. . . ."

"What? . . ." Her body was crying out for the feel of his tender-harsh hands; only her anger that he was leaving her on the desert, tied up, kept her from straining toward him.

"Go to sleep," he growled, uncoiling in one lithe movement to stand over her. With the set sun and a sky full of fiery red and gold clouds at his back she could not read his expression. She started to question him, but anticipating as much, he stuffed his handkerchief into her mouth and tied it securely. He bound her feet and she watched through wrathful, spitting green eyes as he pulled on his

clothes and buckled his gunbelt around his narrow hips, his eyes
already remote and engrossed with the plan she could see had replaced everything else for him. Damn him!

It wasn't until all the daylight had faded and night was reality
that she realized the precariousness of her position. Maybe the
next face she would see would be an Indian's! Worse yet, maybe
he didn't intend to come back for her. Maybe she would be left
there to die, helpless, naked, alone, with only the desert creatures
to keep her company—the scorpions, snakes, Gila monsters, spiders. . . . She shuddered. And only one thin blanket over her.
She had heard her uncle and his riders talking about the deadly in-
habitants. Now all those names she had forgotten were there—like
nightmare creatures—all the worse because she did not know what
any of them looked like. Or which was the most deadly . . .

Would an Arizona spider be worse than a scorpion? Or a snake?
She shuddered at memory of that enormous Gila monster that had
waddled off, wagging its fat, blunt tail. Did it take large bites out
of a person? Or inject venom? She had visions of being eaten alive
one bite at a time by monsters of such ugliness that her mind
veered off into numbness.

Stop it, fool! Even if it is true, it serves no purpose. But by midnight, when the cooling ground was alive with crawly things that
had eyes that seemed to glow in the inky darkness, she finally gave
way to her terror, crying like a small child, and none of her bravery
helped in the least.

Dallas Younger woke up first and knew even before he opened
his eyes that something was wrong. He lay there, still warm in his
blankets, listening to the shriek of the birds, feeling the sun on his
face, and his black brows knit into a frown in his handsome, sensual face. He sat up abruptly and looked around at the camp. The
fire had died to cold ashes; men still slept in their blankets. *Why
the hell hadn't the night guards woke them at sunrise?* He came to
his feet, pulled on his boots, roaring for his men to get the hell up.

A piece of white caught his eye, a note torn from butcher paper
and slipped around one of the buttons on his shirt. Growling, he
ripped it off his shirt and read it with his mouth dropping open. It
was written in the same hand as the note on Caswell two days ago:

Younger, this is where I'm going to put a bullet. Keep a close eye on
your belly. Cantrell

"Where are those goddamned sentries?" he bellowed, paling perceptibly. Cass Ewell, who had walked out a distance to relieve himself, hollered, "Over here!"

Emmet Wilson, one of the two who had been charged with first watch, was dead—his throat cut from ear to ear. They found the other guard less than fifty feet away, probably lured out by some sound, maybe even Wilson's dying.

"Stupid bastards—serves them right for being so damned careless!" Younger snarled. "Saddle up! Then spread out and find his trail. I want that bastard! When I get my hands on him he's going to be praying for death a long time before he gets his wish!"

Ward Cantrell left his horse at the stream, took off the saddle, tied the horse securely next to the girl's mount, and then moved as silently as an Indian over to the blankets. He slipped off his boots, lay back with a sigh, and heard a soft, muffled sob that caused him to look sharply at the figure huddled next to him.

"Hey, you all right?" he whispered, reaching out to smooth her hair out of her eyes. Her face was wet with tears and felt cold and clammy under his hand. Christ! Now what? He untied the gag and then her hands and feet and took the silent crying girl into his arms. He'd thought she would be sound asleep—not crying like an orphan left to die somewhere.

"Hey, what happened? Did something scare you?" Jesus. She was cold as death all over.

"Hey, are you all right? You're all right. Just scared," he whispered, brushing at her face gently. But she only shivered uncontrollably and huddled her slim body against him, trembling. In the moonlight, which now silvered the sheer walls of the canyon, her face was like wet marble and as cold. He lowered his head and pressed warm lips against her cheek, brushing tears away with his warm hands.

"Hey, don't cry. Everything is all right. You're okay. Nothing bad is going to happen to you." But he could see she wasn't responding. Tears kept spilling down her cheeks, and she was shivering like she'd taken a chill.

"Did something bite you, a snake or something?" She didn't respond, just kept crying as if he weren't there. He pulled the blankets back and inspected her all over to be sure, but there were no signs of injury, no swellings or bumps anywhere. He took his clothes off and pulled her back into his arms to share his body heat. Even without the blanket he was warm. Her cold body felt good against his, and it seemed natural to slip inside her and begin moving slowly. And just as natural to kiss her wet face and then her cold lips until he felt them become warm and responsive. He continued the gentle rocking motion until he felt her beginning to relax, her cold limbs becoming warm and pliant instead of cold and stiff.

Leslie woke with a strange headache that lasted until noon and finally receded. She ate whatever he gave her that day, did what he told her to do almost like a mechanical doll. She felt strangely bemused and confused but grateful he didn't keep the rope around her neck. By the time they had stopped for the night she was exhausted but almost back to normal emotionally. She looked at him strangely then, as if she were trying to remember something. She had a vague recollection of a nightmare filled with nameless terror and then nameless, faceless comfort. Had she dreamed it or had he made love to her again—for a long time, gently, with warm kisses and soft murmurings?

She couldn't tell by his actions today. He was remote, cool, efficient—the same as before. If he had comforted her, if she had needed comfort, neither one of them seemed willing or able to talk about it. Maybe it had been merely a nightmare.

She couldn't tell anything from his reactions. His clean-shaven face was as impassive and stoic as any Indian she could ever imagine. She would like to know, but she couldn't imagine asking him about it, and they were still traveling too fast for conversation.

The land was no longer level. They rode through hills now— small hills and great rolling hills, through wild canyons, basins, and valleys, sometimes crossing narrow streams. The land was still gray and brown, still strewn with rocks and cactuses and small tufts of grass—the very same type of land as before but turned on end, receding off into ominous-looking mountains. Sometimes she saw live things, but she had no idea what they were—just small slithery things. One second they blended into their surroundings, into the rocks they sat on; the next they slithered away—disgusting!

CHAPTER
SIXTEEN

They made camp this time next to a dry stream bed, and Leslie watched Ward take a shovel from his assortment of packs and begin to dig until water, murky and sluggish, bubbled up.

"How did you know there would be water there?"

"Guessed." He built a small fire, opened a can of beans, and heated water for coffee. He moved deftly and with an economy of motion that Leslie found fascinating. The artist in her saw him as one of the simple rustics used by so many painters, herself included, to enhance a landscape. She leaned back on her elbows, her legs stretched out in front of her, covered by her tattered gray riding gown, and amused herself by planning a landscape with the simple pots and pans, the brown of Cantrell's clothes, the yellowed desert sands, the orange glow of the small crackling fire, the blue sky turning fiery red and purple as the sun lit the clouds from underneath. She could use bravura brushstrokes for the sky and clouds, but she would need a finer brush to capture the unexpected refinement of feature she saw in this bandit: the thick, curling, honey-colored lashes fringing his fine blue eyes, the rich smoothness of his lips, the handsome angles of his face. . . . In this light she would use ocher to simulate teak for the symmetrical sweep of his dark arms, where muscles swelled and tapered with masculine strength and competence. She would have to balance the fiery, evanescent sky against the dark and warm tonality of the man.

Art was her first love, and no matter how much she might personally despise Cantrell, she could not help framing him in various poses. He had a lithe, striking form. With his tawny, flaxen hair and his azure blue eyes, set in a warm, sun-bronzed face, he would tempt any painter. The artist in her did not need to judge his personal worth. He would serve as a decoration, a mannequin only.

She felt very superior thinking her fluid, lofty thoughts, denying his manhood in the bargain, but she soon tired of her diversion. After they ate he used one of the tin pans and washed from his waist up, then shaved, scraping the red-gold stubble off his lean

87

face with a wicked-looking blade he carried in a sheath behind his gun. She had never watched a man at his toilet before and found this fascinating. She forgot that she hated him and that he was a killer and began asking questions.

"How long have you been a train robber?"

He glanced at her, his face darkened with a scowl. "Three, four years," he finally said.

"What happened to your girlfriend? The one on the train?"

He grinned, remembering that little Belen had gone back to Mexico in a fit of temper brought on by her jealousy during the train robbery. "You two didn't exactly hit it off," he said, ignoring her question.

"What did you do before? You haven't always been a train robber, have you?"

He chuckled. "Seems like I have." He sighed and put down the razor. He rinsed his face. He'd been a hunted outlaw for six years, doing whatever he had to do to survive and little else. The world was full of people who could spot a fugitive on sight. Honest work was damned hard to come by. The closest thing he'd had to a legitimate job was when he worked for the Que Ti Qua Ranch, enforcing Colonel Goodnight's Winchester Quarantine to keep fever-bearing herds of longhorns from crossing the Texas panhandle. Mostly that had involved riding from point A to point B, armed to the teeth, looking dangerous enough to discourage trespassing, and occasionally leading a herd down a designated trail to avoid contaminating the local stock. It hadn't been legal, but the law had deliberately ignored the activity because it successfully protected the ranchers in the panhandle. . . .

"Hey, remember me?"

Ward grunted. "What the hell are you doing? Writing an article?"

"I'm here at your insistence, not my own, and I'm bored. You don't need to be ashamed of your past. There's no way you could impress me."

The look he gave her was one of bitterness. "What do you want to hear? That I'm lower than a mineshaft? Well, I am. I rode with the Jackson Hole Gang in Wyoming, fought with McSween in the Lincoln County range wars, enforced illegal quarantines. Rob the T and P at least once a month. I do whatever pays the best until it stops paying, then I move on."

"So who's paying you to kidnap me?"

"Once in a great while I do charity work," he said grimly.

"Charity work! If this is your idea of benevolence . . ." She was speechless. Finally recovering, she asked, "Is there nothing too low for you?"

"I don't dig post holes," he said, grinning suddenly.

"You mean you don't do anything that consists of honest toil." She shook her head and the wind picked up tendrils of her dark hair and fanned it over her face. She brushed it back with a slender hand. "I despise men who can't do anything useful. Being an outlaw is another way of avoiding responsibility, or not doing the drudgery that each one of us has to do for survival."

Ward laughed. "You look like you know a lot about drudgery. Your smooth, white hands have never pushed a plow."

Leslie flushed. There was too much truth in his words. She decided to change the subject. "Is that El Paso accent of yours real?"

"It's real enough, I guess."

"You must have attended school somewhere. Did you graduate?"

Now he picked up the rag he had been using as a towel and wiped his face. "I almost graduated from Harvard, but I was expelled three months before," he said, grinning, because he knew she wouldn't believe the truth.

"I suppose there are ways you could have heard of Harvard. . . . Where did you really go to school?"

"Long Branch Saloon, class of '82." There was a kernel of truth in his words. His career as an outlaw had started in the street in front of the Long Branch in Dodge City six years ago. . . .

"Ahhh," she sighed. "It suits you somehow."

"So does your outfit."

She looked down at her torn riding habit and back up at him in surprise. "What?"

"You're the kind of woman who can inspire a man to rip the clothes off her back." His eyes narrowed, and she saw muscles in his cheek bunch and writhe. "It's amost dark, little one. Come here," he said, tossing the rag away from him.

She swallowed and her frosty lime-green eyes widened. She could feel her heart thumping heavily in her chest, much faster than it should, and fought to control the fear, or whatever, that was causing her distress. She instinctively backed away from him, scooting off the blanket. She did not want a repeat of what had happened last night. She could not explain what had happened to her in his arms. It defied logic and reason as she knew it. A stranger had taken over her body, some dark demon-creature that knew nothing of traditional morality, personal pride, integrity.

Now, sitting tensely before this man she had hated, this man who had killed innocent men and forced himself on her, she felt breathless. She swallowed and flushed and looked away from the sharp light in his piercing blue eyes. She stood up, either from nervousness or in preparation to bolt, and he took a step toward her.

"If you run I will put the rope back around your neck. If I put it on again, it stays." His voice was quiet and unemotional, but she knew he meant it.

He was too close to her. Too close. Leslie licked her lips, and for the second time since he had taken her, he saw tears sparkle in her eyes. She had eloquent eyes, and now he could read her torment plainly. She was almost too direct; it would be impossible for her to lie successfully.

"That's not fair," she whispered, turning her back.

"Kidnapping is inherently unfair," he said softly, moving to stand before her, so close she could feel the threatening warmth of his body. "It won't do you any good to run or fight," he said softly, coaxingly. "It'll just make it harder on you."

Leslie heard him with relief. At last! Something she could recognize in all that vague and fearful confusion. She turned defiantly, her eyes flashing. "I should be like you? Do whatever is easiest? Most convenient? Well, I'm dreadfully sorry, Mr. Gunfighter, Mr. Train Robber, Mr. Kidnapper, but I can't take the easy way out just because it might save me some pain or inconvenience. I have integrity, and I'm going to fight you, because not to fight would fill me with shame, and I can abide anything except that."

Ward reached out and touched her cheek, and, amazingly, she didn't draw back. Then she closed her eyes, as if from weakness, and he could feel her pulse begin beating wildly. Trembling started in her stomach, near her spine. He was so close she could feel the heat from his body.

"Please," she whispered.

Ward saw and understood—not completely or with definition, but at a more fundamental level. He felt a sudden resentment. He should teach her a lesson, all about lust and hypocrisy, but she was too vulnerable. Most females had no well-thought-out philosophy. If you took away their belief or their habit of obedience, they were adrift in a rudderless ship on a vast, bewildering sea.

He wanted her, but not enough to risk being responsible for her downfall. She reminded him of too many things he'd thought he had left behind. This girl with skin like satin represented all that he had fled eight years ago.

"Don't bother to run. I'm not in the mood for war." He caught her arms and dragged her over to the blankets. She began to fight against him, but she was incredibly strong. He tied her hands behind her, gagged her to stop her outraged cries, and then tied her feet while she glared with hate over her shoulder at him. When she was trussed up like a Christmas package, he lay down beside her and began to stroke and caress the smooth curve of her slender back. He smoothed the hair off her face and felt her become still, watchful, under his hand. He knew what she expected. Why disappoint her? He lowered his head and kissed her throat and the firm swell of her breast. There was enough cruelty in him to enjoy the shudder of fear that rippled through her.

It cost him something to leave her—to relinquish that satiny warmth—but he covered it well. "Sorry I can't stay with you, but I'll be back soon. You'll be safe. I wouldn't leave you if there was any real danger." He covered her and left, and it was full dark before her anger left her to be replaced by uncontrollable terror.

Dallas Younger posted three guards for his remaining seven men to sleep in peace. They didn't expect a visit tonight. No one would dare pull a stunt like that two nights in a row.

"Harris, Leonard, Sanders, you got first watch, and I don't want any fallin' asleep, you hear? You keep moving and keep an eye on each other. Anything out of the ordinary and you call out, you hear?"

"Gotcha, boss."

"Right!"

"Hell yes!"

"Keep in plain sight of each other so's there can't be any slip-ups!" Younger warned.

It was almost midnight, with chill winds moaning out of the hills, when a bank of slow-moving clouds obscured the almost-full moon that had arced overhead. Sanders, who had walked out the farthest from the campfire, heard the tiniest sound, whirled around, ready to cry out, and felt his nose and mouth covered by a hand with the grip of steel.

Neither Harris nor Leonard saw Sanders drop. Harris had reached down to pick up a billet of wood. He did that every time his path crossed one. It paid off. No one ever had to make a special trip looking for twigs and branches when he was around. He had mentioned what a good idea this was to the other two, but they never paid any attention to anything. He straightened and searched out his two comrades, exactly as he was supposed to do.

He saw Sanders straighten up, adjusting his rifle to carry it more comfortably, and continue the arc he had been making from the fire out to the east and then back toward the horses, then to the fire again. Sanders was too damned predictable to be a good sentry! That's the first kind a mad-dog killer like that Cantrell would go after! Himself, he just did something different every time. He wasn't taking any chances on getting his throat cut!

Harris adjusted his armload of firewood and watched with tight-mouthed disapproval as Sanders lit a cigarette and Leonard, who was always out of tobacco, walked over to join him. Harris was of half a mind to wake Younger and tell him they were messing up! Damn them! They couldn't even obey a simple directive! Harris was an old army man himself, until he had been found guilty of rape and murder. But it wasn't his fault. He hadn't known they counted those filthy squaws as people. They should warn a man—not just decide to hang him for one lousy mistake. He'd done the only thing he could have done under the circumstances, and that was to kill three guards and escape. He still couldn't figure out what all the fuss had been about. He'd been a good soldier—damned good! The girl had only been an Indian! A damned Crow, at that! Wasn't worth a damn! Certainly wasn't worth a good soldier's life!

Those damned clouds covered the moon again, and Harris couldn't decide if he should risk getting Dallas Younger awake and all hot under the collar about the way Sanders and Leonard were messing up, probably getting together to nip on the bottle Leonard always kept hidden!

They were still out there together. Probably getting drunk! He should wake Younger, but he was hell on men when he was mad, and he hated being waked up in the middle of the night. And everything did look all right. Harris saw Sanders coming toward him, and he could tell he'd been right about the bottle. Good thing he hadn't gotten Younger up—they had decided to share with him!

The man he thought was Sanders took a full swig of the whiskey and passed him the bottle. Harris tilted his head back, and let the fiery liquor burn a warm trail down to his stomach.

"That hit the spot!" he said gratefully, passing the bottle back. He adjusted his armload of billets carefully.

Sanders tucked the bottle into his hip pocket; Harris turned to resume his path back to the fire with his billets and found himself caught in a vise of steel, his mouth and his nose clamped shut. He clawed for his gun and felt a white-hot pain at his throat—the last memory he would ever have.

Man and wood crumpled to the ground, and Cantrell slipped noiselessly to the sleeping forms scattered around the campfire. He searched each sleeping face until he found Younger, bent down and pinned a note, which he had written while it was still light, onto Younger's shirt, and then slipped back into the night.

Seven down. Seven to go. Then Younger.

With difficulty Ward Cantrell found the place he had left the girl. There was no stream to follow tonight and no moonlight now to help him. It surprised him that he felt such urgency to get back to her. He knew she was safe there. He had spent years sleeping in the desert, mountains, plains, and nothing had ever threatened him, except an occasional flea or tick. She was probably crying again, and it gnawed at him, making him impatient with himself, but he had no choice.

His decision had been made for him days ago. He would abide by it even if it meant his own death. The men who could do what he had seen at that small farm, to unarmed women, an old man, and a boy, deserved to die. He would kill them without pity or mercy. He felt no guilt—no more than if he had killed a rabid skunk. The only requirement he had was that they be awake and that Younger, who had led the raid, know what was coming so he could sweat about it. It was too bad the girl got hurt, but she couldn't be allowed to change anything.

He found her and his camp when he was almost ready to give up and wait for morning. If her horse hadn't whinnied, he would have missed them altogether. She was ice cold and completely unresponsive. He quickly untied her, undressed her and himself, and held her as close as he could, kissing her face, her eyes, her mouth, until he felt her begin to respond.

Any remorse he had would be not for the men he had killed but for this slender female who trembled uncontrollably in his arms. . . . She was sweet and curving, delicate and pure. He made love to her while she was still clinging to him like a trusting

child, and that even managed to twinge the conscience he didn't
think he still had.

CHAPTER
SEVENTEEN

He woke her before dawn, and this time, because she was naked
and she knew she'd been fully clothed when he tied her up, she
knew that something had happened. The dream again, but apparently it wasn't all a dream.

Cantrell saw her sweet mouth tighten into an angry line. "You
tricked me," she said, looking cross and irritable.

"Correction. I took advantage of you. That's what I'm supposed to do," he said patiently. "You're a hostage, a victim. Or
had you forgotten?"

Flushing angrily, her pretty chin came up in that stubborn way
she had. "I thought there was supposed to be honor among
thieves, or some such code."

"You asking to join me? Or are you trying to lay down rules of
conduct for relationships with hostages? A guide for all us uneducated types?" He tilted his head back and looked at her through
narrowed eyes, his expression wavering between bitterness and
anger. He had awakened in a strange, rancorous mood. "Might as
well forget it," he said grimly. "Most of us don't read anything
but our own wanted posters, else we would be into real crime—be
lawyers, politicians, and railroad tycoons—where the real money
is."

"I guess we're lucky you can't read. You'd be really dangerous
if you could," she said caustically, beginning to jerk on the clothes
he had belatedly tossed her.

The small rolling hills had turned into mountains. She was seeing real trees now—fir, spruce, pine, and oak—scattered but slowly, very slowly, becoming dense, forestlike. They were leaving
the desert behind, climbing into more heavily wooded sloping terrain that looked wild and uninhabitable. They moved slowly, picking their way through the brush and rocks. The air was rich with
pine and musky animal smells. Occasional pine cones littered their

path. The sun was still high overhead, but mostly they rode in the shade.

Now she was seeing small furry animals—jackrabbits, the riders on her uncle's ranch had called them. And more slithery things. Cantrell didn't talk much, but as they rode he occasionally shot at a jackrabbit. She noticed with chagrin that he did not miss. Maybe he didn't try the hard shots. Soon there were four rabbits hanging from the horn of his saddle.

When the sun began to sink below the horizon, she noticed that he changed course. They were going east now.

"Where are we going?" she asked tiredly. She had been drooping in the saddle for miles.

He turned and looked at her for practically the first time. Her pretty face was streaked with dust and sweat beneath the protecting hat he had taken off one of the men he had killed. She had braided her long black hair and wrapped it around her crown. Wispy hairs framed her dirty face. She looked exhausted, and he realized for the first time that she had been subjected to a ride that would have killed most women. "You've had a pretty rough time of it, haven't you?" he asked softly. This first sign of compassion from him unnerved her. A lump formed in her throat, and she just sat there, too sore and tired to move, wondering what he was thinking.

Ward was thinking about what he had to do that night and that he didn't want to leave the girl tied up on the desert again. Her reaction to it was too damaging. He could tell she didn't understand any better than he did what happened to her, and the effect lasted into the next day. Besides, if something should go wrong and he didn't make it back . . . That creamy white skin was too good for buzzards. It was time to get rid of her anyway. If Younger caught up to them, there would be a hail of gunfire. . . . Every time they had stopped to rest the horses, he had scanned the horizon, and each time Younger was nearer. He'd been a fool to save her boyfriend for last.

They rode until the sun was setting. Leslie dragged in the saddle, too weary to complain and too stubborn to beg him to stop. He grunted, and she looked up, amazed to see a small adobe house with a thatched roof squatting under a band of cottonwoods. Three days without ever seeing another person had almost convinced her they were alone in the world—that there was no other life in Arizona—if they were still in Arizona.

The adobe hut was built next to a natural artesian seep where water bubbled up and sparkled like liquid black pearl in the dusk. The family that spilled out of the rude shelter, once they saw that Cantrell came in peace, looked more Indian than Mexican. The man had a pointed head with a black thatch of hair that looked as stiff as straw. The woman had small, sullen eyes and thin, corded arms. There were four children with round, solemn eyes. They looked like chicks peering from behind the mother hen's drab feathers.

Cantrell negotiated with the man in a guttural Mexican dialect. Money and two of the rabbits changed hands. The man spoke rapidly to his wife, and she quickly gathered some things from the house. The man hitched a small burro to a cart and the family clamored into it.

"What are they doing?"

"They're leaving." He walked over to stand beside her horse. "Follow them. They'll lead you into town."

His eyes were unreadable. She could feel her heart begin a heavy, muted pounding in her chest. This should have sounded like deliverance, but it felt like rejection. "What if I don't want to be led to safety?" she asked, her voice low.

He frowned as if he didn't understand.

"Send them away," she whispered.

Ward could feel a pulse come alive in his temple. He wanted her, but he also realized that even though she had been virginal, she was still Younger's woman and, being woman, capable of more treachery than Younger could ever imagine. And even if he could trust her, he knew she wouldn't be safe if Younger caught up to them. With a dozen men shooting at him, no one would be safe. He shook his head. "No."

Leslie knew she was insane, but something was driving her. Something primitive and totally unmanageable. She leaned down quickly, before she could change her mind again, and touched her lips to his, part of her dazed by what she was doing and part of her exulted by the quiver that went through his lean, rock-hard frame.

Taken by surprise, his tawny eyebrows crowded his piercing blue eyes, but she wasn't frightened now. She turned her head slightly so their noses would not act as barriers and pressed a shy, tentative kiss on his bottom lip. He searched her eyes, frowning his lack of understanding at her and then he turned and motioned the man away. He lifted her out of the saddle, and she slid into his arms.

His lips claimed hers, and he groaned as if this were the last thing in the world he wanted, but his lips were clinging to hers, warm and demanding. His hands pulled her tight against him, and she could feel the hardness of his thighs against her own.

The Mexican family scampered into the wagon. Her arms lifted to twine around his neck, and she felt him lift her and carry her inside. The small hut smelled of beans. The bed he laid her on was a mattress of corn husks covered by ticking.

Silken lashes darkened her cheeks. Her lips were parted, expectant. He brushed his lips against them and then against the smile lines on her soft face. She tasted of alkali dust and made small mewling sounds against his ear. He kissed her awkwardly at first and then hungrily, glad her usually stormy green eyes were closed. When he could force himself to let her go, he backed away from her and began to undress himself. She unbuttoned the row of buttons on her tattered riding gown and then sat up, shrugging out of the gown, exposing the whiteness of her small breasts. She looked so tender and trusting as she looked up at him. Moving into her arms, he had the awful feeling that she was different for him. Most girls were little more to him than a flash of white skin, an open mouth. . . .

He was right. Their lovemaking was tender-fierce, hungry, a wild mating that left them both exhausted.

She couldn't tell if she had been asleep or not. The room was dark. A coyote yipped into the night. He was stirring. His hand found hers, and she lay there quietly, content until he raised up on one elbow and brushed the hair away from her face. He lowered his head, and his lips nipped at hers, then moved on to brush against her eyes, cheeks, ears, and throat. She would have believed herself incapable of response so soon after that starburst of sensation, but she was wrong. He kissed her until she was flushed and shaking, until she was so engrossed in her own body's response that she barely noticed when his lips slipped down to her breasts and then her belly. His mouth was there, dragging a shuddering, in-drawn breath through her, burning her blood into steam to scald and plunder her before she could move to stop him. With diabolical skill he brought her all the way up, and when her body was convulsing with shock waves of ecstasy he buried himself deep inside her to bring them both soaring upward again, clinging together as if the whole world would drop away and leave them, and then, unbelievably, it did. At the moment of heart-stop, the world fell away. She would have screamed if his mouth hadn't stifled her cries.

"Oh, oh, oh, I never knew, I never knew. . . ." she whispered, gasping.

"So now you know," he whispered, brushing black curls off the sweet oval that glowed with luster even in the almost dark room.

He was still on top of her, their limbs still meshed, warm, sweat-sheened together, his hands still tangled in the silky black mass of her hair. He groaned and buried his face in the warmth at her throat, then pushed himself away from her.

He stood up. "Where are you going?"

"You don't need to know that," he said, pulling on his pants. "I'll be back, but if something should go wrong, follow the wagon tracks into town. We're near Flagstaff. You could make yourself useful. Cook those rabbits. I'll be back in time to help you eat them."

CHAPTER
EIGHTEEN

Leslie woke up slowly, disoriented, blinking at the rough adobe ceiling. She frowned, remembering that he hadn't come back to help her eat the rabbit she had cooked.

"Unnn." That sound, like a grunt of pain, had come from the room on the other side of the canvas.

"Cantrell?" she called out.

A soft curse was her only answer. She scampered off the bed and dressed herself as quickly as she could, her heart pounding with sudden fear. Running her fingers through her hopelessly tangled hair, she brushed aside the canvas over the door opening. Cantrell was seated in a chair with his back against the wall. Relief flooded her. "What are you doing?" she demanded, moving so she could see his face.

"I was hoping you would sleep awhile," he said, ignoring her question.

"Oh, my . . ." she gasped. He was frowning down at his left shoulder, trying to poke into torn flesh with a sharp knife. Bloody skin, bruised and burned around the edges, gaped. His shirt and pants were soaked in blood.

"What happened?" she demanded.

He hadn't looked at her yet. Now he lowered the knife and sighed as if he had finally found something he couldn't do. His eyes were momentarily desolate. He searched her face and sighed again. "Don't be scared. It's not as bad as it looks."

"How did it happen?"

"I failed," he said simply.

"Are they close?"

"Close enough, I guess."

She felt sick, but she was determined not to fall apart. "What are you trying to do?"

"Get a bullet out."

"I'll do it."

He looked at her skeptically. She took the knife from him and considered it. To her, probing inside his shoulder with something that sharp was insanity. It almost guaranteed that more damage would be done. She went to the pan on the basin, washed her hands with the stinging lye soap she found there, and then returned to his side.

"You ready?" she asked.

Her creamy white skin had paled at least two shades, but she looked game, so he nodded. She had to force herself to touch the gaping red tissue, to push her finger into the warm ooze that had been his shoulder. Her stomach lurched, turning inside out. She groped in warm flesh, fighting the faintness that threatened her. Cantrell had set his teeth against the pain, but beads of sweat popped out on his forehead, and all traces of his tan were gone. She was about ready to give up when she felt something sharp and jagged. She had to force two fingers into the wound to pry the flattened bullet out of there. At last, shaking, she withdrew; the bullet dripped blood as she dropped it on the table and collapsed into a chair.

He expelled a loud breath. "Jesus!" he groaned.

"Getting shot is dumb," she said to cover her own anxiety.

"I know," he said ruefully. He glanced at his wound and sighed. "We need to clean this thing," he said slowly, as if dreading the thought of it. "Get that bottle of whiskey out of my saddlebags."

Leslie complied. He nodded in encouragement and she uncapped the bottle. "You ready?"

His blue eyes were bleak and weary from so much pain. He dragged in a breath. "Maybe I'd better lie down."

He walked unassisted to the bed. Panting with the effort, he lay back and nodded at her, and she lowered the bottle. At the last second he turned his head away. She slowly poured the fiery liquid all over his shoulder, using her fingers to open the burnt edges of the wound. Cantrell dragged air into his suddenly convulsing lungs through tightly gritted teeth, his body stiffening, arching, and then at the very last, when the breath escaped out of him in a low, anguished moan, he fainted.

"Oh, God!" Leslie groaned. She threw her arms around him, sobbing. His skin was dry and hot. In panic, she searched his wrist for a pulse, found one, faint and thready, and sighed. At least he wasn't dead. And momentarily he was not in pain. But what would they do now?

Her mind refused to function. His head was turned away from her. His profile and the graceful column of his sturdy neck tempted her. She used her gown to wipe the beaded perspiration off his face, then lay down beside him and pressed her face against his. He looked so helpless. She reached out to smooth the hair off his forehead and ended by pressing her lips there. His skin had a salt, manly smell that was like a narcotic to her senses. She held him blindly, from some need that she couldn't name, until she felt him stir, then she slowly moved away.

He opened his eyes, tentatively, as if he feared consciousness might produce more pain. "We have to go," he said. The look in his eyes, still pain-weary but determined, told her it would do no good to argue.

CHAPTER
NINETEEN

"Where are we going now?" Leslie asked, watching him carefully. He had mounted easily, but his face looked gray and he hadn't moved since he got into the saddle.

Ward barely heard her words. Black fog, swirling dizzyingly in his head, threatened to engulf him. Don't move, he cautioned himself. Take deep, even breaths. All that blood will grow back—in time. Unfortunately, he didn't have much time. Younger had gotten reinforcements from somewhere. They could not all be Powers men. Maybe a local posse? Had Powers or some local sheriff wired ahead? Be plenty of men who wouldn't mind collecting a reward, maybe two of them, if Powers was as mad as the Texas and Pacific Railroad.

The ground under his horse came slowly into focus, and he kicked the big black gently, very gently.

Leslie watched him warily. He had lost a lot of blood, and he swayed a dozen times, but he stubbornly refused to fall.

Much later, they topped a rise and saw a narrow dirt road winding around the mountainside. The air felt cool and crisp, even at midday. They must be fairly high up in the mountains. The smell was crisp and resiny.

The sky overhead was filled with roiling, tempestuous clouds, so low they were almost within reach—threatening to unleash their pent-up fury in the heat and passion of a summer thunderstorm. Mists swirled over their heads, augmenting the tension within her. She was torn between fear and anger at him for beginning something that could only end in death for him and possibly for her as well. The angry, lowering clouds, the threat of pursuit, the heavy, charged atmosphere, all combined to frazzle her usually steady nerves.

Ward swayed, fighting spiraling waves of nausea and weakness that had combined with an abominable frailty that threatened to overwhelm him. The hills and valleys before him surged sickeningly. It was an effort to speak. "Okay, this is where we part company."

"Here?" She looked around, puzzled. "I don't see any Indians."

"Flagstaff is around that bend. You'll be safe there."

She looked where he pointed, frowning, her smooth forehead rutted with worry. "But what about you?"

He had turned his horse to leave her. He had no energy to fight her, but he forced himself to sit straight in the saddle. "I'm going to cheat you out of your revenge. You can't have everything, little one," he said huskily.

"What about the Indians?"

"They'll just have to suffer."

"Where will you go?" she asked, strangely unwilling to let him ride away.

"Friends," he lied, nodding in another direction. "They'll take care of me." His face was gray, damp, set in determination. His clothes were dirty, bloodstained, torn. He kicked his horse gently, as if he didn't dare jar anything, and she felt a strange ache in her chest. Without thinking, she turned her horse, leaving the trail to follow him.

He stopped. "What are you doing?"

"I'm going with you!"

"No . . ." He frowned fiercely.

"You can't stop me—you're too weak. Besides, I'm not through being a hostage. You're supposed to trade me for your freedom. I read books, you know. I know how it is done. . . ."

"Christ!"

"Cantrell, look!" she cried in sudden alarm.

A party of riders came into sight from the direction of Flagstaff, saw the two of them less than two hundred yards from the trail, and urged their mounts into a run, beginning to fire.

Cantrell spurred his horse and Leslie did likewise, following him down what looked like a natural trail around the mountain. They flew through a dark corridor of pines with the low-hanging branches slapping at them. They came out of the dense foliage and were on another trail, this one more clearly defined. Without slowing his horse, Ward searched the hollows and crests, looking for a way to evade their pursuers even though he knew it was only a matter of time. The horses, especially his, were used up.

Ward saw another knot of riders and recognized Younger at their head. Pursuit behind him and in front of him. He had one split-second to regret he hadn't traded horses with the girl, and then reached for his rifle, urging the black forward at even greater speed. He heard the girl scream his name, but his mind was already focused on what he was going to do. He wrapped the reins around the pommel, lifted the rifle into position, and began to fire into the knot of riders, scattering them.

Leslie couldn't believe her eyes. Cantrell had gone crazy! He looked like one of the wild bandits in a Salvator Rosa painting. His hat had fallen back on his shoulders, his blond hair gleamed in the sunlight, and he was riding straight into the arms of at least a dozen firing men. Bullets spanged up dirt and rocks all around him. Men were falling, horses rearing and screaming, and then a bullet caught Cantrell's big black in the chest and both horse and rider went down.

Fear that had held her stunned and immobile now sent her flying forward. She didn't see anything except that lean sprawled form. Someone shot at her and she heard someone else yell, "You fool! That's Leslie!"

She would have thrown herself on the ground beside Cantrell if someone hadn't caught her arm and jerked her aside. Horses milled everywhere and dust blinded her.

"Where the hell do you think you're going?" That was Dallas Younger's voice, snarling at her. She turned, jerking her arm out of his steely grip.

"He's hurt!" she said without thinking.

"Damn right he's hurt! If he ain't dead, he's gonna be a lot more hurt before I get through with him!"

"No!" she shouted, springing at Younger, her eyes glazed with fury, her nails curved into talons.

Like an enormous grizzly, Younger shoved Leslie aside, flinging her into the dirt with a look of rage and mistrust that reminded her finally which side she was supposed to be on.

"Get that bastard on his feet!" Younger bellowed. Two men pulled Cantrell's limp form up, holding him by the arms, and Leslie had to bite back the urge to tell them again that they were hurting him. While they were dragging Cantrell toward a furious Younger, the other group of riders who had been pursuing them joined the melee, jerking their horses to a halt just a few feet from where Leslie was struggling to her feet.

"Who's in charge here?" Their leader, a tall, barrel-chested man with a silver badge catching the light, dismounted stiffly and stepped forward. He had a rumbling, sonorous boom of a voice.

"Who the hell wants to know?" Younger demanded.

"My name is Geronimo Nieves, Sheriff of Coconino County. I have a warrant for this man's arrest."

Geronimo Nieves had the most battered-looking face Leslie had ever seen. He had two scars, one slashing diagonally across his right cheek and another dividing his chin. His face was darkly tanned except for those two white slashes flashing like lightning on a dark night. His ears were gnarled, and his nose looked permanently flattened.

"Won't be necessary, Sheriff," Younger said, ignoring the outstretched hand. "We'll be taking care of him ourselves."

Younger dismissed Nieves with a wave of his hand and walked over to where Cantrell hung limply between the two men. He jerked Cantrell's head back and watched it fall forward lifelessly.

"The bastard still alive?"

"Barely."

"Get him awake! I want him to enjoy every goddamned minute of this!" he snarled.

A third man took a canteen off a horse, and they leaned him back and poured the water on his face while Leslie struggled not to scream at them. Her heart was beating furiously.

"This bastard killed eleven of my men," she heard Younger telling Nieves.

"Maybe more," Bass Wimer, a big man with a dull simian look, said, pointing to two who lay sprawled in the dirt and two more who sat nursing their wounds and groaning.

"You know why he done it?" Nieves asked, glancing from Cantrell's slumped form to Younger's furious face.

"Crazy, that's all," Younger growled. "Kidnapped my woman, and when we followed, he sneaked back and surprised us."

Leslie was watching Cantrell with fear and foreboding. They handled him roughly, pouring water on his head and slapping him, and only despair over the reality of their situation kept her from rushing forward. He groaned finally, and his eyes blinked open, fever bright and unfocused. They stood him up, one on each side, holding him with his arms twisted back, and she groaned.

"Well, well, well, so you've decided to join us." Younger sneered. "How are y'all feeling now, Cantrell? How's it feel to know you're the one about to die, bastard?"

Younger stepped closer to his prisoner and sent his fist crashing into Cantrell's face. "You're going to be real sorry you didn't kill me back there," he said. He hit him again, causing a gash to open up along his cheekbone, and this time Leslie cried out shamefully, begging him to stop, not even realizing she had until Younger turned on her, letting his eyes rake over her like she had no clothes on. He came to her side and dragged her away from the tree she had sagged against.

"Did this man rape you?" he demanded with a snarl.

"No!"

"No?! Does that mean he didn't rape you or he didn't have to?" Younger asked, his face dark with fury.

"Get your hands off me!" she hissed. "I won't be talked to like that by you or anyone else!"

Younger glared at her angrily. "You're pretty uppity considering what you been doing with Cantrell."

Nieves stepped forward, placing himself beside Leslie. "Let her be," he said quietly.

Younger shot her a look full of venom. He dropped her arm as if it burned him and turned his attention back to Cantrell's limp form. "Wake that bastard up! I want him to know it when we hang him! Get the rope!"

Men were rushing to comply.

Leslie turned to Nieves. "You're not going to let them hang him, are you? He's a train robber. There's a reward for him—but not dead." She was improvising now, desperately. "Please, Mr. Nieves, stop them. This is all a mistake."

Younger placed the rope around Cantrell's neck, and they brought the horse forward, steadying Cantrell's slumped, lifeless form.

"Please, Mr. Nieves!"

She had a strange accent. He looked at her appraisingly. "You're not from out here are you?"

"I'm from Massachusetts, but please, stop them. They're going to hang him!"

Cantrell was sagging in the saddle they had forced him onto, still unconscious. His face was shiny with bruises; blood trickled from half a dozen cuts. She had the insane urge to take his battered head and hold it to her breast. She knew that if she lived to be a thousand years old, nothing would ever move her as strongly as that sight.

Younger's men positioned the horse and rider under a sturdy limb and threw the rope over it. Three men braced themselves, and Leslie felt her heart stop and then lurch wildly and sickeningly.

"Hold on here!" Geronimo Nieves finally stepped forward. "I'm taking this man in so he can stand trial."

"Like hell you are!" Younger roared.

Nieves held out his hand, and one of his men slapped a shotgun into it. He pointed it at the three men holding the rope. "Drop that rope or you'll die with him."

"He hangs, damn you!" Younger snarled, lunging forward to slash at the horse, sending it forward. Nieves fired point-blank into the three men and the rope slid through their fingers. Leslie threw herself forward, trying to reach Cantrell, but Younger caught her, jerking her against him, peering angrily into her face before he flung her away from him with a curse. "I'll deal with you later."

The horse Cantrell had been on lurched forward, and he fell to the ground unharmed except for the fall, which must have been painful. Fortunately, he was already unconscious. Heart pounding wildly, she sagged against the tree while the sheriff and his posse loaded Cantrell across a horse and left without further incident. She watched until they were out of sight, then turned her attention to the men who had been shot.

"Get 'em on their horses," Younger snarled. "Ain't no use trying to doctor 'em here."

He grabbed Leslie's arm and put her forcibly onto her horse. His gray eyes were flat, unemotional slate. She'd never been afraid of Younger before, but now, suddenly, looking into those relentless, angry eyes, she realized that he no longer considered her a lady. She felt the steely grip of his hand on her arm, and knew soul-shaking, gut-deep fear.

CHAPTER
TWENTY

The ride to Flagstaff, with four wounded men, was slow, but Leslie barely noticed. She felt immune to her surroundings, dazed, as if her mind had gone numb. Her head was filled with an angry buzzing sound, and her heart was beating far too hard. Her hands on the reins trembled as if they belonged to someone else, perhaps a fearful old woman. Surely they could not belong to Leslie Powers.

The sun was still bearing down on the trees that grew thick and green to the very edge of the rutted red clay road. It shone on the pale pink rocks that jutted out of the mountain, on the men who rode all around her but hopelessly separate from her. The air was cool; even though it was midday the weather had a crisp mountain feel to it. September? Or was it October? She would have recognized October in Wellesley. . . . Could she ever get back there? How many thousands of miles lay between her and her past? She sagged in the saddle with the hopelessness of it, so much distance, so many miles stretching out. . . . She could not imagine ever finding her way back there.

Occasionally Dallas Younger glanced angrily in her direction, and she felt drenched in the hate lashing out at her from his dark eyes. It was another pressure on her numb brain, but she did not ask herself what right he had to hate her. She accepted his hate. An angry buzzing sound in the distance was growing louder now, so loud she could no longer hear the sounds of their horses' hooves smacking into the hard-packed dirt road.

Flagstaff was a lumber camp. The town was much smaller than

Phoenix, without the boisterous air of a cowtown. A town of workers. The shrill whine she had been hearing was the saw from the sawmill, out of sight. Flagstaff did not seem real to her. Merely a small noisy town at the base of a massive mountain whose topmost peaks were already dusted with a thin cap of snow. No railroad there. Heavy wagons loaded with trees that had been reduced to naked poles rumbled past, heading for the source of that shrill whine.

Younger dispatched his men to see to the wounded while he took Leslie to the only hotel in town, the Orlando, which was a tall, awkward rectangle of a building, two-story, with the inevitable awning. He signed the register as if he would take out his anger on it, and then took her by the arm, roughly, to lead her up the stairs to her room. He unlocked the door and then turned on her, his dark eyes narrowed with fury.

"What did you do, fall in love with that bastard? He was going to sell you to the Indians! Didn't you know that? To a bunch of filthy Indians who live on reservations like so many dogs penned up! He didn't take you because he fell for your big green eyes and your milk-white skin!" He caught her shoulder, and she cried out instinctively, angrily, twisting away from his hands.

"Get your hands off me! You either treat me as a lady or leave me alone!" she snapped.

A sneer spread across his face, curling his lips down. "Pretty high and mighty for a piece of used goods, ain't you, missy. A lady don't do what you did."

Younger was rewarded with a white-hot flaring of passion, a starburst of heat that lightened, then darkened, her eyes. Fury blinded her to everything except his sneering face. The rage, fear, and frustration that had been building for days exploded. Her arm seemed to move of its own accord. She didn't realize she had hit him until she saw the stunned look on his face and felt the pain, like a burn, on the palm of her hand.

She should have been afraid, but she wasn't. She felt a surge of joyousness at the way it felt when she hit him. Her muscles seemed to swell with strength. With unbounded energy. This was what she had been needing—someone to strike out at, someone to take out fear, anger, and frustration on.

She lunged at him as if she really believed she could kill him, as if she thought she was seven feet tall and weighed three hundred pounds, the way some of those lumberjacks had looked on the wooden boardwalks below.

He didn't seem to notice her wonderful strength. He took hold of her with rough hands, glaring into her face like he had always hated her.

"You won't be so high and mighty when I get through with you, missy," he growled viciously, jerking her around and shoving her at the door he had unlocked.

Leslie staggered into the room, finally caught her balance, and faced him again, her face pale but defiant. "Get out of my room! You have no right to be in here!"

Dallas Younger's face was a mask of hatred, his voice a sneer of condemnation. "I was willing to marry you, you little slut! I have every right! He took something that belonged to me, something I was saving. I was gonna marry you—proper—in a church! I was gonna treat you like a lady! You weren't a little whore till he got his filthy hands on you."

He slammed the door, closing them in, and it sounded to Leslie like the closing of a tomb. His eyes were filled with fury, revenge, and lust, and it was all directed at her. She stepped back, opened her mouth to scream, and he lunged at her like an enraged panther, knocking her onto the bed that dominated the small, barren room.

Her scream turned into a gasp of panic that he shut off with his hard mouth while he forced her down onto the bed. She fought like a wildcat, her eyes spitting fury, but he was just as determined as she and far stronger. His hands ripped her gown aside. Screaming, she slashed at his face, trying to take his eyes out. She missed, but clawed a bloody furrow down his cheek. He slapped her hard and she reeled away from him, barely feeling it, and came at him again, teeth bared, nails curved into claws.

"Ow! Dammit! You . . . damned cat!" He yelled, backing away.

"Get out of here!" she screamed hysterically.

"All right!" he shouted, backing away from the fury in her green eyes. "All right."

Geronimo Nieves paced back and forth in the outer part of the jail until the doctor came out, closing his black bag.

"Well, Ben, he gonna make it?"

"Reckon that's between him and his maker. I stopped the bleeding. He's lucky he wasn't awake for that. *If* he has a strong constitution and *if* he don't get infected and *if* he ain't already lost too much blood . . ."

"How soon can we move him to Phoenix?"

"Can't say—three weeks or a month, maybe. What's he charged with?"

"Eleven counts of murder, kidnap, and rape."

"Should've just let them hang him," Ben grunted.

"Now, Ben, you know I couldn't do that any more than you could let him bleed to death."

"Yeah, yeah, I know, but maybe I wonder how smart we are sometimes," he growled, waving his hand disgustedly. "See you later tonight. I'll look in on him to make sure the bleeding doesn't start up again."

"Thanks, Ben. Night."

The ride back to Phoenix with a sullen Dallas Younger and a cadre of crippled gunfighters was far from pleasant. Leslie would have welcomed any sort of natural disaster to distract her from the outrage that still bubbled and boiled within her, but the weather was disgustingly pleasant.

They had been riding for a long time—she couldn't tell how long. The sun was high overhead, preparing to start its descent toward the horizon, which was far off and ragged with the silhouettes of majestic fir and pine. They were in a high, rough canyon, traveling south. Copses of aspen and oak, brilliant with their burnished autumn golds, yellows, and reds, were fiery against the somber green of the conifers and the smooth swirls of pink sandstone cliffs.

At last she found something she remembered. The configuration of trees that overlooked the Powers fortress. She had been riding numbly for hours . . . or days—she couldn't tell which—and suddenly they were on the narrow dirt road that led through the trees . . .

They descended the long, slow incline impatiently, as if all of them were eager to get back. Halfway down the road she saw the gates of the fortress swing open, and her heart did tiny flip-flops. Another confrontation to be gotten through before she could start that long trip back home. So many miles back . . .

Her uncle came out onto the long porch, shading his small, narrowed eyes from the sun. She returned his look, expecting some sort of greeting but ready to take him on as well as Younger, if need be. Mark Powers merely turned and walked into the house. She and Younger followed him to his office, and by the time she

reached there it had dawned on Leslie that her uncle was not exactly overjoyed to see that she was safe. He looked from Younger's sullen face to hers.

The scene that followed was not believable. Mark Powers was
stiff, formal, and deaf to anything she had to say. He cut her off by
holding up his hand, and then nodded to Dallas Younger to tell him
what had happened. He listened gravely and shut Leslie off angrily
when she tried to interrupt.

"That true?" he asked, squinting at her suspiciously. "You
talked the sheriff into saving that bastard Cantrell?"

"Yes, but . . ."

"Speak when you're spoken to, Leslie," he interrupted, his
eyes as bright and hard as jade, his mind closed against her. "You
sure he raped her?" he asked, turning to Younger.

Younger's sensual mouth curled into a sneer.

Something snapped in Leslie's head. "Why ask him?" she
screamed, oblivious to ears that might be pressed against the walls
of her uncle's study. "Don't you think I would know?" She
pointed at Younger. "He's the one who tried to rape me!"

"What did the sheriff do with Cantrell? What did he do with that
bastard?" Powers demanded, ignoring her.

"Nieves took him to Flagstaff. Said he'd bring him to stand trial
when he's well enough to travel," Dallas replied, also disregarding the girl who faced them like an angry tigress.

Leslie still couldn't believe her uncle meant to ignore what she
had told him. She faced him, incredulous but still determined, demanding his attention. "What are you going to do about this man?
He hit me, ripped my clothes, and treated me in an abominable
fashion."

Mark Powers pursed his lips into a tight little wrinkled slit.
"That true?" he asked Younger, who still looked sullen and
snarly.

"I reckon," he said gruffly. "She came at me like a damned
wildcat."

"You still willing to marry her?"

Younger's eyes raked over her. He was furious with her. He
shouldn't have anything to do with her, but like he had told Sam,
even second-hand the way she was, she was still half owner of the
whole Powers spread. "Yeah, I reckon so," he said finally. "I'll
probably be sorry."

Leslie was speechless.

"We'll take care of it when we ride into town to watch 'em hang

Cantrell. Maybe Saturday. They'll be bringing that bastard in to stand trial. She'll have to identify him.''

''Won't be that soon. We roughed him up pretty damn good.''

Angry words trembled on Leslie's lips, but none found voice.

CHAPTER
TWENTY-ONE

The mountains were hulking gray shadows behind a brilliant display of aspen trees flaming red and orange in the early-morning air. The sun was a pale gold ball in a hazy sky. Clouds sailed overhead on a stiff wind that smelled of sand and sage and whipped her riding hat, threatening to send it sailing away. It felt good to be out of the house and on a horse again with crisp wind on her face.

October first. She couldn't believe she had been in Arizona less than two months. It felt like years. She was dressed in a very smart black and white hound's-tooth riding gown with a jaunty black hat trimmed in white ribbon and a showy white egret plume. She looked very stylish. Dallas Younger had looked at her strangely, but she noticed that he had taken great pains with his wardrobe also.

Since they were going to town, she assumed Cantrell had survived, unless this trip was for the sole purpose of marrying her to Dallas Younger. Leslie rode sidesaddle next to Annette, who had come along to act as Leslie's maid of honor. Annette rode, but it did not come naturally to her. She grumbled at every step of the horse, as if her protestations would somehow inspire the gentle mare to be more considerate of her.

The women had each packed a bag, cramming all they could into them. Leslie knew what she was going to do. Her uncle and Dallas Younger would be furious—maybe they would kill her—but they would have to do it in front of the whole town.

The majority of the population of Phoenix was lining the wide dusty street when Geronimo Nieves rode into town with his prisoner.

"He don't look like no mad-dog killer to me," a tall, lantern-jawed man in front of the saloon sneered.

"Killed twenty men in cold blood!"

"Naw! Twenty? I heard it was closer to thirty."

"Hell, he didn't kill no thirty men. Powers ain't missing no thirty men."

"He shoulda killed 'em all. Then he wouldn't be here!"

Ward Cantrell ignored the hundreds of pairs of eyes that watched him. His fierce blue eyes raked over the crowd, looking for Younger, who was nowhere in sight. He heard some of the comments, but his face gave nothing away. His muscles tightened involuntarily. He would rather have a snake like Younger out where he could see him, but since he wasn't exactly in control anymore, he forced his muscles to relax. There wasn't a hell of a lot he could do about anything, dragging chains on his hands and feet. The horse he rode was probably tired of them too.

The slow procession reached the jail, and Ward waited for the word to dismount. He was learning patience. Three weeks in jail had taught him something six years of outlawry hadn't—the value of freedom. But, he thought dryly, if Powers and Younger have their way, I won't have long to worry about freedom.

The first few weeks in the U.S. cavalry had taught him the value of keeping his thoughts to himself. His company had been blessed with a burly drill sergeant who believed that everything he said should be received with reverent respect. After watching two recruits being pounded into the turf for twitching with mirth at sheer unadulterated ignorance being verbalized, control quickly became automatic.

Now if he felt anything at being paraded through the street like a circus animal, it didn't show on his lean face or in his still military carriage as he dismounted.

The jail was bigger than the one in Flagstaff, and the cell they put him in had a window, for which he felt a rush of gratitude. Ward settled back on the lumpy mattress with relief. He was still shaky. The ride had taken the last of his reserves. Sleep came easily, like pulling down a shade.

While her uncle was at the hotel desk, arranging for a block of rooms, with hers in the middle, no doubt, she strolled to the window near the open door. She only wanted to glance out, but two of Younger's men broke away from the rest and followed her. Irritated, Leslie shot a disdainful look at Younger and walked out the door. The two watchdogs moved in closer. What would they do if she bolted into the street? She didn't find out because she was arrested in her tracks by a shrill female voice:

"Is that her? The one who was kidnapped?"

"Sure Lord looks like her!"

"That's going to be some trial! I wouldn't miss it for the world!" The woman was tall and buxom with sharply etched features and eyes that looked Leslie over as if she were one of the women of ill-repute that congregated in the saloons.

"I heard two men discussing it with my husband just last night, and one of them was a barrister. He said that trial could go on a mighty long time. They'll drag everthin' out into the open—strip her bare. You mark my words. Find out what really happened!" The second speaker was short and stocky with a sturdy, self-satisfied look about her.

"Do tell! Skinny little thing for a Powers, ain't she? Probably asked for it! She has flirty eyes—I've seen her type before!"

"Ain't that the beatingest thing you ever heard of? I wouldn't want my husband on the jury. I just hope they don't let *her* attend church with decent folks."

The other woman laughed, a prim, sanctimonious sound. "I doubt if she spends time in churches—else she wouldn't have ended up the way she did."

"Did you see Cantrell? Right pert handsome man, if I do say so myself. . . . Bet she could tell some tales!"

"Kin tell he's a killer by the eyes. He looked my way just onct, and I felt the chill all the way to my bones. He'll hang—no doubt about that. My husband said he was withholding judgment—probably because he hates Powers!"

"Kept her long enough, didn't he?"

The heavyset woman snickered, and Leslie had the urge to walk over there and rip the woman's gown off so she would know how it felt to be stripped naked in front of a whole townful of people. Anger burned inside her. They hadn't once acknowledged her, except as an object to be talked about! She watched their backs as they walked away, feeling stunned by the force of her own reaction. If she'd had a gun, she would probably have shot them both.

As their voices faded, she heard one of them remark, " 'Bout the only good thing Powers does is to get rid of some of the riffraff that drifts into town. They'll hang Cantrell. Serves him right."

Cheeks burning, Leslie turned abruptly and walked back inside the Bricewood, oblivious to the contrast of the cool, sky-lit Garden Courtyard that served as the lobby of the hotel. Palms ten feet high swayed gently. Fans hung down on slender, almost invisible cords and stirred the tepid air, swaying the graceful fronds of the ferns that were interspersed between palms and clusters of chairs.

Her room was on the second floor this time. Annette helped her bathe and slip into a cool green organdy gown, a frosty lime color that matched her eyes and had long sleeves and a high neckline with a crisp white collar. The gown was frilly and lacy with intricate pleats falling gracefully from the bustle. She chose a small straw hat with a white velvet ribbon trailing down behind her, barely damaged at all by the crush of her satchel. Annette recombed her hair and pinned it in a mass of artful curls off her slender white neck. By the time they were finished, Leslie's heart was pounding frightfully, and she barely cared what she looked like.

They dawdled so long with her toilet that Younger was banging on the door before they were ready. They let him wait. When she finally went down to the lobby, he and her uncle were with Sheriff Nieves. She recognized his scar-slashed face immediately.

"Leslie, the sheriff here wants you to identify the man who kidnapped you before he goes back to Flagstaff."

"Very well," she said docilely, turning smoothly as she deliberately ignored the arm her uncle offered her.

Younger had changed his shirt. She had to admit that he really wasn't a bad-looking man, just despicable. Leslie walked beside Sheriff Nieves at the head of the procession, ignoring the eyes, hostile, curious, or indifferent, that watched her.

The jail was a block and a half away. The men chatted desultorily, but Leslie wasn't listening. Her heart was pounding so hard she thought she was going to shake apart from it. Would the jail be a good place to make her stand? Would Nieves help her again, or would they all treat her like her uncle had? She was faint with fright and fear by the time they got there—breathless and half-terrified—but determined nonetheless.

Another lawman met them at the door. He looked like a schoolteacher who had by some accident of fate become a sheriff in a small town. He seemed confused by so much authority. He introduced himself as Sheriff Tatum, and then introduced Kincaid and Nieves and turned to her. "Miss Powers, I'd like to present Chantry Kincaid the Third. He owns most of the Texas and Pacific Railroad. He's here to pay the reward if Cantrell here is his train robber.''

Kincaid took Leslie's hand and held it in a protective embrace while his clear green eyes engaged hers in mutual appraisal. She met his piercing gaze proudly, determined that she would not be cowed by anyone in Phoenix no matter who they were or what they thought of her. She nodded stiffly, and he patted her hand, taking her by surprise.

Kincaid was imposing and darkly handsome—probably in his mid-thirties, and she detected none of the condemnation she had expected to see in his eyes. They were clear and admiring. Leslie relaxed ever so slightly and noticed that while he might look like a pirate of a man, he was dressed in the height of fashion, even for the East—wearing an English "lounge suit" of blue serge with the popular wing collar and black silk scarf instead of the more cumbersome cravat. Altogether a comfortable style, and he wore it exceptionally well.

"How do you do?" she murmured, grateful she had on gloves so he couldn't feel how cold her hands were in spite of the heat.

"This must be quite distressing for you, Miss Powers. If I'd been thinking, I would have brought my wife along." He had a pleasant masculine voice. She found it surprisingly reassuring.

Leslie shot him a grateful look that Kincaid did not miss. Her response made him wonder if anyone else had bothered about her feelings. Powers had never impressed him—except as a man who was probably more accustomed to using women than taking care of them. He cursed himself for not bringing Jennie. Leslie Powers looked like she could use some female support. He hoped that this wouldn't take too long or be too unpleasant for her.

"Might as well get on with it," Sheriff Tatum said.

Kincaid stepped back, blocking Powers and Younger to allow Leslie to precede them into the jail. It took him only seconds to realize that Younger and Powers were acting as if they had forgotten Leslie Powers was a lady. Kincaid could feel his anger rising.

Nieves and Tatum took their lead from Kincaid, ignoring Powers and Younger in deference to the young lady. Kincaid was one of the most influential men in the territory. His financial holdings included a shipping line; the Texas and Pacific Railroad, with offices here and in San Diego; and a chain of hotels, including the Bricewood West, which boasted appointments unheard of in the West. He built hotels along his tracks to rival those in large eastern cities, and he was rewarded with vast profits. People paid the extra money to stay in luxurious surroundings. There was something exciting about eastern comfort on the western frontier. And it was no longer impossible. Railroads were tying the states and territories together more effectively than anything else could ever have done. The refrigerator boxcar had made it possible to transport anything that ice could preserve. The West was no longer cut off from the conveniences that made life enjoyable.

Men rarely ignored Kincaid. And now he was treating the Powers girl with every respect due a young lady of substance. Tatum could do no less. He smiled at her. This was his opportunity to show Mr. Kincaid, who was also active in town politics, that he was doing a good job. As the host sheriff, he cleared his throat and interrupted the several low-voiced conversations that had started up.

"Well, I guess you know what we're here for, but I'll say it officially. Miss Powers is here to identify the man who kidnapped and uh . . ."

Kincaid scowled him into silence.

"Excuse me, ma'am. Uh . . ." He turned toward the cell where Ward Cantrell lay stretched out on the thin mattress, his eyes closed. "Cantrell! Stand up! The lady's going to take a look at you!" Cantrell came up easily. He was thinner, and his nose had a new hump in it, but the eyes, those sky-blue, pitilessly cold eyes, jolted through her like a shock wave. He looked more like Alexander the Great than a train robber. Even in his ragged, dirty clothes, with his hair longer and wilder than she remembered it, he had the kind of bearing that was unmistakable.

Or had she read too many nickel novels? His eyes never flickered. He just looked at her in that opaque, unemotional way he had about him and she turned away, frowning.

"I'm sorry, Sheriff Tatum; that isn't the man who kidnapped me." Her voice was clear as a bell and very firm in the sudden silence.

"Wha—?" Powers turned on her. Younger grabbed her arm and jerked her back around to face Cantrell. "Take another look!" he snarled. "That *is* the man!"

"No, it *isn't*!" She jerked her arm free. "Sheriff, I would like to make a complaint of my own, though, against Dallas Younger and my uncle. They are trying to force me to marry Mr. Younger, and I have refused. I am half owner of the Lazy P Ranch, and if they can force me to marry Younger, my uncle and he will have full control. I am asking you to intervene in my behalf before they force me into marriage with a man I despise."

"You little baggage!" Younger stepped forward menacingly as if he were going to hit her, and Kincaid dragged Leslie back and placed himself between them, but not without noticing the reaction of the prisoner. There was murder in those blue eyes for Younger.

"That's enough," Kincaid said flatly, staring coldly and unflinchingly at Powers and Younger.

Leslie could feel the hate like a tangible cloak surrounding her. Thank goodness for Kincaid! He stood protectively close while the sheriff from Flagstaff who had been there at the capture questioned her.

"But Miss Powers, this is the man you were with," he insisted gently, in deference to Kincaid's protective posture.

"I know that, Mr. Nieves. Don't you remember what I told you? I said, 'That man is a train robber. There's a reward for him.' "

Nieves frowned. "That's right, by Jove, that's what she said! But—how did you get away?—How did you happen to be with him?"

"The kidnapper left me at the road and went south. I saw this man and started to ride toward him when I saw you. He fled and I panicked. I thought perhaps you were bandits. . . . I had no idea why he ran away. . . ."

"How did you know he was a train robber?"

"I recognized him. He robbed the train I was on."

"That right?" Nieves asked, turning to Cantrell. "You a train robber?"

Ward Cantrell's eyes gave nothing away. They flicked over her once, bringing a warm flush before he chuckled. "You'd try to steal meat from a grizzly, wouldn't you?"

"Now wait just a goddamned minute! This man's name is Cantrell! He rode right into my camp, killed my men, and threatened to cut my throat. He signed a note telling us he was going to sell her to the Indians. He signed it Cantrell," Younger ended furiously. "Cantrell!"

"D'ya have the note?"

"Hell, no! My word is good enough," Younger blustered.

" 'Fraid not," Tatum said gallantly, earning him a reward when Leslie smiled at him. " 'Fraid, Mr. Younger, that courts only act on evidence, either hard evidence like that note, or an eyewitness account. We have a witness who says this ain't the man," he said, enjoying Younger's rage, since there was nothing he could do to him at the moment. Everyone knew Younger always kept up the pretense of staying on the right side of the law.

"Ask him how he got shot," Younger demanded. "One of my men shot that bastard up in the mountains."

All eyes were on Cantrell then. Leslie held her breath, praying Kincaid, who was standing protectively close, couldn't hear her heart pounding in the stillness. But Kincaid was engrossed in Cantrell. Ever since he had entered the jail he had been thinking that he knew Cantrell from somewhere, but so far he hadn't been able to remember from where.

Tatum grunted. "Check 'round—we'll probably find out there was another train robbery that day."

Younger wouldn't be stopped. "He wounded four of my men in front of your eyes, Nieves! You saw him go riding at us like some fiend out of hell! Do you deny that?"

Cantrell let his eyes, still cold blue, but now with glints of amusement flickering in the depths, rake over the red-faced Younger. "Guess I'm the excitable type, Sheriff. Men in front of me, shooting at me, men behind me, shooting at me—I guess I took it personally. Didn't realize they had me mixed up with somebody else," he drawled coolly.

"You lying bastard! I'm gonna get you for this!" Younger snarled viciously.

"I may not be unconscious next time, Younger," he said quietly, his husky voice steely. Cantrell dismissed Younger and turned his attention back to the girl, wondering what had made her decide to lie for him. He had been shocked to learn that she was Powers's niece. Sounded like she had troubles of her own with both Younger and her uncle. There was real loathing in her pretty eyes whenever she glanced at either of them. He saw her sweet face, so fresh and tense, and knew that he had been worrying about her. It had been blind and hidden from him until now, but seeing her so crisp and demure and ladylike freed him from some burden he had been carrying without knowing or being able to identify it. All dressed up in cool green organdy that matched her defiant green eyes, she was a vision of rare loveliness. Her cheeks, as velvety smooth as carnation petals, were flushed with warm rose. She looked as if she had survived with little permanent damage to her fine feminine spirit, and he felt a surge of relief in that knowledge.

The thought of her at Dallas Younger's mercy did unaccountable things in his chest.

Younger wasn't about to give up, but it was Powers who stepped forward. "Sheriff, my niece lied about that man not being the one," he said stoutly.

Tatum sighed heavily. "Cantrell ain't going no place. Even if he ain't the one, she identified him as a train robber. I'll be checking through all the warrants. Mr. Kincaid here's been looking for Cantrell for some time himself. From what I hear about Cantrell we'll get enough to hang him anyway."

"You'd better see to it! My niece may have been taken in, but I damn sure ain't! I mean to see justice done!"

Powers and Younger turned and stalked out the door.

Tatum faced Leslie, clearly flustered. "Now—uh—Miss Powers, ma'am—about that—uh—complaint of yours, ma'am."

"I'm willing to drop it if you can guarantee that Mr. Younger will not be allowed to molest me while I am in Phoenix. I intend to leave town as soon as I can get a train out of here," she said firmly.

Kincaid smiled admiringly and offered her his arm. "Miss Powers, my wife and I would like to invite you to be our guest for the duration of your stay in Phoenix. I can assure you that no one will molest you again. If you would be so kind, we can go directly to the bank and arrange for a transfer of the reward money to your account. I'm in your debt, Miss Powers."

Leslie glanced at Cantrell, saw the flush of anger come into his face, and then looked quickly away, wondering why the thought of her going with Kincaid should evoke a reaction in his stubborn eyes where very little else did.

"You're very kind, Mr. Kincaid, but I couldn't accept a reward. But I do accept your hospitality. I must confess that I feel the need of your protection."

CHAPTER
TWENTY-TWO

"Mr. Kincaid, I want to apologize for airing the family laundry and putting you in an awkward position. . . ."

Kincaid shook his head. "Please, Miss Powers, don't be embarrassed. I know something of your uncle. People don't choose their relations. I only hope that you weren't too badly treated.''

They were on the sidewalk now, and Leslie squinted against the brightness of the sun as she looked up into Kincaid's face. "I didn't tell the sheriff everything, Mr. Kincaid. My uncle will not be satisfied until Mr. Cantrell is dead. . . . What will happen to him now?''

Kincaid noted the quiver in her voice and the sudden paling of her cheeks. Gossip that she had fallen in love with her kidnapper had reached him. Everyone in town had heard about Younger's anger at her for trying to save the outlaw from being hanged on the spot in Flagstaff. Kincaid instinctively felt pity for her. Not just because she was so young and so lovely; the West needed young women with the fire and spirit Leslie Powers had exhibited. Unfortunately, the West was so raw and in such a hurry that its justice was oftentimes as crude as it was abrupt. He felt sorry for her, but he didn't want to give her false hope.

"I'm convinced in my own mind that Cantrell is the leader of the gang that has been robbing the Texas and Pacific. I'll have some of my men who've seen him come in to take a look at him. I, uh, expect, with all the other things he's wanted for, he'll spend a good many years behind bars.'' He stopped short of telling her that Cantrell would probably hang. No sense upsetting her at this point. He took her arm and steered her toward his carriage. "Do you need to pick up anything before we ride out to the house?''

"I have some bags and my lady's maid, if you're sure your wife won't be upset. . . .'' She was remembering the women who had talked about her that morning in front of the Bricewood West. What if Mrs. Kincaid were one of those?

"Nonsense,'' he said, helping her into the buggy. "Jennie will love it. I'll drop you at the house and come back for your things.'' Leslie Powers was obviously determined to do whatever had to be done—she was spunky as hell—but he wanted to spare her another confrontation with her uncle so soon.

"Thank you. I'd appreciate that,'' she said gratefully, settling back against the upholstered seat.

He slapped the reins on the horse's flank, and Leslie steadied herself as the carriage moved away from the jail. She ignored the eyes that followed their departure. The warm sun felt good to her. It seemed to ease her trembling. She sat back, relieved that the confrontation with her uncle and Younger was over.

They were passing through a part of town that Leslie had not seen from the windows of the Bricewood West. Here streets were laid out in the familiar New England grid that she was so used to, lined with row upon neat row of sturdy homes. She could hardly believe her eyes. She had thought the town consisted of the hotel, the livery stable where her uncle had left the horses, and the wide street lined with saloons and stores that she had ridden down in the parade.

"Oh," she sighed, "this is like a real city!"

Kincaid chuckled. "You sound homesick."

"I guess I am," she admitted. "What are those?" she asked, pointing at trees with blue-green, spiny branches that reached twenty-five or thirty feet into the air, lining the dirt road on either side of them, providing filtered shade.

"Paloverde trees," he chuckled. "I wanted tree-lined roads for Jennie. We transplanted them from the desert."

"You certainly went to a lot of trouble. You must love your wife very much."

"When you meet her, you'll understand," he said simply.

Leslie fell silent, glancing at the houses, which appeared to be smaller versions of the spacious rectangular structures of New England, half-timber, half-clapboard, with steep roofs and tiny casement windows, except they had exterior chimneys instead of the central chimneys of New England. The eaves projected more, and the houses looked stark and uncomfortable perching on flat grassless lots, sometimes separated by fences, sometimes not. Most of them were two- and three-story—ungainly, top-heavy, and boxy. They were the kind of houses she was accustomed to, but they looked so forlorn here, surrounded by sand, rocks, and Paloverde trees. One was a perfect copy of the cozy, white-washed Dutch houses with their stone gables and projecting eaves. One was modeled after the rural Jacobean English houses. She recognized the grandiose baroque style, the geometrical gables, exterior chimneys, and stair towers. Inside she could almost see the elaborate moldings, carved balustrades, massive wooden doors, and arched doorways crowned with delicate fan windows. No doubt there would be four rooms to each story. Next door was an elegant, boxlike brick structure of classical Georgian style.

If she closed her eyes so she could not see the strange trees, and the stark lots, if she nestled these houses in imaginary spruce, willow, and ash trees, she could be back in Massachusetts. But even without that assistance she had to admit that this was a real neighborhood. It lacked the classic precision of planned eastern communities, the roads were not paved or even cobbled, but it was apparent that this had not been a random happening. She could hardly believe it.

"Is this . . . I mean, how long have these houses been here?"

Kincaid laughed. "Not very long. This happens to be my first humble attempt at subdividing land. What do you think of it?"

"Why, it's marvelous, but where did you find so many people who could afford nice houses? I mean, it is not exactly Boston, but it's not Phoenix either."

"When I came here the first time in 1882—that's when the railroad reached here—there were two thousand people. It was a pleasant little community that had just been incorporated into a city. For miles all you could see was sand and rocks, relieved occasionally by clumps of ocotillo shrub, cactus, and a few Paloverde trees. Now there are almost four thousand people. I imported many of them myself, to run the hotel, the railroad, the bank, my ranch. In 1864 this was nothing more than a site where a man by the name of John Smith pitched his tents for a hay camp to fulfill a forage contract for the army outpost at Fort McDowell. They named it Phoenix because this town was built on the ruins of an Old Indian pueblo.

"Actually it was a more pleasant town before the railroad, because now we get the cattle drovers who are a wild bunch. In 1882 we already had a school house, two churches, and the first ice factory in the Arizona territory. I remember when old Abe delivered ice in a wheelbarrow for seven cents a pound."

A wagon with children in the back, staring at them with solemn eyes, rattled past, raising a dust cloud.

"We lived at the hotel then, and Jennie was anxiously awaiting the birth of our son," he said over the noise of the wagon. "The Phoenix Hotel had a swimming pool behind it with a canvas roof. She spent half her time sitting in the water and the other half sipping iced tea. I really shouldn't have let her stay here. I should have sent her north where she would have been comfortable, but she wouldn't hear of it. I had to be here, so she felt like she had to be here. We've never been very good at separations."

"How many children do you have?"

"Two."

"Which one of these houses is yours?"

"We're almost there. Jennie wanted to get as far from the stockyards as possible. We have corrals that hold two thousand head, and sometimes the wind shifts."

They passed a row of houses, these more elegant than the rest. Then he slowed the horse and nodded at the house on the corner, facing south. It was like nothing she had seen before: it looked like the Spanish missions she had seen, except there was a simple elegance in the lines that marked it as a home.

"That brick is called adobe. It's made from the clay of this region. We fired it in a kiln we transported from Minnesota."

"It reminds me of a monastery."

He laughed. "That's because I stole a lot of my ideas from the Jesuits. It gets very hot here. I used foot-thick adobe walls to keep the heat out and recessed the doors and windows under a generous roof overhang so that the sun doesn't shine on them. It helps."

The front of the house had a series of curved arches opening onto a deep porch. Inside, there were two massive mahogany doors that looked as if this pirate of a man had stolen them from some feudal castle. The roof was red tile and gleamed in the sunlight. Kincaid chuckled at her silence. "Total freedom encourages eccentricity. I must admit that I was tempted to do something modern, but Jennie prefers either Classic Greek Revival or Gothic, so we compromised."

"What do you call it? I've never seen anything even remotely like it."

"I stole my ideas from the Indian pueblos, the Jesuits, and our neighbors to the south—the Mexicans."

"It is magnificent! You designed this yourself?"

"You are very kind. I am an engineer . . . with aspirations. I don't believe architects create. I think they compile. The first job of any good designer is to discover what works well in the area where he intends to build. The second is to organize those things into a design. Heat calls for thick walls and that generous overhang."

"Oh! That's very good. You know . . . when I was on the train, coming here, I talked to a young man named John Loving. He called you a visionary. I can see that he was right."

"John is very kind. I have imagination. I don't know if that qualifies me as a visionary, but I can't help remembering something I learned in school about Major Stephen Harriman Long, a man who explored far more territory than Lewis and Clark, and gained almost no fame for it, because he was consistently unimpressed. He toured the richest farming region of the eastern seaboard, around Lancaster, Pennsylvania, and found it depressing. I believe the words he used were 'sinks of dissipation and debauch-

ery.' When he reached the site of what would be Chicago he wrote
in his journal that it was unfit for either commerce or agriculture.
He was later given credit for convincing Americans that the Great
Plains was a desert. He saw mountain ranges merely as obstacles.
A man totally without imagination. I look at a desert and imagine
any number of possibilities. All it takes is a little water, a road,
maybe a railroad, and cities sprout like mushrooms. I think in
quarter-acre lots. It is an occupational hazard. Leave it to me and
the entire continent past the Mississippi River will be subdivided.''

"I prefer your vision to many others I've heard. I am tired of fat,
fashionable frame houses. I think I like your western architecture.''

"That's partly why I'm here instead of in New York. The East
has become exhausted, sluggish, and inhibited. Here we have
space to be innovative and the opportunity to build whole cities in
a decade. We are not tied to a uniform ceremonious style or any
other style. I prefer western barbarism to eastern philistinism.''

"You have real plants! A real garden!'' she cried, noticing the
shrubs for the first time.

"My wife is from New York. She insists on the civilizing influence of a thoroughly irrigated garden around any house she lives
in.''

"It's so beautiful!''

"Then why the tears?'' he asked gently.

"You're very observant,'' she smiled, dabbing quickly at her
eyes. "It just made me homesick, that's all.''

"Where are you from?''

"Massachusetts, Wellesley,'' she sniffed.

"Beautiful country.''

She sniffed again. "Yes.'' Oh, God! She missed it so much!
Now that she was letting down she felt tears crowding up and
struggled to control them.

Kincaid opened the door and a white-haired woman with deep
dimples and smiling eyes was standing in the entry hall as if she
had been waiting for them. There was an almost cavelike feeling of
coolness the moment Leslie stepped inside.

"Good afternoon, Mr. K.''

"Afternoon, Mrs. Lillian. Is Mrs. Kincaid home?''

"In the library, sir.''

"I want you to meet Leslie Powers. Leslie, Mrs. Lillian has
been with the Kincaid family since I was born. She raised me, my

brothers and sisters, and ran the family practically single-handed. She is also the repository for the Kincaid family history. Though I admit that there are parts of it she's been ordered not to discuss, for reasons known only to a few,'' he said, chuckling.

Mrs. Lillian smiled and Leslie was completely enchanted with the woman. She looked the perfect grandmother, from her silver-gray hair to the frilly pinafore over her blue silk gown.

"Don't listen to him, my dear. I have never been good at re-membering what I'm not supposed to discuss."

Mr. Kincaid threw his head back and laughed. "Well, at least you are honest," he said.

"Welcome to the family, my dear. If you need anything at all, please let me know. I'm always around. The children do not take all my time by any means." She patted Leslie's hand and turned. "I'll go tell the missus you're home."

Leslie turned her attention back to the interior of the house and had to control the urge to gape. It was a dream. In the front part the ceilings were at least thirty feet over her head, open to the roof, but the back half of the house had two stories. Sweetly curved stairs seemed to float on the air, so gracefully were they designed. Somehow the long roof-overhang had given the impression that the very house was hugging the ground, almost blending into it.

It was light, airy, open—not anything like she had expected from the massive, heavy look of the outside. There were tall narrow windows that reached all the way up to the ceiling, and while she could tell that sunlight did not fall directly on the windows, except in early morning and late evening, the rooms were not dreary, even at midday.

"This is the *sala grande*," he said with a sweeping movement of his right arm to indicate the spacious area to her right that looked like a ballroom. Crystal chandeliers hung on long chains from the high ceiling. Simple wicker furniture and potted palms similar to the ones she had seen in the lobby of the Bricewood West were scattered around the enormous room.

"What does that mean, *sala*?"

"Spanish for parlor or large room," he said, smiling. He liked her direct questions. Too many girls either would not have been curious or would have pretended they knew. "Straight ahead is the library, and the room to your extreme left is Jennie's music room."

Leslie turned, following the sweep of his hand. From inside the music room, the ceiling looked like it had been made in a waffle iron: recessed squares separated by raised dividers. One enormous window dominated the far wall. It was shaped like a tall, narrow cupola, coming to a point at the top like a triumphal arch. It was at least twelve feet wide and twenty feet tall. Clear leaded glass, with diagonally cut panes, was set flush with the outside wall of the house. Since the walls were so thick, it was deeply recessed into the wall and framed by a wood cornice. Sheer cream-colored lace curtains were pulled back by velvet ribbons, softening the harsh sunlight. Except for a few chairs, an elegant white Steinway grand piano was practically the only piece of furniture in the room. A mirror twelve feet high and as wide as the north wall, probably thirty feet long, brought a gasp to Leslie's lips.

"Oh," Kincaid said, "the mirror. My wife was a ballerina before we married. She still goes through her routines every day. Says she feels better. . . ."

"How marvelous!"

"That's why there's no rug in here. She needs good solid hardwood."

"The floor is beautiful. The whole house is beautiful." She did not exaggerate. It was a house designed to lift spirits as high as the ceilings.

They walked slowly toward the back of the house, and she caught sight of paintings on the staircase enclosure. It was an art lover's paradise. She felt dizzy with so much to look at. Dozens of paintings, hung on blind cords, were artfully arranged by someone who had an eye for proportion.

"How cleverly you hang them! Oh! That has to be a William Prior! My mother had one. Isn't his modeling exquisite? Did you know he is one of the most skillful portraitists in New England? He was a Bostonian, and he could paint flat-featured portraits or excellent rounded features—whichever the client could afford. He is the only artist I've ever heard of who put style on a class basis—only his wealthiest customers would pay for the refinement of modeling the features, or I guess people who were acquainted with the more academic proficiencies of European artists. Oh!" She stopped, suddenly self-conscious.

Kincaid chuckled. "I take it you enjoy art." He seemed relaxed, and not the least put out with her. The nicest smile!

"My mother was an artist and an art teacher. I paint, but not well enough to earn a living at it. She was listed in *Who's Who of American Painters*," she said proudly. "I want to be one of the best landscape artists in America. I studied art at Wellesley, but I want to study in Europe.''

''My wife is the collector. Get her started and she will talk your leg off.''

The library was decorated in celery green with none of the weird grandeur that was so prevalent in the homes of the rich. The walls were papered with soft green silk, and the draperies were of the finest green brocade. The room had a light, fresh look about it that was unlike the heavy, overripe opulence of the period. There was none of the heavy velvets, in deep, rich colors made from the new aniline dyes that were so violent and so popular. Nor did the room have the appearance of being overcrowded, as was the fashion. There was a feeling of sparse elegance in the Kincaid home.

CHAPTER
TWENTY-THREE

They found Mrs. Kincaid seated at a small writing desk beside a tall, narrow, elegantly draped window. She glanced up, smiling. ''Just a moment, please. If I don't write this down, I will forget it.'' She wrote quickly and then stood up. ''That's done! Thank goodness,'' she said, walking quickly toward them.

''Jennie, love, I'd like you to meet Leslie Powers.''

''Oh, Leslie! I'm so happy to finally meet you,'' she said, smiling warmly, directly, into Leslie's eyes so there could be no mistake about how she felt. Relief flooded Leslie, and she smiled.

''How do you do, Mrs. Kincaid?''

''Please, Leslie, call me Jennifer or Jennie.''

''Oh, no, I couldn't presume . . .'' Leslie demurred.

''I insist. Unless, of course, you want to insult me,'' Jennifer said, smiling.

''Oh, no, I would never want that. . . .''

''Good, then it's settled.''

Jennifer was a head shorter than her handsome husband. Her waist was slim and her body supple. She went up on tiptoe and kissed his cheek, then smiled at him.

''Well, I was delighted to receive your message about our

houseguest. Do they have your train robber in jail now?'' she asked, her voice a delight to the ear, pleasing, well modulated.

Kincaid grinned. ''Sure looks like it.''

''Thank goodness, Chane,'' she said, turning to Leslie. ''He has fretted about that for years. It will be a relief to worry about something else.'' She paused suddenly. ''I can be informal to a fault,'' she said, shaking her head. ''You would probably like nothing better than an opportunity to rest and collect your thoughts, and we stand here making small talk. Come, Leslie, I'll show you the way to your room.''

Leslie followed obediently, noticing that while Jennifer was striking as a still portrait, she was even more striking in motion. There was tremendous energy in her—it was apparent in the way she carried herself. She had hair the color of pale summer wheat, highlighted with streaks of silver, a glory of shiny, shimmering tresses drawn back from her dainty ears in cascading curls. She was blessed with radiant skin the color of old Brussels lace, and her cheeks were warmed by a hint of plum that echoed the deep purple of her eyes. Jennifer Kincaid was most assuredly not the type who would make cutting remarks on the street about a total stranger. Mr. Kincaid had not had to explain Leslie's predicament. Jennifer was naturally compassionate.

''Jennie, love,'' Chane said to his departing wife. ''Leslie is an artist. She was admiring your collection.''

''Oh, how wonderful!'' Jennifer flashed Leslie an excited smile. ''Tell me what you think of these,'' she asked, taking Leslie's hand and leading her to the east wall.

The room they called the library was a combination art gallery and reading room. One wall was devoted to books, one to a fireplace, and the other two to paintings hung all the way to the ceiling, which was twelve feet high. The variety and quality of paintings took Leslie's breath away. There were two Rembrandts, three Claude Monets, two Van Goghs, several Orozcos. Enthralled, she walked the length of each wall, her eyes wide with wonder, like a small girl on a holiday.

Jennifer smiled and took Leslie's hand again. She led her to a collection that was very special to her and waited while Leslie absorbed what she was seeing. The look on the younger woman's face was all that Jennie needed to know that the two of them would get on famously.

''Oh! I've always wanted to own one of these! They are original

Patroons! The old Dutch families of New York hoard these like the very devil. How did you ever?''

Jennifer laughed. ''I happen to belong to one of those old Dutch families. I am the one who is currently hoarding them,'' she said gaily. ''My maiden name is Van Vleet. This painting here is of my great-great-great-grandfather Jonathan Van Vleet. It was done in 1710. That is Peter Van Vleet, my brother. He was seven. It was painted in the Patroon style, but as I'm sure you know, the Patroon painters existed only until about 1730, more or less. A friend of the family, Christopher Chambard, could mimic the style. Isn't it adorable?''

''Yes. And what a manly-looking seven-year-old! Did your brother live up to the promise?''

Pain flickered in Jennifer's eloquent violet eyes, and Leslie groaned. ''Oh! I'm sorry! Please forgive me. I'm so forward. My mother spent years trying to keep me from asking inappropriate questions, to no avail. . . .''

''No, please. It's just that I haven't seen my brother for eight years. I don't know if he is alive or dead. . . .''

''I'm so sorry.''

''Don't be. Please.'' She quickly changed the subject. ''This one is by De Peyster Manner. See the ships in the background. They belonged to dear old Moses. He was a very successful merchant. Moses Van Vleet, my great-great-grandfather. What a pompous dullard he looked!''

Leslie was entranced by the primitive beauty and the vivid colors. ''Have you ever seen so much innocence and contentment? You would feel, looking at that painting, that that man could not possibly give short weights in his store!''

''You're right!'' Jennifer agreed, laughing. ''Maybe that is why the Dutch, who were shrewd businessmen, liked the Patroon painters! Maybe at one time this hung in the window of his establishment right next to the Bible!''

They both laughed.

''Let me show you to your room. You must be tired.''

They climbed lush carpeted steps, elegantly curved, to a spacious hallway and a large comfortable bedroom with a small balcony that overlooked a surprisingly green lawn and garden in back of the house. Leslie shook her head in disbelief. The trees and flowers could have come directly from Wellesley. Under the noonday sky, the lawn was apple green, partitioned with English hedges, neat rows of local flowers she didn't recognize, and all carefully manicured. A high stone fence enclosed the garden. A spacious barn, carriage house, and stables in the same style and adobe as the house were ringed at the northern perimeter by a row of tall trees that afforded privacy.

"Oh! It's so lovely!"

"Thank you. Arizona's concessions to a New York girl!"

"I had no idea Arizona made concessions! I thought this was a hopeless desert."

"You have no idea how deep Chane's engineers had to go to find year-round water!"

"China?"

"Almost!"

They laughed again and Leslie squeezed her hostess's hand. "Jennifer, I want to thank you for being so nice and for taking me in. I truly appreciate it! I can't tell you how much," she said shyly.

"It is our pleasure. We love having a guest. Just relax and don't worry about a thing. Let us take care of you. Chane didn't say . . . Are you Mark Powers's daughter?" Leslie could tell by Jennie's face that she was not impressed with Mark Powers.

"He is my uncle. I came here to try to settle my father's estate. But Uncle Mark . . ." Her throat tightened, and she felt tears stinging behind her lashes.

"Charles Powers was your father?"

Leslie waited in silence. If Jennifer had disliked him as well, she wouldn't be able to bear it. There was a lump in her throat and a sense of rampant dread in her chest.

"Yes," she said tremulously.

"I didn't know him personally, but Chane said he was a fine, decent man."

"Thank you," Leslie whispered gratefully. She realized in that moment that while she hadn't known her father, she had created a wonderful, warm fantasy about him that she was still emotionally attached to. She really wouldn't have been able to bear it if Jennifer had smashed it with a careless word.

"Leslie, do you need anything? I'll be going to Bauer's later to do some shopping. If you don't feel like venturing out, make a list. I'll pick everything up."

"Thank you, but if your husband sends my bags and Annette, I'll be fine."

"Do you have any plans?"

Leslie shook her head. "I don't know what I'll do. I used most of my money to come here to try to settle my father's estate, but I don't think my uncle intends to give me a cent."

"Well, my husband is pretty good at business matters. Something will turn up." Jennifer smiled reassuringly. "Would you like to meet the children?"

They were beautiful and extremely polite, treating Leslie like a princess. The boy was dark-skinned and black-haired, with green eyes—a miniature pirate like his father—and the girl was a delicate, creamy blond with striking blue eyes, elegantly fringed with thick lashes.

"Oh, she didn't get your eyes," Leslie said, without thinking.

"Nor Chane's," Jennie laughed. "Actually, she has my brother's eyes." Pain darkened her eyes momentarily and then she brightened. "Blue is better anyway. No one trusts a woman with purple eyes."

Leslie admired the toys that they wanted to show her and then allowed Jennifer to rescue her and take her back to her room. "They liked you. I think they would keep you all day, talking your leg off," Jennifer laughed.

"Thank you. They are adorable. I don't usually like children," she admitted.

Jennie laughed, "I admire your honesty. Few people like children, except their own, and not always then. I told Chane I would have his children on one condition—that the boys looked like him and the girls like me. I had nightmare visions of great, hulking females and delicate, fragile boys. . . ."

They laughed, and Jennifer left to let her relax. Leslie tried the bed. Two bounces told her it was as comfortable as it looked. A painting caught her eye, and she went to stand before it. She stood there a long time, studying the dark, warm, tonal style, the directness of the presentation, with a growing sense of excitement. She knew the artist! She was sure of it!

Trembling in her eagerness, she turned the canvas and searched for an inscription—finally found it in the top right corner. "Girl at the Piano to Jennifer with love, Theodore Robinson." It was he! In her excitement, she reacted by habit, looking for her mother to share it with.

Art had always been the center of their life together. Meals were rarely on time; household chores, laundry, even shopping, were done haphazardly, or to accommodate their schedule, which revolved around lighting.

"The house is here to serve us, not vice-versa!" Margaret

would say emphatically when her friends who did not paint would look askance at the cozy clutter of paint pots, brushes, and drying canvases.

Leslie grew up with the resinous smell of oil paints and turpentine, eating cold meals, and loving it. She despised clocks and schedules and felt truly sorry for friends whose lives were meticulously regulated.

There had been many times when she'd been summoned from classes for a "family emergency" that turned out to be a chance for the two of them to rush across town to chat with some visiting artist, and at least as many times when she'd skipped school altogether to see a show or a collection. When there was money enough, which was very seldom in the early days, they would purchase tickets to Boston, pack a big basket of chicken, wine, cheese, and fruit and stay overnight in the city, visiting the art museums from the time they opened in the morning until closing time at night. They would ride back on the Pullman coach and arrive in Wellesley late at night. Leslie remembered walking in the very middle of the wide, dark streets, hurrying through shadowy, scary aisles, her small hand tucked warmly inside her mother's.

Now her mother was dead and Wellesley, Massachusetts, was thousands of miles away, shrouded in shadowy mists, unreachable. Even the memory of those green and pleasant hills seemed like a dream. She was filled with a vague sense of anxiety. By publicly denouncing her uncle, she had broken her last family tie, as bad as it was. She felt the way she had after the funeral, when she had walked back in the house and seen the canvas her mother had been preparing for her next painting. . . .

She didn't realize she was crying until Jennifer, who had come up to bring her a tray, pulled her into her arms and began to stroke her back. "You've had a rough time of it, Leslie," she crooned softly. "Let the tears fall; let them come. Don't fight it. There, that's better. A good cry will do wonders, there, there. . . ."

Jennifer held her closely while great, gasping sobs shook her slender body. It seemed much later when Jennifer moved to dry Leslie's tears, after the worst had passed.

"Feel better now?"

"I feel drained," she said, shuddering. "I never cried before, not until after my mother died. Now I seem to be crying all the time. It isn't like me. I just don't cry," she said, shaking her head, still sniffling.

Jennifer sat down on the bed and pulled Leslie down beside her.

"You lost both your parents in a short time; you were betrayed by your uncle and kidnapped. You have tremendous strength, or you wouldn't have survived all that. You must be reeling emotionally." She paused and patted the slender hand that was lying limp in Leslie's lap. "I remember when my parents were both killed. At the time I seemed to be coping with everything, doing what had to be done, going about my life the way I thought I had to do, until one day I realized that I had just been keeping myself busy so I wouldn't have to realize they were really gone. It was very difficult," she sighed. "You loved your mother very much, didn't you?"

Leslie nodded, feeling her bottom lip tremble.

"Your mother loved you very much as well. And being a mother myself now, I realize that if I should die suddenly, I would want my children to have a good cry—one time only—and then do whatever they had to do so they could remember me with happiness. A mother loves her children as long as *they* live, not just as long as she lives. When I die I want my children to be happy, not sad, as soon as possible. Your mother would want the same for you. Love wants only love for payment, not unhappiness nor tears." She hugged Leslie and changed the subject. "Maybe you've been holding too much inside. I remember when I was about your age, I began tearing up at the slightest provocation. I discovered that I was in love."

"With Mr. Kincaid?" she asked, sniffing.

"Yes."

"But he is so perfect for you. . . ."

Jennie laughed. "It didn't seem so at the time. Falling in love with him was equivalent to the worst disaster imaginable. You see, I thought he had been responsible for my parents' deaths. It was far more complicated than that even, but suffice to say, he appeared to be entirely unsuitable."

Leslie felt new tears welling up into her eyes. She felt sure suddenly that everyone in the world knew that she had tried to protect Cantrell. She would never live it down.

"I'm sorry, Leslie," Jennie said softly. "I'm so dense sometimes. I didn't realize . . ."

"It's all right," she said quickly.

"Do you love him?"

Leslie shrugged, feeling desolate. "No. I don't know. At first I hated him. Then I felt confused. I didn't want them to hurt him. I don't want him to hang."

She looked up, blinking back tears. Jennie smiled and pulled her into her arms again. "You are a very honest young woman. Sometimes people don't understand such honesty. That was the case when I fell in love with Chane. Even my brother didn't understand. He . . ." Jennie stopped, unable to continue.

"What happened?" Leslie asked, pulling away to search Jennie's wide purple eyes, now clouded with pain.

"I don't know. He disappeared eight years ago, only days after my marriage. I haven't seen him since. I don't know whether to grieve for him or to be furious with him. . . . And so I have done both—for eight years."

"You love him very much. . . ."

Jennie nodded. "I love him the same way I love my children, with the same unreasoning passionate possessiveness. . . ."

She sighed heavily. "As a child, he had the most expressive face. When he smiled he could light up a room. When he glowered, he could dim the sun. I always knew what he was thinking—we thought alike. I blame myself. Because I knew he suspected I was in love with Chane—and I didn't try to explain to him." Tears welled in her dark eyes, and she tried to blink them back, continuing as if she couldn't help herself.

"I was angry. I said stupid, stupid things to Peter, forgetting how much he loved me. I forced him to leave. It was all my fault."

Jennie's voice was choked with pain. Leslie wanted to stop her, but she felt helpless to intervene. "I was so self-centered," she said bitterly. "I didn't take into account that he hadn't recovered from our parents' deaths, that he was in pain and struggling with his own survival. You see, Peter was so stoical that he fooled me. He could turn to stone, become unreachable. And sometimes he used that to trick me into thinking all was well." She paused, covering her face with her hands. "He must have been in such pain, thinking I had fallen in love with the man who had caused our parents' deaths. . . . Peter loved them and it was obvious he worshipped me. I could see it in his eyes even when he didn't want me to. I should have known that I couldn't keep hurting him the way I was. There is no justification for me, because you see," she said, wiping the tears off her cheeks, "if I had talked to him, everything would have been fine between us, but when I first fell in love with Chane, I refused to explain my actions, because I couldn't—I didn't understand them myself."

Leslie sighed and Jennie dragged in a ragged breath and patted Leslie's hand. "I'm sorry. I didn't mean to tell you all that."

"Please don't apologize. I feel honored that you did."

"So!" Jennie said, standing up and becoming brisk and cheerful. "You must be hungry. Eat something," she said, waving at the tray, "then you can take a nap. That will help you to acclimate yourself. If you're like me, nothing ever looks quite so bad after a meal or a nap. Mrs. Lillian prepared this special tray for you so you can spend some time by yourself . . . if that suits your mood. If not, come downstairs for dinner. I'll leave it up to you."

Leslie smiled in gratitude.

Jennie found Chane in the kitchen fending for himself while Mrs. Lillian fussed at him for stealing food.

"I need to talk to you."

Chane sobered instantly. He took her arm and led her into his study. When the door closed, Jennie faced him. "I want you to save that train robber."

Chane looked at her as if he didn't quite believe his ears. "You want me to save the man who has been robbing my trains?"

Jennie shrugged. "Yes."

"But why?" he said, incredulous and frowning. A muscle bunched in his cheek, and Jennie reached out to touch it.

"Because Leslie is in love with him. She's a bright, sensitive, warm-hearted young woman. If she loves him, he can't be so bad."

Chane threw back his head and laughed. Jennie waited patiently while he sobered. "You're serious, aren't you?"

"Yes," she said, the light in her eyes steady and determined.

He shook his head. "The paper gets wind of this, they're going to think I've lost my mind."

Jennie smiled. "You'll do it?"

He grinned and held out his hands in helplessness. "For you, love, I would give up my entire fortune, but," he said, sobering, "don't expect a miracle. At this moment the prosecutor is deciding whether he has enough evidence to try Cantrell on eight counts of murder, mayhem, kidnapping, and train robbery or on just a hundred or so counts of train robbery."

He sighed. "God knows what else he's done." He shook his head. It was typical of Jennie to allow her ready compassion to rule her in these matters, but it could only cause her more pain if he wasn't able to save the young man. "I'll do what I can," he said. "But I'm not able to perform miracles."

"Of course you are. I can't wait to tell Leslie exactly how you did it."

"Dammit, Jennie." He laughed. "This is serious."

"I know, but you'll think of something."

"Well, don't say anything to Leslie. It will only hurt her more if I fail."

CHAPTER
TWENTY-FOUR

Chane arranged for Leslie Powers' luggage and her lady's maid to be delivered to the house, and then headed back to the jail.

"Sheriff, I'd like to talk to your prisoner."

"Cantrell?"

"Please."

"Help yourself."

Kincaid walked over to the cell where Cantrell's lean form was sprawled on a cot.

"Cantrell, I'd like to talk to you," he said quietly.

Ward shoved his hat up off his nose. "So talk."

"Leslie Powers said Younger intends to kill you. I would like to know why."

Ward considered telling Kincaid the truth, but his stubbornness refused to let him do that. Kincaid was not his friend. He was still the same man who had caused the deaths of both his parents. Nothing could change that, not even the fact that he had married Jenn. But he would keep him in mind, because he did want Younger and Powers punished for what they did to the Mendozas. If he found that he would not be able to deliver that vengeance, he would tell him later. For now he only shrugged. "Maybe I know too much about Powers's activities—or—" He shrugged. "Maybe she's wrong."

"What is Powers afraid of?"

"That's between me, Powers, and Younger," Ward said flatly.

"I think I could help you if you would trust me."

Ward Cantrell came to his feet then and walked over to the center of the cell. His cold blue eyes locked with Kincaid's. "I don't want anything from you, Kincaid—ever."

Chane frowned, his straight black brows crowding his piercing hazel eyes. There it was again—that feeling that he should know this man. They stood eye to eye, Cantrell insolent and dangerous, from his warlike stance of a gunfighter to the curl of his lips and the steely glint in his narrowed blue eyes. He was a warrior, body and soul—there was no doubt about that—but that didn't explain Chane's feeling that he should know this man. But where? When? If he knew, would it explain why the man had concentrated so intensely on the Texas and Pacific?

Chane cursed the inadequacy of his recall, wondering how he could face Jennie if he failed. He groped for some way to motivate this young hellion.

Recognizing Kincaid's frowning thoughtfulness as a warning, Ward turned away.

"I wasn't," Kincaid said succinctly to Cantrell's broad back, "planning to *give* you anything, except a chance to earn your freedom." He was more than a little irritated. "Somehow I had thought a man facing the gallows would be a little more reasonable."

"Save your breath, Kincaid," he drawled, his husky voice freighted with contempt. "I don't want your help."

"I did some checking around, Cantrell," Kincaid said slowly, ignoring the man's obvious dislike. "You have the kind of experience I'm looking for. You know men, and you know how to lead them. Before you came along, that bunch you put together never did anything right. You turned them into one of the most effective outlaw gangs in history—never got caught—except that time they tried that bank job without you."

He didn't mention Cantrell's reputation with a gun. His own experience along those lines kept him quiet. Cantrell had worked his way right up the line—he was a target now for every would-be gunfighter who wanted to make a name for himself. But he was something more because he chose his fights. He turned down men he didn't want to kill and even managed to make friends of some of them. He had charm and apparently intelligence as well. That was what had been bothering him about this thing with Powers. Why would a young firebrand like Cantrell suddenly turn into a vigilante? He wasn't the type. Wilcox's report was filled with incidents that would seem to prove he didn't get serious about anything—not guns, horses, or women—he took what was easy and what fell his way. He did not go looking for trouble.

"You know a hell of a lot about me, don't you?"

"I get monthly reports. . . . That's why I think it would be a waste of time and money to let you rot in jail for ten to twelve years."

Cantrell scowled. Anybody but him; anybody but Kincaid, he'd snap at the chance. He'd been everything there was to be, done everything. He didn't mind the idea of wearing a badge and taking his chances against rustlers or bad men, but he wouldn't work for the man who had caused the deaths of both his parents and dishonored his sister, even if he did marry her later.

"No deals with you, Kincaid," he said flatly, turning back to his cot.

"Think it over," Chane said, feeling a mixture of anger and frustration.

Kincaid left the jail and found his attorney, Winslow Breakenridge, in his office. He spent ten minutes with him and then went directly to the governor's office in the back room of Bauer and Stanton, General Merchandisers. Governor Ed Stanton was in a meeting with three men seated casually around a large mahogany desk that was Ed's only concession to his high office. He had been appointed governor of the Arizona Territory by the president, had been elected for one term, and was already worrying about being reelected. Chane waited only a few seconds before Stanton looked up, saw him, and excused himself to come out of the small room.

They shook hands, smiling like old friends who enjoyed each other's company.

"You pretty busy?"

Stanton grinned. "Talking bullshit—just between me and you," he said in a low voice. "These gentlemen are trying to persuade me that we should move the capital to Tucson."

Chane chuckled. This tug-of-war between the residents of Tucson and Phoenix over the site of the capital had been going on for years. Endless behind-the-scenes haggling, such as this visit by Tucson's finest, was only part of the politicking that went on.

"Don't they know they don't stand a chance as long as you live here?"

Stanton grinned. "They figured that angle already—offering me a governor's mansion."

"Seriously?"

"Sounds serious."

"Guess we'd better up the ante," Chane said, only half joking. There were many benefits that befell Phoenix because it was a state capital, primarily economic. The Arizona Territory now had two colleges, one at Flagstaff and one at Tempe. With the capital here, it was almost guaranteed that the next one would be in Phoenix. Young people would no longer have to go back east to get educated. The ones who could afford it still would, because of the status it bestowed on Phoenix's wealthier residents. That wouldn't change. Men still liked to demonstrate their superiority to their surroundings.

"When can you get away? I need to talk to you," Chane said. "Saratoga Club in ten minutes be all right?"

The Saratoga Club was a private saloon in the Bricewood West, frequented by card-carrying members only. The memberships had been Kincaid's gifts to the men who owned businesses and ranches around Phoenix. It encouraged their patronage, and the exclusivity was strictly maintained. The atmosphere was deliberately circumspect, even dull, but it was restful. There were no women allowed. No rowdies allowed either. Peers met there and were assured they were special. It was a bastion of old-boy politics on a raw frontier. And it was good business. It did not pay its way financially, but it more than paid for itself in other ways, when Kincaid could find the time to visit there. The gossip was always revealing, the more so because the men who frequented the staid bar felt like compatriots.

Men waved and nodded as Chane made his way to a table. The walls were paneled in ornately carved mahogany. The bar occupied a place of prominence in the center of the big room for gentlemen who liked to stand while they drank. Clouds of blue smoke swirled gently, stirred by the large hanging overhead fans. Small round mahogany tables, each with two or three leather captain's chairs, clustered in front of the bar. Glasses were raised, gold coins clinked on the hard marble surface of the bar, and the men nonchalantly flicked cigar ashes into the deep maroon pile of the carpet.

Stanton was only ten minutes late, a record for him. He was always late because people stopped him anywhere and everywhere to tell him their problems. He was totally approachable by stranger and friend alike, and he loved to talk.

He dropped into the chair opposite Chane, and a waiter was there magically with his usual drink—whiskey and milk.

He took a sip of his drink. "My ulcer needed that," he sighed, leaning back. "What brings you out this time of day? Hotter'n hell out there, isn't it?" he asked, appreciating the relative coolness of the staid, dimly lit Saratoga Club. He reached into his pocket for his nail clipper.

"There was a meeting of the Cattlemen's Association here last night," Chane began slowly, careful not to point out that Stanton hadn't been there. Chane knew Stanton always spent Monday nights with his mistress, Kate Fletcher, at her place, to reward himself for being an attentive son-in-law, father, husband, and uncle all weekend. Wednesday nights he rewarded himself for working so hard and Friday nights to fortify himself for the long weekend ahead with family and ritual.

"Ahh, I see. Anything important?"

"They appointed me as a committee of one to let you know how unhappy they are that nothing has been done about the cattle rustling, which has been getting worse every week," he said, exaggerating only a little. He knew Stanton would believe every word because the morning's paper had carried a story along those lines. The *Gazette* hadn't mentioned his committee assignment, because he had just invented that.

"Damn!" Stanton growled, letting his displeasure show in the angry darkening of his already florid face. "You're the third man today to tell me that," he growled. "If I weren't sitting in this cool room, enjoying this life-saving concoction, I would kick your ass," he said gruffly. "Now how the hell am I going to get out of this?"

"Why don't you appoint a special ranger unit to concentrate on the rustling hereabouts?"

Stanton scowled at his friend. "Terrific idea—except where the hell do I get the money to pay for it?"

Chane quickly calculated the cost. At forty dollars a month, a half-dozen men only cost two hundred forty dollars. Even for six months it was under fifteen hundred dollars. A small price to pay if it made Jennie happy. "I'll donate the money, if you keep quiet about where it came from."

"Why the hell you doing this?" Stanton asked suspiciously.

"Because, they are stealing my cattle, remember?"

"Oh, yeah," he sighed. "But who the hell do I hire?"

"Gotta be someone with real leadership ability. A man who can take charge," Chane said, as if he were mulling it over. "You really can't let this rustling continue. They're getting too blatant. They cleaned out Frank Jones—didn't leave him a steer. The ranchers want every last one of them caught and hanged."

"Go on," Stanton said.

"I think I've found the man who can find out for us."

"Who?"

"Ward Cantrell."

"That gunfighter that kidnapped the Powers girl?"

"She came into town today with her uncle. Said he wasn't the one."

"Humph!" he snorted. "Have my doubts about that. What do you know about Cantrell?"

Chane grinned. If he told him everything, Stanton's ulcers would go into convulsions. "Lawmen possessing the ideal mixture of fearlessness, expertise with firearms and lily-white morality are damned hard to come by. Two out of three is the most we could hope for," he said dryly.

"So I'll be careful not to ask embarrassing questions," Stanton said, grinning before he settled down to business. "Cattle is big business," he mused, frowning, his florid, heavy-jowled face intent with thought. "All right," he said slowly. "Suppose I agree. We've got too many problems. Cantrell's wanted for killing a passel of Powers's men. If what I've heard is true, he's wanted in Wyoming. He's wanted for robbing your trains. He's probably wanted in other places for no telling what else. Even if I gave him a full pardon, that might just be for the little stuff. How would we handle that?"

Chane sighed. "I don't know. I talked to Winslow Breakenridge. He says we have to let him stand trial. But he thinks that no one is actively looking for Cantrell on those old charges. He thinks that after the trial, you could, in the interests of the territory, commute his sentence if he agrees to provide certain services to the territory."

Stanton snorted. "Great! The judge sentences him to twenty years breaking up boulders in the hot sun or to hang, depending on the mood old fire-and-brimstone Cadwallader is in, and there's no doubt what Cantrell will decide. That's no choice! You offer a man a deal like that, and he'll choose life over death any day. But as soon as he's out of sight, he'll run like hell! We'll never see him again," he said flatly.

Chane frowned. "In theory, you're right. But Cantrell is a man of honor. I feel it. I don't know why, but I'm willing to guarantee it. If he says he'll do it, he will."

Stanton shook his head, grimacing before he took another sip of his drink, set it down, and began pushing at his cuticles again, fairly caressing the shiny nail clipper he always carried.

"You aren't going to like this," he said heavily, "but I think it's too damned risky."

Chane nodded. "I agree that there's some risk, but we're just about pushed up against the wall. If you don't do something about the rustlers, you'll never get elected again—not even as a dogcatcher."

Stanton groaned. He dearly loved being governor. It was a position that provided unlimited opportunities and prestige. Even his wife never questioned him about his many absences. She knew and accepted that the governorship made extreme demands upon his time and energies.

"I can't just pardon the man who has been robbing and killing my people," he snorted.

Chane leaned forward. "So they hang him, everyone cheers, and five minutes later he's forgotten. But you, my friend, still have a problem. Men like me keep complaining to you about losing cattle. Men might even start saying rude things about your leadership abilities."

Stanton frowned. "Is that a threat?"

Chane shook his head in denial. It had been close, he thought, amazed at himself. Was he so besotted with Jennie that he would even stoop to blackmailing his friend to please her in a whim? He didn't even like Cantrell. He was suddenly remembering a casual remark he had overheard once about his being henpecked. Anger flushed through him. It wasn't justified. He loved Jennie and wanted her happy. That did not make him henpecked. But something hardened in him. Cantrell was a grown man. He had damned well known the penalties when he began his career as an outlaw. He could damned well take what was coming to him.

Angry at himself, he stood up. "I'll see you later, Ed."

"Whoa! Wait a second," Stanton ordered. "This is pretty important to you, isn't it?"

Chane sighed. "I don't know."

Stanton nodded. "Let me think about it. That reminds me. I've always wondered why this Devil's Canyon Gang only seemed to rob you. Have you given that any thought? Maybe he knows you?"

"What are you implying, friend?" Kincaid asked dryly.

Stanton chuckled. "Sounds pretty bad, doesn't it? But you have to admit—most outlaw gangs hit banks, stagecoaches, anything they can."

Chane sat back down. He sighed and picked up his drink. "I've thought about it. I had Wilcox working on it from that angle. He checked out everyone who resembled the description we had for the leader of the gang. That's how we picked up Cantrell's name, but we couldn't trace him back more than five years."

Stanton laughed. "He looks older than that!"

Kincaid grinned, and they both fell silent.

"You sure he could do the job?" Stanton asked.

"I'd stake a lot on it. I had Wilcox give me a full report. Cantrell is a born leader. He prefers to go it alone, won't follow man or beast unless they were already going where he wanted to go. He doesn't do anything he doesn't want to do. He's no good-time-Charlie who goes along for the ride. Like I said, his history only goes back five years. There's no telling what he did before that."

"Please," Stanton said, reading Chane's mind, "my ulcers are bleeding already."

"You have sort of a strange relationship with your nail clipper, too," Kincaid grinned, nodding toward Stanton's hands, where he was absently pushing at his cuticles with the blunt edge of the clipper.

"This may seem strange to you, but it never gets headaches."

"You should have married it."

"No. I should have stayed single. I was never this horny when I was single."

Ward Cantrell had several opportunities to regret turning down Kincaid's offer of help. The sheriff increased the number of deputies who were always on guard, and he was given a court date—two days away. An attorney by the name of Winslow Breakenridge, placid and smooth as a frozen lake, appeared out of the blue to announce that he had volunteered to be his counsel during the trial. He asked a lot of questions Ward either couldn't or wouldn't answer and left the jail, shaking his head sadly. "I'm *your* attorney, Mr. Cantrell. If you won't trust me—I can't help you."

The trial, since it was only for train robbery, was poorly attended. Leslie Powers was not called upon to testify. Apparently Kincaid had seen to it that her presence would not be needed. Ward was grateful to Kincaid for that. Leslie had been through enough already.

The trial was held in the Garden Courtyard of the Bricewood West, which seemed ironic to Ward. The room was packed with Kincaid's special agents. Ward recognized Ben, Three Fingers, and a couple of others from the last train robbery. Breakenridge sat beside him at the table facing the judge's makeshift bench. Kincaid stood in the back of the room and watched him with cool, unreadable eyes. The whole thing was totally predictable. It took four hours. The jury was out of the room for only twenty minutes, but there was no doubt in Ward's mind what their verdict would be.

Guilty. The foreman looked right at him when he said it. The judge nodded, asked the defendant to stand, then read him the sentence: hanging, to be carried out at sunrise tomorrow. Ward didn't even flinch; he just stood there listening to the drone of that sanctimonious voice with a fresh wave of bitterness choking him into silence. They led him past Kincaid and a heavyset man with silver-streaked gray hair and a heavy florid face he didn't recognize, and he stopped.

Kincaid nodded. "Nasty break."

"You got tobacco on you?"

Kincaid passed him the makings; Cantrell rolled a smoke with deft brown fingers and passed the makings back.

"Got a light?"

Kincaid handed him a small box of matches. Cantrell ignited one match with his thumbnail, held it to the cigarette with a steady hand, and then looked up, bringing the full force of his cold blue eyes into play.

Cantrell held out the matches, dropped them into Kincaid's hand. Chane held out matches and tobacco, offering them back to him.

"No thanks, Kincaid. If I want anything from you, I'll ask," he said quietly, coldly.

Kincaid watched him walk away before he turned to Stanton. "Well, what do you think of him now?"

"He's got guts. There's some fire in that boy. His hand didn't even quiver."

"He'd kill me right now if he had even half a chance."

"You saw that, too, huh?" Stanton grinned.

Chane nodded. There was still something about Cantrell that bothered him, aside from his impending death and Stanton's unwillingness to commit himself to pardon him. There was a quality he saw in Cantrell that he saw in his son—an unwillingness to bend. Unfortunately, not bending could mean breaking instead. That was why the trait bothered him in young Chantry. Such stubbornness was rarely rewarded by society.

Stanton must have read his mind. "Looks pretty cocky now, but that young man has just been ushered to the gates of hell. It'll take him a little time to realize it, but when he does he could crack under the pressure."

Kincaid shrugged. "I've been wrong about men so many times. I've seen what looked like brave men who had to be carried to the gallows, kicking, screaming, and crying like babies. I've also seen little wimps who walked up the steps and put the noose around their own necks. So don't ask me to tell you which way he will do it," he said gruffly.

Stanton grunted. "Did you decide yet?" Chane asked, wondering how he was going to stall Jennie again.

Stanton shook his head. "I'm still thinking about it. I gotta see which way the wind is blowing."

Chane cursed his friend's political bent, but he knew there was nothing more he could do. Jennie and Leslie would just have to live with it, whichever way it came out.

Ward Cantrell had never been given to soul-searching, but with the promise of death at sunrise, he knew he would not sleep. "Anybody you want to see?" the sheriff asked after dinner.

Ward thought about his sister, but that was out of the question now. He couldn't make peace with Jenn without crawling to Kincaid, and there was absolutely nothing in it for Jenn. All he would be giving her would be a chance to grieve. She didn't need that. He knew, at least on one level, that Jenn would rather see him than not, no matter what the outcome, but he was too practical to indulge himself at so great a cost to her. There was nothing anyone could do to save him now, and no reason to open old wounds. Jenn had no doubt made peace with his disappearance. She had earned her right not to be disturbed again.

The first hours of the night were spent in denial—he could not believe that tomorrow morning he would die. He prepared for bed in the usual manner, ignoring the small table the sheriff had moved into his cell, ignoring the paper, inkwell, and quill. He laughed to think that he was supposed to want to write letters at a time like this.

About nine o'clock, a wagon rattled to a stop outside, and he moved to stand so he could watch. Two men leaped down and unloaded a long pine box. They carried it inside and put it down on the floor beside the door. The sheriff and his deputies were noncommittal, but the two delivery men looked significantly at him. He felt the first faint stirring in his chest. He walked to the window and looked out. The incessant hammering had stopped hours ago. Now, in the dim light of the street lamps, he could see the gallows where they intended to hang him. He glanced back at the long pine box. All the preparations for his death had been made. Everyone except him had accepted it. He sat there for a long time, looking at the box, and finally the realization sank in that even though he was alive now, and even though it felt like it was permanent and unconditional, these men had the power to end his life. He had never felt uncontrollable fear before, but now he felt himself quaking inside. He really was going to die. This was not a bad dream.

Once he accepted that fact and measured his own helplessness, those emotions gave way to more anger and bitterness. Rage swelled up inside him. If he could have, he would have torn that small cell apart, but he suddenly realized the futility of it.

It was not until the guards had gone to sleep and the moon had arced overhead, that he settled into acceptance of his death and his sister's importance to him. Then he desperately wanted to see her. He was grateful that he didn't have the option to send for her, because he would be forever ashamed of himself for subjecting her to that. Besides, he remembered, she was a Kincaid now. There was still bitterness there, but he did not blame Kincaid for what had happened to him. Kincaid may have speeded up the time schedule so that he would hang tomorrow instead of next year, but there would be no real difference. He was still a nobody, going nowhere. One more year wouldn't have changed anything.

Once he faced that, he knew what had been bothering him for the last year. Now that it was too late, he could admit that he wanted to do something with his life—something to look back on with pride. Maybe that was why he had been hoarding half of the money from his share of every job. He decided he would give his sister the key to his safe deposit box. That way, in case she was staying with Kincaid out of necessity, she would have a way out of the marriage. There was enough money there to give her a new start.

Thinking about Jenn and his family always reminded him what a failure he was. At least there was no one there to verbalize that fact, or tell him what was expected of a Van Vleet. They would hang him in a few hours, and it wouldn't even be noticed in Phoenix, much less make the news in New York. If it did, he could see the *New York Times* headlines now: "Scion Of Once Wealthy Van Vleet Family Hanged For Train Robbery." There were people in New York who would enjoy that tremendously. Dying in anonymity had some advantages. At least Jenn would be spared that final indignity. He hadn't spared her much else, he thought bitterly, suddenly despising himself for his stubbornness.

CHAPTER
TWENTY-FIVE

Ward sprawled on his bunk, staring up at the plastered ceiling and wondering if there was anything he could have done differently so that he wouldn't have ended up here, waiting to die.

Could he have stayed in New York? Instead of joining the cavalry? It hadn't seemed so at the time. Too many things had happened that last year in New York. His parents had died, both shot with the same gun. It had been touted as murder and suicide, but he and Jenn had known that their father had been driven by Chantry Kincaid III to that final act of desperation. Then Jenn had by some inconceivable process fallen in love with Kincaid. And he had incurred Kincaid's ire by proxy and had been beaten so brutally that he still carried the scars. And even before he had recovered, Jenn had married Kincaid, without even bothering to tell him.

He had joined the cavalry. Simone had begged him to take her, and he had. Could he have changed his fate by not leaving the service? Would that have changed the outcome of that fateful day in June of 1882? He searched for a beginning, and his mind always came back to that night when he came home to find Simone sobbing into a pillow, sprawled across the bed in the small house they shared. . . .

"Hey, what's wrong?" he asked, moving to her side.

"Nothing, everything," she said tremulously, sniffing noisily.

"You want to tell me about it?"

"No . . . yes . . . I don't know," she wailed.

He lay down beside her and took her into his arms. Her lips were salty, trembling, and cold beneath his. He kissed her for a long, slow time, until her breathing changed, settling down into rhythmic looseness that indicated a mood he could handle. When he finally lifted his head, she smiled shakily.

"You're going to hate me," she whispered.

He looked at the luminous delicacy of her face, seeing the tears glisten on her cheeks and the flicker of pain in her wide brown eyes, and felt that same sense of wonder he always felt when he looked at her. "I love you," he whispered, leaning down to brush the tears off her cheeks.

"Hold me." She sighed. "Please hold me."

He held her close to him. "Tell me what's wrong."

"I'm . . . I'm . . . pregnant," she blurted.

"And?" he prompted.

"You don't want a baby," she said. New tears brimmed in her dark eyes and spilled over, cascading into the dark hair that fanned out on the pillow. He brushed gently at the tears, letting the relief he felt ease some of the tension that had been building up inside him when he thought there was something serious wrong.

"Of course I do," he whispered. He held her close, feeling the trembling in her slender form. He had no family left of his own, except Simone. Simone was all he had, all he wanted. She was good and loving and loyal, and she had no one except him.

When they had come west two years before, they had brought her mother with them because she had tuberculosis. She had seemed to get better, but she had died eight months ago. And while it was true that he had never actively wanted a baby, and also true that this might not be the best time in the world, since he was scheduled to be officially mustered out of the army in ten days, he was also sure that he could find some way to provide for them.

"We'll manage just fine with a baby," he said firmly. "Why wouldn't we?"

She cupped his face in her hands and they were cold and trembling against his warm skin. "You aren't angry, *chèri*?"

He searched inside himself to see how he did feel about it. His father had always been too busy for him. His mother thought boys belonged in school—the farther away the better, probably. Only Jenn had really seemed to love him. If he had any feelings about the matter, it was probably just that his son would not grow up like that. He would have two parents who cared about him, and he would go to school only if it was within walking distance from home. His son would not learn riding and hunting from strangers and teachers. There were some things a boy should learn from his father.

He must have scowled, because Simone's face registered alarm. "Peter, *chèri*, what are you thinking about?" she asked.

"I was just thinking that I don't want our son to be a bastard."

Tears sprang into her eyes. "But what can we do about that?" she said, the last words dissolving into a wail of sheer anguish.

"We can get married," he said firmly.

Now Simone covered her face with her hands and burrowed into the pillow as if she would hide herself there. "No, no, you don't know . . ." she moaned, turning away from him.

"Know what?" he demanded.

"I-I don't know enough to be a mother," she wailed.

He chuckled softly. "How do you know that?"

She reached under the pillow and pulled out a tiny blue sock that was dirty from so much handling and strangely misshapen. It had an extra bulge on one side, and the soft, thick yarn still hung from it. Deformed and tiny, with strings hanging from the toe, it seemed so pathetic that he couldn't help himself, the laughter bubbled out of him, surprising him.

"See?" she wailed, covering her head.

"Well," he said, stifling the laughter as best he could, "that's not so bad for a first try. You'll get better. You have months to practice." He kissed her until she forgot her misery, and they made love. Life seemed full and rich.

The next day was his day off. He bought two tickets on the stagecoach, and they went to Dodge City and got married there so no one in Fort Dodge would have to know that they weren't already married. He didn't want anyone throwing that up to her.

Two weeks later, when he was standing in line in the bank in Dodge, waiting to cash his last check from the army, he noticed two white men outside hazing a big, black soldier named John Trayner, while at least a dozen laughing men egged them on.

"Hey, nigger! Come outta that store! Your skin may be black as the ace o' spades, but your liver is lily white! Come out here this minute 'fore we come in there and drag you out!"

The big Negro, an aide to one of the officers at Fort Dodge, was justifiably reluctant to tangle with drunken white men, especially in Dodge City, which was one of the wildest towns in the West. Dodge was the end of the line for all the crews that drove cattle up the trail from Texas, and those southern boys didn't cotton to smart-alecky blacks.

"Yassah, I's coming out, suh!"

"Yassah, yassah!" a tall, lanky, raw-boned man in a large black Stetson mocked him. "You make me sick, nigger! Ain't no wonder they use manure like you for fertilizer back home."

"Reckon he wouldn't even make good fertilizer!" the other one laughed. He was a pale, red-haired Georgian who had gained notoriety because of his habit of refighting the Civil War every time he got drunk. "Hey, nigger! This your wagon?"

Sergeant John Trayner, whom Peter knew as an industrious, hardworking man, with a wife and two small children at home, peered out of the doorway of the general store, his eyes round with fear. He hadn't worn a sidearm, probably because he was only coming into town for supplies. There was undoubtedly a rifle in the wagon, but with those ruffians where they were, the rifle might as well have been a hundred miles away.

"Nawsuh! Belongs to the army," Trayner said, still holding a fifty-pound sack of flour he had been in the process of carrying to the wagon the man was pointing at.

"You hear that, boys? This here is a nigger wagon! Hey! Y'all come on! Let's take us a ride in a nigger wagon!"

Men up and down the wide dusty street lounged about in chairs tilted back against the storefronts. Other men stood in small clusters. They could have been talking about the heat, or the lack of rain, or the news they had read in the *Dodge City Expositor*. Now they stopped talking and turned to watch.

Six of the men who had been shouting encouragement now left the shade of the sidewalk and scampered aboard Trayner's wagon. The one who had started the hazing stood in the back of the deep wagon bed. He leaned down and picked up a bag, held it up for Trayner to see, then pulled his knife and slashed the bag, laughing as the contents spilled out. The other men yelled lustily and laughed as the black man dropped the sack he had been carrying and plunged off the sidewalk to save the rest of his supplies.

"Yuh can't do that. That's gov'ment property!" he shouted, his rage overcoming his desire not to cause trouble. Before he could reach the man, the wagon started to move, whipped by one of the rowdies who had taken up the ribbons.

"Who's gonna stop us, nigger?" the one with the knife shouted, laughing at the helpless look of rage that had transformed the black man's face. "Who's gonna stop us?"

Trayner no longer realized that they were all armed and he wasn't. He ran as fast as he could after the wagon and the jeering men. "Stop! Yuh can't take that wagon!"

"Come and get it, nigger!"

The driver whipped the team as the men in the back all laughed and mimicked the black man. One of the men began throwing the sacks and boxes of tins out of the wagon, trying to trip the man who ran after them. Another man grabbed tin cans and began pelting the Negro with them.

"Them's gov'ment property! Stop that! Come back here with that wagon!" he yelled, jumping deftly over the sacks of flour and sugar they threw in his path, fighting his way through the shower of cans.

Peter was just coming out of the bank when the wagon came even with him, the men howling and laughing with insane boisterousness. Peter was shoving his money into his trousers pocket when he saw one of the men draw his gun and fire. Trayner stumbled and dropped, and Peter didn't think beyond the moment. He drew his own gun, fired, and hit the one who had shot the unarmed soldier. The man flipped out of the wagon and lay motionless on the ground.

A yell of outrage rose up from the men in the wagon. The driver *whoaed* the racing horses to a halt, and the men in the wagon bed dropped down, clawing for their revolvers. Peter dived behind a water trough and returned their fire. He saw one man hit—he was flung backward, screaming.

Someone in the wagon called out to the driver to get that damned wagon moving. Peter saw Trayner begin to inch his way out of the wide, dusty street. A man in the wagon lifted his head and pumped another bullet into Trayner. Peter fired almost simultaneously and the man stood up, pivoted, and fell headlong out of the wagon as it began to move forward again.

Peter ignored the receding wagon and rushed to the fallen man's side. Trayner was breathing slowly with an audible rattle. Blood had already soaked through his clothing and was spilling into the dirt, turning dark brown.

"My wagon," he groaned. "They got my wagon."

"The army can get your wagon back. Here, let me help you."

"Aaahhh . . . no, please, Cap'n. Hurts too bad to move."

"Jesus! I didn't think. I'll go for the doctor," Peter said, cursing himself.

"No." Trayner gripped his arm with desperate strength. "No, won't do no good, Cap'n Van Vleet. I'm a goner, me. Gotta say something to you, though," he panted raggedly, gasping as the pain hit him in waves now. The rattle became more pronounced, and his face was the color of clay, gray and damp.

"My wife," he gasped, "she's a fine, proud woman. It would hurt her to know how they shamed me. She comes from a proud

family, wif brave menfolks. It would hurt her too bad. Tell her
. . . Would you . . . tell her I died like a man, please, Cap'n?''

Peter's chest felt clamped by a vise. He was remembering the
pretty brown-skinned woman who would have to receive that message. He remembered her as a hardworking woman and a good
mother. He felt a weariness inside him. She didn't deserve this,
but neither did John Trayner. Peter nodded, gripping the cooling
black hand. ''I'll tell her,'' he said, his voice thick.

''Cap'n Van Vleet . . .''

Peter didn't bother to remind him that he wasn't a captain anymore. He was officially out of the cavalry now.

''Yes, Sergeant Trayner.''

Trayner smiled at the title of respect. He opened his eyes, and
they were unfocused and glazed with pain. ''Tell her, Cap'n,'' he
panted around the deep rattle in his chest, ''tell her that I love
her.''

Peter nodded. He didn't have to ask if he should send for her.
John Trayner was too proud to be subjected to that final indignity—
having the woman he loved see him lying in the street like a stray
dog that had been shot for stealing scraps.

''I'll tell her, Sergeant,'' he said gently.

One of the spectators shouted that the wagon was gone, and men
merged into the street, silent and curious. Snake Edwards, an army
scout and a good friend of Peter's, helped move Trayner to the
shade of the sidewalk. Someone went for the doctor, but Trayner
died before the doctor arrived.

Peter closed Trayner's eyes, covered his face with his vest, and
then stood up. There was an unnatural stillness inside him, as if he
had not fully realized what had happened.

Snake spat a stream of tobacco into the dirt and shook his head.
''Sure wish you had'na butted in the way you did.''

Peter frowned his lack of understanding. ''What?''

''Didn't change nothing. He's dead just like he woulda been if
you'd minded your own business, and now you got yourself a peck
of trouble. Those men are on the vigilance committee. They'll
either come back here and get you themselves or put a price on
your head—won't be nothing you can do about it.''

Peter shook his head. ''The vigilance committee? I thought that
was just storekeepers and property owners.''

''Used to be—at the beginning. But the crews coming up the
trail got rougher and wilder until the honest men, even in a pack,

couldn't handle 'em. So's they let in some of the wild ones and then some more until now the wild ones control.''

"So what now?" Peter demanded.

"Depends on how mad they are . . ." Snake shrugged, his lean face noncommittal. "But I wouldn't stay around waiting if I was you. I'd get my woman and head out of town, far as I could get.''

"Run? From a bunch of drunk cowpunchers? There wasn't a man in the bunch. They were a pack of snot-nosed kids," Peter said, incredulous.

"Those *kids* would as soon kill you as look at you," Snake growled. "You've been holed up too long with your pretty little wife. You're out of touch, Captain."

CHAPTER
TWENTY-SIX

They borrowed a wagon and took John Trayner home. Peter broke the news to his wife as gently as he could, and then he and Snake carried Trayner in and laid him on the floor of the small, well-scrubbed parlor.

"How did it happen, Captain Van Vleet?" she asked, holding herself stiffly as if her dignity were the only thing left between her and utter and final hopelessness.

"Your husband was attacked by a pack of sneak thieves, Mrs. Trayner. They killed him and stole the wagon and supplies."

Her dark eyes searched his face to see if he was lying to her. Then she looked away. "Was he . . . did he suffer?" she asked softly.

"No, ma'am. He died quickly," he said.

She stooped down and touched her husband's hand, lying cool and limp across his chest. "Did these thieves . . . did they shame John?" She looked up at him, and he could see something hardening and coiling within her at the thought of strange men shaming her husband. She knelt on the floor beside his body protectively, and Peter could see her convulsing with fury and violation, speechless with the welter of emotions that were threatening to overwhelm her.

"He had no reason for shame. He did all that he could have done, Mrs. Trayner," he said, his voice strangely thick.

She swallowed and closed her eyes, fighting for control. "You see, John was a good man, a gentle man. That's why I loved him so much. My brother and my father are brutal, hating men, Captain. I never understood them before."

Dragging in a deep breath, she stood up. "Thank you, Captain. I'd best get busy and tend to John."

"Mrs. Trayner, if there is anything either I or my wife can do . . ."

She nodded as if she understood, but he could tell by the look in her eyes that she would never ask. "Thank you, Captain. I think it fitting that he be dressed in his best uniform, don't you? I'd best get him cleaned up before the children come home from school. You'll excuse me, please, Captain. They'll be here soon, and I don't want them to see him such a mess."

When Peter had turned the wagon and snapped the ribbons, sending the horses leaping forward, Snake, who was doing his best to hold on to his seat, asked, "Where we going now?"

"I'm going to ask Simone if she will come stay with Mrs. Trayner, then I'm going back to town to settle this thing."

Snake rolled his eyes and shook his head. "You're hauling about one brick short of a load, boy."

"I don't give a damn. You tell me who else will stay with her. She needs some female companionship, dammit."

"I ain't questioning that. I'm questioning how smart it is for you and Simone. Those boys weren't play-actin' this afternoon. They're meaner'n poison."

The house was neat and orderly and smelled of the strong lye soap Simone used to clean, but Peter could tell immediately that the place was deserted. He also knew that it would do no good to go looking for her. She had many friends in Fort Dodge. She could be anywhere. He searched his memory to see if he could remember what she had said that morning. She usually told him what she was planning to do, but, husbandlike, he usually didn't listen too closely.

They returned the wagon to its owner and spent the afternoon going from saloon to saloon looking for the men who had killed Trayner. It was nine o'clock, almost full dark when Peter decided they might as well give up their vigil and return home. Snake insisted on riding with him. "You were lucky, boy. Those men could have made a lot of trouble for you."

"Wonder what happened to them."

"Maybe somewhere sleeping off their drunk. Don't rightly understand it myself. Any other time they woulda been right back, raring to finish what they started," Snake grunted.

There was a light burning in the cabin, lighting the windows with a warm, cheery, luminous glow that shone out at him and quickened that little leap of gladness he always felt when he saw the house he and Simone shared together. It was an automatic but welcome response. He smiled into the darkness.

As they drew closer, Peter became aware that something did not feel the same. It was elusive and oppressive. On the surface everything looked like it always did, but the smile faded and he slowed his horse, tightening his legs around the animal's heaving sides. His eyes narrowed as he tried to penetrate the darkness. They drew closer, and the same nerve-end tingle that had made him such an effective Indian fighter now sent an alarm racing along his nerves. He reached out to signal his friend.

"Get down!" he hissed, throwing himself sideways off his own horse just as bullets whined over his head, puncturing the air where his body had been only a split-second before.

The night was torn apart by gunfire. Peter dashed for the cabin. His hand was on the door when he heard Snake drop. He spun around and threw himself in the direction of the sound. Bullets were spewing up a cloud of dirt and dust that blinded him. Gropingly, he located his friend, and with bullets spanging and whining all around them, he dragged him into the cabin. He kicked the door shut and crawled over to the table to put out the light and froze in mid-breath. Simone's arm, clearly visible through the doorway into the bedroom, dangled from the bed onto the floor, white and limp.

Ignoring the crash of gunfire that filled the small cabin with frightful, strident concussions, he crawled into the bedroom. Simone was naked, sprawled across the bed. Her pale skin was blotched with bruises. Her throat gaped where a knife had opened it. The bedclothes were drenched in her blood. The smell of it was sweet, intimate, and cloying in his nostrils.

Peter curled over, unable or unwilling to breathe, his lungs filled with heaviness and clamped by icy bands. Forgetting the men outside, he stood up and pulled the coverlet over Simone, as if that simple act would somehow comfort her. He huddled there on the floor, holding her cold hand, overwhelmed by a welter of emotions, blaming himself. If he had been here . . . If he hadn't left her alone . . . If he hadn't gotten involved in something that wasn't his problem . . . If he had listened to Snake, found her, and left town instead of trying to play the hero . . .

"Come out, you nigger-loving bastard!" a loud voice called out to him. "Light those torches! He'll come out then."

Snake groaned, and Peter roused a little. He forced himself to crawl back to Snake's side. He didn't bother to put out the lamp. The shooting had stopped momentarily. Snake's eyes were glazed and unfocused. He had taken one bullet in the stomach and one in the chest, high up. Blood mixed with a frothy spittle dribbled from his mouth, creeping toward his ear.

"Simone . . . okay?" Snake whispered.

"Yeah," he lied, moving to wad his vest up and put it under Snake's head.

"I need a . . . drink."

Peter crawled to the cupboard where Simone kept their lone bottle of whiskey, tucked it under his arm, and scooted back to Snake's side. He uncapped the bottle and held Snake's head so he could take a swallow. Snake groaned, then coughed. The ragged, tearing sound in Snake's lungs grated through him the way chalk grated on a blackboard, setting every nerve in his body on edge.

"That's better," Snake whispered. "Now, boy, you get the hell outta here. They're gonna burn this place."

"I'm not leaving you," Peter said firmly.

"I'm a goner, boy. You git. Before it's too late."

Peter shook his head. His eyes fell on something small and blue. It was the baby bootie. Without thinking, he put it into his pants pocket. Snake groaned, and Peter clamped his teeth together, praying for an end to his friend's pain. He felt numb and insulated against his own feelings.

"Gimme another drink."

Peter held his friend's head, let the whiskey trickle into his mouth. Snake started to cough—a ragged, tearing ugliness that twisted inside Peter like some crazed reptile, coiling and lashing. Snake's hand groped for his, and Peter held it tight. Snake returned the pressure for a second, and then his eyes rolled back in his head. The rattle of his breathing stopped. Peter sat on the floor of the lighted cabin, holding his friend's hand. He didn't know how long he sat there. The firing had stopped, and he could hear the sound of a few crickets chirping off in the distance as if this were any normal evening.

A hoarse yell rent the stillness. There was the crash of glass breaking, and a torch arced into the room, sailed over his head and struck the lamp, to send kerosene spraying over the other half of the room.

"Come on out, nigger lover!"

Another voice joined the first. "Get a rope! Bring a rope with yuh! We're gonna hang this lily-livered bastard." Others joined in, until a dozen men were yelling obscenities.

The flames caught and leaped up, illuminating the inside of the cabin and filling the small room with a wild roaring sound like a waterfall, close up. Heat slammed into him like a wall that could not be walked through. Peter stood up slowly and walked to the mantel, where his shotgun hung. He scooped up a handful of shells and loaded quickly. He knew he couldn't get all of them, but he was sure he could get some of them before they got him. Flames were licking at his legs; he walked toward the door, the shotgun hanging alongside his right thigh.

"Here he comes! Wing him! We're gonna hang that nigger lover! Teach him a lesson!"

The men were either drunk or overeager. Three of them rushed forward, ignoring or not seeing the shotgun. Peter waited until they were close together, melded into one tight target, and then he swung the gun up and pulled both triggers. The men flew backward as if they had been jerked by hidden wires. The night was shattered by the crash of answering gunfire. Peter reloaded and kept walking. Two men to the left of Peter stood up and yelled. Peter swung around and they caught the twin blasts in chest and belly. A man to the right of Peter panicked and stood up to run. Peter dropped the empty shotgun, drew his revolver, and shot the man in the back. At that point, it turned into a rout, with Peter clearly outlined against the burning house, his gun blazing. When the hammer landed on an empty cartridge, he was the only one standing.

They weren't all dead. He could hear someone groaning, but the fine white fury had drained out of him. He could hear the roar of the fire and smell the acrid, heated smoke, but he could not feel the warmth. He holstered his gun, walked slowly to his horse, mounted stiffly, and kicked the horse into a trot.

He didn't have a single scratch on his body. He rode most of that night, only stopping when the moon set and it was too dark to continue without endangering his horse. He had no food or water. He unsaddled the mare, tied her close to a lush patch of tall grass, and gathered twigs to build a small fire to take the chill out of his bones.

Blind to the threat of pursuit, he kicked a small depression in the earth, arranged the dried limbs and bark, and reached into his pocket for a small tin of matches. The fire caught, and he sat down, shivering with a mixture of shock, exhaustion, and cold. Damp wood popped and crackled in the flames. A coyote yipped in the distance, and the mare snorted in response. Stars blinked overhead. The fire leaped, spreading warmth and light. Something on the ground caught his eye. Puzzled, he picked it up and recognized the small misshapen bootie that Simone had struggled over. He had touched it without recognizing it, but now a whole passel of memories rushed into the void of his numb mind as if they had been somehow attached to the yarn. He was seeing Trayner and Snake dying, Simone and his unborn child dead, and Mrs. Trayner's grief, with sights and sounds and smells and the helplessness and anger all mixed up together so that he felt paralyzed. The memory cut like a razor into soft flesh until it grated against the bone, and he groaned softly and doubled over, unable to free himself from the pain of it, rocking with helplessness.

Two days later, when he stopped at an isolated ranch house to buy supplies off a settler, he heard that ex–army Captain Peter Van Vleet was wanted for the murder of his wife, her lover Snake Edwards, and eight members of the posse who had tried to capture him.

He couldn't get honest work because someone always recognized him. The blaze of silver-streaked flaxen hair made him an easy target. Easy to describe. Easy to recognize. And once he had started running, there wasn't any way to stop.

Now Ward Cantrell, the former Peter Van Vleet, stood by the barred window, looking out at the dark, quiet shapes of the buildings outside the jail, smelling the sage from the desert, letting the soft night winds cool his face, feeling that perhaps there hadn't been anything he could have done, except be someone else entirely. Someone smarter and wiser and more cautious . . .

He could hear a dog yipping off in the distance and the faint sounds of dance hall music. The sky was beginning to lighten on the eastern horizon—dark purple instead of black. Purple, a few shades darker than Jennifer's eyes.

At twenty he hadn't been able to forgive Jenn for falling in love with Kincaid, but in the last eight years he had learned a lot about women. Too many of them didn't seem to have any control over whom they fell in love with. Sometimes a man's just standing in the right place at the right time seemed reason enough. Too bad he hadn't bothered to recognize this fact about women earlier so that he could have forgiven Jenn before he died. . . .

That thought brought a sardonic gleam into his eyes and a smile to his lean face. They couldn't help themselves any more than Leslie Powers could stifle the passion and fire in her wild little body. She was all woman, definitely unique in the best sense of the word, and every inch a lady.

Leslie Powers. Her name conjured up a well of turbulent emotions, not the least of which was guilt. He had wronged her in every possible way. He had taken her virginity, destroyed her reputation, and left her vulnerable to Younger and others like him. And amazingly, after all that, she had faced them in the jail with courage that bespoke an indomitable spirit. She had shown herself as a woman who would not be cowed. There was something very rare in that one. It was unfortunate that he had met her too late and under the worst possible circumstances.

He sighed. Had he fallen in love with her? Was that why his heart leaped when she walked into the jail?

He closed his eyes, unwilling to answer either question. There was nothing he could do about it now. He glanced at the eastern sky. The horizon had lightened to violet. It was almost time.

His heart constricted. Realization was like a net closing around him. Fear was like a wild thing inside him. *He did not want to die. He wanted to live!* He gripped the bars, pressing his face against the cold metal, eyes closed, fighting for control.

He had faced death many times before, but this, locked up and waiting to be executed by men he hated, was the worst. Much worse than when Mama Mendoza had taken him in. He'd lain on her lumpy pallet for days in a near coma, wracked with fever and pain. Then death would have been a relief. On the field of combat it would have been at least quick. It was a very different thing to contemplate your own death by hanging. It was a simple thing to die after a lengthy illness and quite another to die when you were young and healthy and the blood in your veins could still sing at the mere thought of a pretty girl.

He watched the sky turn from violet to gray; then he sat down at the small table and took up the quill.

Dear Jenn,

There is far too much to say and too little time to say it in, but I feel compelled to tell you that I left New York in a childish fury when you married Kincaid, and I realize now that it is I who should have begged your forgiveness. Forgiveness for judging you harshly and for waiting until it was too late to come to my senses and to realize that no matter what has gone before, we are still brother and sister. I hope when you think of me it will be without bitterness. I love you more than anything or anyone. Please forgive me. I was and still am a stubborn fool. By the time you read this letter I will be dead. There is no way I can explain all that brought me to this moment, except to say that I did the best I knew how to do. It just didn't work out. Please take care of yourself. It gives me comfort to know that you are happy, so please endeavor to stay that way. The key is to my safe deposit box at the First National in Phoenix. Use the money in any way that will increase your happiness. I love you.

Your brother,

Peter

He reread the letter, put the key inside, and sealed the envelope. Then he fished a small leather pouch out of his trousers pocket. He painstakingly opened the drawstrings and pulled out a tiny blue sock that was soiled and misshapen. His fingers smoothed it out so that the extra bulge almost didn't show. The yarn was gritty with age and wear. Beneath that, in the bottom of the pouch, there was a delicate gold locket. He opened the locket and Jenn's smiling image stared out at him. Clasping the two objects, the small sock that Simone had struggled and despaired over so long ago and the locket he had taken without Jenn's knowledge, he slowly walked to the bunk, and lay down to wait for Arizona's justice.

When the two deputies, neither of whom he had seen before, came for him, he carefully concealed the locket and the tiny sock in the pouch and gave it and the letter to Tatum's night guard. He asked the man to deliver them to Mrs. Kincaid.

"I'm going that direction about ten this morning. That be soon enough?" the man asked.

"Sure. Ten is fine."

CHAPTER
TWENTY-SEVEN

Malcomb stopped before Mrs. Kincaid and bowed slightly, proffering his tray. His expression clearly said, "Who could be sending anything as disreputable as this?" Jennifer looked from his haughty eyes to the cheap envelope and stained leather pouch, then raised her eyebrows in acknowledgment of his unspoken question.

Though he considered it a dreadful imposition, Malcomb was accustomed to delivering pleas for help from women less fortunate than his mistress. Many times she ordered him to saddle a horse so she could ride to some adobe hut and console a woman who had lost a child or a husband. As much as he disliked it, he dared not refuse to bring her anything that was sent to her, for fear of incurring her quick wrath. Her husband's employees and their families were her family.

She lifted the envelope off the tray. "Where did this come from?"

"I know not, madame. The deputy said nothing except that it was for you."

"Deputy?" Her four young guests were talking freely. Jennie walked to her desk, picked up a letter opener, slit the long edge of the envelope, and a key dropped out. She stooped to pick it up, then sat down at the desk, her skirts flowing out around her in graceful sweeps of shimmering silk.

She unfolded the letter and her heart leaped with excitement and joy as she recognized the bold script—it was Peter's handwriting. She would know it anywhere. She read the letter quickly, and the glad light faded to be replaced by disbelief and then anguish.

Sensing something out of the ordinary, the young women fell silent, watching her. They saw Jennifer's cheeks pale, saw the letter crumple in her fingers, and heard Jennie's low moan. Leslie rushed forward and knelt in front of the stricken woman, her eyes beseeching her.

"He's dead," she whispered. "My brother is dead." She clutched the letter, her wide, purple eyes filling with such pain that Leslie could feel tears welling in her own eyes.

161

There was pandemonium as the others rushed to Jennie's side, two of them bursting into sympathetic tears. Details were forgotten as they helped Jennifer up to her bedroom.

Chane came in at eleven o'clock, content with the way things had gone with Cantrell. The young man wasn't going to forgive him soon, but he had accepted the governor's alternative and agreed to recruit and lead a special force of rangers to catch the rustlers who were preying on the ranchers' stock. They had leveled with him about the dangers involved, and Chane had recognized the same traits in Cantrell that he knew so well in his brother, Lance. Tell him it was a job that couldn't be done, that good men had died trying it, and his blue eyes filled with dancing lights. His husky drawl had been like hearing Lance. "I'm sure you're right, Kincaid, but since my choices seem to be temporarily limited, I guess I'll try it."

Ed Stanton had been tickled. "I should have known you could pull it off. You gave him a challenge he couldn't resist."

"I may have also signed that young man's death warrant."

"God! I feel a hundred years old when you say 'young man' like that. I'm going to have to see Kate to find out if I'm still young enough."

"Do that."

Chane was still smiling when he handed Malcomb a stack of mail. "Where is Mrs. Kincaid?"

"Upstairs, sir. She is being seen by the doctor."

"Matt is seeing Jennie? For what?" he demanded, alarm flooding into him. Jennie was not prone to sudden illnesses. "Has she been hurt?"

"Her brother died. She became quite upset. We thought Dr. Wright could help. . . ."

Chane could see the question in Malcomb's eyes. "That's fine," he said. "You did well." Chane took the stairs three at a time. Leslie and three young women he knew only casually were clustered in a sympathetic knot, whispering in front of Jennie's door. Dr. Matt came out, spotted Chane, and came forward, meeting him at the top of the stairs.

"She'll be all right. She's in shock. She wanted you, and now that you're here, she'll be fine."

Chane brushed past him. Jennifer was on the bed, tears slipping silently down her cheeks into the silvery blond tresses at her temples. He knelt beside her.

"Jennie, love, I'm so sorry," he whispered, gathering her

gently into his arms. She pressed close to him, new sobs racking her body. He moved onto the bed, and she huddled against him, crying silently, her body jerking with the force of her convulsions. He stroked her hair, kissing her face and aching with the need to take this burden of pain off her slender shoulders. He barely remembered Peter; the young man had avoided him because of their misunderstanding, but he knew Jennie had loved him far out of proportion to his apparent worth.

She cried and it was a terrible thing to watch—there was such fierceness and rage in her crying—as if Peter had betrayed her by dying while they were still estranged. She was convulsed with fury and violation, crying raggedly, like a stricken wounded creature, unable to speak, like a mother who had lost a dear child, wailing her pain. He held her as best he could until the worst of it had passed, and she collapsed in his arms, silent tears still slipping down her cheeks. He kissed them away and brushed the soft damp hair off her swollen, reddened face.

"How did he die?"

Jennie sighed, exhausted. "I don't know. It said that by the time I received the letter he would be dead. Oh, Chane, you don't suppose he . . . committed suicide, do you?"

"When did the letter come?" he asked, puzzled, since he had personally picked up their mail.

"One of the deputies brought it."

"Oh." He subsided, accepting that explanation.

"Hold me, Chane," she whispered, her silky voice husky and trembling.

He moved to comply, pulling her closer against him, as responsive to her now as he had been eight years ago when she had walked into his well-ordered life, captured his heart, married him, and then smashed his life down around his shoulders. Only days after they had married, her brother had been beaten, and she was carried off by one of Chane's enemies. He had searched madly for her, and found her only when Commodore Laurey, who hated him, was ready for him to find her. Only after photographs of Jennie, naked and flawlessly beautiful in the arms of another man, were delivered to the Bricewood East in New York City. Heartbroken and betrayed, he went to the address given to retrieve his wife. But once there, he found she was not the same woman he had loved and married. She was holding a gun, which she fully intended to use to end his life.

"Do you remember the day I found you, after you were kidnapped by Laurey?" he asked, his lips against her ear.

Jennie shuddered. She remembered opening the door eight years before and finding Chane there, unshaven and disheveled, his dark eyes filled with a mixture of pain and the lingering hunger he wasn't altogether able to hide. She had still been so thoroughly under Laurey's spell, so filled with his lies and his drugs, that she had almost killed Chane. As if it were only yesterday, she could see his narrowed hazel eyes, hear his strained voice.

"How many ways can you kill a man, princess?" Then his voice hardened. "Either shoot that thing or put it down."

As she thought of what she believed he had done to Peter, how his hired thugs had almost killed her brother, her finger trembled on the trigger, aching for the strength to do what needed to be done. Chane reached up and tapped the center of his chest, where she could remember laying her head, listening to the reassuring thud of his heart. His husky voice was deliberately cold and taunting. "Too low, Jennie. Raise the barrel and point it a little more to the left. The large arteries are here."

He was giving her information as unemotionally as any physician. If she pulled the trigger the way his forest-dark eyes were daring her to, he would never use that tall, lean, clean-muscled body to lure another girl to her death. One tug of her trembling finger, and she would avenge her mother, her father, and Peter with one swift bullet.

She and Peter truly believed that Chane had been the cause of their parents' deaths. Peter had come home from Harvard before the end of the school year, expelled for cheating, the president's letter said. And only weeks after his homecoming, Reginald Van Vleet had killed his wife and then himself, leaving a note that said he had lost everything because of proxies Vivian Van Vleet had signed over to Chantry Kincaid III. She had found their bodies in the study, read the note, and hidden it from the police. Then she and Peter had set out to avenge their parents by bringing Kincaid to his knees. It might have worked, except that she had fallen in love with him, become pregnant, and allowed herself to be married to him. She had been so ashamed of her weakness for Chane that she hadn't been able to tell Peter. Then, before she could correct that terrible omission, Peter had been beaten by men who purported to be working for Chane, she had been kidnapped, and Laurey had spent days drugging her and telling her lies so she would kill Chane when he came for her. She hadn't known until later that they had taken photographs of her with another man and given them to Chane so he would hate her as much as she seemed to hate him.

She didn't know Peter had found out about her marriage to Kincaid until after he had disappeared. By then it was too late. They searched for him, but they did not find him.

It was no wonder she almost killed Chane that day. Facing him, believing all those lies, she knew she had to pull that trigger. . . . His bronze chest, warm and sturdy, swam before her eyes, and she imagined his blood pumping out of torn arteries and felt a wave of nausea sweep over her. She flung the gun away from her and turned away, covering her face with her hands.

"What's the matter, Jennie? No guts? You can't do anything in a straightforward manner? Would it help if I turned my back?"

She turned on him then, her eyes flashing purple fire, all hint of velvet smoothness gone—she was a tigress, poised for attack. "You dare mock me! The man who never, ever takes care of his own dirty work!"

"I'm not going to ask what you mean by that. Your actions defy my understanding. But I don't want to understand what makes you tick. I only want to be insulated from your treachery. You'll understand if I have Steve take care of you, won't you?"

"Oh, yes!" she screamed. "That's your way! The Kincaid way. You certainly wouldn't handle these nasty little details yourself." For just a second she was tempted to give him the gun and make him do it himself, but not even anger could carry her further against the scorn she could clearly read in his eyes. She actually believed he had come there to kill her.

What a twisted, painful time that had been! Only their love had kept them coming back together, searching for the kernel of truth they both knew existed in their emotions for each other. Her love for Peter should have saved him as well. . . . Fresh tears streamed down her cheeks. Peter had never had a chance, not really. Everything he believed in, his whole world, had been ripped away from him. Even she had abandoned him. . . .

"Jennie, love, please don't cry. I didn't mean to bring up painful memories," he whispered, tightening his embrace. He felt her pain keenly, but he could not forget that he had a great deal to be thankful for.

Jennie was one of a kind. There could not be another woman anywhere who could inspire as much love as she did despair. Now she was in pain, and there was nothing he could do except hold her and encourage her to remember her brother with love and let him go.

"You were so close to Peter. . . ." he whispered.

Jennie nodded against his chest. "He was much more than a brother. He was my best friend. I could tell just by the look in his eyes that he was so proud of me—of everything I did. I loved him so much. He had beautiful eyes—very expressive. I always knew exactly what he was thinking. When he smiled he could light up a room. When he glowered, as he often did, he could blot out the sun. He was like a young princeling—girls were crazy for him— but he was cautious. He had a good mind, a good sense of humor." She sighed. "I always compared him to Alexander the Great because he was wonderfully competent. He could do anything: sailing, fencing, languages, dancing, riding, shooting. Everywhere men needed to be good, he excelled. He could have been anything he wanted to be." New tears welled up, and he kissed them away.

"Oh, Chane, darling," she said, faltering, "I would give anything if I could have seen him, talked to him. . . ."

Chane nodded. "I know, darling."

They were silent for several moments. "Did you know he graduated from St. Cyr with honors?" she asked.

"St. Cyr in France?"

"Yes. . . . It was the West Point of France, attended by some of the most brilliant young men on the Continent. He was outstanding in the classroom and on the field. He quickly became a champion with a broadsword, an épée, even a pistol."

"How long was he there?"

"Two years. Then he joined the French cavalry. They sent him to Saumur."

Chane whistled. "I'm impressed," he said softly. "That is *the* finest cavalry school in the world. I rode two hundred miles fourteen years ago to watch a demonstration of their drill practice."

"They are very impressive on horseback. They start with the best horsemen and make them into something really special to watch. They turn away ten men for every one they accept. They only bother with the *crème de la crème*."

"Why did he come back to the States?"

"We were still doing things as a family. I had a chance to star in *Aida*, so Father talked him into hiring a replacement to complete his commitment to the French cavalry so he could graduate from Harvard. That was highly unusual, but Harvard accepted the transfer conditionally, to be based on their testing of his academic skills. Of course, they wanted to do it for Father because he was one of their most generous supporters, but even stuffy old Harvard was impressed after they tested him." The smile faded and Chane could tell that another dark memory had encroached.

"What's wrong?"

"That was strange, that last six months he spent in New York. Something was wrong, but he wouldn't talk about it. Then our parents died, and neither of us seemed to be able to cope with all that was happening to us. By the time I met you we had grown so far apart we almost never talked. He was like a stranger." She sighed. "And I guess my tumbling into your bed didn't help matters—"

"That reminds me," Chane interrupted. "I know this won't help a lot, but Cantrell accepted Stanton's offer of a pardon in exchange for catching the rustlers. . . ."

"Ohhh." Jennie sighed. "I'm so glad. Leslie will be so pleased."

"She knows. She was up this morning. I would have told you as well, but you were sound asleep. . . ." A knock at the door brought Chane's head up. He kissed Jennie and strode to the door. Malcomb's stern face was puckered into a frown.

"There's a young man downstairs who says he needs to see Madame. He was quite insistent."

"Did you get his name?"

"No, sir. He asked if Madame had received a letter earlier. When I told him she had and was very upset he said he had to see her."

Chane glanced at Jennie, who had curled into a tight shivering ball without him to hold her. *She has been through far too much already,* he thought grimly. "I'll come down."

The young women had departed. The house was quiet. Ward Cantrell was standing in the entry hall, his tan Stetson in his hand. When he saw Kincaid his blue eyes narrowed into flinty chips.

Chane stopped in front of the younger man. "What can I do for you?"

"I need to talk to Jenn."

"Jenn?" Chane could feel his eyebrows crowding his narrowed eyes. He didn't like this familiarity.

"Mrs. Kincaid, then," Cantrell said, flushing but stubbornly determined that he would not be sent away.

"She's not able to see anyone. She just lost someone who was very dear to her."

"I know," Cantrell said grimly. "I wrote that letter."

CHAPTER
TWENTY-EIGHT

Leslie Powers succumbed to the many entreaties of her new friends and decided not to run like a scared rabbit back to Massachusetts. Mr. Kincaid hired attorney Winslow Breakenridge to represent her, and he convinced her that with a little time they could force a settlement of her father's estate. So Leslie accepted the Kincaids' offer of hospitality and prayed for a speedy resolution to her difficulties.

Jennifer seemed to recover rapidly from the loss of her brother, saying they hadn't been close in a long time—it was just such a terrible shock. Life went on as usual. The Kincaids moved in the diamond glitter of a Phoenix Leslie had never seen before.

The fifth night she was there the Kincaids had a dinner party to launch Leslie into the mainstream.

Mr. Kincaid had insisted on paying Leslie the reward for Cantrell's capture. They had ignored her protests, refusing to listen to her disclaimers. Jennifer finally prevailed by telling her that Ward Cantrell was an old friend of hers and that the reward was actually for saving his life when Younger tried to hang him.

"Please accept it, Leslie. Ward is a very dear friend," Jennifer pleaded, her purple eyes filled with warmth. "It is important to me. Really, it is."

Leslie finally shrugged helplessly. "How could anyone refuse you?"

Jennifer laughed and pressed the money into her reluctant hand. "Now, let's go shopping. You're feeling much better, and I've planned a small dinner party for tonight. Let's buy ourselves new outfits—top to bottom!''

Jennifer's enthusiasm was infectious. They shopped all morning. Leslie found a lime-green satin gown, cut quite low in front with gathered sleeves that fell in smooth fullness toward the elbow. The skirt started just under her breasts and fell in graceful gathers all the way to the floor in front and trailed after her in back. Very Grecian in its long clean lines. The skirt was decorated with gold embroidery, very delicate and intricate. No need for corset or bustle under this creation!

Annette put her hair up in a Grecian style, like a beehive, with heavy ringlets falling down the back, tiny ringlets around her face.

Leslie found herself seated next to Chane's business associate, Tim Summers, and wondered if Jennifer had taken up matchmaking also.

"You are absolutely ravishing, Miss Powers," he whispered, his black eyes warm with admiration.

A week of Jennifer's support and Dr. Wright's medicines and salves had restored much of Leslie's confidence and vitality. She had managed to retain her dazzling smile, but the weeks of uncertainty had left their mark, at least inside, and she regarded Tim Summers speculatively. She had seen him on two other occasions, deeply engrossed in conversations with Chane, and now the thought came to her: Was he, since he was Chane's valued friend, privy to all the details of her story? Did he perhaps think, as her uncle had, that once the loaf is sliced, anyone can have a piece?

Everyone in Phoenix knew Leslie had been kidnapped by a man who had held her captive almost a week. Only Jennifer's subtle but nonetheless powerful influence over the female population had stopped overt displays like the one in front of the hotel, but she still, even in recall, smarted from the sting of that deliberate affront, and kept her voice cool as she answered him. . . .

"Thank you, Mr. Summers."

His smile was magnetic. He was an attractive man with lustrous black hair, fair skin, and black eyes that reflected perfect self-confidence. A man serene in the sure knowledge of his own worth, from the excellent cut of his custom-tailored suit to the deep cleft in his firm chin.

Leslie noticed that she was receiving covert but envious attention from at least two of the young female guests, and her natural female competitiveness asserted itself. The next time he leaned close to whisper a compliment, she giggled and was rewarded by more begrudging smiles. Tim Summers was, apparently, a desirable catch. She could understand why—his coloring was striking, and he *did* have good strong features and beautiful manners. Jennifer had said only the day before how hard he labored and how much Chane depended on him. In five years he had worked his way to the top of the Texas and Pacific Railroad Company.

Tim was attentive throughout dinner, barely taking his eyes off Leslie, keeping her wineglass full, and with very little prompting, telling her interesting tidbits about life in the Wild West. He was a transplant also, having been born in Newark, New Jersey.

Jennifer watched her guests with growing relief. She had taken great pains with this party to introduce Leslie to Phoenix. She had imported a ten-piece orchestra from Chicago, ordered cases of French champagne, and stolen Chane's head chef and three of his assistants from the Bricewood West. They spent the day preparing trays of delicacies from the shipment of special foods. This party was proof that the railroad was more than a minor convenience to her. Chane's wonderful refrigerated boxcars carried shrimp from New Orleans, oysters from Boston, caviar from New York.

The Texas and Pacific had changed the face of the American continent. Phoenix was a burgeoning metropolis compared to what it was before the railroad. Now citizens who could afford it had all the necessities and many of the luxuries that were available in the most sophisticated eastern cities.

Before her guests arrived, Jennifer had appraised the accommodations with the critical eye of a woman raised in Paris, London, Vienna, and New York City, and she was pleased. As a Van Vleet, she had moved in the highest circles of society with the Astors, the Belmonts, the Vanderbilts, the Waldorfs, and hundreds of minor luminaries who revolved around them. Now, as the wife of one of the most powerful men in the Arizona Territory, she had deliberately forced the matrons of Phoenix into a corner where they either had to snub the Kincaid family or accept Leslie. If attendance at the dinner party was any indication, Leslie would not suffer at the hands of narrow-minded hypocrites any longer.

This party pleased Jennifer tremendously. In New York City there were any number of arenas for launching a debutante and carrying on the usual mating rituals: the Academy of Music, Delmonico's, or the Patriarch's Balls held at various mansions, but here in Phoenix the most useful tool was still either a dinner party, a dance, or a combination of both.

Caroline Astor might bank a room the size of the Coliseum in roses and orchids and invite the famous "Eight Hundred" to introduce one of her daughters to society. The first families of New York City did not scrimp on their own. Jennifer could remember when her friend Carrie Astor married Orme Wilson. That had been a wedding celebration to remember. The gifts had been valued at over one million dollars at a time when factory workers earned twelve dollars a week. It should have dismayed her, but she had always been part of that world. She took their extravagances and their social rivalries in stride.

In Phoenix, Jennifer had raised a few eyebrows herself. Her own attempts to create a civilized home for herself and Chane had caused a minor uproar in the town—not on a scale like the first families of New York—but it had been controversial. There were at least two dozen families in town who were wealthy, and five of the women were extremely competitive. They had screamed the loudest of all. When Chane built their home, new homes had sprouted overnight. If Jennie gave a party, she could count on at least five other women trying to outdo her.

Now, with Leslie's future at stake, she was looking forward to some lively competition, because if the rumor mill ground accurately, her predictable peers had already launched into their rivalry.

Five parties were scheduled for the coming two weeks.

Jennifer watched impatiently for her brother. She saw Tim's determined interest in Leslie Powers and enjoyed it on one level. Partly because it would point out to Peter—oops, she corrected herself, to Ward—that Leslie was a very desirable young lady.

Tim Summers leaned close to Leslie, whispered in her ear, and Leslie smiled. What were they talking about? Jennie sighed, wondering if she had made a mistake inviting Summers. What if Leslie fell in love with him instead of Ward? Where was Ward anyway?

"Grew up around railroads," Tim was saying. "Newark lies in the path of most direct routes to New York City. Nearly all the trunk lines have terminals in Jersey City, which is only a few miles from Newark, so it was natural that I would become interested in railroads. There are fortunes to be made in railroads, and a smart man who knows how can beat out the competition. You have to get in first, get a stranglehold on the territory, then keep out competition."

"Sounds very dog-eat-dog," Leslie said.

"It is. You have to get them before they get you," he said, his black eyes shining with missionary zeal.

"Are you good at getting them?" she asked politely.

"Good enough," he said with satisfaction.

When the gaily chattering group moved into the library for after-dinner liqueur and coffee, Tim stopped her abruptly.

"May I call you Leslie?"

She nodded, transfixed by his eyes. He had the most opaque eyes she had ever seen—like black sponges—light and images obviously went in, but nothing came out. The pupils were not distinguishable from the dark irises. Somehow that made her uncomfortable.

"I would like to ask Mr. Kincaid for the privilege of calling on you, if you do not object."

How formal he was! Leslie had the wild urge to laugh. She had been kidnapped, held prisoner for days, maligned on the streets by hateful women, and because of the Kincaids' influence, he was treating her as if nothing had changed, as if she were the same lady with the same impeccable reputation she had enjoyed before.

"Mr. Summers, I am not exactly . . ." She stopped, struggling for words.

"Please call me Tim."

I am no longer a child, she thought angrily. *As a woman who has lost the magical power of her virginity, I am not someone you could be seriously interested in, and since I am not in the mood for an amorous affair at this time and may never be again, I advise you to look elsewhere for your entertainment.*

But aloud she said, "I'm sure there are many women in Phoenix for you to choose from, Mr. Summers. You have been more than kind. I am truly honored at your interest. And I sorely regret misleading you, if I did, but I am not prepared . . ."

For the first time she saw a reaction in the midnight pools. His black eyes flared with a starburst of crystallized heat. He turned abruptly and left her standing there while he made his excuses to Jennifer, then retrieved his greatcoat from Malcomb.

Furious, Tim closed the door behind him. One of the cats that hung around the Kincaids' stable meowed plaintively and he looked down. It brushed against his ankle. In a rage, he kicked it in the ribs as hard as he could. Howling in pain, the cat limped into the bushes.

He was on the lawn, heading for his horse, when Leslie opened the front door.

"Mr. Summers. Tim!" He stopped and waited for her in grim silence. Apparently his intensity extended into his personal life as well as his professional life. She stopped about three feet from him, feeling the chill night air, feeling slightly ridiculous. "Why are you leaving?"

"Because you have prejudged me," he said softly, vehemently. "Because I haven't a chance with you. Maybe no one does—I don't know—but I resent being placed among that group of people who have hurt you by their callous disregard for your feelings. I resent the fact that you assumed because of your unfortunate experience that I could only be interested in you either as a casual light of love or a charity case. I see no reason to stay under those circumstances." There was anger and tension in every line and angle of his handsome face and lean form. He was furious, and somehow the intensity of his emotion finally stirred a response in her. He turned on his heel to leave.

"Please don't go," she said to his back.

He turned slowly and she could see him relax slightly.

"I'm sorry," she said softly. "Please feel free to call on me if that is your wish."

He came back every night she allowed him to. Within a week he admitted that he was in love with her. There was no doubt about her recovery after that. She was still female, still effective. She bubbled with life and new happiness. She had survived a terrible ordeal and come out whole. She felt older but more capable. She was grateful to Tim for bringing her back.

She let him kiss her a week later, then he proposed to her, and she refused, gently.

"Leslie, darling, think about it."

"No. I don't want to be married. I'm only nineteen, and I would be a dreadful wife. I would rather paint or manage an art gallery than run a house."

"We'll have a housekeeper. I can afford it. I'm a rich man, darling. You won't *be* a housekeeper. You'll be my little jewel. My princess."

He was easy to manage, but she could feel the pressure building. He wanted her, and she was stalling him. She didn't want to get that deeply involved, to risk pregnancy—or worse yet—marriage!

Kincaid entered the comparative dimness of the Texas and Pacific offices with relief. It was hot as hell outside, especially for

November. He had just left his brother-in-law. It had been three weeks since Ward Cantrell had admitted to being Peter Van Vleet. They had done a great deal of talking. Hearing Peter's version of the events eight years before had amazed and vaguely horrified him. It was a miracle they had all survived. His mission today was a result of their talks. He was going to begin the process of helping Ward sort out all of his legal problems.

"Good morning, Mr. Kincaid."

Chane's eyes searched the large room, darting from desk to desk. The large office was well lit and seated four young men who worked under Summers, handling all of the administrative detail it took to operate a railroad. Kincaid did not involve himself with the daily operations. His interests were in creation, not maintenance; that was why Summers was such a godsend to him. He seemed to thrive on all that trivia. The men smiled and nodded.

"Sorry, sir. Over here."

The sound must have reverberated. Chane turned, frowning. When he saw the young man who had stood up, a smile lighted his dark face.

"Is that you, John?"

"Yes, sir!" John Loving came forward with a broad smile making deep dimples in his chipmunk cheeks.

Chane held out his hand. "Good to see you. I sure don't get over here very often, do I? Are you liking your job?"

"Oh, yes, sir," he said with as much enthusiasm as he could muster.

"How do you like Arizona?"

"Oh, well, it's certainly not New York, but I'm learning to adjust."

"Did you come alone? No family?"

"Yes, sir. My folks are still there. I really miss them."

"Come out to the house for dinner. I'll have Jennie fix your favorite dishes. She'd love to see you again."

"Thank you, sir. Any time you say."

"Good. I'll have her set a date."

Kincaid passed on through, and Loving followed him with his eyes. It was plain to see that Loving held him in the highest regard.

Tim Summers was in his shirt sleeves, up to his elbows in paperwork, when Kincaid leaned in the doorway.

"Good morning. Got a second?"

Tim looked up and smiled, coming to his feet. "Always. Have a seat. What can I do for you?"

"I need a complete list of all losses we've suffered that could be tied back to the Devil's Canyon Gang."

Tim frowned. "Okay. I'll put someone on it immediately. May I ask what's up?"

Chane hesitated only a second. Tim Summers had been with him for five years. He was a hard worker, competent, and bright. He decided to trust him.

"The gang's leader is making restitution."

"Cantrell? Where would he get that kind of money?"

"He inherited it."

"So he pays us back. Does that end it? I mean—isn't there still the problem of some broken laws?"

"Yes, but Governor Stanton commuted his sentence and made a deal with him. I agreed, on behalf of the railroad, to drop all charges. Cantrell agreed to make restitution, and Stanton decided, based on all that, to take him back into the fold. In addition to that, Cantrell's inheritance was quite substantial. He's a millionaire now. That looks like a pretty solid guarantee that he won't be robbing any more trains."

Tim frowned. "Maybe my Calvinist forefathers are still haunting me, but wrong is wrong—no matter how much money a man has. Some of the biggest crooks ever had millions."

Chane grinned. "You're absolutely right, but Stanton isn't going to give Cantrell something for nothing. Cantrell has agreed to clean out the rustlers that have been giving us so much trouble. It's a fairly common practice."

"Hire a thief to catch a thief?"

"Something like that."

"But—he has been an outlaw for a long time. He must be wanted other places."

"He's not being actively hunted anymore. He dropped out of sight, as far as they are concerned, years ago. If nothing stirs them up, they aren't going to push it. Later—when he's squared away here—he can see about settling with them."

"What's he wanted for?" Tim asked casually.

"He's wanted in Dodge City for ten counts of murder."

Tim whistled.

"No definite charge. He's wanted for questioning. He fought on the winning side in one of their range wars. About a month after he rode away the other side got reinforcements and regained control. They owned the sheriff, and they had a grudge against Cantrell so they issued the warrant. If he got picked up and turned over to that faction, he'd never make it to the jail alive.''

Tim grinned boyishly and shook his head, sighing. "Hard work does have its rewards. At least I don't have a lynch mob dogging my heels.''

"True.''

"We'll get that figure for you right away,'' Tim said crisply.

"Good.'' Chane stood up. "Oh, and send notices to all our offices to cancel any rewards we posted for any members of the gang. And, Tim, this isn't common knowledge.''

"Yes, sir. You can count on me. I'll take care of everything.''

"Thanks.''

His next stop was to see his wife.

"Jennie . . .''

"In here,'' she called, loudly enough for Chane to hear her.

"What are you doing in here?'' he asked, his frown changing to a smile at the sight of her on the floor of the unused guest bedroom, her voluminous skirts fanned out around her, surrounded by boxes of family portraits, tintypes, and small souvenirs.

She glanced up and her eyes were unusually dark and solemn. "I don't know exactly. Trying to validate a memory . . . or perhaps dispel a perception. . . .''

"About what or whom?''

"Peter . . .''

Chane closed the door to assure privacy. "What about him?''

Jennie sighed. "He's changed so much. . . . I hardly know him. . . . He's so . . . so . . . aloof, so filled with resolute masculine purpose. He's one of them . . . the way you were . . . Oh, how I hated that . . . when you wore a gun. . . . Do you remember the first time I saw you in your western clothes . . . how horrified I was. You had the same look of competent masculine arrogance he has. The same spirit of lawlessness. He appears so uncompromising . . . so unreadable . . . with such deadly skill. . . .''

"Did he say anything to hurt you?'' he demanded, anger rising in him instantly and hotly.

"No, no,'' she sighed. "I almost wish he had. . . .''

"Why?''

"I was a stranger to him. . . . He was polite. He tried to do everything exactly right so as not to hurt my feelings. But he felt nothing for me except perhaps guilt. If he loved me, it was in the abstract.''

Scowling, Chane dropped down beside her and picked up one of the tintypes. It had mellowed into pinkish brown tones. A younger Jennie stood beside a handsome young man—blond, dapper, open of visage, with good humor smiling out of his bland eyes. She was right. There was little of Peter Van Vleet left in Ward Cantrell, a man who projected pure animal power and prescience. A man whose narrowed blue eyes could bristle the hair on a man's neck at twenty paces. A man who could lead an outlaw band, kidnap a woman, and kill ten men in cold blood.

"It's no wonder I didn't recognize him," he muttered.

"Nor I . . ." Jennie whispered.

Chane was stunned. He searched her face. Under his scrutiny the beautiful, coolly composed face he carried in his heart began to quiver in anguish. Pierced to the quick, he pulled her into his arms. "Jennie, love," he whispered, breathing in the sweet feminine fragrance of her silky hair. He had mistakenly thought her the happiest of women since Peter's—Ward's—return.

"Is there anything I can do?"

She shook her head. "Not unless you can turn back the clock. Trade a cynical man, purposely brash and aloof, for a warm-hearted, playful young man who isn't afraid to love. . . ."

Chane frowned his puzzlement. To his eye, Cantrell had done what any man confronted with a startled, stunned, and then weeping woman would have done. He had held her tenderly and with obvious consideration. He started to say as much, but Jennie stopped him with a frown.

"I know . . . I know. It meant nothing! Because he felt nothing more for me than he feels for any woman in distress. I wasn't real to him!"

Chane chuckled, his green eyes filled with a mixture of sardonic amusement, love, and desire to understand. "There's nothing particularly unusual about that among men of Cantrell's ilk. . . ."

"That is exactly my point. Peter *is* Ward Cantrell. He has become *a man of that ilk*. I admire him tremendously, but I also hate it. I admire the strength that allowed him to survive, but I hate the barriers he has erected, the cold calculation I can see in his eyes on occasion. He weighs everything, risks, rewards. . . . It is too easy to see the roots of his military experience—his easy military carriage, his ability to *take a necessary action*, as they say. At some point a man like that stops being a man and becomes something else. I don't want Peter to be that way. In one sense, though, it was as if we had never been apart, but in the most important sense he was accommodating me. . . ."

"So?" he asked, frowning. That seemed acceptable to him. Why shouldn't Cantrell accommodate his sister? It was the least he could do after all these years.

Anger flared in her violet eyes. "So how would you like to be accommodated? What if we made love and you were fully involved and I was being *accommodating*? . . ." she said, making the word sound like an insult.

Chane chuckled. "I've always been able to find ways to get your full attention," he said, his eyes darkening.

"But what if you couldn't?"

He frowned. "I guess I'd be concerned. So what do we do now? What do you want?"

"I don't know! I . . . I guess I want him to feel his own joy or pain, his own homecoming."

Chane took her hand and kissed it, groping for words to comfort her. He was remembering the way Ward Cantrell's husky voice had thickened, finally failed, when he related the events leading up to Simone's death, how his eyes had hardened into arctic chips as he told the story of the Mendoza family. There was no doubt in Chane's mind that Ward had been through holy hell since he had last seen his sister. While Jennie had grown in her ability to love, nurturing two bright children, Ward was struggling to survive, had been forced to put love aside. Maybe he should explain those incidents to Jennie, but he wanted to spare her. . . .

He kissed her palm and then her lips. "He'll come around. . . . It'll take time. . . . Unfortunately, I don't want him any different yet—he's got a job ahead of him that will require all his nerve and skill."

"I don't mind his toughness. But he's so unreachable. I don't think he expects to survive this. . . ."

Chane laughed. "There, my love, you are wrong. There is a finely honed survival instinct beneath that nonchalant, devil-may-care facade. What you see is Ward's bone-deep belief in his own ability. Some call that arrogance. I call it self-confidence. All he lacks now is the strength he lost when he was wounded. I've ordered him to rest for a minimum of two weeks. By the time he leaves Phoenix, he'll be in top form. Even now he's like a cat—lean, wiry, and indestructible—but there's no depth to it yet. He needs a little more time. I know men. I'll know when he's ready. . . ."

"Do you think he still loves me?" she asked, her bottom lip quivering.

"I know he does. If he hasn't shown it to your satisfaction, I can only assume he can't peel back eight years of reserve in a day or two. Give him time. If it came easily, you wouldn't give a damn for it anyway, if I know you. . . ."

Jennie sniffed, but a smile broke through the forlorn look. "Humph. A lot you know. . . ."

Relieved, he kissed her. Jennie hadn't changed much in the almost nine years he had known and loved her. If anything, she had become more exacting, but in the direction of personal relationships, not in material matters. She was still blithely unconcerned in that regard. Possessions were not essential to her, but the happiness of her close circle of loved ones was singularly important. He gave daily thanks that so far their life together had not been marred by any significant loss.

Fortunately, Chane had always been able to give Jennie everything she needed. Now he frowned. In the future he could give her almost everything . . . except her brother's safety . . . and her brother's love. . . .

Annette and Jennifer clustered around the mirror in Leslie's bedroom, admiring Leslie as she posed.

The new red satin gown was far more sophisticated than anything she had worn before. It had a plunging Parisian-style neckline, a chiffon vestee that hugged her breasts, tiny cap sleeves, and saucy flounces over a pert tournure that nipped the waistline. The fabric, which was a very fine silk, fell into a short train in back, emphasizing the slenderness of Leslie's waist and hips. What would Tim think, Leslie wondered, seeing me in such a provocative style?

Annette had created a confection of a hairstyle to complement the cosmopolitan gown—masses of curls twisted into a smooth, high-crowned coiffure that exposed her slender swanlike neck. With the elbow-length gloves that were *de rigueur* for evening wear, Jennie knew there was not a man alive who would not yearn to press his lips at the base of that graceful alabaster column. Leslie looked totally self-confident, as if she could face anything, whether it be the matrons of Phoenix or Ward Cantrell. . . .

Jennie, a hopeless romantic, believed with or without provocation that Leslie was meant for her brother. She did not spend hours plotting ways to get the two of them together, but her creative mind, so keenly focused on Peter's welfare, gave bonuses. This second event was for the express though covert purpose of introducing Ward to "society," in effect bestowing upon him any protection and benefit that her and Chane's considerable influence could afford him.

Ward, upon hearing about it, was skeptical. Chane shrugged. "It can't hurt anything, and it *might* help." With Chane's endorsement and backing, Ward reluctantly agreed to attend. Should she tell Leslie that Ward would be there? Or should she allow her house guest to discover him for herself?

"Do you think it is wise, with my tattered reputation, to wear such a flamboyant color among strangers?"

The gown in question was Jennie's. Her laughter was a typically throaty, well-modulated, sultry release of notes that routinely caused women's mouths to tighten with disapproval and envy. "Why not nail our colors to the mast? If people don't like it, we don't need them. As a *danseuse* and later as an opera *diva*, I found that people respect you more if you are not wishy-washy. That dress is smashing on you! It would be a crime if you *didn't* wear it!"

Even Leslie's dainty kid slippers, low-heeled for dancing, were bright carmine red. Black hair, black gloves, and that shamelessly red gown . . . Even if she were not vain, the look in Jennie's and Annette's eyes would have satisfied her completely.

"No one else could wear that particular shade of red so well, *mademoiselle*!" Annette said frankly; then, upon realizing her faux pas, she blushed and stammered an apology to Jennie, who brushed it off with a forgiving smile.

"She's right, you know. I ordered the gown and never wore it for that reason." Jennie smoothed the skirt over Leslie's hip. "This gown does marvelous things for your complexion. With your green eyes . . ." Jennie sighed. "I hope the other young ladies will not be too badly injured by your presence tonight."

"I, for one, hope they are devastated!" Leslie said, her eyes lighted with mischief.

The unexpected reply delighted them. "Bravo!" Jennie cried as the three women burst into peals of wicked laughter.

When they were alone, Leslie turned to Jennifer.

"I'm really grateful to you and Chane for all you've done for me. I . . . I'm not good at saying things, but I just wanted to let you know that if you ever need me, it will give me great pleasure to assist you in any way I can. . . ."

Pleased and flattered by the genuine sincerity she saw in Leslie's lovely green eyes, Jennie smiled and took her hand. "We've loved having you. I . . . we both . . . hope you will consider staying here . . . making our home yours on a permanent basis. Both Chane and I want you to know that we consider you family. If you have any needs at all, we will be hurt if you do not let us know. If we can help you in any way . . . it is our wish to do so."

Leslie flushed with a sudden urge to cry. "I can't tell you how much your support means to me. . . ."

Jennie squeezed her hand. "It's not necessary that you do so. To us it is only necessary that you are happy."

Something hard stirred in her chest. "Thank you so much."

To change the subject Jennie said what had been on her mind for a long time. "I'm amazed daily by your resilience and strength. I say this because I have been through a similar experience and know some of its consequences. You've been through so much these last weeks and months. Perhaps when you are ready I will share some of it with you. Remember that I, too, have been through a great deal.

"But now I will give you the advice my agent gave me on my first professional appearance. When you face the harridans of Phoenix in your red gown, there is only one thing you must remember—don't let them hear your knees knocking."

Leslie laughed. "This reminds me of my mother's adage for preparing me for my modest debut into society: 'Social courage is a contradiction in terms: it means a strong desire to be accepted taking the form of elegant indifference.' "

"What a singular analysis! Had I champagne at hand, I would toast your mother's wit *and* her beautiful daughter!" She lifted an imaginary glass. "To Leslie Powers, who is living proof that a woman is exactly as happy as she decides to be."

"Hear, hear!" Leslie cried, getting into the spirit, even as she wished, contrarily, that she were either a better actress or truly happy.

CHAPTER
TWENTY-NINE

Debbie Denning had an unruly mass of reddish brown hair that curled like a short, woolly cap around her pert face. Her skin was a healthy, tawny color, made vibrant with rosy cheeks and large, lively brown eyes that sparkled with intelligence and vitality. Jennifer had invited Debbie to meet Leslie the day before the ball, so the young women were no longer strangers to each other.

Jennie's orchestra played rousing waltzes and brisk polkas. So much so that no woman could dance every dance. Leslie and Debbie were temporarily alone, Tim and Winslow having gone to the heavily laden banquet tables along the south wall of the *sala grande*.

"Are you beginning to like Arizona now?" Debbie asked, pausing to cast a critical eye at the enthusiastic couples dancing past.

"Not Arizona, no. But perhaps this house, these people. I love this house. It's a house that a person can feel safe in. . . ."

"There is something so special about this house," Leslie said, "It's exactly like they are. Don't you feel it?"

"You like the Kincaids, don't you?"

"Yes, I do. Mrs. Kincaid, Jennifer," she corrected herself, "is like my mother. Independent, interested in a great many things, and very energetic. She glows with an inner delight, as if she understands everything around her and likes it anyway."

Debbie nodded appreciatively. "That's very good! You've caught the essence of her. And Mr. Kincaid?"

"The rock of Gibraltar, solid, warm, protective, and endlessly reliable."

Debbie was silent, awed by the picture Leslie painted with her words. Then—

"You *are* an artist. You see with an instinctive, undistorted clarity and passion. . . . Is it always this easy for you to reach to the heart of people?"

Leslie laughed. "No, sometimes I can't see beyond the first

182

layer of skin.'' She was thinking now of Cantrell—for the first time—wondering suddenly what was beneath that iron reserve he hid behind. Man or only a clever imitation? But she stopped herself. This was no time to think about Ward Cantrell. . . .

The Kincaids' ballroom glowed with the timeless elegance of classic design. It was awash with party colors, alive with talk and music, ablaze with candle glow, illuminating the vibrant energy of a hundred young women flirting with two hundred young men.

The dance followed only days after the dinner party. Leslie was astonished by the amount of work the staff had accomplished in such short order. People began arriving on foot and in carriages, women in their carriage bonnets and wraps, the men in their clawhammer tailcoats, frockcoats, and Stetsons. They filled the house by eight o'clock and threatened to overflow into the garden. The Kincaids greeted each guest by name, warmly, and made it plain to Leslie and probably them as well, that they were keeping track of who was treating Leslie Powers with the respect they had decided she deserved, and who was not.

It was their intention to introduce Ward Cantrell with the same careful attention to detail. Unfortunately, Ward was either late or had decided to forgo society. Jennie fretted inside. Fortunately, her stage training assured that it was her secret. Not even Leslie suspected. There were times when Jennie felt terrible keeping their young house guest in the dark about Ward and his significance in their lives, but Chane assured her of the absolute necessity for secrecy. ''The fewer people who know, the better. We cannot afford to have the name Peter Van Vleet bandied about. The authorities in Kansas would be only too happy to reissue those murder warrants.''

The men were all in black, but the women burst forth like the colors of the rainbow. Champagne flowed, diamonds glittered, and Jennifer felt unaccountably proud of her small victory. No one dared snub Leslie! She had been accepted!

Jennie searched for Chane in the festive crowd. She found him near the outer fringes of the dance floor, heading toward Tom Wilcox. Tom had worked for Chane for many years. He was the head of the security division of Chane's various enterprises. A totally nondescript man who was loyal, hardworking and seemingly able to blend into any background without effort.

''Good evening, Jennie,'' said a familiar voice.

''Ed! How nice you could come.'' She gave him a chaste, ceremonial kiss befitting the governor of the territory, and he smiled.

He was robust and jovial. A diamond ring sparkled on his hand, drawing attention to a glass of strangely tinted milk.

"You couldn't keep me away. Jennie, you've outdone yourself this time."

"Oh, isn't it lovely? I'm so proud of this town, these people."

"You did it."

"But they came!" They chatted amiably until the governor saw Kincaid and Wilcox part. He excused himself and caught Chane before he could disappear into the melee of dancers and revelers. They came together at the entry hall of the *sala grande*.

"You treating your ulcer again?" Chane grinned, his green eyes twinkling.

"Milk looks like hell at a party doesn't it? Folks are going to lose confidence in me. What's happening with our boy?"

"He has a lead. He thinks there's a definite possibility that the line we built to the new silver lode is being used at night to move stolen cattle."

"I'll be damned! Now why didn't we think of that?"

"Too old-fashioned, I guess. I'm not used to the idea yet. I can't adjust to the thought that my cattle are being rustled and moved in my trains."

Stanton shook his head. "Jesus, God! What will they think of next? Does he have a line on who's behind it?"

"No. That's why he's back in town. He wants to spend some time at night going through the railroad records to see if he can unravel it."

Stanton nodded, but at that moment was pulled away by a town matron eager to gossip with the governor.

Chane expelled an angry breath. He didn't like Cantrell's latest report. This new possibility meant that someone he trusted, someone in a position of authority in his company, was stealing him and all the other cattlemen in the area blind. But the first report of Cantrell's activities had pleased him. The young firebrand was running true to form. He had assembled the toughest cadre of rangers the Arizona Territory had ever seen and had managed to turn them into a team. Five men, all ex-bandits and outlaws themselves, two of them sworn enemies of Cantrell's, and he had taken charge. Wilcox was still shaking his head over that.

Chane could hear him telling it:

"He gives an order to them to follow him and then he just takes off. Doesn't look back to see if anyone is following him or not—he rode right into a bunch of suspected rustlers. Well, let me tell you,

I was worried. Here he is taking on five men all by himself. The others sat their horses awhile, looking at each other like they couldn't believe it, then one of them kicked his horse forward and they all followed him into the fray! They been following him ever since. They could have just let him get killed, but I think they were afraid he'd take them by himself and they'd look like cowering sissies. He has that kind of blind confidence. After two weeks, when he tells them they are going to do something, they know they will. They don't know how, but they don't question him. He has picked a second lieutenant already and is bringing him along, a young Wes Hardin type named Dusty Denton. They hit it off right away. Denton is smarter than the average bad man, spent some time with the Jackson Hole gang in Wyoming. I think Cantrell rode with them for a while too—maybe at the same time, but I can't prove it.''

"*See that you don't,* " Kincaid had told Wilcox with a wry smile. Ed Stanton's ulcers would have grandchildren.

Chane saw Cantrell with Sandra McCormick on his arm. He would have given a great deal to know how he had managed that one. Sandra was one of the prettiest girls in town. A slender golden-haired girl with big smoky gray eyes. He had seen her around town with different young men, usually Winslow Breakenridge. Winslow was a good attorney, but he didn't appear ready to settle down. He walked out with Sandra and Marybelle Lewis, sometimes Elizabeth Cartright. The rest of the local girls were unremarkable, except Debbie Denning, who was new to Phoenix. Debbie was something special, almost like a member of the family the way she fit right in and made herself at home. But then Jennie had a way of doing that—making everyone feel comfortable. He had been married eight years, and it still amazed him how his thoughts always came back to Jennie. . . .

"Hi, Mr. Kincaid," Cantrell said, almost grudgingly. They were still uncomfortable with each other.

"Evening." He nodded. He had deliberately put himself in their way because he wanted to talk to Cantrell. He had thought of more questions he wanted to ask since their talk this morning.

"Trinket, you know Mr. Kincaid. . . ."

"Hello, Sandra."

"Evening, Mr. Kincaid. Nice party," she said, smiling.

She was clinging to Cantrell's arm in a possessive way, certainly not conducive to giving him up so he could talk business with one of the old fogeys.

"Enjoy yourselves," Kincaid said. He knew when he wasn't wanted. He watched them disappear into the throng on the dance floor and turned to seek out Ed Stanton again.

"How long has Powers been ranching in this area?" Chane asked when he and Stanton were alone.

Ed frowned, pulling bushy salt-and-pepper brows down in a heavy ledge of concentration over his narrowed gray eyes. "Oh, ten years, maybe more."

Chane scowled. The T & P reached Phoenix in 1882, six years ago. About four years ago we built the spur line to my brother's silver mine. There doesn't necessarily *have* to be a connection. . . .

"How long has Powers been doing so well? He's running close to ten thousand head of cattle, if Wilcox is right about his estimate. Ten thousand head and better than fifty men."

"Four years, more or less."

"About the time we started losing cattle, wasn't it?" he asked dryly.

The orchestra played the stilted, mincing music for a quadrille and then a minuet, but only a few brave dancers participated, so Jennifer reminded the orchestra leader to play lively tunes—mostly waltzes. This was not New York City!

Leslie danced with Chane, Tim, then Winslow Breakenridge, her new attorney, and was just being returned to Tim's side when she saw a tall, tawny-haired man in an elegant black frockcoat who looked like Cantrell. Her heart didn't cease its mad thumping and she didn't realize she was staring until Tim caught her look and turned to Winslow Breakenridge, who was there with Marybelle Lewis.

"Who's that with Sandra McCormick?"

Winslow searched the crowded dance floor until he found the pretty blonde. "An ex-client of mine—Ward Cantrell."

Leslie felt the blood drain from her face. It was him.

"Are you all right, Leslie?"

"Dance with me, Tim." She sounded tinkly and brittle as she talked, and she had the wild irrational impulse to run upstairs, lock her door, and cry. But why should the sight of him with a girl in his arms have that effect on her? He was nothing to her.

The dance ended and Tim steered her toward Jennifer. He was due to dance with his lovely hostess.

Too late Leslie recognized the man standing beside Jennifer. "Leslie, Tim"—Jennifer caught Leslie's hand and pulled her close—"I would like you to meet someone. Leslie Powers, Timothy Summers, this is an old friend of mine, Ward Cantrell. You both know Sandra, I'm sure."

Leslie heard herself murmuring the proper "how-do-you-do's," even making small talk, but she could feel nothing except the clamor in her body. In a black silk frockcoat with white silk waistcoat and white linen shirt, Ward Cantrell was cool and handsome in a way she had never dreamed. He had been attractive before, but now, set against a sumptuous background, dressed in the right clothes and looking negligently at ease with both, he was like a young prince. Everything about him bespoke a noble lineage. Even the tint and texture of his clean-shaven face looked as if it had been chosen for him with infinite care.

The lean and dangerous look was still there, especially in his eyes—they moved over her like a warm caress—and she saw tiny glints of mischief in the azure depths.

Sandra McCormick didn't once take her eyes off Ward's face. He accepted her adoration as if it caused him not even the mildest surprise. Apparently he was used to quick conquests. That shouldn't surprise Leslie. He looked like a young Apollo descended from Olympus, not a train robber and kidnapper. Her heart was shaking her entire body.

She hadn't missed the affectionate look Jennifer gave Ward. Jennifer was so obvious when she liked someone—she probably wasn't even aware she had taken his left hand and held it all during the introductions.

Leslie didn't know why or how it happened, but when the music started up again they were alone.

"May I?" he asked.

Why not? Neither one of them seemed to be good at small talk. It surprised her that he danced well, though.

He grinned down at her. "You're a real little beauty with your face washed, Leslie."

Leslie flushed. Was he deliberately reminding her of that time they bathed in the stream?

"Thanks," she said dryly. "I thought you spent all your time murdering and pillaging."

"I've stopped."

"You've stopped?"

He chuckled softly. "I'm not murdering anybody now, am I?"

"Can we hope this trend will continue?"

"I can be bribed."

"Is that how you got out of jail?"

"Blackmail," he whispered, brushing her cheek with his lips.

"Stop that!" she hissed.

"Jealous boyfriend? Tell him we're old friends."

"I don't consider you a friend . . . ."

"Too bad."

"Why aren't you in jail?"

"I forgot how much you nagged. Jail was too dull." He shrugged negligently. "I complained and Mr. Railroad gave me a job."

"A job? What do you do?"

"Guard the trains."

"Does he know about you?"

"Everything."

His hand on her bare back was causing a muted ache down the entire length of her body. She lowered her lashes and pretended to be engrossed in watching the dancers all around them while she tried to analyze it. She had danced with a dozen men in the last two hours, and not once had she been aware of a man's hand on her back unless it seemed to move threateningly close to something he shouldn't be touching. Now, as if she didn't have enough problems, she was tingling all over because this outlaw put his warm hand on her bare back.

As if he had read her thoughts, Ward moved his hand slowly up her back to firmly cup her shoulder, sending a sharp hungry pain through her belly. *Damn him!*

"You have the silkiest skin, Leslie," he whispered, pulling her closer. "Let's get out of here," he said, his warm breath tingling on her cheek.

Leslie groaned inwardly. She couldn't believe she was actually considering it! Damn him! What did he think? That he could kidnap her and then drop in and seduce her whenever he felt like it?

"I happen to be with Tim Summers. He's a very nice man. And you happen to be with Sandra," she said waspishly, feeling her cheeks stain with color.

"I don't consider that a condition. You sound like it has an incubation period or something. Is it contagious?"

He was laughing at her now. She could feel the fury bubbling in her veins. "I'm not going to play games with you, Ward Cantrell, and I didn't tell the sheriff you weren't the one just to help you. I was . . .''

"I know why you did it," he said evenly, his eyes holding hers. He had added that to the list of reasons why he was going to kill Younger.

Leslie forced her lips into a smile and pretended to be distracted by the gaiety and laughter all around them. Damn him! Why did he have to look like he cared?

They danced in silence for a while.

"I'd still like to show you the stars, Leslie."

"No thank you," she said evenly.

The dance ended, Cantrell concentrated his charms on Sandra the rest of the evening, and Leslie couldn't help noticing how effective he was. By midnight Sandra allowed Ward to take her out into the moonlight on the long veranda, and they left shortly after that. There was no doubt in Leslie's mind where they were going or for what. The only questions were why should she notice, and why hadn't she warned Sandra what an unscrupulous bastard he was? But would she have cared? Sandra looked blinded to everything except Cantrell.

Anger and frustration made her reckless. When Tim asked if she'd like to step outside for a breath of fresh air she let him take her out onto that same veranda and returned his kiss with an ardor that pleased him and awakened his hopes and desires.

"Leslie, darling, you take my breath away," he groaned.

"Do I?" she asked, nipping at his earlobe.

"Oh, Leslie, I need you so. . . .''

Leslie returned his kiss and asked him to take her back inside. She danced with a dozen men and feigned gaiety, but underneath she felt a frustration that she could not escape.

Ward's intention was to leave the pretty blonde at her front door and go to one of the saloons to pick up a willing *señorita* for the night. He helped Sandra out of the carriage, and escorted her to the front door of the gingerbread mansion, but she stopped him with a pressure on his arm.

"Ward?" she asked softly.

"What is it, Trinket?"

She searched his face in the moonlight. "I'm not like what you think I am."

What the hell? Ward could feel himself frowning. He hadn't

been thinking about her at all. As far as he was concerned there were only two kinds of girls: available and unavailable. Sandra was the latter.

"Oh, I know what you're going to do," she challenged. "You'll leave me here and go find a girl to sleep with. . . ."

Christ! Girls have changed. Maybe Jenn was right. First that hellcat Leslie and now a passionate little female who reads minds.

Blond Trinket tossed her hair with a touch of shy defiance and continued. "I don't want it to be that way."

"How do you want it to be?"

She was trembling with urgency. She wanted him. . . . He had been like an ache in her blood since she'd seen him with a young Mexican girl, a pretty *señorita* with flashing eyes and an insouciant smile. He had looked like he was trying to leave her, and she was trying to keep him there. He had allowed her to tease him for a while, apparently even enjoying it, but when he was finished, he was finished. Sandra McCormick, Daddy's golden girl, who looked shy and virginal, had watched the way Ward Cantrell had handled that girl when he was through playing with her, the way his lean brown hands had looked biting into the creamy white flesh of her arms before he kissed her and put her aside, and she had been sick with anticipation ever since. His hands had been inexorable, handling her easily—as if the girl had been a toy or an object to be used any way he wanted to use her.

Sandra moistened her lips nervously.

"I want to be the girl you bed," she said softly, her voice almost breaking up.

Ward helped Sandra back into the carriage and took her to the house on Barton Street that belonged to Lance and Angie Kincaid. He had the use of it for as long as he needed because they were in Austin visiting the elder Kincaids, and Yoshio, their houseboy, liked having a guest. He hadn't met them yet, but Jenn had raved about her handsome brother-in-law and his pretty young wife. Apparently the brothers were very close. Lance and Angie were supposed to be away for a month or more.

There was a master suite upstairs that he was using. He stopped at the credenza that served as a bar along the wall next to his bedroom door. The house was well built. Each bedchamber had a sitting room with comfortable chairs, a desk, shelves for books and bric-a-brac. On one side the room was crowded with engravings in bronze: horses' heads and fine-looking horses. There was an elegant Wilton carpet on the floor, its chief color a rich blue, and the curtains and hangings were a delicate amber. A chromo of Whittier's *Barefoot Boy* hung on one wall. The double doors to the sleeping chamber were open. The light from the sitting room spilled into it in a widening wedge.

"Would you like a drink?"

Sandra flushed. She wanted this, but it irked her that he had come directly upstairs to his bedchamber. Didn't he realize that she was a nice girl? A well-brought-up young woman of substance?

"Is it going to hurt?" she asked shyly.

His eyes narrowed in suspicion or irritation; she couldn't tell which. "Haven't you done this before?" he asked, watching her closely.

"Not exactly," she lied. What did he expect? That she would admit it?

Ward's lean brown fingers closed like steel bands around her arm, above the elbow. He dragged her forward abruptly, almost savagely, the look on his face changing from irritation to anger that darkened his eyes almost to violet and roughened his husky voice.

"Rich little girls who want to play around should stay in their own crowd." He turned her loose contemptuously. "I'm sure someone will accommodate you."

Damn! She had guessed wrong. She couldn't believe it. He was furious. She had thought he would be excited—the others had been. The thought of deflowering a cringing virgin excited lots of men. Some of them were so aroused they couldn't do anything; they went out of control. Well, she wasn't about to give up. She would try a different approach. She let the tears spill out of her eyes, let her lips begin to tremble.

"I want it to be you," she said softly, tremulously.

"Is that why you tracked me down and asked me to that damned dance, so you could get your ticket punched, have a little fun, and still keep your lily-white reputation among your fine friends?"

She started to cry in earnest. He was harder than she'd thought. She was going to have to use her hidden weapon. Still crying like a heartbroken child, she began to unbutton her gown. This always worked.

"No," she said softly, shaking her head, "No, I—I—saw you in town yesterday and I wanted you ever since." That part was true—too true.

Suddenly the trembling was real. There was something about this man . . . watching her with a strangely impassive, knowing look in his eyes that frightened her. He wasn't like any of the others. He couldn't be tricked or manipulated.

He reached out slowly, his steely fingers closed around her arm, above the elbow, and she could feel the heat in her belly spreading out like rivers of fire. Her breathing was shallow and painful. Her mouth felt like cotton suddenly, and the pain in her arm, where his warm fingers were biting into it, was sending a sweet savage ache all the way down to her toes. If he sent her away now, she would be sick—violently sick. She wouldn't be able to bear it. If he wanted her to beg . . .

She opened her mouth to say whatever she had to say, but it wasn't necessary. She saw it in his eyes. He knew she had lied and why.

Trembling, she moved close enough to feel the dry tingling heat of his lean, hard-muscled body. Her eyes holding his, she placed his hand over her breast and pressed forward so she could feel the hard pulsing warmth of him against her belly. His hand closed around her breast, its heat wrenching a low moan that strangled in her throat. She reached up to pull his mouth down to hers, but he stiffened, realizing for the first time in his life that while his body was raging with its usual response to a beautiful, willing female, his mind was strangely unresponsive, holding him there, immobile.

He started to ignore the reluctance. She was very desirable, and he hated pain, especially his own—he would have a miserable night if he took her home now—and there was no need to. He owed allegiance to no one. Leslie Powers had made it clear to him that she was not harboring a lingering desire for him. Trinket's flesh against his was warm and insistent, but he disentangled himself.

"What's wrong?" she asked, a small frown puckering the perfect smoothness of her lovely face.

"Nothing." He took her arm and led her toward the door.

She resisted. "What are you doing?"

"Taking you home where you belong . . ."

Desire blurred into the pain of rejection in her wide gray eyes, and he felt a corresponding wrenching within himself. He hated it almost as much as she, but he recognized his mental reluctance as an unwillingness to engage in another relationship with another lost female. He had six years of that behind him. It would be too easy to take advantage of her neediness and too hard to get rid of her after he had. . . .

Sandra peered into his face, saw the stubborn light in his blue eyes, and lashed out at him furiously. Her hand struck him across the cheek once, but before she could repeat the blow, he grabbed her arm and held it.

"Let me go! You bastard! Don't hold me! I hate you! I hate you!" But he didn't relent, and she couldn't. She glared at him with hatred until tears blurred her vision and she collapsed against him, sobbing. She cried bitterly.

Strangely, he could have made love to her then; she had become real. His mind would have found the energy for him to cope with her needs afterward. . . . He pulled her close and let her sob out her frustration on his shoulder. When the storm had passed he wrapped her in one of Kincaid's long coats and led her outside. In the buggy she would not speak to him—she huddled as far away from him as possible—hating him.

"Take me back to the dance," she said grimly, blotting Ward Cantrell out of her mind. When the buggy stopped, she flung off the coat, leaped down, and ran across the lawn, her cheeks burning with the shame and desperation she felt.

A man stepped off the front porch and headed across the lawn toward her. In the dancing light and shadow from the play of the electric porch light against the trees she recognized Tim Summers. He stopped. "Sandra?"

"What?" she asked sullenly.

"Are you all right?"

He was glancing at the buggy that still waited at the curb, wondering if the dark shape was Cantrell and what had transpired between them that she was fleeing from him so, and if he could somehow use that knowledge to his advantage. He watched her in the shifting light, noting the simmering anger in her eyes, and decided he could.

"Would you care if I wasn't?" she demanded, her voice strangely taut, choked with pain.

He hesitated the way he did when someone asked an unexpected question of him. "Of course I would."

Of course I would, she mimicked bitterly to herself. *Like hell he would.* She wanted to hit him the way she had Cantrell, but she didn't know Tim Summers. There was something intimidating about him. Something about the way he watched her that told her he might not send her away. . . . She dragged in a ragged breath, letting some of her anger subside.

"Are you leaving?" she asked.

"Yes," he said. Leslie Powers would not miss him. She had

begged to be excused and gone upstairs. She did not seem to crave society the way most young women her age did. She had been polite, proper, but not impressed. Her lack of concern over his attentions had irritated him to the point of fury, but he had managed to contain it. Now he saw Sandra, who looked as if she had been rejected by Cantrell, as a possible means to an end. "Would you like to go back inside, or would you rather go for a ride?" he asked, watching her closely.

"A ride," she said without hesitation.

They rode out to the river, which flowed about half full this time of year. The moon streaked the quietly flowing water with a wide silver band that twinkled and shimmered. Sandra moved close to him, and he put his arm around her and lifted her face to kiss her.

Normally he would not have considered Sandra McCormick a woman to spend time with. He had a natural contempt for her type. They reminded him too much of his mother, who had been the bane of his life until her death four years ago. He had lived in fear that she would track him down and visit, showing the world that he was not what he appeared, that he was only the son of a woman who couldn't seem to keep her gown down around her ankles, where it belonged. His father had abandoned them when he was six; the reasons were not clear in his mind, but he believed it was because of her. She'd had the same look of vague self-interest bordering on madness that reminded him of Sandra and most young girls. He had hated his mother, but Sandra excited him in some strange way. The excitement was a heady overwhelming experience, but when he was not under the influence of the moment he preferred the sort of class that was apparent in Leslie Powers. He had been irresistibly drawn to her level gaze and her well-developed sense of self. She was not impetuous and experimental. Sandra, if not for her father's wealth and position, would be a common strumpet like his mother, like most women. But he had Leslie now. If he were going to woo and win Leslie, it would take patience and the ability to weather a long sexual dry spell. Leslie had made it clear to him, however demurely, that she was not interested in a casual romantic liaison. Sandra could give him the edge he needed, the ability to endure a prolonged courtship.

To Sandra, his kiss was nothing in itself, but the contact of a man she considered powerful had the ability to draw out the dark poison that had welled up in her at Cantrell's rejection. Now she shuddered and relaxed, allowing the warmth and nearness of this man to cleanse her. She didn't care about the consequences of her actions. She was numb to everything except the compulsion that was driving her blindly forward, toward the satisfaction that she needed.

Sandra touched Tim intimately as if she knew him well, and felt him shudder. His kisses grew wetter and more hurtful, but it didn't matter; the only thing that mattered was that he not abandon her, and she knew how to assure that. . . .

Without warning his hand tangled in her hair, hurting her. "Oww!" she cried out, arching backward.

"Promise me something," he growled.

"What?" she whimpered, squirming awkwardly.

"Promise me that you will not tell anyone that you have been with me, ever." His voice was taut, angry, as if she had already betrayed him. Shame flushed through her. His hand was still tight in her hair, but she forgot the physical pain in light of this new demand. She should leave him, refuse to let him touch her, but strangely, her body was responding to the pain. An ache started in her loins, and she groaned in dismay. Mistaking the pitiful sound for protest, he tightened his hand in her silky blond tresses.

"I promise," she whispered, shamed to the core.

"I mean never, never tell anyone. Do you understand?"

"I understand. . . ."

"You'd better. If you know what is good for you . . ." His voice was hard, frighteningly hard and cutting. In spite of everything, the secret place between her legs throbbed insistently. Tears of shame, fueled by a dark pool of ugliness swelling inside her, spilled down her cheeks.

She made one pitiful move to get out of the buggy, to prove to herself, if no one else, that she still had pride. His hand dropped to her breast and clamped around it like a vise, causing her to cry out in anguish.

"Shut your mouth, slut. Unless I tell you to open it." There was no further opportunity to assert herself.

CHAPTER
THIRTY

Ward Cantrell was at every party Leslie went to for the next week, but he didn't ask her to dance again. She watched him with Sandra, Elizabeth Cartright, Marybelle Lewis, and her anger seemed to grow each time she saw him. After almost a week of his presence in Phoenix society, the women were talking of nothing else. He had become an item.

"My father said he made an extremely large deposit at the bank."

"Heavens! All that and money too? I can't believe it!"

"Where did he come from? I mean, I would like to know where they cultivate such devilishly attractive young men."

"Don't laugh! Elizabeth is still in shock. I don't think the poor girl knows what hit her, and he's already moved on to the next girl."

"Where do you go to queue up? I don't care if it is for a short engagement."

They were being deliberately blasé, but Leslie felt her temper rising. Damn him! He had seduced Sandra that first night. They left the dance early, and anyone who saw her could tell just by looking at her now that she wasn't the same girl. Shy Sandra had been replaced by a girl who was very much aware of her body, as a source of pleasure and as a weapon. Ward had taken her out twice and then showed up with Elizabeth Cartright while Sandra was becoming a Venus's fly-trap. Men were buzzing around her like flies around a honeypot. She was a woman now—you could see it in the swing of her hips and the look in her eyes.

Elizabeth and Marybelle, and then Ward had flitted back to Sandra like a stallion with a herd of mares to service.

Leslie was furious. He would go his merry way, but those girls were ruined! He had destroyed their reputations, and he obviously didn't even care for them.

Sandra was at the refreshment table with Phoenix's most exciting young bachelor. She was clinging, laughing, and teasing— almost as engrossed in him as he was in his drink!

196

The dance tonight was at the Lewis house. Amboy Carlton Lewis was the manager of Kincaid's Bricewood West. Lewis had been in hotel management for twenty-five years—an assistant manager of the Bricewood in New York City. He probably would have remained an assistant manager the rest of his life—good jobs did not open up very often—if Kincaid hadn't offered him this job.

The Lewis house was typical for the period if not for the location. The formal parlor, reading room, and dining room were laid out in tandem along the back edge of the house. The rooms did not have walls separating them from one another. As was the custom the year before when the house had been built, the rooms were separated by decorative doric columns, and the furniture was arranged as if the walls were there. Now the furnishings had been pushed back along the walls opposite the veranda. It was chilly outside, so the several sets of double French doors that opened to let in cooling night breezes were closed. Only one set of doors at each end of the long row of rooms was open to provide ventilation for dancers.

Thank goodness Charles Frederick Worth had dethroned the hooped cage and the crinoline. Leslie Powers's gown was a vision of restraint. She had no desire to look like a walking version of someone's overdecorated drawing room. She was wearing a peacock-blue silk faille gown by Worth. It had been forced on her by Jennie who had never worn it, claiming it did terrible things to her complexion. Leslie did not believe it for a minute, but who would refuse Jennie when she wanted to do something? And it was perfect for Leslie. The peacock blue brought out a smoky blue-green look in her eyes that she liked. The décolletage was a little extreme, the waist wonderfully tiny and belted with a wide velvet ribbon, but the bustle was smaller than most and had a saucy pert look to it that was marvelously flattering. The skirt was pulled tight over her slender hips, hugging her figure and then bursting forth in back into a waterfall of flounces and ruffles, falling into a short train. She loved it!

Leslie and Tim made their way to the punch bowl, and Leslie heard Sandra's irritating voice.

"Ward, darling, please say you'll come tomorrow night. It's so important to me," she pleaded prettily.

"Don't push so hard, Trinket. I'll make it if I can," he said absently, his cool blue eyes scanning the crowd.

Marybelle Lewis and Winslow Breakenridge joined Ward and Sandra, and Winslow dutifully asked Sandra to dance. Marybelle had him well trained apparently. As soon as Sandra was gone,

Marybelle moved in on Ward, wanting him to dance with her, and Leslie heard herself almost with shock.

"Well, well, Ward Cantrell. Fancy seeing you here." She smiled sweetly and insincerely as she practically dragged Tim toward them.

"Leslie. Summers." Cantrell nodded curtly at Tim, then dismissed him and let his eyes go back to Leslie.

What female could resist warm blue eyes that so openly told her how beautiful she looked? She might hate him but . . . he did look handsome—even in a somber black frockcoat that looked like all the others around them, counterpoint to the brilliant colors of the females.

Since mass production had begun with such a passion in the 1860s, fashion was accessible to all. The frockcoat Ward wore was of the finest, softest wool, and the fit across his broad shoulders and around his narrow waist was impeccable. The cut of the lapel was slightly different, though, suggesting that perhaps his suit was a French cut. But where would a lout like Cantrell get a French-cut frockcoat? Unless it belonged to Mr. Kincaid's brother. But if it did, would it fit so perfectly? The trousers were custom fitted too, from the same soft wool. Even the shoes looked like the softest, shiniest leather. If she hadn't seen him the other way, dressed in rough clothes, with guns around his waist, she would almost believe he *was* a gentleman.

The music started again, a waltz, and Tim, always the gentleman, held out his hand to Marybelle, who had no choice but to take it. Leslie suddenly felt too nervous and keyed up to stand there inventing small talk. She looked at Ward almost angrily, and he held out his hand, his azure blue eyes narrowed speculatively. Leslie lifted an eyebrow at his damned arrogance, and his lips almost lifted in a real smile as he swung her out onto the dance floor.

"You dance exceptionally well, Mr. Cantrell. I thought you were only a train robber. . . ."

"Liar. Everyone in Phoenix knows I am an *old friend* of the Kincaids. . . ."

"Was that bitterness? But why should you be? The Kincaids are exceptionally well received everywhere."

Ward's eyes flicked over her, taking in the elegant blue gown she wore. He rarely looked at women in detail. He saw that they were attractive or not. His eye did not notice geegaws and ribbons—only whether or not they enhanced or detracted from the vision. And it was apparent to him that Leslie, with her eye for color and detail, did not fall into the trap that caught so many women.

She looked fresh, small, and delicately made, but with a curious richness and spirit in the way she held herself that caused a tiny spark to leap instantly alive in him. In contrast, he was remembering the way she looked that last morning. There'd been something completely defenseless about her then.

"Did you sleep well?"

"How I sleep is no concern of yours, Mr. Cantrell."

"Sorry," he said, retreating with a grimace.

She was instantly contrite. If they had to engage in this charade to convince Phoenix society that they were both respectable, upstanding citizens, it would be better if they could at least enjoy the conversation, wouldn't it? In repose, Cantrell seemed calm and formidable—as calm as a ray of cold sunshine and as formidable as a typical military officer—manly and up to his duty.

"So you made quite a splash in Phoenix society," she said. "You charmed poor Sandra quite out of her head. The town is teeming with gossip about your being a friend of the Kincaids. . . . You haven't tripped over your spurs once. That is quite an accomplishment. You must be proud," she said, not mentioning he had also seduced the willing Sandra. "I thought you were only a simple train robber."

"A good train robber is a jack of all trades," he said. "Besides, I only worked at that a few hours every few months. The rest of the time . . ." He shrugged, letting it drop.

"You were in pursuit of ladies fair and pastures green," she said, finishing his sentence.

"No more than you are," he replied, leaning his head back and looking at her through eyes that were mere slits.

She ignored his remark. "Now that you are no longer devoting all your energies to seducing the lucky *señoritas*, word gets around. It is very fashionable to be pursued by you."

A smile tugged at those perfectly etched, insolently sensuous lips. "I thought young executives were all the rage now," he drawled.

Leslie blushed, and Cantrell lifted an eyebrow, while tiny glints of amusement danced and flickered in his eyes like starbursts of summer lightning. Something wild and hungry, like an invisible current, passed between them. A pang of hopelessness stabbed into Leslie, and she articulated what had enraged her.

"Young executives have a future. No woman in her right mind

would deliberately get involved with a man who could be hanged by the neck at any moment.''

His eyes stabbed at her, and she quailed before their intensity, before the power and maleness of him. He did not believe himself vulnerable to man or beast, but she could not forget that he had been within minutes of being hanged when Governor Stanton finally commuted his sentence.

His arm relaxed its hold around her waist, and that careless, handsome smile came over his face, transforming it again. ''You're right,'' he conceded.

Leslie didn't know what had passed between them, but she felt dazed by it. They seemed to lose the ability to enjoy jabbing at each other after that exchange. She danced in silence.

''I'm glad to see you didn't suffer any permanent damage,'' he said softly.

Why did Cantrell always remind her they had been intimate? Didn't he ever forget? ''No thanks to you,'' she said sourly. She was tempted to tell him that Tim Summers had called on her every evening since she met him. Would Ward Cantrell care that they sat in the music room after dinner and carried on pleasant, civilized conversations? She with the still life she was painting, Jennie at the piano, and Mr. Kincaid chatting desultorily with Tim, who kept stealing unobtrusive glances at her.

''You're the most beautiful woman in the room,'' he whispered, his hand tightening around her waist.

''I'm surprised you had time to notice,'' she said, hating herself the moment the words were uttered. Stop admitting you watch, dammit!

''I don't usually waste time admiring women who are out of my league,'' he admitted. ''Train robbers don't work as steady as young executives.''

''By design, I'm sure.''

''So,'' Cantrell said, changing the subject again, ''you're walking out with Mr. Dull.''

''He is not dull,'' she defended.

''Sorry,'' he said, his eyes filled with that sharp light that jolted through her like the electric current she had felt at the state fair in Boston. ''You're walking out with your dashing young executive,'' he corrected.

''He is not dull!'' Leslie repeated, instantly angry at him for being so damned observant.

Ward quirked his eyebrows and grinned. ''God forbid anyone

should even suggest such a thing,'' he said, his eyes filled with superior knowledge.

He had known the moment he had seen her tonight that any contact with her would be a mistake. The sight of her, cool and lovely in a peacock-blue gown, with her hair pulled back off her ears, but otherwise loose on her shoulders, had caused a hungry ache to race through the entire length of his body. He had hoped he could be as impervious to her as she was to him, but seeing her in her proper setting, armored with all the artillery a lady of impeccable upbringing has, he realized the insanity of his position. Leslie Powers, indignant, with her face set in that imperious, untouchable mien, like some snow goddess cloaked in lacy, crisp fabrics, reminding him of all the untouchable females he had ever known, completely overwhelmed him. In the light of a thousand candles, with her skin so incredibly soft and dewy, she glowed with the purity of an arctic thing. Her gleaming beauty, her extreme femininity, like a young, virginal school girl except for the décolleté gown, her very imperviousness, made him ache to remind her how flawlessly her body could respond to his.

She was so different from Sandra, who pursued him publicly, acting as if they were lovers, as if she didn't remember she was furious with him for refusing her offer.

Seeing the angry set of Cantrell's jaw, Leslie sighed. Now it appeared he did not want to be drawn into conversation, and somehow, knowing that made her absolutely determined that she should be. "So how long have you known the Kincaids?"

He shrugged. "I guess I've known Mrs. Kincaid quite some time. I don't really know Mr. Kincaid all that well.''

"They're very nice, aren't they?"

"She is."

Leslie looked at him curiously. "Don't you like him?"

"I don't feel like I know him well enough to decide if I like him or not.'' A muscle bunched in his cheek, above the lean, square-cut jaw. "He seems to be what she wants,'' he said, shrugging. He pulled her closer, and she bristled, bringing a look of sardonic amusement into his blue eyes.

"Were you in love with her?"

Surprised, Ward looked down at the flying feet of strangers skimming over the smooth marble dance floor. "She married him. I can't change that."

"You didn't answer my question."

"Maybe I don't see that it's any of your business."

Leslie flushed. "I still can't believe they just let you out like that. Do you suppose they can be that irresponsible?"

"Thanks," he said dryly.

"Well, it just seems like you should be in jail somewhere," she said, realizing perversely that she was beginning to enjoy herself.

"Probably should be," he said grimly.

"I'm serious," she said. "Why aren't you in jail?"

"What did the Kincaids tell you?"

"I didn't ask. They mentioned something about a conditional pardon. . . . But I don't really know what that entails."

"Then you know as much as I do about it. Conditional pardon means they have the right to keep me on a short leash while I do their dirty work, then jerk it back when I'm done. If I please them, they might—*might*—lengthen my leash."

"And if you don't?"

"Maybe they'll hang me. I don't know. . . ."

"Please them at what?"

"Guarding the railroad," he lied.

"Set a thief to catch a thief?" She laughed. "How fitting. How have you done so far?"

He shrugged. "My heart's not in it, but they seem to be patient, probably hoping I don't get a better offer."

"They're right to worry. . . ."

Strangely stung by her words, he kept his tone light, teasing. "Maybe I could go straight."

"Why would you?"

"Why not? Kincaid's paying me almost as much as I used to make robbing his trains."

"You just do whatever is easy?" she demanded, contempt obvious in every carefully measured word.

"Don't you?" he asked, glancing at Tim Summers, his husky voice caustic.

"Tim wants to marry me," she said defiantly.

Blue eyes fairly danced with devilment; his low, well-modulated voice was freighted with awe. "A real catch. Think how respectable you will be."

"You, you . . ."

"Bastard?" he asked courteously.

"If the shoe fits . . ."

"There's a lot of bitterness under that satiny little veneer you show the world, isn't there?" he asked softly.

Leslie was strangely breathless. She had danced too many waltzes. "Why should I be bitter?"

"I don't know, but maybe I'll find out," he drawled. They were beside the raised portico where the orchestra played. The french doors opening onto the veranda were only steps away. It was apparent he didn't care who saw him whirl her forcefully out the doors. If she weren't so bemused by the ordeal of dancing with him and trying to carry on a decent conversation, she would have protested, but he gave her neither time nor opportunity.

Once outside, away from the prying eyes of Phoenix's cadre of humorless matrons who watched the young people with envy and suspicion, she turned on him, her eyes glittering like a cat's in the moonlight. "What are you trying to do? Ruin the lives of half the girls in Phoenix?"

"You mean Trinket? What about her?" he asked, frowning.

"Marybelle was Trinket," she corrected him.

He shrugged. "What about her?"

"You've got the whole town talking about her."

"Correction. *She's* got the whole town talking about her. I didn't touch her. . . ."

"I hope your happiness is not dependent upon my believing that."

"No more than yours is."

"Ohhh!" She turned away. "It's a beautiful night, isn't it?" she gritted, her voice painfully brittle.

He didn't answer. He turned her, pulled her firmly into his arms, and set his mouth over hers. Leslie couldn't tell if she cried out or only wanted to. Darkness closed down, shutting her off from reality. Moon, stars, even the strains of music and activity on the other side of the wall, faded out of consciousness. Her fisted hands, white fluttering butterflies against his black coat, made one futile attempt at resistance before they slid up to twine and cling around his neck.

His lips were ruthless and plundering. His hands slid down to caress her back, pulling her against him, crushing her breasts into his warm sturdy chest. This was trial by fire, and Leslie felt herself losing control. He kissed her until her body was aflame and trembling with a recurrence of the hunger she hadn't felt since the last time he held her.

When the kiss ended, he stepped away from her to lean against the banister and roll a cigarette. Trembling, she watched bitterly as his deft fingers quickly and efficiently completed the task. His lean brown hands cupped the blue flare of the match and he shook it out and dropped it. Was there some symbolism there for her? He could light them and he could put them out. What was she to him? Just a girl he had kidnapped once? He wanted her now, though, at least momentarily. But how long did his passions last? A week? Two days?

"Why did you kiss me?" she asked.

"Because I wanted to."

"Why?"

"You keep turning up in my arms, Leslie. I want to know why."

"So, did you find out?"

"Maybe—maybe not." He was holding back now and not sure why. He wanted her, and the kiss told him he could have her, but suddenly he needed more—maybe to punish her for giving herself too easily to Summers.

"Well"—she turned away, hiding the sudden bitterness that welled up within her—"let me know if you come up with anything useful."

She was almost to the door when he stopped her and shoved her against the wall, letting his control drop away, leaning his warm, hard-muscled body into hers, trapping her there while he flicked away the cigarette he had used as a diversion and let his hands cup her face.

"I just thought of something," he said, his voice gruff with some unidentifiable emotion. His warm mouth, only a hair's breadth from hers, brushed lightly over her parted lips, and Leslie had to stifle a groan. Damn him! He was toying with her now, enjoying the effect he had on her! Could those hateful blue eyes see every weakness? Could they see her blood turning to steam because his body was molded into hers, or did his hand, caressing the curve of her cheek, feel the tumult in her traitorous arteries?

"Come home with me, Leslie," he whispered huskily.

"I didn't know train robbers had homes." She was stalling now, praying for strength.

"Will you come or would you like to be kidnapped—for old times' sake?"

"Would what I want make a difference?"

"Try me. It might."

Then so quietly that she almost didn't hear it or didn't believe she heard it: "Give me a *chance*."

She was suddenly quiet, the frustration and confusion of the past days and weeks strangely stilled in her, everything fading except his presence. Even the urge to issue a witty, cutting remark subsided.

His eyes held hers; a rich current of energy moved through him to her similar to the dark flood of passion he normally aroused in her, and yet richer, more peaceful, awakening a hunger for pure, nonsexual closeness with him she hadn't felt before.

A door edged open and a couple slipped out onto the veranda. The girl was giggling nervously, soft and breathlessly, but the young man's voice was low-pitched, urgent. They moved as far away as possible, partly shaded from view by an encroaching tree, and their negotiating continued.

Leslie looked back at Ward. His eyes had not strayed from her face. Behind him, the moon cast a silvery glow on the roof of the stable at the back of the Lewises' property. Small electric lights encased in festive Chinese lanterns lit the garden pathways with colored light. Laughter and music mingled with the sounds of soft wind and an occasional horse neighing. A dog barked. The other couple was silent now, engrossed in each other, unaware of anything else. The smell of flowers from the garden mingled with the dry night smells of sage from the unseen desert.

"Wait here," he said on impulse.

Bemused, Leslie watched as he leaped over the wooden railing and dropped catlike into the soft earth beneath them. He sprinted to a bush, broke off a flower, walked quickly up the steps, and bowed low before her.

"A flower for a beautiful lady," he said softly.

Leslie had seen a hundred expressions on his handsome face—its mobility of expression was part of his attraction—but never this one. He looked like a little boy, his eyes filled with something so sweet, innocent, and youthful that she felt a melting sensation that started low in her spine and swept upward, bringing a flush of heat and moisture so overpowering that she couldn't speak. She blinked back the heated rush of tears, unwilling to let him see how touched she was. She took the flower, a small, delicate native ornament from his warm hand.

"Thank you," she whispered.

CHAPTER
THIRTY-ONE

What would have happened if Marybelle Lewis hadn't chosen that moment to fling open the double doors nearest them and step outside, sending a wide arc of light onto the balcony beside Leslie and Ward?

"Ward, darling," she drawled. "Are you out here?"

Ward stepped away from Leslie, shielding her from Marybelle's sight. "Here, Trinket."

"Oh, sorry to interrupt. Mr. Kincaid was looking for you. I thought you would want to know."

"Thanks. Tell him I'll look him up in a few minutes."

She didn't look like she wanted to leave, so he walked over, pointed her in the right direction, opened the door, and guided her skillfully inside with a firm hand on her small waist that reminded Leslie of too many unpleasant things about him.

"Sorry about that," he said as he returned to her side.

"How many Trinkets do you have?" Then without waiting for him to reply, "They have names. Why don't you use them?"

"I have a lousy memory for names."

She laughed, and it was a soft, bitter sound that probably told him far too clearly that she resented his having so many women that he couldn't remember their names. "Maybe *you* have a terrible memory, but I don't." Furious, flooded with a sudden consuming anger that had kindled when he touched Marybelle's waist in that casual, proprietary way, she stepped away and moved to brush past him, but he caught her arm, pulling her against his warmth and hardness again, his mood as transformed as her own.

His lean fingers biting into her arm were like a narcotic on her senses. She could feel her heart pounding wildly; she wanted him, but she refused to be another one of his Trinkets.

"Let me go!" she hissed.

He leaned down and found her mouth, kissed her lightly, his warm lips searing into her like a shock wave, but she refused to respond. Then, just as abruptly, he relinquished her lips and stepped away from her.

"All right," he said softly, grimly. He opened the door for her, and

Leslie stifled the urge to throw herself against him to tear his hateful eyes out. She forced a smile and stepped back into the pandemonium.

Ward singled out Debra Denning, and she didn't stand a chance.

Debra was her closest friend in Phoenix and too sweet and unsuspecting to deserve what was happening to her. Leslie tried not to watch, but her eyes found Ward Cantrell in spite of her attempts to the contrary, cutting a lithe and graceful figure on the dance floor. The waltz was all the rage, and Ward looked handsome gliding and whirling his rapt partner over the floor.

When the music paused, Ward slipped something into the hand of one of the musicians, they broke into the strains of Beethoven's *Moonlight Sonata*, and Ward bowed low and formally to Mrs. Kincaid. Jennie's face glowed with happiness as he twirled her out onto the floor.

They danced beautifully together, seeming to float in time with the rhythm, swept along by the melody. Couples stopped dancing to watch them. Leslie glanced past Tim's shoulder and found Mr. Kincaid. He was standing alone, watching them with a look of rapt pride and happiness that jangled her nerves. If a man like Cantrell, with his reputation as a womanizer, were dancing with someone Kincaid cared about . . .

Elizabeth Cartright moved to stand beside a heavyset matron Leslie knew only casually. They exchanged pleasantries and then Elizabeth dropped her tone to one that was obviously conspiratorial.

"Mrs. Kincaid and Mr. Cantrell certainly dance beautifully together, don't they?"

The matron lifted her chin and sniffed. "They should. I heard from a very reliable source that they were lovers in New York. Of course, that was years ago."

"No!" Elizabeth gasped, feigning shock.

"Yes. I heard there was a terrible scandal surrounding it, too. Mary Freake, the McCormicks' cook, used to work for the Astors. She told Sarah, my downstairs maid, that the Kincaids separated for quite a spell, and it wasn't that long after they were married. Sounded to me like Jennie may have married on the rebound, regretted it, and just took off. I've heard of that happening before. Of course, I don't know that Ward Cantrell was the reason for that split-up, but she certainly seems quite taken with him for a married woman."

"Mary said the separation was caused by another man?" Elizabeth prompted.

"That she did. Mr. Kincaid took it right hard too, from what she told my Sarah." The matron lifted her lorgnette and expanded her lungs. "Heavens! Well, Mr. Cantrell is a fine specimen of a man. I daresay if he put his mind to it, there aren't many women who could resist him."

Elizabeth sighed. "But one would think a *married* woman would be a *little* more discreet."

Debra Denning and her escort joined Leslie and Tim. The two women listened as Tim and Winslow exchanged greetings, then Debbie winked at Leslie. "I imagine the mothers of all the single females in town are giving thanks this night that Mr. Kincaid had the foresight to marry Jennie."

"What do you mean?" Leslie asked, frowning.

"Well, she looks like the stiffest competition around, doesn't she? I'm sure they're all grateful she's already taken."

Leslie frowned Debbie into silence.

"Sorry, I meant no disrespect. The Kincaids are dear friends of mine. I don't believe that dreadful gossip. I know Jennie is totally devoted to her husband. I was being facetious."

"Sorry," Leslie murmured. "Oh . . . well . . . they are attractive together, aren't they?"

"You have truly mastered the art of understatement, Leslie Powers," Debra said, sighing. "Truly mastered it."

"I personally think all that washed-out beauty is overrated," Tim said, reaching to take Leslie's glass from her fingers. "Let's give them something to watch besides blonds." He set her glass on the buffet and swung her out onto the dance floor, and Leslie gratefully lost herself in the music. The sonata ended, another waltz began, and Chane Kincaid cut in on Ward to reclaim his wife. Ward rescued Debbie from Winslow Breakenridge, who was a graceless dancer at best.

When the next dance started Leslie saw Cantrell making his way toward her through the crowd. Tim saw him also.

"Looks like you're about to be singled out for the high honor of the evening," he said, his eyes watching her closely.

"What do you mean?" she asked.

"Cantrell is headed this way to do his duty by you again."

"He has no duty to me," Leslie said, flushing with anger.

Tim laughed. "Easy, darling. No insult intended. I was merely remembering something I overheard to the effect that perhaps Cantrell has eyes for only one, but as a pseudogentleman, he is being careful to dance with a number of young ladies . . . to disguise his real interest."

"Dance with me, Tim."

Ward danced two more dances with Debbie, concentrating all

his considerable charm and attention on her while Leslie danced intermittently, sipping at the champagne Tim brought her.

Debbie smiled a lot, obviously enjoying whatever she and Ward were discussing. He had made another conquest—that was apparent—especially to Sandra McCormick, who watched him with barely concealed petulance.

There was tension everywhere. Leslie felt hot and jangled. Tim was watching her with what seemed like cool speculation in his black eyes. He didn't say anything more, but the tension between them was intolerable.

Before Ward Cantrell could leave with Debra, Leslie allowed Tim to take her out into the moonlight. He kissed her and she clung to him, returning his kiss with ardor.

"Leslie, my treasure, you take my breath away! I love you so. . . . I want you so," he groaned, holding her as if he couldn't possibly let her go.

"Do you really love me, Tim?"

"I love you so much, my dearest jewel, that I am convinced I invented the emotion. I'm wild with despair one moment, elated the next. Awake or asleep I dream of you. Say you'll marry me and end this tumult. Please, darling. Say that you love me. . . ."

It was nice to have a man who didn't chase every female in town. Loyalty deserved to be rewarded. She wasn't willing to marry him, though.

"Where could we go?" she whispered.

"Oh, my darling treasure. Do you mean it?"

"Yes, but where?" she breathed, not daring to examine her impulse.

"My house?"

"Fine," she said, elated that this time Ward Cantrell, womanizer extraordinaire, would watch her leave early, snuggled in a man's protective embrace! She giggled her most sultry champagne giggle when they passed Ward and Debra; she waved fuzzily at her new friend and was rewarded with a flash of narrowed blue eyes from Mr. No Comment before Tim wrapped her shawl around her shoulders, brushed a kiss on her upturned lips, and led her out into the night. Let him look! He might have been the one to awaken her to the pleasures of sex, but she got to decide whom she shared them with!

Leslie shivered at the crisp feel of the chilly night air. It smelled of sage. Night sounds were not audible over the trotting of the horse and the creak of Tim's buggy. The moon had gone down, leaving the road dark except for what light the stars gave blazing down on them. The buggy rocked and swayed, jerked around by the deep ruts in the road.

She didn't have to guess—Tim lived on one of the lots Chane had made available. Two blocks from the Kincaid house and only one block from the house on Barton Street that Jennifer had pointed out as the current residence of Ward Cantrell.

Tim's house was one of those fashionable frame houses she had told Chane she had grown tired of—the clean white rectangular boxes with simple pitched roofs, crisp, painted, and made pompous with engraved cornices and curlicues around the porch and on the support posts. She was reminded of a story she had read in a Chicago newspaper about a firm, in business since 1867, that "is happy to furnish cottages and villas, schoolhouses, stores, taverns, churches, courthouses or towns—wholesale or retail—and to forward them, securely packed, to any part of the country." Was that what Chane had done? Laid out his lots in a typical New England grid and then ordered himself a village? She would have laughed if she hadn't already begun to regret her impulsiveness. Her hands felt cold and clammy, even when she pulled her shawl around her as tightly as she could.

The interior was stark, sparsely furnished, and warm from the heat trapped in the wood. It smelled new, as if no one lived here really. The sound of their shoes on the hardwood floor echoed and bounced around the walls.

"Needs a woman's influence. I'm not here enough to make the place look lived in," he apologized.

"It's no wonder. Mr. Kincaid relies on you for everything."

Tim glowed. "Isn't he amazing? I can't believe my good fortune. I would work twenty hours a day if it was needed."

"What do you do exactly?"

"I'm in charge of the line all the way from San Diego to El Paso. Phoenix is the main office. This is where all the major problems get solved—right here. You need to ship anything at all, see me. I can fix it for you."

"I'm impressed."

He was busy while they chatted. He uncorked a bottle and poured wine into two glasses and led her to the couch in front of the fire.

"You're very efficient, Mr. Summers," she said, feeling embarrassed now. "You must have done this before."

"None of the 'befores' ever mattered, though, Leslie. You feel like the first. There are so many things I want to say to you, so many things I want to do with you. I feel like a schoolboy.'' He put his glass down and lifted her chin.

Tim kissed her long and skillfully, whispering love words. Once, groaning at the effort it cost him to be gentle with her, he held her tightly, shuddering. His powerful reaction stirred something in her. Even if she didn't like him, she would have responded emotionally to such ardor and extravagant praise; but in spite of both their efforts, her body remained wooden and unresponsive. The face that surfaced out of that welter of confusion in her head was the color of teak: an irresistible swell of smooth lower lip, and narrowed blue eyes that picked up the light and sent it stabbing into her heart. So singularly appealing . . .

''Leslie, my darling, I'm going to make you forget everyone except me,'' he whispered, his voice rough with feeling.

What did he mean by that? Everyone? There hadn't been that many! And besides, she didn't need him to make her forget. She was going to forget Ward Cantrell because he was a hopeless womanizer who couldn't be trusted any farther than a beaver in heat!

Tim was kissing her again, this time insistently. She cursed the part of her that was always leaping into situations without any idea how she would get out. Had she needed so desperately to make a statement to Cantrell that she hadn't thought once about the consequences of coming here with Tim?

Now he was urging her up, no doubt to lead her into the bedroom. ''Leslie, my treasure, you are so breathtaking.''

Was that her voice, sounding so whiny? ''Tim . . . I'm sorry . . . but my head hurts so. . . . I think I drank too much champagne. I'm sorry,'' she said miserably. ''Please take me home. . . . I don't want the Kincaids to worry about me.''

Tim, the eternal gentleman, stifled whatever response he felt. ''Of course, Leslie. I forget how fragile you are, my sweet. It has been such a short time, really, since your ordeal. And . . . I'm a patient man,'' he said ruefully, ''as much as I hate it.'' His voice, so urbane, took on a note of forced jocularity. ''Take all the time you need. Argh!'' He yelled like a man being tortured, startling her. ''I can't believe I said that!'' He half groaned, half laughed, dropping his head in his hands in mock tragic despair that wrenched a nervous, grateful laugh from Leslie.

The house was dark when she slipped in the front door with the key Jennifer had given her days before—the one she hadn't needed until tonight. Her bed was cold and haunted. She shivered between the cold sheets, staring at the star-silvered balcony, watching the intricate, spidery leaves of the trees being whipped about by the chilling night winds. Tim was forgotten.

In memory, she was back on the veranda, fighting for her very life. His mouth was set in grim purpose. He could have been facing Younger . . . except for the look in his eyes. . . . That one fleeting moment . . .

"Why did you kiss me?"

"Because I wanted to. You keep turning up in my arms, Leslie. I want to know why."

Did he know now? Had he spent the night making love to one of his Trinkets and feeling empty?

Damn! She should not let Ward kiss her. Just the memory of it, and she was throbbing with that strange weakness and lethargy his kisses and his presence awakened. That wild, impetuous feeling his touch caused was only an ache now—a long, sweet ache that didn't stop. Suddenly she was remembering another time and she could hear her own words, half-strangled with the remnants of passion, half-dazed: *"I never knew. . . . I never knew. . . ."*

In memory, he was a flash of blue eyes, warm teak skin, a certain musky male smell, his hands tangled in her hair. She could not forget the way he groaned and buried his face in the warmth of her throat, then pushed himself away from her.

He was always pushing himself away from her. He might not be interested in her, but at least someone was. Tim wanted to marry her. Tim loved her.

"Leslie, darling," he had counseled, "it takes time and practice to learn to respond." If only he were right about that. Her instinctive angry response was stifled by the gratitude she felt to Tim for graciously allowing her to renege on an implied consent. Thank goodness for Tim and his wonderful sense of humor, his consideration, his support. She would work harder in the future to deserve him.

Without warning, a heavy thrill ran down her nerves—half pleasure, half pain, obliterating thoughts of Tim. Was the flower still in her quickly discarded gown, tucked between deep ruffles?

It was there—small, wilted, and fragile—almost as fragile as the moment when she imagined that unbelievable look on Ward's face—indescribable yet so reminiscent of sweet, innocent youth that she felt the melting sensation again. He had looked so open, so vibrant with feeling . . . like a young boy with his first crush.

Was it that expression that had started in her this heavy, mindless will to connect with him, to be close to him? Was it the memory of that expression, once gone, erased as if it had never existed, that had wrought such a fury in her when he touched Marybelle Lewis in that smooth, suave, careless, entirely characteristic way?

She wanted to toss the flower in the waste paper basket, but it was so delicate, so sweetly formed, so fragrant, that in the end, even though she chided herself for it, she pressed it between the pages of a book.

I will not become one of those horrid spinsters who hoard books with pressed flowers, she thought savagely. Ohhh! That would be *intolerable!* She closed her eyes and gritted her teeth. Damn you, Ward Cantrell. I hate you. *I hate you!*

Kincaid watched his chance and finally caught Cantrell without one of the girls clinging to his arm.

"I would ask you to step out on the veranda, but I'm afraid you wouldn't respect me in the morning," Chane said softly to Ward while they both gazed out across the sea of swaying bodies on the dance floor.

"What the hell am I supposed to call you?"

"Call me Chane."

"That seems a bit familiar for an outlaw and a railroad tycoon, don't you think?"

"Did Jennie tell you that your parents left each of you over a million dollars?"

"She mentioned it but I still don't understand."

"The letter about the bankruptcy was the fake—not the letter from me. I did write your mother a note thanking her for her proxies—standard courtesy letter—didn't even remember it. The letter advising your father that loss of those proxies had resulted in financial disaster for them was written by Latitia Laurey after she killed them. It was supposed to provide the incentive for your father to have killed your mother and then himself."

"Christ! Twisted but cunning. We fell for it—especially me."

"Unfortunately, by the time the assets could be inventoried and their solidity verified, you were gone. Jennie placed ads in newspapers, wrote letters to every contact she could think of. She always expected to hear from you."

"I transferred money to the bank here. As soon as you give me the amount, I'll make reimbursement for the money I stole."

Chane nodded and they fell silent, each lost in his own thoughts.

Ward was remembering seeing Latitia Laurey that one time at the Palace Theater, through the one-way mirror. Recalling the way she had behaved in that room with Kincaid when she didn't know she was being observed, it was easy to believe she was a woman driven by a powerful, twisted sexuality. After she had been arrested, Latitia had confessed that she had had an affair with Vivian Van Vleet. Ward cringed at the knowledge that his and Jennie's mother had . . .

He cut off those thoughts. Vivian had tried to break off the affair, Latitia fought with her, and Reginald Van Vleet had overheard enough to scare Latitia into thinking he would expose her. Unwilling to live with the fear of exposure, Latitia killed him and then Vivian. Commodore Laurey's hatred—inspired by his fury at Kincaid for costing him millions of dollars in a business transaction, and fed by Latitia's pain when Kincaid rejected her for Jennie—had grown into an obsession. When the truth came out, Laurey and Latitia had both been sentenced to life in prison.

"I'll call you Mr. Kincaid in public."

"How long do I have to stay in town to satisfy . . . Mrs. Kincaid?"

"That depends on how you're feeling. If I allow you to begin riding hard before you have fully recovered and something happens to you, my life won't be worth a plugged nickel. Are you getting impatient to be on with it?"

Ward expelled an angry breath. "Yeah."

"Sounds like you've already begun," Chane said, slanting a look at the younger man, and not missing the simmering hostility evident in every line and angle of his lean frame. Not even fine clothes could hide the leashed tension he was controlling with an effort.

Could Leslie's leaving early with Summers be the cause of this? Chane wondered to himself. Had Cantrell fallen in love with the girl in the time they spent together? He didn't probe, because it was apparent that Cantrell was not in a mood to answer personal questions.

"Wilcox tells me you may have a lead on how our cattle are being rustled, and who is doing it," Kincaid ventured.

Ward sighed. "Not who. Though I suspect Dallas Younger and Powers. I've scouted a little. I'm convinced they're using your spur line to move stolen cattle, and then shipping them like any other herd. I mentioned that I've sent telegrams to some friends and acquaintances of mine. The last one should be riding in any day now. Did you ask Stanton if his offer of amnesty could be stretched to include them if they're willing to work?"

"I think so. What are your plans?"

"Nothing fancy. We'll catch Younger with some stolen cattle if we can. If that doesn't work, I'll round up a herd and try to make contact with the person in your office who is being so accommodating."

Chane quirked his eyebrows in approval. "Sounds simple enough to work all right," he mused, his mind tracing the steps and then projecting the various outcomes.

"Dallas Younger and three of his 'special force' are mine," Ward said, his voice hard, as if this point were not negotiable. "I have a score to settle with them. The rest of them—I'll leave their fate to you. If you want them alive, we can scare billy hell out of them and let 'em run or bring 'em in. I don't care either way."

"Doesn't sound like that oath you took soaked in very deep," Chane said, chuckling, then he sobered under Cantrell's glowering look. "Use your instincts. There are some men who'll run like a coyote until dark and then come back to kill you as soon as you go to sleep."

They watched the dancers in silence. Then Chane glanced at his young companion. "Be careful of Younger. He's no four flush. He's a real gunfighter—fast, fearless, and cool as the north side of a January gravestone. I saw him draw once in Tombstone. He can't be rattled by talk or threats."

Ward stiffened, and the anger that had been seething under the surface since Leslie had left with Summers boiled up now, seeking release. "If I need my diaper changed, I'll let you know," he said furiously.

The look and tone jarred Kincaid. Frowning, he sorted their conversation in his mind. Then realization hit him. This man who stood beside him as sturdy and solid as a young oak was the same kid who had hated him eight years ago. Peter hadn't forgotten their old animosity and resented being treated like a child. Peter—Ward, he corrected himself—was a man now, with a man's competence, strength, and scars. And he didn't want anyone, especially his sister's husband, to forget that. Pride surged in him. Peter was a man—one he grudgingly admired; but in his eagerness to protect Jennie from worry or pain he'd almost forgotten that.

He cleared his throat. "I didn't see the gunfight between you and Dodge Merril, but I heard about it," he said, glancing at Cantrell's fierce profile. "Dodge was rated with the best. I heard you gave him draw advantage and still put two slugs in him." He paused for a second. "Younger's probably not as fast as Dodge, but I can't help worrying about you." Chane moved so that Cantrell had to look at him. "I know you don't want my advice, but I need you to understand my position. My wife has been mourning

your loss for eight years. Oh, it's true we had a good life, because
your sister has tremendous energy and heart, but there was always
that cloud that I could see behind her eyes, that eternal waiting and
hoping that would surface in little things, and then as time drew on
and you didn't show up, in bigger and bigger things. The only
comfort I could offer her was that you were obviously alive because my people would have known if you weren't. Now I won't
have that to help me. If something happens to you now, she will
know it, and knowing it will kill something in your sister that
won't ever come alive again.''

Chane expelled an angry breath. "And, dammit, I got you into
this. It's me Jennie will blame if something happens to you. It could
destroy Jennie or our marriage or both if you are killed. You can get
mad if you want to, dammit. But I have too much to lose. You *will* be
careful of Younger, or by God I will assign a half-dozen men to your
tail, and *they* will take care of you," Kincaid threatened.

Ward met that furious green gaze, and it was apparent his
brother-in-law meant every word. There was fury and strength in
those hazel green eyes and an equal amount of angry stubbornness.
But that was not the deciding factor. Ward was moved by Kincaid's description of his sister's plight. Somehow he had thought
that she grieved him for a week or two and then went about her
life. Learning that she had carried his loss for the full eight years
sobered him to the realization of what he had done to her.

"Thanks for the tip about Younger," Ward said.

Chane dragged in a ragged breath and relaxed a little, knowing
he was at least partially forgiven. "I only mentioned it because I'm
not sure I could beat Younger, and I was considered pretty good in
my prime."

"You were a ranger—Texas Rangers are noted for their short
primes. If you lasted at all, you had to be damned good."

Chane grinned. "What is this, respect for the elderly or admiration for law and order?"

It was Ward's turn to get serious. "Maybe both. I've, uh, been
meaning to tell you that I'm grateful for the way you've taken care
of Jenn. I was a fool. I've always been too stubborn for my own
good. If there were any way I could make it up to her, I would do
it," he said, meaning it.

Chane nodded and they were silent for a while, watching the
dancers. "Use your judgment with the rest of Powers's hired
hands. If they're following Powers's and Younger's orders, scare
hell out of them and let 'em run. If they're likely to hang around

making trouble . . ." His words trailed off. He was remembering how hard life was for a range-riding cowpuncher. Sometimes a man got tired of moving from range to range looking for an honest man to work for. He'd personally known some good men who put up with a crooked spread for a while. A man could do that as long as they didn't ask too much from him personally. He should have known that Cantrell, of all men, would think of that angle.

"Consider it done," Ward said quietly.

Ward found his hostess and thanked her. He located Blueberry in the welter of horses and carriages in the front yard. Mounted, he turned the horse toward the house on Barton Street, sorry he had gone to the social.

The wind was cool and dry against his skin. Seeing Leslie with a man who could offer her all the things she needed and deserved had forced him to face some hard truths about himself and her. She was strong, fiercely loyal to the man of her choice, and accustomed to life's better offerings. She was not a woman who would settle for a man living under a cloud, even if she were physically attracted to him. Bright, vibrant, passionate, she could and would walk in the sunshine.

The horse snorted. The lighter outline of the Kincaids' stable loomed before him. He stabled the animal, unsaddled him, and did the chores he hated doing in the rotten mood he was in. After he changed clothes he would walk to the offices of the Texas and Pacific and continue the task of going through the books, in hopes of finding some clue.

There was a light in the library—a bright yellow line beneath the door, shining into the hallway. He opened the door slowly. Trinket and the blue-eyed girl whose interruption had infuriated Leslie were sitting on the sofa, smiling at him as if he should have been expecting them.

Scowling, he pulled his coat off and tossed it over a chair. Blond Trinket was standing in front of the fire that Yoshio, the Kincaids' houseboy, had laid. Ward walked to the buffet along the wall and poured himself a drink. He tossed it down, felt the hot jolt of the whiskey, but beyond that—nothing. The mood that had started when Leslie turned him down for Summers was still in him. "Ladies." He inclined his head. "What's going on here?"

"We wanted to see you," Sandra said.

Ward had visions of a posse breaking down the door to rescue the two of them and shook his head. "See me in the daytime. Are you crazy?"

Sandra stood up and walked toward him. "We wanted to be with you."

Normally he would have appreciated all the trouble they had probably gone to so they could come here to surprise him. "Does your father know where you are?" he demanded.

"We sneaked out. Please, Ward, don't be angry. I need you tonight," she said, stepping against him. "I was miserable at the dance. You didn't pay any attention to me." She slipped her arms around his neck and buried her face against his chest. "Ward, darling, I belong to you. Please let me stay."

Ward glanced at the other girl, and she shrugged and looked embarrassed, not sure what part she was supposed to play. He disengaged himself and walked back to the sideboard, smelled the decanters, and then poured himself another drink, stalling for time. He tossed down half of it, enjoying the heat that spread out inside him. "Do either of you want a drink?"

"No." There was something in the way she said it that brought his head around. Sandra had wiggled out of her gown and stepped away from it, leaving it in a heap behind her. She looked like a sleepwalker, and the other girl, instead of looking shocked because her friend was naked except for her jewelry, looked equally dazed. She was barely breathing. He had the wild impulse to walk out of that house and never return. How had she managed to undress so fast? What happened to the usual accouterments that women wore?

She slipped into his arms, and his impulse to flee vanished. Warm body with the feel and smell of female always worked. His body knew what to do—even when his head was completely confused. She lifted her lips and dragged his head down to meet them, and the dark knowledge of the body took over.

That's the way Denton found them: Ward still in his black suit, Sandra McCormick naked and breathless in his arms. A beautiful dark-haired girl on the sofa watching them. Denton stopped in the doorway, his mouth gaping like a catfish.

Dusty Denton, born Robert Buckmeister Denton, had been on this wild frontier for seven years, almost as long as Ward. He knew that in the Territories the standards of morality had relaxed to a remarkable degree, but there were limits, and these looked like daughters of respectable residents. He had seen the females who weren't. He also knew that in any group of people, females included, there would be a certain percentage who did not obey the rules—even when they were from good families and knew them all by heart. He'd met his share of women like that. It had never mattered whether they were from rich families or poor. Morals didn't seem to understand class boundaries.

In large eastern cities the netherworld of the criminal elements who lived off the scraps of society were tucked away in distant parts of the city. Nice women were not exposed to that sort of thing. Here, saloons, dance halls, churches, and brothels existed side by side—each influencing the other. Sharp lines of demarcation between good and bad got blurred. Cattlemen branded mavericks, gunmen shot men in the streets, prostitutes got married and went to church regularly.

Frontier natives did not have time for lengthy courtships. Men lived and died with surprising suddenness. Alive one second, dead the next. Frontier towns did not breed gentility—in its men or in its women.

He had no guarantees either. He could be dead tomorrow. Or the next day. Kincaid and the governor had carefully explained the risks and rewards. He decided to follow Cantrell's example, whatever the risk.

There was a moment of stunned silence before Ward spoke, his husky voice smooth as velvet in the stillness. "Which one do you want?"

Nobody breathed. The muted ache that had begun when Ward had kissed her spread downward, turning her knees to rubber.

Dusty Denton almost strangled in his attempt to remain as calm as Ward looked. A beautiful naked girl, in a room with two fully clothed men, turned his blood into steam. His voice sounded hoarse. "The blonde."

Sandra turned back to Ward. "Are you serious?" she whispered, her eyes enormous in her face. She was tingling in spite of the sudden fear that turned her heartbeat into a heavy thumping in her chest. She was on fire—all over. She knew by the quiet knowledge in his blue eyes that Ward could tell. Something relaxed in her, secure in the knowledge that she didn't have to pretend with him.

Ward shrugged. "Do you want me to be?"

Something was born in Sandra's eyes, something primitive and vibrantly alive. "Yes," she said softly. "I belong to you. You can give me away if you want to."

Ward leaned down and kissed her, but he could tell she had already transferred her passion to the other man. She turned obediently and walked into the young man's arms.

Denton looked like he might double over with the sudden ache her solemn, wide-eyed compliance caused in him. He shot a look at Ward, who picked up his glass and was draining it. A cry for help, but the girl took his hand. He followed her out of the room.

Ward turned to Blue-Eyed Trinket. Excitement and fear mingled in her eyes. He could see the pulse in her throat. He took her hand. "Come on, I'll take you home."

"No," she said, the sound small and frightened, but defiant as well.

He hesitated. Leslie was in Tim Summers's bed. He had known by the defiant look in her angry green eyes. He might as well enjoy himself. He damned sure wasn't going to become a monk because she rejected him, but even as he said it, a part of him recoiled. He definitely would not become a monk, but he also could not make love to another woman tonight. Not with the pain of Leslie's rejection so fresh.

His grip tightened on the girl's arm.

"Yeah," he said, forcing a grin. "I knew you were teasing."

Frowning, she allowed herself to be led away.

"Where's your coat?" he asked.

"I didn't remember it. We left in sort of a hurry."

Ward took one of Lance Kincaid's out of the closet and put it around her shoulders. "This should keep you warm till I get you safely home."

CHAPTER
THIRTY-TWO

Just before noon on Saturday Tim Summers stopped beside John Loving's desk. Loving stood up quickly.

"Yes, sir?"

Summer's cold black eyes raked over him, making John squirm inside. This last month on the job was the most precarious in his career. His confidence in himself was badly shaken.

"Come into my office," Summers said curtly.

He knew by the tone of Summers's voice that he was in trouble. Loving followed quickly. Summers poured himself a cup of coffee and sat down. John remained standing uncertainly. Summers didn't usually allow him to sit.

"Sit down," Summers said crossly. "I hate having to crane my neck to look at you."

Flushing, John took the seat across from Summers's desk. He resisted the urge to loosen his collar, forced himself to endure the cold stare of his boss, but he couldn't control the reddening of his face.

"I saw that memo you wrote to Jack Frazier telling him to buy from Smith Mercantile instead of Bauer's." There was barely controlled fury in Summers's black eyes. The angry set of his features stunned John Loving.

"But that's what you told me to do," he blurted.

"I don't give a damn! When I tell you to do something, I want you to do it—not write memos about it covering your ass!"

Summers picked up a letter. "Mr. Summers has directed that in the future we purchase all uniforms from . . ." he quoted sarcastically from the memo; then he threw it savagely at Loving. "What the hell are you trying to do—set me up?"

"No, sir," John said miserably.

Summers slammed his fist on his desk. "From now on, I want to see any correspondence you write before anyone else sees it—do you understand that?"

"Yes, sir." John's face was dusky red all the way down to his collar.

"Wenton came to see me this morning. Apparently you are trying to mishandle the feedlot as well."

"I am?" John asked, frowning.

"You are! We make a good part of our income there, but we won't if you keep operating it the way you seem to want to."

"What should I be doing?"

"You should be shipping the big herds first—the herds that are too big to hold in the pens."

"But, sir." John paused, frowning. "I mean, why?"

"Because, dammit," Summers gritted, "we can hold the smaller herds in our feedlot and charge them twenty cents a day for feed per steer. The big herds always stay outside of town anyway until time to ship. We don't have the capacity to handle them, except on a pass-through basis."

"But in Dodge City, when I worked there, we made it a practice to hold all herds four or five days, regardless of size, to prepare them for the trip. It increases their chances of survival, improves their weight for sale, and it was fairer. We shipped them on a 'first-in first-out' basis. . . ." His voice trailed off.

Summers's black eyes were boring into him. "Mr. Loving, we are not here to play Santa Claus. We're supposed to be making money," he said flatly.

"Yes, sir."

"Do I need to repeat these instructions again?"

"No, sir."

"Do you think you can handle this without writing a memo?"

"Yes, sir."

"Good. Do you know Simon Beasley?"

Loving flushed. Summers knew he did. Everyone knew Beasley. "Yes, sir. He's the buyer for Consolidated Can Company."

Summers nodded. "That's right. Any herd he owns can be shipped immediately—no waiting."

John swallowed. He knew better than to ask why. If Summers wanted to tell him, he would, but apparently his eyes gave him away.

"Why?" Summers asked for him. "Because Mr. Kincaid relies on me to see that the right people are taken care of. I don't expect you to understand local politics, Mr. Loving. Just to do as you are told. Is that clear?"

"Yes, sir. Is that all, sir?"

Summers stood up, giving the signal for Loving to do likewise. "If you have any trouble, you come to me and no one else. Is that understood?"

"Yes, sir."

After taking Sandra home, Ward didn't sleep until almost dawn. The combination of pain over Leslie's rejection and frustration triggered by Sandra's deliberate attempt to arouse him kept him tossing and turning until the sky paled into luminous gray. He slept an hour or so and went for a ride.

The fierce running of the powerful horse, its hooves skimming the levels, skirting the scrub and creosote, leaping narrow gullies, plunging headlong across the desert, brought Ward's muscles into play and helped cool the fires that raged in him. He let the stallion run until a semblance of sanity returned and the sun was growing hot. Then, slowing the heaving bay, he wiped the perspiration off his forehead and turned the big horse back toward Phoenix.

He found Jenn in the music room, singing as she played the elegant Steinway, her voice sultry and golden with a hint of thrush that was as pure as a bell, a mixture of perfect tone and vulnerability that was appealing and provocative. She was alone in the room. He leaned down and kissed her cheek while she smiled serenely and continued to sing to him. In a soft navy-blue morning gown she was so lovely, so shiningly cool, clean, and feminine, that he felt five years old again.

She ended the sonata and stood up. Ward didn't think. He pulled her into his arms and buried his face in her soft hair. For the first time since they were reunited he felt the warm glow of love at full surge. It had worked in him like a tide, slowly and remorselessly building, only now to crest. It was as if he had not really seen her before. Had not connected this woman with the one he'd rejected. He hugged her as if he dared not let her go for fear of losing all that he lost before, losing it again, irrevocably.

His need was like a balm, drawing a barb out of her heart. A dam burst within her as well, releasing the tears she hadn't cried when she could have, tears of joy, love, and long years of heartache streaming down her cheeks, tears held back because to shed them might increase her sense of loss, might somehow cement that loss or precipitate it. "Peter, Peter, Peter, I'm so glad you came back," she whispered, trembling, holding him as tightly as her arms could hold him.

"So am I, Jenn. So am I." His husky whisper was filled with pain as deep and wide as her own. She clung fiercely to him, soaking up the comfort, letting his nearness heal her wounds. She drifted in a daze of happiness. The two people she loved most in the world were becoming friends, and Peter was truly back—the way he had been before all the trouble.

Her voice was strained and husky with emotion. "When you left New York I blamed myself the way you are blaming yourself now. I know how awful it is to lose people you love . . . and to blame yourself for it. Please try to see that you . . . you can't." Muscles in his lean brown jaw bunched, and she reached out to touch his warm cheek, groping for the words to ease his pain. "If you had died instead of Simone, would you want her to blame herself? Or would you want her to make a new life? Find a new love?"

He turned his head away, but she had her answer. "Why are you so forgiving with the ones you love and so hard on yourself?" she whispered. "I love you," she said fiercely. "I know you far better than anyone else does—even you—and I know that you always did the best you could. . . . You're strong, and you love deeply . . . but you're not God. You can't save everyone you love. Someone deliberately killed each of them. If they hadn't accomplished it then, they would have picked another time. You can't stand guard over the ones you love."

His eyes looked bleak, ravaged, before he closed them, clamping his jaws together the way she had seen him do from childhood on up, refusing to cry, trying to reject the comfort she offered him. Jennie put her arms around his waist and hugged him hard, burrowing her cheek into the crook of his neck. He was rigid. She felt the heavy pounding of his heart beneath the firm, warm muscles. "I would give anything to make you realize how special you are," she murmured.

He laughed and it was a bitter sound. "Some men are blessed. Everything they touch turns to gold. Everything I touch dies. . . . I've failed at everything it's possible to fail at. Face it, Jenn. I'm not what you think. I walked in the house one afternoon only minutes after Mother and Father were killed. I led my friend into a trap and got him killed. Simone died because I was in town acting like a goddamned hero. Mama Mendoza, Isabel, Pedro, Grandpapa . . . I almost got Leslie killed. . . . Everything I touch." He sighed, as if too exhausted to continue.

"That's the most outrageous piece of rationalization I've ever heard!" she said, suddenly angry at him. "Did you ever stop to think that in the last eight years thousands of people died without your help? How on earth do you suppose they managed it?"

Ward shrugged, looking sheepish. "Are you implying I could be less than perfect?" he asked, a touch of his usual humor returning.

"You are so stubborn," she whispered, hugging him again. "And so powerful. I'm feeling sorry for those poor misguided souls who think God arranges these things. What should I tell them?"

She felt a shudder ripple through his lean body. He had changed in so many ways. He was broader of shoulder, harder, and more capable . . . and stubborn as ever. His eyes hid more from her. "Well, whatever you do, don't fall in love with Elizabeth Cartright. We can't afford to lose her—no one in Phoenix would ever know what anyone else was doing."

Ward laughed and it was the sound of pain overflowing into mirth. "Maybe I could make a living hiring myself out to fall in love with people's enemies. I could get rid of women, children . . ."

He could joke about it now, but she knew he was protective of women and children. As a child he was willing to give his most treasured toy to comfort a friend, then stoically take a tongue-lashing from their nanny or their mother for "losing" it. His generosity knew no boundaries. A beggar's pain was as real to him as his own. Others could look through such unpleasantness. Ward could not. Wherever he went he usually arrived home with empty pockets. Now if she was interpreting his morose mood correctly, he was determined to spare Leslie Powers. Jennie decided to appeal to his generosity. "Are you saying that you don't care for Leslie?"

"What? How the hell did she come up?"

"I just want to know. Would you break her heart? What if she loves you?"

"She doesn't, and she won't if left to her own resources." Ward sighed. "I have nothing to offer Leslie Powers. She's a lady, accustomed to a different life. She is horrified by me and my past—and rightly so. I'm horrified by it, but I have to live with it; she doesn't."

"Could you be wrong about that?"

"No."

"How wonderfully omniscient you've become," she said dryly, lifting her eyebrows. She leaned back against the circle of his arms, unwilling to let him go just yet. "Will you have lunch with me?"

Ward chuckled. "You haven't changed a bit, have you? Tears in your eyes and you're still hungry. How much ballet practice do you put in, anyway?"

"Three hours"—Jennie shrugged—"more or less."

"You are incorrigible."

Her laughter was a golden tinkle of notes that warmed him, putting all his devils at rest. Jennie came up on tiptoe to kiss him, and that is the way Leslie found them: Jennifer so soft and lovely, a perfect cameo in profile; Ward so lithe, sturdy, and handsome—and both of them so engrossed in each other that they didn't notice her, frozen and mute in the doorway. She turned to leave, and Jennie saw a movement out of the corner of her eye.

"Leslie, dear, were you looking for me or Ward?" she asked, pleased with herself for remembering not to call him Peter.

Leslie didn't look at them directly; she pretended to be gazing toward the kitchen, looking for something, but Jennie didn't move out of Ward's embrace. They seemed unaware of the picture they presented. Thank goodness Chane hadn't caught them this way, she thought, turning. Aloud she said, "No, I was going out. I just wanted to let you know."

The laughter had gone out of his eyes. Now they were impassive, watchful, cool, where before they had been filled with warmth and probably love. He was wearing a blue linen shirt, open at the throat, and tight-fitting black corduroy pants with a gun strapped to his right thigh. His thick wheat-colored hair was wind-blown, but the medallion-sharp features were disgustingly pleasing to look at.

"Won't you have lunch with us?" Jennie asked.

"No, thank you, Mrs. Kincaid." She gave them her brightest smile, tossing her heavy black mane of curling tresses, and demurred. She didn't consider the polite invitation. She knew instinctively she did not want to come between him and one of his women. "I'm going riding with Debbie. She's probably waiting for me now."

"Have fun. Be careful, dear."

Leslie threw them an insouciant wave. She did not expect to have fun. Her hope was that she was not thoroughly miserable. If she hadn't agreed days ago to go riding with Debbie, she certainly wouldn't consider it today. She had tossed and turned half the night, only to have her sleep, when it finally came, tortured by dreams of Cantrell making love to her. After what she had just seen, she was grateful she hadn't confided in Jennifer about Cantrell.

Debra was in a good mood, lighthearted and gay. They rode to the foothills on the east.

"Are there Indians around here?" Leslie asked.

"Probably a few strays, but they're harmless. The majority of them are on reservations. I suppose there could be danger if a band of renegades left the reservation and decided to make trouble. My father says that doesn't happen anymore."

The air was crisp, clean, and redolent with the odor of sage. It was a particularly pungent smell that Leslie was slowly learning to love. At first it had been unpleasant.

On top of a hill, with gentle breezes blowing and the warm sun on their shoulders, they ate the lunch Debbie's mother had prepared for them. White clouds sailed overhead like Spanish galleons. The panoramic view Leslie sketched from the mountaintop was breathtaking. The desert sparseness was rugged and wild, stretched out endlessly under a stormy sky without being intimidating, because she could not believe it was real. It was as dreamlike as her response to the knowledge that Cantrell was in love with Jennifer.

"I hate to mention this, Leslie, but I think we'd better start back. I need to be home by three."

Leslie sighed. "As I do."

Back in town, they stopped at the corner of Main and Front

streets to say good-bye. Buggies rattled past; horses snorted and stamped along the streets in front of the stores, which were doing a brisk business. Children let out of school loitered in front of shops and played in the dusty road.

"Will you be at the McCormicks' dinner party and dance tonight?" Debbie asked, stroking her horse's damp neck with a gloved hand.

Leslie nodded, fighting the urge to say she was sick of parties. It was disloyal and ungrateful of her. Jennie had gone to a great deal of trouble to arrange for her friends to give these parties in her honor.

A small surrey, white-fringed and sparkling in the sun, pulled up next to them and stopped. Elizabeth Cartright was cool and lovely in white organdy.

"Hi! You two plotting what you're going to wear?"

"Not exactly," Debbie said, squinting into the sun.

"Everybody will be there. Personally, I wouldn't miss it for the world! I'm dying, absolutely dying, to see who Ward Cantrell brings. I heard the most delicious rumor, and, darlings, if it is true, *if* it is true—" She stressed "if" significantly, leaning forward and looking both ways as if she feared being overheard. "And mind you," she continued, "I'm not saying it is, because *frankly*, it would be insanity for a certain young matron we all know, absolute insanity!" She ended breathlessly.

Debbie looked at Leslie, her brown eyes exaggeratedly wide and amused. "Heavens!" she said innocently. "Who could he *possibly* bring? . . ."

"It will rock this little desert dump back on its heels," Elizabeth said knowingly.

Leslie stifled a sarcastic remark. Elizabeth smiled archly and condescendingly, savoring her scandalous secret, her brown eyes fairly dancing with mischief. "You don't know?" she asked. "You really haven't guessed?"

"We haven't the foggiest, for heaven's sake—not the foggiest! So why don't you just tell us. Because I have to go. I promised to be home by three," Debbie said irritably.

"You're both blind! I mean really, actually, totally blind! He's going to bring Jennifer Kincaid."

"I don't believe it!" Debbie said vehemently. "Jennifer Kincaid is a lady, and she is in love with her husband! She would never . . ."

"My, are you naive! Married women cheat all the time. I could give you names and dates," Elizabeth said smugly.

"Some do. She wouldn't," Debbie insisted. She turned to Leslie. "You live with them. Have you seen anything that would make you think she would do that?"

"Absolutely not," Leslie lied with matching vehemence.

Elizabeth shrugged and *giddahupp*ed her horse. Leslie said good-bye to Debbie and watched her leave. She waited several seconds before she turned her horse toward Barton Street. She knew which house, because Jennifer had pointed it out to her. Bathed in sunlight, with a cluster of soaring, showy aspens dropping their fiery autumn leaves, the two-story white frame house was homey and charming. A shiny-leafed vine crept and twined its way along the roof line of the porch that ran across the front and around the side of the house.

This house was immaculately maintained, though not of recent origin. It had an air of permanence about it. There was real grass beneath the leaves that scattered in the wind. The vine had grown the length of the long, deep porch.

Seeing this house, so charmingly New England, with its clapboard siding and its steep roof and neatly framed casement windows, she could imagine a crystal epergne with sweets nestling in its dangling cups, a pair of dumbwaiters hoisting vintage wines from a well-stocked cellar, a tearoom awash with sunlight, or sparkling china set ablaze with candleglow. Its solidity bespoke gracious living.

A hundred yards away, a house, framed but not roofed, was surrounded by chaos—the lot strewn with mounds of dirt, stacks of bricks, and racks of lumber.

It was apparent that this was not one of Mr. Kincaid's instant houses. From here the mountains on the east rose with high craggy peaks and wooded slopes.

Maybe Ward wouldn't be there. Her heart was making a terrible racket in her chest. She tied the horse at the hitching post, determined to brazen it out. She owed the Kincaids too much to let her own revulsion stand in her way. But even so, the walk up to the door was a heart-stopping experience.

Her knock was answered by a wiry little Oriental with black-rimmed, tortoiseshell spectacles and sleek black hair parted in the middle.

"Yes, prease?"

"Is . . . Mr. Cantrell in?"

"Yes, miss. Come in, prease." He stepped back, bowing from the waist, then led her into another room to wait.

She was in a library with an enormous seascape on one wall, so realistic she could almost smell the ocean. It drew her irresistibly. It was surprisingly good! The plasticity and atmospheric color were the creation of a supremely gifted artist. It had radiance of light, resonance of tone, dramatic mood, and tremendous imaginative meaning.

She was transfixed, gazing in rapture. She could almost feel the spray on her cheeks. She prayed she really could—maybe the burning would stop. It was foolish to feel flushed and scared just because of a man she despised.

"Good afternoon."

Where had he come from so silently and quickly? She turned abruptly, swallowing, trying to arm herself.

"Hello."

A small pulse started in his temple. She was wearing the black and white riding habit she'd had on when she stopped at the door to bid Jenn good-bye before her ride. The smooth velvet was almost as black as the wind-blown tresses that fell to her waist. She was lovelier than ever. Her cheeks were flushed with warm color, and her hair was a fog of wispy curls framing her forehead and ears. Her skin glowed with the exertion of her ride.

"Can I get you something to drink? Tea? Anything?"

"No, thank you," she said, stalling. "Do you know the title or the painter of this?"

"That's very good, isn't it? It's by Washington Allston. According to Yoshio, he painted it for the Kincaids when Chantry the First was a sea captain. The story is that dear departed Chantry saved Allston's life. It's called *The Rising of a Thunderstorm at Sea*. You paint, don't you?"

"My mother acquired a rather formidable reputation. I hope to follow in her footsteps."

"What genre?" He didn't realize he had said something very untrain-robberish until he saw her eyebrows quirk up.

"What genre!" she repeated, realizing she had not adjusted to all the information she had about him. Yesterday Jennie had mentioned that before he left New York he had been a stockbroker. Somehow, thinking of him as growing up in New York, going to school with Jennie's brother, and working on Wall Street was unsettling, but she answered him. "She taught naturalism, a little luminism, but I'm starting to lean toward impressionism. It's all the rage in Europe. Unfortunately, America is still so colonial. It will be ages before the schools here teach it.''

An awkward silence ensued. Since she didn't know how to begin, she glanced around nervously, saw they were alone, and blurted it out.

"I came here to ask you to . . . because I . . . I want you to give up your relationship with Mrs. Kincaid.''

Ward frowned, not sure he had heard her correctly. ''What?''

"Because it's hurting her. People are talking about her and you. This is a small town. It could ruin her. She has a good marriage. She loves her husband. You don't need her. You have more girls than you can keep track of now.'' She stopped. Blood was staining her cheeks. She was breathing hard, completely unstrung, and he just stood there, looking at her with his blue eyes strangely impassive.

"Why do you care?'' he asked, hiding his surprise.

"Because they've been good to me. They're good people. They don't deserve to be gossiped about.''

Ward flinched at the earnestness in her green eyes, the vibrant emerald color of sea foam on a sunny day. He ran his hands through his rumpled hair, smoothing the tawny thatch into some kind of order. He had been sleeping—to make up for working at the T & P office most of the night.

"Your trust is a wonderful thing to have, your ladyship. It makes me yearn to deserve it.''

"Oh! Don't try to act as if you only do despicable things because I suspect you of them. You were doing despicable things long before I met you.''

Anger kindled in his eyes, crackling like tiny white flames in the depths, but Leslie didn't care. "If you care about her, you'll give her up.''

Everything was forgotten now—his desire to spare her, his guilt at the way he had wronged her, everything except the implied insult in her earnest request. He stepped toward her, and part of him knew better than to give in to the sudden fierce urge to hurt her the way she had hurt him, waving her saucy good-bye as she clung to her lover's arm, but another part of him didn't care.

"Why should I give her up? She's a beautiful woman. You saw us together. Did she look like she was trying to escape my clutches?''

Leslie's cheeks paled, and her breath caught in her throat.

"How can you be so callous? She's married . . . with a family.

How can another conquest be as important as that? Besides, she's older than you. Don't you care about anything?''

"She's only three years older, in the prime of life actually. . . . Jenn is a very beautiful woman,'' he growled, enjoying the tension in every line of Leslie Powers's flushed face and slender body. "And in answer to your question, no, I don't care billy hell about anything.''

Trembling, she started past him.

His arm shot out and stopped her in mid-stride. "What's your rush? I thought you wanted to help your friends.''

Her green eyes looked him up and down, flaring with scorn and fury. "No one can talk to you. You are an animal. All you ever think about are your own needs.''

That strange light flared in his eyes, darkening then lightening the blue, from violet to sky-frost, turning them as cold and flat as his husky voice. "Then let's talk about something that interests me,'' he said grimly. On one level he knew he was about to send his life spiraling out of control again, but he didn't care. He would have continued even if he knew that in the next second he would be killed for it.

"Like what?'' she demanded, glaring at the hand around her wrist, impeding her escape and increasing the rapidity of her heartbeat. A small, tingling current moving from his warm flesh to her own made it impossible for her to think or move away.

"Like a trade.''

"What kind of . . . trade?'' she asked, her voice breaking.

"How much of a sacrifice are you willing to make to save your friends from disgrace?'' he asked, his eyes darting from her furious eyes to her heaving breasts. The riding gown was demure and ladylike, but he remembered only too well the provocative tilt and swell of her small, firm white breasts. The memory caused an ache he could not control. He wanted to hurt her, to see the same sort of pain in her wide green eyes he had felt last night. Nothing short of that would satisfy him. She tried to pull away from him, and his fingers tightened around the soft flesh of her upper arm. "Or am I the only one who is supposed to suffer?'' he asked softly, hatefully.

"What do you want?''

"I want you.''

CHAPTER
THIRTY-THREE

"Is this some sort of joke?" she asked, her lips stiff, her heart pounding like a rail setter in her breast.

His lips quirked up at one corner, his tawny eyebrows lifted, and she knew even without the look in his eyes that it was no joke. She couldn't breathe, couldn't think. She felt flushed with heat and fever.

"You want to save your friends, don't you? You already know what a bastard I am. I do whatever is easy, remember?" She thought she saw a flash of bitterness in the cool blue depths before he smiled hatefully, mockingly. "You're as beautiful as Jenn is, in your own way. I'll accept a substitute, if you cooperate"—he paused, watching her intently—"fully."

Leslie swallowed, moistened her dry lips, her eyes darting around the room as if searching for an avenue of escape.

Ward Cantrell watched her intently, coolly, hiding the bitterness he felt.

"What . . . ?" She couldn't bring herself to finish the question. She was too agitated: struck mute by his presence, his incredible demand, and her own surprising response.

"What do I want?" he asked tauntingly, finishing her question for her.

She nodded, unable to do more.

"I want you to be my mistress," he said softly. "My willing mistress."

Oh, God! She was collapsing inside, and it took all the courage, pride, and stubbornness she had to keep him from seeing it. She never should have come here! Ever! Let Jennifer make her own mistakes! Maybe Chane didn't care if she took lovers! Chane had seen Jennifer and Ward dancing together, too. Maybe the Kincaids had a modern marriage. Leslie wanted to flee, to run as far and as fast as she could, but she felt rooted to the spot.

Apparently he wasn't going to give her a chance to flee or respond. His hand came up, lifted her chin, traced the curve of her jaw, her cheek, her temple, scalding her with warmth and that in-

232

definable ache that his touch caused. His fingers slid through her hair, twisting into it, holding her head still, as if he actually believed she was capable of resistance; he leaned forward slowly, his eyes never leaving hers, until his mouth closed over hers and she couldn't tell whether her eyes closed or blindness had been added to insanity.

She felt swept away, free floating, on fire, responding in spite of herself to his terrible, punishing kiss. But why should he want to hurt her? It didn't matter, though. His mouth couldn't hurt her the way his actions did. At least when she was in his arms she could forget his other women, give herself up to weakness and wanting.

Leslie couldn't remember how she got back to the Kincaid residence, up to her room. She fell across the bed and buried her burning face in the pillow.

Ward Cantrell was the worst kind of fiend—murderer, train robber, wrecker of reputations and marriages—and she had agreed to become his mistress to save Jennifer! Shame flushed through her like a stain. She would never be clean again, and the worst part was not that he had demanded that price or even that she had agreed to it. The worst part was that she wanted it. In spite of everything she knew about him—she wanted it!

She couldn't cry. Maybe people who sell their souls to Satan don't cry. That would be too simple. Oh, God! What had she done? One kiss and she had agreed. She could still feel the way his lips burned into her. It was diabolical. All he would have had to do was ask. She would have consummated their bargain on the spot if he had wanted it. Fortunately he didn't have the same lack of control she suffered from. He had kissed her and sent her away. If he behaved himself at the party tonight, she would be expected to receive him graciously. He would tell her where. . . .

"I'll expect complete cooperation, Leslie. Otherwise no deal."

"Do you love Jennifer?" She had seen the shame in him then, and somehow his knowing how wrong his love for Jennie was softened her. There was conflict in his narrowed blue eyes as well before he finally said, "I've loved her for a long time. I'll need your help."

Leslie leaped off her bed and ran to the window, too agitated to lie quietly. The garden and stable area were deserted. Unseen starlings, flickers, and wrens argued in noisy exchange, the bold, dominant cactus wren, with its raucous cries, sounding like the

winner. Nothing moved in that precise, neatly cultivated oasis. A
cat sprawled in a sunny nook, daring the birds to believe his act of
indifference. Sounds of young Chane and Amy playing in some
part of the house mingled with the bark of a dog in the distance.
Youngsters played in the vacant field behind the stable, squealing
in glee and outrage. The sun was moving toward the western horizon. Leslie held on to the railing with hands that were white with
tension, dreading the party that night. She couldn't possibly keep
seeing Tim while she was, even secretly, Ward Cantrell's mistress. She would have to tell Tim that she didn't want to see him
again.

She cursed the fates that had brought her there, only to let her
fall under the spell of a man with no sense of responsibility, no future, no compassion, no morals, only a diabolical touch that left
her too weak to resist him.

Ward had watched Leslie Powers depart, slim, proud, defiant,
and turned away. He had gotten his revenge—she was terrified and
repelled, but she had agreed to be his mistress. If it didn't hurt so
bad, it would be funny.

He poured himself a double and drank it. Not even the burn and
jolt of good whiskey could dispel his bitterness. The one girl he
wanted, he had to blackmail into his bed; the others he could have
just by forgetting to lock a window or a door.

He would tell her after the dinner party that he had no intention
of accepting her noble sacrifice, but she deserved to sweat a little.
He hadn't forgiven her for Summers.

That brought a sardonic smile to his lips. Unfortunately she
didn't need or want his forgiveness. She would love whoever she
wanted to love and do one damn fine job of it, without any blessing
from him.

The McCormicks' invitation was for a formal dinner party. Leslie knew Sandra McCormick only as one of the girls Ward called
Trinket. Seeing the house, like a gingerbread mansion, with
turrets, verandas, gables, and loggias, she thought she had been
transported to the Black Forest. "You would expect to find a
house like this tucked away in some Alpine Village," she murmured to Tim, taking his hands as he helped her disembark from
the phaeton he had rented for the occasion.

They walked quickly up the first concrete walk Leslie had seen in Arizona. The house and grounds were ablaze with light. Uniformed footmen helped occupants from the line of carriages that slowly crunched forward on the gravel concourse leading up to the house. A virtual army of stiff-collared waiters were on hand to assist. Leslie couldn't believe she was still in Arizona. This was like a night at the opera.

Six lavishly set tables were strategically placed amid potted palms and crystal chandeliers. Leslie and Tim were escorted to a table where Elizabeth Cartright chatted with her escort, Winslow Breakenridge. Sandra introduced her gentleman friend as Dusty Denton. They sat next to an empty chair that Sandra was trying desperately to ignore.

No one inquired as to whom it was for—Sandra was as transparent as the diaphanous chiffon wrapper she wore around her slim shoulders. But even agitated, Sandra was lovely, Leslie had to admit. She wore a fashionable, dark brown satin gown that brought out the healthy golden tones of her skin and hair and emphasized her gray eyes, making them look smoky and mysterious.

Leslie wore an elegant black velvet gown that hugged her slender curves and made her feel older. "Leslie, darling," Tim had said as she descended the Kincaids' staircase. "You take my breath away! I can't find words to pay tribute to the way you look tonight—older surely, sophisticated undoubtedly, mysterious, provocative. I could go on and on."

He had taken her hands and smiled down at her. "But what happened to the Leslie of the teasing smile and the sunshine?" She had forced a sunny smile to stop the outpouring of compliments.

"I'm in disguise, Tim! Can't you tell?"

The Kincaids made their entry together, without Cantrell, and Elizabeth looked haughty but undaunted. Cantrell arrived late, and Elizabeth leaned forward and whispered to Marybelle that Jennifer had apparently decided to play it safe. Leslie burned with the urge to tell her off, but she couldn't bring herself to say anything. She felt strangely subdued.

Cantrell looked subdued as well. He accepted Sandra's gush of gratitude silently, nodded to everyone around the table, and sat down. Leslie looked up into his eyes and was not prepared for the jolt of reaction they caused in her. The blood began to pound in her chest and throat, and she felt weak with the tension and fear that had consumed her since her visit to his house. That singular look that he flashed her—a mere quirking of eyebrows and flexing of certain face or eye muscles—communicated volumes. His eyes were filled with tiny glints of recognition that seemed to demand and evoke a response from her. Tonight, for whatever reason, his power and her response were painfully intensified.

Little was expected of her conversationally; the men at the table were engrossed in a discussion precipitated by Winslow, who had said that Prescott, up north, was the most sophisticated town in Arizona.

"What makes you say that?" Tim demanded. "We have a sizeable colony of easterners here in Phoenix. I doubt that you'll find a more sophisticated group than what is seated around this table." He eyed the others with obvious satisfaction. "Denton, where are you from originally?"

"Massachusetts."

"Cantrell, where do you call home?"

"Upstate New York."

"You see," Tim said, "even *they* were exposed to civilization at one point. We are all *émigrés*, so to speak, living on a rude frontier, but doing it in style. For the most part," he said, looking pointedly at Cantrell and Denton.

Winslow chuckled, a superior, condescending sound. "Almost fifty percent of the people in Prescott are hard-core easterners, and wealthy."

"Are you sure about those figures?" Tim demanded.

Winslow nodded, his smile smug. "Are you ready for this? Prescott does not have a single church."

Tim was undaunted. "So they are pagans. That does not necessarily make them sophisticated. If you want to talk blatant paganism, let's talk San Francisco, where houses of ill-repute are considered necessary by the city fathers to insure the safety of their daughters."

Leslie barely listened. She was too painfully aware of Ward's presence across the table from her. She had felt vulnerable and exposed ever since he had kissed her. Now, seeing him, she feared that he had reconsidered and realized that he couldn't give up Jennifer, that maybe he had decided to compromise by being more discreet in public. What was he thinking? Did he find her at all attractive? Or only a nuisance to be dealt with?

Ward was trying not to think. Leslie Powers was by far the loveliest girl there. Even with a cloud hanging over her head she managed to look composed and totally feminine. He had contemplated numerous ways to torture her for her lack of trust, but now he couldn't bring himself to use any of them. A woman willing to sacrifice her own honor to save his sister's was not someone he could torment. Funny he hadn't realized that ahead of time.

He tried to concentrate on Blond Trinket, but that was too much like reading the labels on a row of identical tin cans; there were no surprises. He vowed that as soon as he could get Leslie alone he would tell her he had no intention of taking advantage of her, then leave Phoenix. He was tired of resting and recuperating. He longed for a return to the rougher, simpler life of the open range: canned beans and uncomplicated *señoritas* who did not linger in a man's mind, making him feel dissatisfied and irritable.

Dusty Denton had brought word that Doug Paggett and the rest of the men he had summoned were assembled in Buckeye, and that their scouting the mountains to the north had paid off. They had located pens that could be used to load stolen cattle onto Kincaid's trains. Unfortunately, the books had revealed nothing out of the ordinary. Either the man kept a separate set of T & P's books, or the entire operation was handled without the knowledge of anyone in the main office. That seemed a remote possibility, but no more remote than that Kincaid, who was a good judge of men, could be that wrong about someone working for him.

The party bubbled like champagne all around her, but Leslie felt locked away by her own feelings. She knew Ward had been raised in the East, but she had still expected him to embarrass himself with the complicated array of dishes, glasses, and silver, but he didn't seem aware of the opportunities he missed to humiliate himself. Maybe some people are just born knowing everything they need to survive, she thought.

"What school did you attend, Cantrell?" Tim asked, causing Leslie to jerk alert, completely attentive.

Ward glanced at Dusty, then Leslie and Tim. He smiled, and his eyes came alive with mischief. "Radcliffe," he said.

Dusty Denton, who should have been expecting it, because he alone at the table knew how close that was to the truth, choked on his wine. Dusty and Peter Van Vleet, now passing as Ward Cantrell, had known each other when they were young, dumb, and unable to conceal things from each other. Peter had helped him through biology, and he had stood guard in the cold while Peter stole his first kiss from Dusty's cousin behind the boathouse at Dusty's parents' house. He and Peter were senior students at Harvard University until Peter was caught by a surprise bed check with two naked Radcliffe College students fighting in his bedroom at three o'clock in the morning because they had both climbed in his window on the same night. The two girls were taking turns, and Peter was half-dead from lack of sleep. He had been, until the previous month, a serious student, studying until lights out, falling like a rock into his bed, and sleeping until reveille. Until little Kim, and later her friend, started climbing in his window. If he hadn't been so bursting with the exuberance and sexual energy of youth, he would have known better. He'd been a fool to let it continue, but Dusty, flushing with the memory of his own reaction to Sandra McCormick, knew only too well that a man's automatic defenses didn't work against warm-skinned naked girls who slipped into a man's arms.

Old Elliott, who had just happened to be Harvard's president and the father of one of the girls, got his revenge by expelling Peter four months before graduation. The reason that he gave in the letter to Peter's father, who was a Harvard alumnus and a heavy contributor, was cheating, the most dishonorable type of expulsion any family could suffer. But Peter didn't find out about the trumped-up charge until he was back in New York, and the events of his homecoming rendered it unimportant.

Sandra, who had been thumping Dusty on the back, grabbed the wine bottle from a hovering waiter and offered to fill anyone's glass.

Tim frowned. He couldn't tell if Cantrell was making fun of him for asking or if the man didn't know Radcliffe was a girls' college and was merely trying to impress them by using the name of a prestigious eastern school or if he was subtly reminding them what a ladies' man he was. Tim's expression wavered between delight at such ignorance and incredulity. He could barely control himself. "Ahhh, a serious student!"

Cantrell endeavored to look humble while accepting Tim's sardonic praise.

"Many of us," Tim said, tongue in cheek, "who attended less prestigious schools had some difficulty qualifying. I'm curious. With its being one of the most elite universities in the country, was being accepted at Radcliffe difficult in any way?"

Ward shrugged. "Well . . . yes and no."

Tim waited, controlling the sense of expectant delight.

"Well, you know how thoroughly they examine and scrutinize everything from your bloodline to your family's bank account," Ward drawled.

"Yes, yes . . ." Tim said, egging him on.

"Well, scholastically I was acceptable, financially my family was acceptable, my mother was a Radcliffe alumna. Unfortunately they approved everything except my . . . uh . . . excuse me, ladies . . . gender."

A flush darkened Tim's cheeks as he realized Cantrell had led him on a fool's errand, and he had blithely followed.

Before Tim could reply, Marybelle giggled. "I'll bet if you *were* accepted, you would have been the most sought-after roommate in the dormitory."

"What did you major in?" Sandra asked, joining in.

"Public service," he said, grinning. Eight years before, when he was expelled from Harvard for what he considered bad judgment bordering on stupidity, it hadn't seemed so funny.

Summers refused to be put off. "What kind of work do you plan to do, Cantrell?"

"Whatever comes easy," he said, wondering what Summers was getting at. Everyone in town knew he was working for Kincaid. No one outside of Chane and Jennie knew he was sworn as an Arizona ranger. His cover story had been in the newspaper as well as on half the lips in town.

"Are you still nursing that grudge against Mark Powers and Dallas Younger?" Tim asked, taking a sip of his wine and eyeing Cantrell from beneath hooded eyes.

"Did I have a grudge against them?" Ward asked, alert now that the questioning was showing purpose.

"Didn't you?" Tim paused, looking significantly at Winslow Breakenridge. "I heard Younger knocked you down during the fiesta days' parade. Didn't you try to save Leslie when her horse reared? I was sure someone told me you were talking about killing them both. And with your reputation as a gunfighter I don't imagine you make idle threats, do you?"

Ward chuckled, his eyes going to Leslie. "I have made threats ranging all the way from idle to outrageous—and that just covers today."

The girls laughed their appreciation, and Leslie flushed, remembering the implied threat in their bargain.

"Seriously, though, Cantrell, I did hear that Younger is making threats about meeting you—what do you gunfighters call it?—in a showdown," Tim persisted. "What will you do if he challenges you?"

Ward shrugged. "I'll decide that if it happens. I haven't noticed him looking for me in broad daylight."

"You mean he might try to bushwhack you? Kill you from ambush?"

Sandra frowned at Tim. "Don't be so morbid. This is a party—not a wake. Anyone like another glass of wine? Ward?"

Small talk resumed, and Leslie noticed that Ward neither drank nor ate much.

When they all moved into the grand ballroom to dance to the imported orchestra, she avoided Cantrell. He seemed fully recovered from his gunshot wound, perfectly capable of supporting not only his own weight but also that of the girls who seemed to cling much too tightly and closely when he danced with them. She stood as much as she could and then excused herself.

Unexpectedly, Leslie found herself alone in the elaborately mirrored powder room with Sandra McCormick. The blonde shrugged, as if she too could not imagine how this had happened. They made small talk for a moment, politely, then Sandra faced her purposefully.

"Do you love Tim Summers?" she asked abruptly.

Leslie frowned her displeasure. "I . . ." she began uncomfortably, aware that Sandra was her hostess, and she did not want to be rude to one of the Kincaids' friends.

"Sorry," Sandra said quickly. "You don't have to answer." The look on Leslie's face was ample reply.

Leslie read Sandra's face as well and tried to correct the impression she knew Sandra had gotten. "I like him a lot. I'm not a person who falls hastily into love," she lied.

Sandra laughed. "And Ward Cantrell?" she asked, flushing with pleasure because for a change she had the upper hand in a conversation. Leslie Powers was far more affected than her ladylike exterior seemed to indicate. In sudden sympathy Sandra reached over and patted Leslie's hand.

"You don't have to answer that either. You don't lie well at all. I thought you would." She paused. "You know, I decided days ago that I hated you, but I guess I don't."

"What made you change your mind?"

"I don't know exactly. I guess because you're as confused as I am in some ways. Oh, I didn't mean to insult you or anything."

Sandra meant it. There was something so pitiful about her apology; she truly believed that no one could possibly be as confused as she was. Leslie's heart went out to the other woman. She shrugged. "It's okay. I'm sure I'm just as confused as you, maybe more so," she admitted.

Sandra smiled and it was a real smile, full of warmth. "No one could be that confused."

"Except me," Leslie said, feeling strangely touched.

Sandra swallowed, as if struggling with tears. Her eyes were strangely bright. "We can't both win, can we?"

Leslie sighed. She didn't know if winning would mean being loved by Ward or learning to live free of him, but neither seemed possible at the moment.

"You don't have to answer. I know he doesn't care for me. I just make a fool of myself because I can't help it."

"You've not made a fool of yourself," Leslie protested.

"You haven't seen everything," Sandra said, pain clouding her gray eyes. She lifted her chin as if that would somehow rearm her, then she shrugged. "I didn't mean to say so many . . . revealing things. I hope you will forgive me."

"Of course," Leslie said, meaning it. "That's a lovely locket you're wearing," she said to change the subject. The intricate Chinese dragon design in the center of the unusual gold and enamel locket had caught her eye.

"It was a gift from my aunt. Would you like it?"

"Oh, no!" Leslie said, slightly horrified. "I wouldn't dream of taking it."

Sandra shrugged. "Suit yourself. It means nothing to me. Well, shall we go face the old biddies for a while longer?"

Leslie laughed. "Might as well."

When she told Jennifer about the singular conversation Jennifer smiled her slightly ironic smile. "What did you make of it?"

"I knew not what to make of it."

"That is just as well. With your genial nature you are much too prone to give generous interpretations to everyone's actions. A line from a Henry James play I did once has stuck indelibly in my memory. 'My dearest Emma, do not pretend, with your sweet temper, to understand a bad one, or to lay down rules for it: you must let it go its own way. . . .' And I fear that is what we should do with this. Leave the interpretation to time. Then and only then will we be able to guess at its meaning, if there is one."

Leslie frowned. "Surely you don't think that aimless encounter had some deeper meaning?"

"My dearest Leslie, do not pretend, with your sweet temper, to understand a bad one."

CHAPTER
THIRTY-FOUR

Through the sprawling leaves of a potted palm, Leslie saw Dallas Younger in the spacious entryway, hat in hand, speaking to the McCormicks' butler. He was presentable in a dark frockcoat, but he looked out of place among the elegance and sophistication of the gingerbread mausoleum. She stopped dancing abruptly.

"What's the matter, darling?" Tim asked, his pale, handsome face reflecting his concern for her.

"Dallas Younger. What's he doing here?" she demanded.

Tim craned his neck, peering through the palm leaves.

"Looks like he has business with Mr. McCormick."

Leslie would not be led back into the strains of the music. She watched as Younger talked to McCormick. Soon Sandra joined them, took Younger's hand, teased and cajoled for a few moments, and led him onto the dance floor. Ignoring the looks of the curious, Younger danced as if he purely enjoyed the opportunity. Cantrell, standing beside one of the double doors that led outside, watched, his handsome face impassive.

During dinner he had looked strangely vulnerable, reminding her of the Ward who brought her that one fragile flower. She'd had the feeling, vibrating to his nearness, that she could search him out and find him instantly—even in a dark cave packed wall to wall with men—the way mother bats return unerringly to their young. Maybe his damned arrogant body sent out signals to her.

Now, with his thumbs hooked in his pants pockets, even the slim horizontal shadow under his smooth bottom lip added to the impression of barely contained rebelliousness and cold passion. He was a hellion, a maverick, and he definitely looked the part tonight; even in very correct evening attire he exuded an aura of controlled recklessness that was as much a part of him as his silver-streaked, tawny hair and those insolently sensuous lips.

For all that he did not appear agitated, there was a definite threat in his stance that caused her to shudder. She cast a questioning glance at Tim, wondering if he had somehow known ahead of time that Younger might be dropping in, but, preoccupied by his conversation with Winslow Breakenridge, his face reflected no guile.

Ward searched the room for Leslie, wondering how she was taking Younger's arrival. The urge to confront the man was strong in him, but this was not the place. He was an officer of the law, sworn to maintain order, not destroy it.

Patiently, Ward waited until Younger had relinquished Sandra to a young man he didn't know. Younger made his way back to McCormick's side; Ward walked onto the dance floor and took Sandra out of her partner's arms.

"Ward, well, sir . . . it's about time you deigned to dance with me." Her cheeks were unnaturally flushed, and her eyes were sparkling with excitement.

"Did you invite Younger here?" he asked, swinging her into the rhythm of the waltz.

"He had business with my father. I only invited him to stay. He's very handsome, isn't he? Are you jealous?"

"I realize you're all grown-up now, and you probably don't want any advice from me, but if you're smart, you'll stay away from Younger."

"You are jealous!" she said triumphantly.

"I'm trying to warn you," he said quietly. "I've had some experience with Younger. He plays rough." Her eyes sought out Younger's villainously handsome face, took on that strange glazed look, and he cursed himself for a fool. He had probably only succeeded in making the bastard irresistible to her.

"Look, Trinket, would you trust me in this? Younger will hurt you, possibly kill you. Do you understand what I'm trying to tell you?"

"What?" She frowned at him, her lovely gray eyes clouded with confusion.

"The man is dangerous. He could *kill* you."

A sudden understanding and shame filled her eyes. She seemed to sag in his arms. They were near the open doors to the veranda. He danced her outside.

"Are you all right?" he demanded, setting her down.

In the dim light from the party she began to cry. He sat down beside her and put his arms around her. When her sobs had subsided, she stood up and burrowed into his arms. "I'm sorry," she sniffed. "I didn't mean to cry all over your jacket."

"That's all right."

"Why do I do things like that? And like Dusty? And like what I wanted to do with you?'' she demanded, furious at herself and shamed to the core.

Ward shrugged. "You're looking for love."

She sighed. "That sounds so simple when you say it."

"Finding love is never simple," he said, reaching into his pocket for his handkerchief.

"I'm going to die," she said suddenly. "I know it. I'm going to die in some horrible way and I'll never find anyone to love me."

"That's hogwash."

She shuddered. "No, it's true. I know it in here," she said, touching her stomach. "I'll die and be completely forgotten, as if I never existed. . . ." New tears welled up in her eyes, and Ward sighed, feeling helpless.

"You aren't going to die," he said, groping for some way to handle this. He looked around, wishing there was someone he could turn her over to.

"You'll forget me. Everyone will. They'll go to my funeral and say phony things about what a nice girl I was, because no one ever knew anything about me. You're the only one in the world who even knows me." Sobs bubbled up and shook her slender body. "You'll forget me too. I've always known that I would never live to be twenty."

Ward shook his head. "That's nonsense. You're going to live to be a hundred. This is a hard time for you. But you'll find someone to love."

"Do you have a cigarette?" she demanded.

"Not with me."

She was deeper than he had thought. Of course, she would have to be, since his original impression was that she had all the depth of butcher paper. He felt closer to her suddenly. He had the urge to tell her that Younger had killed a nineteen-year-old girl, but he was no longer completely sure it had been Younger. There could have been another man involved. Some shadowy figure behind both the killings and the rustling. And anything he told Trinket would be all over town. There would be hell to pay, and no way to prove it to anyone's satisfaction.

He felt frustration and a growing sense of his own helplessness. Nothing he could do or say would make a difference to her. She was so hungry for a man of her very own that she would settle for anything, as long as it was exciting and would horrify her father. For a moment, when she was crying, he had felt hope, but he knew by the look in her eyes that neither shame nor tears mattered to her. Only her need mattered. She was a female first, a person second.

"Would you like to dance?" he asked.

She sighed. "I would like a cigarette, but since you don't have that, would you do me a favor?"

"If I can."

"Promise me that you won't forget me."

Jolted by the intensity of her need, he nodded. "I promise." He held out his arms to her, she moved into them, and he swung her into the rhythm of the music. They danced for a moment on the veranda, and then Ward edged them back into the main ballroom. When the dance ended, he left her to search for Leslie.

"Tim took her home. I think Younger's turning up here had something to do with her sudden headache," Winslow said, quirking his heavy black brows.

Tim drove Leslie home and offered to stay with her, but she convinced him that she needed to be alone. He kissed her and left reluctantly. She asked Annette, who was still up, to prepare a bath, and forced herself to try to enjoy it in spite of her jangled nerves.

"Not feeling well, *mademoiselle*?"

"My head hurts frightfully," she lied, sighing.

The bath helped a little. She put on a gown, brushed out her hair, pinned it up because the night had stayed unaccountably warm, and lay like a board on the bed, holding herself half off the mattress with her elbows. Sleep did not come, so she paced in the moonlit room, cursing herself for leaving the social because now she would have to wait until tomorrow to find out if he had started a fight with Younger or gone home with one of his Trinkets or, worse yet, embarrassed Jennifer in some way. He was capable of anything.

She walked to the balcony. The moon was up, silvering the treetops and casting shadows beneath them. A dog or a coyote howled in the distance, and a breeze whipped her gown around her legs. The smell of sage mingled with the fresh garden scents. Cantrell would not come here. She was safe now from any threat he might have posed her if she had stayed at the party. On an impulse, she shrugged out of the nightgown, let it drop, and walked to the full-length mirror next to the french doors that led into her private bathroom. The pale silvery moonlight slanting into the room lighted her breasts and cast shadows beneath them that accentuated the

slenderness of her waist. Liking the fragrance of jasmine her bath
had imparted, she lifted her arms, posing, wondering how her
body compared to the bodies of the women Ward Cantrell had
known. . . . Her in-curving waist was taut, flaring into slender
hips and long, slim, well-shaped thighs. Perhaps her breasts were
too small and her body too skinny . . .

She heard a sound on the balcony and turned in time to see a
shadowy form loom suddenly, filling the doorway. Leslie drew
back, gasping, her heart lurching.

"Christ!" Ward whispered, his husky quiet voice rich with consternation.

She faced him—a sweet, curving ivory wand in the moonlight
that slanted into the room—and he leaned against the door frame,
groaning. "Leslie . . ." He knew he had to tell her he was leaving
town, that he had only come here to release her from their bargain,
but the rapid rise and fall of her small tip-tilted breasts struck to the
core of him.

"I should have known you would make this as difficult as possible," he said grimly, stalking past her to rip the coverlet off the
bed. He wrapped it around her but did not step away. His strong
hands used the fabric like a net to pull her close.

"Difficult? . . ." she repeated dumbly, frowning down at her
naked breasts, left exposed to her view, her mind so befuddled that
even the revealing hardness of her nipples did not faze her. The
heat of his body so near, the warm masculine scent of him, added
to her confusion. He groaned huskily and pulled her close against
him. Without his hands to hold the coverlet between them it fell
away, covering only her back. The rough feel of his clothes against
her sensitive flesh sent a shudder through her slender form. She
was breathing far too fast. Light-headed, she leaned weakly
against him.

"Leslie, dammit." Arms tightened around her trembling body;
one warm hand slid up her arm to tangle in the raven tresses, scattering the pins, fanning the fragrant mass around her shoulders.
The urge to bury her face against the warm, manly crook of his
neck and shoulder was irresistible.

All he had to do was touch her and that hard knot of heavy pain,
coiling like a snake in her belly, brought her hands up of their own
volition to pull his head down. His fingers tightened in her hair,
pulling her head back, and slowly, as if he were trying to stop himself but losing, his mouth closed over hers, and she was lost,

drowning, oblivious to everything except her primitive, undeniable need to couple with this man.

"No . . ." he groaned softly, his breath a feather against her cheek. His fingers encircled her wrist so tightly she cried out.

"Owww! What?"

"Don't do that," he growled, moving her arm back so he could capture both her hands. He dragged in a heavy breath and expelled it. "You have to listen to me," he panted, "because if you don't, all my good intentions are going to dissolve."

"I'm listening," she breathed, taking a fiendish delight in the sure knowledge that having her naked in his arms was more painful for him. Unable to resist the urge to torment him, she squirmed against him, wriggling around so that her hands were behind her, his arms around her again. He groaned, like a man lost. His mouth found hers, at first tentatively, as if he really didn't want to kiss her again, and then hungrily, his hands sliding up her arms to close over her shoulders, as if he didn't dare touch her anywhere else.

Forgetting her desire to torture him, she arched into the lean, hard warmth of him, pressing her body shamelessly against his, aware only of his touch, which satisfied a hunger that had lain dormant in her for too long, but satisfied it only a little. The tasting seemed to feed the hunger, so that it swelled and grew in her, becoming uncontrollable. Trembling, clinging to him, she pulled his head down, wanting his kisses with a fierceness and hunger that seemed bottomless.

"Leslie, love," he groaned. "Please look at me."

Why was he pulling away from her? Why was he talking when he could be kissing her? She buried her face against the hardness of his chest and felt the heavy hammer of his heart, matching her own. She sought his mouth, but he caught her face between his hands.

"You have to listen to me," he panted. His voice was husky and harsh, and his hands, holding her face, were harshly possessive.

"What?" she murmured sulkily.

"I want you, Leslie," he whispered against her face, his breath warm. "I want you more than I've ever wanted any woman, but I can't take you by trickery or deception. I just came here to tell you that I am not romantically interested in Jennifer Kincaid. I never was. I only said that because you made me so damned mad. And to punish you for choosing Summers over me." He paused, panting as if he had run a mile. "I have to go. I'm leaving Phoenix."

"Go?"

He buried his face in her hair. Air escaped from his lungs, making a sound low and filled with pain. His arms tightened around her as if he couldn't bear to let her go. "I just came to tell you so you would understand."

"So go," she crooned insincerely, pulling his head down to continue the kiss he had interrupted.

"Did you understand a word I said?" he demanded, resisting her, holding her arms in a fierce, viselike grip.

"You want to go. So go." She shrugged with perfect feminine wile, her chin lifted, her lovely eyes hooded, mysterious, not willing to let him see the joy that had flooded her that he was not involved with Jennie, that he never had been.

"I *have* to go," he whispered. "I forced you once. I can't do that again, dammit. You have to come to me of your own free will. Do you understand that? I have to know that I didn't trick you into anything."

Flushed with her own power, she laughed softly and reached up on tiptoe to kiss his neck. His hand tightened on her arm, biting into the soft white flesh, and even that pain felt wonderful to her, because she understood the reason for it.

"I'm trying to do something that you will think honorable, dammit," he growled, furious with her.

"I'm not interested in your honor. Just be yourself, Cantrell," she whispered.

"That's what I'm trying to do," he said grimly. "I'll be back in one week. You know where the other Kincaids live? If you want to see me, come to me there . . . or send a message and I will come to you."

"And what if I don't come?" she whispered. "What if I asked you to take me for a ride instead?"

"When?" he scowled.

"Tomorrow . . ."

Saturday. Could he wait one more day to join the men in Buckeye? She held her breath, waiting, until he sighed and said, "Where?"

"I don't know. . . . I just thought that if you wanted to be honorable . . . a ride is a very honorable thing to do."

Tim Summers went back to the dance after he left Leslie at the Kincaids' front door.

"Where's Cantrell?" he asked of Winslow Breakenridge, who was refilling his glass from the enormous silver punchbowl.

"He was with Sandra for a while—renewing their little love affair. Then he disappeared. Where's Leslie?"

"She wasn't feeling well. I took her home. I think Dallas Younger's showing up here upset her."

Winslow laughed. "Or Cantrell's jealousy over Sandra's obvious infatuation with Younger."

"Leslie and I are practically engaged. She has no interest in Cantrell, except as a curio. He's a little different—that's all."

"Bully for you. I personally would worry about any girl he showed an interest in."

"What makes you think he's showing an interest in Leslie?" Tim demanded.

"Love is blind!" he laughed. "Haven't you noticed? He calls all the women Trinket except Jennifer Kincaid and Leslie."

"So?"

Winslow laughed. "A trinket is a pretty bauble of little value. . . ."

Tim searched the dance until he determined that Ward Cantrell was no longer there. He tried to ignore Winslow's taunting remarks, but there were too many things he couldn't forget—like the brooding look in Leslie's eyes whenever she saw the blond outlaw.

He signaled Dallas Younger, and they drifted into a deserted corner where they could speak privately.

"Was Ward Cantrell the man who kidnapped Leslie?"

"Hell yes! You didn't believe that story of hers, did you?" Younger's face turned dark with fury.

"As a matter of fact, I did," Tim said, his face grim. It had never occurred to him that she would lie about that. Knowing that she had changed everything—especially his evaluation of her reaction to Cantrell's presence. It explained why Cantrell had gone to the Kincaids' as soon as he got out of jail, and Leslie's reticence about making a commitment to marry him. She was either stringing him along, hoping to snag Cantrell, or trying to make one of them jealous. Or perhaps she knew that Ward Cantrell was a rich man. Maybe little Leslie was a golddigger.

He pulled Sandra aside and whispered instructions to her, then left the party, barely stopping to thank his host, and drove back to the Kincaid mansion. There was no carriage or horse around, and the house was dark. He stationed himself in a heavy grove of trees where he could watch both entrances, concealed by the shadows of the tall trees that shaded the house from the desert sun. He didn't have long to wait.

Cantrell let himself out the front door and headed, at a brisk walk, back toward Barton Street. Tim didn't bother to follow. He went directly to his own house, took paper and pen in hand and composed two letters, both basically the same, describing Cantrell in detail and telling the sheriffs of Dodge City, Kansas, and Cheyenne, Wyoming, where they could find Ward Cantrell.

He sealed the envelopes and prepared them for posting first thing in the morning. Then he headed toward town, secure in the knowledge that the letters would go out on the seven o'clock train and would reach their destinations within the week. He only had one more small chore. . . .

CHAPTER
THIRTY-FIVE

It was as if the whole of Arizona conspired to produce a perfect day. The sky was a dazzling blue. Large white mountains of clouds scudded quickly overhead without blotting out the crisp sunshine. The wind on Leslie's face was cool, pleasant. Even the horse she rode seemed to have developed a perfect gait. The heavy smell of sage hung in the air like incense. Leslie rode astride her horse in a carefully chosen white blouse and a navy blue riding skirt and bolero, with a fashionable hat to protect her face and arms from the sun. She had long ago shed the coat she was wearing when he called for her, so early that only Mrs. Lillian was there to wave good-bye to them. Was there an undertone of approval in Mrs. Lillian's eagerness to provide them with such a lavish lunch?

Leslie felt freer than she had since coming to this awesome place, no longer intimidated by the mind-boggling size of its deserts and mountains, and strangely accepting of herself and her reasons, still hidden from her, for suggesting this excursion.

Cantrell, riding beside her on Blueberry, was wearing a blue shirt that echoed the blueness of his eyes and complemented the warm teak tones of his skin. He made a lithe, striking figure on the big bay horse, and when he smiled at her, his eyes narrowed with appreciation; it was as if they had become two different people, existing for just this one day.

Ward looked younger, more open. She could almost believe, looking at him, that she'd never known him before. Maybe because he really talked to her. There was no holding back, no falseness between them. Unless this was another kind of falseness. But Leslie didn't want to think about that possibility.

They stopped in a marvelous tree-shrouded canyon with a wide, shallow river running through it. They were surrounded by bright pink volcanic canyon walls soaring a thousand feet over their heads.

Head propped on her right hand, she lay on a blanket spread over soft grass while he unsaddled the horses so they could graze. Upstream, where the river was divided by a sand bar, a white-tailed deer walked tentatively to the bank and lowered its head to drink from the cold, sweet water.

"What is this called?" she asked when he returned to drop down beside her.

"Arivaipa Canyon. In Apache it means 'Little Running Water' because even in August the river doesn't go dry, like everything else."

High above, yellow-blossomed century plants dotted the scrub-covered mountainside. On the edge of a pink cliff streaked with black, a rock formation loomed up, looking like a man with pack ready to step up into the sky.

"The Hohokam used to till this as far as you can see."

"How?"

"Stone hand tools."

"What did they grow? Rocks?"

"Grain, vegetables . . ."

"What happened to them?"

"A number of things. I guess what finally drove them away was a massacre not far from here. Chief Eskiminzin surrendered to the soldiers at Camp Grant, asking that his people be allowed to live peacefully in their old home in the canyon under the soldiers' protection. They agreed; the Indians settled, and they began to cultivate the lands, until the people of Tucson became upset by reports of wildcat Apache raids on defenseless white settlers. Folks from Tucson got up a big party of men, almost a hundred and fifty whites, Mexicans, and Papago Indians, and rode into Arivaipa and wiped out the entire village—men, women, children, old people—all except for a few children they sold as slaves.''

Leslie shuddered. ''Were they punished?''

''No. It raised a storm back east, but the guilty were tried and acquitted by local juries. Guess it showed, more than anything else, that folks were tired of worrying about the Apache.''

''Are we safe here?''

He nodded, smiling at the look of unease that had clouded her lovely face. ''That was sixteen, seventeen years ago. The Indians haven't been much of a threat since the war.''

''You weren't here then, were you?''

''In April of 1870, I was twelve years old. We lived in New York, on Fifth Avenue at Fifty-seventh Street.''

''Tell me about your family.''

''My mother was beautiful, vivacious, ambitious, and infamous by the time she was twenty-two. She was the second generation of American women of society to make the stage a profession. From what I hear she was damned good at it too, though I have to admit I wasn't too wrapped up in her accomplishments. I was—don't be shocked—a little self-centered at that time,'' he confessed, a sardonic smile lighting his lean face. ''I preferred polo, horse-breeding, and horse-racing—anything at all to do with horses.''

Leslie laughed, ''Well, your interest in that area has served you well.''

''Early job training, with prescience.''

They laughed and it was easy, unstrained camaraderie, as if they had called a truce.

''Are you hungry?'' she asked.

''I'm always hungry.'' He grinned. ''Suit yourself.''

But he didn't eat much, while she was famished and showed it by eating two chicken sandwiches, some cheese, a piece of pie, and topping it off with a glass of warm milk that hadn't quite survived the trip. It had been cold when Mrs. Lillian sealed the quart jar that morning.

''Ohhh, that was wonderful,'' she said, sighing.

He leaned against the trunk of a tree and closed his eyes. ''Wake me anytime,'' he said, chuckling.

Leslie rummaged in a bag she brought with her. ''What are you up to now?'' he asked drowsily.

"I'm going to draw you . . . if I can find my charcoal."

"Sort of a busman's holiday, huh?"

"Something like that . . . You don't mind, do you?"

"Not unless it can be used as evidence against me."

She laughed, a golden tinkle of notes; he smiled, and for just a second he was the same man who had picked the flower in the garden and handed it to her with a bold flourish. The breath caught in her throat, and she wondered crazily if she would ever forget that one moment when he revealed himself to her. Was she doomed to spend the rest of her life waiting breathlessly for another glimpse? Part of her was irritated that she could so easily be hooked. In the scheme of things, what possible significance could a fleeting glimpse have when measured against all that she knew about him? But today, with her lying on a soft blanket beneath a spread of gnarled oak limbs, under a crisp cloud-filled sky, with a warm breeze on her face, and a full stomach, with the smell of a picnic hovering around them, it was as if the scales had tipped. Leslie could not fully remember anything beyond this moment.

She sketched quickly, doing a caricature that came out quite well actually. She portrayed him with wickedly narrowed eyes, a wide jaw, an exaggerated pout on his lips, and two guns in his hands. They laughed about it, and she lay back to relax. His hand found hers, and her eyes closed. She floated in her own shade of darkness while his lean fingers played over the palm of her hand, explored her fingers, her thumb, then intertwined fully and became still, so that only the tingle of a small pulse, moving like a current from his skin to hers, was noticeable to her. She was moving into uncharted territory now, a small voice warned her, but it was ignored, drowned out by the more insistent hunger in her body. If only he wouldn't be so tender with her. She could withstand his gruffness and his insolence.

"Tell me about your childhood, Leslie. I have a hard time visualizing you as a child," he said, his voice husky and low, as he surrounded her hand in his two warm ones.

"I was very boring as a child. I was bossy, generous, and I held grudges. Every mother has a favorite story. . . . My mother said that when I was about two years old she told me not to touch any of the things on the low table in the parlor. She said I looked her in the eye and touched each one. She slapped my hand after each defiant touch, and when I was all done, every single item thoroughly touched and me just as thoroughly punished for it, I lost interest in that table and never bothered it again. What would you call that? Principles? Or the lack thereof? I'm not sure.''

Ward laughed. ''I'd call that a well-defined sense of justice. If I ever have another baby . . .'' He stopped with a slight grimace.

Leslie looked at him with a question in her eyes, and he shook his head, a scowl darkening his brow. ''You might just as well tell me. . . . If you don't, I'll imagine something ten times as bad. I promise you that,'' she said softly, reclaiming his hand, since he had let hers go.

He sighed. ''I was married about seven years ago. My wife was expecting a baby.'' Haltingly at first, and then more easily, he told her about the events in Dodge City, everything. She held his hand, using it to prompt him when he faltered, unaware that she did. She had doubted his honesty before, but not this time. She listened, and a layer of resistance peeled away, like bark off a tree.

''So, you were a captain in the army one day and a hunted fugitive the next? That must have been quite an adjustment.'' She was fighting back the urge to fall sobbing into his arms. Part of her needed it. She had listened with much pain and not a little remorse. Her generous nature insisted now that she confess.

''Yeah.''

''I've wronged you, Cantrell. If not publicly, then at least in my own mind. I conjured up all sorts of images of you living a life of sloth, irresponsibility.''

''Perhaps I have.''

''Maybe, but it wasn't your choosing. It's almost like a fairy tale.''

''Fairy tales have happy endings.''

''How did you know that?''

He laughed. ''I went to Harvard, remember. They cover things pretty well. I think they called it English Literature.''

She blushed. ''I never really believed you.'' She paused. ''Tell me. Harvard educations do not come inexpensively. How could you give up a world of privilege and live like a Mexican sheep herder?''

''No choice. You would be surprised what you can do under those circumstances.''

She was remembering her own immersion into his life, the days after he kidnapped her. She nodded. "So you were swooped up in the daily struggle to survive. What did you do at first?"

"Bled a lot," he said ruefully.

"Were you injured?"

"I was feeling sorry for myself."

"How did you decide to become an outlaw, I mean, to rob trains, that sort of thing?"

"I got hungry," he shrugged. "Let's walk," he said, coming to his feet with that lithe grace that characterized all his movements, pulling her up with him.

Above what Cantrell called Arivaipa Canyon there was a bend in the creek. Squat, scrubby trees hugged the far shoreline. In the shadow of the canyon wall, the shallow water glistened royal blue in the afternoon shade, silver in the sunlight. Soft grass grew up to the gravel that lined the creek. The Pinaleno Mountains loomed on the north. She remembered the name from their ride around them earlier.

"Look," he said softly.

She followed his pointing finger and saw a small gray cat padding out to the water about a hundred yards away.

"That's a bobcat. The mother is not far away." He watched it until he saw it rejoin the rest of the litter and then, taking her hand, he led her directly to what he wanted her to see. Things his sharp eyes uncovered while she was otherwise occupied.

He showed her a fox's lair, an eagle's nest, then led her up a steep hill so they could watch the litter of bobkittens at play. When they were back down the hill, she laughed. "That was wonderful. You've had a good life, in spite of everything, haven't you?"

"I won't permit it to be otherwise, Leslie. I'm too selfish to waste my life anymore. I'm not willing to spend it being miserable."

"Me either."

"So what do you see in Summers?"

She shrugged. "Tim's intelligent, very handsome, entertaining, and not very demanding."

"And doesn't turn up on any wanted posters. That's important to you, isn't it? Someone predictable . . . someone you can take charge of, be in control of. . . ."

"I guess so. I lived with my uncle for a couple of months and experienced what it was like not to be in charge, to be out of control of my life. It was intolerable! But why did you say that? You don't know me that well."

"I've seen you take charge too many times not to have noticed."

"Take charge," she cried. "Like when?"

"You don't remember?" he chided. "When I tried to send you off to Flagstaff."

Leslie flushed. "I still don't see how that . . ."

"Sure it does. As soon as you got your bearings, within two days of my scooping you off that road, you were calling the shots."

She grinned, unaccountably proud, but still seeking proof. "Well, you _could_ have misunderstood."

"My foot! I got the distinct impression that you engineered everything, even when I thought I was seducing you, it turned out to be for your benefit."

He was more perceptive than she had thought. Pleased far more than she wanted him to know, she shrugged, unable and strangely unwilling to deny his accusations.

"Younger was closing in on you then, wasn't he?" he asked, his eyes narrowed.

"My uncle wanted me to marry him. Perhaps it did cross my mind that if I were no longer virginal, he might not think me marriage material."

Raucous birds cried overhead, and Ward hooted with delight. "You're one in a thousand. . . . Can't fault your logic. Though I have to admit it piques my vanity a little."

She laughed. "Good!"

"Good? You're a heartless little wench."

"Healthy."

"True. I never cared for any woman who wasn't at least as selfish as I."

"Selfish?"

"Sure. Selfishness is healthy. You've got that well-developed sense of your own worth that's most becoming in a woman."

"How did you reach this conclusion?"

"I can see it all over you. You're too busy with your own interests to prostrate yourself at any man's feet. You paint, you read about painting, you study technique, you tote that little sketch pad with you everywhere you go. You don't really need people all that much, though you are perfectly charming when you're with them.''

"You are far more observant than you appear.''

He laughed. "But then I would have to be, wouldn't I?'' he said, mimicking the time she used that same line to insult his intelligence.

"*Touché.* '' She laughed. "I'm curious. What makes my selfishness so attractive to you?''

"Few men have time to be a woman's whole life.''

"You certainly think of everything, don't you?''

"Not usually.''

"Is this different for you?''

"Did your mother teach you to be so direct?''

"I don't think so. Does it bother you?''

"I've answered questions today no one has dared ask me before.'' He paused. "I've told you things I didn't tell my attorney.''

"Winslow? I can understand that.'' She laughed and mimicked Winslow's stilted speech and mannerisms.

When they stopped laughing, Leslie leaned against the tree they were standing under and looked up at him. Cantrell's eyes darkened.

"So when are you going to take charge and kiss me?'' he challenged.

"What happens if I don't?''

"Then I might risk life and limb to kiss you.''

"I'm not that fierce,'' she whispered.

"That sounds like something Sitting Bull might have said to Custer.''

"Do you feel like Sitting Bull?''

"Custer.''

"Ohhh! Poor thing.'' She sighed. "Forgive me if I don't fully believe you.

"What was the happiest time in your life?'' she asked to change the subject.

"You ask more damn questions . . .''

"Do I?'' she teased. In that second, with his eyes narrowed against the sun and his jaw clenched in mock consternation, he looked every inch the sturdy, capable army captain. Why hadn't she guessed? Perhaps because she knew so little about *real* outlaws? Had she supposed they were all so clean-shaven, so articulate and capable?

Listening to him as he told her about one of the early settlements he'd been to, she could detect the hint of his almost vanished eastern accent. Or had he perfected that El Paso drawl so thoroughly that only the most suspicious listener would catch the almost imperceptible New England twang?

"There was no law there," he said slowly. "No occupation but labor, no government, no taxes, no public debt, no politics, only an old man who kept records in a ledger of births and deaths, performed the marriage ceremonies, baptized the children, and granted the divorces on request."

"Why did you like it so much?"

"It seemed like heaven to me. By the time I got there I had been running so long. . . . They were so innocent, so cut off from civilization that they hadn't even heard of me."

"Why didn't you stay there?"

"Nothing lasts forever."

His voice was quiet and deliberately expressionless, just as it had been when he had told her about Simone and his friend Snake. She had a heavy, smothering pain around her heart. Was it for the pain he had suffered? Or only because the sun striking the smooth, healthy teak of his skin made her want to put her lips against the sensuous smooth swell of his insolent bottom lip?

Of a sudden she took off her wide-brimmed straw hat and threw it into the air with all her strength. It sailed smoothly upward, caught a draft from the mountainside, and flipped over and over, bouncing wildly on an air current, causing her to cry out. "Oh, my hat! My hat!"

He laughed and strained upward with his arms in a futile, enthusiastic way, shaking his head.

She began to run after it, and he followed, laughing at the playful shrieks she uttered unconsciously, bobbing and darting under the diving, soaring hat, talking to the hat as if it were deliberately defying her. Unexpectedly, it came slicing downward, right at her. She dodged and squealed. By the time he reached her side she was kneeling, bending forward to retrieve the battered straw. Her neck, exposed by the hair falling to one side, gave him a sharp pang. Her breasts swung slightly in her blouse, the slender arching curve of her back was beautiful and strong. She wore no stays.

She looked up into the dark, warm look in his eyes, and her excitement stilled. She stayed on her hands and knees, looking at him, her eyes going tender before her usual defiance reasserted itself. She tossed the hat at him, and he caught it, going down on one knee. She grabbed for it, but seeing her intent, he darted away, keeping it from her. She darted around him in a mad, playful fashion, laughing. She was small and agile, quick as lightning. He pushed her aside, but she came leaping back at him, making up in energy what she lacked in height and weight. She almost fell, then shrieking with delight, she stumbled away from him only to surge back, floundering tumultuously, wild with joy. They dodged and darted, laughing until they were both breathless, then collapsed on the grass.

The hat lay beside them on the matted, tussocky grass, forgotten. "Oh, that was wonderful!" she sighed.

"You half killed me," he groaned.

"Poor thing . . ."

"Look who's gasping for breath."

"Is this a case of the pot calling the kettle black?"

Panting, he rolled over and pinned her loosely, his hands on either side of her breasts. "Dallas Younger couldn't have caught you."

"No," she said, becoming still, knowing what he meant, surprised that he had worried about her situation with Younger at all. He didn't move, but her hands, sliding around his lean waist, felt the slight tremor inside him. His body, usually so like a weapon, hard and implacable against her, relaxed. The heavy feeling in her heart melted. Her blood, roused from the romp and the long walk in the warm sun, surged deep inside her, making her aware of herself as a woman, aware of her power and his.

"I'm glad," he said softly. "I hated the thought of you at his mercy."

His sincerity touched her. Her heart felt crushed in a burning grip, so that she was speechless.

"I should have known you would whip him."

"I didn't humiliate him too badly."

He grinned broadly, his eyes lighted with mischief. "He was lucky to get away with his life."

She laughed, enjoying his obvious pride in her accomplishment, arching backward, her small breasts touching his chest, burning into him like fire-tips.

His lips on her throat, soft and warm, did not surprise

her. His words were tortured, almost inaudible: "Leslie . . . love . . .''

The river rushed noisily beside them. The air was clean and fresh, smelling of pine and resin and river smells. The sun was warm on her skin.

Kissing her softly, shakily, he undressed her as if she were not the same woman he had been intimate with in the past. He was gentle, filled with a queer, blind clumsiness. She too was changed. Naked and with open eyes, she received him solemnly, with a sort of blind submissiveness. Their coupling was like submersion in warm water. She was lost, drowned, then caught up in a tornado and whirled around until her senses reeled. She clung to his sweat-sheened back, as if her life depended upon maintaining some connection with him, his warm skin, his hungry mouth.

They lay locked in fierce possession, clinging together as if unwilling to intrude on the mysterious stillness in their bodies. Did she sleep?

"Did you sleep?" His words sounded like an echo of hers.

"I don't know. Did you?" she whispered.

"No." He rolled off her, bringing her with him so that she lay atop him. "I would have crushed you."

They lay quietly, not talking, not wanting to. She fully understood the pain he could inflict now that she knew she cared for him. She didn't say love, even in her mind, but a small warning, like some muted bell, sounded deep inside her, back near her spine, in darkness, like the chill of a foghorn along the frozen eastern coastline.

As if he sensed the change in her, he kissed her, then disentangled himself and pulled on his pants and boots.

"Wait here." He was back in moments, his hands filled with tiny, yellow flowers that he scattered over her half-dressed body. "You deserve roses, long-stemmed red roses, but this is the best I could do."

"It's wonderful; it couldn't be better." She smiled, gathering the tiny flowers in her hands to breathe their fragrance, her strange mood completely dispelled.

The ride back to Phoenix ended much too soon. Was that because she didn't know if she would ever see him again? Or because riding back was like returning to confusion after experiencing a glimpse of clarity?

Was it the look on Jennie's face when Ward nodded his curt

good-bye to her? The sudden flicker of controlled anguish in her lovely violet eyes before she lowered them and took her husband's protective hand? Had Jennie deliberately waited up for them? Did Mrs. Lillian perhaps say something she shouldn't have? But Jennie didn't look envious or resentful. She seemed genuinely happy to see them.

Watching him ride away from the Kincaid house, into the enveloping darkness of midnight, so tall and lean and straight, so manly and up to his duty, she felt that dim, muted bell in the depths of her sounding again, and she shivered.

CHAPTER
THIRTY-SIX

Yoshio met Ward at the door, his typically Japanese face clouded with worry. "I tly to stop her. I tell her you be gone a rong time, maybe not come back at all, but she insist she have to see you."

"Who?"

"Brond Tlinket," he said, smiling at his own savvy.

Ward grinned at the mispronunciation. "It's okay. I'll see her."

"That for sure," he said firmly, bobbing his head. "You see prenty of her. No choice. That's what I'm tlying to tell you. She in your bed."

"In my bed?"

Yoshio nodded, the tortoiseshell glasses hiding the expression in his dark eyes. "You want Yoshio to wake you in the morning?"

"I'm not staying. As soon as I pack I'll be gone until next Saturday, if all goes well. You get to bed." He knew Yoshio went to church on Sunday mornings. He had confided that he was Buddhist but that he enjoyed the ritual in the other church as long as he didn't listen to the words.

"Ward." Sandra pushed the door open, waiting for him.

"Hi, Trinket."

"I waited and waited for you. I thought you cared about me." She was naked and crying, Kincaid's robe wrapped carelessly around her slender body. "I know you didn't invite me here or anything, but I needed to talk to you." Her long blond hair was loose around her shoulders. Her eyes were red and swollen. She looked so pitiful that he didn't stop to wonder what had unsettled her so. His words were gentle, meant to be consoling.

"You were playing with fire. I had to stop you. Dallas Younger is mean in a way you can't even comprehend. He isn't playing games, Trinket. He plays for keeps."

"Liar!" She jerked away from him, screaming that word from the very depths of her, her teeth bared, her movements violent. "No! You bastard! You rotten bastard! You tricked me! You're just like all the rest! Tricking me! Using me! I know what you're trying to do! You're like my father, like all those sanctimonious self-righteous bastards who try to keep me from finding happiness. You make a thousand rules so that no one can remember them all and then punish a man for nothing." She sobbed angrily for almost a minute before she started again, this time jerking free of the hand he put out to restrain her, to pace back and forth shouting and waving her arms.

"Life is a joke! You know that? All I want, all I ever wanted, is to be happy! To have someone who wants me! Me! Is that so much to ask!?. To have someone of my very own! Someone who wouldn't push me away." She fairly spat the words.

"Hey, I haven't lied to you. . . ." He reached for her, to gentle her the way he would a riled-up horse, and she leaped at him, her nails curved into claws. Pain flashed like fire through his cheek. He slapped her hard, then pinned her arms before she could rake his other cheek with her nails.

"What the hell has gotten into you? Stop this nonsense, dammit, or I'll turn you over my knee. I care about you, or I wouldn't have even bothered with you. I meant what I said. You stay the hell away from Younger. He's a dead man anyway, as soon as I get him on my turf instead of yours," he growled, holding her struggling, naked body.

She changed instantly, like a child who gratefully accepts her punishment and then, relieved of both the guilt of the misdeed and the pain of the scolding, is reborn in innocence. "Do you really care?" she asked, snuggling against his chest, slipping her arms up to cling around his neck. "Can I stay with you? I need you, Ward. Please? I'm sorry about your face. I didn't mean to . . ." New tears flooded her swollen eyes. She sounded like a child. Looked like one with her clenched fists pressed tightly against her trembling lips. He let his guard drop, pulled out his handkerchief to wipe his cheek. Blood stained the whiteness. What the hell had gotten into her?

"I'm a working man, Trinket. I'm leaving town now. I won't be back for at least a week," he said gently, trying not to show the impatience he felt. "Behave yourself, and stay away from Younger."

He disengaged himself, took her small hand in his, and led her to the bed. She followed eagerly until she realized he wanted her to dress herself.

Ignoring her, he strode purposefully around the bedroom he had used, gathering his few personal belongings. Sandra, fully dressed now, watched with baleful resentment. His mind was miles away. He was eager to bring this job to a quick conclusion. He had most of what he needed now—men he trusted at his back. It was just a matter of time and a little luck. All they had to do was catch Younger and some of his men with stolen cattle.

Sandra couldn't read his thoughts, but she didn't need to. She could tell what was important to her—he had forgotten she existed—if he had ever known it. . . . Her face, if he had bothered to look at it, was a mask of betrayed femininity.

He stopped to survey the room, checking to see if he had forgotten anything. He pulled out his handkerchief and wiped at his cheek where blood was trickling.

"I'd like a cigarette," she sniffed, wiping her eyes.

He rolled one for her, lit it, and passed it to her.

"Thanks," she said, inhaling deeply.

He watched, fascinated. He'd rarely ever seen a woman smoke. She did it with perfect ease.

"Did you have something on your mind tonight?"

She shrugged. "I don't know. I just didn't want to be alone. Before, I just pretended with everyone. They all think I'm pretty and stupid. I hate it," she said with sudden vehemence, curling in on herself, like a flower closing. "I just want someone to love me for myself."

Ward reached out and touched Sandra's bowed head. Buoyed by Leslie's magic, he felt magnanimous toward the world, especially the pitiful, lost girls. "That's what we all want, Trinket," he said gently. "It isn't easy to find."

Sandra shook her head. "How can you say that? Every woman in town is in love with *you*."

Ward grinned. "That's not real. I'm a novelty to them—nothing more."

Sandra frowned. "A rugged western bad man who looks smashing in a dinner jacket?"

Ward shrugged. "That's all it is. . . ."

"Do you love Leslie Powers?"

His blue eyes darted away. "I've got nothing to offer a woman," he said grimly, meaning it.

"You do love her," Sandra said knowingly.

"The timing is all wrong." He knew exactly how important timing was. He had seen perfectly planned train robberies turn into disasters because of timing that was off a few seconds one way or the other. Timing was everything.

He had a debt to pay to society that might take years. Leslie wouldn't wait for him while he moldered in some prison.

"That is the dumbest reason I've ever heard of. If you love her, you love her. You'll just have to find some way to overcome the bad timing."

Was this the same girl who had just raked her nails down his left cheek? He put questions about Sandra's strange behavior out of his mind. Just as he should Leslie if he didn't want to risk the sort of pain he had suffered when Simone died.

"You said that Younger might kill me. . . . Was that just to keep me away from him?"

"No, it's true."

"Can you prove it?"

"No, I can't," he said, turning to look at her.

She searched his eyes, saw the level honesty there, and shrugged. "So could you be wrong about him?"

He nodded. "I could be, but I doubt it. Just do me the favor of keeping away from Younger until I know, okay?" he asked.

Her eyes skittered off to one side, unable to meet his. He sighed. "Then try to protect yourself at least. Don't be alone with him."

Her eyes were enormous in her face. "I'm not sure I can promise either, Cantrell."

"Well." He sighed. "At least you're honest."

Sandra smiled shakily. "Surprised me as well," she admitted. Something flickered in her gray eyes. She took off the necklace she wore and put it in his hand. "Keep this."

"Hey, I don't wear necklaces," he protested.

"I know, but I don't want to be forgotten. If you have to keep it, it's always going to be in the way, so I know you won't forget me."

"You've got that right," he said ruefully.

"Will you keep it?"

"You sure ask a lot."

"I need a lot."

"All right," he said grimly.

"Just tell her it's from a friend. She'll understand," she said, reading his mind. Smiling, she picked up her coat and turned to leave.

"I'll walk you home," he said.

"No thanks. I can walk myself. Besides, if my father saw me coming in at this hour with a man, he'd have a conniption."

Ward was tired enough that he wanted to accept the out she had given him, but his conscience wouldn't let him. "I'll walk you as far as your yard. He won't see me."

"You shouldn't be nice to me. I don't deserve it," she said, her gray eyes clouded with something akin to remorse.

The moon had set and the sky was dark except at the horizon, where it was turning murky pink. Stars looked like tiny pinpricks of light overhead, already fading. The wind was chill and dogs howled occasionally. Sandra sneaked in the back way, through the kitchen.

"Coming in sort of late, ain't you?" the cook asked, looking up from where she was lighting the tinder in the wood stove to begin her Sunday baking.

"Don't nag me! I'm sick and tired of everybody in the whole world always telling me what to do!" she snarled viciously but quietly, for fear her father would hear and come down. "If you say one word about this, I'll get you! You hear me, you old witch?"

Mary Freake, a pale woman with a tiny pointed chin, backed away from the venom in her mistress's face, nodding in acquiescence. She needed this job, and she'd heard stories about what happened to people who carried tales to that nice Mr. McCormick. "Yes, ma'am. No offense intended, ma'am."

Sandra didn't stop to acknowledge her victory. The servants weren't people to her—they were battlements hired by her father to protect him from her. They came with the house, like furniture. She slipped up the stairs, thinking her angry thoughts. All she had to do was walk back inside this house and she filled up with rage, as if it leaked into her from the air here. She could feel the rage bubbling in her veins.

She fairly flew up the stairs. There was nothing she could do until tonight. Then she would show her father. She would show all of them!

* * *

Sandra slept all day Sunday, only getting up at teatime to bathe and dress herself for dinner. She could get away with almost anything as long as she was pretty and charming to Daddy's dinner guests.

That brought a bitter smile to her young face. How long had she known that? Forever it seemed, but she'd learned it a little at a time. Beginning when she was very young. Her first conscious memory of her father was when her mother died.

"Daddy, Daddy . . ."

"What is it? What do you want?" Sam McCormick asked impatiently, fighting his way back to the surface. He'd been drowning in his own bitter thoughts, reliving that last hour when the woman he loved, who had promised to love him forever, abandoned him to this grief. "Maramee! Oh, God, Maramee, please don't leave me! Please! I love you! I need you!"

Tears had welled in her gray eyes. "I'm sorry, Sam," she whispered.

"Please don't leave me. . . ." He was crying, great silent sobs that were tearing his insides apart. Her hand was so cool. So cool. How long had he been crying? He looked up suddenly and knew she was gone. His whole world ended that day—that moment. Except that the remnants of their life, their world, wouldn't leave him alone.

"Daddy . . . Daddy . . ."

"Sandra—please—go play."

"I don't want to play, Daddy. I want to help you. What are you drinking? Can I have some?"

"Of course not. You're not old enough. Now run along. Daddy wants to think."

"I'll help you think, Daddy. I'll be good and quiet."

"If you want to be good, go outside and play."

"I'll just sit here beside you, okay, Daddy? I just want to sit with you."

"Margaret! Margaret! Would you come get this child!" he yelled to the housekeeper.

Margaret came rushing in.

"Naughty girl! Why do you keep bothering your poor daddy? Doesn't he have enough problems? I'm sorry, Mr. McCormick. I didn't realize she was bothering you again."

"No, it's okay. You can't watch her every second. Maybe I should get a governess for her."

Margaret had picked her up, and she had cried all the way up to her room. She had cried all afternoon and she didn't even know why she did. But she had slowly learned not to bother her father. She had a whole houseful of women to remind her what a busy, important man he was.

Sandra had learned her role well, so that she had become almost invisible. Tonight she suffered graciously and smilingly through the Sunday dinner and after-dinner rituals and then kissed her father's cheek and asked to be excused.

"Of course, dear. Good night," he said absently, turning back to his guests.

Sandra glided smoothly up the stairs until she was out of sight, then ran the rest of the way. She changed her evening gown for riding clothes—a buff-colored silk blouse and a divided riding skirt. She shrugged into a long, full coat and slipped out the back way without being seen to walk the short distance to Tim Summers' house.

"Sandra!" he said, a quick frown knitting his brow. Wariness and calculation clouded his black eyes as he pulled her inside. "Did anyone see you leave? Are you alone?"

She walked slowly into the middle of the large, sparsely decorated parlor, wondering if she had made a mistake coming here. "No one saw me," she said petulantly.

"Did you see Cantrell?"

"Yes."

"Did you do as I told you?"

"Yes," she said sullenly, feeling the dark ugliness of remorse. Cantrell had tried to be her friend.

"Would you like a drink?" he asked, his voice becoming cordial.

"Yes, please," she said, grateful that he wasn't treating her like a bothersome child. Maybe it would be all right after all.

He poured two drinks and led her to the couch. He sat down beside her and looked her over while she sipped gingerly at the drink. She had changed since that night at the river. Before she had been a pretty, if somewhat vapid, young woman. Now, with her breasts swinging free beneath the thin silk blouse she wore, she was very desirable.

"I don't know you very well," she said softly, flushing at the truth in her words even though he had taken liberties with her that still caused a dull ache of shame when she allowed herself to think about it.

"But you can trust me."

"Can I?"

"Absolutely."

"Why did you tell me to invite Dallas Younger to stay and dance the other night?"

Tim hesitated, watching her eyes and the particularly glazed look when she mentioned Dallas Younger's name. He had expected her to ask why she was told to mark Cantrell's face. Since the party, he'd had an opportunity to reappraise his plan, and it had not come up wanting in any serious respect. Except that if Sandra turned up dead, Cantrell might have an alibi and it would be harder to place the blame on him. So Sandra would disappear. Blame would be more easily placed on Cantrell, with no definite time frame to worry about. A hundred men could be deputized to track down Cantrell and hang him. With claw marks on his face and Sandra's locket in his possession Cantrell wouldn't be able to convince an angry lynch mob of his innocence, would he?

He moved closer to her, his eyes darting from her half-opened mouth to her eyes. "Dallas Younger wants you," he said softly to distract her from any more questions.

"He does?" A heavy pulse started in her throat.

"I told him he didn't have a chance."

She frowned, not understanding. "What?"

"Well, you're in love with Cantrell, aren't you?"

Sandra swallowed miserably, remembering Ward's rejection of her and her own duplicity. She shook her head.

"You're not in love with him?" he asked, looking surprised. "Then there is some hope for Dallas?" Tim lifted Sandra's drink to her lips and watched her obediently sip the straight whiskey he had poured into her glass. "That makes more sense, though, when I think about it, since Cantrell has asked Leslie Powers to marry him. . . ."

"He asked Leslie?"

"You didn't know that?" he lied smoothly.

"I thought Leslie was going to marry you."

Tim sighed, looking hurt. "So did I." He waited for the impact to hit her, then he proceeded. "So we've both been rejected, haven't we?" The rest of his plan was clear now. Even if Sandra were found alive, which was unlikely, she was so stupid and gullible that she would think she *had* run off with Dallas Younger. With their agreement, she wouldn't mention him even if she did realize it was his idea.

Pain was bright and sharp in her smoky gray eyes. She was really quite lovely. He set her drink on the floor, put his arm around her, and pulled her close. "Poor baby," he crooned. "Poor sweet Sandra . . ."

She was completely pliant in his arms. His eyes darting from her glazed eyes to the rapid rise and fall of her rich breasts, he reached out slowly, deliberately, and began unbuttoning her blouse. He slipped his hand inside, cupping the silky, heavy swell of her breast, feeling the warmth and the tumultuous pounding of her heart.

Sandra moaned and turned her face away, shamed by the look in his glittering black eyes but unable to stop him.

His fingers moved slowly, insistently, playing with the tiny bud until it was rock-hard, stroking and teasing the sensitive flesh until she could no longer think coherently.

"Stand up and take your clothes off for me," he whispered against her ear.

Sandra was in an agony of wanting, but there was something about Tim Summers that discomposed her. She had taken off her clothes with men before, but then it had been playful or teasing or because she wanted to. With Tim it had to be because he ordered it, and there was something humiliating in obeying him, in watching the twisted, ugly expression in his eyes while she did so. She still had some pride. . . .

"I think I'd better go," she said weakly.

He didn't answer her in words. He caught her hair at the nape and pulled her head back, forgetting himself, forcing a cry of surprise and pain from her half-opened mouth. "I need you, Sandra," he whispered urgently against her cheek. "We need each other. Don't disappoint me."

"You're hurting me," she whimpered.

Tim relaxed his grip on her hair, reminding himself that he had to go slow until he had her where he wanted her.

"Sorry, but you're so beautiful," he lied softly.

"Why are you doing this to me?" she whined, stalling.

"Because Dallas wants you. And because we are alike, you and I. If you insist on meeting Dallas as he wants you to, I might be willing to help you."

Bemused, Sandra gazed into his eyes, the shame slowly dissipating, being replaced by the needy ache that deadened everything else for her. "Please don't hurt me," she said softly.

He helped her up and walked her into the bedroom, his hands possessive and rough around her waist.

CHAPTER
THIRTY-SEVEN

Sunday morning was quiet around the Kincaid household. The family had eaten a late breakfast. The children were upstairs playing in the nursery.

Chane and Jennifer were relaxing in the library before a cozy fire that had been built to take the early November chill out of the air. He was reading the newspaper while she read a book she had started two days ago. They were lost in an easy and companionable silence. Jennie lay curled up on the sofa with her bare feet pressed against Chane's thigh.

Malcomb came to the end of the sofa, gliding on noiseless feet. "Ahem," he coughed.

Chane scowled. The man moved so silently he could never tell where he might appear next.

"Yes, Malcomb."

"The sheriff is here to see you, Mr. Kincaid."

Jennie gave a low cry and sat up. Malcomb closed the door behind him. "Oh, no, could it be Peter? You don't suppose . . ."

"Your brother is fine. We just saw him last night before he left town," Chane reassured her, folding the paper to put it on the table beneath the electric desk lamp with statuary base—an alabaster water bearer surrounded by crystal teardrops hanging from the lampshade. Chane walked the long way around the sofa so he could touch Jennie's shining crown of sleep-tousled curls. Neither of them had gotten much sleep, but she looked cuddly and fresh-faced in spite of it in a purple velvet dressing robe that complemented her wide purple eyes.

"Something could have happened to him," she said, uncomfortably.

His hands closed around the soft warmth of her upper arms. "You worry too much about him and not enough about me."

"No one has a price on your head," she whispered, and there was fear and pain in her eyes, shimmering there.

"Jennie, love, he's fine. More than likely Tatum wants to tell me that more of my cattle have been rustled."

"You're probably right," she said, sighing and putting her head on his broad chest.

"If you press your body against me like that, neither one of us will ever find out what Sheriff Tatum came here to say to me," he warned, his voice turning sensual.

"Then go! Please, and hurry back," she said.

Chane found the sheriff waiting in the entry hall. "Morning, Sheriff Tatum. What can I do for you?" he asked, steering him into the dining room.

"Morning, Mr. Kincaid. I'm here on business, to see Miss Powers."

Chane was instantly alert for all that it didn't show on the surface. "You're here to see Leslie?"

"Yes, sir. About her uncle. Guess you haven't heard. He was found dead this morning about nine o'clock in the livery stable. Found him behind one of the stalls."

"Horse kick him?"

"No, sir. Throat been cut. Dallas Younger's swearing it was Ward Cantrell. He claims Miss Powers lied about Cantrell not being the one who kidnapped her. He's also saying that Cantrell and Miss Powers are lovers. That maybe Cantrell did this so's he could marry her and own the Powers spread." He paused. "This does leave her full owner now."

"Sheriff, I can assure you Miss Powers would not be a party to murder no matter what she stood to gain by her uncle's death."

Tatum flushed, staring at the delicate pattern in the plush carpet beneath their feet. He didn't have nice things himself, but he could appreciate how the brick red pile complemented the rich shine of the mahogany table and chairs.

He did not feel comfortable arguing with a man of Kincaid's stature, but he did have a job to do. " 'Fraid I'm going to have to talk to her anyway," he said, looking Kincaid in the eye.

Chane knew Tatum was a good man trying to do a difficult job, but he wasn't sure Leslie could face Younger's accusations if she had succumbed to Cantrell's lovemaking. She was level-headed and full of spunk, but she was far too honest.

He made a quick decision. He'd seen Tatum in action on other occasions and hadn't been disappointed in any serious respects. Tatum already knew a little about the circumstances leading up to Cantrell's original release and that he had personally arranged it.

"I guess I'd better level with you, Sheriff. Have a seat. Let me take your jacket. Would you like a cup of coffee?"

"Coffee's fine," he said, taking the chair Chane nodded at. When Malcomb had come and gone with the coffee, Chane told Tatum the truth—that Cantrell was Jennie's brother and a rich man in his own right. Coupled with Tatum's prior knowledge that Cantrell had been sworn as an Arizona ranger, the explanation seemed sufficient.

"I'm a reasonable man, Mr. Kincaid. You know that. I'll look elsewhere for the killer, but frankly, it won't help much, my knowing. There must be a hundred men that Younger's talked to since this morning. Any one of them could take a hankering to shoot Cantrell on sight. Seems to me if you want to protect your brother-in-law, you'd better make an announcement or something."

Chane knew the man was right. They'd considered that. But Ward Cantrell was only wanted in Wyoming for working on the wrong side in a cattle dispute. Peter Van Vleet was wanted in Kansas for almost a dozen counts of murder.

"I know your advice is good, Sheriff, but we can't do that yet. We'll just have to pray he stays out of their way."

The sheriff left, and Chane sent Jennie, armed only with the information that Powers was dead, upstairs to break the news to Leslie. He wanted her prepared and composed before she had to face any questions from anyone. Her open, sunny disposition was prone to bantering, teasing, and blunt truths. She might admit her interest in Cantrell, and that could lead anywhere, depending upon the mood of the mob.

Leslie was stunned by the news. She hadn't known Mark Powers at all three months ago; then she had tried to like him and ended up hating him, but she hadn't wanted him dead. Even hearing that she was full owner of the Powers ranch had no meaning for her.

"I could never live there," she said, frowning at Jennie. "Not as long as Younger is . . ."

Jennie saw the frown and understood. "But you can fire Younger now, disband his riders," she said, patting her hand.

Leslie looked stunned by her new power. "I can, can't I? Then I will, immediately." But she knew she still wouldn't feel safe in that house. There were too many memories, and no assurance that Younger wouldn't come back.

Jennie left Leslie to dress and found Chane in the library, holding the paper absently, as if he had dropped into deep thought. He reached up and patted her hand. "Is she all right, dear?" he asked.

Jennie sighed and sat down beside him on the sofa. "She's fine. But I've been worrying. Do you suppose they could blame Pe— I mean Ward?"

"Don't go looking for trouble," he said gruffly, feeling a moment of guilt that he hadn't told her everything, but he didn't believe things were out of control to the point where he and Ward couldn't handle them. "I'll keep my eye on things. Ward's pretty damned good at taking care of himself, you know."

"I know," she sighed, "but I just couldn't stand it if something happened to him."

Her eyes were darkened with pain and worry. Chane cursed the circumstances that kept her in constant fear. Her love for her brother had been a constant threat to their happiness, and he was feeling that threat more each day, not less. He stood up and pulled her into his arms.

Jennie pressed herself against the length of his hard, masculine body. "I love you so much," she whispered, her silky voice barely more than a whisper. They had made love the night before, and she should have been sated with it, but his clean-smelling masculine scent aroused her again.

His warm hand stroked her face. His thumb teased lightly over her lips and then lifted her chin. His mouth was warm and adhesive against hers, clinging softly.

He meant to kiss her lightly, teasingly, but the spark that was always between them caught fire and leaped into brilliance. He took her there, on the sofa, with only a closed door between them and the rest of the family, and her lovely legs wrapped around him, holding him tight against her. She should have protested, but she wanted him with a fierceness that frightened her.

He brought them much too quickly to fulfillment. When he lifted his dark head from her breasts, her lashes were dreamily closed, her carnation-white skin was flushed pink, and her silver blond hair was fanned out on the sofa. She was so appealing to all his senses—he ached with desire to possess her completely, even now, when the proof of his possession was still between her legs. There were times when he felt mad with desire for her. The only time he possessed her completely was when he was making love to her, and those times were too short, even when they made love most of the night. The rest of the time, Jennie withdrew into her own interests: her music or her ballet or their children. For the most part he appreciated her individuality, but part of him still wanted to possess all of her.

"Treacherous little trifle, aren't you?" he asked huskily, using banter to hide the clutch around his heart. "What shall I tell the servants when they discover us like this? That you couldn't keep your hands off me? That I tried, but you were too strong for me?"

"Liar! I daresay one of us is a mess," she said, becoming aware of the warm moisture between her legs. She didn't relish the thought of explaining to Malcomb what the new stain on the sofa might be.

"I love you, Jennie," he whispered, the teasing banter completely gone. "I love you so much it scares hell out of me. . . ."

Jennie pulled his head down to hers, sighing with the happiness she felt. "I love you, Chane. I have never loved you as freely as I do this minute. It's so wonderful, I feel free to really love you now that Peter is back with us. And safe . . ."

Something must have flickered in Chane's eyes. Alarm showed in her wide violet eyes, and a small frown puckered her usually smooth brow. "He will be safe? You wouldn't lie to me about that, would you?"

"He will be safe," he said with far more certainty than he felt. She sighed and held him close. Chane closed his eyes, listening to the beat of her heart against his ear. There were times during the last eight years when he had actively resented Peter's intrusion into their happiness. Now, by her own words, Jennie admitted that if anything happened to Peter, it would sabotage their happiness. Chane couldn't help but be resentful.

Chiding himself for his selfishness, he sat up, retrieved the nightshirt from the floor, and pressed it between her legs, enjoying the way she dragged in a ragged breath and closed her eyes as if expecting more. "If you are trying to tempt me, it's working," he said softly.

"Oh! You . . . you . . . *man*! You are tempting me!" she said, slipping the gown under her hips.

Thus freed, he put on his robe and stood up. He was feeling a pressure to walk downtown and see just how bad things were.

"Is everything all right?" she demanded.

He cursed the closeness of the bond between them at times like this; it was too hard for him to fool her. He reverted to a ploy that always worked. He turned her over and slapped her on the bottom. "Listen, wench, if you don't stop trying to seduce me, I'm going to call Malcomb in here. Now get dressed." He fled the room before she could recover and figure out his real motives for leaving the house.

Tim rushed to Leslie's side as soon as he heard the news about her uncle. He was loving and solicitous. Common sense dictated that Tim was by far the more suitable choice for a husband. She enjoyed his company; he was a thoughtful person and a good conversationalist. Later that afternoon he came by again to take her riding.

"You need to get out of the house. It'll do you good, darling."

"Thank you, Tim. I feel a bit confused. I don't remember Uncle Mark from my childhood. And we didn't get along very well when I was staying at the ranch."

"Don't feel guilty, darling. Relatives are like historical monuments—it's nice to know they're in place, but they're best enjoyed from a distance."

They rode out in Tim's elegant little surrey, Leslie admiring the scarlet and gold of the early-November landscape. Orchards on either side of the road were alive with color. The afternoon air was cool. Soon winter and snow would mantle those northern mountains.

They passed the last farm, and the landscape grew rougher, the thickets beside the rutted road more dense and impenetrable. Clouds, like fat cottonballs, scudded across the blue sky, threatening to bring rain. Except that she had learned they practically never did. Trees in an orchard on their right were tipped with vibrant red and other bright touches of color, proving that even though it was warm during the day, the nights were cold enough to slow the sap in the trees.

"You look beautiful, Leslie," he said, glancing at her as he held the reins loosely in his capable hands.

"Thank you," she said.

"You look exceptionally lovely for a girl with a headache," he smiled.

"I don't still have a headache," she said, looking at him coolly, not liking his insinuating tone.

"Did you sleep well?" he asked.

"Very well, thank you."

He tilted her chin up and kissed her lightly, ignoring her instinc--tive withdrawal. "It shows, darling."

Leslie thought she must have imagined that momentary change of tone. The rest of the afternoon Tim was charming and entertaining. She enjoyed his anecdotes, laughing frequently. It felt good to be so carefree.

They stopped beside the river to walk. He took her hand. She glanced at him but didn't take her hand back. She was still under the influence of Ward's lovemaking and hadn't decided what role to play with Tim. Could they be friends? Or would he want her to declare her feelings for Cantrell? She almost laughed. She would be glad to do that, if she knew what they were.

Undecided, she did nothing. Tim was possessive and loving, and while he let her know that he loved her and wanted her, he exerted no pressure on her. He was so unlike Ward in that regard. At times Ward's mere presence was an almost unendurable pressure. She felt disloyal riding and chatting with Tim, but Ward hadn't made any commitments to her or asked for any from her. They walked to a grassy knoll under a tree and paused. Tim smiled into her eyes, his pale face handsome. "So here you are again, in the center of a maelstrom."

"What?"

"Your name is on every tongue in town. Surely you knew."

"No, I didn't know. What are they saying about me?"

Tim closed his eyes in remorse. "Kincaid is protecting his womenfolk, isn't he? And I . . . Oh, Jesus!"

"You might just as well tell me. Otherwise I will have you take me home so *they* can tell me."

Tim looked miserable. "They are saying that you and Cantrell are lovers. That he killed your uncle so that the two of you will be full owners of the Lazy P."

The color drained out of Leslie's cheeks. "Do you believe that?"

"Of course not! If I thought for a second that you have a lover who kills everyone who gets in either of your ways, would I be standing here?"

"Why are they trying to blame this on Cantrell?"

"Because your uncle's throat was cut. That is Cantrell's trademark, my love. That's the way he killed a number of Younger's men."

"He's also a gunfighter. Does that mean that every man who is shot was killed by him?"

Tim laughed. "You don't need to convince me, love. I am convinced he's innocent, just as I am equally convinced that he is *not* your lover. I happen to know that Sandra McCormick spent the night with him last night. And I told the sheriff as much this morning when this whole thing got started. God knows I have done all I can to help the man."

Tim took her home at five o'clock, and his kiss was short but ardent.

"I have to go to Tucson on business tomorrow morning, but I'll be back Tuesday, latest. I'll miss you dreadfully, my love. Try to think of me," he said, kissing her again.

Too bad she couldn't respond. It would certainly have simplified her life if she could have felt the tumult of passion when Tim kissed her instead of Ward.

It wasn't Tim's fault that by the time he arrived at any stage in their relationship, Ward Cantrell had already ruined it for him. Comparing Ward to Tim was ludicrous. Like comparing a race horse with a plow horse, a Renoir to a child's drawing, a lying, cheating bastard to a decent and honorable man!

CHAPTER
THIRTY-EIGHT

Monday morning, when John Loving reached the feedlot, the sharp, heavy smell of cattle assailed his nostrils. There was a crowd—actually two distinct crowds—facing one another in grim silence, waiting for him. He was reminded of the adage that the mob has many heads but no brain. All John Loving could see for sure about the men waiting on the edge of the maze of pens and cattle runs was that they were armed to the teeth and potentially explosive.

The feedlot foreman, Will Wenton, was lined up with Simon Beasley, opposing a cattleman by the name of Hank Morrissey. They were standing at the entrance to the loading chutes, below the ramps that climbed up to railroad car level. A train was waiting, chuffing its black smoke into the air. Cattle lowed and bawled.

John walked into that fearsome crowd like Daniel going into the lion's den. There was no way he could win this. The messenger's words still rang in his ears.

"Mr. Loving, you'd better come quick! There's trouble down at the feedlot! Hank Morrissey's been waiting ten days, and he says his steers'd better move out today or else."

"So why don't we accommodate him?" John asked quietly.

"Because Mr. Beasley bought Aaron Wellman's herd, and he wants to ship today."

"Wellman's cattle have been in the feedlot four days, haven't they?" John said. It wasn't really a question. He knew they had. He also knew that Beasley from Consolidated Can Company was a snake, but that Summers had ordered him days ago to allow Beasley to ship his herds on a priority basis.

"All right, I'm on my way." The acres of pens where the cattle were held for fattening before shipment were two blocks south of the office—two long blocks.

When Hank Morrissey saw John Loving, he left the others and came forward. He was about thirty-five, wiry from hard work, with a clean-shaven, weather-beaten face. Beasley and Wenton exchanged smug looks, but they stayed where they were. They knew Loving had been carefully instructed by Summers.

"I've been waiting to ship for ten days, Mr. Loving. I got a hundred head here, and I'm losing money every day they stay here. A couple more days and I'll have to give that herd to Beasley just to stay outta debt!"

John stopped, a light dawning slowly. It cost him something to keep his face impassive, but he managed it.

"Did Beasley make you an offer for your herd?"

"Sure! Two dollars a head cheaper than I can sell them for in Chicago, even with transportation and normal feedlot costs! The bastard!"

"I guess I'd better hear both sides," John said uneasily. They walked to the edge of the two factions. Men grumbled low, threatening remarks, but they moved back to let him pass.

"What's the trouble here?" John asked.

"No trouble. I have a reservation to ship a hundred and fifty steers today and Morrissey is protesting."

"Is that right?" John asked Will Wenton, who was looking belligerently at Morrissey.

"That's right," he said smugly, rocking back on his heels. "Had that reservation a week, he did."

Morrissey swore vehemently, and the men behind him began to mutter threateningly. "That's a damned lie! He couldn't've had a reservation, 'cause he just bought that herd yesterday."

John considered that for a few seconds. "Can you explain that, Mr. Wenton?" he asked reasonably.

Wenton, a man with a protruding stomach that made him look more pregnant than fat, glanced uneasily at Beasley. Simon Beasley, a swarthy heavyset man with an expensive frockcoat and diamond-studded cravat, chewed on a half-eaten unlit cigar and grunted. His small eyes glittered at Loving.

"I can," he said smoothly, mouthing the cigar. "I have a contract to ship a certain amount of beef on certain days of the month. I reserve my boxcars ahead of time like any good businessman would."

"That right?" John asked Wenton.

"Yes," he said smugly.

John turned to Morrissey. "You heard. It's our policy to honor reservations. I'm afraid there's nothing I can do except guarantee you personally that you can ship tomorrow."

Wenton and Beasley exchanged glowering looks.

"You can't do that!" Wenton exclaimed.

"Why not?" John asked, his look reminding Wenton that he was still the boss.

"Why, because you cain't! That ain't your job, for one thing. And Mr. Beasley has those cars reserved for tomorrow, too."

"What is he shipping?"

Morrissey spat angrily into the dirt at Beasley's feet. "He thinks he's shipping my herd! But I'll starve before I'll let him have 'em!"

Beasley motioned his men forward, and John saw the signal and faced Beasley squarely.

"You cause any trouble here, Beasley, and I'll change my mind and see that Mr. Morrissey ships today—not tomorrow," he said firmly.

Beasley's swarthy face took on a dusky red hue. "You're overstepping yourself now, Loving. Your boss ain't gonna like it when he hears about this," he said grimly.

John Loving knew Beasley was right about that. He'd had too many close calls with Summers already. This would cost him his job, but he didn't care. It would be a relief to be rid of it. The Texas and Pacific wasn't run like the rest of Kincaid's operation. Maybe there was something about the political infighting that always accompanied railroads that had brought out a streak of greed. But that wasn't his problem. Not after today or, more particularly, not after Tim Summers got back from Tucson tomorrow night. Morrissey would ship tomorrow if he had to personally load those cows across Wenton's and Beasley's fat carcasses.

"But that will be too late to help you, won't it?" John Loving asked quietly, enjoying the incredulous look that came into both their eyes.

Beasley considered Loving's ultimatum, finally shrugged. He could ship today, see Summers tonight, and ship tomorrow, too. This snot-nosed kid was just trying to placate Morrissey and save his own ass.

"All right," he growled. "We'll do it your way, for the time being."

Morrissey's riders were grumbling to themselves, not sure yet if they were going to back down or not.

"You guarantee we ship tomorrow?" Morrissey demanded.

"You have my word," John said.

Morrissey dragged in a frustrated breath. "All right," he said, signaling to his riders to disband.

Wenton gave the signal to start loading Beasley's herd, then spat into the dirt at John's feet. "You're asking for it, ain't you? Summers ain't going to like this."

"He won't be back until tomorrow night. Shall we take the problem to Mr. Kincaid and let him settle it?"

Wenton paled and lowered his eyes, looking from side to side. "Naw, we'll do it your way. You're the boss," he said grudgingly.

"Where's Morrissey from?"

Wenton's eyes narrowed. "He's from Pleasant Valley."

That figured, John thought. If he were local, he'd know enough to complain to Kincaid personally, but Wenton and Beasley were probably careful not to pull this guff on local ranchers. He had half a mind to go to Kincaid and tell him, but he knew he wouldn't. He had to play it out now.

John Loving was at the feedlot before seven o'clock the next morning. Morrissey and all his hands were there, too—armed to the teeth—but it wasn't necessary. Beasley didn't show his swarthy face.

When all his cattle were loaded, Morrissey relaxed and turned to John, his clear gray eyes level. He stuck out his rough brown hand. John gripped it.

"Thank you, Mr. Loving."

"You're welcome," John said, feeling slightly foolish. A man shouldn't have to go through this kind of rot just to ship a herd, but his hands were tied. He'd spent a bitter night; he finally decided he didn't want to work for Kincaid anymore. He was either crooked or blind, and either one was inexcusable. He'd written out his resignation before he'd gone to work. It was on Summers' desk.

Morrissey frowned. "Are you going to lose your job over this?" he asked, squinting into the sun that was just coming up.

"No. I quit."

"I'm sorry."

"I'm not. I can work other places," he said, meaning it.

"I'm sorry for the railroad—not you. You'll do all right anywhere."

"Thanks."

Hank Morrissey went to the Bull Whiskey Saloon to wash some of the residue of frustration out of his system. He had been in town almost two weeks, so he knew some of the faces by now.

"Howdy, Hank, name your pizun. I'm buying." Sam Shibbel slapped the bar.

"Whiskey, Sam, and thanks."

"Did you get rid of that herd, or should we have the biggest damned cookout this side of Austin?"

"I got rid of it, but it's the last time I'm shipping Texas and Pacific," Hank said grimly.

"They got you there. Ain't another railroad till you get to El Paso."

"How the hell can they get away with this?"

Shibbel shook his head. "I've known Kincaid, the feller that owns most of the T and P, for nigh onto six years, to speak to, and he didn't seem like the type. Shoulda known better. All them high-tone swells is crooked as the day is long. That's how they got rich," he said disgustedly.

Morrissey downed his drink and turned to leave. "Give him my regards—the bastard!"

Shibbel laughed. "We ain't that close."

Riding in the Kincaids' heavily sprung brougham toward the church at the west end of Van Buren Street, she felt weighted down and hot. God! How she missed her Massachusetts. The town of Wellesley was spread on a carpet of green. Trees would be brilliant with autumn, and the wind would be cool with smells of wood smoke and burning leaves.

Sweltering at ten o'clock in the morning, on her way to a funeral, Leslie lifted the black veil and dabbed her perspiring face, hating the formality of mourning clothes. She felt like a hypocrite in the borrowed black gown, with its low bustle and its too-full skirt that ballooned out over her hips. She had left her acceptable mourning gown at home, never guessing she would need it again so soon.

The street they were on was lined with a shallow fringe of two- and three-story buildings. There was a depressing conformity of style in the way the gaunt, squarish buildings each had a door and two windows and a porch roof or awning that jutted out like bulky eyelashes demurely lowered.

The broughham swayed around a corner, and Leslie got a glimpse of the road ahead of them. It was a ribbon of glistening dust-colored sugar flowing between the clapboard false-fronted buildings whose weathered wood was fading even as they passed.

The desert seemed more hospitable than this town. She imagined people staring at the sleek Kincaid carriage, thinking angry, accusing thoughts about her. She unconsciously pulled her veil down, straightening it protectively. She even hated the thought that they had occasion to think about her.

In passing all this hodgepodge of shabby buildings, only the Bricewood West, with its French Second Empire version of the palazzo style, showed a very unPhoenixlike dignity. There was something so incongruous about the way it sat so smugly, as if it knew something about this town that no one else knew. Gazing at it now, as the carriage rocked past, she had the feeling she had never really seen it before. Maybe she hadn't seen any of Phoenix before.

They reached the church a few minutes before ten. Mrs. Kincaid walked with Mrs. Lillian and Annette, while Chane escorted Leslie to the gravesite, where the clean, precise pine box already waited beside the open grave. By now, Leslie knew about making arrangements, having been forced to cope with her mother's death, but she was grateful to Chane for taking care of these for her. He had arranged for the church sexton to dig the grave, the local carpenter to build the box, and the livery stable owner to deliver the body in a horse-drawn glass-sided hearse. On the whole, the arrangements were far more primitive than her mother's, but embalming had not spread to the West on a large-scale basis yet.

She saw faces she recognized: Tim Summers, Winslow Breakenridge, some riders from the Lazy P, Dallas Younger, some cattlemen whose names she did not remember, and a few merchants.

Mr. Kincaid had engaged Reverend Abercrombie from the First Presbyterian Church to officiate at the burial. He had paid a formal call on Leslie the day before. He came forward and greeted her warmly, with ceremonial solicitousness that made her grateful now for the black veil that covered her face.

The words spoken were few, and it was apparent that Reverend Abercrombie had never met Mark Powers. The last time she went to a funeral, it was her mother's; it had been followed closely by another death, her father's. Was this funeral again only a prelude to another disaster?

Tuesday afternoon at four o'clock, only six hours after Mark Powers's funeral, four riders from Happy Slocum's Sleepy S found a stranger hanging from an oak tree on their land. There was a fire nearby and a running iron still hot. They cut the man down and found a note stuffed in his vest pocket. It was a warning to all rustlers to clear out of the territory, that Ward Cantrell was taking over the rustling of cattle in the Salt River Valley and that there wasn't room for competition. It was signed tersely: Cantrell.

Word reached town by five o'clock, and rumors were flying. Cattlemen feared that rustling was being organized like crime had been in large eastern cities for years. Men were coming in singly and in groups to ask the governor to deputize a special posse to hunt Cantrell down. Losses to rustlers had instantaneously doubled, at least in their minds.

Sandra McCormick, missing and presumed kidnapped, only added fuel to the fires that were burning. She had been gone since no telling when; the maid had found her bed unslept in on Monday morning. A thorough search of the town turned up nothing. Sam McCormick was convinced Ward Cantrell had taken her. He announced a reward for her return and the capture of the person or persons who had taken her. The town buzzed with excitement.

Elizabeth Cartright made a special trip to see Leslie on Wednesday while Debbie was visiting. Elizabeth, with her penchant for gossip, could talk of nothing else.

Brightly gowned and stylishly coiffed, the three girls made a striking picture to Chane as he strode past the library, looking for Jennie.

"Well, frankly, darlings," Elizabeth said, smiling knowingly, archly, "I think I was wrong about one thing in this whole little episode."

Debbie shot Leslie a weighted look. When Elizabeth Cartright admitted she'd been wrong about something it was a red-letter day.

"I think Ward's little flirtation with Jennifer was a trick to make Sandra jealous."

Leslie shook her head wearily. Debbie's lips curled into a patient smile, and she glanced at Leslie. No sense trying to stop her. When Elizabeth wanted to say something she would say it. Arguing with her would only give her more opportunities to snipe and speculate.

"Apparently it was Sandra he was after all along. The thing with Jennifer"—she whispered her name, looking at the door guiltily—"was just to upset Sandra, to remind her she had serious competition."

"*Serious compet*—?" Debbie couldn't help herself.

"Of course, darlings, don't you realize? A married woman is *the* most serious competition a single girl can have. Why, heavens, I thought everyone *knew* that! She's older, experienced, and best of all, she's safe. Even if he gets her in trouble, she has a way out—she's already *married*! What could be better than that? All fun—no fear!"

"I'm sure there must be *some* drawback—else why would a man ever chase an unattached female? They do, you know," Leslie reminded her dryly.

"Of course, darlings, of course they do. When they decide to settle down. Maybe, just maybe, Sandra and Ward have eloped—no—no—not likely. More likely he has taken her into the hills to continue their affair without interruption. Can you imagine that? Mistress to the chief of a rustler gang! Think of the *experience* she is having! If it all weren't so *sordid*, I would probably envy her. After all, he is a very *attractive* outlaw."

"Are you disappointed that he didn't take you?" Debbie asked.

"Heavens! What a question! I'm as outraged as anyone over the whole sordid mess! I simply find it fascinating, that's all! It is one of the most exciting things that has happened since Leslie was kidnapped and ra—" Elizabeth clapped her hand over her mouth in horror. "Oh, Leslie, *darling*! *I'm sorry*! I would rather bite my tongue off than remind you of your unfortunate experience!"

"I'm sure you would," Leslie said smoothly. *I would rather you had, too.* Had Ward really carried Sandra off?

Tim came over after dinner with his own ideas about Sandra's abduction.

"I don't think she went with Cantrell."

"You don't?" Somehow that surprised her. She hadn't expected Tim to rush to Cantrell's aid again.

"No, not really. But you saw what an impact he had on her. She changed overnight." He laughed. "I mean *overnight*." He grinned admiringly. "I wouldn't mind having that kind of an impact on a woman."

Leslie stiffened.

"Can you imagine what he does to cause all these girls to fling themselves at him the way they do?" Tim asked, smiling warmly, leaning forward to brush a kiss on her cheek. When his black eyes were lighted with warmth it was hard to tell what might be going on behind them. . . .

Tim lifted her chin, brushed a kiss on her parted lips. "I'm glad *you* aren't one of his Trinkets," he said, his black eyes still narrowed with smile crinkles. Did she only imagine it, or had the sable warmth of a second ago been replaced by cool impervious ebony?

Feigning pique, Leslie lowered long silky lashes and lifted her chin provocatively. "Why, Mr. Summers, I do believe you are beginning to take me for granted. Was that a left-handed compliment or an outright insult?"

Tim grinned and the warmth was back as if she had imagined that tiny flicker of emotion. "I could just be counting my blessings, couldn't I? After all, I didn't lose my girl. It wasn't *you* he carried off."

Smiles were getting harder to come by. This one took its toll. Thank goodness he pulled her close to kiss her. Too bad she couldn't stop thinking. *Respond. Don't think.* But she did.

"Tim, please, people are still dropping in to pay their respects. The funeral was only yesterday."

"I'm sorry, darling," he said contritely. "I forgot you're still in mourning."

Any excuse, even a phony one, was better than nothing. She accepted her reprieve gratefully.

Sandra McCormick waited two days in Powers' fortress for Dallas Younger—two of the longest days of her young life. The Mexican women who still ran the place as if Mark Powers would walk in any moment were cordial and accepting, having become accus-

tomed to Younger's and Powers' women. To them this one was no
different, except younger and fresher-looking. Most of the white
women who came to the ranch were plump, brassy, and laughed
too loudly. This one still had the bloom of youth and the nervousness.

Younger rode in on Tuesday night about ten o'clock. Sandra's
heart began to pound wildly. What would she do if he sent her
away again? She'd been secretly infatuated with him since she had
seen him in town three years before. She had pursued him in the
same fashion she had Ward Cantrell, except she'd only been sixteen then, and Dallas Younger had laughed at her and sent her
away. "No, dice, sweetface. I know a hanging tree when I see
one. Your daddy's too big, and you're too little. Come back when
you're all growed up," he had drawled, his slate gray eyes mock-
ing her.

Well, here she was. Would he think her grown-up enough now?
Had he told Tim he wanted her, or had Tim only told her that so he
could misuse her? She still carried bruises from Tim's lovemaking. He had said terrible things to her and worse things about her.
At the time it had heightened her excitement, but she hadn't been
able to look at him afterward. She had almost refused to go to
Younger after that. What if Ward was right about Dallas?

She could see him at the foot of the steps, hear his men greeting
him, hear his heavy step on the porch, feel the flush of embarrassment. Her bravado, that dazed sort of mindlessness that allowed
her to function, almost failed her completely. What if he laughed
at her and sent her away? After all she had done to get here. She
hadn't left a note for her father, hadn't told anyone. She must have
been insane to let Tim drag her off that way.

The yearning and dreaming over Dallas Younger's dark, handsome, virile image all those years must have made her crazy.
Damn Ward anyway! If he hadn't disappointed her . . .

Younger—tall, broad-shouldered, almost as lean-hipped as
Ward, but harder-looking—stopped just inside the door when he
saw her standing there. His dark brows formed a heavy ledge of
disapproval over his bold eyes and hawklike features. His sensual
lips quirked up at one corner, as if he were chewing a toothpick.

"Hi, Sweetface. What y'all doing here?" he asked gruffly.

Sandra thought her heart was going to stop. It lurched crazily,
then thundered on. She couldn't think of anything to say. "I came
to see if I'm all grown-up," she said thickly, her lips trembling so
she had to bite them.

"You alone?" he asked, looking around suspiciously, his eyes narrowed now, watching her intently.

"I've been here two days, waiting," she said expectantly.

"I thought you were Cantrell's girl," he said harshly. "He bring you here?" He had heard the rumors about Cantrell's kidnapping her. He'd gone to Powers' funeral and, being a practical man, he knew he wouldn't be working for the new owner. He had stopped to pack some things, take any cash Powers had left lying around, and head up into the hills to take over the rustling operation firsthand. Since he couldn't use Powers' backing and the ranch as a base, he expected he'd be moving on soon anyway. Talk in town was that rustling, with Cantrell making his brags and the furor that caused among the honest ranchers, wouldn't be easy work anymore. He and Cedar Longley had talked about that on the trip out.

He stamped his feet as a matter of habit and began to take off his gloves. She looked terrified, but he had to admit that she was a pretty little doll, nervous as hell, but determined. He'd recognized her type years ago. She wanted a big daddy. Well, he thought, smiling, she'd come to the right place, if she was on the level.

He walked into the center of the room, took off his Stetson, his gloves, his coat, and threw them at the sofa.

"Come here," he growled.

She walked into his arms blindly, her blood a deafening roar in her ears. She was on fire even before his harsh mouth found hers. His powerful arms crushed her against his hard chest, and after a few seconds of measuring what he thought of as her sincerity, his hands found her breasts and began teasing and tormenting them while he kissed her.

When he finally lifted his dark head, she was limp and shuddering with ecstasy, her blouse gaping open, pulled down at the shoulders, exposing her full, round, thrusting breasts. He lowered his head and buried his face between the silky globes.

"I reckon you'll do," he growled, picking her up to carry her into his bedroom.

CHAPTER
THIRTY-NINE

Wednesday morning Kincaid saw John Loving in the tobacco store. The store reeked with the roguish smell of fine tawny tobaccos artfully blended. John was leaving as Chane paused, momentarily blocking the narrow doorway.

"John! How are you?" Chane asked, smiling warmly.

Loving looked at him with uncustomary coolness in his intent gray eyes. "Fine, thank you."

"I talked to Jennie about that dinner we discussed; can you come on Saturday? She's looking forward to seeing you. You know how Jennie loves to talk about New York." While it was true he and Jennie had discussed John's coming to dinner, Jennie had not agreed that it should be this Saturday. She was taking Ward's new troubles hard. It was his idea, upon seeing John, that it would do Jennie good to entertain someone who would get her talking about New York, take her out of herself.

A muscle bunched and writhed in Loving's jaw. He couldn't believe Kincaid was so out of touch with what was going on in his own town. "No, sorry," he said politely. "Give my regards to Mrs. Kincaid, though." Loving nodded coolly and stepped around his former employer.

Frowning, Chane watched him walk stiffly away. A cloud of dust at the south end of town caught his eye. It looked like a dozen or so riders in a big hurry. Other men stopped to watch. Within minutes the center of the wide, dusty road was filled with rearing, milling horses and shouting men.

"We've found Cantrell! We've found that bastard, and he's got the girl!"

Chane pulled one of the men aside. "What's happening?"

Red Barnett wiped his sleeve across his face and spat into the dust beside his horse's feet. "Cantrell and about six, seven men are in Buckeye. Beasley is offering a reward for any man who rides in there and takes Cantrell."

"Beasley?" Chane demanded. "What the hell does the Consolidated Can Company care about Cantrell?"

"Don't know," he said, spitting a long arcing stream of tobacco into the dust. "But you add his reward to McCormick's and they've got my full attention," he drawled.

"Did you actually see the girl?"

"No, but Beasley did."

"If he said he saw Cantrell with Sandra McCormick, he's lying!" Chane shouted, trying to be heard over the din. "Cantrell is a sworn officer of the law."

"A lawman! Bullshit!" a man beside him interjected. "That's like leaving a grizzly to guard honey! Stanton fell for that un, he's gettin' senile!"

Others joined in the laughter. Chane spent an hour going from man to man, making sure they knew that Cantrell was a sworn officer of the law and that there would be penalties for interfering with him, but there were too many hot heads, too many men who shouted him down, repeating the cant that had been bandied about ever since Powers's death, Sandra's disappearance, and Cantrell's unfortunate departure.

Jennie and the children were waiting lunch for him. He kissed Jennie and knelt to hug the children. Jennie was distracted. Worry clouded her lovely eyes. He had kept as much from her as he dared.

He was agitated about the events of the morning, but only one seemed acceptable to discuss with Jennie. The coolness and strangeness of that encounter with John Loving was too unusual to ignore. "I ran into John Loving at the tobacco store this morning. He refused my invitation for dinner Saturday."

Jennifer frowned. "He did? Did he seem all right otherwise?" she asked, taking her place at the table.

"No," he said, seating her and then the children.

"Do you suppose things aren't working out for him at the office?"

"I don't know. I haven't been near the place to speak of in weeks. I'm concentrating on the revisions to the blueprints for the hotel we're building in San Diego. You know how I am when I have an opportunity to be creative. I've been so engrossed with that project. . . ."

"Chane, I think you should talk to John. Find out what's wrong."

He scowled. "I guess I'd better."

"Have you heard anything about Ward?"

"Nothing from him directly. Just the usual rumors started by people who don't have anything better to do."

Leslie joined them at that point, and Chane was grateful for the diversion. In another moment, Jennie would have begun to question him.

To Leslie, looking at them around Mrs. Lillian's charmingly set table, all seemed serene. The fragrance of fresh flowers, grown with painstaking care by the Kincaid gardener in a small greenhouse beside the stable, mingled with the rich smells of warm bread, ham, and coffee. China and crystal gleamed. Jennifer was cool and lovely in a crisp yellow batiste morning gown. Her usually warm smile was subdued.

The children greeted Leslie gaily; she hugged them and then sat down.

"Good morning." She smiled, taking her seat at the table. Leslie wore dark blue in deference to her uncle. Chane sat at the head of the table. Jennie had once said laughingly that wherever he sat, that *was* the head of the table. Jennifer sat on his right, Leslie on his left, nontraditional but very "Kincaid" seating arrangments; Amy sat next to her mother, and young Chane next to Leslie.

But before the meal could begin, Malcomb was at the door to the dining room. "Excuse me, sir. Governor Stanton is here to see you."

Chane cursed inwardly at the fresh wave of pain that darkened his wife's eyes as she tried to gauge the seriousness of Stanton's news from the tone of Malcomb's voice. "Relax, love," he said, squeezing her cold hand.

The men went into the library and Jennifer sighed. "Another high-level conference about Ward Cantrell."

"What do you think they will do?" Leslie asked, sipping her coffee, trying not to show her concern.

Eyes haunted, Jennifer shrugged. It would please her tremendously if Leslie would admit she was in love with Peter—Ward, she corrected herself. Then they could suffer together instead of apart, both trying to pretend only an acceptable level of polite concern. She wanted to tell Leslie the truth. Leslie wouldn't tell anyone. But Chane was so adamant, telling her that Ward's life could depend on her silence.

The devil in Jennifer couldn't resist testing Leslie's reactions. "The Cattlemen's Association is threatening to offer a rather sizable reward for Cantrell—dead or alive—I heard." It was only a rumor, and one that Chane had managed to squelch, but it served its purpose. Leslie looked properly stricken in spite of her attempts not to. Leslie trusted Ward's competence to evade capture, but the thought of another reward, dead or alive, added to the other two, frightened her. Jesse James had been shot in the back of the head by his best friend for ten thousand dollars only a few years ago.

A cold heavy lump formed in Leslie's chest. He wouldn't stand a chance. Too many people would want that money. Someone should warn him. He could ride away . . . be safe.

"Chane said he's absolutely sure Ward had nothing to do with either Powers's murder or Sandra's disappearance. I've known Ward a long time. I know he is a man of honor. . . ."

Leslie barely heard her. Jennie didn't know the same Ward Cantrell she knew. He had killed Younger's men, kidnapped and seduced her, and had spent the night with Sandra after spending the day making love to her. The part of her that wanted to believe in him was starved for details that would repudiate the damning evidence against him, but they were not forthcoming.

Chane came into the room before she could reply. Jennifer turned her attention to him. "Was it bad news? Is Ward—?"

"He's fine, as far as we know."

"Were you able to talk him out of the reward?"

"Yes," he said firmly. "We're calling another meeting of the cattlemen tonight. I'm sending a rider out to the ranches to let the owners and operators know. I'm sure Ward's been framed. It's unfortunate that he left town at the same time all hell broke loose. He'll be fine, I'm sure," he said, forcing an optimistic demeanor. "But with murder and kidnap charges being bandied about, even Stanton is nervous, and I vouched for Cantrell."

Jennifer's face drained of color. Things must be more serious than she'd thought. She knew by Chane's look that when he said, "I vouched for Cantrell," he had told Stanton that Ward was her brother and that it was barely enough to sway him.

"At least they are going to hold off until tonight," she said worriedly. "Will that be enough time?"

"Not unless the sheriff finds Powers' killer, or Sandra reappears. The town is hanging mad, and Ed is first and foremost a politician. He's not going to go against public sentiment.

"Word just reached town that Cantrell has taken over the town of Buckeye. They're talking about an alternate plan now—a big posse to ride in there tonight, rescue the townspeople, and bring Cantrell and his men to justice." He had softened that considerably for the women's benefit. The mob he saw, which apparently was still growing, would not bother to bring anyone they caught back to town for a trial.

Wheels began to turn in Leslie's mind. Winslow Breakenridge had assured her that if she needed money, she could draw on her uncle's bank account. He had arranged it with the bank.

After lunch, she rode into town with Chane, who said he was going to the railroad office to talk to Summers about Loving. Chane suggested she stay home and let him take care of her errands for her, but she insisted.

The town was strangely quiet. He was grateful that the streets were cleared of lynch mobs—probably because the eager vigilantes were home preparing for their big ride.

They parted on Van Buren Street.

Leslie went directly to the bank and sought out Harvey Aspen, the president.

"Well, good afternoon, Miss Powers." He smiled. She was, since her uncle's death, one of his biggest depositors. "What can I do for you?"

"Good afternoon. I want to find out how much money I can withdraw from my uncle's . . . my . . . account."

Harvey Aspen's prim banker's face puckered into a frown. He didn't like withdrawals, especially by women, but unfortunately he couldn't prevent them.

"How much would you like to withdraw?" he asked cautiously.

"Ten thousand dollars," she said tentatively. "Is that much available?"

"Haarrumph. Well, uh, yes, there is . . ."

"Good! That should be fine. I would like large bills, please." She smiled, breathing a sigh of relief. Apparently Winslow knew exactly what he was doing.

"It's dangerous to carry that much money in cash."

"I'm not going far," she reassured him smilingly. "I'm going to invest it, so please don't say anything."

"Invest it? Here?"

"Mr. Kincaid is letting me buy some stock."

"Ahh! A wise investment! We can make a simple transfer."

"And spoil my fun? Oh, no, I want to do this personally. Miss Freeman always told us if it was worth doing, it was worth doing personally. In money matters, she said, it is best to handle those very personally."

"Who is Miss Freeman?" he frowned.

"A very dear friend and president of Wellesley College. You

wouldn't know her, I'm afraid. But there was some scandal about her having a love affair with the president of Harvard. Sort of a long-distance, mail-pouch type of affair.''

She chattered incessantly, so that by the time the transaction was finished, he was glad to see her leave even though a good portion of "his money" went with her.

Financing arranged, her next stop was the railroad ticket office. She avoided the central administrative offices, where Tim worked, and studied the ticket schedule.

"May I help you, miss?"

"I'm new in Phoenix," she said, smiling prettily. "How much does it cost to go to Tucson?"

"Five dollars."

"How far is Tucson?"

"A hundred and thirty miles by rail."

"Could I see that on a map?"

"Course you can, ma'am. One thing a railroad ticket office always has is a map," he said proudly, glad he could so easily impress this pretty girl.

He brought the map out, and Leslie spotted Buckeye immediately. It was about twenty miles downriver on the north side of the Gila, the same as Phoenix. That should be easy to find, even for her. She thanked him profusely, and then rushed home to change into riding clothes.

Her uncle had sent the rest of her things before he died. She was surprised, but realized he was probably glad to be rid of them.

The weather was decidedly crisp for Arizona. Perhaps there *would* be a winter clime. In Wellesley, horseback riding had been popular for both sexes. She had all the winter-weight paraphernalia. She chose her favorite riding habit—London smoke-colored cloth with beige cambric jacket, long sleeves, a full skirt over petticoats and riding trousers, to allow her to ride astride. No lady would ever be seen in just the trousers—too unfeminine! Around her neck a brooch secured a rich brown stock that complemented the beige of the jacket. Over her right breast was an embroidered horseshoe and the intials LMP. Dark patent-leather boots with silver spurs, a beige felt tophat trailing a long flowing veil of pale beige, and brown leather gauntlets completed the ensemble. With a warm cashmere coat behind her saddle, full enough to cover her legs in case it got colder before she reached Buckeye, she felt prepared for anything.

She wrote a short note to Jennifer, took a fast horse from the stable, and left without seeing or talking to anyone.

Kincaid's office in the Bricewood West could well have been described as chaste in its furnishings. The major piece of furniture in his office was a conference table twenty feet long, which he used to spread his drawings on. Next in importance was a drafting table, then a large, cluttered desk, and lastly three large, comfortable leather chairs.

At the moment Kincaid and Brian Perry, his chief architect, were in a huddle over drawings they were working on in the center of that long table. A loud knock on the door, which had been left open, brought Kincaid's head up.

Ed Stanton stuck his head in the door and rapped again.

Kincaid straightened, wondering if it was more bad news.

"Come in, Ed. You know Brian here, don't you?"

The three shook hands. "I just stopped by to see if you have a couple of minutes to spare," Stanton said jovially.

Brian Perry gathered up three of his tools from the scatter of papers. "I'll be next door figuring those cubic feet of air space requirements."

"Thanks, Brian."

"I won't keep you long," Stanton said as Kincaid closed the door after Perry and motioned him to a chair.

"No problem. I needed a break, and so did he. Looks serious."

Stanton frowned. "Could be. Could be nothing, but I thought you would want to know. A rancher by the name of Hank Morrissey is talking real bitter about the treatment he got from the Texas and Pacific."

Kincaid let his breath out slowly. He had feared worse—much worse. If he weren't afraid of insulting his young brother-in-law, he would have ridden out himself to bring him in. Tell him to call off the whole thing. This was no time to try to solve something as simple as cattle rustling when the whole countryside was up in arms, ready to shoot him down on sight. It still amazed him how this whole mess had come about. A week ago everything had been fine. Now . . . God only knew how it would all end.

But apparently Cantrell was not what was on Stanton's mind.

"What happened?"

"Seems your people held him up in the feedlot eight or ten days, letting other herds that arrived after him ship out, charging him for feed until he was about bust. Reckon the last straw came when Simon Beasley bought a herd that had only been in the pens four days and shipped 'em right out. There was almost a shootout. Wenton says if he hadn't been doing some tall talking, there would have been bloodshed.''

Chane scowled thoughtfully, his green eyes narrowed. "I guess I'll pay a visit on Summers. Get his side of it. Was that all you heard?''

"Yes. I knew you'd been tied up with the rustlers and your other business interests." He didn't mention that he was also feeling a little guilty about not being as helpful as he could have been regarding Jennifer's brother, but business was business.

"Thanks, Ed. I appreciate it. Did you ride over?''

"Walked. Dr. Matt says I have to *walk* my ulcer, not nurse it with milk and whiskey.''

"Good. I'll walk to the office with you.''

When Tim Summers came back from lunch Kincaid was waiting for him.

"Afternoon, Tim.''

"Good afternoon, Mr. Kincaid!" Tim smiled warmly, his face lighting with pleasure. "What can I do for you?''

"Information.''

"Let's go into my office. Have you time for some coffee?''

Chane waited until they were both seated with their coffee cups before he continued their conversation.

"What's our current policy for getting herds in and out of the feedlot?''

"We've found that we have the best success in shipping steers that have at least four, five days to rest after a drive. Gives them a chance to get back the water they lost on the trail and cuts down on losses by death. Their weight is better, too. Everyone benefits.''

"Do we ever hold up a herd longer than that for any reason?''

Summers frowned, his black eyes filling with indignation. "Not on purpose," he said grimly, "but I had a problem with my new assistant.''

"What kind of problem?''

"Nothing deliberate—I don't think. Mostly just inattention to detail and an inability to follow simple instructions." He paused, looking apologetic. "I had to fire him. He caused a serious problem with a man named Morrissey. There was almost a range war from what I heard," he ended in disgust. "But let me assure you, Mr. Kincaid. I'm not trying to pass the buck. I take full responsi-

bility for my entire staff. I called him in as soon as I got back from
Tucson, as soon as Wenton told me what had happened. I hope this
hasn't embarrassed you too badly. I had a feeling I should have
sent someone else to Tucson, but I like to do the important things
myself. And I knew you felt strongly about hiring a good manager
for the Tucson branch office.''

"You did fine.'' Chane nodded. "We don't keep anyone's cattle over five days?''

"No, sir!'' Tim said crisply. "And that only to increase their
chances of surviving the trip.''

Kincaid stood up. "Good, Tim. Thanks for the coffee.''

"My pleasure, Mr. Kincaid.''

CHAPTER
FORTY

A cold November morning slowly turned into a warm afternoon as
the hooves of Leslie's horse thundered over the dry, hard earth.
She rode parallel to the watercourse, keeping the wide silver-gray
shimmer of the river in sight. Galloping at a comfortable pace, she
admired the tangle of alfalfa that grew along the river banks, so
different from either the ocotillo, cactuses, tumbleweed, or orchards or farms she passed.

She had made her decision precipitously and regretted it at least
a hundred times in the last two hours. She was making a fool of
herself. He would probably take her money and use it to keep his
mistresses! What if she found him with Sandra? *Hello, Ward! Just
rode over with a wedding present for you two—and to let you know
there are six hundred angry men coming here to kill you.* The sight
of Sandra clinging to Ward would probably bring such a hot flush
of rage that she would kill him herself. *Good afternoon, Ward!
Should I rip out your throat first, or would you prefer I mangled
some very vital parts of your arrogant young body, you bastard?*

Buckeye was barely a settlement. There were four buildings,
mostly lean-tos. She didn't see anyone, but there were six horses
standing in the shade of a weathered two-story building. A faded
sign whispered *Hotel.* The paint, when the sign was new, had been

black; now it was hardly darker than the gray wood. A shaggy, long-haired red dog dozed on the porch.

She reined Kincaid's powerful racy Arabian to approach the building with the horses and the dog slowly, realizing afresh how insane she must be. What if he wasn't there and a pack of bandits raped her and stole her money?

Damn! Why did she have to care what happened to him? He hadn't given her any commitments. A day of love, a few tender words, some lingering good-bye kisses, and here she was, making a blessed fool of herself! Why?

Only because she couldn't bear to see Jennie suffer so grievously? Or did part of her still nurture the hope, blind and pitiful as it was, that Tim was wrong about Ward and Sandra?

At some point a woman gets tired of asking herself questions she can't answer. Why shouldn't she come if she wants to? In any event, she was here! She gave herself a good talking to—about cowards dying a thousand deaths—but it didn't help. Her heart was still hammering madly in her chest, and she felt like a foolish child.

Ward and Dusty rode into Buckeye late Sunday morning. The wide dirt road was deserted except for a Mexican woman driving an oxcart away from the small store. She was broad and swarthy, with a flat, unemotional face that reminded Ward of Mama Manuela and revived the empty ache in his chest.

They tethered their horses in front of the only two-story building in the settlement. There were two *vaqueros* lounging at a table just inside the door and one man behind the bar, sleeping, his feet up, his sombrero pulled down, the wide brim reaching all the way to his fat belly. It smelled of cigarette butts and whiskey.

The scrape of their boots on the rough wooden floor stopped the snores and brought the man's hand up to shove the sombrero back, revealing a round face with small deep-set eyes, thick lips, and a heavy mop of stiff black hair. When he saw Ward his eyes came alive. "*Señor*, Ward! Welcome!"

Grinning, Ward exchanged greetings with the beaming man. Dusty watched in silence, not understanding the rapid Spanish.

"It has been a long time!"

"Yes, it has, friend. Too long!" Ward agreed.

"Mama! Come! *Señor* Ward has come!"

A short, smiling woman with a face that glowed with perspiration and pleasure shuffled out of the kitchen, wiping her hands on her apron. "*Señor* Ward!"

They hugged, and the woman clasped his face in her two hands, smiling at him. "You're too skinny. You need some good home cooking. What is Manuela doing? Starving you? Or are you chasing the girls too hard? Is that why you carry these marks on your face, *hombre*?"

At mention of Manuela's name, Ward's smile faded, and he straightened. Carmen Castenada looked from Ward to her husband.

Ward sighed. "Manuela is dead," he said gently.

Quick tears sprang into Carmen's eyes. Ward told them about the Mendozas and what he suspected of Powers' involvement. When he finished, Cruz, who was patting his wife's shoulder, spoke.

"You will stay here. I can get *vaqueros* to ride with you. Powers must not go unpunished for this!"

"We can't stay here. We don't know what to expect from Younger and his gang. They may run—they may come after us. I'm not going to endanger any more people than I have to."

"Then what will you do?" Cruz asked.

"We don't have a plan. Except to get Younger—whatever it takes."

"Make this your headquarters. We have many contacts that will be of use to you, *Señor* Ward."

Ward looked at Dusty. "What do you think about using this as our base?"

"Suits me fine. No one could get near here without our knowing about it."

Ward frowned. He didn't like bringing war to a friend's home, but Cruz was a smart man and a valuable ally.

"We can try it," he said slowly. "If things get hot, we can stay away from here—pull any pursuers off to the north toward the yellow pine country." Dusty agreed.

"Good! It is settled! You, Señor Ward, will sleep in Juanita's room. She is gone to Sonora, married to a wealthy *haciendado*," he said proudly. "Your friend can have the room next to Juanita's."

They ate Mama's excellent rice, beans, tamales, and corn cakes, and Ward caught up on news of the Castanadas and their mutual friends.

When the rest of Ward's men rode into Buckeye, the welcome

they received was vastly different from the one they had gotten the day before. The welcome mat was out.

Doug Paggett, who had accepted this opportunity to earn a pardon, was grinning when he took Ward aside.

"Hey, *compadre*! You should have been here sooner. We got the full treatment yesterday. Cool courtesy and hot chili! I mean *hot*! Today—we're family."

Ward grinned. "I'm glad you came."

Doug shrugged. "What the hell? 'Lowed I've tried everything else—don't work out—what'd I lose? A couple of weeks."

Ward didn't mention the small matter of survival. "None of the others wanted to try it, huh?"

"Naw, my mama didn't raise no lunkhaids. This boy knows better. Without you they'll end up as tree ornaments. But they don't know that. Nate sees as how he's the brains. I'm happy to be out of it."

"Did you learn anything while I was in Phoenix?"

Doug took off his hat and ran his hand along his ear, which had collapsed at the point of an injury, so that the top half-inch of it flopped over. "Larned myself not to stick my head up."

"Christ! How'd you get a gotched ear?"

"Ran smack into six riders herding about sixty cows into a ravine. Lookin' guilty as hell. Opened fire right off. Low-down ornery galoots stampeded that blamed herd practically right over us. Felt a tolerable amount of gratitude to make it back here with my pelt intact."

Ward looked disgusted. "They got away?"

"We were lucky not to get killed!" Doug protested. "Hope you didn't sprain your back humping all the girls in Phoenix while we were busting our asses," he said bitterly.

"You complain more than a woman," Ward said, shaking his head.

"Figures you'd know that. It's been so long I almost cain't remember what they're like."

Ward cuffed him lightly as Dusty joined them.

"Good chow," Dusty said.

"You shoulda been here yesterday. Chili—Montezuma's revenge!" Doug said dryly, grinning ruefully.

"Did you get a line on how many riders Younger has?" Ward asked.

Doug frowned, becoming serious. "Hard to tell—maybe twenty, but they keep moving. Looks like they're pulling back into the mountains. Looks like something's fetching it to a close. We saw tracks going north. Not too many coming back. They ain't exactly deuce high with me.''

"What are we going to do?" Dusty asked, watching Ward.

"I want to catch Younger or some of his men with some cows that don't belong to the Lazy P. Any cattle moving north?"

"Yeah, some, I reckon." Doug nodded.

"When was this?"

"Yesterday morning."

"What'd you do today?"

Doug looked disgusted. "I was feelin' kinda low-spirited about how I hadn't been doin' enough, so we checked on that train—to see if it was makin' any runs."

"Was it?"

"Naw," Doug drawled. "Looks like they're aiming to see the deal through to the last turn of the card, but I don't know. If they're using the blamed railroad to move 'em, they should be shipping some ever' danged night."

"You're right. Unless something happened to their contact in the Texas and Pacific."

"You didn't find nothin' going through them books?"

"The only thing that would seem to support our theory is that earnings didn't go up this year. Units transported went up, overhead went up, but not profits."

Dusty nodded. "That makes sense. The Texas and Pacific is absorbing the cost of transportation. What does it cost to ship a steer back east?"

"Two dollars a head."

Doug grinned suddenly. "Maybe the old Devil's Canyon Gang had somethin' to do with that. Payrolls were up forthwith—paying all them special agents to ride around on his trains pretendin' they knew what they was doin' when they didn't know any more than a range bull."

En masse they spent two and a half days scouring the countryside for any sign of illegal activity but found nothing. About noon they saw the agreed-upon smoke signal from Cruz. He was waiting for them on the porch.

"Bad news, Señor Ward," Cruz said, pursing his heavy lips. "You have wasted much time because my lazy friend whom I depended upon was drunk. *Señor* Powers is dead. *Señor* Younger stayed in Phoenix for the funeral. He and his men left only last night."

"That explains a lot," Ward said grimly. "How did Powers die?"

"His throat was cut, cheeeech."

"They know who did it?"

"I think not, *mi amigo*. You are the one they look for."

Ward frowned. "There's more?"

"*Sí*. Word among the *gringos* that you are taking over rustling. That you hanged another rustler for working in your territory, *Señor* Ward. The townspeople are forming a *muy grande* posse to ride you down. And"—he paused significantly—"a beautiful *señorita* is missing and they think *secuestrar ella*."

"I kidnapped who?"

"I did not find out her name, but apparently she was to be your *novia*."

Cold bands clamped around his chest. That could only mean that Younger had Leslie. Either Younger or the mysterious head of that gang—the name Younger's man would not divulge, even with a knife to his throat. The thought of Leslie at the hands of the man or men who had killed Isabel chilled his blood.

"Sounds like we've been framed," Dusty growled.

Doug nodded. There was general agreement among the others who had clustered around, listening in silence.

Dusty spoke first. "I say we ride north into the mountains, find their rabbit hole, and wipe 'em out. I think we've wasted enough time."

"There are only six of us," Ward said. "I think Younger has forty, fifty men—all told."

"Forty? Jesus!" Doug exclaimed.

Dusty grimaced. "Let me repeat myself. I say we ride south into the desert and give them Sonora *señoritas* a run for their money."

"Layin' up in Charlie Tarbell's Eagle Hotel in Tombstone ain't exactly the same as facing Dallas Younger and his pack of wolverines," Doug drawled.

"Don't sound like the same idee to me!" Boisterous men howled their agreement.

Ward ignored the good-natured exchange. "I don't think rustling is their only source of income. I think if this mountain hideaway exists, one man could ride in there, but not six."

"One man! Who?" Dusty demanded.

"Me," Ward said quietly.

"Whew! I was afraid he was volunteering me," Doug drawled, dragging his hand across his brow.

"And what are we s'posed to do in the meantime?"

A commotion out front caused all heads to turn.

"Hey, boss! One rider coming in!"

The men exchanged looks and strode quickly to the window. Ward and Dusty recognized her at the same time. Dusty motioned the men back to the bar.

Ward was a master at hiding his emotions from others, but he couldn't ignore the leaping in his blood at sight of Leslie Powers riding into his camp. Relief that she was safe flooded through him first and then pride. She was so fetching, so alive, and so singularly female. In that fancy riding habit and tophat with her hair twisted up into a wind-whipped topknot beneath it . . . and her cheeks flushed from riding . . . she was incredibly lovely. There was a hungry reaction all through his lean frame. But why was she here?

CHAPTER
FORTY-ONE

Cantrell stepped out into the slanting sunshine on the porch and moved forward to lift Leslie down from her mount. And once she was in his arms, it was only natural that he kiss her half-parted lips, stilling whatever utterance she'd been about to make.

All her fears and doubts dissolved in that warm, strong embrace. When his tawny head finally lifted she was weak and breathless in his arms.

"Leslie, love, what the hell are you going here?" he asked huskily.

"Could we talk somewhere?"

"Sure." He led her into the dim interior. It was ordinarily a combination saloon, dining room, and hotel. Now it was an armed fortress—guns, rifles, hard-faced men in various positions. No one seeing that room of desperadoes could miss the tension and the deadly coolness of their demeanor. They were armed and ready to do battle. She recognized Dusty Denton, cool and sturdy with a level, piercing gaze. There were others like him—all young, lean, determined. How had they come to this end—waiting here to die? But they wouldn't die until they had killed a number of their enemies—faceless men who would leave behind wives and daughters to weep and wear their widow's weeds. She could have wept with the sudden sweep of emotion that rose up in her. How futile it all was!

Ward's room was at the top of the stairs to the right. It was the logical place to take her. She followed silently, thinking her riotous thoughts, resenting him for being so willing to expose himself to danger and death. Angry, selfish thoughts trembled on her lips, seeking release, but he pulled her inside, closed the door, and she was engulfed: lost, drowning, and suddenly not caring. His mouth closed over hers, demanding and reclaiming everything: her will, her body, her soul. There was no chance to protest. He undressed her and took her there on the bed that stood alone in the middle of that forlorn shabby room, with soft breezes flapping the cheap windowshade and gold sunlight yellowing the floor and his hair.

And somehow, making love in an armed camp, to a man who would very likely be dead tomorrow, reduced everything to basics. There was no need now to pretend she didn't want him, no need now to hold back.

Urgent. Fierce. Tender yet savage. They were both hopelessly caught up in each other's spell.

Remembering the tension she'd felt until she'd been recognized brought it all home to her. He knew the risk he was running! Why did he stay? Nothing he had ever done made sense to Leslie—except this. But even this couldn't go on forever. Even the wildest, sweetest flame, once it had flared into brilliance, burned down.

Snuggled safely in his arms, with a glorious flush still tingling through her, she could almost forget.

"Leslie," he whispered.

"Hmm?"

"I can't let you stay here. We're moving out soon."

"I came to warn you. There's a posse forming to run you down. They're coming tonight to free the town and hang you."

"What for?"

"For rustling and because they think you killed Mark Powers and kidnapped Sandra McCormick."

"How did Powers die?"

"Someone cut his throat, and Younger told the sheriff it was your trademark. I don't think they believe me anymore about your not being the one who kidnapped me—the sheriff looks at me funny . . ." Her voice trailed off.

"Why do they think I'd kidnap Sandra McCormick?"

"She was your girl . . ." Leslie stammered.

"When did she disappear?"

"Her father said she had dinner with him and his guests Sunday night, went to bed early, and was gone the next day when the housekeeper checked. Not a trace."

"When did Powers die?"

"They found him Sunday morning at the livery stable. His body was in the stall your horse had been in—at least that's what Elizabeth said."

"You came to warn me?" he asked softly, so amazed that he forgot to mention that he hadn't been keeping his horse at the livery stable.

She couldn't answer him in words. "I brought some money. I thought if you . . . if . . ." She couldn't say, "I'm trying to bribe you to run away with me." Even she had too much pride for that. "I mean—it's too dangerous for you to stay here." Her voice trailed off. He hadn't even tried to help her—hadn't uttered a single word to make it easy for her.

Ward was stunned. The woman he had kidnapped and robbed of her virginity, leaving her vulnerable to every wagging tongue in the Territory, had come there to save him. Not even knowing for sure that he hadn't killed her uncle and run off with another woman. Not even asking.

Now, when she would have moved away to dress herself, his hands stopped her, pulled her close to him, kissing her eyes, cheeks, forehead, lips . . . nuzzling tenderly at her neck. "Leslie, my love, my own sweet love . . ."

Did she only imagine that husky whisper?—skin to skin, his hands on her face, holding her as if she were the most precious thing he had ever touched?

Trembling, she gave herself up to this new experience. Allowed him to immerse her in tenderness, her body moving in perfect counterpoint. He made love to her again, and this time his touch was a balm, a drawing-out of old pain, a healing. Tears wet her cheeks, and his lips found them. He gave her the assurances she needed with his body. No matter what happened, she would have this hour, this day, to remember. A warm, soft, perfect moment . . . encapsulated in time, memory, flesh.

Did she sleep? Or only lose track of time? The sun, slanting in at the window, had sharpened its angle. Alarmed by the approach of sunset, she remembered why she had come there.

"Ward, you must get away. A posse is coming to hang you," she whispered against his cheek.

He didn't answer. He was immersed in joy, first that she had come here at all and second that she would run away with him.

"What could be more important than your own survival?" she persisted. "Those men are not going to give you a chance to deny anything. Don't you see?" She sat up, her sense of urgency returning. "They'll take you any way they have to. They'll shoot you or hang you, whatever they have to do. There's a reward for you, dead or alive."

Ward rolled onto his back, frowning. He had lived as an outlaw for six years. For the first time, he had an opportunity to start over. If he ran away there would be no life worth living anyway. No Leslie. He had no choice. He could either die now, fighting for his and her future, or he could run away and die by degrees, as he lost first her concern, her respect, and then her love.

Ward's silence was deafening. What was he thinking now? What a fool she was? Probably. She bit her bottom lip and let her eyes rove around the room they shared. There was a bureau on one wall and a small table with a lacy shawl draped carelessly so that it hung down halfway to the floor. Cream-colored lace that would look very pretty over long black hair. Leslie could feel a coldness settling into her lungs. It spread out, making her breath tingle and ache in her throat. He made love to her in the room he shared with another woman!

Leslie couldn't look at him, couldn't even speak. Mutely, she turned away, fumbling with the clothes he had nearly torn off her body moments ago, feeling her nakedness painfully, and remembering the fears she had suppressed riding into this dust-whipped little town. She could almost laugh now. She expelled a shuddering breath, ignoring the warm hand that caressed the curve of her back—or tried to ignore it. How could he look so relaxed? Didn't he care that by tomorrow he'd probably be dead? She had a sudden vision of him on that big black horse, bare-headed, riding straight into that pack of shouting, shooting men. No one knew better than she what a reckless hellion he was. Or what a rotten cheat! But this, making love to her in his girlfriend's bedroom, was going too far!

She was determined to be as cool about it as he was.

"They are mad enough to hang you on sight. Rustling can't possibly pay all that well. I brought some money. If you leave now, you can be away from here before they arrive."

"Does anyone know you came here?"

"No."

"Whose cattle did I rustle?"

Leslie looked at him sharply. "Don't you know?"

Apparently even Leslie believed that one. He shrugged. "Seen one cow you've seen them all. How did they find out it was me?" he asked instead.

"I guess it was the subtle way you issued that challenge to all the other rustlers to clear out of your territory. Hanging one of them didn't help your image any. I don't know all that much about rules of conduct for rustlers chief, but it seems you have outraged everyone—ranchers, rustlers, even the little old ladies."

"Those are the ones to watch out for," he said wryly, "the little old ladies. They'll get you every time."

The cold ache was gone now. All she felt was a strange sense of numbness. He wasn't interested in running off with *her* even if she paid him. That much was clear!

Leslie stood up and began reaching for her clothes. Ward watched her, completely entranced with the delicious sight of silky skin—creamy white all the way to the bone—and that luxurious mass of midnight-black hair cascading halfway down her back. Perfect cone-shaped breasts with rosy red nipples that he could almost feel against his lips. He would like to spend the day making love to her but . . .

He frowned. He had to somehow get free of this neat little frame someone had constructed for him. He hadn't issued a challenge. Who would gain by killing Powers? Or kidnapping Trinket?

His mind was a hundred miles away, Leslie could tell by the look in his eyes—they were smoky blue in the shabby room. White pitiless sunshine streamed in the undraped window. A shade pulled halfway down was flapping gently in the afternoon breeze.

She straightened and walked to the vanity, picked up the shawl to feel the texture of the lace, and saw Sandra McCormick's locket lying on the dusty wooden table. Ward stretched, languorously, and she noticed the scratches on his face, the ones she hadn't bothered to ask about when she arrived, because she'd been too caught up in her overwhelming response to him.

The intricately engraved Chinese dragon on the gold and enamel locket seemed to glow with a perfect, terrible light.

He *had* lied to her! Perhaps only indirectly, since she didn't ask questions . . . but surely allowing her to believe he didn't know about Sandra's disappearance. . . . She picked up the locket and walked to the bed.

Eyes closed, he was still sprawled like some pagan lord, his lean body completely relaxed. Words trembled on her lips, but she dared not speak. How could he answer her? He would either lie or tell the truth. If he said yes, it is Sandra's, then she would know he had taken her. If he said no, it wasn't Sandra's, she would know he was lying to her. Either would be equally damning, because neither was acceptable to her. The room was suddenly cold and tawdry-looking, like she felt. A great place for a quick, meaningless encounter.

Trembling, she cautioned herself to take her lead from him—to keep it light and get the hell out before he inspired her to do anything else stupid.

"Well, sir, was that satisfactory?"

Ward frowned, his eyes narrowed, and one corner of his mouth pulled down. How did he manage to look so damned reserved and sensuous at the same time? It had to be his mouth, the way it could look so kissable and yet so insolent—like now.

"Very," he said softly, watching her intently.

"Good," she said briskly. She had finished dressing, but her hair was still loose. It swung in a fragrant, heavy mass when she leaned across the bed to pick up a small reticule he hadn't noticed before. He picked up a tress of her hair, trapping her there within easy reach.

Leslie forced one of those sunny smiles Chane and Jennifer raved about, leaned forward, and kissed him very quickly on the nose. "Excellent. Then this should take care of it." She let the money sprinkle down on his thighs. "I have to go now, love. I'm sure you will agree I have kept my part of the bargain. There is ten thousand dollars there. You can live like a king for a long time on that—almost anywhere except Arizona." She laughed.

His hand fell away from her hair. He seemed to go still all over as if he were turned to stone. He didn't move—didn't change expression. He just looked at her without speaking, and she could feel the pain spreading out in waves around her throat and chest and knew she had to get out of there fast.

He picked up one of the hundred-dollar bills, then a thousand-dollar bill. His impassive mien didn't change, but the look in his eyes did. The blue cooled inexplicably, turned opaque, unresponsive. He lifted one eyebrow questioningly, and she forced a little trill of laughter.

"I'm defining a new market for myself. That's a new term I learned listening to Tim talk. We're—getting married soon. I really can't continue being your mistress—but you deserve to be compensated. A deal's a deal." She shrugged as if money matters always embarrassed her.

"Thanks, but as you can see"—he gestured casually to the shabby room—"I have everything I need."

He was right about that anyway, she thought bitterly. She ached all over just looking at him—Apollo—sprawled in naked abandon.

She turned away, a smile curving her lips, shrugging. "Well, keep it anyway. I don't need it. As Tim's wife I will have everything I need. Who knows? You said once, maybe you could go straight. Why don't you try it? You might even like it."

"I tried that once," he said softly. "People won't let you up— once you're down." Did she detect bitterness in that husky quiet voice?

She was at the door now, and he was still on the bed, naked, his left arm folded under the back of his head. A ray of sunshine hitting the window just right sent a shimmer of brightness across the bed, backlighting his still form so that he was only a silhouette: Apollo, the sun god, framed in gold.

She paused, knowing better but unable to help herself, and her mind was filled with craziness: "A lighted chamber, a darkened court." The phrase "Chambre Ardente" flashed into her head from some forgotten history lecture, and she could see the Courts of Cardinal Lorraine, in those dark ages before the Revolution, where prisoners were tried in torchlit chambers, the judges' faces carefully hidden from the hapless men and women they judged. Those people had known instinctively, as she did now, that you could expect no mercy from a judge who hid his face from you.

It reminded her of the way Cantrell had always hidden his real self from her. Or had she only refused to see?

"So long, Cantrell."

Ward picked up one of the bills and blew her a kiss.

"Thanks, hellcat."

CHAPTER
FORTY-TWO

Leslie was home by dinnertime.

"Did you have a nice ride?" Jennifer asked, smiling at her wind-flushed cheeks. "It was a lovely day for it."

"Beautiful," Leslie said, forcing a smile. She had resented all that autumn splendor because it didn't suit her mood. But maybe, she conceded, there wasn't a climate anywhere that would satisfy the needs of a woman who had just been ravished, impoverished, and rejected.

Jennifer was sensitive enough to catch the insincerity in her less than jubilant reply.

"Are you all right?" she asked, looking at Leslie closely.

Leslie sighed. "I don't know," she admitted wearily.

"Would you like to talk about it?"

She shook her head, and even that negative response was a lie. She did want to talk about it—desperately—but there was no one she could turn to.

Jennifer might be one of his mistresses. How could she know? Even Chane, whom she trusted instinctively, was off limits because she might slip and incriminate his wife. Even Debbie was suspect. She had gone out with Ward, but fortunately she didn't brag. Certainly Tim wouldn't appreciate hearing about her love or hate relationship with another man.

Tim came after dinner that night and took her for a ride, and this time when he kissed her she responded exactly as he wanted her to. She couldn't lie, but she snuggled closer into his arms, and that was answer enough. He wanted her, and she needed someone who wasn't just using her. His love was a soothing balm, at a time when she desperately needed comforting.

"Leslie, please say you'll marry me," he pleaded.

The instinctive denial rose, but Leslie stifled it. She had already told Ward she was going to marry Tim. She could do a lot worse.

"All right," she said softly.

"Do you mean it?" he asked incredulously, holding her away from him to let his black eyes burn into her.

"Yes, of course," she said weakly.

"Oh, darling, you've made me the happiest man in the world!"

When he took her home he made a big production of asking Chane for her hand. Chane's warm green eyes jolted her like a physical shock when he turned from Tim to her. She felt exposed—the whole facade she had erected to hide behind peeled away under that piercing look.

"So you've made your choice?" he asked gently.

He knew! She felt like a traitor now. What was he asking her? Since Ward is in trouble, you've chosen Tim? Her chin lifted defiantly. Let him think it! He didn't know Ward—not really. But she writhed inwardly under his scrutiny. Was he really as disappointed in her as she imagined?

"Yes, I think marriage is still a valid choice," she murmured, smiling.

"Well, if you're sure, then of course you two have our blessing," he answered smoothly, graciously, bending down to kiss her cheek. "I'll find Jennie. She's going to be thrilled at the prospect."

The announcement of their engagement did not need to appear in the newspaper. Word was all over town instantly. Everyone knew! And she was wearing a one-carat diamond solitaire.

"It's beautiful, Tim, but it looks so expensive."

"I've had nothing to spend my money on before. All I ever did was work and save it. Now I have you, my darling. I want to dress you like a queen, set you in a beautiful mansion, frame you like the rare masterpiece you are, show you off to all my friends."

He went on, but she wasn't listening. Why did she suddenly feel like a possession?—the most prized treasure of all, but still only an acquisition?

Dusty Denton watched the lovely black-haired creature rush out of the hotel, her cheeks flushed with color. He waited patiently for Cantrell to come down. In two minutes Ward was coming down the stairs tying his guns down, one on each thigh as he strode into the room.

"Get ready to ride out," he said flatly as Dusty came to his feet, his gray eyes watchful.

Dusty nodded to the others and they began to comply.

Ward passed on what Leslie had added to what they already knew.

"What's the plan?" Dusty asked when he had finished.

"I want you and the rest of the men to gather up as big a herd of mixed brands as you can in three days and drive them to that point where the rustlers load 'em onto the railroad cars. By the time you get there, I should have something arranged. I'm going to pay a visit on Younger."

"Alone?"

Ward grinned. "You're not afraid, are you? I realize it gets scary out there at night, but if you all stay close together . . ."

"Graduated from Radcliffe, didn't you? You know what I meant." He grinned.

Ward had already dismissed him from his thoughts. There was a mood of controlled brutality that he was going to work off on someone. It might as well be Younger. He didn't need a sorceress to tell him where Trinket had gone. She'd be lucky if she wasn't dead.

Dusty interrupted, still trying to stop him from going it alone. "Boy, she must be some girl—spends two hours up there and turns you into a one-man army."

"You should see what I've done in the last three days," Ward said dryly.

"Just hearing about it was enough to scare hell out of me."

"Me, too."

Ward left, and Dusty joined Doug Paggett at the bar.

"What the hell is he up to?" Dusty asked.

"I don't know. Did he look like he'd been shot or anything?"

Dusty scowled angrily at Doug.

"No," Doug said, shaking his head, "I'm not joking. The last time he got real quiet and cool like this and took off all by himself we found out later it was because he took a bullet in the back when we were running from a posse. We didn't see him again for months. He almost died. Hadn't been for an old Mexican woman finding him in the desert he would've."

"Why do you suppose he did that?"

Doug looked at the tiny dust cloud that was all they could still see of Ward Cantrell.

"He couldn't keep up. I guess he didn't want to slow us down."

"You suppose it was the same woman I heard him telling the

Castenadas about? He asked them to send a priest to bless the grave.''

''I don't know. I didn't know she was dead.''

That mood of bitter passion still menaced Cantrell—growing darker and more vicious as he rode toward the Powers spread. Dusty hadn't wanted to separate, but they knew each other well enough now so that he had accepted Ward's mood and his decision as final.

Fate played strange tricks. Dusty Denton had grown up with him and graduated from Harvard in the class Ward had been expelled from. This was the third time his and Dusty's paths had crossed. They rode with the Jackson Hole Gang in Wyoming at the same time, and now they were both trying to earn a pardon.

Dusty's story was almost as bizarre as his own. He had inherited a ranch in the Texas panhandle about a year after he got out of school. He and his cousin took a trip to Lubbock to look over his holdings. He didn't intend to stay, just to find out how much to sell it for, but his cousin got into a fight—a simple fistfight over a girl who smiled at him once too often. The other man drew a gun and shot Jonathan Denton in the chest. Jon was unarmed. When Dusty found out he went to the sheriff and demanded that justice be done, but there was a mob on the other side, and the sheriff was too timid to buck it. So Denton issued his own challenge for the other man to meet him in the street—Texas-style—even though he had never worn a gun around his waist. He bought a gunbelt, gun and bullets, and spent less than an hour practicing his draw before the showdown. He was a practiced marksman with a hunting rifle, and he discovered he was just as good with a handgun. He wasn't as fast on the draw as the other man, but his opponent's first shot missed. By then Dusty had his gun out. He fired one shot, and Red Dooley fell—dead before his head hit the ground.

The Texas rangers chased him out of Texas, and he couldn't go home because the sheriff wired the police in Boston. He discovered that nothing spreads faster than bad news. The only solution was to travel in places where there was even less law than Texas.

Dusty hadn't been a close friend of Ward's at school or in Wyoming, but he was developing into one now. If they both managed to survive this. . . .

Ward stopped himself with a frown. He was no Jack Hays, ranger hero. He was more a Poggin, the kind to die with his back against the wall, both guns smoking and only one bullet left in the chamber. When he took this job he hadn't expected to survive it—just to die in a manner more of his choosing. He wasn't a coward or a quitter; if he could survive it, he would. But survival hadn't been a condition then, and it certainly wasn't one now. He hadn't gotten emotionally involved with a girl since Simone, and now that he was, he felt the loss as frustration and fury: frustration because he was trapped by circumstances that made it impossible for him to pursue her and fury that she was too eager to grab the gold ring!

He pushed the big black relentlessly, and the exertion of a wild, heedless ride brought all the muscles in his lean frame into play. The exercise and the rhythmic pounding of hooves flying over the desert finally worked its magic, and after an hour he slowed the horse, finally beginning to relax.

He settled down to a ground-eating pace that was more comfortable for his mount. The killing mood—the cold, deadly passion of the gunfighter—was in him now, and he knew it. He had felt the icy flicker of foreboding too many times—before too many confrontations—not to recognize it now. But always before he had resisted it. Now he welcomed it—goading the horse forward when it slowed its pace across the desert, ignoring the splendor of the sunset that was turning the sky into a panorama of coral and purple.

Dusk found him on the hill overlooking Powers's fortress. The same controlled rage that had brought him there in headlong flight, cooled his nerves, now that he was in sight of his goal, hardening them with grim purpose. He rode the rest of the way slowly, deliberately, expecting Younger to be waiting for him. To all outward appearances he rode coolly, casually, but to a man familiar with his type, the very coolness of his demeanor was warning enough.

He stopped at the gate to Younger's walled sanctuary, drew his gun, and fired twice into the air. He could hear the scuttle and yell of men in startled awareness and then a voice:

"Who goes thar?"

"Cantrell."

"What the hell do you want?"

"Younger."

"He ain't here anymore. Picked up his things and left last night."

"Then you won't mind if I come in and look around, will you?"

There was a short conference and then the gate screeched open on rusty hinges. The man doing the talking looked like any honest range rider. He wasn't one of the men who rode with Younger; and he wore no gun. Most cowboys didn't, though.

"Come ahead."

There was a man in the lookout tower with a rifle trained on Ward as soon as the door swung open. It followed him all the way to the house, and Ward knew it would be there when he came out, if he came out. If these men believed he had killed Powers, they weren't showing any signs of it. He didn't believe Younger was gone, but it was possible. Younger knew exactly where he stood with the new owner. At the porch he stopped, dismounted, and faced the man who had greeted him at the gate.

"Did Younger have a girl with him when he left here?"

Slim Whitman watched the man's eyes—cool, merciless blue—and was suddenly glad he wasn't Younger. "Yeah. A pretty, blond girl. She waited here two days for him to come from Phoenix, then they grabbed a few things and hit off for the mountains."

"Talk in town has it that I killed Powers and made off with the girl," he said, watching the man's face for any sign.

"Reckon they must be wrong, then," the man said coolly.

Ward considered the answer and then nodded—much to Slim's relief. "Did he take any men with him?"

Slim felt no special loyalty to Younger. He'd had his own doubts about the gun-toting foreman and his special riders. "You want to set a spell? About dinnertime," he said laconically, waving to the man in the tower to lower the rifle.

"Thanks."

Ward shared the simple fare with twenty or so cowhands, and then he and the man who had finally introduced himself as Slim Whitman moved out to the porch to enjoy the whir of crickets and the trill of a few birds before the cold night winds made it too unpleasant.

They talked about numerous things, all seemingly inconsequential, but in short order Ward had gotten a picture of an operation similar to the robber baron Cheseldine's some years back. Slim was perceptive. He was one of the spread's regular hands, not privy to any crooked deals, but he had sharp eyes and a quick mind, and apparently he had sized Ward up and made his decision. Else Ward could have gotten a bullet from that tower without warning. When Ward stood up to go, Slim put out his rough hand, and Ward took it. A grin spread across Slim's lantern-jawed face, then quickly disappeared.

"I never shook the hand of a gunfighter before."

"What makes you think you have now?" Ward asked, flashing a grin of his own.

"I know. Plumb smooth, like satin. Can tell you don't rope steers, mister. And I reckon it ain't like that from wearing gloves."

Ward hadn't worn a glove on his right hand in six years. The man didn't expect a reply, and none was offered.

"Younger and the girl left alone. The other men who worked special for him rode off a day earlier—heading for Morristown. They didn't say that, but that's the direction they always go. We hear 'em talking."

"Much obliged."

"My pleasure, Cantrell."

Ward started to leave, paused. "When is your new boss taking over?"

"Reckon not for a week or so. Younger said she's planning on marrying some hotshot railroad man in a few days—probably don't know a cow from a gelding," he ended disgustedly.

"So long, Slim, and thanks for your hospitality."

CHAPTER
FORTY-THREE

Sandra and Younger arrived in Morristown Wednesday afternoon. It was barely more than a settlement: a dozen buildings and a few shanties. From a distance, with gusty winds whipping up the dirt into sheets to throw against the weathered walls and a shutter banging insistently, it looked like a ghost town. Only the horses, standing patiently in the cold mountain air, added a touch of life.

Younger led her past gaunt buildings where she saw shadows of faces peering through the water-stained, dust-coated windows, to a wood-frame house at the northernmost edge of the village. They dismounted; she had to fend for herself. Dallas bellowed an order, and a raw-boned, slow-moving red-haired man ambled out and took the horses around back while they went inside.

There were four men inside, playing cards and drinking. A tired-looking woman in a shapeless gown was cutting vegetables for a stew.

Sandra felt her face flushing as every eye in the place roamed
over her body, even the woman's. Sandra was wearing the silk
blouse and riding skirt, but no undergarments of any type. Dallas
wouldn't permit it. Said he didn't like nothing getting between him
and what was his. She had the feeling they all knew. A muted
throbbing in her loins quickened her breath.

The men were seated at a table that someone had thrown a
rough blanket over. Cards and money were scattered around. The
blanket hung down crookedly, almost touching the floor where it
wasn't impeded by someone's lap.

Dallas waved a careless hand at her. "Boys, meet my little
sweetface." He turned back to her carelessly. "What's your
name, sweetface?"

"Sandra."

"That mean-eyed cuss thar is Cedar Longley. The man to his
right is Pick Sitwell. His brother was the one who took our hosses
when we came in. The sleepy one thar is Bass Wimer and the big
burly lady's man is Texas Jack Jones."

Sandra nodded. Cedar Longley, she'd heard that name before.
He was Younger's second lieutenant. Pick Sitwell had sly, furtive
eyes that made her want to see if her blouse was buttoned. He was
lanky and raw-boned like his brother. Bass Wimer had a dull, list-
less look in his eyes that didn't look like it would last. He might
burst into some act of violence if he ever came fully awake. Texas
Jack Jones had bold black eyes that made her belly feel strange and
tight, like it did when Dallas touched her. Even when he resumed
his lazy-lidded concentration on his cards she could still feel that
stirring in her belly.

"Y'all be good to this little sweetface, ya hear?"

There were various comments, some lewd, as to exactly how
good they would like to be, and Sandra reddened painfully. She
had been raised a lady, and knew the exact degree of her own
shame. No lady would be where she was now. Leslie Powers, who
looked the epitome of a gentlewoman, except for the flashes of
spirit that bespoke a fiery temper, would never allow herself to be
paraded in front of such crude range bums. But Leslie Powers did
not have her problems or her needs.

There was scraping and rearranging of chairs as Dallas sat
down, and then the card game resumed. No one noticed that Dallas
had forgotten to introduce the woman, Bass Wimer's wife, who
turned away in disgust. Sandra was forgotten as the men became

engrossed in sporadic conversation. She wandered over and asked the woman if she needed any help.

Cold gray eyes flitted over her. "Don't reckon the likes of you would be able to do anythin' I'd find tolerable, much less helpful."

Sandra flinched and wandered around the room, ending up behind Younger. She was an outsider; even that tired old hag had something that made her belong. She reached down and began rubbing Dallas's shoulder. He responded, so she pressed close to his chair and let both hands rub his shoulders and chest. That took her mind off her loneliness, and he seemed to enjoy the attention. The stew smelled good, but Sandra had lost her appetite. The ache in her loins was throbbing insistently. She could see the men letting their bold eyes stray over her body. Part of her realized how crude these men were in comparison to the men her father expected her to associate with, but she was too needy to take her shame seriously. Shame was an almost necessary part of getting what she needed from men.

Lightheaded from the rush of events, Sandra started having visions of herself naked among these six rough-looking men, doing their bidding, being the center of attention, and by the time the old hag served the stew, she barely touched it. The playing seemed to go on and on. Sandra stayed at her post caressing Dallas and accepting the looks of the other men until she was in agony. She leaned down and whispered in his ear.

"Dallas, honey, can we go to bed soon?"

She ignored the derisive snort from the man next to Dallas.

"I'm winning, sweetface. I cain't leave now."

"Please, honey, I need you," she whispered desperately. "Please."

"Please, honey," someone mocked her. "Please, Dallas honey." Dallas cuffed him lightly, and they all laughed. Play stopped and the one across from Dallas swore crudely: "Hey, Dallas, take her in that room and give her what she wants, then come on back. We'll still be here."

"Hell, yeah! We'll listen—yell if you need any help."

They laughed. Dallas stood up and yawned elaborately, joining in the fun. Sandra didn't look at anyone, especially the other woman, as she turned.

"Reckon I could use a nap. Come on, sweetface. We'll give the boys a break. They been losing long enough."

Sandra was on fire. She ignored the cacophony of crude remarks and followed Younger into the small bedroom that was separated from the main room by a curtain. Her hands trembled on the buttons and almost tore the skirt off. He only slipped his guns and pants off and they fell across the squeaky bed. She wanted him inside her—hard and big and rough—but he was teasing her, only pressing between her legs, refusing to go inside while he kissed her hungry mouth and squeezed her breasts. Soon she was groaning, pleading with him.

"What d'ya want, sweetface?"

"I want you," she gasped, writhing beneath him.

"You want Dallas?" he prompted.

"Yes, yes, I want you, Dallas!"

"Say it, baby."

"I want you, Dallas."

"Say it louder, baby. I cain't hear when ya whisper."

"Oh, Dallas, Dallas! I want you!"

"Louder, baby, who d'ya want, sweetface?"

"I want *you*, Dallas."

That was loud enough to bring a chorus of ribald remarks and a crude cheer from the other room, but she was too far gone to notice.

Dallas kept Sandra at fever pitch for twelve minutes while the men in the other room made bets about how long it would go on. Pick Sitwell won the bet when they heard her orgasmic gasps and cries exactly nine-twenty-three by Bass Wimer's watch.

"Ride 'em, cowboy!" Pick yelled triumphantly while the others cussed, becoming even cruder with their remarks.

Younger came out in three minutes, and Bass won that bet on both counts: that it would be under five minutes and that he would be alone.

Dallas took his place at the table amid back-slapping and more raucous remarks. The initial uproar died down slowly because the men were steamed up. About midnight the talk grew more serious.

"Heard anythin' from the boss?" Pick asked Younger as he dealt.

"Naw. He's keeping low for a while. We're jus' gonna round up all the steers we've got hidden in them ravines and drive 'em down to the pens so's they can be loaded and shipped."

"Hell, don't sound like you need us for that," Pick snorted.

"Probably don't, but it's something to keep you from drinking, gambling, getting on one another's nerves, and killing one another," Dallas said.

Pick looked to the others defensively. "We been gettin' along fine, ain't we?"

"You always get along fine for the first three days. Then the trouble starts. You're worse'n a box full of locoed gnats! I cain't leave you alone for longer'n that. You always get into trouble. Remember those goddamned Mendozas!"

"Hell, that wasn't our fault. We was jist doing what the boss wanted us to."

Younger threw down his cards, a scowl turning his handsome face dark. "Wal, you done a damned sloppy job of it, too! I took the rap for that with Powers. That was about the stupidest piece of bad work—leaving that gunfighter alive and killing off the women, the old man, and the kid!" That had rankled for a long time. "Stupid goddamned bastards!"

Pick dropped his cards. "We didn't know about the gunfighter. We'd a got him fust off if'n we did."

"Stupid damned bunch!" Younger growled, letting his eyes rip over them. "We been fighting that bastard ever since!"

"Hell, you're jist upset cause it's you he's after."

" 'Twarn't our fault anyway," Bass Wimer interposed. "We coulda handled that more convincin'-like, 'cept the boss was horny for thet gal. He likes it when they're crying and scared. Things jist kinda got outta harness after that."

"I reckon you could say that, all right!" Dallas growled, deciding to drop the subject. "I'm moving up to the camp at dawn. Y'all be ready to ride out."

"Shucks, boss, we figured you was gonna leave us here with the filly," Bass whined in pretended or real agony.

"Aw, hell!" Dallas growled. " 'Sides, you got yourself a woman. Cooks a right good stew, she does."

"Man don't live by stew alone," Bass grumped.

They played one hand in silence, then Texas Jack Jones, the big burly Texan, leaned back in his chair and eyed Younger. Texas Jack had a deep, sonorous voice and usually spoke slowly and carefully. Because of his reputation for a quick gun and a short temper, when he spoke, men listened.

"Wal, now, Dallas, I reckon if that hongry yelling went on much longer tonight you woulda had a problem on your hands."

Dallas leaned back, grinning. "What might thata been?"

Texas Jack kept a straight face. "A couple more minutes of that

pretty little filly yelling about how good you was and I was gonna
go in thar and let you hump me," he drawled.

They roared with laughter.

CHAPTER
FORTY-FOUR

Sandra was treated like a celebrity when she appeared for breakfast. The men made a big show of making room for her at the table
and taking care of her needs. For the first time in her life she felt
important in her own right—not just because she was Sam McCormick's daughter. She didn't mind the crude remarks. It was all part
of belonging.

They left together in a cohesive pack just as the sky was turning
from gray to pink. The cold was bitter, and frost was everywhere,
covering the hills with white. As Dallas Younger's woman, she
rode at the head of the pack, beside her man. There was a new confidence in Sandra now. She had a man who was really a man, and
he treated her like a woman. Two days' growth of beard only
added to his attraction. He was rough, and he looked it, but when
he caught her look and grinned, there was a hint of pride mixed
with the desire that burned between them.

They were going deeper into the mountains now. The sun
slowly melted the frost that crunched under the horses' hooves,
and the ride became more bearable. Dallas had found her a coat
like the men wore, and only her legs were cold. "We'll fix that
when we get to camp. Little Doug has some pants that should fit
you right fine."

They stopped at a wide, shallow stream. They dismounted and
drank upstream from the horses. The men wandered off to relieve
themselves, and Sandra did likewise.

Everyone came back except Bass Wimer, so Dallas yelled for
him to get his butt back so they could leave.

"I found something," he yelled, the booming voice that had
earned him his nickname echoing and bouncing off the surrounding mountains.

Dallas shook his head in irritation. "Damn fool! He's gotta be
the stupidest son of a bitch west of the Pecos!"

"He's hauling a short load all right," Texas Jack drawled, spitting in disgust at a rock.

Bass Wimer came out of the trees, carrying a long slender pole. It was two inches thick and almost symmetrical, as if it had been planed by a carpenter.

"Ain't that purty?" he asked proudly.

"What the hell you gonna do with a stick ten feet long?" Younger demanded, raising a disgusted eyebrow.

"Make things," Bass said defensively.

"Shit, put that thing down and let's ride."

"Aw, dammit, Dallas, let me keep it. It cain't hurt anythin', and I need it."

"Jesus Christ!" Younger shook his head. "All right, but you see to it."

"Thanks, boss."

Sandra looked back several times to see how Bass and his stick were faring. He carried it like a lance for a while, then across his saddle like a tightrope walker she'd seen once. He did whatever he had to do to keep it.

As the trail grew rougher and narrower, Sandra fell back until she was riding in front of Bass. All went well until they broke out onto a wide grassy meadow. The group was in single file with Sandra and then Bass and his stick, carried across the saddle like a balance pole.

Dallas held up his hand and turned in the saddle. Did he see something? She couldn't tell. He was too far ahead for her to read his expression. Bass stopped, pulled out his red paisley handkerchief to mop his brow, and was almost unseated when his horse reared. Bass heard the whirring rattle of the snake, but he never saw it. The horse came down and lurched forward into a dead run. There were too many things happening at once. The horse to control, the hankerchief in his hand, the stick across the saddle. He didn't make it in time. The stick caught Sandra across the middle of the back. She screamed and fell to the side, one foot caught in the stirrup. Her horse caught the stick on the back of the head and bolted, dragging her along.

Pick Sitwell, the closest one to Sandra, lunged off his horse but couldn't reach her in time. Texas Jack was on the wrong side of Sandra's horse. If he thundered up beside her runaway mount, his horse would trample her. Dallas could see the problem instantly. He got into position and was there when the big speckled gray came by. He caught the reins and jerked the horse viciously until it stopped. He held the head down. "Get her foot outta there!" he yelled.

Cedar Longley reached her first, freed her boot from the stirrup, and dragged her out of reach of the horse's hooves. Dallas turned the horse over to Pick and rushed to Sandra's side.

She was unconscious but breathing. He made a hasty examination, his hands feeling for broken bones, crushed places.

Bass Wimer ran up, panting. "She all right?"

Dallas couldn't remember later what happened then. Something snapped inside him, and the next thing he remembered, Texas Jack and Cedar Longley were pulling him off Wimer's limp body. He vaguely remembered hitting him, and his fists were both scuffed and sore, but he had no recollection of Wimer's response. Did he fight back?

Sandra came awake, groaning, and he went to her.

"You all right, sweetface?"

"What happened?" She looked around in a daze. Wimer was limp and bloody; the horses and men were all scattered above her. Had they been attacked?

"Is everybody all right?" she asked.

"Bass and his damned stick! He hit you, sweetface, and then your horse. The horse bolted and dragged you."

She looked around wonderingly. There was real concern in Dallas Younger's eyes—in all their eyes. They really cared about her! She felt tears well up in her own eyes and saw the response in his eyes, and it gave her a sense of power she hadn't felt since the time she had scarlet fever and everyone spoiled her because they thought they had almost lost her.

"Did you do that?" she asked softly, taking his hand and kissing the scuffed knuckles.

"I reckon. I thought he'd killed you. I musta hit him a hundred times, the way my hands ache." He shot a grim look at Wimer, who was beginning to groan and roll over. "He ain't going nowhere, though. I can get him again later. He'll be around."

Younger spoke so matter-of-factly that Sandra nearly beamed. He really cared for her! Now she rode the rest of the way beside Dallas. If she couldn't keep up, they slowed down. She was in heaven. All she had to do was grimace and she could bring the tightening into his handsome face and the anger back into his eyes.

* * *

Sheriff Willie Slaughter opened the letter with the Phoenix post-mark on it slowly. He read it and sat frowning, gazing out the window of the jail aimlessly. He stared at the livery wagon standing in front of Barnard Bros. Photo Graph Gallery.

"I'm going to King's place," he said to the deputy, who lounged in a chair across the narrow room, his feet up, reading the morning newspaper.

"Be gone long?"

"Naw."

Slaughter put on his hat and walked carefully across the wide, deeply rutted main street of Dodge City, sidestepping a wagon and then a buggy with a man and woman perched precariously on the narrow seat.

The interior of the Oriental Saloon was dim until his eyes adjusted to the difference. He could make out Frank Lovell and Wyatt Roundtree playing the faro bank, Frank keeping cases while Wyatt socialized with the dealer and the lookout. Men slouched at the bar over their social glasses. He heard one man joshing his friend about checking to see how come the end of his neck was all haired-over like that. The man did have a very impressive head of hair. Slaughter always admired that, since his own hair had disappeared, leaving only a ring of fuzz around his neck and ears.

Three boys were piking at a monte game, and ten drovers sat around a long table eating together, one of them complaining about the cost of yardage at the feedlot. He could hear the righteous indignation in the man's voice: "I'll not ship any more cattle to this town until they adjust their yardage costs. Listen! For two bits I can get myself a room with a nice clean bed in it, plenty of soap, water and towels, and I can stay there for twenty-four hours. And their stockyards are way the hell out there and they want to charge me twenty cents and let my steers stand out in the weather."

Slaughter stopped at the far end of the bar where Jack Fuller was standing, wiping absently at the bar.

"Morning, Jack."

"Morning, Will, you drinking this early?"

"Naw, I came to see your boss. He in?"

"In the back." He nodded toward the bead-covered opening that led down a narrow corridor and then out into the alley.

Slaughter found the office he was looking for, a large room on the left side of the corridor that looked like a lawyer's office or some rich politician's office instead of just the owner of a Dodge City saloon. He'd been in this office many times, collecting his share of the take off the gambling tables. It was customary. He kept law and order, and King gave him a cut. Saved them both some time and trouble.

John King was something of an enigma for Dodge City. He was the richest man in town, the best dressed, and black as the ace of spades. He owned the Oriental and three other establishments in town. The Oriental was one of the fanciest saloons in the territory. The bartender, Jack Fuller, had been imported from one of those fancy hotels back east, and he could make any mixed drink a man could ask for, as long as he had four bits to pay for it.

Today King was dressed in a very expensive fawn-colored suit that few other men could have afforded. The finest wool, soft as a baby's bottom, and impeccably cut. He was a massive man with thick neck, burly arms, but narrow through the hips. Store-bought clothes would have been ridiculous on that enormous frame. Slaughter could imagine buttons straining and popping off to leave gaping holes where that shiny black skin would glare out. King's face was as much an enigma as the rest of him. The features were brutal, heavy, reminding Slaughter of a prize fighter who had been brutalized once too often, but the eyes—there was no explaining them. They could have belonged to a teacher, someone smarter than he ever met. And there was no doubt John King was tough. He had made a place for himself by sheer brute force five years ago. He had stuffed this town's pride and ignorance down its own throat. He no longer had to prove himself or apologize for his color.

He looked up when Slaughter tapped on the doorjamb.

"Yes?" he asked curtly, his intelligent brown eyes jolting Slaughter with the reminder that they did not belong in that taciturn, brutal face.

Slaughter cleared his throat self-consciously. "I got a letter today about that outlaw you've been looking for—Ward Cantrell."

Impatience was replaced by interest now.

"Oh, where is he?"

"Phoenix, Arizona."

"Are you going after him?" King asked politely.

"Me? Hell, I'm no gunfighter. I ain't never faced a man like Cantrell." Slaughter paused, feeling foolish. "There's a big reward for him. Fifteen hundred dollars. I thought that was why you wanted to know."

King didn't reply. His brown eyes watched Will Slaughter as if he were not seeing him anymore.

Slaughter shifted uncomfortably. He didn't understand what

was going on. He had expected King to be grateful, but now he looked like he was remembering something it would be better he didn't remember. He wouldn't have come, except years ago King asked him to let him know if Cantrell or word of him turned up. He worked for the man, so he remembered that request.

John King had been the most feared bounty hunter in five territories but had given that up after he amassed enough money to buy his first saloon. A number of fugitives were damned glad he had, too. He brought back every man he ever pursued. Mainly because King was a bloodhound on a trail. His massive frame never tired, and he would not give up. He had a reputation for being fast with a gun, and people suspected he had an abiding hatred for white men. He never went after blacks, Mexicans, or Indians. It was said he could track a snake over granite. People claimed he was really the devil, pretending to be a black man to trick unsuspecting white men into crossing him.

"Are you going after Cantrell?" Slaughter asked.

King dragged in a deep breath. "How much is that reward?"

"Fifteen hundred. Dead or alive."

It would not be worth the trouble for so little money, to disrupt his life here, his business, leave his woman. But he had a personal score to settle with Cantrell. He stood up heavily, weighted down by his thoughts that had taken such a bitter turn.

"I will go, but I don't want any competition."

"You got my word."

King was towering over him, broad and stalwart. Slaughter had the urge to back away or hold up his hands, but the man did nothing.

"When does the next train leave here for parts south?"

"Twelve noon. You gonna be on it?"

"Yes."

CHAPTER
FORTY-FIVE

Ward rode through the bitter cold without feeling it, made camp ten miles north of the Powers spread, but found after his long, eventful day that sleep did not come. He was coiled like a spring inside, ready to meet and kill Younger.

He stared at the stars, traced the passage of clouds blocking the view, and watched the moon rise above the horizon. He listened to the yip and howl of coyotes off in the distance.

I'm defining a new market for myself. That's a new term I learned from Tim. We're getting married soon. . . .

He should have followed his instincts and slapped that condescending smile off her face. What a little hypocrite she was! One minute she made love to him wildly and with such abandon that he was half mad with desire for her, and then, for no reason, she changed into Winslow Breakenridge.

Ward closed his eyes. The thought of Leslie married to Tim Summers was unbearable. Why had she ridden to Buckeye and brought him money if she didn't love him? And if she had ten thousand dollars, why did she need Summers? If security were so damned important to her, why would she give it away?

He could see her long black hair fanned out on the pillow, framing her pale face. Her lime-green eyes half-closed, her seductive, kiss-swollen lips were provocatively parted. Her slender body beneath his own was enough to drive him mad.

He forced himself to stop seeing her, but he was outraged that she could spend such a long time making him love her so she could prove beyond doubt that she felt nothing for him. He had the terrible feeling that he would live the rest of his life alone, remembering her, married to Tim Summers.

Angrily, he closed his fist around a rock and threw it. To hell with her! And to hell with the governor's damned amnesty agreement. Bookkeeping was their problem, not his. He didn't give a damn whether they wiped his record clean or not. He could live in England or Europe under any name he chose. All he needed was money, and he had more than enough if he lived to be two hundred years old.

The only people who needed his services were the Mendozas, and theirs was the only debt he cared about paying. He had killed eight of the men who slaughtered them, and he was going to kill the last four.

He tried to concentrate on that goal, but kaleidoscopic flashes of memory haunted him. Was she as frankly sensual with Tim Summers? Did she take her pleasure as openly and as joyously with Summers as she did with him? Why had she waited naked in her room that night after the party? Could anyone be that high-minded? That she would sacrifice herself for a friend's reputation? Or ride twenty miles to repay what she considered a debt, and stay to give herself wholeheartedly, with wild, sweet abandon, before sprinkling her money on him?

Try not to hurt Younger. I may have to marry him. A day later she refused to leave when he tried to release her. She was a mass of contradictions. Even her actions today: first the melting, then the ice. Had she come to save him or only to buy him out? "As Tim's wife I will have everything I need," she'd said.

There was a certain sureness in the outcome of his life now. He couldn't expect to ride into Younger's camp, kill him, and ride out again—not alive anyway. He would die tomorrow, and Leslie would get married and live happily ever after.

He lay back and closed his eyes. Regrets accomplished nothing. At least tonight he didn't have to write any farewell letters. He'd said his good-byes this afternoon.

Sleep came at last and then dawn. The sun crept over the horizon and lit a bank of thunderheads from beneath with brilliant color, turning them and the sky a fiery orange and red. Ward saddled his horse and headed north. There had been good forage. Blueberry felt good. His stride was powerful, rhythmic, impatient. Ward gave him his head, and the stallion stretched out for a good long run that suited Ward's mood perfectly. He was ready for action—tired of waiting.

Morristown nestled in a steep-walled, bowl-shaped ravine formed by two mountains. A stream, barely more than a trickle, cut through the notch. The buildings were east of the almost barren watercourse, probably because spring snows swelled that trickle to a torrent. The residents had apparently learned respect for the river's path, avoiding it scrupulously.

As the sun set, Ward tethered Blueberry near tall grama grass and climbed the rock-studded ridge that overlooked the settlement. He watched from a vantage point on the slope of the mountain west of the small hamlet. There was no activity to indicate Younger was there. He rejoined Blueberry and rode boldly in.

The saloon was a run-down shanty, but it was in better shape than most of the other buildings. It smelled of wood smoke, bourbon, sweat, and cigars.

"Evenin', stranger." The bartender wiped the glass in his hand mechanically.

"Evening. Whiskey."

"Kinda off the beaten track, ain't yuh?" he asked after Ward downed two drinks slowly, appearing to be deep in thought.

"I don't pick where I work—just who I work for."

"And who might that be?"

"Don't reckon that's any of your business," Ward said non-committally, smiling to soften the rebuke.

The man nodded, accepting that. He could tell he was one of Younger's men, but he must be new, since he hadn't made a bee-line for Bass Wimer's place on the north end.

Ward finished his drink, paid the man, then paused, smiling sheepishly. "Younger leave this morning?"

"What's it to you?"

"Just trying to decide how much hell I'm gonna catch for making him mad."

" 'Bout twelve hours' worth."

Ward grimaced in pain. "Much obliged."

CHAPTER
FORTY-SIX

"Oh! It is so exciting! A real wedding at last. We haven't had a formal wedding in eight months. Can you believe that?" Elizabeth Cartright gushed. "Eight months!"

Leslie believed it. She felt nothing but envy for anyone who wasn't getting married in a few days. But she would die before she let Elizabeth know it. She had never been willing to submit her innermost thoughts to public scrutiny. Fortunately Elizabeth didn't require an answer, just a listener.

"Think how exciting it will be. You will be a young matron! That opens all sorts of doors! You'll share secrets with other young marrieds, and learn all about their secret affairs, who belongs to whom, so to speak. Oh, how I envy you! Tim is so *handsome*. I *adore* fair-skinned, black-eyed, black-haired men. They look so *intense*, don't they? And he has such a *nice* smile. It is obvious he absolutely *adores* you."

Leslie fretted over the pretty bouquet she was supposed to be making as a pew decoration and finally put it aside. Wedding preparations were tedious, boring, and a bloody waste of time. She was too nervous to work on trifles. She needed something—maybe a ride. And here she was, trapped with Elizabeth. A person could die listening to her talk about how wonderful everything was. Why didn't she let each person decide for herself what was wonderful and exciting about her own life? The way Elizabeth gushed, it was no wonder denials sprang into Leslie's head faster than she could stifle the flow.

Tim *was* going to be a good husband: considerate, loyal, faithful. He *was* handsome. It was just that his black eyes only looked friendly when he smiled, and too often he stared and then they looked unaccountably cold and unfeeling. It wasn't his fault, though. He had a lot on his mind. Kincaid kept him extremely busy. Leslie caught herself before she could follow that thought with *thank goodness*. In one week she would be married—how incredible! It had seemed so right, telling Ward Cantrell of her decision, but trying to live it was another matter altogether.

Damn you, Cantrell! Damn you!

A day's ride beneath low-hung, slow-moving thunderheads was endured before Younger's party reached the secret camp. Sandra was pale and weak. She had a bruise on her back that jarred each time the horse put a hoof down.

The string of tents trailing down the mountainside from a weathered gray house with a steep roof was a welcome sight. She was half-frozen, tired, in pain. Dallas lifted her off and carried her inside.

Men seated at the table playing cards stood up, scraping their chairs on the wooden floor. "She hurt?"

"Yeah, where can I put her?"

"There's a cot in the bedroom thar."

Dallas carried her through the main room while the others came stomping in, taking off their coats, exchanging greetings with the three men inside the house. They were more of the same rough lot that were becoming so familiar to Sandra: gunslingers, outlaws, range mavericks—trail trash, her father called them.

He put her down on a cot in the bedroom that opened onto the right side of the common area that was used as kitchen, parlor, and dining room. Tired as she was, she couldn't sleep. Dallas rubbed her back with horse liniment cut with butter. With her head on his arm, snuggled against his warm body, her last thought before sleep claimed her was that no one had *ever* been so good to her.

"Dallas, Dallas, wake up. . . ."

Younger opened one red-rimmed eye and glared balefully at Pick Sitwell.

"There's a messenger here from the boss. Won't talk to anyone but you."

"All right," he growled, disengaging himself gently from the sleeping girl and coming easily to his feet. He pulled his boots on and ran his fingers through his disheveled black hair, moving purposefully now that he was awake.

The messenger was Slim Parker, a tall stringbean of a man Dallas had seen many times before in that role. Neither of them acknowledged the other. Dallas appeared at the door; the messenger started off walking, and Dallas fell in beside him. It was habit. They didn't need to appear casual here in the midst of Dallas' own camp, surrounded by his men.

"The boss wants you to come see him."

Dallas hid the angry reaction that came instinctively to him and shrugged. "I thought I already had my orders. I was going to drive the herd down to the pens so we could ship 'em."

"He said he wants to talk to you—alone. He didn't mention any other plan."

Dallas cursed to himself. It would take a day to get down there and a day to get back. "All right," he growled. "Get yourself a fresh hoss and grab a bite to eat. I'll be with you in a minute."

The sun was just coming up, turning the sky near the eastern horizon misty rose. Clouds were gold on the bottom, like the leaves of aspen trees on the canyon floor. Dallas found his second lieutenant, Cedar Longley, pulling on his pants.

Dallas respected Longley in a way he did few men. It was Cedar who had led Younger into this old Apache stronghold; Cedar who placed the lookouts. Longley, son of an old Indian agent, had been raised on Indian reservations till he was twenty. His father was present at the signing of the Guadalupe Hidalgo Treaty, which made the U. S. government responsible for keeping the border Indians under control, and Cedar could tell surprising stories about the Apache as the feudal robber barons of the Southwest. He had watched them take regular and ritualistic tribute from settlers who chose to buy their safe passage rather than fight for it. For fifty years the Apache controlled the passes and looked with contempt upon the white tillers of the soil who lived in their wattled stick houses, plastered with mud and roofed with sticks and branches in the style of the Indian and Mexican arbors.

Younger's tone conferred that respect now. "I gotta go back and see the boss."

"What for?"

"Don't know."

Longley's face was dark, his cool blue eyes speculative. "You think he's getting cold feet?" he asked.

"Could be. Things are getting tolerable warm in these parts, what with Cantrell and his riders harassing our men and making brags that are firing up the ranchers. Hell! We ain't stole half as many cattle in the last two months as we been used to, but loose talk is causing so much hell ranchers are exaggerating like crazy."

Longley frowned and stood up. "We ain't had a chance to talk, what with the girl being hurt and all, but I guess now's just as good a time. The boys ain't going to take it lightly if he's figuring on going straight and leaving us out in the cold."

Younger nodded. "I reckon the boys won't be alone. I'm not taking kindly to the idea either. Ain't no reason why we couldn't continue just like usual once we kill Cantrell."

Longley nodded. "We're of a mind, then," he said with satisfaction.

"Drive 'em to the pens jest like we planned. We'll ship this herd whether he likes it or not."

While a man readied his and the messenger's horses, Younger drank coffee and ate bacon and biscuits.

"Tell Sweetface for me," he said, swinging into the saddle.

"Sure thing, Dallas, and you tell him for us."

"You betcha."

CHAPTER
FORTY-SEVEN

The sun was shrouded behind pale, cloudy vapors. The air was chill but dry and bracing. A horseman rode into Younger's mountain camp, the horse's hooves kicking up dust and eliciting angry shouts from men trying to shave along his path.

Cedar Longley, from his vantage point at the table, recognized the man as one of the sentries posted along the trail. He stood up.

By the time the rider reached the main building he was on the porch with his hat on.

"Rider coming," the man yelled, jerking his horse to a halt. The animal stamped and pawed the ground, kicking dust into the air.

"Alone?"

"Yeah."

"How's he moving?"

"Real casual-like, but he seems to know right where he's going."

"What's he look like?"

"Packing two guns, slung low. Blond dude—looking relaxed as hell."

Cedar Longley grunted. Ward Cantrell—it could be no other. An uneasy vibration raced through his lean frame. Cantrell was here to meet Younger and the last three survivors of the original band who had participated in the raid on the Mexican family—Bass Wimer, Pick and Rand Sitwell. Bass was just stupid. He could be led anywhere by anyone, and once he got caught up in the excitement, he would do anything. Pick and Rand were just plain mean. The two raw-boned twins had probably enjoyed every second of it.

Longley had been an outlaw since he was twenty-one, but he had never raped or murdered women. He had the real gunman's intolerance for needless cruelty. He would kill, but only in self-defense. And like all gunmen he knew the names and faces of all the really dangerous men: King Fisher, Sam Bass, Dusty Denton, Dallas Younger, Lance Kincaid, Ward Cantrell, Ben Thompson, Bat Masterson, Clay Allison, Wyatt Earp, and Temple Houston. At least half of them were already dead. Cedar didn't know any old gunfighters. Even the best of them met their match sooner or later. He'd heard about Cantrell first-hand because a friend had ridden with the Jackson Hole Gang the same time Cantrell had. According to Cedar's friend, Cantrell had split the gang down the middle. He was a born leader and when he stood up to their chief over a deal he wouldn't be a party to, half the men backed him. They woulda seen the bloodiest shootout in history if Cantrell hadn't convinced him that he was fast enough to kill him and three of his men before any one of them got a shot off. He was backed by Dusty Denton and a dozen others almost as good. Denton was greased lightning on the draw too. Rumor had it he could put three holes in the Ace of Diamonds—never missing that big diamond—from twenty paces.

Longley expelled a heavy breath. "Let him come."

"I'll pass the word."

"Do that." Longley, a big, rangy, solid-looking man, was famous for his eyes. They were dark blue and shot daggers that effectively discouraged opposition. He was a Texan, like Younger and Texas Jack Jones, with the Texan's inbred sense of fair play. He wouldn't condone having a man like Cantrell shot from ambush any more than Younger would if he were there.

He went inside and strapped on his guns.

"Hey, boss, what's up?"

"I reckon Ward Cantrell's on his way in here."

"Well, hell! Stop him!" Pick Sitwell came to his feet, almost knocking the table over, spilling coffee everywhere. "He ain't got no right riding in here in broad daylight like he owns the damned place!"

"Won't hurt to ask him his business then, will it?"

Rand Sitwell left the room and came back with his own gun. "Reckon we know what he wants," he said grimly, tying the holster down with a slender rawhide around his right thigh.

Pick and Bass Wimer were already wearing their guns.

"How many men with him?" Rand asked.

"None."

That should have been reassuring, but somehow it had the opposite effect. Pick Sitwell paled two shades, leaving the freckles standing out like tiny cherries floating in milk.

"He's crazy riding in here alone. Ain't no way he can get out alive. We got forty men here."

"Maybe he ain't worried about getting out. Reckon he's just interested in paying a call on the men that killed his friends," Longley said significantly.

"I don't reckon I like your tone, Longley. We was following orders, same as anyone in this gang follows orders. Jest doing what we were told."

"Then you won't mind explaining that to Cantrell. He looks like the understandin' sort."

"Like hell he does! I saw him once in Cheyenne—the day he met and killed Mad Dog Masters. He only understands one thing and that is that he don't brook no opposition."

"Reckon you got a problem all right," Cedar drawled.

"What!" Pick growled, coming over to glare into Longley's face. "I got a problem? I thought we were in this together."

"I don't hold with killing women and kids—nor even old men

waiting 'round to die. You pick your work and you pay the price. I'm a rustler, and I've been worse, but I got limits," Longley said quietly, inexorably.

"Well, ain't you something! All of a sudden, with one of the deadliest guns in the Territory riding in, you got scruples! Shit! You're scared—same as us!"

"I ain't denying that. I'm just warning you, the three of you are on your own."

"You yellow bastard!"

"Practical, maybe. He's got no business with me or any of the others."

Pick grabbed a chair and threw it at the wall, smashing it into a dozen pieces. "Bunch of fine friends you turn out to be." He faced the other five men in the room. "Y'all feel like this two-bit rustler here?"

Their silence spoke for them. They knew the raids on the honest ranchers, like the one on the Mendozas, were on a volunteer basis. Even among the hardest bunch of outlaws, most of them wouldn't participate in wiping out families. It spoke badly for this gang that twelve of the original fifty men had been willing to do it.

Ward had ridden hard the previous day and made up some of the twelve-hour lead Younger had on him. By the time the sun was up an hour he could see the rustler camp. A half-hour later he was there.

He rode slowly and casually, using the opportunity to observe the rustlers' hideout. It was cleverly hidden, comfortable and secure. If he hadn't been following fresh tracks, he wouldn't have found it. Fears that Denton would stumble into the camp and take on Younger's gang were permanently laid to rest.

Younger, or someone, must have had some army experience. The camp was laid out like a military encampment, with one main building and a string of tents straggling down the mountain. It was set in a ravine that branched off in four directions, like a well-planned rabbit hole—plenty of exits, but only one comfortable way to approach, and that well guarded. He had been aware of the sentries for the last five miles.

The house was old and weathered, and Ward guessed that that was where he would find Younger and his pack of killers. The thirty or so men who stepped away from their tents to watch his slow passage looked like run-of-the mill outlaws, little different from cowhands except that they lived by the gun now.

Ward saw signs that this was only a summer camp. First snow

would find this bunch on the move, probably heading down into Sonora.

Riding slowly, he appraised every face along that tent-strewn route, recognizing some of them on sight. They were all of a breed not vastly different from himself. A couple of them nodded when his narrowed blue eyes caught theirs and held for an instant. He recognized three men from the Lincoln County range war, one from the Pine Tree outfit.

He passed the last tent and turned his attention to the weathered gray house and its occupants. When he reached the steps to the porch, he dismounted, dropping the reins.

No one came out, so he went up the steps, his hands brushing the gun on either thigh. Only the scrape of his boots sounded in the stillness. Even the birds had stopped singing, as if they too were anticipating danger. He stopped at the open door and pushed his Stetson back with his left hand.

There were nine men in the small cabin in sight and a possibility of more behind the two closed doors. He almost smiled at that. They must have me overrated, he thought ruefully. Nine men should be able to do the job.

Longley saw that flicker of amusement in the steady blue eyes and felt something of what Cantrell must be feeling now. He stepped forward slowly. No one was making any sudden moves. "You got business here, Cantrell?"

Ward nodded. "With the slime that killed the Mendoza family."

Boots scraped as men moved out of the way, leaving three men alone in the center of the room. Ward hid his surprise that it had been so easy to single them out. The two raw-boned redheads and the fat one with fresh bruises on his meaty face had ridden in the parade, but he wasn't sure he could have picked them out. Apparently no one was covering for the three, exposed by the move toward the far walls.

"I got business with them," he said. "And Younger."

"Younger ain't here."

Ward accepted that. If he were here, he'd be where the action was, not hiding in a bedroom. "He take the girl?"

"Naw, she's still sleeping." Longley nodded toward the room on the right.

His questions answered, Ward turned his attention back to the three he came for. "You want to do this outside?"

"We ain't going to fight you, Cantrell. I ain't no gunfighter."

"I didn't come here to *fight* you. I came to *kill* you. Don't matter that you don't fight back—can if you want to—it ain't a requirement of mine."

Pick sputtered. "You mean you'd just shoot us down like mad dogs."

Cantrell nodded, watching them coldly, no sign of mercy in those pitiless blue eyes. "Just like you handled the Mendozas," he said flatly.

Pick nodded. "All right," he said, expelling a heavy breath. "Outside, then." Cantrell would either have to back out or turn and walk out. If he turned . . .

Longley knew Pick too well to turn his back on him, but apparently Cantrell didn't. He turned; Pick and the others clawed for their guns. Cantrell's turn changed into a full circle, and somehow by the time he was facing them again, both guns were smoking. The explosions rolled one on another until only Cantrell was standing. The floor was littered with the three men he had come there to kill. The sharp, piercing smell of gunpowder was strong.

Cantrell crouched in a posture of readiness, his guns pointing now at the others. "Who's in charge here?"

Longley stepped forward. "Reckon I am."

"I'm taking over this outfit. You got any objections?"

Longley thought about that for a moment. Younger was already talking about moving on to greener pastures. He knew Cantrell's history. He was a good man to ride with. Planned his jobs carefully, executed them well, didn't kill people in the process; no one died in his train holdups.

Longley shook his head. "No objections from me, but maybe some from Younger when he gets back."

"Good." He looked at the others now. "Which one of you do I have to kill to make this stick?"

Texas Jack Jones was the first to break the spell. He stepped to the side and picked up his hat. "I ain't never been too partic'lar who I work for. I'll go tell the boys."

With his exit, the tension began to relax.

"When do you expect Younger back?"

"Two days at the soonest."

"Pass the word. We're moving out in two hours, with the herd you're holding in that blind canyon," Ward said tersely.

Cedar Longley looked askance. Cantrell was crazy. It was one thing to ride in there past forty armed men to kill three men he wanted, but another thing entirely to ride out as the leader of that gang. The man had more guts than good sense. Or he didn't give a damn what happened to him.

Longley shook his head slowly. His eyes were clear—respect mingled with disbelief. Reckon your cards are about dealt out. Cain't hardly wait to see how this turns out. Your life ain't worth a white chip as it is. . . . Out loud he said, "Will do, chief."

Ward nodded and holstered his guns. He knew exactly how long that was good for—until Dallas Younger returned. And he knew that Cedar Longley knew it also.

"Is the girl all right?" Ward asked, starting toward the bedroom. Longley nodded. "You taking that over too?"

"You have any objections?"

"None atall."

The train pulled into Phoenix at eight o'clock Friday morning. John King stood and picked up his satchel. He stopped beside the conductor.

"Which way to the jail?"

"Down that street. You can't miss it."

Sheriff Tatum was not a small man, but he felt small next to the massive black man who stopped beside where he was tacking up another wanted poster.

"You're the sheriff?" The voice had a cultured eastern accent that didn't look like it belonged on a big strapping black man with the battered face of a professional fighter.

"That's right," Tatum nodded.

The big Negro held out his enormous hand. "My name is John King. I'm from Dodge City."

Tatum looked at the hand, then at the man's eyes. He slowly held out his hand.

"Matthew Tatum." He'd never shaken hands with a Negro before. He resisted the impulse to wipe his hand on his pant leg. "What can I do for you?"

"I'm looking for Ward Cantrell. You know where I can find him?"

A light dawned in Tatum's eyes. Now he knew why that face looked vaguely familiar. There had been a story about John King in one of those fancy eastern magazines. The man was a bounty hunter. He was the one who hounded the Shiner brothers until they killed themselves rather than keep running or be caught by King. The man was implacable.

"Everybody's looking for Ward Cantrell," he said heavily.

"Half the town is out right now. If they find him first, maybe you can cut him down and take him back."

"What did he do?"

"I don't know that he *did* anything, but folks think he kidnapped a girl, murdered a wealthy rancher, and rustled some cows."

"How come you're not with the posse?"

"They got seventy men. That ain't a posse. It's a lynch mob. They don't need me," Tatum said flatly.

King nodded. "I'm staying at the hotel I noticed on the way here—the Bricewood West. I'd appreciate it if you'd let me know if you hear anything that would be helpful to me." He took out a fifty-dollar bill and stuffed it in Tatum's vest pocket.

Tatum pulled the neatly folded bill out and looked at it. That was a month's wages for him. He shook his head and gave the money back.

"You'll hear before I will," he said tiredly. "This town ain't got any secrets, especially about Cantrell."

John King thanked him and headed back toward the hotel.

Sheriff Tatum finished nailing up the posters and then got his jacket and walked over to see if Chane Kincaid was in his office.

CHAPTER
FORTY-EIGHT

"What time is the boss going to meet me?" Dallas asked.

"Ten o'clock tonight—the usual place."

Younger and Slim Parker separated at the river. Younger rode into town alone just after sunset, stabled his horse, Maverick, and walked to the Red Eye Saloon to kill time and listen to the talk. Friday nights were lively. There was the usual stir when he entered. He had admirers and those who carried grudges, but there were few men who would publicly denounce him—he had survived too many gunfights for that.

The gossip was about Cantrell: his challenge to rustler gangs, his kidnapping of Sandra McCormick, and how mad everyone was because the governor hadn't appointed a special cadre of rangers to hunt him down. Whole ranches had stopped normal operations to join unofficial posses. Everyone was outraged. If they caught him, they would hang him first and ask questions later. Or shoot on sight. Younger grinned at that—his sentiments exactly, except in his case it was a necessity.

Younger ordered a steak and sat down at a table alone with his back to the wall so he could watch both entrances. He was halfway through the steak, listening idly to the talk around him, enjoying the gaiety and the stimulation a crowd provided, when a pretty, young dark-haired girl approached his table.

"Howdy," she said tentatively.

"Howdy yourself," he replied, grinning appreciatively.

She was young and fresh-looking, not brassy or belligerent like some of the older women were.

"You in the mood to buy me a drink?"

"Set yourself down and we'll see." He nodded to the bartender for two drinks and leaned back, grinning. "Don't recollect seeing you here before."

"I ain't been here long—about a week." Her eyes roved over him, lingering on his broad, furry chest. "You sure are a good-looking dude," she said admiringly.

"You like 'em big and rough, do you, sweet thing?"

She giggled and tossed her hair. "My name's Peggy. What's yours?"

"Dallas Younger."

Her eyes widened. She cocked her head at him. "You one of those dangerous Texans I been hearing so danged much about?"

"Who you been hearing about?" he countered.

"Oh, you and Ward Cantrell."

"Cantrell ain't no Texan. He's no Texan—none atall!"

"How come you say that?"

"I know a phony Texas accent when I hear one, sweet thing. He can drop it and does too damned often for it to be real."

"He's a phony gunfighter, then?"

Dallas shook his head. "I didn't say that either. The men he's killed are just as dead. I reckon he's a gunfighter all right—he just ain't from Texas."

"I thought all the really dangerous men was from Texas," she laughed.

"That's 'cause those damned Texas rangers hound a man until he has to leave or hang. You didn't sit down here to listen to my life story, did you, sweet thing?"

"I sat down here to do whatever you wanted me to. If you want to talk"—she shrugged— "well, that's fine by me," she said, smiling archly.

"And if I want to go upstairs?"

She laughed breathlessly, and he tossed a coin on the table and took her arm.

Peggy enjoyed Dallas Younger thoroughly. He was exactly what he appeared: a simple man who took his pleasures when and where he found them. No fancy stuff for him. His loving was as straightforward as he was.

At nine-thirty, Dallas disengaged himself and dressed.

"You don't forget me, Dallas, honey," she said, fingering the twenty-dollar gold piece he had tossed onto the bed. "Next time you're in town ask for Peggy, you hear?"

"Right, sweet thing."

Younger sauntered through the saloon, waving and nodding to acquaintances. He left the noisy saloon, but the raucous sounds of laughter, piano music, and loud talk followed him halfway to the livery stable where he had left Maverick.

The stable boy was asleep or gone. Younger walked through the big barn, lit now by one kerosene lamp hanging from a support post, to the stall where his horse waited.

"Howdy, Maverick. You enjoy that grain, did you?" He reached for the saddle that was draped over the gate, and just as he did, a noise behind him, like the crunch of straw underfoot, brought his senses surging alert. He threw himself sideways, using the momentum of the saddle swinging down to help. He fell, rolled, came up with his gun in his hand, only to hear the sound of footsteps running into the dark alley.

He holstered his gun, cursing himself for not getting a look at his would-be assailant. He took the lamp off the post and looked around the barn floor for footprints, hoping he would recognize some peculiarity. But the straw that had probably saved his life didn't provide footprints. A gleam of metal led him to a buck knife half-hidden by straw. He picked it up, tested the blade, and flinched when its razor-sharp edge nicked his thumb. Probably the same knife that had killed Powers. He stuck it in his boot, saddled Maverick, and led the horse outside before he mounted him.

Summers was waiting for him beside the old line shack. "You're late," he said testily.

"Had a little problem."

"Anything serious?"

"Naw. What's up?" Dallas demanded.

"Slight change of plans. We aren't going to be moving cattle over the Texas and Pacific anymore. Too risky now. I want you to drive this herd to El Paso and ship them on Crocker's line."

"El Paso! That's eight hundred miles."

"I know how far it is," Summers said caustically. "Do you have a better idea?"

"We're rustlers, not drovers. Mexico's closer if you don't care what kind of price you get for them."

"Mexico's fine. I'm through with rustling. When this is over, scatter the gang."

"What if they don't want to be scattered? We've had a pretty comfortable set-up here for a long time," Dallas said.

"Then kill them! I don't care how you do it—just do it!" he said vehemently, his pale face reflecting his intensity.

Dallas kept his face impassive, but he was remembering that Powers had been killed when he was no longer useful. Now that Summers was marrying the Powers girl, he didn't need the gang anymore—or Dallas. Dallas started to point this out to Summers, but the sound of a rider approaching at a rapid rate brought both their heads around.

"Did anyone know you were coming here?" Summers demanded, his eyes like black pearls in the moonlight.

"Only Parker—he told me to be here."

"I can't afford to be seen with you," Summers said angrily. He moved into the abandoned line shack, and Younger stepped away from the door and moved to stand in the shadow of the building. The rider was only Parker, but he looked agitated, riding the horse almost into the side of the shack before he could stop him.

"Whoa, dammit, whoa!" he shouted, swinging down. "Dallas, it's me, Slim!"

Younger stepped around the corner, putting his gun away. "What you all lathered up about?"

"Hell to pay up at the camp! Texas Jack sent a rider down to let you know what happened. Smoky said Cantrell rode up there and killed three men: Rand and Pick Sitwell and Bass Wimer. He's looking for you, Dallas. And he's taken over the gang. They're driving the cattle down to the pens starting first thing after Cantrell got there. Smoky almost killed a hoss getting here! I found you as fast as I could," he panted, sagging against the wall.

"That worthless two-bit bunch of bastards!" Summers swore, coming out of the building. "Forty goddamned men up there and they let him ride in, kill three of their friends, and then start giving orders! I don't want those cattle at the pens! I want those pens destroyed! Not a trace!'' he said vehemently.

"That don't solve our immediate problem," Dallas drawled, watching Summers.

"Go on," Summers said grimly.

"Looks like Cantrell has decided to be your new partner—cutting me out. Don't look like he wants to be told to take those cows and stuff 'em."

Summers controlled his fury with an effort. "If you have an idea, now is the time for it," he said grimly.

Dallas grinned. Summers was an arrogant bastard. He was enjoying seeing him sweat. "Cantrell is in one hell of a precarious spot. He's got almost forty men behind him, driving five hundred head of stolen cattle, and he's all alone. Soon as I show up—don't matter what he's doing—those men are mine. I take him on, and it's open season on Cantrell. He's a dead man."

"Are you absolutely sure of that?"

"Hell, yes, I'm sure. They're a good ole bunch of boys, but there ain't a leader in the lot. I step back into the picture, and they'll follow me."

"I'm going with you. I want to be sure Cantrell is dead. No slip-ups this time."

Younger raised one eyebrow, but he resisted the urge to remind Summers that he was the one who made the mistake that put Cantrell on their backs in the first place. "When d'yuh want me to brace Cantrell?"

"Soon as possible. I want this behind me. I'm getting married in a few days, and I want that bastard dead! I'm tired of him messing around in my business."

"We can cut 'em off about sunset tomorrow, before they move out of the brakes, if we leave first thing tomorrow morning."

"All right, I'll meet you outside of town at six o'clock in the morning."

Friday night and not even Tim was around to help her fight off the doldrums. Monday the creamy white lace Jennifer had ordered would arrive and they could start work on the wedding gown, but now . . .

Jennifer came into the parlor where Leslie was putting the finishing touches on a sketch of the mountains to the north.

"Where's Tim tonight?" She had just come downstairs from

tucking the children into their beds. Jennie had changed drastically in the last week. Her lovely purple eyes were haunted, forlorn, filled with worry, pain, fear. She had faint blue circles under her eyes, like bruises. It was almost physically painful for Leslie to look at her. She felt embarrassed, as if she were prying into family secrets.

Jennifer was able to hide her pain for brief social intervals, but it came back quickly, stronger than before, as if the poor thing were crumbling under the strain.

Leslie saw this as proof that Cantrell had lied about his relationship with Jennie. Had he also lied about how he fell into outlawry? Not that it mattered any longer. She was finished with him, but she hated being taken in by a cheat.

"Tim had a business meeting. He left at eight-thirty. He said if we were up, he would stop afterward."

Jennie sighed and slipped into a chair, depression showing in the uncharacteristic lethargy that seemed to have seeped into her very bones. "I don't see how you do it," she sighed. "Every time I look at you you're doing another painting, or finishing a sketch. Don't you ever get moody?"

Leslie grimaced. "Moodiness is a luxury. People with few interests are moody. Those of us with work we love experience different degrees of tiredness." She stifled the urge to remind Jennie that she used to be one of the busy ones, before her obsession with Cantrell.

"I guess you'll be waiting up for Tim then. Would you like to play gin rummy? Chane won't be back until almost eleven. He had another meeting with the governor about the rustlers. I know I'll never be able to sleep," she said nervously.

"I'd love to play rummy," she lied. She would do anything to help Jennie. She owed her so much, both her and Chane. In truth, she had lost interest in painting as well. But she continued out of desperation. It was easy to hide behind her work. There were times when she did enjoy it. There were other times when she took her rage out on the canvas. She worked because not to work was unthinkable, because she knew that this too would pass, and when it did, if she had worked hard, she would have something besides her scars to show for it.

They moved to the table. Jennifer brought out the cards and shuffled them. She dealt each of them ten cards and turned a ten of clubs face up. "You go first," Jennifer said.

They arranged their hands, and Leslie drew a card from the

stack, pretending to concentrate. "Any news about Cantrell?" she asked casually.

Jennifer looked thoroughly miserable. Her hand trembled as she took a card. "Only bad news so far. Sam McCormick has increased the reward. He wants Ward tarred and feathered *before* they hang him," she said bitterly.

"Why is he so sure Ward took her? She's a big girl. She could have just run away." Since leaving Cantrell in a jealous fury, she had thought of six ways he could have gotten Sandra's locket.

"I guess because she chased him so. She was so infatuated with Ward. Anyone could tell."

"She looked just as infatuated with Dallas Younger to me," Leslie said defensively. She had gone over that scene at the hotel in Buckeye a thousand times. She watched Ward's reaction over and over, and she still could not be sure he had taken Sandra. Wouldn't he have looked guilty? Wouldn't he have tried to hide Sandra's necklace? Unless he hadn't expected her to follow him there—and of course he hadn't. If he *was* innocent, where did he get the scratches? She always came back to that.

Jennifer's lips tightened into an angry line. "I know it wasn't Ward. I've known him too long. He's not a sneak thief. If he wanted a woman, he would announce it to the world."

Leslie lowered her eyes, embarrassed and miserable for her friend. Had Jennie forgotten that Cantrell had kidnapped her?

Jennie saw Leslie's expression and stopped. "You think me batty, don't you?"

"No, of course not," she said gently, biting back the urge to say, "But I don't see how you can be so sure he's innocent."

"He had a good reason for taking you," Jennie said, as if reading her mind. "Those men killed four people he loved!"

"What?"

Jennie stopped, alarmed that she had blurted a secret they had agreed needed to be kept until this business was settled. "I guess there's no help for it now." She sighed and told her the story of the Mendoza family's murder.

"I never knew . . ." Leslie whispered when Jennie, eyes brimming with tears, ended her recital. "He never told me."

Jennie patted Leslie's hand. "To retell it is to relive it. He told Chane because he had no choice. They were going to hang him."

Leslie bit her tongue to keep from replying. She was moved to tears by the story of the Mendoza family, but that did not change the major issue between the two of them. She could forgive many things, but infidelity was not one of them. It was an unforgivable crime between a man and a woman. She was immovable in that regard. Ward Cantrell could be champion to any number of Mendoza families, honest in every other respect, but if he could make love to another woman after that day at Aravaipa Canyon . . .

Confused and frustrated, Leslie covered her face with her hands. "Why can't he just stay away from women?" She didn't realize she had spoken aloud until she heard Jennie.

"She chased him!" Jennifer said, instantly angry. "You won't see too many men who toss aside beautiful women who throw themselves at their feet. Most men will allow a woman to make as big a fool as she wants of herself." Jennifer laughed suddenly, a brittle, tinkly sound that bordered on hysteria. "You'll think me foolish," she said, new tears welling in her eyes, "but I really think Ward is in love with you."

Lime-green eyes widened, and the last vestige of color drained out of Leslie's cheeks.

"Oh," Jennifer said, "I know he isn't like Tim, always showering you with attention, flattery, and gifts, but I could see the reaction in him the second he saw you, or someone mentioned your name. I'm equally sure he was careful not to let you know, but he can hide very little from me. I've known him too long. He acted very much like Chane did when we were in love but our problems were keeping us apart."

Jennie sighed, responding to the implacable look on Leslie's face. "I'm sorry. It's just that I am so worn out from worrying about him. It seems I've worried about him so damned long." Tears began to stream down her cheeks, and she buckled forward, covering her eyes with her trembling hands.

Alarmed, Leslie moved around the table and put her arms around her. "There, there," she whispered, feeling helpless.

Jennie huddled against Leslie's shoulder, sobbing. After a time, the gasps turned into sniffs and then into shuddering indrawn breaths. At last, she raised her head and smiled weakly. "I know he didn't take her."

Contrarily, Leslie remembered his response when she asked him if her lovemaking had been satisfactory: that husky-quiet "very" and the look in his suddenly opaque blue eyes, as if he were expecting a twist of the knife. Well, she hadn't disappointed him, had she?

Leslie was suddenly trembling. She stood up. "I'm tired. I think I'll take a bath and go to bed, if you don't mind."

"Of course, dear. We both need rest. There won't be much time next week with shopping and fittings and then the wedding and honeymoon, will there?"

Unfortunately sleep did not come. At eleven-thirty she finally got out of bed, wrapped a blue silk dressing robe around her, and started down the stairs only to be stopped by masculine voices coming from the first floor, from the direction of the library. She was at the top of the stairs. The library door opened, and she stepped back into the shadows. She was in no mood to see anyone now.

Chane and Tim stopped in the entry hall.

"When will you be leaving for Tucson?" Chane asked.

"Early. My business should be completed in two or three days and I'll catch the first train back."

"Don't rush. These family things come up. Take your time. You've earned a vacation."

"Thank you, Mr. Kincaid. I really appreciate all you've done for me."

"Nonsense. You work hard. I'm going to hate losing you."

"Well, maybe we can still be useful to each other, even after I take over the ranch."

"I'm sure we can be. Then you'll be a customer, if all goes well."

Tim laughed. "Of course. I forgot that." Then his voice sobered. "Unless Cantrell has already stolen all my cattle," he said grimly.

Chane, a scowl darkening his handsome face, held out his hand.

"You'll tell Leslie for me, won't you?" Tim asked.

"Of course. Have a good trip. Give your aunt our regards."

"Thank you, sir."

The front door closed, and Leslie slipped back into her bedroom, the urge for a glass of milk forgotten. Tim was going away on business—a family problem. Relief swept over her. She had no problem going to sleep after that.

CHAPTER
FORTY-NINE

Leslie woke long before dawn. She lay quietly, listening to the sounds of birds coming awake. Her window was half-open and she shivered slightly, wondering if the cold had awakened her. The sky was a luminous gray, becoming lighter in a cloudless dawn. Yesterday's clouds, which had looked so threatening, were gone, leaving the air crisp and fresh. She felt good, like a weight had been lifted off her shoulders. She stretched and rolled around in the bed, enjoying the freedom and the delicious tingle of good health. Too bad her head was still so confused.

Maybe a ride would straighten that out. It had worked before. She got out of bed and dressed in a simple buckskin skirt that Jennie had given her for riding astride—it had been her sister-in-law's. Apparently Angie didn't cotton to all those fancy riding habits most women wore. With a pale green cambric blouse and the cashmere coat—why not? No one would see her anyway. Mrs. Lillian was in the kitchen. She stopped for muffins and bacon, even stuffing some in her pockets for later.

"Tell Mrs. Kincaid I'm going for a ride. I'll be back before lunch."

"You be careful, dear. Remember what happened to that other young lady."

Leslie smiled. I should be so lucky, she thought.

"I'll be fine. Mr. Kincaid insists I take one of the guns from the stable with me. Don't worry. He taught me how to shoot it."

Leslie chose the big white Arabian again because she liked his gait and he was in a stall instead of loose in the corral.

Saddled up, with the gun in a holster hanging from the pommel, she headed north. Even with Dallas Younger no longer around—he was gone, Tim said, probably in New Mexico or Nevada looking for work—she still wouldn't ride west toward her ranch. She enjoyed riding toward the mountains. It gave her a special sense of freedom, and today she was glad to be alone.

The sky turned clear blue and it was warm enough so that she rolled the coat up and put it behind her saddle. Two hours of the big horse's rhythmic stride and her absorption in the ride burned away her strange mood.

She turned the horse back toward Phoenix about to kick him into a run when she saw a tiny speck between her and the distant town. She stopped, leaning forward to stroke the horse's sleek, wet neck.

She had good eyes, but the riders, if the speck was riders, were too far away: just a tiny cloud of dark vapor, but something flashed a warning at her.

"*You be careful, dear. Remember what happened to that other young lady.*" She looked for cover and found it less than a hundred feet away. There was probably no need for this but . . .

She stifled her doubts. It would cost nothing but a little time to be careful. She waited a half hour before they came into sight. Recognizing them, she stiffened in surprise and rushed to cover her horse's mouth so he wouldn't snort and draw attention to her.

Dallas Younger and Tim Summers! What an unlikely duo! Especially since Tim had told Chane he was going to Tucson about family problems! Tucson was the other direction.

Her heart was pounding, a heavy ache in her chest. She was afraid, stunned, but she didn't know why she should be. Tim could have a perfectly reasonable excuse for riding north into the mountains with Dallas Younger.

Could she follow them and find out what they were up to? She waited until they passed out of sight, and followed at a pace calculated to keep her well behind them. The tracks were plain in the soft, sandy loam. It should be no problem to follow them as long as they didn't see her.

By sundown the cattle, stretching back as far as Ward could see, had begun to settle down to the drive. It would take time before they adjusted fully, and the drive—four days—would be over before they made it. Cedar Longley was in charge. He was the closest thing this bunch had to a trailwise drover who knew where they were going.

Ward didn't stay in one position long. He rode lead and then drag and then rode ahead to see if the cook had found a suitable place to stop for the night. The heavily laden chuckwagon was already camped.

Dinner was simmering over the cook fires and Sandra lay on a pallet under a tree with blankets pulled up under her chin. When she saw Ward she came up into a sitting position.

"You can't hold me prisoner forever," she said angrily.

Ward dismounted and poured himself a cup of coffee. "I don't intend to. I'm taking you home, where you belong." He hunkered down between his horse and the campfire.

"I don't *belong* at home! I belong with Dallas. He isn't anything like you said. He's nice, and he loves me."

"After you explain to your father that I didn't kidnap you, you can go anywhere you want, with anyone you please," he said flatly.

"That's all you care about, isn't it? That's all you ever cared about! You never cared about me—just your own skin!"

Ward grinned. "It has been on my mind."

"Don't you dare laugh at me!" she yelled, coming to her feet. "You won't think this is funny when Dallas gets back! He'll kill you! He's not going to let you get away with this! Even if you did kill him, which you can't, 'cause you're not good enough, the others would kill you."

"Got it all figured out, don't you, Trinket?" he asked, still grinning.

"You're crazy. You can't possibly survive this! Why aren't you worried? Why don't you just ride away before Dallas comes back, and save yourself. I don't really want to see you die," she said, her eyes dropping away from his.

"I am worried," he said evenly. "I think you've got it figured right."

"Then why are you smiling?"

"Why not?" He shrugged. He stood up, reached into his saddlebags, and tossed her the necklace he was carrying for her. She frowned at him, fingering the chill necklace until a light dawned in her eyes. He was giving it back so she could give it to someone who would survive her. Someone who would be around to remember her. But now that Dallas loved her she no longer felt like she was going to die. She felt invincible.

Slowly, still looking into Cantrell's eyes, she fastened the necklace around her throat. They didn't talk anymore. Ward finished his coffee and rode back to rejoin his herd.

The sun had just slipped beneath the horizon, and the sky was ablaze with gold, red, and purple clouds when Dallas Younger spotted the herd milling around as the riders tried to drive them into a blind canyon to hold them overnight.

"Whoa," Dallas said softly. "Whoa, Maverick."

"So, we finally come face to face with Cantrell," Summers said, a feral light glittering in his black eyes.

"No holds barred," Dallas said grimly, checking his gun. He spun the cylinder, broke it, and added one bullet where he usually carried only five. It was a safety precaution to keep an empty chamber under the hammer when he wasn't expecting trouble.

"What are you going to do?" Tim asked.

"Wait till they settle them steers down and most of 'em are around the cookfires eatin'. I reckon that'll be as good a time as any to face him."

"Your men behind him and you in front of him." Summers grinned with satisfaction. Younger was a better man than he had thought. Too bad he didn't need him any longer. He chuckled. "Too bad I can't watch firsthand."

"I thought you were riding in with me," Dallas said, a frown pulling his straight black brows down.

"You know I can't afford to have that many people know who I am," he said testily, looking at Younger as if he weren't too bright.

Dallas Younger's cool dark eyes swept over him. "What did ya come along for?"

"To make sure Cantrell is dead. I told you that once, and I don't like repeating myself," Tim said, his tone harsh, cutting.

Dallas grunted to himself, thinking, *or to finish me off if I survive killing Cantrell?* Ever since Powers's death he had been thinking like that. Last night when someone had tried to cut his throat—the same way Powers died—his suspicions had multiplied.

Since Cantrell had killed every member of Summers's special troops, only Slim Parker and he knew who the real head of the gang was. It would be no problem for Summers to get rid of the trusting Parker. With himself and Parker dead, Summers would be in the clear for good. No one could tie the murders or the rustling back to him. He could marry Leslie Powers next Saturday and be a rich and respectable man.

Dallas settled down to wait for the right time. Dusk came, the sky turned smoky gray, and the riders wandered in one by one to the cookfires that burned like three beacons in the distance.

Finally Dallas stood up and mounted his horse. Summers maintained his stance by the oak tree he was leaning against.

"Mount up," Dallas said tersely.

"What did you say?" Summers shot him an incredulous look,

his pale face mirroring the disruption Younger's insolent command caused in him.

"I said mount up. I'm taking you with me. If you're worried about your reputation, you can go in as my prisoner. No one will know except me that you're not."

"This is ludicrous! You don't need me," he protested, fighting for control. He was furious, but this was not the time to vent that fury. He would settle with Younger later—after the man killed Cantrell.

"Mount up," Dallas said softly, inexorably, drawing his gun smoothly to aim it at Summers's chest.

Tim hid his venom behind his usual calm mask as he strode to his horse. He mounted. They rode boldly down the incline into the camp. There was still enough light so that one of the men, looking up from his bowl of beans, yelled: "Hey, it's the boss!"

Dallas heard Sweetface give a glad cry, and grinned before he settled down to business. He singled out Cantrell and decided how he was going to proceed.

No one made a move to slow their progress. Summers rode in front like a hostage. There was complete silence when they stopped beside the cookfire Cantrell stood in front of.

With the fire between them, Younger and Cantrell faced each other.

"Welcome back," Cantrell said quietly.

Younger trained the gun on Cantrell's broad chest and grinned. "It's good to be back." Then, without taking his eyes off Ward, he said, "Hey Cedar, you here?"

"Over here, boss."

"Good. I want you to take all the boys and get that herd moving again."

"What?" Tim asked incredulously, turning on Younger.

"You better learn to keep quiet," Dallas growled.

"What do you think you're doing?" Summers asked vehemently, ignoring Dallas's warning.

"The boys are going to drive those steers to the railroad so I can settle my business here and join them," he said coolly.

Cedar Longley looked at Dallas, saw that he meant what he said, and shouted an order for the men to get moving. There was a scramble of activity, some grumbles about the change, as men put down their bowls and coffee cups and began to run for the remuda and their horses.

Sandra came forward from the shadows. "Dallas, honey, I'm staying with you, aren't I?"

Dallas frowned. He had forgotten her momentarily. "I reckon," he said finally. "Don't move, though. Stay outta my way." She was behind Cantrell, between him and the chuckwagon but far enough to Cantrell's right so she was out of the line of fire. "Summers, go stand by Cantrell so I can keep an eye on both of you without straining too much."

Tight-lipped with fury, Tim complied. They waited like that while Longley and the others saddled up and moved out to start the cattle moving again. The cook started to move the wagon, but Dallas told him to leave it. He nodded and ran to find himself a horse. Soon they were gone, leaving Tim, Sandra, and Cantrell waiting silently across the fire from Younger, waiting for him to make his move.

CHAPTER
FIFTY

Ward turned and grinned at Summers. "You can relax now. No one can hear you anymore."

"What do you mean by that?" Summers asked, contempt showing in the oily glitter of his black eyes.

"You're Younger's boss. It was a good ploy, but no longer necessary. I knew two days ago. I just didn't realize I knew until you came riding in here."

"How did you know?"

"You're the one who had something to gain by killing Powers and framing me, and you were the one in Kincaid's office with the pull to cover your tracks."

"Too bad you found out too late, isn't it, Mr. Cantrell?"

Ward shrugged. "Better late than never."

"Not in your case," Tim said, his voice taut with fury. He turned to Younger. "Kill him," he snarled.

"Not until you tell him I didn't lead that raid on the Mendozas," Dallas said.

"What the hell difference can that make to a dead man?" Summers demanded angrily.

"It makes a tolerable difference to me, Summers," Dallas drawled. "I don't go around killing helpless women and kids. I got my pride. It happens to be important to me."

"Shit!" Summers sneered. "You're a killer. What difference could three or four more make to you?"

"I don't reckon you savvy gunfighters, Summers. I ain't never killed an unarmed man," Dallas said stubbornly.

"He's helpless. That's as good as being unarmed," Summers sneered, pointing at Cantrell.

"I ain't killed him yet," Dallas said significantly.

"Well, what the hell are you waiting for?" Summers snapped.

"For them to get good and gone," he said, nodding toward his riders. "Or did you forget, we're still protecting your image? Might as well have a cup of coffee. We'll be here a spell."

Ward backed up slowly and leaned against the chuckwagon. All these weeks he was after the wrong man. Dallas Younger was exactly what he appeared to be: a thoughtless ruffian and a gunfighter-turned-rustler, but not a murderer. He should have known. Summers had left clues. He hadn't seen them because he was thinking of him as Leslie's lover. That was reason enough to hate him; apparently it clouded his mind as well.

In his mind's eye he saw Leslie, slim, proud, defiant. *As Tim's wife I will have everything I need.* She was unaware of her lover's complicity. He knew that without question. Leslie Powers could not condone dishonesty in anyone associated with herself. She was a victim like the others.

"Hey, Trinket. Who took you to the Powers spread?"

Sandra's eyes widened in surprise at being addressed. She looked mesmerized by events. "Why, he did," she said, pointing to Summers.

Ward laughed. "I guess Summers is going to have to see to it that none of us gets away from here alive."

"Don't listen to him, Dallas. He's trying to confuse you," Tim said, shooting a reassuring look at Younger.

The herd was moving now. Conversation stopped. The rumble of hundreds of steers running was like thunder, loud and continuous, moving closer. They were almost a half-mile away, but sound traveled far in the clear mountain air.

Leslie stopped at the foot of the hill, ready to turn back. Dusk had come too soon and she lost their trail. Even by continuing in a straight line, she didn't find them. She felt frustration and anger at herself for staying too far back. If she weren't so timid . . .

She turned the horse, unwilling to continue the search. A low rumble, like distant thunder, stopped her. What on earth? She turned the horse and forced it to climb the hill. She could see from there if it wasn't already too dark.

The hill was little more than a hump between mountains, but once she gained the uppermost hummock she saw a black mass of cattle, shaped like a triangle, moving slowly, at a safe distance. In the foreground, a covered wagon stood tall and ghostly pale beside three fires. She recognized Sandra, Tim, and Younger, but cursed the encroaching dusk, wondering if that lean tawny-haired figure beside the fire could possibly be Cantrell.

There was a sudden urgency in her. She had to know the meaning of this bizarre meeting. She spurred her horse and rode boldly down the hill. The wagon was at least two hundred yards away. They couldn't hear one horse over that growing rumble. She rode within fifty yards of the wagon, then dismounted, remembering to take the gun. Leaving her horse with reins dragging, she walked the rest of the distance, to come up from behind the wagon.

She thanked the noise of the herd for covering her clumsy attempts to be stealthy. She was panting by the time she reached the tall covered wagon Kincaid had called a Conestoga.

She took a few seconds to catch her breath and bring the gun up into position. Then she peeked over the seat. At first all she saw was Dallas Younger with a gun, facing her. She moved slowly to the other end of the wagon, slipped around to the front, and peered over the edge of the low wagon bed. This time she saw Ward, Sandra, and Tim. Sandra was facing her, wearing the neckace she had admired at the dance, the same one she found on the vanity in Ward's room in Buckeye.

She stepped back, trying to still the sudden pounding of her heart. Ward Cantrell *had* run off with Sandra! What a monumental liar he was! Or an excellent evader. She hadn't asked. He had pretended innocence and she had fallen for it. Fool! Idiot! Now Younger was probably going to kill them—even Tim. Poor Tim. Of all the people who might deserve to die violently he certainly was not one of them. He was gentle, dull, and boring—the perfect administrator and bookkeeper.

Leslie leaned against the wagon, trying to get control of her pounding heart and shaking hands. She *had* to save them. Before she lost her nerve, she dragged in a ragged breath, lifted her chin, and stepped around the side of the wagon.

"Drop your gun, Mr. Younger," she said firmly, both hands gripping the gun as hard as she could to keep from trembling.

CHAPTER
FIFTY-ONE

"Drop it! Or I shoot!"

Dallas Younger considered the alternatives. If he turned toward her Cantrell would draw. If he shot Cantrell she would shoot him. Could she hit him at twenty paces? She sure lord looked like she thought she could.

He dropped the gun into the dust at his feet.

"Tim, get his gun!" Leslie yelled, moving away from the wagon so she could cover the others.

Summers moved swiftly to comply. When he had Younger's gun in his hand he waved it at Younger. "Get over there with the others," he said tersely. He motioned Leslie to his side, drew her trembling body against him with his free arm and gave her a hug. "Thanks, darling, you just saved my life," he said gratefully.

"What are we going to do now?" she asked, turning in his embrace to face the three in front of the wagon.

Summers considered that for a moment in silence, reassuring her with the warmth and pressure of his body. He would kill all three of them, but he mustn't let her see it happen. She was idealistic and trusting now, but if she thought him a rustler and murderer, her stupid ideals would turn her against him. She must keep thinking of him as a model of perfection—at least until after the wedding.

"Leslie, darling, I want you to go for help."

"I can't leave you here . . . with them," she protested.

"Darling, it's necessary. I can take care of everything now." He gestured with the gun at Cantrell, and Leslie dared to look at him for the first time. "Throw down your guns, Cantrell. Do it!" he said vehemently, with barely controlled viciousness. "Do it or I'll drop you where you stand!"

In the firelight Ward's eyes were in shadow, but Leslie saw the flexing of smooth muscles in his cheek as his left hand unbuckled the gunbelt at his narrow hips. Even knowing all she did about him, the life force in him—so vital and commanding, so resolutely masculine—urged her toward him. She shuddered at her own weakness. His eyes were probably spitting hate at her. Thank goodness she couldn't see them!

"Hey, Dallas," Ward drawled, "how long do you think he'll wait to kill us after she leaves?"

"Reckon about five minutes," Dallas said, "until she gets out of earshot."

Summers felt Leslie stiffen in his arms and cursed savagely to himself, That smart-aleck bastard!

"Don't listen to them, darling. They think all men are as vile and corrupt as they are," he said smoothly.

"You aren't going to kill them, are you?" she asked, searching his face for any sign.

"Of course not. I'll hold them here until help comes. But you must go, darling. I'm counting on you to bring help."

"I lost my horse. I don't know if I can find it again," she said, stalling for time.

"Take mine."

Reluctantly, Leslie walked to his horse and mounted, still holding the gun she had forgotten she had. She rode up beside Tim, he smiled to reassure her, and she slowly walked the horse around the end of the big Conestoga.

Summers heard the horse break into a gallop and breathed a sigh of relief. As obedient as she was beautiful. A few more minutes to give her time to get out of earshot and then he could kill them and end his problems forever.

The rumble of the herd diminished to a low roar. They had stayed a quarter-mile away at the nearest point. Now the bawl and moan of the cattle was almost gone. None of the others knew him as Younger's boss—only these three.

Younger could tell by the oily glitter of Summers's eyes that he was almost ready. Younger had faced at least as many men over a gun as Cantrell. He shot a look at Ward and saw that he knew too.

"Hey, Cantrell, if I rush him, do you think you can drag one of those guns up in time to kill the bastard before he kills my baby?"

Summers laughed softly. "Don't waste your time. I'll shoot Cantrell first, then drop you like a pole-axed steer. You may be big as a bull, but you can't survive a bullet through the forehead."

Dallas shrugged. "Reckon he's got us dead to rights."

"Looks like it," Cantrell drawled.

"Where the hell did you learn to sound like a Texan?" Dallas asked suddenly.

"I studied a little French in school," he said, grinning. "Anyone who can learn a French accent can master a Texas drawl."

"I'll be damned."

Summers sneered. "You two going to hell as friends?"

"You ready to send us?" Ward asked. "You think Leslie is far enough away by now so she'll never know? What are you going to tell her, anyway?"

"That you tried to rush me, of course."

"How are you going to explain killing Trinket?"

"A stray bullet," Tim said smoothly. "A terrible, tragic accident."

Sandra began to whimper and moved closer behind Younger. "That's okay, Sweetface. He's gotta go through me first," Dallas drawled.

Summers sneered. "Now aren't you gallant? I'm going to shoot Cantrell first. I've been waiting a long time for this." He aimed the gun at Ward's broad chest and began to squeeze the trigger slowly. There was a look of triumph in his cold black eyes. His lips lifted in a smile.

"Say good-bye, Cantrell."

Ward dived for his gun. Dallas charged toward Summers. There was a crash of gunfire just as Ward's hand reached the smooth handle of the Colt, and he knew he was too late, but strangely he felt no pain.

He continued the motion, came up into a crouch, ready to fire. Summers toppled forward as if he had broken in two at the middle. Younger stopped, as startled as Ward.

They both turned at the same time and saw Leslie, her face pale and glowing, her eyes wide and staring, before she crumpled forward in a dead faint.

Ward walked over and turned Summers with a kick of his booted foot. With the gun trained on Younger now, he knelt and felt Summers's throat for a pulse. Finding none, he took Younger's gun out of the dead man's hand and stuck it under his belt. He slowly straightened, facing Dallas.

Dallas Younger took a deep breath. He and Cantrell had been working up to this meeting for a long time. He kissed the girl and put her away from him. It was time to die, and he didn't relish waiting around for it.

"Cantrell," he said softly, contemptuously, "you know if I was holding that gun, you'd be dead by now."

Ward grinned. "Well, you're not holding the gun, are you, Dallas?" he asked softly.

"What's the matter, Cantrell? You too yellow to shoot me? Or just too vain? Don't want folks to know you killed an unarmed man?"

There was admiration in Ward's blue eyes now—and respect. The man had more guts than he'd expected. Maybe those stories about Texans and their courage weren't just tall tales after all.

"Well," Ward drawled softly, "I have an extra gun here." He tossed Younger's gun at him. Dallas caught it smoothly, his handsome face breaking into a grin. He looked at Ward, then down at the gun, fondling it slowly, almost lovingly, brushing the dirt off before he slipped it into the empty holster on his right hip.

Cantrell, gun under his belt, walked to where his gunbelt lay, leaned down, and dragged it up. He strapped it around him, holstered the gun and then faced Younger, his stance seemingly relaxed, his right hand hanging casually at his side.

"I'm waiting, Younger," he said quietly.

Sandra's hand flew to her mouth to stifle a sob. They were crazy! Both of them! Only moments ago they were chatting quietly, conversationally, about joining forces to take Summers; now they were facing each other coldly, their eyes narrowed and glittering with their intent.

The tension was too heavy, too stifling. Sandra couldn't move—could barely breathe. "No, Ward, please," she stammered. "No, Dallas, honey, no, please," she pleaded.

"Hush, Sweetface," Dallas said softly, holding up his left hand in a signal for her to stop pleading. His eyes never left Cantrell's eyes. That was where the first sign always showed—not in the hands.

They faced each other tensely for long seconds, then Ward dragged in a slow breath and relaxed visibly, straightening only slightly, but it was enough. Younger saw the change and knew what it meant. He too had the gunman's instinct to kill, but the moment had passed. There was relief mixed with regret. Now he would never know who was faster. Too late for regrets, though. Younger dismissed Cantrell, turning abruptly to face the girl who was frozen in fear.

"You coming with me?"

Sandra looked at Ward, then at Dallas. There was the slightest hesitation before she nodded.

"Well, come on, Sweetface. Let's get the hell outta here."

Ward grinned. "I wouldn't go south if I were you. There's a posse waiting for that herd."

"Much obliged," Younger said, taking the girl's arm.

Ward watched them leave. He sighed. He'd never make a good ranger. Kincaid would be disappointed.

CHAPTER
FIFTY-TWO

Leslie woke up slowly. Her eyes blinked, then focused and she could see. Stars floated like diamonds in an inky black sphere; the rhythmic sound of the horse's hooves against the earth drummed in her ears, and cold wind whipped her feet. She slowly became aware that she was on a horse, being carried across the saddle, wrapped in a blanket and cradled like a babe in strong arms. Her cheek rested on a rough vest that smelled of dust, leather, and sweat, but through all that she recognized the man who held her. There was a scent: a faint, salty, lemony, musky smell that had an irresistible appeal for her. It seemed to pervade her senses—even her ability to think.

"Ward . . ."

"So you're awake at last."

"Where are you taking me?"

"Into the mountains. You're a hunted outlaw now, just as I am."

"Ohhhh!" That pitiful little cry constricted his heart.

"Then I . . . killed him?" she asked softly.

"Yes."

Leslie groaned and turned her face into his chest, burrowing there as if to hide from that terrible truth. She had killed the man she was going to marry to save an admitted killer, kidnapper, train robber, and probably rustler.

The enormity of it staggered her. But fearing that Tim *was* going to kill Sandra, Dallas, and Ward, she had dismounted, slapped the horse into a run, and hurried back to the wagon. She had watched and heard everything until she had mustered her courage in time to pull the trigger and send that bullet slamming into his body. Remembering the stunned disbelief on his pale face when he looked at her with the knowledge of his own death full upon him . . . She would never forget that. . . .

Shuddering, she turned her face and burrowed it into Cantrell's warm body. Ward held her close against him while she fought the revulsion and sickness that came with realization, but he knew that struggle well, and that no one could share it with her. He pulled the blanket closer around her and brushed a kiss on her smooth forehead.

Far off thunder rumbled, and finally Leslie wriggled around until she was riding astride in front of him. Pulling the blanket tight around her, she watched the sky and the sparkles of lightning. How long did she ride thus, shuddering with the memory of her evil deed?

They rode until almost dawn, Leslie alternately sleeping and struggling with her conscience and Ward watching the trail for signs he recognized. At dawn, when the sky was slowly turning pale gray, he found what he was looking for: a small one-room cabin he'd built two years ago when he was in need of solitude. It sat on a level shelf halfway up a mountainside, almost hidden by tall trees. He dismounted and helped Leslie down to stand beside him.

"Where are we?"

"Mountains north of Phoenix. If we get lucky and those clouds dump some rain, we'll be safe from pursuit. No one will find us except by accident. We'll be safe until spring."   .

"Spring?" she asked incredulously, looking from the lowering black clouds to Ward's face. He was serious. She had never seen him more distant. She could tell by the bleak coldness of his eyes that she could never go back. She was a hunted outlaw now, just as he was. His expression confirmed the finality of it.

Why did she do it? She knew what Ward Cantrell was. She knew he expected to die a violent death. She knew it when she walked through that armed camp in Buckeye. She had sensed it in him when he had first kidnapped her. She shivered in the cold, knowing it would be easier to say why she kept breathing. She could no more allow Tim to shoot Ward than she could hold her hand over flaming coals until it burned off.

Ward led the horse behind the cabin. Dawn changed the gray to blue above the towering pines and firs. A grove of aspen trees surrounded by gold, silver, and red leaves carpeted the mountain with warm color; lofty blue-green firs soared upward to be obscured by swirling blue mists, damp viridescent spears piercing the sky. The air was cold, thin, moist. Pine trees scattered pine cones like acorns. The air was redolent with the resiny smells of pine, fir, sage; the earth beneath her feet was spongy with dead pine needles—brown and slippery. The horse snorted from behind the cabin, and it was an eerie, heavy sound in all that stillness. A bird answered from high overhead and Leslie shivered again.

"Come inside. I have a fire started," he said gently, taking her arm. She was still in shock; it showed in her eyes and the way she moved.

Leslie looked up, her eyes solemn. "Why are you doing this? Helping me escape?"

"You saved our lives. Why not?"

Leslie gasped. She had forgotten the others. "What happened to Sandra and Dallas Younger?"

"They escaped."

"But Sandra . . . Why did you let him take her?"

"It was her choice."

"She chose it? She wanted to go with that animal?"

" 'Fraid so."

"How could she? He's so rough, so . . . so . . . crude!"

"Some women like their men rough," he said quietly.

"But . . . she can't possibly find happiness with a man like that! He'll never be true to her; he'll never be able to give her anything."

Ward shrugged. "Maybe that's enough for her." He turned and walked into the cabin. Leslie followed slowly, wondering what he was thinking about.

Ward was wondering if Dusty and Doug had cut off Cedar Longley and the herd, if Kincaid would get the note he left on Summers' body, and if that would be enough to save Leslie and himself. Summers was a respected man in Phoenix. Would anyone, even Kincaid, be willing to believe that Summers was a crook? This paralleled too closely the events in Dodge City. Was that why he had carried her into the mountains instead of returning to Phoenix? Was history about to repeat itself? This time at Leslie's expense? Or would they assume *he* killed Summers?

"Ward?"

"Hmmm?"

"What are you thinking about?" she asked.

"Nothing."

He spread the blankets on the floor in front of the fire and told her to lie down. He covered her with more blankets and then carried in the saddlebags and began unpacking utensils and food to make a meal. Apparently he had raided the chuckwagon. He had everything he needed, and soon she smelled bacon, coffee, and biscuits.

They ate in silence. Leslie had to force herself to take the first few bites and then her appetite came alive and she was ravenous. She'd had only muffins since breakfast yesterday and was half-starved. She ate until she was embarrassed.

"It's a good thing I cooked plenty," Ward said, grinning.

That was the first real expression she'd seen on his face. He was unusually quiet and thoughtful. He seemed to be waiting, locked away with his own thoughts. Was he remembering when they had been together in Buckeye? Immediately afterward, when she was safe at home, in her room, surrounded by friends who cared about her, alone and miserable nonetheless, she had remembered the tension in that armed camp, the grim faces of the men, and wondered if that flash of hardness she kept seeing was bitterness. But why should *he* be bitter? Why should his cool blue eyes look as bleak and cold as a winter snowscape? What did he want from her?

She shook her head miserably. He had never offered her anything. He had tricked her and taken advantage of her—what did he expect?

Ward caught himself frowning into the fire and forced his muscles as well as his face to relax. This wasn't going to work. His instinctive reactions—so deeply distrustful of authority—had sent him off into the mountains instead of back toward Phoenix, where she belonged. Except he wasn't sure he could go back there, ever. Would they believe him about Summers? The town so far hadn't been exactly receptive to ideas of his innocence. It was only their word against Summers' reputation as a leading citizen. Even with Leslie insisting she had shot Summers, they might not believe her. They could conveniently assume it was another attempt on her part to protect him. He knew the way they'd slandered her after that confrontation in the jail.

"What are you thinking?"

"Nothing."

"Yes you are."

"What would you like me to be thinking about?"

"I don't know." She shook her head sadly and then lifted her

chin. Her green eyes flashed with the richness and depth of emer-
alds. "You know what I would really like?"

Ward shook his head. With her eyes sparkling and midnight-
black hair foaming out around the pale oval of her face she was
Leslie Powers, the imperious lady again—not a trace of shock left
to pale those sweet-curving cheeks.

"No, what?"

"Just one time, Ward Cantrell, I want you to tell me the truth."

His face looked grim and purposeful, as if he could walk away
from her and never look back. But part of her didn't care. It felt
reckless, willing to say anything and take the consequences.

Clutching the blanket around her, she faced him defiantly. "All
right! What's on my mind is that I thought you loved me. Then I
went to Buckeye and you made love to me in the bedroom you
shared with Sandra."

"Is that why you? . . ."

"I saw her necklace on your vanity. And tonight she was wearing it!"

His voice was low, expressionless. "She gave me the necklace
in Phoenix because she was convinced she was going to die. She
said she wanted me to keep it so someone would remember her after she was gone. I gave it back to her because it looked like I had
the lifespan of a snowball in hell."

His husky words sobered her. "She wasn't with you?"

"That's right. She was with Younger. Your damned lover took
her to Younger."

"Tim?" she asked, frowning. "Why would he do that?"

"To frame me. So you and everyone else would believe I kidnapped her. He wanted me dead. Summers killed Powers and the
Mendozas."

"Ohhh . . . Tim?" She felt weak suddenly. Weak and stupid.
But she had to know everything. "But there was another girl in
Buckeye. I saw her shawl. . . ."

"If there was a shawl there," he said gently, "it belonged to
Juanita Castenada, the owner's daughter. She was married last
month . . . before she moved away."

Pale and lovely in the firelight, Leslie was supremely doubtful
of Cantrell's motives, his integrity, probably even his parentage,
and yet, in spite of her misgivings, he felt compelled to protect her
splendid, brave spirit. Even though she obviously didn't trust him,
he was determined that he wouldn't let her make a fool of him

again. He reached out and touched her cheek. ''There was no female in that room or any other with me except you.''

Cantrell's touch weakened Leslie's resolve against him, and she resented that it should be so. She didn't reply. She was watching his eyes, wishing she could read them more clearly. Part of her was vibrating to his nearness and his restrained anger. But another part of her was equally determined to get at the truth. She was tired of worrying and waiting. ''Were you lying to me about Jennifer Kincaid?''

''Which time?''

''How many times did you lie to me about her?'' she demanded angrily, clutching the blanket around her. ''When you said you were not romantically involved with her!''

''That's the truth.''

''But there were other lies?''

''You accused me of some things that weren't true and I allowed you to believe they were. I don't think you can blame me for that.''

''Will they hang us?'' she demanded suddenly.

He poked at the fire, a grunt of laughter escaping from him in a gust. ''I suppose it depends on who we run into first, but with Summers out of the way, maybe the mob will lose its steam.''

''Ward?''

''Hmmm?''

''I can't run away,'' she said softly. ''I'm going to have to go back and face whatever has to be faced.''

Without warning he pulled her into his arms, holding her as if the sheriff were already trying to pull her away from him, and Leslie knew she was in love, and the knowledge that it had come too late filled her with sadness and unshed tears.

''What's wrong?'' he asked, his lips nudging her cheek.

She laughed. What could she say? The man I love is an outlaw! A killer. Wanted by the sheriff. And I'm about to hang for murder. . . .

''Hey!'' That half-hysterical laugh told him volumes. He shook her and then folded her in his arms again. ''I'm not going to let them hang you,'' he said huskily.

''What about you?''

''Me either.''

''I have to go back, you know.''

Ward's heart felt like it would burst. He pulled her closer, cradling her face in the crook of his neck and shoulder. She was insane, insisting on her right to be hanged. But insane or not, she had bewitched him from the very beginning with her passionate pursuit of her noble ideals. Her courage and honesty and spirit had shattered his defenses and played havoc with his unwillingness to fall in love.

"Then we'll both go back," he said.

"No, Ward! You can never go back there. I have a chance. You have none." She clung to him tightly, trembling in spite of his warmth. "They'll hang you."

"Would you care?" he asked, holding her away from him so he could search her eyes. His own were strangely dark.

"I would die," she said.

"Then stay with me here . . . for one week."

"Why?"

"One week to remember and I'll tell them I shot Summers."

"No!"

"Why not? It won't make a difference for me. I've killed other men."

"No! I will not permit it. Never!"

"Because you don't want to spend a week with me?"

"No," she whispered. If she were going to prison or to hang, she would still want that week.

"Will you stay one week?"

"If you promise not to try to stop me from turning myself in."

"I promise," he said, burying his face in the fragrant black mass of her hair.

The week slipped past like a butterfly flitting from flower to flower, sampling the sweetness of the nectar until pleasurably sated. They teased and played and made love, pretending they had forever, and Leslie only fretted occasionally about the future. At those times she watched Cantrell closely, but if he was aware he lived under a cloud, it was not discernible. Except for a moment after he had saddled their horses for the long ride back. His blue eyes—so clear and untroubled this whole week—darkened as he lifted her into the saddle. In that second she felt the reluctance and tension in him, but no shirking. A lump rose in her throat. Cantrell would face whatever had to be faced, but she hated the fact that their future was now beyond their control.

CHAPTER
FIFTY-THREE

"Leslie, wake up, dear. The sheriff is downstairs. He wants to talk to you."

Leslie covered her head and groaned. The sun streaming in the window hurt her eyes. She opened one eye and squinted at Jennifer, who was smiling delightedly at her.

"Oh, no! I'm such a mess," she groaned.

"You look wonderful," Jennie said, smiling as if she meant it. "The sheriff will wait, but you had best be up and dressing."

Leslie's heart constricted with fear and alarm. "Where's Cantrell?" she demanded.

"He's downstairs with Chane and some gentleman."

Leslie struggled upright in the bed, looking so confused and scared that Jennie pulled her into her arms and hugged her. "I'm so glad you're safe!" she said. "We were so worried about you. Except I knew he would save you."

Annette came in with a rustling of petticoats and excited exclamations in mingled English and French that went on the whole time Leslie bathed and dressed. Jennie withdrew, probably in self-defense, promising they would talk later.

"Have you seen Mr. Cantrell?" Leslie asked when Annette finished putting the last pins in her hair.

"Oui! He is so handsome! *Magnifique, no?"*

"Where is he?"

"Downstairs! With him!"

"Him? Who?"

"Him! John Loving. He's here. In ziss house!"

Leslie grinned in spite of her fear. "So you finally got him here?"

"Oui!"

"Well, what are you doing up here wasting your time with me?" she demanded.

Annette shrugged. "He was busy with Mr. Kincaid, zee sheriff, zee governor, and some man I do not know. He scare me *so* bad."

"Scared you? Who?"

366

"*Oui!* I opened zee door, expecting somezhing ordinary, and *he* is zere! Staring at *moi* with zee meanest face I have evair seen. Like he as soon shop off my head as say hello." Annette shuddered.

"Who is he?"

Annette shrugged. "John King."

"Where's he from?"

"I do not know. . . . Such good English . . . unless . . . Is Canvas a place to be from?"

"Canvas? Kan . . .sas?"

"*Oui!* Kan . . . sas! That is good, no?"

"No," Leslie said grimly, cursing herself for coming back here. They had him! There was no turning back now. She was regretting so many things suddenly. And remembering what Ward had said when she railed at him for refusing to give her his seed. When she said that man-made laws couldn't take away her right to have his baby: "They can take everything," he'd said quietly, inexorably, "even my right to live."

Her heart was pounding so loudly she could feel it in her toes. Annette stepped back to admire her handiwork, and Leslie stood up. Her heart fluttered at the base of her throat. She might never see him alone again, never feel the warmth of his skin against her own.

"Ready, *mademoiselle?*"

No! No! She wasn't, but she nodded calmly in spite of that nerve-end jangle that threatened to betray her.

At the top of the stairs, she paused. Deep masculine voices were coming from the library. *Here goes. Please, legs, don't collapse. If he can face this, I can too. . . .*

She negotiated the stairs in a sort of breathless daze and stopped at the door of the library, watching them before they became aware of her presence.

They were clustered around the fireplace, sipping from coffee cups and looking pleased with themselves. She found Ward instantly. Annette was right. Clean-shaven, wearing a dark blue shirt and dark trousers, he was Adonis incarnate. Just the sight of him, leaning against the far side of the fireplace, his mouth set in that look of sensual reserve that she knew so well, was enough to double the force of that pounding in her breast. He hadn't seen her yet. He was watching Kincaid and a strapping, well-dressed Negro man, warily, it seemed. Annette was right about the man. He had the most terrifyingly brutal face she had ever seen. Her heart almost stopped.

The governor and the sheriff were there also. But her eyes went back to the Negro. There was something ominous and frightening about him.

Ward glanced at the door and their eyes met. His seemed unusually dark and unreadable—without the slightest trace of sardonic amusement. Her eyes moved down that lithe familiar form and widened. He was not wearing a gun. Did that account for the unusually solemn cast of his handsome features? But why shouldn't it? Ward Cantrell was a warrior, and a warrior should not be stripped of his weapons without a fight. Leslie writhed inwardly with the knowledge that he had laid down his guns and submitted to this civilized form of humiliation for her. Because he loved her. The realization that she had taken the man she loved and reduced him to this, that he should die or be imprisoned like an animal for deeds he could not help, was more than she could bear. The pain spread out in ever-widening waves until her chest ached and her throat felt rigid with anguish.

Ward saw the pain reflected in her wide green eyes. "Let's get this over with," he said to Kincaid.

Chane came forward to take her arm. "Leslie, join us, please."

They paused in front of the governor. "Leslie, you remember Governor Stanton, Sheriff Tatum, Reverend Abercrombie. Frank Johnston is president of the local Cattleman's Association. Doug Paggett and Dusty Denton are friends of Warden's. I'd like you to meet John King, from Dodge City, and John Loving, the new manager of the Texas and Pacific Railroad."

Leslie glanced quickly at Ward, but he was concentrating on his coffee cup, his eyes averted from hers.

"Yes, there've been some changes taking place while you were away," Chane said, smiling at John Loving.

Loving's face broke into a glad chipmunk-cheeked smile of greeting to Leslie, but John King only watched her impassively. She forced herself to nod at each of the men. She wanted to go to Ward, touch him, reassure herself that he was all right, but Chane had a firm grip on her hand.

"Ahem!" Sheriff Tatum cleared his throat, looking around the room at the other men. "I guess since Miss Powers is here, we might as well begin. Would you like to sit down?" he asked solicitously.

"May we offer you tea or coffee?" Chane asked.

"No, thank you."

"Very well," he said, nodding at Tatum.

The sheriff asked a great number of questions, and she answered them honestly, casting glances at Ward to see if somehow she might be saying things that were damaging to him; but he only watched her quietly, his eyes as unreadable as before.

When she felt dizzy with so many questions, Tatum sighed with satisfaction and Governor Stanton stepped forward. "Miss Powers, it gives me great pleasure to present you with these checks for capturing Sandra McCormick's kidnapper and the leader of the rustlers that have been preying on honest ranchers hereabouts for the last three years."

Horrified, she looked from the governor to Chane. "You don't understand," she said, "I didn't capture Cantrell—he saved me! I killed Tim Summers to keep him from killing Sandra, Cantrell, and Younger. . . ."

"That is correct," the governor said, smiling at her.

Leslie sighed. "No, you don't understand . . . I killed Tim because he said he was going to kill them. I didn't capture Cantrell!" she insisted.

Governor Stanton smiled. "Perhaps an explanation is in order. Chane?" he asked, passing the buck.

Chane grinned. "Leslie, you are a heroine. Tim Summers *was* the head of the rustler gang."

"But . . . but I thought Cantrell was the . . ."

The governor smiled benignly. "Mr. Cantrell is an Arizona ranger, Miss Powers. His job along with Dusty Denton, Doug Paggett, and the others was to smoke out the real rustler chief."

Chane took her hand. "When we discovered you'd ridden off Saturday, Sheriff Tatum and I took a posse out looking for you. We came upon Denton and the others the next day after they had recovered the herd from Summers' and Younger's men. We saved the herd, but most of the rustlers escaped over the border."

Leslie barely heard him. She was stunned. An Arizona ranger! Ward knew from the very beginning she wasn't going to hang for killing Tim! He knew *he* wasn't in any danger of hanging either! Rage bubbled in her veins. What a monumental liar he was! She would kill him with her bare hands!

She turned on Ward, her eyes spitting fury, poised like an angry tigress, but he came forward and caught her hands before she could spring at him.

"Wait, Leslie. There's more. We might as well get this all out in the open," he said grimly.

"That happens to be more than enough!"

"I have to go back to Dodge City to stand trial for murder."

Anger forgotten, her eyes went to John King and stayed there. She could feel her insides collapsing. Her hands dropped to her sides.

"They'll hang you . . . ." she whispered, fear squeezing so tight she almost could not speak.

The man named King stepped forward. He nodded. "There is hope, Miss Powers, else I wouldn't be taking him back."

"Hope? How can you say that?" she gasped.

"The men Captain Van Vleet killed murdered my brother-in-law, the captain's friend, and his wife. The captain only killed after gross provocation, Miss Powers. He only killed in self-defense. I have . . . um, you might say . . . encouraged two witnesses to come forward who will testify to his innocence."

Leslie closed her eyes and covered her face.

Ward sighed. "We should have talked this morning, but you were so tired. . . ." Ward's jaw clamped shut, and she could see the muscles in his lean cheek writhing as he decided how to proceed. The thought of him standing trial again, possibly going to prison and hanging, was insupportable.

Chane took her hand. "He'll have good counsel, Leslie. He'll have the support of his family and Mr. King this time. We think that will be enough to tip the scales in his favor."

"What if you're wrong?" she demanded.

"We have to start somewhere," Ward said softly.

"I think we'd best leave these young people alone," Kincaid said, herding the others out of the room.

Leslie barely noticed them. Her eyes were riveted to Cantrell's face. Ward nodded at her, his eyes filled with that sharp light that dazed her. His fingers closed around her arm, above the elbow.

"You were a ranger this whole time?" she whispered.

"Since the day after my trial."

"You knew you wouldn't hang."

"No. I didn't know that. If I failed . . ."

"Why didn't you tell me about Tim?"

He shrugged. Bitterness flickered in the blue depths. "Would you have believed me?"

She was watching him intently, her eyes riveted to his. "There's more, isn't there?" she whispered.

Ward took a deep breath. This *could* get him killed.

"You remember when I told you that I wasn't romantically involved with Jenn?"

Leslie could feel her heart slowing down, like an engine preparing to stop. She looked quickly at Chane, but he was closing the door behind him. They were all gone except Ward.

She shook her head. There was cruelty and cruelty. To tell her now that he lied about loving her . . .

She backed away from him, her eyes spitting, cat green. "Don't touch me! I don't want to hear about the other women in your life."

She backed slowly away, and he followed, stalking her the way he would an animal he meant to kill.

"Leslie, didn't you ever wonder why I kept punishing you?" he asked softly, inching closer.

"No! I don't want to hear it."

But he was determined that she would hear it. His face was set in grim, unwavering purpose. She backed into the wall and gasped. She was trapped! But what had she done to bring out this streak of implacable cruelty in the man she loved? Why was he determined to tell her he loved another woman?

"Leslie," he said softly, "Jenn is my sister."

She couldn't speak. Her jaw dropped. Her head began automatically, involuntarily, to shake from side to side, denying what she would not hear.

The clock on the mantel ticked loudly in the sudden stillness. Everyone had left the room. It was only the two of them now. "You tricked me!" she said incredulously.

"I didn't mean to. I pretended to accept your noble sacrifice to punish you for not believing in me. . . . I never meant to collect on that bargain. I was going to tell you at the dance, but you left. I only came here that night to tell you I was leaving Phoenix."

"Oh! What a liar you are!" She jerked her arm free and grabbed one of the books off the shelf beside her and hit him with it. "You beast! Oh! How I hate you!"

"Ow! Leslie, stop it!" he howled, ducking.

She was like a panther, darting and striking at will. He was helpless against her. The only alternative was to run, so he did, with her behind him, screaming invectives.

Jennifer heard the loud commotion and left the children with Mrs. Lillian. She had wanted to be with Chane when they told Leslie the truth, but a cry of pain from Amy had sidetracked her. Little Chane had tripped Amy, and she cut her lip. He was almost as upset as Amy was. It took both women to get them calmed down and patched up.

When she could leave them she sought out Chane.

"What happened to Ward and Leslie? I thought they were going to. . . ."

Chane grinned, his hazel eyes filled with mischief. "I guess that will have to wait until *after* she kills him."

Jennifer laughed, a low, sultry gurgle that still sent tingles up Chane's spine. "Was she very angry?"

"Well, just a little," he said. "Nothing Ward can't handle, I'm sure."

"I hope he's as humble as you are."

"I didn't notice any humility as he ran past here—only a well-developed survival instinct."

"Do you think she'll catch him?"

Chane grinned, his warm green eyes twinkling. "I'm sure of it. He ran for her bedroom."

CHAPTER
FIFTY-FOUR

Leslie ran to the door of her bedroom and stopped, panting from the wild run up the long, curving staircase. The room looked empty. Hadn't she seen his leg and boot disappearing into this very room?

She walked slowly inside, looking quickly from side to side. The sound of the rug being compressed under a heavy foot brought her whirling around.

"Oh!"

The door slammed shut. He was between her and the door, coming toward her slowly, his blue eyes reflecting a strange satisfaction, as if now *he* had *her*.

Unthinking fury surged up, blocking out reason. She lunged at him, her nails curved into talons.

She would have scratched him too, if his hands hadn't caught her wrists and forced them down behind her back. He pulled her hard against him, taking both wrists in one hand so he could use his other hand to capture her head and hold it still.

She felt like a crushed rose. Furious, she squirmed and twisted, trying to get loose, but she was helpless. He leaned down and set his mouth over hers.

Leslie was determined that she would not respond to his kiss. He had tricked her again. Lied to her, laughed at her, held her up to public ridicule. What had Jennie thought? Knowing everything?

But the hard pressure of his lips, burning into hers, pressing her mouth open, forcing her head back . . . her anger was dissolving into heat, her body coming alive, as if his touch stripped away her protective covering—leaving her exposed to him, to his hands, his lips, his will. . . .

No fair! How could she ever get an accounting from him for his outrageous actions when fear for his safety left her so needy for him? He kissed her endlessly, until she forgot everything except her love for him.

He relinquished her lips. Panting, she pressed her face into his shoulder and felt the scar tissue from the injury he had received the last night she was his captive. She kissed him there, breathing the warm, manly fragrance into her nostrils.

So many memories . . . They crowded into her head, blinding her. She could see him on the corn husk mattress in the small hut after she had taken the bullet out of his shoulder—unconscious, with his face turned away from her, the sturdy column of his neck tempting her. How could a man so strong, so enduring, look so vulnerable?

She had reached out to smooth that tawny thatch of silver-streaked flaxen hair off his forehead and ended by pressing her lips there. Finally, losing all control, she had held him blindly, helplessly, until he stirred.

A vision of his lean form hanging limply between Younger's men as Younger pounded his face into raw meat, brought a helpless groan from deep in her throat. He'd had tinges of those bruises in jail. . . .

And yet he had let Younger go.

She hadn't expected to see Ward again after the jail. Certainly not dressed in the height of fashion, framed against the sumptuous background of the Kincaids' *sala grande*, looking negligently at ease while her heart pounded so loudly she feared she would shake apart from it.

Remembering the confused impulses of fear and pride she'd felt, seeing him beside the fireplace, across the library, a prisoner, she'd thought, a warrior disarmed and waiting to be executed . . . only to find out he was Jennie's brother—why hadn't she guessed? She'd had clues. The way Jennie couldn't quite bring herself to turn loose his hand. Jennie's instant recovery so soon after her brother's death. Chane's look of rapt pride and happiness when Ward and Jennie danced together. She'd been blind.

But he helped blind her. The unselfconscious way he held Jennie in his arms that day . . . She could see herself. Heavens! How foolish she must have seemed to him, going to the house on Barton Street, asking him to give Jennie up.

It *had* been bitterness in his husky voice when he taunted her: "I only care about myself. That's what you said. Why should I deprive myself of a choice female like Jenn?"

When she tried to leave, he stopped her with that look in his blue eyes and the warm pressure of his hand on her arm. In her extremity she had called him an animal, accusing him of any vile thing she could think of, and that strange light flared in his eyes, darkening and then lightening the blue before he said, "I want you." By the time his hand tangled in her hair, pulling her close for that terrible, punishing kiss, everything inside her was collapsing: pride, stubbornness, courage.

But . . . she hadn't been honest with him either, had she? Maybe if she'd told him why she went to Buckeye . . . Later, up at the mountain cabin, if she had admitted she was afraid to go back to Phoenix . . .

She jerked away from him, as far away as she could get in the steely circle of his arms.

"Now what is it?" he asked, recognizing the look in her defiant green eyes.

"You could have told me a week ago that neither one of us was in any real danger of hanging."

"Not me. I didn't believe it. In case you don't remember me, I'm the one with no excess of trust."

"You could have told me you were a ranger."

"To what purpose? When things don't work out, people have a way of conveniently forgetting their promises. Stanton is a practical politician. If the mob chose to believe Summers and Younger over me, he wouldn't have had the guts to tell them I was working for him. . . . I didn't know *what* to expect when I got here. They could just as easily have been waiting to hang me."

"You didn't know?"

"On my sister's honor," he said solemnly.

"Jennie's your sister?"

"All my life . . ."

"There was no girl at Buckeye?"

"Only you."

"Why didn't you come here right away? Didn't you want to know if everything worked out?"

"Desperately. Unfortunately I wanted us to survive more. I thought a week would give things a chance to settle."

She gazed out the window, remembering the low, deliberately expressionless tone of his husky voice the day he told her about Simone and his friend Snake. No, he wouldn't have an excess of trust that all those angry townspeople would believe him just because he was innocent.

"How did John King find you?"

"Someone wrote a letter to the sheriff in Dodge City, describing and naming me. King said he had guessed years ago that Ward Cantrell was really Peter Van Vleet. . . . He had asked the sheriff to keep an ear open for word of me."

"Tim . . ."

"What?" Ward asked, frowning.

"Tim may have been the one . . ."

Ward's lips tightened. "Could be. We'll never know." He was silent a moment. "I'm glad this worked out for Doug and Dusty and the rest of the men who agreed to help me. Stanton was so pleased he pardoned all of us." Leslie murmured her agreement, and they fell silent.

Sounds filtered into her consciousness. Two birds were arguing back and forth in short, raucous spurts of sound. She heard voices outside, in the garden. A horse whinnied and another answered. A dog barked.

"Cantrell?"

"Yeah?" Did she detect wariness in his reply?

"I love you." Her voice sounded taut, strangled, not like her. He held her away from him and saw the tears streaming down her lovely cheeks. Her eyes were dark, the pupils dilated, welling with new tears.

"Leslie, Jesus . . ." He pulled her into his arms and held her tightly, feeling hers and his own pain keenly. She sobbed against his shoulder, her arms moving up to cling around his neck. "Leslie, love, please don't cry. . . . Hey, I can't stand it when you cry. . . . I love you. Don't cry. . . . Everything is going to work out."

She was trembling uncontrollably. "I was so mean to you! You were so brave. . . . You could have been killed. You could have died."

"It's all right now. Hush. I love you."

"I never trusted you. I was going to let him shoot you. . . . I almost did. . . ."

"But you didn't. When it mattered, you came through for me." She kissed him softly, breathing him in.

"Don't worry," he whispered. "We'll find some way for you to make this up to me."

"Ohhh! You are incorrigible. Now that I know your type . . ." she began threateningly.

"It won't help. I trick you every time."

She laughed, her tears forgotten. "I might get smarter as I get older."

"Lord, I hope not," he growled ruefully.

"But then I would have to, wouldn't I?"

Laughing, he cut her off with the only weapon he had, kissing her into forgetfulness. He undressed her and came into her slowly, groaning her name.

"Leslie . . . I love you so. . . ."

She held him close, reveling in the sensations of love: his husky voice murmuring love words, his body dissolving into hers, her bones melting into fiery liquid. She couldn't remember hating him, only loving him. And she would do it all again for him. For this.

About the Author

Joyce Brandon was born in Farmersville, Texas. When she was fourteen her family moved to Fresno, California, where she completed her education. Her first published novel, THE LADY AND THE OUTLAW, won two national awards, including a finalist award from the Romance Writers of America's Golden Medallion Contest—the most prestigious award offered to romance authors. In addition to her writing Joyce travels extensively, teaching her chosen vocation to others and lecturing at colleges, universities, and national writer's conferences. Joyce and her husband John make their home in Fresno, California.

Corporate Strategy
and
Financial Analysis

Managerial, Accounting and
Stock Market Perspectives

John Ellis

Lecturer in Strategic Management, Bournemouth University

and

David Williams

Head of Planning, Bournemouth University

658.15

PITMAN PUBLISHING
128 Long Acre, London WC2E 9AN

A Division of Longman Group UK Limited

© John Ellis and David Williams 1993

First published in Great Britain 1993

British Library Cataloguing-in-Publication Data
A catalogue record for this book is available
from the British Library

ISBN 0-273-03796-X

Typeset and Illustrated by 🐟 Tek-Art, Addiscombe,
Croydon, Surrey.
Printed in Great Britain by Bell and Bain Ltd., Glasgow

The
publisher's
policy is to use
paper manufactured
from sustainable forests

CONTENTS

PART V   THE GENERAL FRAMEWORK REVISITED

PREFACE

Why another book assessing strategic direction?

This book uniquely seeks to interface managerial, accounting and stock market perspectives in terms of the strategies that companies follow. Few books explore in any detail the linkages between strategic and financial imperatives. There are many texts on strategy which include the odd section or even chapter on financial analysis, and many financial texts which have a section or chapter on strategy. Beyond such superficial introductions, however, there is no single text which offers an integrated coverage of these two key areas and in addition links both areas to the question of stock market assessment.

The book is written to help the reader overcome the division between strategic direction, financial analysis and stock market assessment. As such it provides a practically useful framework for analysing companies in terms of their managerial, accounting and stock market perspectives. The genesis of the book comes from the authors' experiences of trying to assist managers and aspiring managers to link issues of strategic management with their financial outcomes and the associated stock market assessment of company performance. The widespread inability of managers to do this often leads to an unbalanced decision-making process whereby decisions as to the strategic direction of the organization are decoupled from an appreciation of financial issues.

All too frequently financial analysis is seen as a specialist area of expertise to be left to the accountant, who understandably has little appreciation or perception of the wider strategic needs. This unbalanced view lies at the heart of much of management education in the UK where personal development and learning is focused on individual disciplines or functions. The recognition of the need to develop general management skills at all levels of management lies at the heart of the current text where different perspectives of business are linked in an integrated and holistic way. Only by such an approach do the authors believe that a full appreciation of the implications of strategic decisions can be made.

In the light of the previous comment the text aims:

- to enable managers and those who aspire to management to understand and use the linkage between strategy and finance in a manner which aids their decision-making;
- to provide an intellectually rigorous but highly practical guide to current and prospective managers as to how they may undertake research on a chosen company to link the assessment of alternative strategic imperatives to future financial and stock market performance.

How the book is organized

To achieve the aims listed above the text is based around a simple but nevertheless very powerful framework which provides the central theme. The framework, which will be explained in detail in Chapter 1, is based around a triad with three separable but linked components assessing strategic direction, financial statement analysis and stock market assessment. Each of these three components in turn is divided into three elements, with each forming the subject of a single chapter.

Whilst the power of the general framework comes from understanding the interconnectedness of the triad, the book is organized to enable the reader to choose his or her own point of entry to the model. Whilst most readers are likely to begin by considering how to assess a company's strategic direction and why, it is perfectly feasible and acceptable to wish to start with, say, either the financial statement analysis or stock market assessment. For this reason each of the three main parts of the book are provided with a single page introduction listing the key features to that part of the book, with a diagram showing how the three chapters in the part are linked together.

Each chapter starts with a section on *context*, which explains the coverage of the chapter and indicates some of the major topics included. Every chapter introduces a range of appropriate tools and techniques, and illustrates these through the use of 'real' companies. Emphasizing that the book does provide the reader with the means to apply the tools and techniques themselves, a single company, United Biscuits (UB) plc, is used to show how an analysis and evaluation of a major company can be undertaken. In addition to using UB to illustrate many aspects of the text, in excess of fifty other companies are used as examples at different points in the text. It should be stressed that none of these companies is chosen to illustrate either good or bad practice, but simply as way of bringing to life key issues raised throughout the book.

For those managers applying the tools and techniques developed in the text, access to information sources should be relatively easy and data plentiful. Those outside of a company will need to rely on external information sources and for this reason the techniques examined do not assume that anything other than publicly available information will be available to the manager or researcher undertaking the analysis. As a consequence the techniques developed in the text may be applied to competitors, or by investors seeking to invest on the stock market. Throughout the text the term researcher or analyst is used generically to describe any individual or group either inside a company or outside wishing to assess an organization. At the end of each chapter the reader is provided with a *checklist* itemizing some of the key areas of the text which need to be applied in practice.

John Ellis & David Williams

ACKNOWLEDGEMENTS

A text such as this which links theoretical concepts with actual businesses and the challenges they face would not have been possible without the help of many people. Foremost amongst these must be those individuals at United Biscuits plc who have not only allowed us extensively to use material culled from the company's annual and interim reports, but have also given us every assistance when we have requested, say, press releases, preliminary statements and business histories. We would wish to make clear, however, that the views expressed in the text on the company are the authors' own, and do not necessarily reflect the company's position. Indeed this general disclaimer applies to all the company examples used, with the responsibility for the views expressed remaining with the authors and the authors alone.

Acknowledgements are also due to staff at the Biscuit, Cake, Chocolate & Confectionery Alliance who provided us with statistics on the biscuit industry in the UK. More locally, contacts at Robson Cottrel Limited, Stockbrokers, Bournemouth, and in particular Mr Roger Parsons, Managing Director and Mr Tony Oliver, Associate Director, were of invaluable assistance in providing advice and information on a number of aspects concerned with the stock market.

Over many years colleagues and students on the Dorset Business School MBA and Postgraduate European Management Programme have provided invaluable help and insights on many aspects of the book, as have many of the panellists from industry and commerce we have used to assist in assessing the presentations participants on these management programmes have been asked to make on companies and their strategic direction. To all these individuals we owe a debt of gratitude.

Without the persistence of our publisher, Dr Penelope Woolf, however, this book would never have been finished, and to her we say a personal thank you.

Finally, to our parents and families who have suffered from the unsociable hours and general lack of quality time they have had to endure during the writing of this book we owe a special thanks, and in particular to our partners Susan and Anne who have been left on their own for so much time.

PART ONE

The General Framework

As illustrated below, this book:

- offers a **general framework** for analysing corporate strategies, combining strategic, accounting and stock market perspectives
- provides the user with **multiple points of entry** to analysing companies
- demonstrates step-by-step **how** to assess strategy, finance and stock market performance
- text incorporates **latest** accounting requirements for UK based companies, **up-to-date** versions of stock market assessment and **current thinking** on strategic direction

Part I	The General Framework
Part II	Assessing Strategic Direction
Part III	Financial Statement Analysis
Part IV	Stock Market assessment
Part V	The General Framework Revisited

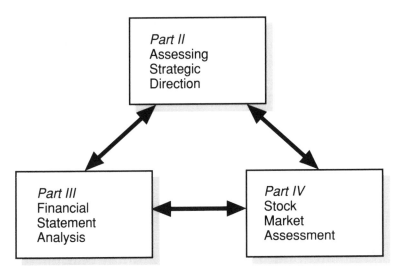

Figure 1.1

CHAPTER 1

Introduction

This chapter is designed to offer the reader an introduction to the general framework around which the book is based, and how its three component parts - assessing strategic direction, financial statement analysis and stock market assessment - are interlinked. The role of each of these three components in the overall assessment of a company is explained, and in turn how each of the three areas can be subdivided is discussed. Specifically, this chapter is arranged in the following sequence:

- *the general framework*
- *assessing strategic direction*
- *financial statement analysis*
- *stock market assessment*
- *the general framework revisited.*

The general framework

The general framework to the book is illustrated in Figure 1.1. This emphasizes that the overall assessment of a company, its strategic direction and financial outcomes is dependent upon an analysis and evaluation of each of the three parts of the triad, namely assessing strategic direction, financial statement analysis and stock market assessment. Figure 1.1 is deliberately drawn as a triad to highlight the interdependence and relatedness of the three areas, and to indicate that the relationship between them is not sequential, or that one component is necessarily more important than the other two.

The essential core of the book is that undertaking an assessment of a company's strategic position and direction requires both a synthesis and an evaluation of non-financial factors (e.g. quality of management, products, markets, industry, broad context, etc.) and financial factors (e.g. profitability, cash flow, debt levels, etc.) in order to be able to fully assess the company and its likely future stock market performance. Further, the stock market performance of the company will influence managers' decisions and hence the strategy and financial performance of the company. The interrelatedness of these three areas therefore lies at the heart of the market economy and the functioning of publicly quoted companies. Unless this is understood by managers inappropriate actions are likely to result, with poor performance the expected outcome.

Using Figure 1.1 the text explicitly links managerial, accounting and stock market perspectives in terms of the strategies that companies follow. By combining these areas in a uniquely powerful way insights are generated which, by only viewing one area of the general framework, would otherwise be missed. In practice the overemphasis on either corporate or business strategy by teachers of strategy on the one side, and finance issues by accountants on the other, means that the critical linkage between the two areas is insufficiently examined. Similarly, the somewhat secretive workings of the financial markets means that even if the link between strategy and finance is recognized, the further link to the stock market performance is not normally considered.

The text is designed to enable the reader to identify and assess the strategic direction of a company, to consider past and current financial outcomes and to link these together with the stock market assessment of the organization which by its very nature looks to the future. Whilst this sequencing of the topics is adopted by the text, the reader should remember that the three areas are interrelated and discontinuity can be triggered by critical change factors in any one area. It is not necessary to follow the chapter order laid out in the book, and the reader is at liberty to start elsewhere in the text if they believe they have a more immediate need or it is more convenient. Nevertheless, the essential point to remember is, notwithstanding the starting point, the need to achieve a full overall assessment requires the individual components of Figure 1.1 to be joined. Failure to do this brings the likelihood that the assessment reached is unbalanced with the inherent risks of inappropriate decisions being taken.

The relationship between the different aspects of the general framework are illustrated by a spine of worked examples, and in particular by showing how the various elements of the analysis can be related to a single stock market quoted company, United Biscuits (UB) plc. The application of the different techniques to UB illustrates how the general framework can be applied to any quoted company using external data sources. Similarly, the internal analyst or consultant is able to apply the same techniques to an unquoted company in order to assess their current and future position.

Assessing strategic direction

Each of the three components of Figure 1.1 itself subdivides into three components. How Part II, Assessing Strategic Direction, is subdivided is shown below:

Part II Assessing Strategic Direction
Chapter 2: Assessing strategic capability
Chapter 3: Taking action to add value
Chapter 4: Finding information on companies and their markets.

Each of the three component chapters of Part II in turn provides an interlocking triad which again emphasizes the interrelatedness of the parts. Chapter 2, Assessing strategic capability, shows the reader how a company, its business situation and strategy can be assessed by employing a range of tools and techniques. Differences in corporate and business strategies are examined and accepted frameworks on competitive advantage and competitive analysis extended, with the latter being illustrated with reference to the European biscuit industry. The importance of the quality of a company's management is stressed and how this may be assessed from an external perspective explored. Once a company's current position has been assessed, Chapter 3, Taking action to add value, considers what options are available to managers seeking to enhance the value of their organizations and at the same time protect themselves from takeover. The analysis contained in Chapter 3 is derived from the application of a number of basic financial principles, with more quantitative aspects of the approach to be examined in Chapter 10. Both for the internal or external analyst of a company, evaluating the current position and assessing what actions might be taken requires an appropriate information base to work from. Chapter 4, Finding information on companies and their markets, explores both what information is required to carry out the necessary analysis and where this information can be found.

Financial statement analysis

Another component of Figure 1.1 is financial statement analysis which is covered in Part III. The three components of this area of analysis are listed below:

Part III Financial Statement Analysis
Chapter 5: Accounting for profit Chapter 6: Accounting for cash Chapter 7: Comparative financial analysis.

Starting with a consideration of what is profit, Chapter 5, Accounting for profit, takes the reader through the key elements of the profit and loss account by using clear and concise explanations and worked examples. The chapter illustrates a range of techniques used to flatter reported profits, and examines the impact of the latest accounting requirements for UK companies and investors. Emphasizing the role of cash and how it differs from profit, Chapter 6, Accounting for cash, examines a company's cash flow statement and shows why having a cash generating business is so vital. The chapter generally emphasizes the importance of cash rather than profit, a theme which is returned to in Chapter 10. The third chapter of the triad on financial statement analysis, Chapter 7, Comparative financial analysis, discusses how meaningful inter-company comparisons can be made against the context of competition becoming increasingly lytransnational. Recognition that, for many companies and sectors, direct comparisons with competitors is difficult leads to the question of how to select companies for comparative purposes. Chapter 7 offers a general framework as to how this might be done.

Stock market assessment

The final element of the triad illustrated by Figure 1.1 is stock market assessment which is covered in Part IV. Again this has three component chapters as shown below:

Part IV Stock Market Assessment
Chapter 8: Share price movements Chapter 9: Short-term share valuation Chapter 10: Long-term share valuation.

Chapter 8, Share price movements, offers a general framework for assessing movements in share prices, emphasizing the distinction between new information which can be labelled continuous, and information which may be classified as discontinuous. The emphasis in Chapter 8 is on providing a general description of share price changes, leaving the more detailed assessment of such changes to the following two chapters. Chapter 9, Short-term share valuation, considers what methods are used by analysts and investors interested in assessing the value of a company's shares on the basis of expected short-term financial performance (up to two years). The chapter contains an illustrative analyst's report to show what features of a company's performance investors often focus attention on. By contrast, Chapter 10, Long-term share valuation, examines the valuation of shares on a longer-term basis and illustrates how shareholder value analysis can be employed. The chapter also shows how strategic choice can be explicitly assessed in terms of financial outcomes and how this is related back to the analysis contained in Chapter 3.

The general framework revisited

Part V The General Framework Revisited
Chapter 11: Some concluding thoughts

The book is concluded in Part V with a focused chapter, highlighting ten issues for consideration when carrying out the assessment of companies and their businesses. Each of the ten points suggests key areas for the practical employment of the general framework introduced at the start of this chapter, and the choice available to the researcher when using the approach in a specific context.

PART TWO

Assessing Strategic Direction

As illustrated below, this part:

- explains the importance of **crafting strategic direction**, and distinguishes between **corporate** and **business unit** strategies;
- illustrates how to undertake a **business audit**;
- focuses on the **quality of management** to adding corporate value;
- identifies what **strategic action** management needs to take to enhance shareholder value and to avoid the threat of takeover;
- gives the reader a choice of using a **top-down** or **bottom-up** approach to analysing companies and their competitors;
- explores **what information** is required to carry out the necessary analysis and **where** such information can be found.

Part I	The General Framework
Part II	**Assessing Strategic Direction**
Part III	Financial Statement Analysis
Part IV	Stock Market Assessment
Part V	The General Framework Revisited

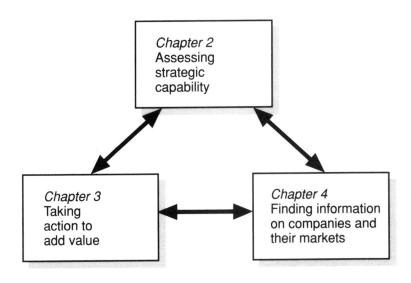

CHAPTER 2

Assessing strategic capability

Managers continue to face ever more turbulent competitive markets. Management action thought appropriate for one period of time quickly becomes dated and unless organizations can recognize critical change factors and react rapidly, underperformance is generally the outcome. To avoid the destiny of decline a first order requirement is for companies to have strategic capability. This is the ability and means to be proactive and to take action which adds value to the organization. The assessment of an organization's strategic capability is the focus of this chapter, which covers the following topics:

- *crafting a strategic vision*
- *corporate and business strategies*
- *undertaking a business audit*
- *quality of management*
- *corrective adjustments*
- *advantages of a 'strategic approach' to managing.*

The chapter begins by considering how strategy is crafted and why having a clear direction is important to the organization. The distinction between corporate and business strategy is then examined, and key requirements at both levels reviewed. The concept of competitive advantage is developed and previous discussion on the topic extended. Alternative product market strategies are discussed, and how to examine these in relation to the broad context as well as the industry/sector and company contexts is considered. The importance of good quality management is a theme which runs throughout the text, and discussion of management styles and capability is considered in detail, together with the question of corporate governance. Recognizing that even successful management teams need to modify their chosen strategies, reflecting organizational learning and the ever-changing external environment, introduces the idea of corrective adjustments. The chapter is concluded with a checklist of factors to be used in assessing the strategic direction of companies.

Crafting a strategic vision

The title of this section is deliberately chosen to convey to the reader the strong judgmental element as to how a company evolves its strategy. Rather than viewing the process as a carefully planned and rationally structured activity, it should be understood that strategies often emerge from the organization's learning in a way which was not previously intended. To provide a starting point it is perhaps helpful to define the term strategy. Dent (1990) notes that the term comes from the Greek *strategos*, meaning the general, and suggests that organizational strategy relates to a 'grand design', something of significance to the overall pattern of an organization's activities.

This definition is perhaps timely because it suggests that organizational strategies in their broadest sense provide a guide or sense of direction to the organization. The idea of an organization needing a vision as to where it needs to go and what it is trying to achieve is a key part to crafting a strategy. Without vision or direction, organizations tend to be ineffectual. It is all too common to find companies and management bereft of ideas. There is no future in playing safe and doing nothing. Vision and risk go together. Risk must be recognized, and judged acceptable to both managers and shareholders.

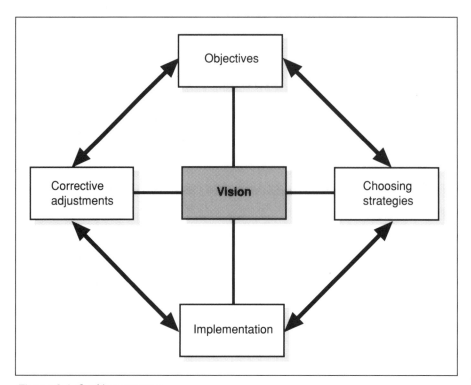

Figure 2.1 Crafting strategy

The key elements to crafting a successful strategy are illustrated in Figure 2.1. Crafting strategy requires management to successfully combine the following five elements:

- vision
- objectives
- choosing strategies
- implementation
- corrective adjustments.

Whilst in practice each of the elements are strongly interrelated, it is helpful initially to consider each separately. Beginning with the *vision*, it has been established that this sets the overall direction, infusing the organization with a clear sense of purpose. The vision is often a general statement or shared understanding of the overall direction or goal of the organization. The vision, or direction of the organization, however, needs to be translated into clearly articulated objectives to enable specific outcomes in pursuit of the vision to be defined. Without such *objectives* the vision is often too general and incapable of being made operational. The objectives provide outcomes against which the organization can monitor its own performance and progress. By determining objectives management is then able to consider what strategies will enable the organization to achieve its desired outcomes. Setting challenging but achievable objectives prompts the emergence of a results orientated climate, and helps guard against organizational complacency and strategic drift.

Choosing strategies occurs because an organization may have a number of genuine alternatives from which to choose in seeking to achieve its objectives. Alternatively, in some circumstances, the choice may be limited to only one strategy which is capable of delivering the desired outcome. An organization's strategy for achieving its objectives consists of those actions and approaches already taking place and anticipated to continue, together with any new strategic actions about to be decided.

Implementation of strategies, although theoretically a separate element, in practice is considered with the choice of strategies. Where this involves significant change from previous policies, implementation is often the most difficult part of crafting a successful strategy. Unless strategies can be implemented the vision will not be achieved. In practice the implementation of strategy is a highly skilled and complex task, revolving around the management of resources, particularly people.

The process of crafting strategy is ongoing and requires constant evaluation and a decision whether to make *corrective adjustments*. Whatever the direction set and strategies pursued, adjustments will be required which both reflect changed external circumstances and the organization's own learning. Frequently, for example, the actual implementation of a strategy results in the organization modifying its objectives, and possibly also part of its vision, as it learns from doing.

Whilst each of the five elements described above and illustrated in Figure 2.1 is critical, the process is far from sequential in practice. Each stage of the process seeks to inform the others and the manner of moving to an agreed set of outcomes requires a number of iterations. Further, it is perfectly possible to make inappropriate decisions at any point. For example, it is possible to have a clear vision which has been delineated into specific objectives, but to choose inappropriate strategies for achieving the objectives, or being unable to implement them successfully. Indeed, to be successful the strategy must be implemented in a manner which is judged to be both effective ('doing the right things') and efficient ('doing things right' – that is at minimum resource cost).

Successful companies tend to be those with well crafted strategies, which contain a vision of where the company is going, but are equally able to translate the vision into operational actions which enable specific objectives to be achieved. Equally, however, once the direction is set and strategies adopted, successful companies respond in a flexible manner to changed events, often by making a series of small, but nonetheless important, adjustments over time. The idea of strategies being periodically determined and never adjusted until the next agreed review date is at variance with reality. In practice organizations and their managers are continuously adjusting their strategies and objectives in the light of more recent information. For example, the latest information on the economic conditions in a company's main product markets may indicate that demand, rather than increasing, is stagnant, thereby requiring a review of objectives or the means of achieving them.

The key point with regard to crafting strategy is that the process is inherently dynamic, and as new information is provided the organization assimilates this and makes adjustments. Of course, there is no guarantee that such adjustments are a sufficient response to changed circumstances. The examples of companies who either have failed to appreciate the degree of change required or have proved incapable of responding are well documented. Occasionally circumstances may change to such a degree that the organization's vision may require review. This might occur if the survival of the organization is in question. All of this is not to deny the importance of crafting strategy, but to make clear the fluidity of the process.

Whilst for brevity the five elements to crafting a strategy have been described sequentially, the development or refinement of the vision may begin with any one of the components to crafting a successful strategy. Hence the reader will have noted how the separate elements are shown as strongly interrelated in Figure 2.1. Organizational learning from, say, the failure to successfully implement a chosen strategy might, for example, lead to the vision being modified, or the decision to choose an alternative strategy to achieve an unchanged outcome. Certainly the reader should be aware that the process is rarely driven from the top in a simple sequential manner.

For the analyst or consultant looking at the organization the challenge is to identify what strategies have been crafted, the extent to which a clear direction has been established, and whether this has been translated into specific objectives and strategies. Further, given the business context in which the organization is operating, what is the likelihood of chosen strategies resulting in acceptable levels of business performance? What level of risk is involved, and is this acceptable?

If the indications are that the organization lacks a clear vision, and indeed shows no evidence of being able to develop direction, the likelihood is that the company is, or will be shortly, underperforming. Such a scenario is likely to say much about the company's current management resource. Crafting a strategy has much to do with the quality of a company's management and this topic will be examined in depth shortly.

Accepting the need to craft a strategy, including its successful implementation, how does the individual outside the company go about identifying a company's direction and assessing capability? To answer these questions let us consider United Biscuits (UB) plc. As we indicated in the first chapter, UB will be used throughout the book to illustrate how many of the key concepts introduced in the text may be applied in practice. In the following discussion it is helpful to note that UB is a medium-sized international food manufacturer whose principal activities include the production of biscuits, savoury products (e.g. crisps and peanuts), chocolate and sugar confectionery and frozen foods.

Obtaining the necessary information to assess companies is a prerequisite before the analyst or consultant can begin work. A full description of how to find information will be given in Chapter 4. For the purposes of this point in the text, it is sufficient to note that much helpful information about how a company is attempting to craft its strategy may be obtained from reading its annual and interim reports over a number of years and tracking press and informed comment on the company. For UB the following discussion draws strongly upon these sources. The company's 1991 Annual Report, published in March 1992, includes a Group Strategic Review (p.9), which highlights the overall direction of the company:

Our prime corporate objective is to become a world leader in snackfoods.

The statement above provides evidence that the company's overall direction is about expanding its activities in order to become a world leader in snackfoods.

UB's Group Strategic Review, published in the first quarter of 1992 as part of the Annual Report, provides evidence of how the company is seeking to achieve its overall corporate objective by stating that the company has a clearly defined strategy and wishes to develop the company's activities 'by doing more of what the company does best in more places.' In other words, the company is attempting to increase the geographical scope of its activities and in particular has set itself a number of clear strategic priorities in relation to its principal business activities. Chief amongst these are:

...we will develop our biscuit and savoury business world-wide with particular emphasis on Europe, North America and Asia Pacific.

...we will build our confectionery business concentrating initially on the large and growing European market.

... improved returns on the investment in our frozen and chilled food operations.

1991 Annual Report, March 1992, p.8.

With respect to the previous discussion on crafting strategy the priorities listed above may be considered to be the objectives the company has set itself in trying to achieve its vision. Geographical expansion is an objective in respect of the company's biscuit, savoury and confectionery businesses, although the focus of the latter is limited to Europe. The strategy with respect to the company's frozen and chilled food operations is by contrast one of consolidation. Consolidation in this context reflects the need to raise the profitability of the frozen and chilled food business.

Reference has already been made to the fact that organizations continuously adjust strategies in the light of more recent information about, for example, external market conditions. A consequence is that there is much to be gained by appreciating the recent business history of the organization in order to understand how the organization has reacted to changed events and the extent to which modifications to its direction have taken place. Again, an understanding of the relevant background can be achieved most readily by reviewing a company's annual and interim reports over, say, a five-year period and tracing the changes to the company direction and the reasons advanced. Illustrating this point, compare UB's statements above with what was written approximately six months later in the group's 1992 Interim Report (published September 1992, p.4):

> During this difficult time we have not been deflected from our clearly defined strategy. Whilst a major cost containment programme has been initiated throughout the Group, we have continued to invest in the long-term future of the business achieving further manufacturing efficiencies; improved quality; wider and more cost-effective distribution; and imaginative product development. In addition we have continued to explore acquisition and development opportunities in our areas of strategic priority.

Whilst stating that the group's strategy remains unchanged, the text suggests some change to priorities. Whilst still seeking to grow and develop, the group has initiated a major cost containment programme across all its activities. Clearly, understanding the reasons for this change is an important task for the analyst or management consultant. One of the questions to ask is the extent to which the group planned to make these adjustments to its strategy or whether circumstances have forced the change on the company. Implicit in the statement above is the fact that the company has been faced with difficult trading conditions during 1992 reflecting downturns in its principal product markets.

The discussion above should not be taken to imply necessarily a weakness to what the company was stating earlier. Rather, it represents the continuous process of updating and adjusting a company's direction and strategies in the light of more recent information. Indeed, the failure to respond to external changes is one of the principal reasons for the underperformance of businesses, and ultimately corporate failure. As with many areas of management action it is a question of balance, between making adjustments to unforeseen events and having to correct poorly crafted strategies. The latter may involve a company making major changes of direction.

Corporate and business strategies

Whilst in practice there are strong links between corporate and business strategies it is helpful to define them separately and to understand what the business is attempting to do at the two different levels. The two levels of strategy arise from the fact that strategy at the corporate level is about the corporate centre, or headquarters team of a group company, which owns the individual business units or companies who are primarily concerned with producing or distributing goods or services to markets. The key concern with corporate strategy is how the corporate centre manages to add value to its business units, a process which has been described as corporate parenting (Goold and Campbell, 1987a). At the business unit level the key requirement is crafting a sizeable and sustainable competitive advantage. The relationship between corporate and business strategy is illustrated by Figure 2.2.

Where a company is diversified to the extent that it operates in more than one business area, there is automatically a distinction between corporate and business activities. In practice most companies quoted on the major national and international stock exchanges around the world are diversified to the extent that they operate a significant number of different businesses. For those companies labelled conglomerates – for example, Hanson plc, BTR plc, BET plc – the number of businesses operated is very large, and the diversity of activities very broad. More usually, quoted companies have a number of different 'strategic legs' to their business, suggesting that they might operate in, say, three or four distinct business areas.

As Figure 2.2 illustrates, a company's corporate strategy is primarily concerned with three key areas of potential added value:

- portfolio management
- corporate core competences
- enhancing business unit performance.

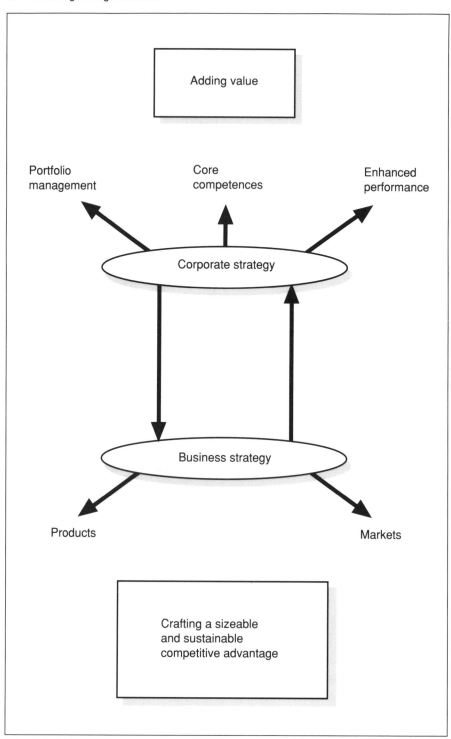

Figure 2.2 Corporate and business strategies

Portfolio management

A key question to be decided as part of the organization's corporate strategy is the overall scope of its activities. Whilst organizations may begin life as single business entities, the majority of quoted companies are multi-activity businesses. Correspondingly, for these companies – but also very often for small businesses – the question arises whether the scope of the organization's activities should be changed. Should the company seek to develop new business activities, possibly by acquiring a company, or alternatively divest itself of some of its current activities? Responding to this question in the context of a number of takeover bids to 'unbundle' diversified, and often poorly performing conglomerates, Goold and Campbell (1989) commented :

- A company should add a business to its portfolio *only* if it believes it can create more parenting value in relation to the new business than other potential bidders.
- A company should divest a business in its portfolio when it believes the business will perform better as an independent company or as part of the portfolio of some other company.

The principles identified by Goold and Campbell provide a framework as to when a company should seek to add to its portfolio of businesses, and when activities should be divested.

Core competences

What then are the core competences that the corporate centre can bring to bear on the portfolio of business units contained within the business group? A headquarters team may possess a special set of skills which can be applied to the business unit to enhance performance. Hanson plc, the acquisitive industrial conglomerate, for instance, on acquiring a company installs an experienced team of its central staff to assist management at the business level to raise performance. Alternatively, the corporate centre may be able to develop synergies (2 + 2 = 5) between different businesses in the portfolio. Prahalad and Hamel (1990) have recently highlighted this question and advocated the need to develop core competences as the focus of strategy at the corporate level. Organizations are urged to build the necessary strategic architecture (structure, systems, management styles, etc.) to enable skills contained in the different business units to be combined and core competences developed. This is seen to be particularly important for businesses competing on a global basis, and is an issue which is developed further in the next chapter.

The emphasis in seeking synergies is the need for corporate management to avoid viewing the organization as simply a collection of discrete businesses. This point in turn raises the question of what is the most appropriate management style to employ to enable such synergies to be exploited.

Enhancing performance

The work of Goold and Campbell (1987b) found that in managing large and diversified companies there was not one correct way to manage a company's business units. Rather the authors identified a number of alternative approaches using different combinations of two management levers: planning and control. Consequently the approach adopted was contingent on a number of factors which could be clustered under two headings, namely the *nature of the businesses* and the *resources of the organization*. The nature of the business focused on the shape of the portfolio of business, the size and length of payback on investments and the competitive environment. Similarly, the resources of the organization include the financial condition of the organization, the personality of the chief executive officer and management skills possessed by senior management. Three principal management styles were most commonly found in practice, namely: strategic planning, strategic control and financial control. Each of these styles had particular strengths in terms of certain aspects of performance, but no one style was superior in terms of all elements of business performance.

Strategic planning was most appropriate where there were significant interdependencies between different business units, but was relatively poor in delivering short-term financial performance. Strategic control led to delegation of strategic direction to the divisional and business unit level, and an attempt to reconcile long-term and short-term objectives. Finally, financial control tended to result in strong financial performance in the short-term, but at the expense of longer-term investments and linkages between business activities. A clear exposition of the characteristics, portfolio implications and performance of the three principal strategic management styles is provided in Table 2.1.

Drawing together the three components of corporate strategy – portfolio management, core competences and enhanced performance – the overriding need is that strategy at this level must add value.

Business level strategy, as Figure 2.2 illustrates, is about how businesses compete in their chosen product markets, and whether they are able to craft a sizeable and sustainable competitive advantage. Sustainable competitive advantage is about the ability of a company to compete in its chosen product markets in such a way that it is able to achieve superior performance and profitability when compared to its competitors over a period of time. It is not a short-term gain brought about by temporary business conditions, or solely the benefit of being able to spot a business position before any one else does. As Cronshaw *et al.* (1990) demonstrate, 'market positions can always be replicated by competitors, and what others can do cannot be profitable for long.' Next plc, the UK fashion retailer, provides a classic example of why market positioning in itself is insufficient. In the 1980s Next realized that the market for ladies' fashions provided new opportunities for segmentation based upon appealing to the 'successful woman' and offering coordinated fashions, or edited retailing as it was known. Next having seen the market opportunity soon found itself

Table 2.1 *Corporate management style*

Strategic planning

Characteristics
Corporate headquarters is deeply involved with management at the business level in formally planning strategies. Emphasis is strongly on the planning lever to influence the direction of the business. Centre may provide clear direction to the business unit. Control of the business unit involves using both strategic (e.g. investment, market share) and financial goals.

Portfolio implications
Approach tends to be employed when there are significant linkages between business units which require coordination, and where a significant part of investment needs to be undertaken on a long-term basis. The strategic planning style tends to require a narrow portfolio of business enabling the centre to gain a detailed understanding of the individual business areas.

Performance
Short-term financial performance may suffer to the extent that the organization takes a longer-term view. Lack of emphasis on financial performance may result in poor cost control. Planning process can be highly time consuming, with the centre losing objectivity. Business unit management may become frustrated by interventions by corporate management in their business.

Strategic control

Characteristics
The strategic development of the business is left to divisional or business unit management. Centre does not set direction to business, or seek to coordinate synergies between business. This is left to the divisional level. Capital projects generally initiated by the business. Businesses expected to make detailed reports to the centre in relation to performance.

Portfolio implications
Likely to be most appropriate where business activities are spread over a number of separate business areas where individual business plans can be self-financed by the business unit. Strategic control may be used with a more diverse portfolio than for the strategic planning style.

Performance
Style attempts to provide a balance between longer-term (strategic) and shorter-term (financial) goals. Maintaining the balance between the two is, however, difficult. Cooperation between business units may be ineffective in exploiting potential synergies.

continued overleaf

Table 2.1 Cont.

Financial control

Characteristics
Strong delegation of responsibility by the corporate centre to management at the business unit. Budget process, and agreeing budget with the corporate headquarters, is critical. Budget becomes a 'contract' between corporate and business levels of management. Strong emphasis on short-term payback for projects requiring investment. Thrust is primarily on the financial controls. Financial performance monitored in detail by the centre.

Portfolio implications
Approach has been used by a number of industrial conglomerates to maximize financial performance from a widely diverse portfolio of businesses. Business units are treated as being autonomous to the extent that linkages between different business areas are not exploited. Some commentators question the extent to which the style is appropriate for technology driven businesses requiring long-term investment. Style most commonly found with businesses operating in mature or declining industries.

Performance
Style tends to maximize short-term financial performance, but at the expense of organic growth. Long-term investment opportunities may be lost, and linkages between business units not developed. Business level management has a strong incentive to 'achieve' agreed budget.

Source: Authors based on Goold and Campbell (1987).

---

growing rapidly and taking market share from the existing competitors in the market-place, notably Marks & Spencer plc, the largest retailer of ladies' fashions in the country. Initially Next gained *first mover advantages* and built up a significant market position. Competitors were, however, forced to take action to protect their position, and what Next had done they copied, with the result that Next's competitive advantage was undermined.

Fashion goods, including clothing, are notoriously susceptible to the cycle of demand experienced by Next, whereby temporary consumer endorsement is soon lost when fashion changes or other competitors respond. Next in this example enjoyed a temporary competitive advantage, but did not build upon its initial advantage to achieve a sustainable competitive advantage. This case emphasizes that first mover advantages in themselves may not yield anything other than a temporary advantage to the company.

How can a long-term sustainable competitive advantage be achieved? Since the term was introduced by Porter (1980) there has been considerable interest in generic strategies – actions applicable to a wide range of business situations – which would enable a business to develop a competitive advantage and register an above-average level of performance. Porter's initial work suggested that generic strategies were one-dimensional, with companies either seeking to develop competitive advantages based on differentiation (being unique) or cost.

Subsequent work by a variety of authors (e.g. Gilbert and Strebel (1988), Cronshaw *et al.* (1990)) has questioned different aspects of Porter's approach. Consequently whilst the idea of competitive advantage remains an important concept, the manner in which it may be achieved has undergone considerable revision.

In seeking to develop a sustainable competitive position it is possible to suggest that management needs to have recourse to five dimensions, whose manipulation can be used to develop competitive advantage. The five dimensions identified are:

- differentiation
- cost
- scope
- time
- competitive linkages.

The five dimensions are not necessarily mutually exclusive, and management will need to recognize and reconcile tensions between, say, the extent of differentiation and cost. Baden-Fuller and Turner (1992) have described these choices as the dilemmas of seemingly irreconcilable opposites. Management's objective is, however, to develop multiple sources of competitive advantage which are difficult or costly to replicate. Further, companies need to understand that the competitive environment is inherently dynamic and the changes in, say, the external context can, in some instances, rapidly undermine the basis of a competitive advantage previously developed. This emphasizes once again that companies which cease to develop and become inflexible are sooner or later – and generally sooner – likely to be displaced by their competitors. Further, once a company has lost its competitive advantage it is likely to require a disproportionate effort on behalf of its management to turn the organization around and regain a previously held position. The history of individual business shows all too clearly that many companies, once they have lost their competitive edge, subsequently find it impossible to rejuvenate their old or develop a new basis of competitive advantage.

The five factors listed above and illustrated in Figure 2.3 operate at the level of an individual or interrelated group of product markets. Applying the dimension of *differentiation* reflects the firm's intention to be unique in some way within its chosen product market. By adopting a strategy of differentiation the firm is seeking to achieve a premium price for its products. For value to be enhanced the additional price received should not be wholly offset by the additional costs incurred in being unique. This requires that the basis of the differentiation must be something that the company's customers want and are prepared to pay for, otherwise the strategy will not add value to the company. Further, the basis of the differentiation must be sustainable reflecting perhaps an established brand or technological feature which is difficult to replicate. To this end established product brands or business formats with associated customer goodwill, if effectively maintained by appropriate management action and reinvestment, can yield above-average returns for their companies over the longer term.

The second dimension of competitive advantage is *cost*. By seeking to be a low cost supplier a company is able to offer lower prices than its competitors, or maintain prices and enjoy higher profit margins. This can lead to the virtuous circle of improved profitability, additional reinvestment and further cost reductions. Costs may be reduced by a variety of management actions including concentrating production on a smaller number of sites, investment to increase efficiency by substituting capital for labour and the introduction of flexible manufacturing systems, allowing companies to benefit from the automation and flexibility of production. For some industries economies of scale in distribution and marketing are more critical than production economies, whilst in other industries spending on research and development is the key.

In practice companies cannot simply focus on cost and neglect differentiation, unless they are operating in commodity markets where quality is standardized and price is the only thing that matters. Even for a product such as basic steel, quality and delivery times will be important elements of the purchase decision. Hence managing the dilemma between quality (differentiation) and

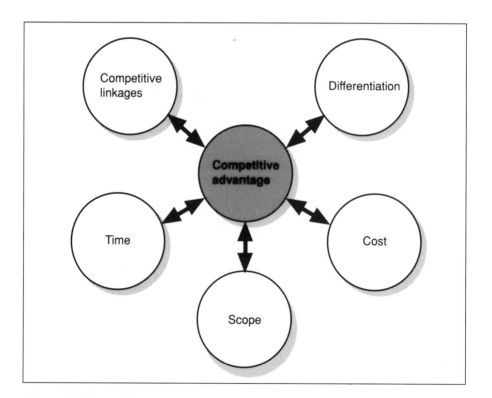

Figure 2.3 Competitive advantage

cost should be a critical area for management attention.

The concept of competitive *scope* was introduced by Porter (1980) and highlights that companies are able to choose whether to operate across a large number of or relatively few product markets. Companies operating across a number of market segments may be described as broadly based, whilst companies operating within a single product market may be described as having a niche strategy. The rationale for adopting a niche strategy is the ability to serve a small part of the total market in a superior manner to the broad-based competitor, and thereby attract sufficient custom to make the strategy viable. For this to happen the size of the niche must be sufficient to offer the basis of economic supply, but be insufficiently attractive to come to the attention of large companies with a stronger resource base. When considering a niche strategy a company may consider segmenting the market either by product and/ or geographical scope. For example, different size companies may seek to supply local, national or international markets.

Recognition of the importance of time as an element of competitive advantage stems from the work of Stalk and Hout (1990) who refer to *time-based competition*. The ability to develop quickly new products from conception to market launch has been shown to be a key element of the competitive process for a number of technology based industries. The ability of Japanese manufacturers dramatically to reduce new product development times and thereby constantly update their product range has been a source of competitive advantage over their western competitors in a number of industries. Unless competitors are able to match the speed of new product development they are increasingly likely to discover that customers find their products outdated. As Illustration 2.1 on the world's consumer electronics industry demonstrates, the ability to develop new products can in turn be a key profit driver for an industry. The consumer electronics industry also illustrates the fact that investment in research and development is risky and does not bring guaranteed success.

The relationship of an organization within the total business system to its supplier and purchasing companies introduces the fifth dimension of competitive advantage: *competitive linkages*. The network of business relationships and how they are managed can be a major source of competitive advantage to the organization. Conversely, if such relationships are poorly managed or neglected then they can seriously undermine a company's competitive position.

In the UK Marks & Spencer's competitive position as a value-for-money retailer is maintained partly by the company's relationship with its suppliers. A close relationship with suppliers enables long-term competitive relationships to be developed and quality assurance continuously monitored. Across the world motor vehicle assemblers are developing ever closer competitive linkages with key component suppliers, who are now undertaking tasks previously undertaken by the assemblers. Both parties have adopted or are in the process of adopting just-in-time (JIT) systems of stock replenishment to improve stock control.

Illustration 2.1

THE CONSUMER ELECTRONICS INDUSTRY

Consumer electronics was one of the growth industries in the 1980s driven by rising consumer spending in the major industrial markets, the development and diffusion of new products, and improvements in production technology reducing the real cost of many new products.

The 1990s have started differently. In 1992 two of the industry's giants, Sony and Matsushita, reported profit falls. Although recession in the companies' major markets was partially to blame, other factors were also important. Not the least of these was the failure to develop new products which the consumer wished to buy.

Increasingly industrial markets were reaching saturation levels with respect to colour televisions and video recorders. Whilst there is some growth left, increasingly demand is not for new products but replacement demand for products wearing out. The companies have responded to this situation by continuing to make model changes and make incremental improvements to existing products. This policy has, however, failed to stimulate demand to previous levels.

The industry is hoping that the introduction of digital audio tape and other new products will correct the situation, but considerable uncertainty remains in respect of future growth levels.

Source: Based on press reports.

On the basis of these five dimensions, the task of management at the business level is to achieve or maintain a sustainable competitive advantage. The dynamics of the market-place will dictate the need for managers to consider how the business will be developed in order to achieve this goal. To assist this process Table 2.2 identifies the principal product market strategies that managers may need to consider.

When examining the options listed in Table 2.2 all strategic alternatives should be examined against the 'base' case of 'do nothing.' The 'do nothing' case represents what would happen if the company's management continued with existing strategies. The other strategic options should then be measured against the base case in order to judge the extent to which the company's position is improved or made worse by adopting an alternative strategy. The outcomes to alternative strategies will need to be compared in terms of whether the option chosen 'adds value'. This concept is explored in Chapter 3, and again in Chapter 10.

To assist the reader in considering alternative options a popular framework for considering alternative strategic options has been introduced by Johnson and Scholes (1993) based upon the three criteria of *suitability, feasibility* and *acceptability*. These are defined as follows:

- *suitability:* does the strategic option fit the needs of the company's situation?

- *feasibility:* is the company able to implement the strategy given its resource base?
- *acceptability:* is the strategy acceptable to the company's stakeholders?

Unless all three criteria are met the proposed strategy will not be undertaken. It is not sufficient for a strategy to be suitable and feasible, it must also be acceptable to the company's stakeholders. In the next chapter it is argued that to be acceptable the strategy must create shareholder value.

Table 2.2 *Product market strategies*

Business strategy	Product market implications
Existing product markets	
Do nothing	Management continue to pursue past strategies. The 'do nothing' strategy should form the base against which all other strategies are evaluated.
Consolidation	Action to strengthen the company's position in its existing product markets.
Withdrawal	Decide to cease to operate in the product market. Management need to consider what is the most appropriate exit strategy. This may be a phased withdrawal from the market rather than an immediate cessation of activities. A company may also withdraw from a market by selling a business to another company.
Market penetration	The strategy is to increase the company's market share. This may be difficult in a mature market, where any growth is likely to be at the expense of competitors. This strategy may bring retaliation from competitors who find their sales falling.
New product; existing markets	
Product development	Management's strategy is to develop new products, but to sell these products in their existing markets.
New market; existing product	
Market development	Existing products are sold in what are for the company new markets.
New products; new markets	
Diversification	Company attempts to move away from its existing product market base by selling new products into new markets.

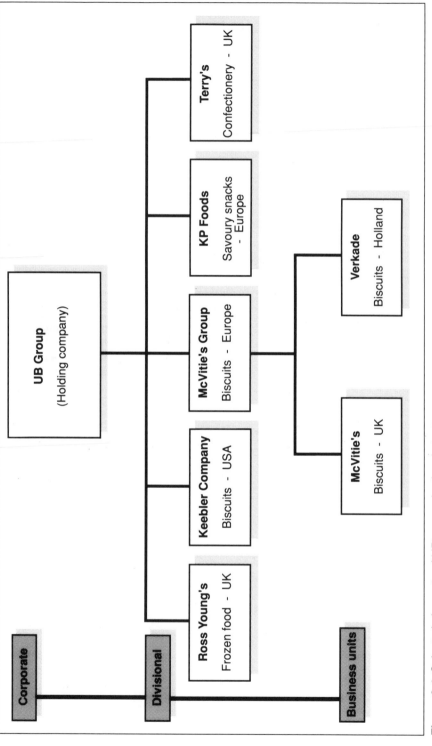

Figure 2.4 Selected elements of UB's organizational structure

To illustrate how Table 2.2 may aid the understanding of a company's product market strategies it is important to consider the strategic priorities identified for UB earlier. The company's stated strategy in respect of its frozen and chilled food operations is one of consolidation, while, in respect of the biscuits group, McVitie's, the strategy being pursued is market development – expanding into Europe. For any company, an important aim for the analyst will be to identify what are the product market strategies of each of the main businesses, and to what extent will these assist the development or maintenance of competitive advantage. To be able to do this the corporate group must be disaggregated by business division. The majority of large companies cluster their individual businesses, known as strategic business units (SBUs), into operating divisions, with each division representing a major area of activity. This form of multi-dimensional organizational structure is widely known as the M-form and is illustrated for UB in Figure 2.4.

UB plc, the group company, organizes its businesses into five main divisions, with a sixth dealing with development operations (not shown in Figure 2.4). It is worth noting that two of UB's divisions – McVitie's (European biscuits) and Keebler (North American biscuits) – operate in similar product areas, but in different geographical markets. This point illustrates that the fact that even though a company may decide to adopt the M-form, the actual organizational structure as it applies to an individual group is for management to determine.

In addition to identifying the principal activities and markets of the business divisions it is important to consider relative size. A company might, for example, operate with four divisions, of which one contributes all of the profit. Information on the turnover (sales) and profit of a company's principal constituent business is to be found in the annual report. The relative importance of UB's five main divisions, using 1991 figures, is given in Table 2.3.

Table 2.3 *UB divisional turnover and profitability 1991*

Division	Turnover (£m)	Turnover % of total UB	Profits (£m)	Profits % of total UB
McVitie's	787.3	26.5	106.7	41.4
Keebler	983.0	33.1	65.6	25.4
KP Foods	504.3	17.0	43.5	16.9
Ross Young	542.9	18.3	27.5	10.7
Terry's	153.4	5.2	14.3	5.5

Source: *UB Annual Report 1991*, March 1992.

On the basis of the figures outlined in Table 2.3, McVitie's was the principal profit driver for the group in 1991, accounting for 26.5% of turnover and 41.4% of profit. Each of the business divisions above, together with the individual businesses contained within, need to be examined to assess the extent to which that part of the company possesses a competitive advantage in relation to the activity and its markets. This requires a detailed review of the relative strengths and weaknesses of the competitive position versus rivals, and the extent to which clearly identifiable external trends may assist or adversely affect the business position. The feasibility and acceptability of alternative product market strategies needs also to be related to the external and internal context of each of the business units to assess whether a strategic option will enable the effective strategic development of the organization. For example, in a mature product market, whilst a strategy of market penetration may pass the suitability criterion, the existence of large competitors who are likely to retaliate will raise doubts as to its feasibility, and in turn its acceptability to stakeholders.

Undertaking a business audit

Recognition of the different *external* and *internal* contexts relating to a business suggests that a thorough business audit should be conducted to assess strategic options and their likelihood of developing competitive advantage. Such an audit necessitates a focus in two dimensions: on three levels of analysis – *broad context, industry/sector* and *company* – and on three time frames – *past, current* and *future*. By combining these two dimensions nine cells identifying different information needs are created.

The first dimension recognizes the need to carry out analysis at three levels:

- *broad context* – identifying trends relating to the general business environment;
- *industry/sector* – identifying competitive forces operating at the level of the industry/sector; and
- *company-based factors* – focusing on how the company manages its products and markets.

The time dimension emphasizes the need to look at the dynamics of the business rather than simply focus on the past or current positions. It is important to understand that the past and present are only important to the extent that they help to make sense of the future. Forecasting forward is the key to assessing future financial and stock market performance.

The generic framework for combining the two dimensions of analysis is presented in Figure 2.5. It shows time on the horizontal axis, and the levels of analysis on the vertical axis. The diagram illustrates how using the two dimensions it is possible to develop a 3×3 matrix to analyse competitive position.

To help interpret Figure 2.5 the key drivers in relation to the three different levels of analysis will now be examined. Analysis at the level of the broad context is designed to identify and assess those change factors which can influence the company's general business environment. For convenience the change factors

The third and final element of analysis focuses on factors related to the individual company. Although the overall nature of the competitive forces have a significant impact on company profitability, variations in inter-company performance within an industry are explained largely by factors at the level of the company. Some of the key areas which should be examined in relation to the individual company include:

- quality of management
- relative market position
- product brands/business format
- market scope
- operations.

A further critical area relates to financial resources and performance, but discussion on this subject is deferred to Part III of the book. The five key factors to be examined in relation to the company-based level of analysis are illustrated in Figure 2.9.

The *quality of management* is a critical ingredient to undertaking analysis at the level of the company. Management is often the key differentiator between those companies able to fashion a competitive advantage and outperform the competition, and those who achieve poor levels of performance. The impor-

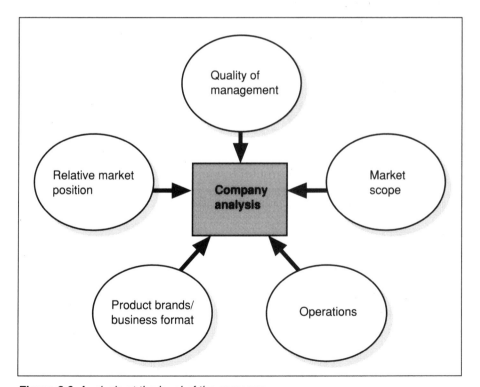

Figure 2.9 *Analysis at the level of the company*

tance of a company's management resource means that this subject is the focus of the next section in this chapter.

A company's *relative market position* assesses the organization's strength and positioning when compared to the competition. Appraisal of a company's relative strength is likely to require both an assessment at the level of the industry and in respect of different market segments. For example, the biscuit market in the UK can be segmented according to whether the product can be classified as a sweet/semi-sweet, plain/savoury or chocolate biscuit. The relative position of biscuit manufacturers varies according to the market segment under review.

A consideration of a company's position in relation to the different market segments is likely to require an assessment of the extent to which, for example, the company has established *product brands*, a business format or a technologically superior product. For fast-moving consumer goods, including biscuits, branded products are a key element of market strength which relates back to the issue of differentiation as one of the key factors which can lead to competitive advantage. Product brands or business formats are often related to customer goodwill, and the extent to which an established reputation can lead to enhanced sales. In the case of industrial products this may reflect elements of technological leadership as well as established market reputation.

Together with assessing a company's relative market position there is the need to consider *market scope*. Does it matter, for example, that the company is strong in some market segments, but weak in others? Equally, to what extent does the company seek to compete on a local, national or international basis? If a company has restricted its market scope will this lead to the company experiencing increased competition from larger players in the future?

The role of *operations* emphasizes the need for companies to be effective in the supply of their chosen products or services, and the need to consider the extent to which the company may be considered to have organized its operations in an efficient and effective manner. Has, for example, the company been investing in new facilities or have these been run down, so that the company's production units are in need of new investment? To what extent does the configuration of a company's operating facilities match the market need, or simply reflect the past history of the organization?

Table 2.6 illustrates how an assessment at the level of the company may be related to the McVitie's division of UB plc.

Table 2.6 *Assessment of company-based factors as related to McVitie's biscuits*

COMPANY
Quality of management   • Management has demonstrated the ability to develop successful new products.   • Company has maintained profitability during period of recession in the UK market.   *Relative market position*   • McVitie's is the market leader in the manufacture of biscuits in the UK, operating in the three main market segments: sweet/semi-sweet, plain/savoury and chocolate coated.   *Product brands*   • McVitie's owns a number of strong brand names, including McVitie's Digestive, Chocolate Home Wheat, Hob-Nobs and Rich Tea.   *Market scope*   • Recent acquisition policies have increased the company's exposure in the European market-place. The company is still predominantly focused on the UK market-place, although less so than, say, three years ago.   • The company's ambition is to increase its share of the European biscuit market from 14% to 25% by the end of the decade.   *Operations*   • The company has invested heavily over the years to increase efficiency and reduce the costs of production.

The factors listed above in relation to the three levels of analysis are not intended to be exhaustive, but rather to illustrate how the framework may be employed to analyse the position of the business and to consider the extent to which there exists a sustainable competitive advantage. How each of the factors listed above, and others, are combined is inherently a matter of judgement. Experience has shown that attempting to quantify the importance of individual factors and then aggregating to provide an overall result tends to lead to spurious and false impressions of accuracy. In the final analysis, all the key change factors have to be given an implicit weighting in the mind of the researcher and a concluding judgement determined.

The need is to recognize the inherently dynamic nature of the framework and the requirement to apply the three levels of analysis to the future. The length of the future forecasting period is a function of the extent to which management and shareholders take a short-term or longer-term view. Chapter 10 explores issues relating to the time horizon required and emphasizes the need in most business situations to look forward for up to five years.

Quality of management

An implicit theme running through much, if not all, of the discussion to this point has been the importance of good management, both at the corporate and business level. Crafting strategy is about management developing a vision and approach which will enable the organization to achieve high levels of performance. Time and again it has been demonstrated that if companies in the same business sectors with similar resources and competitive positions are compared with one another the factor which really explains the differences of performance is management. Why is it that virtually unknown companies continue to emerge to become some of the largest companies in their industries, whilst previously well-known organizations go backwards, are taken over or go into liquidation? One has only to compare a list of the 500 largest public listed companies over a number of years to see this process at work. This is not to deny that companies with strong and established market positions often compete from a position of strength and that competitors face a difficult struggle, but to recognize that even in such situations it is surprising how fast dominant positions can be lost. All of these comments mean that assessing the quality of a company's management is critically important.

For a corporate group, assessing senior management means identifying who are members of the board of directors, and in particular who holds the key positions of chairman and chief executive. Again, looking through the company's Annual Report will enable information to be gleaned on who the members of the board are and what their ages, experience and responsibilities are. Much can often be gained from an understanding of the background of the individuals, including how long they have served the company, what previous positions have they held, and whether they have a background in, say, finance, marketing or operations. An individual's previous 'track record' tells you much about the person and how they operate. It is possible to think of many managers operating with a strategic 'recipe' – a particular way of doing things. A recipe learnt in one company may, for example, be brought to another if the individual moves positions. Most chairmen and chief executives tend to have a particular way of operating, often learnt from many years of business experience and reflecting their own personal characteristics. Interestingly these characteristics may mean that unless chief executives are able to change their 'recipe' and style of management, then their effectiveness is likely to be limited to a particular context.

Sir John Harvey-Jones, in describing business as a marathon, has been quoted as saying:

> The guy who was absolutely first class at sloshing through the mud maybe isn't so good at racing up to the high peaks.
>
> Sir John Harvey-Jones (1992) 'How to run the Marathon Relay', *Investor's Chronicle*, 24 January, p.13.

This raises the question of whether the senior management team fits the needs of the business. A chief executive who was highly effective during the years of expansion in the 1980s may not be the most appropriate leader in more difficult times when cost containment may be more important than product or market innovation. Equally, the person who turns the business around in times of difficulty may need to give way to somebody else to allow the business to grow.

Looking in on the company the researcher should seek indicators of particular management styles, personalities and recipes which may strongly influence the direction and running of the organization. Whilst it is impossible to cover all situations some of the questions which might be asked when seeking to gain an understanding of the management team include:

- Is the management team dominated by a single individual? If so, who is it and what values and beliefs does he/she hold strongly? Strong managers can be highly successful, but they can be difficult to remove, especially if they combine the roles of the chairman and chief executive.
- Does the organization have a problem in recruiting and retaining senior staff as might be indicated by rapid management turnover? This can arise from the problems of working with an autocratic chief executive who refuses to allow others to develop the company in ways with which he or she is not comfortable.
- Has the top team been in place too long, run out of ideas and in need of rejuvenation? Is the chief executive increasingly involved in outside interests, suggesting he or she has less energy to devote to the business? Is there a balance between experience and youth?
- Are the senior staff close to retirement so that there may be a succession problem? Has the existing chairman or chief executive groomed a successor to enable a smooth changeover at the top?
- Have there been significant changes to the board of directors, and in particular changes of the chairman or chief executive, perhaps indicating a movement away from previous policies pursued by the company?
- If there have been resignations from the board, are these due to retirement, or do they signal disagreements amongst the directors on the direction and running of the company? The resignation of senior non-executive directors, in particular, can be a warning sign that all is not well.
- What has been the past track record of the management team? Have they proved that they can manage both in bad times as well as good?

The list of questions above is not exhaustive, nor is it meant to imply that there is necessarily one right way to manage a business. Different personalities and styles can be equally effective. Rather, the list above is intended to help the analyst to question what is the nature of the management team, and to enable a judgement to be made as to whether it has the appropriate mixture of skills and experience. The objective is to provide an assessment of the strength of the management resource, and whether there is a sufficient depth and breadth of management to craft and carry through chosen strategies. In the final analysis it comes down to whether the investor has confidence in the management of the company and its ability to achieve appropriate levels of performance in the future.

A number of the questions above relate to the extent to which a company is dominated by a single individual. Often such individuals are critical to providing the drive and vision for companies, but equally this may come at a price (see Illustration 2.4).

Illustration 2.4

MANAGEMENT STYLES – THE CULT OF THE INDIVIDUAL

The death of the publisher Robert Maxwell and the subsequent disclosure of the extent of the problems with the two public companies to which he was connected – Maxwell Communications and Mirror Group Newspapers – led to the City of London becoming concerned about companies where a single individual was all-powerful.

Similarly, the ratings of Hanson Group plc suffered following concerns about the management styles of Lords Hanson and White, which were exposed in the aftermath of the purchase of 2.8% of ICI's shares in May 1991 by Hanson Group plc. Subsequent debate about the possible takeover of ICI by Hanson focused on the quality of Hanson's profits and its style of management. In particular, the major investment institutions were unhappy about the company's corporate governance, including the number, appointment and power of its non-executive directors. Pressure on the company forced it to state that it would become more open, but not before considerable damage to Hanson's image had been done. Discussion of the succession to Lords Hanson and White was also widely talked about given the advancing ages of the two leaders.

Source: Based on press comment at the time.

Concern about power of executive chairmen and chief executives has led to extensive debate about the role of non-executive directors and the circumstances in which they are able to check the power and actions of an all-powerful executive director (see Illustration 2.5).

Illustration 2.5

CORPORATE GOVERNANCE – THE ROLE OF THE NON-EXECUTIVE DIRECTOR

Non-executive directors are directors who do not have executive, i.e. senior management, responsibilities in the company. Non-executive directors therefore have a part-time involvement with the company for which they are generally paid a fee. Often non-executive directors are executive directors of other companies.

There has been much debate about the value of non-executive directors, given that their involvement is necessarily limited. To be of significant value they must be allowed to play an important part in decision-making. This is not always the case. Non-executive directors, even if they do not normally have a significant input to decisions, may have a crucial role to play in a crisis, when their independence from the company may be important. For example, the non-executive directors were the initiators of the removal of Ernest Saunders in the wake of the developing 'Guinness crisis'.

Source: Authors.

The role of the non-executive director is arguably more crucial in today's business world where executive directors are unlikely to be major shareholders in the company and there is a clear separation between owners and managers. Echoing this theme the Governor of the Bank of England has indicated the need to prevent a concentration and abuse of power in a company, suggesting the need for the 'separation as a general rule of the role of chief executive and chairman' and 'the appointment of independent directors' (FT report, 29 April 1992, p.14). The separation of the roles of chairman and chief executive was highlighted by the Cadbury Committee's report also on corporate governance (see Illustration 2.6).

Illustration 2.6

CADBURY REPORT

The Cadbury Committee on the financial aspects of corporate governance published its final report in December 1992. The Committee's findings emphasized the need for companies to comply with a code of best practice on corporate governance. Some of the key features of the proposed code included:

- a company's board should contain sufficient numbers of non-executive directors, who have the necessary standing, for them to exert a significant influence on the board's decisions;
- non-executive directors should provide an independent judgement on areas critical to the company's future;
- a formal process should be used for the appointment of non-executive directors who should also have a specific term of appointment;
- the contract of executive directors should not exceed three years without shareholders' approval;
- the pay of executive directors should be subject to recommendations by a remuneration committee dominated, or wholly formed, by non-executive directors; and
- a separate audit committee should be established, with clear terms of reference.

Source: Based on press reports on the findings of the Cadbury Committee.

Taking up the theme of the role of the non-executive director, Sir John Egan, Chief Executive of BAA plc and a non-executive director of the Foreign and Colonial Investment Trust, recently discussed some of the roles of the non-executive director in a free-market economy:

> The most obvious role is to ensure that a Company behaves with a high standard of financial probity. Clearly, non-executive directors must, to the best of their ability, make sure through the audit committee that annual and other reports correctly reflect the trading position of the company and the status of the balance sheet; through the remuneration committee that executives are appropriately rewarded and through other committees and the board meetings, that the Company behaves honestly, in line with its stated strategy, and in a manner that they would be proud to describe to their shareholders.
>
> A more difficult role is to monitor the performance of the Company and its executives in relationship to their stated plans and intentions. But perhaps the most difficult is to ensure that the plans of the Company are prudent enough to cope with the volatility of the environment and that the plans can be carried out within the capabilities of the employees and the technical and financial resources of the Company.
>
> Sir J. Egan, 'The Role of the Non-executive Director', in *Report and Accounts, 1991*,
> The Foreign and Colonial Investment Trust.

To consider these questions we turn once more to UB. Again the *Annual Report* provides details of the composition of the Group's board of directors. Brief details of each of the directors are reproduced in Illustration 2.7.

Illustration 2.7

UNITED BISCUITS PLC
MEMBERSHIP OF BOARD OF DIRECTORS

Executive directors – name, age and position:
R.C. Clarke, 63, Chairman
E.L. Nicoli, 43, Group Chief Executive
J.A. Warren, 38, Group Finance Director
T.M. Garvin, 56, President and CEO, Keebler Company
D.R.J. Stewart, 57, Group Company Secretary.

Non-executive directors:
Sir Charles Fraser, KCVO, 63, Vice Chairman of the Board; Chairman of the
   Audit and Management Resources Committees
The Rt Hon. Lord Prior, 64
Lord Plumb, 67
N.M. Shaw, 62
Lady Howe, 60
T.H. Wyman, 62

Source: UB, *Annual Report 1991*, March 1992.

An immediate observation in respect of the composition of UB's board is that non-executive directors outnumber executive directors. Indeed UB were one of the first UK companies to create a board that included a majority of non-executive directors. Further, the roles of the chairman and chief executive are separated, and the company's audit and remuneration committees are formed entirely of non-executive directors (Chairman's Statement, *Annual Report, 1991*, p.5).

What are the business activities or functions represented on the board, and the length of service of members? The number of executive directors is rather small, although understandably so, and contains in addition to the chairman and CEO, the finance director, president of the group's largest overseas subsidiary and the company secretary. The *Annual Report* provides details of the length of their board experience, revealing that two of the executive directors have joined the board since 1989. The two longest serving executive directors were appointed in 1984. Mr Clarke became chairman of the group in 1990, and Mr Nicoli was appointed to CEO in 1991. Collectively this information suggests the composition of the executive members of the board has witnessed a number of recent changes and the management team is comparatively newly formed.

Reviewing the non-executive directors, there appears to be a good balance of individuals, including senior business people, politicians and a solicitor. Further, at least one non-executive director has significant international business experience. The chairman's statement reveals that Lord Plumb is about to retire as a non-executive director and, subject to shareholder approval, Mr Colin Short, finance director of ICI plc, and Mr Robert Napier, chief executive of Redland plc, will become non-executive directors. Overall the impression is that the non-executive group of directors collectively provide a powerful voice in helping the executive directors to manage the company. Certainly they do not look like the token presence of outsiders that is the case in some companies.

Reading through a company's report and understanding the balance of executive and non-executive directors often makes fascinating reading. Many companies do not have the same mix as UB. Take, for example, Ratners' *Annual Report* in 1990, and the governance of the company at that time. Carefully reading the Report of the Directors reveals that during the period covered the company had nine directors, of whom two had resigned and one new appointment had been made. At the end of the year the company had six directors, of which five had service contracts with the company (i.e. they were employed by the company) for the provision of their services as directors. To put it more succinctly, five of the six directors were executive, and only one non-executive. Further, Mr Gerald Ratner held the posts of chairman and managing director. Clearly, Ratners' board at the time had a very different composition to that of UB.

Whilst it is possible to gain an understanding of the organization's main board of directors in the way described above, information about management at the level of the business unit is more difficult to obtain for the external researcher. In many cases, those outside the company may need to consider the performance of the business unit as a proxy for how successfully management has managed. For the internal consultant or manager it is relatively easier to collect information on management at the business level and to make assessments accordingly.

Corrective adjustments

Reference has been made to the fact that corrective adjustments need to be made to the strategies that have been crafted, not least because management's view of needs is continuously being updated with new information. Equally the fact that a strategy is judged a failure or success may or may not be related to the original reasons for selecting the strategy in the first place. What is clear, however, is that many companies do make significant adjustments to their strategies, and emphasis on one approach at any point in time may be replaced by a different set of priorities relatively quickly.

Many senior managers find it difficult to state publicly that inappropriate options were chosen, so unless the current management is different from the team which adopted the previous strategy, a more positive explanation than the honest acceptance of a mistake is generally the view presented to shareholders. This is often witnessed in relation to the overall portfolio of businesses a group company operates. At one point in time the company may decide to move into a new business area, often by making an expensive acquisition, proclaiming major growth opportunities, synergies with existing business and the management potential to maximum profitability as the reasons for such action.

In the event of the strategy delivering less than was expected at the time of purchase the company inevitably talks about 'returning to its core businesses', with the consequent sell-off or liquidation of the previously acquired business. The pressure to take such drastic actions often comes from the management realizing that its shareholders will demand action to correct underperformance, and if this is not forthcoming the danger to the existing management is that shareholders might support a takeover and the removal of the board.

By contrast companies sometimes pursue particular strategies for reasons which turn out to be at variance with those that determine the success of the strategy. Where this happens management are unlikely to disclaim the credit for their action, and present the 'success' to their shareholders as a well thought through and planned strategy.

Periodically it may not be an individual strategy which is changed but the whole vision and direction in which the organization is moving. This most commonly occurs when the organization experiences a 'crisis', often manifest in poor financial figures. At such times there are likely to be significant changes of senior management, on occasions initiated by major institutional investors who refuse to support management unless changes are enacted (see Illustration 2.8).

Illustration 2.8

GRANADA PLC

In May 1991 Granada sought to raise additional finance on the stock market through the mechanism of a rights issue: asking existing shareholders to invest further sums of money in the business by subscribing to additional shares. The company desperately required funds because two of its strategic investments in particular were causing problems. Firstly, its computer services division into which the group had heavily invested was underperforming. Secondly, a more immediate problem was the company's investment in BSkyB, the satellite television company, which required a further injection of capital. As part of the price demanded by the City of London for providing the necessary finance, the then chief executive, Mr Lewis, was forced to resign from the company's board of directors. In effect the chief executive was forced to carry the responsibility of a failed strategy.

Source: Based on press reports at the time.

Advantages of a 'strategic approach' to managing

It should be clear to the reader that the arguments advanced in this chapter are in support of crafting a strategy which provides direction to the organization. This is not, however, to suggest that companies would be advised to adopt a rigid and inflexible approach to the process, or that the emphasis should be on some form of strategic planning as was advanced in the 1970s. Strategic planning at that time tended to place an overemphasis on analysis and insufficient focus on the need to implement and manage change in organizations. The planning approach tended to lead to large bureaucratic structures which produced elaborate plans which inevitably proved unworkable and inflexible. This is not the approach advocated by this chapter. Rather the need to take a strategic approach to managing a business emanates from the following:

- the need to provide guidance to the organization in respect of the why, what and how of strategy:
  - why is the organization seeking to take strategic action?
  - what is the organization seeking to achieve?
  - how is the strategy to be achieved?
- as part of the 'why' of strategic direction, the need to consider the organization's external environment, and the opportunities and threats that arise from it;
- the need for a basis for resource allocation and the monitoring of progress within the organization;
- the need to ensure that strategies can be successfully implemented, by recognizing the role of management in instilling the drive and leadership to the organization;
- the need to review, evaluate and initiate careful reaction and action as appropriate.

Concluding remarks

Whether a strategic approach is adopted or not is very much dependent of the quality of management. Do managers, first of all, recognize the need to adopt this approach? All too often managers focus too strongly on the operational issues and fail to understand and evaluate longer-term trends. How many managers really understand the changing dynamics of their industry? Even if managers do recognize the importance of being 'strategic', how many in practice continue to focus on immediate needs and simply make a series of short-term decisions? Without the discipline to look beyond the present and manage in a proactive and strategic manner the risk of underperformance is high. Companies without a clear strategic vision and the proven ability to craft strategy should be treated with caution and fundamental questions asked. To assist this process the following checklist may prove helpful.

Checklist

- *What is your assessment of the management resource? Is the balance of skills and experience on the board appropriate for the company?*
- *Has management shown itself to be able to perform in bad times as well as good?*
- *Is management proactive or does it simply react to events?*
- *Does the company have a clear strategic vision or direction?*
- *Has the company's vision been translated into clear corporate and business strategies?*
- *Does the company manage effectively and efficiently at the corporate level?*
- *Have you identified the company's principal business divisions and their business strategies?*
- *Do the business strategies adequately take account of the dynamics of the business's external environment?*
- *Will the chosen strategies maintain, or assist in the development of, a sustainable competitive advantage?*
- *Do you believe that the company can successfully implement its chosen strategies?*

CHAPTER 3

Taking action to add value

Managers at both the business unit and corporate levels need to broaden their conceptions of strategy; they need continuously to ask themselves whether management action is adding value to the organization. The value creating potential of any strategic response must be capable of realizing the highest possible value for shareholders. Otherwise, another management team will seize the opportunity to manage the organization's assets, as evidenced by the unprecedented wave of mergers, acquisitions and divestitures that have occurred in the last five years. This chapter looks at the need to create value by reviewing the following topics:

- *managing value: the key to winning strategies*
- *mismanaging value and competitive disadvantage*
- *reconciling creating value and competitive advantage*
- *restructuring: closing the value gap.*

The chapter begins by emphasizing that shareholder value which derives from cash flow returns should be a standard measure of corporate performance, and that as such, it is necessary from the outset to ascertain how management can take action to create net added value. This leads to a review of what is value and how organizations add value, what actions can result in companies mismanaging value, and why value is important to shareholders. Taking action to close the value gap focuses on the strategic choices available to management seeking to enhance shareholder value and secure their own position. Once again the chapter concludes with a general checklist to be applied for the purposes of identifying appropriate management action to add value.

Managing value: the key to winning strategies

Organizations must have a consistent link between formulating and valuing strategies. In companies that treat crafting strategic direction and valuation as separate processes too much concern may be given to issues of product portfolio and market share, and too little to the shareholder consequences of such actions. Winning strategies must meet the test of sustainable and superior value creation.

The essential characteristics of the process of adding value are illustrated in Figure 3.1. Organizations may raise funds either by issuing share capital (known as equity) or by borrowing (debt). In addition, most organizations will have built up reserves from operating successfully in previous time periods and these are also a form of equity. Adding together an organization's debt and equity gives the total funds available for management to employ in the business.

Management will deploy the monies available to fund operations at the corporate centre (e.g. headquarters teams) and at the level of divisions and business units. The role of the corporate centre may be described as something analogous to a financial intermediary, for example a bank, to the extent that funds are allocated between the different businesses in such a way that will generate a return above the cost of capital – the financial return the owners could earn elsewhere for investments of similar risk. Collectively the corporate headquarters and business units will create value to the extent that the cash flows are generated in excess of the expenses of running the divisions and business units.

Figure 3.1 shows that in addition to potential added value, corporate headquarters also incurs costs. From the gross value generated will need to be subtracted the costs of running the corporate headquarters. These costs can be placed into two categories. First, there are the direct costs of running the corporate headquarters, which in the case of highly bureaucratic organizations can be significant. Second, there is an indirect and less tangible cost to the extent that additional management layers may make for poor decision-making and an inflexible organization.

When such headquarters costs have been subtracted from the gross value added by the business units A, B and C, and after adjusting for the cost of capital, any additional cash flow generated by the organization can be said to be creating net added value. Conversely, if costs are in excess of the income generated and there is a negative cash flow, the strategies pursued can be described as destroying value. This shareholder value perspective – the standard measure of corporate performance adopted in this book and presented diagrammatically in Figure 3.1 – is of fundamental significance.

A highly simplified numerical example can be used to illustrate the principles of value creation and destruction. Take two companies – A and B – and consider value creation and destruction for one year only. Company A creates a gross value of £50m in the year and has corporate headquarters expenses of £20m.

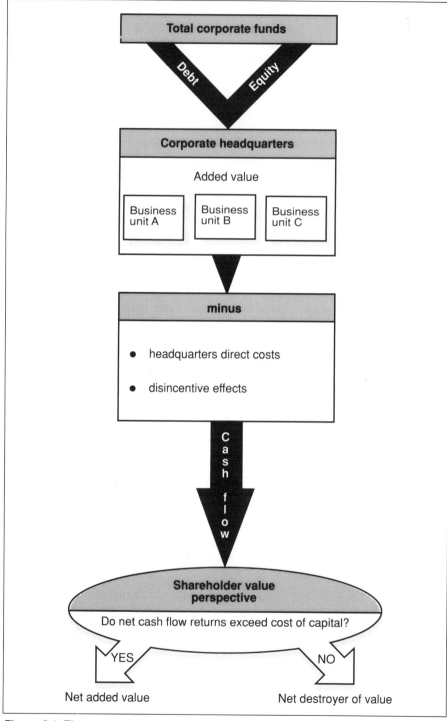

Figure 3.1 *The corporation as a financial intermediary*

Conversely, company B creates gross value of £10m, and has the same central headquarters expenses as company A. For simplicity both companies are assumed to have a cost of capital of £10m. Which company creates value?

	A	B
Gross value added	£50m	£10m
Less headquarters costs	£20m	£20m
Less cost of capital	£10m	£10m
Net value created/destroyed	£20m	(£20m)

Company A is managing to add value of £20m, whilst company B has destroyed value to the same amount. In the case of company B it is possible to draw the conclusion that the organization has either inappropriate strategies, or that management is incapable of implementing them successfully. For company A, whilst value has been created, the question arises could management do any better and create even more value? Illustration 3.1 provides a further example.

Illustration 3.1

SEARS PLC
In January 1988 Sears plc, a major UK retailer, won a contested take over bid to acquire Freemans, a mail order business. In the first full year of the acquisition the profits (£26.6m) from Freemans failed to cover the financing costs (£47m) of the additional debt acquired to finance the deal. In other words, in the first year as part of Sears plc, the newly acquired mail order business was not creating sufficient value to meet its cost of capital, and consequently value was being destroyed. Market reaction to the announcement of Sears' results led to the price of the company's shares falling by almost 5% to 116p. It is of course the case that over a longer time perspective the acquisition may successfully create value, but it certainly did not do so in the first year. Source: Based upon a report appearing in the *Financial Times*.

Successful organizations are the ones which consistently create significant value. Less successful organizations are those companies which create too little value and in the modern economy face the ever increasing threat of takeover. Once again the key to the process of value creation is management. Can the existing management create significant value, or does it require a new management team to unlock value from the business?

Mismanaging value and competitive disadvantage

Managers all too often make poor judgements resulting in either value being destroyed or very little net value being created. To understand why this is the case it is important to focus again on the three key components of crafting a successful corporate strategy discussed in Chapter 2, namely:

- portfolio management
- corporate core competences
- enhanced business unit performance.

With respect to each of these three factors management may make inappropriate decisions which detract from the creation of value. Occasionally, all three factors collectively need adjustment if value creating strategies are to be achieved.

Portfolio management

Discussion in Chapter 2 highlighted the fact that most businesses of any size have a number of 'strategic legs'. For some organizations these different business areas may be strongly related and the company operates with a relatively narrow focus. Alternatively a company may be highly diverse, with its business divisions operating in very different business sectors, each being essentially autonomous of one another. The shape of an organization's portfolio of businesses inevitably raises the question of why and how companies diversify and the extent to which such actions can create value.

The reasons why companies diversify are numerous, but can be grouped under the following four headings:

- risk spreading
- growth
- synergy
- financial engineering.

Risk spreading

Managers are often persuaded to pursue a strategy of diversification in respect of risk spreading. They may believe, for example, that the organization is too dependent on a single national economy whose prospects are uncertain. Hence they may wish to diversify overseas and spread their exposure across a number of geographical markets. Alternatively, they may be concerned that their product base is too narrow, and worry about an excessive reliance on a single product to generate the majority of corporate income. Concern may also revolve around dependence on a single large customer, who if they changed their purchasing pattern could severely threaten the business. This last point is a particular worry of many smaller organizations.

Whilst the arguments advanced above may provide a rationale for spreading risk, a strategy of diversification is itself not without risk. The degree of risk is related partly to the process by which the company achieves its objective of diversifying. Broadly two options are available. The organization may choose to grow organically (internal growth) or by acquisition (external growth). Both means have relative merits and potential risks. If management chooses organic growth, they are deciding to develop an existing business or to start a new business using internally generated resources. Alternatively, by acquiring a company, management are deciding to use external growth to diversify. Illustration 3.2, on internal and external growth, considers some of the contrasting benefits and problems associated with both routes. Equally, some companies vary the means of developing new products or markets using a mix of internal and external growth strategies. Marks & Spencer (M&S) plc has, for example, pursued a mix of strategies in seeking to achieve its vision of becoming an international retailer:

New market entered	Means of achieving market entry
France, Belgium, Hong Kong	Internal growth
United States	External growth
Norway	Franchise operation
Spain	Joint venture with local company

In addition to organic and external growth M&S also has used franchise agreements and joint ventures in establishing a presence in overseas markets. Franchise agreements provide a relatively low-cost, low-risk entry strategy to a market as they are primarily an agreement to allow another party to produce or sell a company's goods, but do not commit the franchisor to the same level of investment that would be required for, say, organic growth. Joint ventures are attempts, in this context, to overcome the steep learning curve inherent in penetrating an overseas market. By combining with a 'local' company M&S is able to gain an immediate and improved understanding of local market conditions and to adapt its trading format accordingly. International diversification, without a clear understanding of local market conditions and business cultures, can be highly risky as a number of companies — for example, Midland Bank and Sock Shop — have found to their cost.

In assessing the desirability of diversification as a risk spreading strategy, it is important to consider for whose benefit is the strategy being pursued? Investors have the opportunity of selecting their own share portfolio if diversification of risk is their prime motivation: they do not need costly corporate managers to do it on their behalf, especially as management are likely to pay a 25 to 35% premium to secure ownership of another line of business. In such circumstances, diversification is obviously a dilution of shareholder value,

Illustration 3.2

INTERNAL AND EXTERNAL GROWTH

Internal growth

Context
Likely to be an option available to management when an industry is still growing, allowing new companies to enter the market, or where the industry is fragmented and not dominated by large companies.

Resource requirements
Organic growth requires the company to develop its own resource base. This can be a particular problem if the company is seeking to expand into overseas markets or into new product areas. A key question is whether the company has appropriate managerial and financial resources to execute the strategy successfully.

Relative benefits and disadvantages
Strategy allows the company to pursue incremental growth and to learn from 'doing'. Risk is correspondingly easier to manage, and there is the option for the company to abandon the strategy before too many resources have been committed and the decision is irreversible. A major disadvantage is that the speed of development may be slow, with initially low levels of market penetration. It can require many years before a company builds a significant presence in a new product or geographical market by using a strategy of organic growth.

External growth

Context
An attractive option to management wishing to enter a mature market, which is already highly concentrated and dominated by a small number of sellers.

Resource requirements
By using external growth the acquirer is purchasing an established operation. The purchase of a new business brings no guarantees of the quality of the resources purchased. The purchased company may be highly successful with good quality management; alternatively, the acquired company may require drastic action to make the business viable. In the latter case, does the acquiring company have the necessary management and financial resources to do this?

Relative benefits and disadvantages
External growth provides the acquiring company with an immediate presence in the market. This benefit of speed is counterbalanced by risk. Once entered into acquisitions are not easily reversed, and certainly not without cost. Post-acquisition management is crucial if an acquired company is to be successfully integrated with an existing organization.

Source: Authors.

---

unless management have developed clear ideas about how to manage or change the direction of the newly acquired business. Hence the pursuit of diversification for the purposes of spreading risk is likely to be primarily for the benefit of corporate management, although whether in the longer term this strategy improves the security of management is an open question. Unless management are able to create superior value from the new line of business, its right to manage those assets will be challenged by others.

Growth

Together with the desire to spread risk, management are likely to pursue growth as a major reason for diversification. Industries tend to move through a cycle of growth, maturity and decline, and whilst some industries can enjoy periods of renewed growth following the initial onset of maturity, at some point in their development the growth of an industry tends to slow.

Management may become concerned that there is a gap between their expectations of growth and the ability of the current business to match these growth expectations. If the current business cannot produce enough growth to meet corporate objectives, some headquarters staff may start looking for higher growth business opportunities. The strategies chosen to overcome the so-called 'growth gap' may not necessarily create superior shareholder value, if they fail to generate sufficient cash flow returns to exceed the cost of capital. This is particularly likely where organizations get into markets their management do not understand, and where there is little organizational fit between the two companies' administrative systems and corporate cultures.

Illustration 3.2 highlights some important aspects of both internal and external growth.

Synergy

Managers of businesses in mature industries either need to seek diversified growth, or they have no opportunity to invest their surplus cash. The challenge and opportunity is to invest in related businesses where diversification can generate synergy – the third motive for diversification. Whilst undoubtedly synergies do exist – situations when two businesses together are worth more than the sum of the parts – they equally should not be taken for granted. In practice operating synergies – for example, increased economies from concentrating production, or the benefits of shared distribution facilities or information technology – do not always meet the claims of management at the time of the acquisition.

Synergy was claimed to be the rationale behind many of BAT's acquisitions outlined in Illustration 3.3. BAT illustrates that in practice it is difficult for companies with unrelated business activities to achieve synergies, and that many of its acquired businesses would perform as well, if not better, as independent or demerged enterprises. It is all too easy for over-diversified companies to include businesses and assets that could be worth more to others or do not return their cost of capital.

In the main synergies are more likely to be achieved where there is some degree of relatedness of the acquired company to the existing core business of the organization. Such relatedness might, for example, be a function of the

Illustration 3.3

BAT PLC

British American Tobacco (BAT) plc, a large conglomerate, was the subject of a major takeover bid worth some £13 billion in 1989. The takeover bidders argued that the company had made some fundamental mistakes in its strategy of diversification. Similarly, many institutional investors found its incongruous mix of tobacco, paper, retailing and insurance difficult to understand.

The company had used the cash generated by its mature tobacco business to fund diversification into sectors which included paper (Wiggins Teape in the UK; Appleton in the USA), financial services (Eagle Star and Allied Dunbar in the UK; Farmers in the USA) and retailing (Argos in the UK; Saks in the USA). At the time of the takeover bid the performance of the acquired businesses had failed to match market expectations, while profits from the core business, tobacco, were lower in 1988 than four years previously. As a result the group's value was less than the estimated worth of the constituent business. It was the value of these parts which Sir James Goldsmith, a well known financier, sought to unlock in leading a takeover bid for the company. It was anticipated that, if successful, he would sell all the businesses, with the exception of tobacco which he would seek to run more efficiently.

Goldsmith's bid raises a fundamental dilemma for the managers of a mature business. Should managers seek to use the cash generated by the mature business to fund diversification into new growth areas, or should they remain with the large but relatively static core business in which they have proven expertise and skills in producing a reliable and abundant flow of cash? The logic of Goldsmith's view is that managers should stick to what they know best, come to terms with a slower and stable growth path, and give shareholders' funds back to the owners in the form of increased dividends over successive years.

Source: Authors and press reports.

---

commonality of product, technology or geographical scope of operation. By expanding into related areas, managers should be able to realize potential synergies, create superior value and enhance shareholder returns.

Financial engineering

The fourth factor driving some companies to diversify is financial engineering. Conglomerate acquisitions depend primarily on financial rather than operating integration to achieve corporate goals. By acquiring underperforming companies and making a one-off gain by shrinking management overheads and eliminating waste, companies may boost earnings per share, particularly if they practise the creative accounting techniques outlined in Chapter 5. Despite rising earnings per share, the underlying economic returns are often weak. The frequent lesson is that continued investment in over-diversified business activities may generate rising earnings, but does not necessarily create value. Unless cash flow returns on diversified investment are above the cost of capital, the organization is a net destroyer of value, and its asset value may be increased by restructuring or 'unbundling'.

Companies, including BTR plc , Hanson plc and Tomkins plc, have made a name for themselves by unbundling underperforming conglomerates. When considering so-called conglomerates the question raised is why do some companies seemingly succeed where others fail? Part of the answer is that while the portfolio of businesses they operate appears superficially to be unrelated there is a common relatedness in the form of the corporate parenting adopted. Take, for example, the case of Tomkins plc, which has grown rapidly in the last few years. Tomkins plc, a highly diversified conglomerate which owns Smith & Wesson (US producer of firearms), Hayter (UK lawn mower manufacturer) and Philips Industries (US producer of windows and doors), has a strategy of reviving underperforming companies in low-technology, mature manufacturing businesses which do not require high levels of capital spending. By setting demanding but attainable targets for the individual businesses, with their formerly large headquarters staff drastically reduced, Tomkins is able to raise business performance and create added value.

The examples of successful acquisitors, including Tomkins, Hanson and BTR, highlight how companies seeking growth by acquisition should look carefully in terms of a pre-acquisition assessment, the acquisition of the target company and post-acquisition management. These three key areas are discussed in Illustration 3.4. All too often the risks of a merger are underestimated, while the anticipated payoffs exaggerated. Any organization contemplating an acquisition must recognize that there is a steep learning curve associated with takeover activity, and that in overall terms the probability of increasing shareholder value is low.

Corporate core competences

The second of the three principal components to crafting a successful corporate strategy is the development of corporate core competences. Figure 3.2 shows that core competences – the collective learning of the organization in respect of how to coordinate diverse technologies and production skills – are an invisible 'thread' that may link seemingly disparate business units. They are also the key drivers behind investing in new markets, quickly entering emerging markets and changing the rules of competition in established markets. Growth opportunities are seen to be less the outcome of managing a diversified portfolio (see previous section), and more about the ability of senior management to manage a portfolio of competences necessary to enable business units to adapt quickly to the challenge of opportunity and change.

This is a particularly demanding task, especially when the organization is structured along headquarters, divisional and business unit lines. In these circumstances there may be considerable under-investment in developing core competences and core products. No individual business unit may feel directly

Illustration 3.4

WHAT MANAGEMENT SHOULD CONSIDER WHEN SEEKING TO MAKE AN ACQUISITION

Pre-acquisition assessment

Undertake a full assessment of the target company before making a bid. Make sure you understand the nature of the company to be acquired and its strengths and weaknesses, including its financial position. Consider to what extent you are in a position to overcome the weaknesses you have identified. Avoid opportunistic purchases, unless you can make an adequate assessment before concluding the deal.

Acquisition of target

The golden rule is not to overpay. Avoid competitive bidding, where there is at least one other company, which has a 'deep pocket', interested in acquiring the target company. Only pay what you think the company is worth to you. Do not be afraid to walk away from the purchase.

Post-acquisition management

Do not neglect this third and critical area for management action. Make sure you have a clear view of what you intend to do with the company. From your pre-acquisition assessment you ought to have an understanding of the strengths and weaknesses of the acquisition. If it has been performing badly what action do you intend to take to raise performance?

Remember integrating a new company into an existing organization can be difficult and should not be underestimated. Marrying different company cultures is not easy.

Source: Authors.

---

responsible for maintaining a viable position in core products, nor be able to justify the scale of investment required to achieve global leadership in some core competence. This prompts Prahalad and Hamel (1990) to recommend that senior management should make a greater time investment in developing an organizational capability – what they call a 'strategic architecture' – that establishes objectives for competence building.

The strategic architecture should force the organization to identify and commit the technical and production linkages across business units that would be absent from a purely diversified portfolio management relationship between senior management and business units (Figure 3.2). If successfully designed and implemented, strategic architecture should also foster the development of distinct skills and capabilities that cannot be matched or easily replicated by other organizations. Consequently, any competitive advantage that results from building distinct core competences and organizational capability is likely to provide sustainable competitive advantage and superior value creation.

In deciding which core competences to build, organizations should ask three questions:

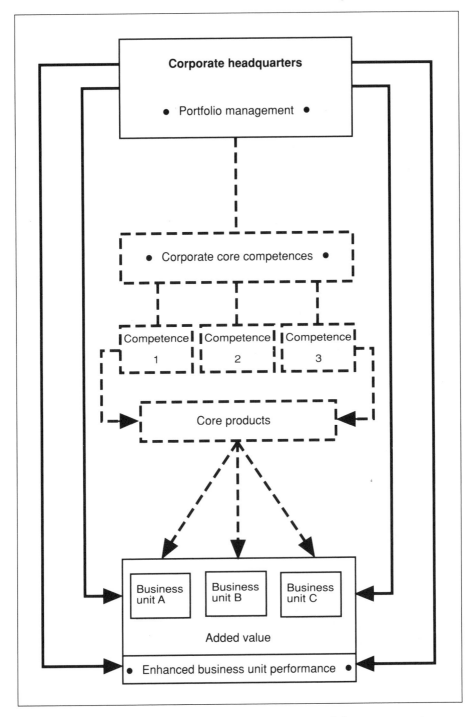

Figure 3.2 *Key components of corporate effectiveness: portfolio management, corporate core competences and enhanced business unit performance*

- First, which core competences will allow an organization to exploit changes in either their own markets or those of others? Such opportunities may occur in the organizational space not occupied currently by any of the business units or may fall partly into a number of business unit domains – and is not served adequately by any of them. Identification of these opportunities can be enhanced considerably if management build the necessary core competences and core products to enable market focused business units to exploit these windows of opportunity.
- Second, which core competences will provide 'gateways' to future markets by enabling the organization to produce successful cross-business products? In technology driven industries, senior management should enunciate the strategic architecture and build relevant competences to secure future growth.
- Third, which core competences will be valuable under a broad variety of industry outcomes, thereby enabling an organization to feel they have more to gain by changing the rules of the industry rather than maintaining existing industry recipes about how to compete for market share?

If companies wish to compete for newly emerging industry sectors, rather than for shares of existing markets, they must look beyond the boundaries of their current business in order to harness the core competences which underpin several of them. Such competences need actively to be developed and continuously enhanced. It is also important to align corporate resources within an organizational setting or strategic architecture that shows how various technological and other developments may coalesce as the new industry emerges.

For core competences to emerge, management attention has to be directed to identifying and building overarching competences and to product/service concepts and standards. Organizations must build networks of alliances which have cumulative corporate, as opposed to a series of bilateral business unit, relationships with different business organizations. Organizations must be clear that the strategy for developing core competences is about positioning the organization in new industries rather than current competitor and industry positioning.

According to Hamel (1992), the question for the next decade and beyond is 'what is your share of new business creation?' Identifying and developing core competences can be critical for the creation of new industry opportunities, for the provision of new strategic perspectives which are of different character from current competition for market position, and for providing a platform for superior value creation well into the next century.

Enhanced business unit performance

Adopting an appropriate management style to enhance business unit performance is the third element in the crafting of a successful corporate strategy (Figure 3.2). The discussion on management styles in Chapter 2 illustrated that there is no one correct way to manage business units. No one style was superior in terms of all aspects of performance. Individual styles were found more appropriate in some situations that others. For example, using a financial control style to manage a narrowly focused technology driven group is unlikely to lead to the required level of investment to sustain performance in the longer term. Equally, the strategic planning style may be too bureaucratic for an unfocused group, for whom a financial control style may be more appropriate.

One of the interesting factors to emerge from reviewing the actions of companies taking over poorly performing groups is that whilst the acquiring company may remove a number of the previous decision-makers, the majority of senior and middle management are often retained by the new owners. Frequently, the same managers who were previously part of a poorly performing business are now able to demonstrate their ability to achieve above-average outcomes for the business. The reason for this seemingly surprising turnaround is very often that managers who were previously dispirited, under the new regime are empowered to take the actions that they were formerly unable to implement, and as a consequence become highly motivated to drive the organization forward. This point emphasizes very clearly that if the management structures and systems are inappropriate for the business context, performance can be enhanced greatly by changing management styles. Where management is weak and defensive, such changes are unlikely to occur without prompting. An organizational crisis may well be required, for example an actual takeover bid, before there is any chance of provoking the existing management to respond.

Although the three elements of crafting a successful corporate strategy have been dealt with individually, in practice the mismanagement of value can stem from a combination of one or more of the three factors depicted in Figure 3.2. In an extreme case value may be mismanaged by having too wide a portfolio of businesses, the inability to develop core competences and an inappropriate management style. It has also been shown, once again, that there is a critical distinction between competitive strategy at corporate and business level.

Crafting successful corporate strategies is a necessary but not sufficient requirement for maximizing value creation. Just as important is whether individual businesses have good product market positions to enable value to be created at the level of the business unit. Weak competitive positions at the level of the business unit are unlikely to enhance an organization's value. Such positions may be described as a competitive disadvantage to the extent that the business continuously earns poor returns and value creation is low or even negative.

Where situations of competitive disadvantage exist management at either the corporate centre and/or at the business unit must consider what actions can be taken to improve the situation and hopefully develop a position of competitive advantage. If this cannot be achieved within acceptable timescales and cost, the question arises as to how the organization exits the business.

Reconciling the creation of value and competitive advantage

The thrust of the argument presented above is that organizations need to add value at the corporate centre and generate value at the business unit level by ensuring the businesses within their portfolio have a competitive advantage. Only by taking action to add value in respect of both corporate and business strategies can the organization be said to be seeking to maximize the total value added.

Given the alleged short-termism of the stock exchange, some commentators suggest that adding value and competitive advantage can be at variance. Commentators subscribing to this view tend to see the two concepts – adding value and competitive advantage – as being mutually exclusive. Reviewing this debate, Rappaport (1992) indicates that those who believe in this view argue that maximizing value is inherently more short term because this is the time period used by the stock market in rating companies, whilst competitive advantage by its nature often requires significant investment and a lengthy time period before the benefits accrue to shareholders. Succinctly, the nature of stock markets results in investors taking insufficient notice of the longer-term investments of the company, which in the short term may not appear to increase the organization's value. This is a view we and others (see Rappaport, 1992) reject. There is little firm evidence that the stock market takes an excessively short-term view of companies, or that investments with prospective payoffs in the medium to long term are undervalued. Pharmaceutical companies seeking to discover new drugs are an interesting case to consider given the substantial research and development spending required for new product development. For pharmaceutical companies the announcement of a break-through in developing a new drug compound, even though product launch is many years away can have an appreciable influence on the share price (see Illustration 3.5).

The linkage between creating added value and share prices is illustrated by Figure 3.3. If an organization is successful in creating superior net added value it will have surplus cash available after meeting all its costs (e.g. costs of running the business units and corporate centre, meeting the cost of capital, etc.) to distribute. The surplus cash can be used in two ways: first, management may decide to reward shareholders by paying dividends; or second, the money can be reinvested in the business. Both actions will be of benefit to shareholders. If dividends are raised, the income component of the return to shareholders is increased. Alternatively, if monies are reinvested in the business and generate cash flows that exceed the cost of capital, the prospect of even greater future dividend payments may be envisaged. Correspondingly, share prices will increase on the expectation of improved future returns and shareholders will again benefit, this time through an appreciation of the share price and the

Illustration 3.5

PHARMACEUTICAL COMPANIES AND SHARE PRICE MOVEMENTS

The share price of pharmaceutical, or drug companies as they are often called, is highly sensitive to the perceived prospects of new drugs which could become, or are in the process of becoming market-leaders. Price sensitive information includes comment by drug regulators in key global markets and news from the company's research establishments. The reaction of investors reflects the very long and drawn out process that drugs have to complete successfully before they are allowed to be prescribed by doctors for their patients, coupled with the huge rewards awaiting the successful development of a new product.

The potential benefits of successful product development can be seen by reviewing the case of Wellcome plc. Wellcome has through its herpes virus drug Zovirax and Retrovir used in the treatment of AIDS managed to command a major segment of the market with the consequent benefit to company sales and profits. Similarly, Glaxo is looking to the development of several new drugs to compensate collectively for the slowing growth of the sales of Zantac, its highly successful ulcer treatment drug. Gross margins for patented pharmaceuticals are reported to be almost 100 per cent.

Just as a company's new product development can boost share price, the prospect of a competitor developing an improved product, or the expiry of patent protection and the introduction of generic drugs, can depress prices. Similarly, the prospect of the regulatory authorities either preventing the sale of a product or alleging the abuse of a dominant market position is likely to have an adverse impact on potential sales and hence investor sentiment.

Sources: Based on press reports and industry sources.

opportunity of making a capital gain if they choose to sell their shares. As Figure 3.3 shows, if organizations improve their value creating ability, shareholders, the owners of the company, will directly benefit.

For poorly performing companies shareholders will have grounds for complaint. Companies adding little value will be unable to increase their dividend stream appreciably, or generate significant funds to reinvest in the business. Consequently, the share price is likely to remain depressed given poor current and future dividend prospects. Where companies are actually destroying value, management will be unable to pay dividends, except from reserves, or maintain investment levels in the business without seeking additional external finance.

Divergence between the market's valuation of a company and management's view may arise for a number of reasons, including differences in knowledge about the company and its prospects, and how these are evaluated. Certainly the stock market does not have perfect information, and managers are often in the position of having more up-to-date knowledge of their businesses than the market. Information differences between the stock market and managers can lead to a perception gap.

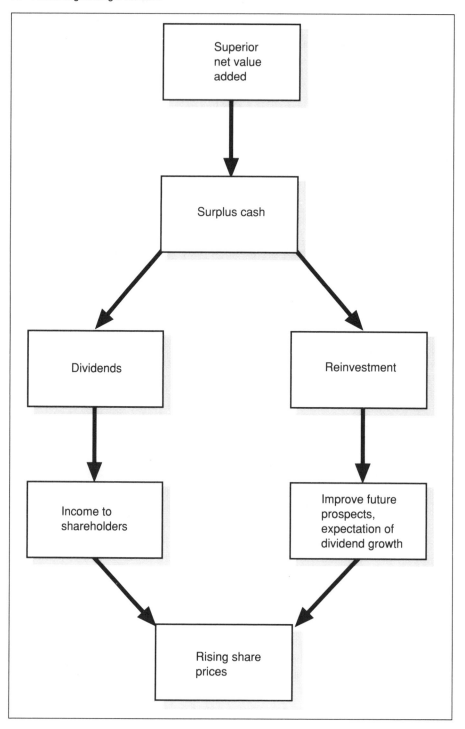

Figure 3.3 *Relating value added to share prices*

The perception gap, illustrated in Figure 3.4, may be either positive or negative. If the market price is below the current value of the company as known to management, the position results in a positive perception gap. Conversely, if market price is above the current value of the company a negative perception gap exists.

Where a positive perception gap exists it suggests that corporate management have been poor in communicating with the key influencers – brokers, major investing institutions and financial press – of the stock market. In some instances, senior managers neglect the public relations part of their job, so that the market is not particularly well informed about what the company is doing and its prospects. If this is the case an appropriate public relations strategy should be able to improve market sentiment towards the company leading to an improvement in the share price. It is not uncommon for managers and the market to disagree about the correct valuation of the company based on how each evaluates the fundamentals of the business. In extreme circumstances where management feel that the market does not understand their business, or persistently undervalues it, management may decide to repurchase the shares and become a private company again. Virgin plc provides a good example of a company which has pursued this course of action.

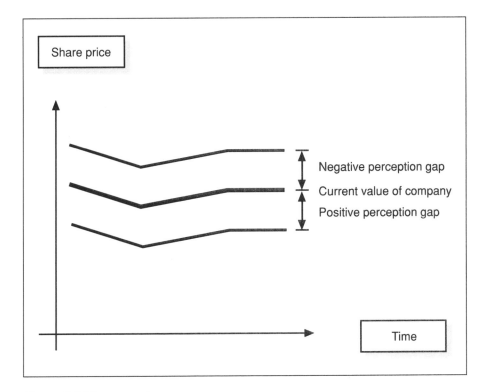

Figure 3.4 *The perception gap*

An insight into how managers value their own company may be gleaned by observing whether directors in the company are purchasing or selling shares. If directors are consistently purchasing shares this may be a good indicator that they believe future prospects for the company are attractive and that the current share price is an undervaluation. Alternatively, if directors are constantly reducing their holdings this may indicate that they believe the current share price is in excess of the actual value of the company. To assist in this task, the weekend edition of the *Financial Times* newspaper publishes a weekly list of companies for whom directors have made large share purchases or sales.

Where a negative perception gap exists and market price is in excess of current value, management will have considerable difficulty in justifying the existing share price. The excess of market price over market value may reflect investor expectations as to the likelihood of either the incumbent management or a corporate raider taking action to improve shareholder value. The market is anticipating that if the company itself does not improve the performance of its assets and realize value, possibly by demerger, then it is likely to become the target for takeover. Hence the share price discounts the market's view of future events.

To illustrate how value may be unlocked in a takeover consider the case of Imperial Chemicals Industries (ICI) plc. During 1991 ICI, Britain's largest chemicals company, was at the centre of speculation concerning a likely takeover bid being received from Hanson plc, an industrial conglomerate with a reputation for purchasing companies either because it believes them to be under-managed or it considers current management to be over-extended. Post-acquisition, Hanson attempts to sell promptly those parts of the newly acquired business to buyers prepared to pay premium prices, and installs financial controls to make the retained businesses add more value.

On 14 May 1991, Hanson acquired 2.7% of ICI's share capital sparking intense debate as to how much the company was worth if all its businesses were sold separately to strategic buyers, companies wishing to develop their existing product market positions. Estimates in the City of London ranged from £12 bn to £16 bn, as analysts sought to calculate ICI's true break-up value. ICI's board of directors considered the company's market valuation to be £16 bn.

Working with the highest valuation of ICI at the time, it is possible to illustrate the process by which an acquirer considers a potential company for the purposes of 'unbundling'. The value of £16 bn represents the gross value of the company, and reflects the expected future earnings of the different constituent businesses within the group. For example, the strongly performing pharmaceuticals business was valued in excess of £8 bn, whilst both bulk chemicals and paints where expected future earnings were lower were priced respectively at just over £1 bn each.

If ICI could be broken up for £16 bn what would be the gain to the unbundler? By purchasing ICI the acquirer would have to repay existing net debt of some £1,750 m, and pay minority interests £450 m. Minority interests reflected joint ventures between ICI and other companies, with both parties having a claim on the value of the respective business. By deducting net debt and minorities from the gross value, the value of the assets to the acquirer would be £13,800 m:

		£m
Gross value of ICI		16,000
Net debt	1,750	
Minorities	450	
		−2,200
Net value before tax		13,800

Further, on the sum remaining the acquirer would have to pay tax. For illustrative purposes a notional tax penalty of 10% is assumed, leaving a break-up value of £12,420:

	£m
Net value before tax	13,800
Notional tax penalty at 10%	1,380
Break-up value	12,420

To gain control of a company an acquirer must bid for the company's issued share capital. Whether existing shareholders will be tempted by the bid will depend on the price offered. The higher the price the greater the probability that shareholders will accept the bidder's price. The total cost to the bidder will therefore be the price at which the shares are purchased multiplied by the number of shares outstanding. On 13 May, prior to Hanson building a stake in ICI, shares in the company were trading at £11.00, valuing the company at £7,765 m. Hanson purchased 2.7% the next day at £11.75, and by 16 May the share price had risen to £12.47.

The extent to which the bidder has to pay over-and-above the pre-bid price is referred to as the bid premium. It is the premium the acquirer has to pay to gain control of the company. As Table 3.1 shows, a 20% bid premium to the share price on 13 May would result in Hanson bidding for ICI at £13.20 per share. A 30% premium would raise the price further to £14.30 per share, and a 35% premium to £14.85. Clearly, the extent to which a bidder needs to tempt existing shareholders with a premium will have a material effect on whether unbundling is a profitable activity.

Table 3.1 illustrates how the cost of purchase influences the return to the unbundler. Starting with a pre-bid price of £11.00, if the company's share capital could be purchased at this price, then the total cost of acquiring ICI would be £7.765 bn. Press reports at the time suggested that Hanson had some £7 bn in cash available to fund the bid, leaving £765 m to be financed by debt. With a gross value of £16 bn, the break-up value as previously calculated is £12.42 bn. Hanson would have to pay advisers fees of, say, £130 m and interest on the additional debt amounting to £61 m, based on a rounded after-tax rate of 12%, together with repayment of the £765 m loan debt. These last three items

Table 3.1 The restructuring of ICI

Economics of potential restructuring or reshaping ICI plc, summer 1991	Initial share price (£11.00)	20% share price premium (£13.20)	25% share price premium (£13.75)	30% share price premium (£14.30)	35% share price premium (£14.85)
	£m	£m	£m	£m	£m
Market price of ICI	7,765	9,318	9,706	10,094	10,482
Financing of bid:					
Cash	7,000	7,000	7,000	7,000	7,000
Debt	765	2,318	2,706	3,094	3,482
Gross value	16,000	16,000	16,000	16,000	16,000
Less debt	1,750	1,750	1,750	1,750	1,750
Less minorities	450	450	450	450	450
Net value before tax	13,800	13,800	13,800	13,800	13,800
Less tax	1,380	1,380	1,380	1,380	1,380
Break-up value	12,420	12,420	12,420	12,420	12,420
Less advisers' fees	130	130	130	130	130
Less after-tax debit interest	61	190	220	250	280
Less debt finance	765	2,318	2,706	3,094	3,482
Value remaining	11,464	9,782	9,364	8,946	8,528
Potential 1 year return (%)	63.8	39.7	33.8	27.8	21.8

result in a further £956 m (£130 m + £61 m + £765 m) being subtracted from the break-up value to leave the acquirer with £11,464 m, for a cash outlay of £7,000 m. Assuming the company can be broken up in one year this would lead to a return of 64% (i.e. £11,464 m/£7,000 m × 100 = 64%). This looks highly attractive when compared to other investments, although the degree of risk has not been considered.

Moreover, for companies such as Hanson the market will expect a premium to the pre-bid price as the reward to shareholders of relinquishing control. Table 3.1 illustrates that as the bid premium increases the potential return to the acquirer decreases. At a 30% share premium, which is not uncommon in the market for corporate control, the annual return to the acquirer is down to 28%. The bid premium may rise to 35% if, for example, another company enters the bidding, with the annual return being reduced to 22%.

Whilst these returns sound attractive, there are considerable uncertainties inherent in the calculation. The break-up value of the company may prove, for example, to be an overestimate of the prices other companies will be prepared to pay for the constituent businesses. Certainly at the time of the Hanson purchase of a minority shareholding in ICI there was considerable divergence of opinion as to the value of the different businesses. Much of this reflected the different assumptions analysts made with respect to how fast the businesses could be sold and the extent to which recession in the chemicals sectors would make businesses attractive to buyers. Although Hanson declined to make a formal takeover bid for ICI, the underlying message is clear: at the time ICI was not doing as well, and was not worth as much, as its unbundled asset value.

Restructuring: closing the value gap

Management have little option but to manage value in a superior way, otherwise others will displace them and do it anyway. Companies which manage value well do not need takeover defences to protect them from acquisitors. Raiding a company which manages value effectively would be pointless. There would be no destruction of value to reverse, large corporate overheads to cut, or businesses that could be sold to others for relatively high prices. Those who manage value well can keep the gap narrow between potential and actual value creation. Conversely, large performance gaps and the need for restructuring are likely to occur where management fails to generate additional value. The size of the value gap is a measure of how much management needs to do in order to achieve the highest possible value for shareholders.

By taking all or some of the value enhancing actions a potential acquirer would undertake, management can close the size of the value gap. As Figure 3.5 shows, closing the value gap necessitates consideration of three sets of strategies:

- strategies to improve operations
- strategies based on acquiring or disposing of assets
- financial engineering strategies.

These three sets of strategies will be considered sequentially to add to the reader's understanding. In practice, however, companies may be forced to adopt all three strategies simultaneously, particularly if time is short and the organization is facing a takeover bid.

If we assume for simplicity that there is no perception gap of the types depicted in Figure 3.4, then management needs to become skillful at 'raiding' themselves to generate additional value. In the simple example portrayed in Figure 3.5, the current share of the fictitious company is valued by the market at £1.10. If management undertake *internal improvements* – for example, increasing revenues, decreasing unit costs and reducing corporate overheads – cash flows would increase and the share price might rise to £1.40. The next step is determining the long-run cash flow returns from *external improvements* – for example, liquidation, disposals and acquisitions – which would push the share price a further £0.30 to £1.70. Finally, *financial engineering* – switching to higher debt financing, with tax benefits derived through the deductibility of

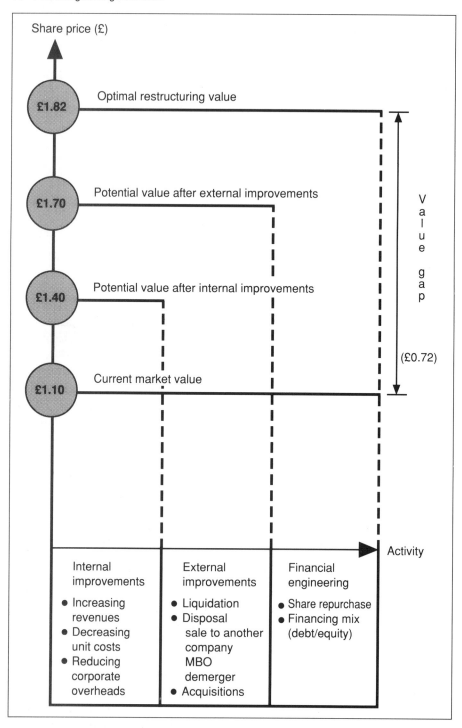

Figure 3.5 *Closing the value gap*

interest payments – may bring about a modest share price increase from £1.70 to £1.82. The value gap is £0.72 – the 65% difference between the market price of £1.10 and the potential price of £1.82.

The maximum value of the organization, the integration of the internal and external improvements together with the benefits of financial engineering, is the optimal restructured value. Corporate raiders profit by capturing the difference between current market value of the organization and its restructured value. While the numbers depicted in Figure 3.5 are purely hypothetical value gaps of around 65% are not uncommon.

Strategies to improve operations

Strategies to improve operations are the actions management can enact which do not require the acquisition or disposal of businesses. Included under this heading are all the strategies that could be pursued to raise the value of the organization on the basis of retaining all the businesses currently constituting the group.

To assist exposition action at the corporate and business levels will be described separately. At the corporate level improving operations should focus on (a) developing core competences, and (b) enhancing business unit performance. Actions in both of these areas need to focus on improving performance and removing the reasons why in the past it has been poor. Existing management might well consider what actions an acquiring company could undertake to improve performance of the corporate centre. For example, there may be the opportunity to remove a substantial corporate overhead by cutting headquarters staff which directly and indirectly detracts from the value added by the business. Equally such action might be accompanied by a change in management style to unlock the potential of the individual business units. Senior management may need to recognize that some actions can have an almost immediate effect, whilst others take longer to have an influence on the organization.

At the business level the emphasis should be on improving competitive performance. Management needs to recognize that this may require both actions which can have an immediate effect, and those which are likely to take much longer to generate increased value. The most immediate actions normally will be focused on reducing costs and raising revenue. In every organization, however well run, there is generally some scope to 'take out' costs which may have become inflated by relatively easy business conditions or undemanding management. This said, it is important that management do not axe parts of the business in pursuit of cost reduction in a way that undermines the basis of the company's competitive advantage. For instance, faced with difficult trading conditions management might be tempted to cut R&D spending, which, whilst unlikely to have any effect in the short term, may have considerable repercussions in the longer term. Hence any cost reduction strategies adopted must not be at the expense of the long-term competitive position of the business.

Raising revenue may result from action to provide short-term support to products in order to maintain or enhance their market position, which may lead to a significant benefit to earnings. Alternatively, product rationalization may take place, with weak product lines being discontinued and resources switched to support product lines with stronger market positions. The basic requirement is to identify key cost and revenue drivers, those elements of the business which have the greatest influence on value creation, and whose careful management will lead to a significant increase in value.

Strategies based on acquiring or disposing of assets

As Figure 3.5 shows, the second set of strategies that management will need to pursue in reducing the value gap relates to the acquisition or disposal of corporate assets. Evaluating the potential of the business units contained in the company's business portfolio and the extent to which they are capable of adding value through the development of competitive advantage raises the question of deciding which companies should be retained and which should be divested or liquidated.

Businesses with strong product market positions where a competitive advantage exists or is capable of being developed are likely to be retained, while businesses with weak product market positions with little likelihood of developing a competitive advantage should be divested or liquidated. In reaching these decisions, strategy at the corporate and business levels is brought together. Decisions to retain or divest a business will reflect both the view of their competitive potential at the business level and how the activity fits in terms of the overall portfolio of businesses, the development of core competences and the management styles used to manage the individual business units.

Action to strengthen the competitive position of businesses to be retained could include the acquisition of additional companies to build critical mass in the chosen product markets, or entering into strategic alliances where competitive advantage cannot be assured by the business remaining independent. In many cases the imperative to enter strategic alliances is driven by the increasing globalization of markets, examined further in Illustration 3.6.

Management needs to divest or liquidate a business if it is unable to create sufficient value to justify its retention, or it is considered that the business's performance will be improved by becoming an independent company or part of the business portfolio of another organization. In extreme cases the need may not be to diversify the business, but to close the operation down and put the business into liquidation. Where a business is to be sold management may be required to take action to prepare the business for sale which might, for example, include limited investment.

Once the decision has been taken to divest a business the question then arises of how this is to be done. In most instances the most likely mechanism is to find another company to purchase the operation as a 'going concern'. The most

Illustration 3.6

GLOBALIZATION – THE FOOD INDUSTRY

International factors impinge on companies and industries in a number of ways. A key issue is the extent to which companies need to consider operating on a global basis in order to be competitive. Following the work of a number of writers (e.g. Levitt, 1983; Porter, 1986), it is conventional to distinguish between industries organized as *international* or *multi-domestic* industries, and industries termed *global*. These two types of industries effectively establish the extremes of a continuum along which individual industries may be positioned.

An international or multi-domestic industry is one which operates primarily on a country-by-country basis, recognizing the specific needs of the national market, and being able to achieve any significant scale economies by operating on a national basis. Historically, retailing has been a national industry, reflecting the different cultures of individual countries as embodied in the tastes and purchasing patterns of consumers. To the extent that an industry is organized on a national basis international competition is likely to be less important, unless foreign-owned companies enter a specific national market.

The food industry provides a case study of an industry where competition is increasingly being organized on a global basis. Globalization in the food industry is being driven by two sets of factors – the convergence of consumer tastes, and the pursuit of economies of scale. Across the world, whilst some national differences remain, the trend is towards the convergence of consumer tastes. As consumers become more homogeneous increased opportunities arise for pan-national branding, allowing manufacturers to brand on a regional – Europe, North American and Asia-Pacific – if not on a global basis. With consumer demand for food growing relatively slowly in many product markets, manufacturers are seeking to enhance the earning power of their existing brands, as well as engaging in new product innovation in an attempt to stimulate sales.

The slow growth of market demand and the increasing power of large retail buyers has led to the intensity of rivalry amongst food manufacturers increasing. Faced with such competitive pressures companies have invested heavily to raise levels of efficiency and to reduce costs. Companies operating across national boundaries have been able to concentrate production facilities in order to rationalize costs and gain economies of scale. A necessary condition for these benefits to be realized has been the development of pan-national brands, which has also enabled marketing efforts to be concentrated to the benefit of sales.

Both the convergence of tastes and availability of production and marketing economies has resulted in greater industry concentration. Nationally based competitors are increasingly facing competition from truly global companies. Even where differences of national tastes remain, global companies may mix partial globalization strategies with strategies designed to meet the needs of the local (national) market. Lorenz (1986) refers to this concept as *customized global marketing*. Unless nationally focused competitors have some way of protecting their market, they face an unequal fight to maintain profitability and

continued overleaf

ultimately to survive. National food manufacturers have two options. Do they seek to become global players, or do they remain focused on a national market, following, say, a niche strategy or becoming an own-label producer for large food retailers? Companies choosing the first option will need to pursue a strategy of growth by acquisition given the maturity of food markets worldwide.

In the context of UB's desire to become a world leader in snack foods it is clear which of the options the company's management has chosen. Acquisitions over the last decade have resulted in the establishment of a North American base (Keebler Company) and expansion into Europe. Increased penetration of the Asia-Pacific region has been more recently enhanced with the company's announcement in November 1992 that it was acquiring the snack business of Coca Cola Amatil (CCA), the Australian drinks company, for a consideration of £195.5 m. The acquisition of CCA enables UB to claim leadership in two out of the three major regional markets in the world – Europe and Asia-Pacific – when compared to its global rival PepsiCo, with whom it is contesting leadership of the world snack market. Although in a weaker position than its rival in the important North American snack market, the growth potential is considered greater in Europe and Asia-Pacific.

The acquisition of CCA provides an example of a cross-border acquisition, a characteristic of takeovers and mergers likely to be more common for the food industry over the next decade as companies seek to establish global positions. In Europe a further impetus to this process has been provided by the establishment of the Single European Market.

For the food industry the momentum behind takeovers and mergers is likely to be driven by the economic fundamentals of the industry, which may in the future provide fewer opportunities for 'unbundlers'.

Source: Authors.

advantageous price for the selling organization is likely to occur if a strategic buyer can be found who is prepared to pay a considerable premium to acquire the company in order to, say, strengthen its existing business operations.

The case of UB purchasing Ross Young, the frozen food producer, from Hanson plc in 1988 provides a good example. UB needed to add to its existing frozen food operations in order to achieve sufficient size to be competitive. At the same time Hanson plc was 'unbundling' Imperial Tobacco, a company that it had previously acquired and which had tried unsuccessfully to diversify away from its dependence on tobacco. Hanson was able to sell the Ross Young business to UB for £335 m, a premium price which might not have been achieved without the company's strategic imperative of achieving critical mass in the market for frozen foods.

By contrast UB sold its restaurants, comprising Wimpy, Pizzaland and Perfect Pizza, to Grand Metropolitan plc in October 1988 for £180 m. In deciding to sell its restaurant business UB recognized performance was poor and felt that the costs and prospects of developing a competitive advantage did not justify retention of the businesses within the group.

It is important to recognize that the final price paid for a company is the outcome of a process of negotiation and bargaining, reflecting the needs and the motivation of both parties. A distressed sale by a business in some difficulty, for example, places the seller in a weak position. Conversely, companies such as Hanson plc appear to be able to seek out strategic buyers and negotiate attractive prices for their shareholders.

As Figure 3.5 illustrates, divesting strategies may include management buy-outs (MBOs) and demergers. MBOs were popular in the expanding economic conditions of the 1980s when finance was readily available for companies with attractive prospects. Using the MBO route is another method of empowering existing managers to run a business they know well. Providing the financing is structured carefully, and prospects for the business foreseen, MBOs have a good chance of success. Some MBOs have proved that performance can be raised quickly enabling the company to be floated on the stock exchange after a relatively short period of independence. Taunton Cider, which returned to the stock market in the summer of 1992, provides a good example of this process (see also Illustration 3.7).

Illustration 3.7

EXPRESS FOODS – A MANAGEMENT BUYOUT

On 4 November 1992, Grand Metropolitan plc announced its UK cheese and food services business, Express Foods, was being sold to a management buyout team. The purchase of Express Foods for £96 m would enable the business to become an independent company once again.

Grand Metropolitan had decided to dispose of Express Foods as the business no longer fitted with its strategy of focusing on the expansion of a range of international branded products.

Source: Based on a report appearing in the *Financial Times*.

Demerger of parts of an organization by floating a new company on the stock market has proved another route to divesting assets in a way which leads to improved performance. In many cases it is only the emergence of an actual bid that promotes management into the necessary action. For example, the prospect of Hanson plc bidding for ICI plc prompted management in the latter group to announce plans to split the organization into two companies through demerger. Likewise, the difference between Goldsmith's proposed 'unbundling' and BAT's subsequent 'reshaping' of its diversified portfolio differed only in scale and style.

Similarly, Rank Hovis McDougall, the food manufacturer, when subject to a bid from Hanson plc, announced plans to demerge the company. This has been referred to by some commentators as the 'fall apart defence' – whereby existing management promise to do the things that the predator is threatening to do, and break the company up. To accept this defence requires a belief that incumbent management will act successfully, and that corporate renaissance as opposed to relapse will take place.

Whilst takeover bids represent some of the most dramatic events in the history of organizations, not all companies require the emergence of a takeover bid to act to enhance value. Financial institutions can force changes in both corporate strategy and top management, although this usually only occurs when there is an organizational crisis, as witnessed by Granada plc in 1991. In other instances, managers have proved capable of breaking up organizations with inconsistent parts, as shown in Illustration 3.8.

Illustration 3.8

COURTAULDS PLC

In 1989 Courtaulds plc announced its intention of dividing its business into two independent companies: one based on chemicals, and the other on textiles. Each company would have a separate stock market quotation. The company's Chief Executive Officer, Sir Christopher Hogg, and his management team had recognized the different skills and disciplines required to manage two different clusters of companies.

The chemicals business had a very strong international emphasis, was technology based and considered the most dynamic part of the Courtaulds group. By contrast textiles were fashion oriented and focused on the UK market. Textiles had also suffered from the perception of being the less dynamic part of the company. The formation of the textiles division into a separate entity would enable employee morale to be raised and management to have a single focus in managing the new company.

Courtaulds' decision to demerger itself was a recognition of the difficulty of managing diversification, and that specialization was a source of competitive strength.

Source: Based on *Financial Times*, 31 October 1989.

Financial engineering strategies

The third set of strategies available to managers seeking to close the value gap are known as *financial engineering strategies*. Financial engineering is a highly complex area and only the broad principles will be discussed. Opportunities may be available to improve the financial management of the business by, for example, reviewing the balance of debt and equity finance. Under UK tax laws interest on debt finance can be offset against pre-tax profits, making it advantageous to finance at least part of a company's capital requirements using borrowings. Equally, a company may have the opportunity of using currency or interest rate swap arrangements to reduce the cost of capital further.

Whilst financial engineering may be helpful, in most instances the greatest value enhancing opportunities lie in terms of improving existing operations and taking action to acquire or dispose of assets. The fictional numbers used in Figure 3.5 emphasize this point, with 16% of the share price increase attributable to financial engineering, and 42% respectively to internal and external improvements. It should be noted these latter two areas – internal and external improvements – should in particular be the focus of management's efforts to narrow the value gap and avoid the risk of takeover: allowing others to do what they should have done in the first place.

Financial engineering strategies are often a key consideration for corporate raiders when deciding on what is the optimal way of financing a takeover bid. Should a takeover bid be launched an important issue for the shareholders of the respective companies is who will benefit most from the removal of a value gap? Will the shareholders of the take over target predominantly gain, or will the benefits be more evenly shared between the owners of both companies. To illustrate this question consider the case of Rank Hovis McDougall (RHM), which was subject to two takeover bids in the autumn of 1992. Prior to a bid being received shares in RHM had been languishing, with market sentiment

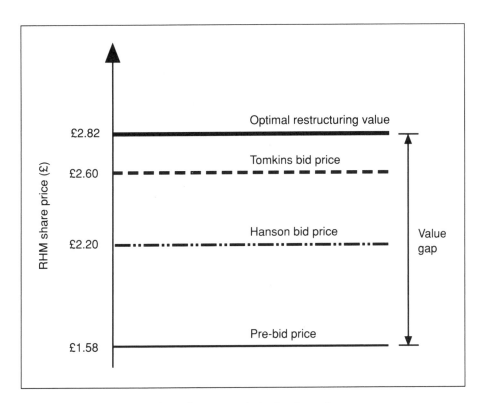

Figure 3.6 *RHM: closing the value gap and sharing the gains*

unfavourably disposed towards the incumbent management team. The first offer for RHM was launched by Hanson plc on 5 October 1992, with a bid of £2.20 per share. Speculation following Hanson's bid was that the market would demand a higher price of, say, £2.50 per share before the bidder could be confident in securing control of RHM. Before Hanson's initial offer was raised, Tomkins plc entered the bidding offering shareholders of RHM £2.60 per share on 29 October 1992. At this price Hanson declined to increase their offer, and allowed their bid to lapse.

The fundamental question is how much is the company really worth and who stands to gain from the takeover of the company? At the time of Hanson's bid, City analysts suggested that RHM was worth some £1,000 m, equivalent to £2.82 per share. Given that RHM's shares were trading at 158p prior to a bid being received this suggests that the value gap for the company was worth some £1.24 (£2.82 less £1.58). As Figure 3.6 illustrates, Hanson's initial bid would have resulted in the benefits being shared equally between the shareholders of Hanson and RHM, with each company gaining 50% of the maximum restructuring value of RHM. If Hanson had been forced to raise its bid to £2.50 then RHM's shareholders would have gained almost 74% of the value gap. In the event Hanson did not raise its bid following Tomkins decision to bid for RHM at £2.60 per share. As Table 3.2 shows, at the price Tomkins was offering RHM shareholders, the majority of the value gap would have accrued to existing shareholders in RHM. The lower the bid price in relation to the size of the value gap, the greater the benefit to the shareholders of the acquisitor. Conversely, in a contested bid where a high price is paid relative to the value gap, the benefit is distributed in favour of the shareholders of the target company.

Table 3.2 *The distribution of the gains from restructuring RHM*

	Hanson bid at 220p		Hanson bid at 250p*		Tomkins bid at 260p	
RHM	62p	50.0%	92p	74.2%	102p	82.3%
Hanson	62p	50.0%	32p	25.8%	—	—
Tomkins	—	—	—	—	22p	17.7%
Value gap	124p	100.0%	124p	100.0%	124p	100.0%

*This is for illustrative purposes only. Hanson did not raise its bid following Tomkins' offer.

Market reaction to both the Hanson and Tomkins bids is instructive in gauging whether investors believed the takeover of RHM would have been likely to increase or dilute respective shareholder interests. Whilst generally the market accepted the logic and price of Hanson's initial bid, the reaction to Tomkins' higher offer was generally negative. On the day Tomkins announced its offer, their share price fell by 19% as investors expressed concerns about the fullness of the price it was paying for RHM and the extent to which the proposed bid reflected a change in corporate strategy. Tomkins had previously focused on acquiring engineering companies. Concerns were expressed that RHM represented both a change of scale – when compared to the company's previous acquisitions – and entry into the food industry, where the company had no previous experience. By comparison Hanson's decision to allow its bid to lapse and not attempt to bid above Tomkins was accepted by the market as the correct strategy in order to preserve shareholder value.

The case of RHM illustrates once again the risks involved in corporate takeover, and the need to examine closely whether the action being pursued will increase shareholder value. As noted earlier any action to take over a company can result in value being destroyed. All companies, when they are seeking to diversify, are vulnerable to the extent that there are risks involved, and this is true whether the action is being taken by an unbundler or is being pursued by a company seeking to become less dependent on a mature market. In all these cases management needs to ask itself one question: does the action proposed add value? (See also Illustration 3.9.)

Illustration 3.9

BRITISH TELECOMMUNICATIONS PLC
The recently privatized company British Telecommunications (BT) plc is expected to build a sizeable cash mountain in the 1990s as the cash it earns exceeds the costs of running the business. As cash builds up, the question arises as to what the company might do to enhance shareholder value.   The company could, for example, increase dividend payments, or repurchase its own shares. Both actions would benefit shareholders and distribute the value the company has created to the owners.   A danger to shareholders is that management may be tempted to pursue a strategy of diversification which, if unsuccessful, would result in value being destroyed rather than created.   Source: Based on *The Financial Times*, 2 November 1992.

Concluding remarks

Companies diversifying in the 1990s are likely to be more carefully scrutinized than ever was the case before. Investors will need to be convinced that such action will indeed create value, rather than has been too often the case in the past that value is destroyed. There is no place for management who do not manage their organization from the perspective of creating value. All strategic actions at the corporate and business levels require managers to consider the extent to which value is being enhanced. Companies who maximize value creation will be successful not only in competitive terms, but also in delivering returns to shareholders. The link between successful corporate and business strategies and shareholders' return is clear: managers ignore it at their peril.

By using the framework presented in Figure 3.5, management can determine the optimal value of the company – the sum of all the internal, external and financial engineering improvements. As noted earlier, raiders profit by capturing the difference between the current market value of the company and its optimal restructured value. Closing the value gap necessitates a thorough self-evaluation of the benefits of corporate and business unit strategies. This leads us to suggest that businesses which are more valuable as part of another company's portfolio or as independent entities should be divested, whilst units that cannot be sold and currently earn less than their cost of capital should be closed down. By contrast businesses with strong product market positions should be enhanced by adopting appropriate internal strategies, and where necessary acquiring further assets. Unless these actions are taken the company and its management remain vulnerable to take over.

Checklist

- *Identify the current market value of the company.*
- *To what extent has the share price changed over, say, the last year?*
- *Does the change in the share price suggest that existing management is able to create significant value, or does it need a new management team to unlock value from the business?*
- *Have directors recently bought or sold shares?*
- *Does the company communicate effectively with its shareholders? Have there been any marked changes to communicating performance recently?*
- *What internal improvements have been taken by management, and/or are in the process of being implemented to add value?*
- *What external improvements – liquidations, divestments – have been undertaken, and have these actions contributed to adding value?*
- *What external improvements – acquisitions – have been pursued to strengthen competitive advantage and thereby increase long-term value?*
- *What actions, if any, have been taken with respect to financial engineering? Have these assisted value creation?*
- *What further strategies can you identify for management to adopt which add value?*

CHAPTER 4

Finding information on companies and their markets

Finding appropriate quantitative and qualitative information on companies and their markets provides the basis on which to assess the organization's strategic direction, to undertake financial statement analysis and to interpret stock market assessment. The chapter is arranged in the following sections:

- *what information is needed*
- *how to go about gathering information*
- *detailed information sources:*
  - *company-based information*
  - *industry/sector analysis*
  - *assessing the broad context*
- *collating the information.*

The chapter begins by ascertaining what are the appropriate data requirements to carry out an external or outside assessment of the value creating potential of an organization, and how such information can be gathered. A detailed listing of appropriate major secondary information sources is provided, focusing on the company, *the* industry/sector *and its* broad context. *Key information requirements are ascertained for each prospective level of analysis according to whether they assist in* assessing strategic direction, financial statement analysis *and* stock market assessment. *Finally, to assist the reader to carry out what can often be a complex and time-consuming task, a checklist to collecting information is provided.*

What information is needed

Figure 4.1 shows that the manager or analyst needs to be concerned with three key information sets which link the formulation and valuation of organizational strategies: assessing strategic direction, financial statement analysis and stock market assessment. These are the three clusters of information, as described in Chapter 1, which enable the value of an organization to be identified. For each of these information sets, data needs to be collected in relation to three levels: the company, the industry/sector and the broad context. With the exception of on-line databases and earnings forecasts, information in relation to all these elements is largely historical in nature. All too often analysts focus on the past, without appreciating the past is only helpful to understanding the present, and the information on the present is only helpful in as much as it helps us to forecast the future.

An added complication is that the diversity of many large companies requires individual evaluations of business divisions and units to be made. Unless analysis is carried out both at the corporate and business levels it is impossible, for example, to gain a clear understanding of the product market position of a business, as well as assessing the strength of the corporate management team. Correspondingly, some of the information needs relate primarily to assessing the corporate strategy and group's position, whilst other questions need to be tackled at the level of the business unit.

It is important to remember that in the final analysis all information on a company has to be collated and an overall assessment reached. Nevertheless, to enable the total information requirement to be managed, Table 4.1 takes the three information sets and levels illustrated in Figure 4.1, and generates nine 'cells', each defining an important information need.

Whilst each of the nine cells in Table 4.1 defines a set of information needs, at the outset it should be recognized that there is considerable overlap between the different areas. Many sources of data provide information in relation to a number of the cells, and the researcher's understanding of any one area or level is likely to be enhanced by knowledge gained overall. For this reason it is important not to confine the collection of data to one information set, or to focus exclusively at one level of analysis. For example, focusing on the non-financial components of the analysis and virtually ignoring the assessment of financial statements inevitably gives rise to a distorted picture. Similarly, focusing exclusively on the financial numbers results in important market and industry information being ignored. From the start it is important to ascertain the links between the financial and non-financial analysis in order to gain a full appreciation of the company's business position.

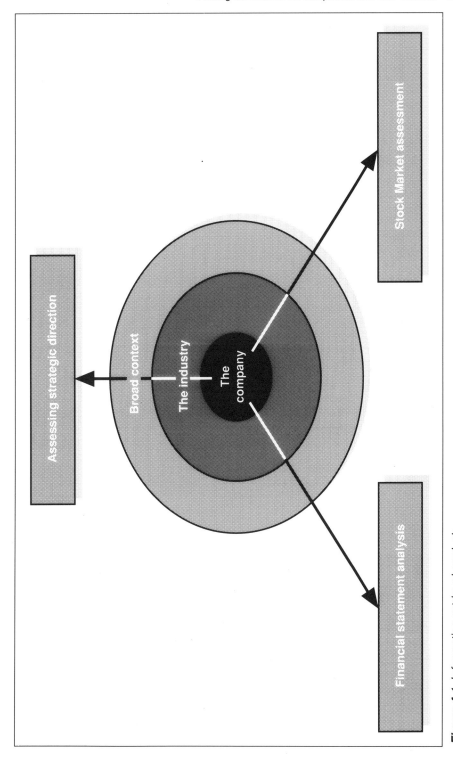

Figure 4.1 *Information retrieval analysis*

Table 4.1 *Key information requirements*

	Assessing strategic direction	Financial statement analysis	Stock market assessment
Company	**1.** Identify and assess corporate and business unit strategies, management resource, product market positions, etc.	**2.** Assessment of current and future outcomes to company's strategies – sales, profitability, cash flow, etc.	**3.** Understand market assessment and rating of the company
Industry/sector	**4.** Evaluate competitive forces and relative strengths and strategies of competitors. Review key industry drivers and likely future pattern of industry development	**5.** Make comparisons with other companies operating in the same or similar product markets	**6.** Compare company's rating to other companies in the same sector. Review performance of sector against overall market
Broad context	**7.** Assess key PEST change agents, i.e. P – political E – economic S – social T – technological factors	**8.** Evaluate opportunities for funding raising (debt and equity), likely tax and interest rate changes, etc.	**9.** Identify movements in overall stock market, and likely future pattern of share prices

How to gather information

Information gathering can appear to be a daunting task. Just as the journalist cultivates information networks and jealously guards such sources, so the researcher needs to become familiar with where information can be found and in what form. Two of the most important developments in recent times are the extent to which information sources are continuously changing with the advent of computer-based data systems, together with the broadening of many UK-based publications to include a much wider European perspective. The knowledge of where to find relevant information and the skill in using the data found is one of the hallmarks of the good company/industry analyst, researcher or strategic manager.

To guide the process of gathering information, Figure 4.2 provides a general framework for collecting and analysing information. It is arranged as a flow diagram. This enables the manager or analyst who is new to the task of collecting information to undertake the necessary work as a series of simple steps. The first step is for the researcher to define both the level of analysis and the information set required. Any one of the nine cells depicted in Figure 4.1 can be chosen, and for illustrative purposes cell 1 – where level of analysis (company) and information set (assessing strategic direction) are configured – has been selected.

Figure 4.2 suggests that once the information need is determined and appropriate cell number selected, the next step is to examine secondary sources of data. Secondary data sources refer to information previously collected and collated. They include, for example, the company's annual and interim reports, industry surveys, government publications and trade journals. Secondary sources should be utilized initially, given that these are often easily accessible and in many instances their use incurs relatively little financial cost. Secondary data sources are particularly relevant to the individual who is seeking to analyse a company and its business activities for the first time and needs to achieve a rapid understanding of a company and its key drivers. As information is collected it should also be analysed. In this way, factors which are relevant (and those largely irrelevant) can be established and priorities for future data collection can be established.

When analysing secondary sources the researcher needs to ask the question: does the data satisfy the information requirement? If the answer is yes, then it should be possible to reach a conclusion. More frequently, the answer will be no. If this is the case the next question is whether additional secondary data is required. Often the researcher will initially examine a sample of secondary sources, and will have the option of reviewing additional sources if the first trawl of information does not satisfy the required need.

Assuming additional secondary information is required, Figure 4.2 shows the next decision is to examine whether, in the light of the assessment made, the information requirement needs to be redefined. Frequently, as information is collected it becomes easier to identify the issues influencing a company's performance. Consequently, the initial information requirement may need modification. This reflects an important underlying principle to all the tasks of data collection, namely the process is iterative with a series of feedback loops at each stage. Each time new information is provided, the need for further information can be reassessed. Eventually, all the critical secondary sources will have to be culled, and if additional information is still required it will be necessary to collect primary data.

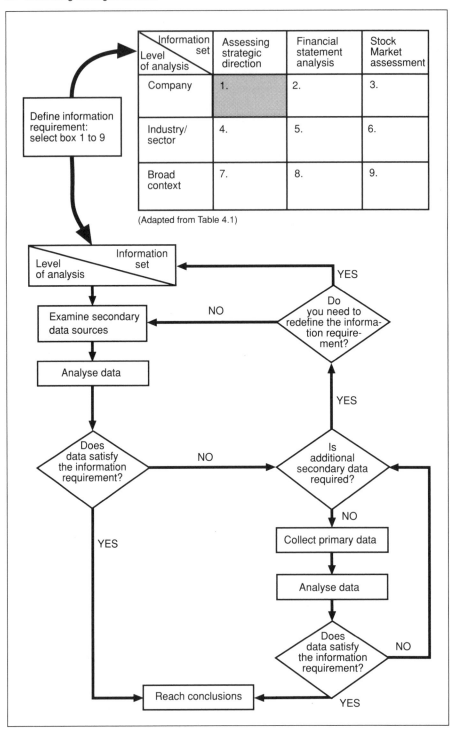

Figure 4.2 *The information gathering process*

Primary data requires researchers to generate their own data to satisfy a specific information need. This might include the researcher surveying a company's customers, interviewing industry experts or observing how the company runs its operations. Primary data offers the prospect of collecting information for a specific purpose, rather than using information already in existence but which might have been produced for a different need. Given the often higher cost, both financially and in terms of time, of collecting primary data, Figure 4.2 suggests that this source is used to overcome any information gaps, or to confirm the validity of conclusions reached on the basis of secondary information.

As with secondary information, primary data needs to be analysed and evaluated in terms of whether the findings satisfy the information requirement. If it does not, it is necessary to go back and consider again what alternative sources of information might be available. Occasionally, primary data may prompt a reconsideration of the information requirement and a further review of secondary sources.

The underlying process, as illustrated in Figure 4.2, suggests a sequence of collecting secondary data before moving on to primary data. Whilst this is broadly the most cost-effective way of progressing, it may on occasions be necessary to undertake both the secondary and primary collection of data concurrently. The risk in following this procedure is that for the researcher who is new to the task there is an insufficient database from which the collection of primary data may be shaped. This can lead either to collecting data which repeats information already available from secondary sources but which the researcher has yet to discover, or missing the opportunity to use primary data methods to best effect by not specifying accurately what the critical questions to be answered are.

The need to verify the quality of data raises the need to make extensive use of *triangulation* (Johnson, 1987, pp. 77–8): 'Triangulation is the employment of different methods of analysis to observe the same database.' Data triangulation involves the use of a range of different sources of information to examine the same findings. In the context of analysing companies alternative sources of information should be employed to cross-check findings and to help identify the extent to which statements are objective. This is particularly important in respect of analysing company inspired information given the inevitable wish of the board of directors to present information in the best possible light.

Whilst recognizing the benefits of triangulation, there is a potential risk for would-be analysts, namely one of collecting too much repetitious information essentially drawn from a single information source. If this should happen it is unlikely that work will progress much beyond the information gathering stage. To avoid this potential problem it is important to seek information which genuinely confirms or adds to the stock of knowledge, and to disregard sources which simply repeat an assessment already known by drawing on the same sources of information.

Detailed information sources

Having identified the information needs in Table 4.1 and the process for gathering data, where should the researcher start? Whilst in practice it is possible to start at any point, and data triangulation necessitates cross-referencing with other data sources, most analysts would appear to start to build up a picture from the 'bottom-up' or 'top-down'. Hence in Figure 4.1 the information set on the company is placed in the centre of the diagram. Corresponding to Figure 4.1 for the 'bottom-up' approach, once information has been collected on the company, it is then possible to move to gaining information about the industry/sector and the broader context. Whilst this sequence of levels provides a helpful way of unpacking information requirements, in practice there is considerable overlap between the levels of information, and the researcher may wish to collect information concurrently once an initial understanding of the key aspects of the company and its businesses has been achieved. Following Figure 4.1 the detailed discussion below of the sources of information is subdivided into three categories:

- company-based information
- industry/sector analysis
- assessing the broad context.

Company-based information

Table 4.2 indicates again the key information requirements to be determined from using company-based information. The focus is on the first three cells depicted in Table 4.1; cells 4 to 9 relating to industry/sector analysis and the broad context are considered later in the chapter.

Notwithstanding a degree of overlap between the three levels of information requirements, Table 4.3 lists the major sources of appropriate company-based information.

Assessing strategic direction

CORPORATE COMMENT

Chairman's statement (annual report)
There is no mandatory requirement for the chairman to report separately from the board of directors, but for many companies the practice is for a separate statement to be made. This is generally a retrospective view of the company and its trading environment over the past year, together with indications of the strategic direction proposed over the near term. The information context is not normally sufficient to generate a firm forecast for the next year, but much can be ascertained from the tenor and tone of what is included (and excluded) from

Table 4.2 Company level analysis – key information requirements

	Assessing strategic direction	Financial statement analysis	Stock market assessment
Company	**1.** Identify and assess corporate and business unit strategies, management resource, product market positions, etc.	**2.** Assessment of current and future outcomes to company's strategies – sales, profitability, cash flow, etc.	**3.** Understand market assessment and rating of the company
Industry/sector	**4.**	**5.**	**6.**
Broad context	**7.**	**8.**	**9.**

the statement. Furthermore, some companies, for example UB, provide separate statements by both the chairman and the chief executive officer.

A company half-yearly or interim statement will also usually contain a statement by the chairman, who will again review the company's trading performance for the first half of the year. An example is provided in Illustration 4.1.

Illustration 4.1

UB PLC – CHAIRMAN'S STATEMENT
Outlook
'We do not expect any significant improvements in the trading environment for the remainder of this year, and we therefore anticipate continued pressure on our margins, particularly in the USA. While the outcome for the full year will undoubtedly fall short of last year's record profits, the resilient performance of our UK and continental European businesses confirms my confidence that our strategy will deliver good returns over the longer term.'
Source: *UB Interim Report 1992*, September 1992.

The directors' report (annual report)

In contrast to the chairman's statement, the content of the directors' report is controlled by company law and the listing requirements of the stock exchange. The requirements of companies listed on the London stock market can be found in the Stock Exchange's *Official Yearbook*. This sets out the listing requirements, known as continuing obligations for companies who are already listed on the stock market. Key aspects of the continuing obligations are itemized below:

Table 4.3 *Major sources of company-based information*

Assessing strategic direction:	
Corporate comment:	
● Chairman's statement	(Annual and interim reports)
● Directors' report	(Annual report)
● Business history	(Company sponsored books)
● Acquisitions/disposals	(Company announcements)
● Trading statements	(Company announcements)
● Newspaper reports	(Business press)
● Hard copy indexes	(*Research Index* and *Clover Newspaper Index*)
● Information retrieval systems	(FT Profile and Textline, ABI-Inform and F & S Index plus Text)
Business unit comment:	
● Segmental analysis	(Annual and interim reports, employees' newsletters, *Key British Enterprises, UK Kompass*)
● Brand or trade names	(*UK Trade Names, A–Z of UK Brands*)
● Corporate parents	(*Who Owns Who*)
Financial statement analysis:	
● Annual financial statements	(Annual report)
● Half-yearly results	(Interim report)
● Summary information	(Extel cards and *Hambro Company Guide*)
● Information retrieval systems	(FAME database)
● Funding announcements	(Company statement)
Stock market assessment:	
● Information retrieval systems	(Datastream and Microview/Microextel)
● Current stock market rating	(Business press)
● Future earnings	(*The Estimate Directory, The Earnings Guide*)

- the requirement to issue an annual report within six months of the end of the financial year to which it relates;
- an explanation of why trading results of the company differ markedly from any published forecast the company has issued;
- a geographical analysis of turnover and profits;
- a statement by the directors of any reasons for significant departures from standard accounting practices;
- the identity of independent (non-executive) directors and short biographical notes;

- the name of any major country in which subsidiaries operate;
- whether the company is 'closed';
- details of debt finance.

A brief example is outlined in Illustration 4.2.

Illustration 4.2

UB PLC – DIRECTORS' REPORT
Some of the topics covered by the directors' three page report, published as part of the company's 1991 Annual Report, were: • acquisitions made during the year • changes in accounting policy • employee share scheme • charitable donations and political contributions • changes to the non-executive directors of the company • status of the company. Source: *UB Annual Report 1991*, March 1992.

Business history

It is always sensible to ascertain if a company has produced a written history of its growth and development. In *A Clear and Simple Vision* (Pugh, 1991), four decades of the growth of United Biscuits are discussed from the company's perspective. The book provides a number of fascinating insights into UB's generic strategy, a rationale for the acquisitive expansion and the criteria adopted (see Illustration 4.3) together with a detailed account of UB's initial failure to build a strong presence in Europe. While the emphasis is on the past, the text helps to provide a perspective on current operations.

Illustration 4.3

UB – ENTERING THE EUROPEAN MARKET
'The criteria for prospective acquisitions (in Europe) were that the target company would have to: • be a market leader or have a number of market leaders in their range; • be operating in an expanding market; • have a quality name; • be well managed and well regarded by the trade; • be profitable.' Source: Pugh (1991), p.76.

Acquisitions/disposals and trading statements

A rich, if irregular, source of information from companies is provided by the announcements they make periodically to inform the stock market of major acquisitions/disposals or to warn of deteriorating trading conditions. These announcements will normally be reported in the following day's business press, which is invariably sent press releases by the company. When a company has made a major announcement it is often possible to obtain a copy of the press release by contacting the company directly. The details contained in the press releases published by a company provide an invaluable source of information to the individual researching a company's strategy. Illustration 4.4 gives an example.

Illustration 4.4

UB PLC – NEW US ACQUISITION

'I am pleased to announce that we have agreed to acquire the leading manufacturer of own-label cookies in the United States, the Bake-Line company of Chicago. The cost is $70 (£47) million in cash, and we will also assume around $5 (£3) million of debt. The transaction will be financed from our existing resources, and completion will take place shortly. Bake-Line will retain its own identity, but will report into Keebler.

'Bake-Line has approximately 25 per cent of the US own-label cookie market, and manufactures its products in a modern, purpose-built bakery which has the capacity to handle further increases in sales.

'With a thorough knowledge of the US own-label business, strong relationships with many major retailers, and its modern flexible factory, Bake-Line is ideally positioned to help UB capitalize on the fast-growing own-label sector of the US biscuit market. In addition, there will be substantial synergy between Keebler and Bake-Line, with the former's strength in brands complementing Bake-Line's own-label expertise.'

Source: UB press statement signed by Mr J. Warren, Group Finance Director, 5 January 1993.

Newspaper reports

In the UK the best single daily source on business matters is *The Financial Times.* As well as providing daily financial and stock market information as outlined later in this chapter, the paper's regular features include:

- an analysis of the largest quoted companies' annual and interim profit announcements. The *Weekend FT* (published every Saturday) provides a list of companies reporting their annual (final) and interim results in the forthcoming week;
- reports on mergers and acquisitions;
- an assessment of strategic direction – the 'Lex' column in particular (see Illustration 4.5 for an example) is renowned for the analytical insights it offers

on companies' strategies, and is to be found on the back page of the paper's first section.

Illustration 4.5

UB PLC – COMMENT BY LEX
The optimistic interpretation of UB's management reshuffle at Keebler is that it will enable the parent to impose stricter discipline over its wayward child. The depressing one is that it highlights just how little control UB has over its own destiny. No matter how well the new chief executive performs, Keebler will continue to be hampered by the brutal reality of the US biscuit and snack markets. Despite being number two in its chosen fields, Keebler remains a comparatively small player with few easy expansion routes. Market terms are largely dictated by the dominant Nabisco. As yet, there is little sign of a truce in the biscuit price war, which has so disfigured Keebler's margins, although economic recovery will clearly help. A similar problem applies to Ross Young, UB's frozen foods business in the UK, which shows a dismal return on assets despite severe rationalization. In both cases, UB's energetic new management must be sorely tempted to cut and run. Yesterday's moves, though, imply a renewed resolve to struggle through. That may be the only viable option given the difficulties of disposing of such assets in current markets. But it also suggests UB's share price will limp, no matter how fast the other half of the business runs. UB's style will be further cramped by high borrowings, which limit the scope for acquisitive growth. Source: Lex column, *Financial Times*, 28 January 1993.

To trace articles published in the *Financial Times* the researcher should consult the *Index to the Financial Times*, which is published monthly. The index is designed to indicate when articles on a company or an industry appeared, and what in general terms was discussed. All the quality newspapers – the *Times, Sunday Times, The Independent* and *The Guardian*, etc. – operate similar indexing systems to the one described for the *Financial Times*. Back copies of the *Financial Times* and other quality newspapers are kept on microfiche by most of the larger business and municipal libraries. At the same time, increasingly newspapers are being stored on CD-ROM databases, which enables in-depth keyword searching.

Hard copy indexes to corporate comment

An index not confined to a single newspaper or periodical is the *Research Index* which is published weekly. This contains two sections indexing respectively company and industry news. Its coverage is not exhaustive, but rather selective from a wide range of newspapers and trade journals. As with another example, the *Clover Newspaper Index*, no indication of the detailed content of the cited articles is given.

Information retrieval systems for corporate comment

Written hard copy indexes are being superseded by new information retrieval systems, and in particular by compact disk (CD-ROM) and on-line databases. Both systems provide not only the opportunity to search for information sources, but also to gain immediate access to abstracts of any information discovered. The speed by which information can be located, and the ability to update the database on a regular basis, offer significant benefits to the users of these systems. Three examples of such information retrieval systems, which are particularly appropriate to assessing strategic direction, are given here.

The FT Profile, which also provides a gateway to Textline, provides the full text to the *Financial Times*. Both are commonly used databases of newspaper and periodical articles. As with other databases they are extremely useful for identifying recent articles and allowing the researcher to select those which are of particular interest. Other bibliographical databases which are available on CD-ROM include, for example, ABI-Inform and the F & S Index plus Text. It is increasingly the case that the full text of articles is available from such databases, and not just a brief synopsis.

BUSINESS UNIT INFORMATION

Segmental analysis

Stock exchange listed companies provide segmental information concerning (a) the turnover, (b) operating profit and (c) capital employed for each substantive business segment and for each geographical area served. This is the only information contained in the annual report which allows insights into whether different parts of the corporate group vary as to their trading performance, and the extent to which operating profits are concentrated by geographical area. Given the dearth of segmental information concerning how different parts of the business perform, segmental reporting is of considerable interest to the analyst. Of course, should management of the company wish to evaluate different parts of the corporate group, their access to internal management information makes the task that much easier to undertake.

By reviewing UB's segmental information for the first half of 1992 shown in Illustration 4.6, the critical comments contained in the 'Lex' column concerning US biscuits (Keebler) and UK frozen foods (Ross Young) in Illustration 4.5 are readily understood. Collectively these two divisions accounted for some 50% of the company's turnover, but only 30% of the trading profits on the basis of the interim results for 1992.

Employees' newsletters may also be of value in looking at business unit performance. UB, for example, has recently looked at a different division in successive issues of its newsletter. The information may be more timely than the annual report, and may give more detailed insights into new product launches and plant reorganization. Additional product information may be gleaned from published sources, including *Key British Enterprises* and *UK Kompass*. Both sources provide information on products and services produced

Illustration 4.6

SEGMENTAL INFORMATION – UB PLC FIRST HALF 1992		
	Turnover (£m)	Trading profits (£m)
McVitie's Group	407.5	47.6
Keebler	508.8	12.1
KP Foods Group	267.2	17.9
Ross Young's	268.2	14.2
Terry's Group	68.9	3.2
Source: *UB Interim Report 1992*, September 1992.		

and/or distributed, geographical scope and trade indexes for large numbers of UK-based companies.

Brand or trade names
Within a particular product/market segment, it is of interest to establish the ownership of brand or trade names. The discussion in Chapter 2 emphasized that brand or trade names could be an important source of competitive advantage. *UK Trade Names* provides a major listing of trade names, but excludes food, drink, tobacco and pharmaceuticals. *The A–Z of UK Brands* offers an overview of consumer brands, their ownership and market sales.

Corporate parents
Although the annual report provides insights into subsidiaries and associated companies, *Who Owns Who* is particularly useful for establishing relationships between companies. Volume 1 lists UK parent companies with subsidiaries and associates, while volume 2 provides an alphabetical listing of subsidiaries with the name of the parent.

Financial statement analysis

Annual and half yearly financial statements
The 'Annual Report and Accounts' is the primary source of accounting data on a company. In the UK the presentation of financial accounting information is based on three financial statements: (a) the income and expenditure of the company for the period (the profit and loss account), (b) the assets and liabilities at the end of the period (the balance sheet), and (c) the cash flow of the company (the cash flow statement). These statements are supported by 'Notes to Accounts' which provide additional information on some of the summary data incorporated in the three financial statements. The information content of a company's accounts is prescribed partly by company law, partly by the Account-

ing Standards Board (ASB), and partly by the requirements for stock market listed companies.

While the information provided in an annual report is of considerable importance, it is normally published three to four months after the end of the trading period to which it relates. Between the publication dates of successive annual reports, a company will publish its 'Interim Report' which relates to the company's trading activities for the first six months of the company's accounting period (see Illustration 4.7 for an example). Interim reports are not usually audited and contain modest amounts of information in comparison to the annual report. By providing information on a company's turnover, profit, tax, dividend and earnings per share, interim reports offer invaluable information between the publication of successive annual reports.

Illustration 4.7

UB PLC – INTERIM REPORT	
Consolidated profit statement, first half 1992	
	£m
Turnover	1525.5
Trading profit	87.2
Interest	17.2
Profit before tax	70.0
Tax	21.7
Profits after tax	48.3
Earnings per share – undiluted	9.7p
Dividends per share	5.5p
Source: *UB Interim Report 1992*, September 1992.	

Summary information

In view of the importance afforded the annual and interim reports, it is not surprising to find a wide variety of hard copy, CD-ROM and on-line information sources carrying financial information. Some of the most readily found are given below, while others will be discussed with the sources listed under the heading of stock market assessment:

- Extel cards probably offer the most comprehensive hard copy financial information service. **Extel's UK Listed Companies** service provides a set of information cards on all companies listed on the British and Irish stock exchanges. Subscribers to the service receive both an annual card offering a detailed summary of a company's financial performance and activities, together with cumulative news cards issued as and when important information on the company becomes available. Other card services offered by Extel Financial Services include:

- **Unlisted Securities Market Service** – information on over 400 companies traded on the stock exchange's Unlisted Securities Market;
- **Unquoted Companies Service** – information on unquoted companies.

- *The Hambro Company Guide* provides an up-to-date printed source on key aspects of the financial performance of major companies. The guide provides details of the five-year financial records of the companies covered and is printed four times a year. It can be found in most large libraries. A companion publication is the *Arthur Andersen Corporate Register* which is a useful source on UK management. Published twice a year, the register offers a management profile of leading companies, identifying executive and non-executive directors and offering a short biographical note on each.

- *FAME (Financial Analysis Made Easy)* is a comprehensive CD-ROM database on both large and small companies, which is updated on a monthly basis. The entries include financial history, ratios and trends, but excludes share price information. The data can be displayed and printed in a graphical format, and the software allows for the manipulation of annual report information to enable statistical analysis to take place.

Funding announcements

In the same way as a company will make announcements about acquisitions/disposals, funding raising operations are likely to lead to the company issuing a press release. Indeed, if the funding development is linked to a major acquisition the financial implications of the company's strategy are likely to be incorporated into a single statement by the company's broker on behalf of the company. Illustration 4.8 provides an example.

Illustration 4.8

UB PLC – ACQUISITION OF CCA SNACKS
Funding the acquisition
'The acquisition is being financed in part by a placing of new UB ordinary shares to raise approximately £80 million and the balance is being financed from UB's existing resources.
'24.1 million new ordinary UB shares are being placed with institutional investors at a price of 332 pence per share.'
Source: Morgan Grenfell press release, 10 November 1992.

Stock market assessment

Preliminary statements

Prior to the publication of the annual report, a company will make a preliminary announcement of its results. A company's preliminary statement will contain a summary of the principal elements of the company's trading performance for the reporting period by including a consolidated profit statement. In addition, there is likely to be a commentary explaining key aspects of the company's performance for the year being reported.

Whilst preliminary statements do not contain the breadth and detail of a company's annual report they do provide analysts and investors with the first details of the company's reported trading performance for the period. As a result it is the release of the preliminary results which tends to be the focus of newspaper comment, with the subsequent publication of the annual report not being reported upon unless it contains major new information.

Information retrieval systems

Most stock market information is held in computer databases, which take their lead from information published in the *Financial Times*. Details of the statistics published in the *Financial Times* and suggestions as to some of their principal uses can be found in *A Guide to Financial Statistics*, 2nd edition, 1989. The advent of computer databases has assisted greatly the ability to review trends in a company's share price when compared to, say, the Financial Times All Share Index. Two examples of the computer services available to anyone wishing to monitor market trends are given below.

- **Datastream** not only holds information on individual companies' accounts, but also offers the option of plotting share price movements to assess relative performance. For the occasional user this on-line service is relatively expensive, although a number of university libraries do have access to Datastream for educational purposes.
- **Microview/Microextel** also give daily share price movements and key performance ratios by accessing information from Extel's financial and stock market database. The computerized database is constantly updated, and also contains information on any changes the company has made to its capital structure. Again the user is given the option of graphing share price trends relative to a sector or the market in total. Similarly, Microview provides company-based financial information and allows inter-company or sector comparisons to be made.

Current market rating

Unless you are interested in continuous dealing on the stock market and wish to access the movements of the market throughout the trading day, the previous day's closing share price as printed in the next morning's newspapers should be adequate for most users. With the advent of personal computers it is relatively easy for individual investors to develop their own company share price databases if they wish to do so, and to plot how an individual share moves relative to the market.

The business sections of each of the quality papers will also carry a report of the main companies featured in the day's trading and the reasons for any change in the share price. These reports together with any weekly review published in the weekend press or *Investors' Chronicle* can be helpful in revealing if a company share price has moved significantly and some of the reasons why.

Future earnings

Reaction to a company's reported performance or any trading statements issued will be made by stock market analysts. These analysts will compare the company's actual performance with their forecasts, and offer judgements on the company accordingly. Their views are likely to be set out in a short written circular with a recommendation – buy, hold or sell – to investors as to what action, if any, they should take. Occasionally, analysts may publish a detailed assessment of the company with an in-depth analysis of its business prospects, the quality of management and other information affecting projected performance. Market analysts' circulars also contain financial projections, including estimates of future earnings.

Analysts' estimates of future earnings are now available to private investors and researchers with the publication of the *Estimate Directory* (Edinburgh Financial Publishing, Edinburgh) and the *Earnings Guide* (Earnings Guide Ltd, Horsham, West Sussex) on a monthly basis. Both publications provide analysts' forecasts of a company's profits, earnings and dividends for the next two years, together with other relevant information concerning relative share price performance, prospective p/e ratios and major shareholders.

It is hard to overstate the value of these two respective monthly publications for keeping abreast of the latest City forecasts for any given company. Both publications cover all UK companies with a market capitalization greater than £10 m, with the *Earnings Guide* also providing entries on leading European companies. While a company's annual and interim reports provide information on the recent past, the forecasts of profits and earnings give invaluable insights into future expected performance.

Summary

To summarize, the principal information sources for company-based information with regard to cells 1, 2 and 3 in Table 4.1 are listed in Table 4.4.

Table 4.4 *Company level analysis – principal information sources*

	Assessing strategic direction	Financial statement analysis	Stock market assessment
Company	1. • Chairman's statement • Directors' report • Business history • Company and unit announcements • Newspaper reports	2. • Company's annual and interim report • Extel cards • Hambro Company Guide • FAME	3. • Datastream • Microview/ Microextel, • Business press • The Earnings Guide • The Estimate Directory
Industry/sector	4.	5.	6.
Broad context	7.	8.	9.

Industry/sector analysis

The second category of information relates to industry/sector analysis, the middle circle in Figure 4.1. Broadly an industry may be defined as a group of firms offering products or services which are close substitutes for each other. Table 4.5 illustrates again the key information requirements at the level of the industry/sector.

Table 4.5 *Industry/sector level of analysis – key information requirements*

	Assessing strategic direction	Financial statement analysis	Stock market assessment
Company	1.	2.	3.
Industry/sector	4. Evaluate competitive forces and relative strengths and strategies of competitors. Review key industry drivers and likely future pattern of development	5. Make comparisons with other companies operating in the same or similar product markets	6. Compare company's rating to other companies in the same sector. Review performance of sector against overall market
Broad context	7.	8.	9.

As with the previous level of analysis, and notwithstanding some overlap between the key information requirements, Table 4.6 lists the major sources appropriate for undertaking analysis at the level of the industry or sector.

Table 4.6 *Major sources of industry/sector based information*

Assessing strategic direction:	
• Competitor strategies	(Annual and interim reports)
• Official government statistics	(Business Monitor Series, Monthly Digest of Statistics, etc.)
• Non-official industry sources:	
– market research publications	(Commercial research bodies)
– trade associations	(CBD directories)
– trade journals	(The Source Book)
Financial statement analysis:	
• Inter-company comparisons	(Annual and interim reports)
• Business ratios	(ICC, Dun and Bradstreet)
• Company rankings	(European Top 500, Times 100, Fortune Top 500)
Stock market assessment:	
• Sector ratings and trends	(Business press, Datastream, Microextel)
• Industry risk	(LBS Risk Measurement Service)

Assessing strategic direction

Competitor strategies

Just as important as reading and analysing a particular company's reported performance (annual and interim reports) and future earnings prospects (analysts' forecasts) is the need to do the same for industry competitors. Competitors may provide important clues as to who is winning the competitive battle, or what is the state of the trading environment. Given the diversity of markets served by large companies such as UB, it is important to define the distinctive product markets in which the major business units operate. With respect to UB, these have been defined as biscuits, savoury snacks, chocolate/sugar confectionery and frozen foods. For illustrative purposes, attention in the remainder of this section will be focused on the United Kingdom biscuit market.

Table 4.7 lists some of the major players in the UK biscuit market, as discovered from some of the data sources identified in Table 4.3. The information contained in Table 4.7 shows that the major competitive brands are not owned by single-product companies, but comprise divisional units of much

Table 4.7 UK biscuit producers – major companies and selected brands

Brands[1]	Company[2]	Corporate parent[3]	Segment
Wagon Wheels Jammie Dodgers Jaffa Cakes	Burton	Associated British Foods (ABF) plc	Chocolate coated Sweet/semi-sweet
Club Peek Frean Cream Crackers Twiglets	Huntley and Palmers Jacob's	BSN NV	Chocolate coated Sweet/semi-sweet Plain/savoury
Cadbury's Biscuits	Premier Brands	Hillsdown Holdings plc	Chocolate coated
Malted Milk Retailer own brand	Elkes Biscuits	Northern Foods plc	Sweet Elkes;/ semi-sweet
Classic Collection Crinkle Crunch	Fox's	Northern Foods plc	Chocolate coated Sweet/semi-sweet
McVitie's Digestive Chocolate Home Wheat Hob-Nobs Rich Tea Carr's Table Water Chedders	McVitie's	United Biscuits plc	Sweet;/semi-sweet Chocolate coated Plain/savoury

1. *A–Z UK Brands*/annual reports.
2. *Kompass.*
3. *Who Owns Who.*

larger business enterprises. All of the biscuit brands listed are produced by companies owned by major multi-business food manufacturing companies – ABF, BSN, Hillsdown Holdings, Northern Foods and UB. By examining copies of the annual and interim reports for these companies it should be possible to discern from a review of the companies' operations important insights about each of the biscuit companies listed. This information can then be used in developing a database on biscuit manufacturers.

Importantly, Table 4.7 contains information on market segments. This relates back to the question of competitive scope identified in the discussion of competitive advantage in Chapter 2. Not all companies will seek to serve the same market segments, and it is important very often to disaggregate down to product markets to assess the relative strength of competitors in different markets. Choosing how to segment any industry may be relatively easy, or may require careful thought.

Just as UK biscuit companies export to mainland Europe, leading European biscuit manufacturers supply the UK market. While it is relatively straightforward to identify the key European players using directories such as *Major Companies of Europe* (Graham & Trotman, 1991), ascertaining appropriate financial data may be more problematic than for UK-based companies. This is attributable to difficulties in reconciling varying European accounting standards in general, and the prevalence of large privately owned companies in Germany in particular.

Official government statistics

To facilitate data triangulation, it is necessary to compare the aggregate picture derived from individual companies with published data at the industry level. The business statistical offices of the various national governments are the prime source for this information. For UK-based industry the Business Monitor Series offers data on past movements in production, exports and imports. As with its European counterparts, the data is compiled at various levels of aggregation. With respect to biscuit manufacturing, these range from a broad definition (food manufacturing) to a narrow definition (biscuits and crispbread). Harmonization of European industry statistics is far from complete. Mort (1992) provides a very practical guide to the numerous statistical offices publishing official statistics.

It is important to be clear why this painstaking collection and collation of industry statistics is so necessary. The following three reasons are perhaps the most important:

- First, as an indication of 'market concentration'. By cross-referencing corporate and business turnover data with associated industry data, it is possible to discern the extent to which small numbers of large biscuit manufacturers dominate the market.
- Secondly, to gain a measure of domestic market size. For any country the size of the domestic market is home manufactured deliveries *plus* total imports *less* total exports.
- Thirdly, as an account of trade flows. A net surplus will occur when domestic production exceeds domestic consumption; a net deficit when domestic consumption exceeds domestic production. A net surplus may suggest that companies based in the country possess a competitive advantage.

Other industry-based information likely to be produced by official sources includes producer prices which will indicate the extent to which the industry is experiencing a change in its cost of producing or distributing goods or services. Producer price indexes assist in the removal of inflation from data covering a number of years, and facilitate an understanding of the underlying trend.

Non-official industry sources

It is regrettable that many of the more easily accessible non-official sources of industry/sector data add little value to government statistics, and may contain major inaccuracies. Thankfully not all commercially produced research falls into this category. The litmus tests for all non-official statistics are 'complementarity' and 'additionality'. The former refers to the ability of the information source to provide a synthesis of the most up-to-date government statistics, thereby saving the researcher much time and effort. The latter refers to highly valuable information that bridges the gap between bottom-up (a company-based approach) and top-down (where a company's identity is concealed on account of the confidentiality of government statistics). Where a non-official information source passes the test of additionality it will add to the researcher's understanding of the industry and the competitive position of key players in the market.

The need to assess non-official sources serves as a timely warning to avoid excessive use of one data source, as well as emphasizing again the importance of data triangulation. Some of the best sources for identifying non-official information sources are as follows:

- Global: *Market Search* is published annually by Arlington Management Publications Limited and is a directory of published research studies on markets across the world. A further source worth consulting is Bell (1989), *Directory of International Sources of Business Information.* For the US, the *US Industrial Outlook* is a very useful source for analysing industries.
- European: *The European Directory of Non-Official Statistics Sources* (Euromonitor) is a useful starting point, together with Mort (1991), *European Market Information: a handbook for managers.*
- UK: Two illustrative examples are *The A–Z of UK Marketing Sources* (Euromonitor), and *The Source Book* published by Keynote which reviews numerous industry/sectors and identifies:
  - trade bodies
  - trade directories
  - statistical and other sources
  - periodicals
  - on-line databases.

Market research

A number of organizations publish a general series of reports focusing on individual industries and sectors, including: Euromonitor, Economists' Intelligence Unit (EIU), Jordans, Mintel, and ICC. Increasingly these organizations publish both for the UK and Europe. For example, Euromonitor publishes *Market Research Great Britain* and *Market Research Europe.* Both publications appear monthly and deal with consumer markets. Further, there are a number of market research organizations which provide specialist analysis of a single sector, e.g. Verdict Research covering retailing. Similarly, the Henley Centre for Forecasting produces a regular publication, *Leisures Futures*, assessing trends in the principal leisure markets in the UK. A number of the major libraries contain collections of at least some of the general industry/sector series, e.g. the Science Reference Library, Holborn, London; the City Business Library, Moorgate, London; the Export Market Intelligence Library, DTI, Westminster, London; etc.

Trade associations

A further non-official information source, generally on individual industries, is provided by the trade associations. CBD Research publishes a *Directory of European Industrial and Trade Associations* which covers all countries of Europe except the UK and Ireland, together with a full listing of domestic associations in a sister publication *Directory of British Associations.* Trade associations vary enormously in their size, resources and publications. Some associations are significant organizations in their own right, for example the Society of Motor Manufacturers and Traders (SMMT), whilst others are much more modest in their scope. Data produced and published by the SMMT is the basis used for evaluating new vehicle sales in the UK, and is regularly commented on by the media. The larger organizations, including the SMMT, produce highly valuable industry-based statistics and/or commentaries on their sector. Where this is the case the company analyst should seek out these sources accordingly.

For the biscuit industry the Biscuit, Cake, Chocolate & Confectionery Alliance (BCCCA) provides detailed statistics of the UK market allowing the analyst to gain a good appreciation of trends in production, consumption and trade. Illustration 4.9 shows some of the industry statistics available from the BCCCA, whose coverage exceeds 95% of UK biscuit manufacturers.

Illustration 4.9

UK PRODUCTION, CONSUMPTION AND NET TRADE FLOW OF BISCUITS AND CRISPBREADS (TONNES), 1988–90			
	1988	1989	1990
1. Home market dispatches	582,000	571,000	576,900
2. Export market dispatches	72,130	75,020	76,580
3. Imports	23,020	29,400	31,360
4. UK production (1 + 2)	654,330	646,520	653,480
Year-on-year change (%)	+2.1	−1.2	+1.1
5. UK consumption (1 + 3)	605,220	600,900	608,260
Year-on-year change (%)	+2.6	−0.7	+1.2
6. Trade surplus	49,110	45,620	45,220
Year-on-year change (%)	−3.3	−7.1	−0.9

Home trade dispatches: added value, 1990	Value (%)	Volume (%)	Value/ vol. ratio
Chocolate coated biscuits	35.5	26.4	1.34
Sweet/semi-sweet	46.8	57.7	0.81
Plain/savoury	17.6	15.8	1.11

Source: Based on *The Biscuit, Cake, Chocolate and Confectionery Alliance, Statistical Year Book, 1990.*

Trade journals

A further related source of information is the trade journal. This may be a weekly, monthly or quarterly publication often written by a small number of people connected closely with an industry. These publications may offer informed comment about some of the latest industry-wide developments including technological change, or simply include social news. Again they are worth checking if only to reject. The *Research Index* discussed earlier covers many of the better known trade publications and is helpful to use in identifying published articles from this information source. Equally, *The Source Book* discussed earlier offers information on trade journals relating to individual sectors.

As with many things the more researchers develop their knowledge of an industry/sector, the more able they are to locate sources of information on assessing strategic direction.

Financial statement analysis

Inter-company comparisons

Once the annual and interim reports have been obtained for competitors it is possible to carry out a comparative analysis reviewing one company's perform-ance against another. This allows the relative performance of different compa-nies in the industry to be assessed. Some of the difficulties associated with ensuring that such comparisons are meaningful will be discussed in Chapter 7 which focuses on comparative financial performance.

Business ratios

Financial comparisons for companies operating in the same industry or sector can also be found by consulting the Business Ratio series produced by the ICC Company Information Service. Reports in this series of publications attempt to allocate companies to particular industries in order to allow peer group comparison. Care should be taken to check the definition of any financial ratio generated, as definitions do vary: ICC also publish an annual publication on all industrial sectors – *Industrial Performance Analysis* – which gives ratio com-parisons for a single financial year.

A rival publication is produced by Dun and Bradstreet International, *Key British Ratios: The Guide to British Business Performance.* This is a compilation of ratios calculated from the audited accounts of UK companies. The informa-tion provided includes performance ratios shown by quartiles and common sized balance sheets and profit and loss accounts. The *Bank of England Quarterly Bulletin* also publishes an annual table of corporate profitability by industry sector.

Company rankings

The Financial Times publishes an annual survey of the European Top 500 companies by market capitalization, providing general information on turnover, profits and return on capital employed. Market capitalization is used to rank the size of companies in order to avoid differences in national accounting bases which affect measures of corporate profitability. Each company included in the publication is allocated to an industrial sector and this can be used to identify the major players in each European industry. The European Top 500 also provides separate rankings of British companies. Other publications offer similar lists on a global and/or national basis. These include, for example, The Times 1000 and Fortune 500.

Some of the disadvantages of using published summaries of industry performance is the extent to which information is out of date by the time it is published. Particularly with regard to comparisons of business ratios at the level of the industry, there are considerable time lags in companies publishing their accounts and information being collected, collated and published. There are also considerable problems in verifying the precise industry definition and its compatibility with the boundaries required by the user. Perhaps the greatest value of such data is the lead they give to benchmarking, a necessary requirement if one company's performance is to be compared with that of competitors.

Stock market assessment

Sector ratings and trends

Stock market assessment of industry performance is of necessity going to adopt a broad industry definition on account of there being a marked absence of large single-product manufacturers and service providers in most areas of an economy. The absence of large single-product biscuit manufacturers is no exception, requiring sector comparisons to be made on the basis of a broad definition of the industry, namely food manufacturing.

This is one of the sectors defined for the purposes of compiling the FT-A All Share Index which is the principal measure of overall stock market performance in the UK. The *Financial Times*, together with a number of other newspapers, reports trends in stock market indices for each sector and the share prices of companies allocated to each sector. When compared to the overall movement in the stock market, the relative performance of a sector against the market can be determined. Historical trends of the performance of a sector against the market are most easily obtained by accessing one of the on-line or CD-ROM information retrieval systems discussed earlier.

Industry risk

The extent to which share price movements in a company or sector exaggerate or understate movements in the overall market is measured by the company's *beta*. A beta of 1 implies that a company or sector's rate of return will correspond to the stock market overall. Shares with a beta greater than 1 are more volatile than the market, while the reverse is true for a beta of less than 1. The London Business School (LBS) Risk Measurement Service calculates betas for all the major UK listed companies and industry groupings, publishing their findings four times a year.

Summary

Table 4.8 summarizes the information sources which can be consulted at the level of industry/sector analysis.

Table 4.8 Industry/sector level of analysis – principal information sources

	Assessing strategic direction	Financial statement analysis	Stock market assessment
Company	1.	2.	3.
Industry/sector	4. • Annual and interim reports of competitors • Official government statistics • Commercially available desk research • Trade associations • Trade journals	5. • Annual and interim reports of competitors • Business ratio reports • The European Top 500, Times 1000, etc.	6. • Business press • On-line databases, CD-ROM • LBS Risk Management Service
Broad context	7.	8.	9.

Assessing the broad context

The third category of analysis is concerned with the organization's broad context. This is the outermost circle as illustrated in Figure 4.1. The broad context is concerned with all the general contextual factors which potentially have an important effect on the organization. Amongst the most important in assessing strategic direction can be political, economic, social and technological factors. Equally, the environment for raising additional capital or likely changes to the tax regime and interest rates could be critical in respect of future financing. Table 4.9 illustrates the key information requirements in respect of the broad context.

Some of the key sources of information available in respect of the broad context are identified in Table 4.10.

Table 4.9 *Broad context level of analysis – key information requirements*

	Assessing strategic direction	Financial statement analysis	Stock market assessment
Company	1.	2.	3.
Industry/sector	4.	5.	6.
Broad context	7. Assess key PEST change agents, i.e. P – political E – economic S – social T – technological factors	8. Evaluate opportunities for funding raising (debt and equity), likely tax and interest rate changes, etc.	9. Identify movements in the overall stock market, and likely future pattern of share prices

Table 4.10 *Major sources of information available in relation to the broad context*

Assessing strategic direction:	
• Economic forecasts • National statistics and trends	(IMF, OECD, NIESR, etc.) (CSO publications, commercially produced reports)
Financial statement analysis:	
• Annual tax and revenue statements • Cost of funds	(HMSO publications, business press) (FT-A Fixed Index Indices)
Stock market assessment:	
• Market forecasts	(Brokers' reports, business press)

Assessing strategic direction

Economic forecasts

Working at the level of the broad context an important starting point is to gain an overall view of future economic developments and how these are likely to influence demand in particular sectors of the economy upon which the business is dependent. Forecasting the future economic context will require judgements about the political context at both the international and national level given that many economic decisions are inherently political by nature, and that international and national decision-making are increasingly interrelated.

Where a company operates in a number of geographical markets an assessment of the broad economic context will require an evaluation of the likely performance of the different national economies. For example, UB has a heavy exposure to both the UK and North American economies, and the future pattern of developments in both economies is therefore likely to have a major influence on company performance. Both the International Monetary Fund (IMF) and the Organization for Economic Co-operation and Development (OECD) provide forecasts for the major economies of the world. Further, a number of UK-based organizations, for instance the National Institute for Economic and Social Research (NIESR) in its quarterly review, offer a commentary on developments in the major world economies as well as providing a detailed assessment of the UK economy. The major finance houses in the City of London also provide regular global and country specific bulletins discussing economic and political factors and how these may influence future prospects. Similarly, the *Financial Times* publishes individual country reports as supplements to its main sections on an occasional basis. These reports invariably provide an assessment of the overall economic/political context to the country, and discuss future prospects. Using a combination of the sources listed should enable the reader to gain an appreciation of the likely future economic performance of the national economy under focus.

National statistics and trends

For the individual not wishing to rely on the interpretation that others have placed on the numbers there is always the option of consulting the official sources of information and assessing recent trends for themselves. Using the UK as an example the Central Statistical Office (CSO) produces a range of publications which may be consulted to gain an understanding of key national trends. For those unfamiliar with many of the sources the CSO's *Guide to Official Statistics* is a useful starting point.

The monthly publications *Economic Trends* and the *Monthly Digest of Statistics* collectively provide up-to-date information on most of the major economic series covering the UK economy. For those wanting information as it becomes available press releases are worth considering, although those of importance tend to be summarized in the following day's *Financial Times*. The publication *Financial Statistics* is a monthly source of financial statistics, indicating, for example, trends in lending and borrowing.

An annual publication offering longer-term series on areas including industrial output and consumers' spending is the so-called 'Blue Book' dealing with *National Income and Expenditure*. There is an accompanying guide to this publication entitled *Sources and Methods*, detailing how information is collected and the likely levels of accuracy.

Complementary to the publication of economic data are the publications providing information on social and demographic trends. These publications are worth looking at over a number of years as information is not always reproduced each year. For the UK *Social Trends*, published annually, is of invaluable assistance when reviewing, for example, lifestyle trends. Information on demographic trends, in addition to the general review published in *Social Trends*, may be found in the publications produced by the Office of Population and Census Surveys. A third publication, *The Family Expenditure Survey*, provides an annual cross-sectional survey on households in the UK and is helpful in reviewing purchasing patterns by different income groups.

Some of the commercial market research organizations cited earlier under industry analysis do from time to time produce broad studies of society highlighting social-economic trends and drawing on government statistics as well as any primary research they have undertaken. These studies, whilst they can be expensive to obtain, can be particularly useful in gaining an overall appreciation of, for example, lifestyle changes within society and emerging fashions.

Financial statement analysis

Budget and autumn statements

Assessing the likely pattern of tax changes requires a review of the political as well as economic climate. The monitoring of government statements can provide important clues to future developments which subsequently are announced in the country's annual budget. For the UK the *Financial Statement and Budget Report* ('Red Book'), published by Her Majesty's Stationery Office (HMSO) and available immediately after the budget statement has been delivered, provides the details of any tax changes, together with the Treasury's economic forecast. Similarly, the announcement of the public expenditure plans, which from November 1993 will coincide with changes on the revenue side, provide an important guide to public spending. Where public spending forms a high proportion of an industry's or company's sales these announcements should be monitored with particular care. This is also the case where a major spending decision by the government is awaited. For example, the future of British Aerospace plc, the UK's largest military aircraft builder, was heavily dependent on the decision on whether or not to build the European Fighter Aircraft (EFA). Prior to a major decision being made, ministerial comment and statements should be monitored carefully.

The Red Book, published at the time of the budget, contains estimates of the government's borrowing requirement for the next financial year. The borrowing requirement and likely pattern of interest rates are two of the key factors which influence the funding environment not only for government, but also for companies. Stockbrokers will use the information on the outlook for government borrowing and interest rates, together with an assessment of the current and future prospects for corporate earnings, levels of savings and indebtedness, to develop a view as to the likely climate for companies wishing to raise additional funds on the stock market. At the same time all the various factors will be collated and a view as to the likely movement of share prices arrived at.

The cost of funds

The economic policies of any government and the decisions which are announced will have a significant influence on the cost of funds to corporate borrowers. Regardless of whether a company is attempting to raise additional funds by issuing shares or by borrowing, if government policies lead to the expectation that interest rates will rise, the cost of funds to all borrowers, including companies, will rise. This is clearly important for those companies seeking additional funds to maintain or expand their operations. The FT-A Fixed Interest Indices published in *The Financial Times* daily offer a broad indicator of the cost of borrowing funds for five, ten and 25 years. By tracking movements in the indices over time it is possible to analyse how the cost of borrowed funds has changed. The average cost of additional borrowings is shown by the current levels of the index.

Stock market assessment

Market forecasts

Just as economists attempt to forecast the future pattern of the economy, so equity analysts employed by the major investment houses attempt to forecast the future levels of share prices. They will collect all the relevant information relating to the broad context and forecast the general level of the market in the future. These analysts – or strategists as they are sometimes called – essentially consider overall trends and do not seek to forecast movements to an individual company's share price. They are primarily concerned with such macro level questions as will equities in general provide a higher return than alternative investments? The findings of equity analysts are published fairly frequently by the investment houses, thereby providing a view of the overall future pattern of share prices.

Summary

Table 4.11 summarizes the principal information sources at the level of the broad context.

Table 4.11 *Broad context level of analysis – principal information sources*

	Assessing strategic direction	Financial statement analysis	Stock market assessment
Company	1.	2.	3.
Industry/sector	4.	5.	6.
Broad context	7. • Forecasts by IMF, OECD, NIESR • Government statistics and publications • Commercial market research	8. • Annual tax and revenue statements • FT-A Fixed Interest Indices	9. • Institutional reports on future stock market levels

Collating the information

A complete list of the principal sources for each of the three sets of information – assessing strategic direction, financial statement analysis and stock market assessment – and the three levels of analysis – company, industry/sector and broad context – is provided in Table 4.12. This draws together Tables 4.4, 4.8 and 4.11. Through carefully collecting and assessing information in relation to each of the nine cells first identified in Table 4.1, the researcher will gain a thorough understanding of the company which is being assessed.

A number of important issues concerning information collating have been noted. First, the order in which the search for information is undertaken is far less important than the systematic route adopted by the researcher. Second, it is of critical importance to link contemporary financial and non-financial information sources. Third, the necessity for data triangulation cannot be overemphasized. It provides a 'fail-safe' mechanism for establishing the robustness of the information set. Four, excessive focus on the past should be avoided. It is more important to collect information about current and future trends, and less critical to review history. Finally, it is essential to collate the material in a sound and sensible manner so that information retrieval effectiveness matches the data collected.

Concluding remarks

The information gathered in Table 4.12 enables the researcher to identify the company's businesses and strategic direction, to make judgements of the company's management, to consider performance to date, and to assess how the stock market rates the organization. From this information the researcher, be

Table 4.12 *All levels of analysis – summary of key information sources*

	Assessing strategic direction	Financial statement analysis	Stock market assessment
Company	**1.** • Chairman's statement • Directors' report • Business history • Company and unit announcements • Newspaper reports	**2.** • Company's annual and interim report • Extel cards • *Hambro Company Guide*	**3.** • Datastream • Microview/ Microextel • Business press • *The Earnings Guide* • *The Estimate Directory*
Industry/sector	**4.** • Annual and interim reports of competitors • Official government statistics • Commercially available desk research • Trade associations • Trade journals	**5.** • Annual and interim reports of competitors • Business ratio reports • The European Top 500, T imes 1000, etc	**6.** • Business press • On-line databases, CD-ROM • LBS Risk Management Service
Broad context	**7.** • Forecasts by IMF, OECD, NIESR • Government statistics and publications • Commercial market research	**8.** • Annual tax and revenue changes and public expenditure • FT-A Fixed Interest Indices	**9.** • Institutional reports on future stock market levels

it an external analyst or internal management, will be able to judge whether the company is maximizing its value creating opportunities or whether there is considerable scope to enhance the value of the organization.

In reviewing how professional analysts go about accomplishing this task it is interesting to consider some recent research which has been carried out. Illustration 4.10 highlights their reliance on company-based information in analysing companies.

To assist in the practical task of collecting information and making judge ments of likely future corporate performance the chapter is concluded with a checklist covering the key issues highlighted in the text.

Illustration 4.10

WHAT INFORMATION SOURCES DO PROFESSIONAL ANALYSTS VALUE MOST HIGHLY?		

A recent survey of the views of investment analysts provides some insight into which sources of information are most highly prized. The survey asked analysts to rate the importance of different data sources on a company for the purposes of investment decisions. The importance of each source was measured on a scale of 1 (extremely important) to 5 (of no importance). The results reproduced below provide some interesting insights.

Sources of information	Mean score	Rank
Preliminary statements	1.27	1
Personal interviews with company	1.48	2=
Interim statements	1.48	2=
Company presentations	1.57	4
Annual reports	1.62	5
Telephone call to company officials	2.10	6
Company public relations	2.29	7
Visits to company	2.33	8
Trade journals	2.38	9
Company literature other than financial statements	2.62	10
Datastream or similar	2.81	11
Industry and government statistics	3.19	12
Other analysts	3.57	13

Source: Hussey, R. and Bence, D. (1992) 'Analysts and the Cash Flow Statement'., *Accountancy*, September, p.138.

Checklist

- *Identify general information needs and potential sources of information.*
- *Plan information gathering, using secondary data sources to gain an overall understanding of the organization and its business.*
- *Consult company-based information to review overall strategic direction, management team and recent financial performance.*
- *Separate the different business activities and determine which industries need to be assessed.*
- *For each identified industry assess competitive trends and the relative position of the company compared to its competitors.*
- *Review broad context to industry sectors and organization.*
- *Collate analysis of individual business activities and undertake an overall assessment of the organization.*
- *Decide whether you believe the organization has been managed in a way which maximizes shareholder value.*

PART THREE

Financial Statement Analysis

As illustrated below, this part:

- seeks to make **access to financial analysis** easy, by clear and concise explanations and worked examples;
- illustrates the impact of **new accounting requirements** for UK companies and investors;
- emphasizes the distinction between cash and profits and why **cash generation** is so critical to a company's future;
- stresses the need to identify appropriate **benchmarks** by selecting other companies for inter-company comparisons.

Part I	The General Framework
Part II	Assessing Strategic Direction
Part III	**Financial Statement Analysis**
Part IV	Stock Market Assessment
Part V	The General Framework Revisited

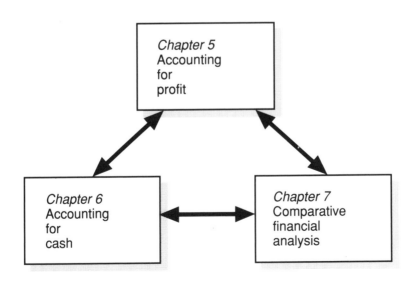

CHAPTER 5

Accounting for profit

The financial reporting of profit provides a key measure of the performance outcomes associated with an organization's strategy. To aid users' understanding of the published annual reports of companies, it is important to assimilate the basic principles which affect the quality of accounts and the clarity of their presentation. External users of published information will wish to appraise themselves of two sets of questions: what have been the financial outcomes to the strategies the company has pursued to date, and what is the financial position of the company at a given point in time? Answers to both of these questions can be found in two of a company's principal financial statements, namely the profit and loss account (P&L) and the balance sheet. The principal topics of the chapter, and their order of appearance, is as follows:

- *examining the profit and loss account*
- *deciding on a definition of profit*
- *balance sheet*
- *enhancing profits at the expense of the balance sheet*
- *new accounting standards for profit*
- *business unit profitability*
- *concluding remarks.*

The chapter begins with an examination of the format of the P&L account and precisely 'what is profit'. Subsequent discussion of the balance sheet also requires an appreciation of its format, as well as the important relationship between the P&L account and balance sheet. Some of the controversial techniques for enhancing profits at the expense of the balance sheet are highlighted. More effective accounting standards for the reporting of profit are considered in some detail, together with an appreciation of how changes by the Accounting Standards Board (ASB) should assist the interpretation of company accounts. The question of disaggregating corporate profitability to provide an insight into business unit performance is shown to be of considerable importance. Once again the chapter is concluded with a checklist.

Examining the profit and loss account

The P&L statement provides a record of the company's activities over a period of time. Most companies use a twelve-month reporting period – this is known as the accounting period. The profit and loss statement details the revenue the company has generated over the accounting period and the costs or expenses which have been incurred in producing such output. As its name suggests, it allows analysts to consider the extent to which a company has been trading at a profit or loss over a period of time. A company makes a profit when its revenue is in excess of its expenses. A loss is made when revenue is insufficient to cover the expenses. A simple numerical example illustrates the point. As Figure 5.1 shows, during a twelve-month accounting period Company A has generated revenues of £150 m and incurred expenses of £100 m, resulting in a operational profit of £50 m. By contrast, Company B incurs expenses of £150 m and generates revenues of £100 m; thereby incurring operating losses of £50 m.

Figure 5.2 indicates the principal items of revenue and expense to be encountered on Company A's P&L account. The company's revenue is generated from its turnover or sales (£150 m). It is from this figure that expenses or payments are subtracted as one moves down the P&L account. While total expenses – cost of sales (£80 m) and overheads (£20 m) – clearly sum to £100 m, only one profit figure – operating profit – matches the £50 m illustrated in Figure 5.1. The different layers of profit illustrate the need to take care when discussing profitability.

Table 5.1 *Pro-forma profit and loss account for Company A (52 weeks to 28 December 1993)*

	£m
Turnover	150.0
Cost of sales (including depreciation of £25m)	80.0
Gross profit	**70.0**
Overheads	20.0
Operating profit	**50.0**
Exceptional items (included to show positioning)	0.0
Profit on ordinary activities before interest	**50.0**
Interest	10.0
Profit on ordinary activities before tax	**40.0**
Tax	12.0
Profit on ordinary activities after tax	**28.0**
Minority interests	4.0
Profits attributable to shareholders	**24.0**
Extraordinary charges (credits)	10.0
Profit for the financial year	**14.0**
Dividends	7.0
Balance to reserves	7.0

Source: Figure 5.2.

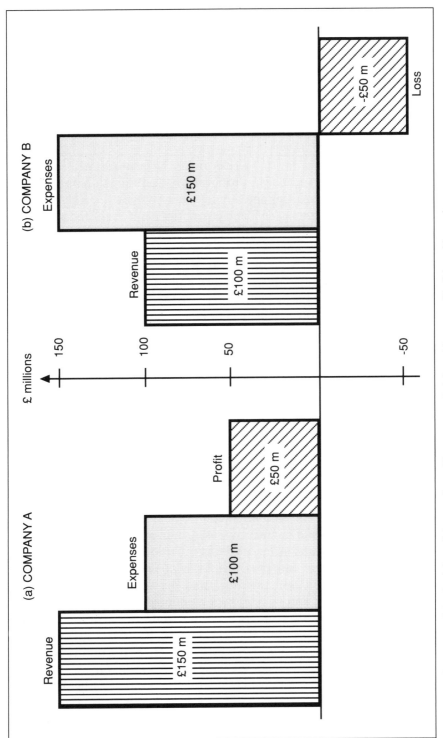

Figure 5.1 *The essential principles of the profit and loss account: (a) making a profit; (b) making a loss.*

A layered format is used for the profit and loss account, with the items commonly expressed in the vertical format shown in Table 5.1. Notice the pro-forma P&L account offers not one, but seven named types of profit, namely gross profit, operating profit, profit on ordinary activities before interest, profit on ordinary activities before tax, profit on ordinary activities after tax, profit attributable to shareholders, and profit for the financial year. The alternative layers each offer different insights into the company's performance. Detailed consideration as to which profit figure to use will be based on the profit levels reported by UB for 1991, to which we now turn.

UB's P&L account for the 52 weeks to 28 December 1991 begins by identifying the company's *turnover*. Turnover (or sales) is the sum the company has gained from providing goods and services as part of the company's ordinary operating activities, excluding VAT and other sales based taxes and after trade discounts. During the 52 weeks to 28 December 1991, UB's accounting period, the company's turnover amounted to £2,660.5 m. From this income the company needs to deduct the *cost of sales*. Cost of sales is the sum of costs incurred in the production of the company's goods and services. For example, for biscuit manufacturing it includes the cost of ingredients, the direct labour costs of running the factory and depreciation on plant and machinery. Depreciation is the amount the company sets aside each year to cover the gradual reduction in the value of a fixed asset which has a limited working life. For example, machinery becomes worn out and obsolescent in time. UB's cost of sales in 1991 amounted to £1,490.8 m, including £75.3 m for depreciation. Subtracting the cost of sales from the company's turnover gives the *gross profit:*

	£m
Turnover	2,660.5
Cost of sales (including depreciation of £75 m)	1,490.8
Gross profit	**1,169.7**

Gross profit represents the company's profit before indirect or overhead expenses have been met. UB's accounts show two major categories of *overheads* – distribution, selling and marketing costs, and administrative expenses. *Distribution, marketing and selling costs,* as the title suggests, is the sum the company has spent, in the case of United Biscuits, on moving its products to wholesalers and retailers, and the associated marketing and selling costs. Distribution, marketing and selling costs amounted to £786.1 m in 1991. *Administrative expenses* cover a range of costs including head office, directors' fees and auditing expenses. In 1991 these costs amounted to £141.4 m. Deducting the cost of sales and overhead expenses from the turnover, and adjusting for other income, provides the company's *operating profit*. This is also known as trading profit or profit before interest and taxation. Other income, a small item, made a positive contribution of £2.7 m during 1991, and includes income from ordinary activities which is not assigned to another heading, e.g. royalties and rents.

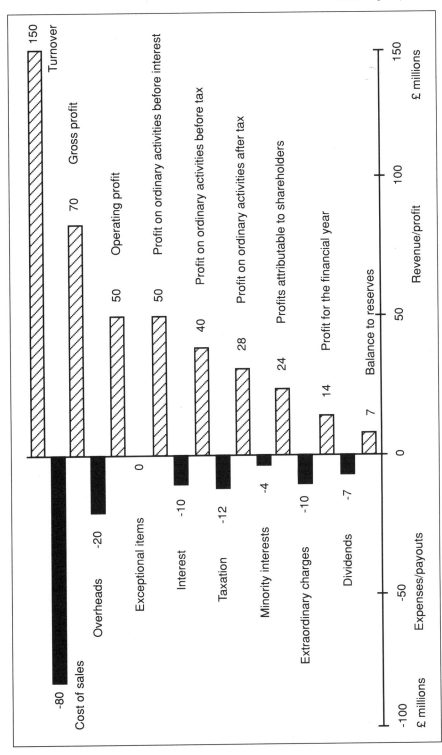

Figure 5.2 *Principal items of the profit and loss account*

For 1991 UB succeeded in generating an operating profit of £244.9 m.

		£m
Gross profit		**1,169.7**
Overheads:		
Distribution, selling and marketing costs	786.1	
Administrative expenses	141.4	
Other income	(2.7)	924.8
Operating profit		**244.9**

Operating profit is shown prior to any adjustment for identifiable *exceptional items*. Exceptional items are defined as material items arising out of the ordinary activities of the business, but whose size or incidence requires them to be disclosed separately if the accounts are to provide a true and fair view of the business. As UB had no identifiable exceptional items in 1991, their position is shown on the P&L account for illustrative purposes only:

	£m
Operating profit	**244.9**
Exceptional items	0.0
Profit on ordinary activities before interest	**244.9**

Profit on ordinary activities before interest is an important figure as it shows how much the company has made from its trading activities. It is calculated before making adjustments for any interest payments on borrowings, profit sharing or taxation.

Interest payments are the next major item of expense. The sum reported on the face of the P&L account is a net figure. In a note to the accounts, which is reproduced below, UB reveals that the company paid interest of £37.8 m in 1991 and received £6.1 m, leading to a net outflow of £31.7 m.

'Notes to accounts' provide greater detail for some of the key lines of accounting information appearing on the face of a company's principal financial statements and should be consulted in order to gain a full appreciation of how a summary figure is calculated:

		£m
Interest payable		
Bank loans and overdrafts	15.0	
Loans wholly repayable within five years	6.5	
Loans not wholly repayable within five years	12.9	
Lease and other	3.4	
		37.8
Interest receivable		
Short-term deposits and loans	2.9	
Other	3.2	
		6.1
		31.7

Source: Note 3, *UB 1991 Annual Report*, March 1992, p.41.

Profit sharing indicates the allocation of profit to employees as part of the company's profit-sharing scheme. Profit sharing has become popular over the last ten years and many companies operate schemes for their employees. The costs to UB in operating its profit-sharing scheme in 1991 were £1.9 m.

Taxation refers to the amount of tax the company is paying. Again only the overall figure appears in the P&L account, with a more detailed breakdown being given in a note to the accounts. Tax on UB's ordinary activities amounted to £65.5 m in 1991:

	£m
Profit on ordinary activities before taxation	**244.9**
Interest	31.7
Profit before profit sharing	**213.2**
Profit sharing	1.9
Profit on ordinary activities before tax	**211.3**
Tax on ordinary activities	65.5
Profit on ordinary activities after tax	**145.8**

Once the company has paid tax it is often assumed that the remaining profits are available for distribution to shareholders, or to be retained in the business. In practice, further adjustments such as for *minority interests* and *extraordinary items* are required to the profit on ordinary activities after tax before issues of distribution can be considered. Minority interests arise when a company partly owns a subsidiary, indicating that other shareholders, who also partly owns the company, are entitled to a share of the profits. For example, UB owns only 50% of Aguia SA, a Brazilian biscuit manufacturer. The figure shown in the P&L account is the amount that has to be deducted from UB's profit to pay minority interests. In 1991 this amounted to £2.3 m. Adjusting for minority interests allows *profit attributable to shareholders* to be calculated. This is commonly referred to as the 'bottom line' figure for profit:

	£m
Profit on ordinary activities after tax	**145.8**
Minority interests	<u>2.3</u>
Profit attributable to shareholders	**143.5**

Before the profit for the financial year can be declared extraordinary items need to be discussed. In 1991 the definition of extraordinary items (subsequent changes are discussed later in the chapter) emphasized the fact that they relate to activities which fall outside the normal activities of the business and as a result were not expected to occur on a regular basis. For example, in 1991 UB's P&L shows an extraordinary charge of £13.4 m. Details of how this figure is made up are to be found in a note to the accounts:

	£m
Loss/(profit) on disposal of businesses	14.1
Deferred tax	(0.7)
	13.4

Source: Note 7, *UB Annual Report 1991*, March 1992, p.41.

The company's decision to withdraw from retail store distribution and various sectors of the ready meals and desserts markets is estimated to cost more than the proceeds realized from the disposal of the assets of these businesses, which after tax adjustments amounted to £13.4 m.

Subtracting extraordinary charges from the profit attributable to shareholders leaves *profit for the financial year*, which in 1991 amounted to £130.1m for UB:

	£m
Profits attributable to shareholders	**143.5**
Extraordinary charges	13.4
Profit for the financial year	**130.1**

Profits for the financial year are available for management to distribute. They have two choices. Profits can either be returned to shareholders in the form of *dividends*, or retained in the business and reinvested. Of the £130.1 m available to management, UB in 1991 decided to pay out £71.7 m in dividends leaving £58.4 m to be used to enhance the asset base of the business. As the balance sheet provides a statement of the company's assets and liabilities, this £58.4 m is described as the *balance to reserves*, and provides an important link between the P&L account and the balance sheet:

	£m
Profit for the financial year	**130.1**
Dividends	71.7
Balance to reserves	58.4

This concludes the description of the P&L account, which for convenience is reproduced in full in Table 5.2. Notice that the P&L account is the consolidated statement for UB, indicating that it covers all the group's operations.

Deciding on a definition of profit

A highly confusing question is which concept of profit does the analyst use? Is gross profit – the largest profit figure – the correct one? Alternatively, should attention be focused on definitions of profit calculated after all expenses have been met? The different definitions serve to emphasize that no single profit indicator is entirely adequate. Deciding on a suitable concept of profit is determined by the information need. If the underlying profitability of the business is the objective in reviewing a company's results, then it is *operating profit* – the profit from the company's trading activities – on which the analyst

Table 5.2 Consolidated profit and loss account, United Biscuits plc, 1991
(for the 52 weeks ended 28 December 1991)

		£m
Turnover		2,660.5
Cost of sales		1,490.8
Gross profit		1,169.7
Distribution, selling and marketing costs	786.1	
Administrative expenses	141.4	
Other income	(2.7)	
Operating profit		244.9
Exceptional items		0.0
Profit on ordinary activities before interest		244.9
Interest payable		31.7
Profit before profit sharing		213.2
Profit sharing		1.9
Profit on ordinary activities before tax		211.3
Tax on profit on ordinary activities		65.5
Profit on ordinary activities after tax		145.8
Minority interests		2.3
Profit attributable to shareholders		143.5
Extraordinary charges (credits)		13.4
Profit for the financial year		130.1
Dividends		71.7
Balance to reserves		58.4

Source: *United Biscuits plc Annual Report 1991*, March 1992, p.34.

should focus. Operating profit is also segmented in a company's accounts by trading activity, and is therefore a key figure in assessing business level performance.

The figure for operating profit does not include either deductions for interest or taxation. The exclusion of these items is made on the basis that interest payments are a function of the company's funding policies and therefore not reflective of the company's trading position. Similarly, deductions for tax are primarily a function of the external tax regime. Often the analyst will be interested in *profit on ordinary activities before tax*, or pre-tax profits as it is more commonly known. This figure takes into account both the company's operating performance and the interest cost of a company's borrowings.

In assessing a company's level of profit a second concept of profit that analysts are likely to focus on is *profit attributable to shareholders*, or earnings as it is often commonly called. The exclusion of extraordinary items from this figure has been justified on the grounds that they were non-recurring items. Hence they are less material to understanding the underlying position of the business and its maintainable earnings over time. This has been termed the 'current operating performance' concept of profit. The difficulty with this approach has been the temptation for companies to report losses as extraordinary, and any windfall profits as exceptional. The attraction of categorizing any losses as extraordinary items is that they are below the bottom line, i.e. the profit attributable to shareholders.

By dividing profit attributable to shareholders by the number of ordinary shares issued, a company's earnings per share (EPS) is calculated. EPS describes the amount a single shareholder would receive if all of a company's profits attributable to shareholders were distributed in the form of dividend payments. Companies have been keen to report continuous growth in EPS since this is a commonly accepted and reported financial ratio.

As a result, complex adjustments have been made to the reported profits to establish continuous growth in the EPS. Since exceptional items (unlike extraordinary) are included in the calculation of profits attributable to shareholders, they appear above the line and therefore influence the EPS. Consequently, a company wishing to window dress their accounts in order to enhance reported performance might wish unflattering financial performance to be recorded as extraordinary items, thereby excluding such transactions from the calculation of the EPS, as in Illustration 5.1.

Illustration 5.1

ALBERT FISHER PLC

Albert Fisher plc, a food processing and distribution company, illustrates the potential problems associated with extraordinary items. For the accounting year 1990/91 the company treated a £2 m profit on the sale of the stake in a joint venture after a recent acquisition as an exceptional item. As this appears above the line the EPS was correspondingly enhanced. By contrast a loss of £6.47 m on a US investment was treated as an extraordinary item, taken below the line, leaving the EPS unchanged.

The company defended its accounting policies on the grounds that the exceptional profit arose directly from its trading activities, whilst the extraordinary loss was caused by a writing off of the company's investment in Pacific Agricultural Holdings, a Californian company not directly related to the group's normal business.

The company's interpretation of exceptional and extraordinary items resulted in a significant increase in profits attributable to shareholders, and all importantly allowed EPS growth to be reported.

Source: Based on a report appearing in the *Financial Times*.

For illustrative purposes only, if the extraordinary items UB reported in 1991 relating to the disposal of businesses are reclassified as exceptional items, then the effect on profits attributable to shareholders is to reduce reported profits from £143.5 m to £130.1 m, a fall of almost 10%. This effect is shown below, with column 1 showing profits as reported, and column 2 extraordinary items reclassified as exceptional:

	Column 1	Column 2
	£m	£m
Operating profit	244.9	244.9
Exceptional items	0.0	13.4
Profit on ordinary activities before interest	244.9	231.5
Interest	31.7	31.7
Profit before profit sharing	213.2	199.8
Profit sharing	1.9	1.9
Profit on ordinary activities before tax	211.3	197.9
Tax on profits on ordinary activities	65.5	65.5
Profit on ordinary activities after tax	145.8	132.4
Minority interests	2.3	2.3
Profit attributable to shareholders	143.5	130.1

The alternative view to focusing on maintainable profits or earnings is the all-inclusive concept. This holds that all transactions influencing the company's profits should be included in calculating earnings per share. As will be discussed later, under the influence of the Accounting Standards Board (ASB) the system in the UK has moved in favour of the all-inclusive concept and away from the idea of current operating performance. This discussion highlights the need to apply judgement to the interpretation of published accounts and to consider carefully what is included and what is excluded in any concept of profit, and which concept of profit is most appropriate to appreciate important components of financial performance.

Finally, a further problem when interpreting profit figures is the use of *provisions*. Companies may make use of provisions to smooth their reported profit. Provisions relate to sums of money the company anticipates having to pay. These may result, for example, from the expected reduction in the value of an asset, or to provide for a loss likely or certain to be incurred, but over which there exists uncertainty as to the amount to be paid or the timing. The subsequent loss can then be set against the provision, reducing the impact of the loss on the reported profits for the year in question. For example, if a company has made provisions in its previous year's accounts amounting to £30 m and records a loss of £35 m in the current year, the effect on the current year's reported profits is only £5 m. If a company makes provisions and finds for some reason they have overestimated the actual costs involved, the unused provisions may be added back in later years to enhance profits, as in Illustration 5.2.

The potential for companies to transfer profits between years by the use of provisions means that the use of this accounting procedure should be examined with care.

Illustration 5.2

HANSON PLC
Hanson plc, the industrial conglomerate, reported pre-tax profits for the year to September 1992 of £1.29 bn. Reported profit reflected the utilization of no less than £469 m provisions. Despite the substantial employment of provisions the announced result was down on the previous year's profit of £1.32 bn, which included provisions of £307 m.   The group's balance sheet indicated total provisions of £4.86 bn. Acquisition of Beazer plc in December 1991 had led to provisions of £1.29 bn being set up, including £670 m for rationalization and changes in accounting policy.   Source: Based on a report appearing in *The Independent.*

The balance sheet

The second principal financial statement provided by companies is the *balance sheet*. The balance sheet shows a detailed breakdown of the company's assets and liabilities at the end of the company's accounting period. It is a statement relating to the financial position of a company on a specific day.

The balance sheet, as its names suggests, 'balances'. The double-entry book-keeping system on which accounts are based ensures that for every *liability* a corresponding *asset* is created. An asset may be defined as a resource of the company and includes fixed assets such as buildings and machinery, and current assets such as stocks and cash. Liabilities are obligations the company has to its owners who have invested money in the company by buying shares, and those from whom the company has borrowed. As Figure 3.1 illustrated, the money a company raises from issuing shares (equity) and borrowing (debt) constitutes the total funds the company has at its disposal.

To see how it is possible to construct a balance sheet, the four steps illustrated in Figure 5.3 and based on a simple numerical example will be used. In Figure 5.3 if company A issues shares worth £100 m, it incurs a liability to the shareholders who have invested their money in the company. In return for issuing the share capital the company will receive £100 m of cash, which is a corporate asset. *Step one* ensures that total liabilities equal total assets.

In order to produce output the company may decide to use its cash to purchase machinery worth £50 m, and a stock of raw materials for a further £50 m. As *step two* demonstrates, the cash has been transformed into two different assets – the machinery, known as a fixed asset, and stocks, a form of current asset. Even after these transactions, total assets equal total liabilities, and this forms the fundamental identity of the balance sheet:

$$\text{Total assets} = \text{Total liabilities}$$
$$\text{Fixed assets} + \text{Current assets} = \text{Issued shares}$$
$$\text{£50 m} + \text{£50 m} = \text{£100 m}$$

Together with shares, the company may borrow funds which are classified as another form of liability. As *step three* shows, if the company borrows £50 m in addition to the shares it has issued and holds the money as cash, the balance sheet identity becomes:

$$\text{Total assets} = \text{Total liabilities}$$
$$\text{Fixed assets} + \text{Current assets (Stocks} + \text{Cash)} = \text{Issued shares} + \text{Borrowings}$$
$$£50 \text{ m} \quad + \quad £50 \text{ m} + £50 \text{ m} \quad = \quad £100 \text{ m} + £50 \text{ m}$$

The linkage between the P&L account and the balance sheet can now be illustrated. The pro-forma P&L account in Table 5.1 showed that after dividends have been paid out of the profit for the financial year (i.e. after all expenses/payouts have been made), the remaining sum of money is known as the balance to reserves. As Table 5.1 showed, a profit for the financial year of £14 m for the year to the end of 1992 resulted in the company paying a dividend of £7 m, leaving £7 m to be transferred to the balance sheet as reserves. Reserves – funds accumulated by the company over time – are a form of liability as technically they are owned by shareholders, and together with issued share capital are known as shareholders' funds. Thus the total liabilities of the company are now shareholders' funds – issued shares, £100 m, and reserves, £7 m – and borrowings of £50 m, a total of £157 m.

The double-entry book-keeping system of accounts requires that if the company liabilities rise by £7 m, assets should also rise by the same amount. Hence, if money is transferred to the reserves, management may decide to hold the money as cash, or reinvest in the business by, say, acquiring more stock. In either case an asset of £7 m is created to mirror the increase in liabilities. Assuming the £7 m is used to fund an increase in stock, after *step four* the company's balance sheet on 28 December 1993 becomes:

$$\text{Total assets} = \text{Total liabilities}$$
$$\text{Fixed assets} + \text{Current assets} = \text{Shareholders' funds (Issued shares} +$$
$$\text{Reserves)} + \text{Borrowings}$$

For the example used as an illustration, the figures are:

Fixed assets	£50m	Issued shares	£100m
Stock	£57m	Reserves	£7m
Cash	£50m	Borrowings	£50m
Total assets	£157m =	Total liabilities	£157m

This simple example illustrates the fundamental principles of the balance sheet and how profits transferred from the P&L account increase the asset base of a company. Conversely, losses reduce the asset base of the company. Hence the P&L account links the balance sheets of two successive periods as shown in Figure 5.4. Based on the example above, this shows that the preceding balance sheet on 28 December 1992 had total liabilities and assets each worth £150 m.

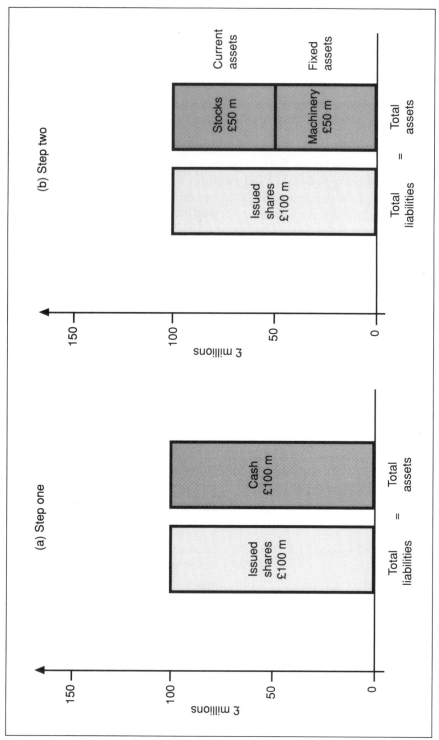

Figure 5.3 *The balance sheet*

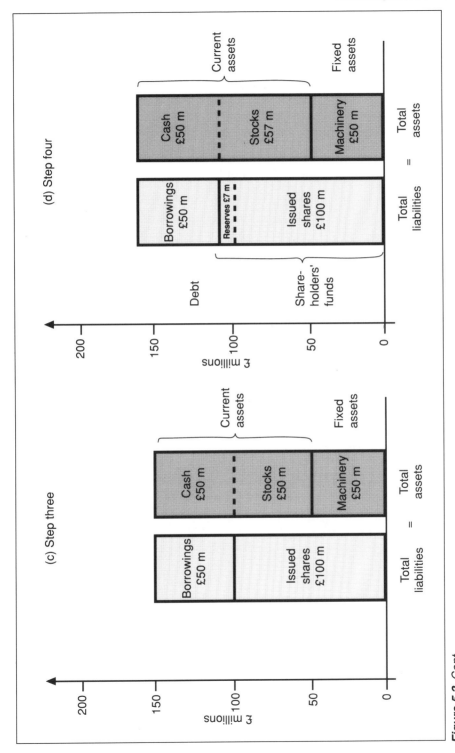

Figure 5.3 *Cont.*

Profit for the 52 weeks to 28 December 1993 resulted in £7 m being transferred to reserves. The balance sheet on 28 December 1993 had reserves of £7 m, and total assets and liabilities of £157 m.

Before examining the actual balance sheet for UB, it is worth summarising what has been established:

Total assets = Total liabilities

Total assets = Fixed assets + Current assets

Total liabilities = Shareholders' funds + Borrowings

finally, the profit and loss account links successive balance sheets.

In relation to the final point the reader should be aware that there are circumstances when financial adjustments are taken directly to the balance sheet, and the associated financial transactions do not pass through the profit and loss account. As a result comparing successive balance sheets requires further adjustments to be made to understand the movement of shareholders' funds. This issue will be examined later in the chapter in the section on new accounting standards for profit.

Whilst the concept of the balance sheet was developed showing total liabilities

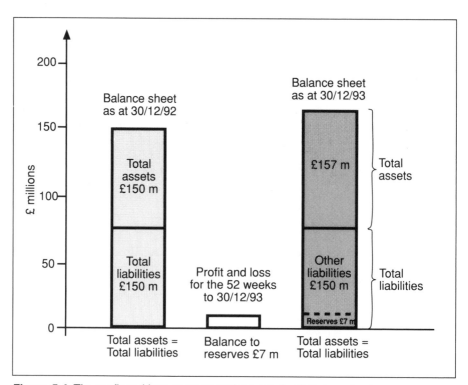

Figure 5.4 *The profit and loss account and successive balance sheets*

and assets alongside each other using what is known as the horizontal format, the Companies Acts require the information to be shown vertically, with total assets first, and then total liabilities. Information for UB is presented in the following order:

- Total assets:
  - Fixed assets
  - Current assets
- Total liabilities:
  - Creditors (to whom the company owes money) – amounts falling due *within* one year
- – Creditors (to whom the company owes money) – amounts falling due *after* more than one year
  - Provisions for liabilities and charges
  - Capital and reserves (shareholders' funds).

An important question when seeking to interpret some of the information contained in the balance sheet is on what basis is the company valuing its assets? The convention in most countries is to value assets according to their historical values. Thus, a machine is placed on the balance sheet at the price at which it was purchased. Reading UB's annual report confirms that the accounts are prepared primarily on a historical basis:

> 'The accounts are prepared on the historical cost basis of accounting, except for the revaluation of certain assets.'
> Source: *UB Annual Report 1991*, March 1992, p.39.

Whilst many assets appear on the balance sheet at historical cost, companies often take the opportunity to value some of their assets by alternative methods. These methods might include valuing assets on the basis of what they might fetch in a sale, at replacement cost (current cost), or according to the value the directors agree to place upon them (brands). This emphasizes the point that the absence of annual or independent valuation, other than by directors, can lead to major problems in interpreting balance sheet items. As a result, at any one time the balance sheet is likely to be an amalgam of assets valued according to their historical cost, current cost and by the directors of the company. Not surprisingly, some analysts tend to treat the balance sheet of most companies with a healthy degree of scepticism:

> 'There is no logic behind the summation of some assets valued at historic cost, revalued several years ago, and other parts of the balance sheet which reflect current values. Despite this, we cheerfully add these numbers together and some people believe they mean something. Some analysts, for example, even base debt/equity ratios on them.'
> D. Tweedie, speaking at the conference, 'Moving Toward Market Value Accounting', quoted in the *Financial Times*, 28 November 1991, p.14.

UB's balance sheet date is 28 December 1991. The balance sheet begins by considering the value of the company's *fixed assets*. Fixed assets is the term applied to assets which are intended to be used on a continuing basis for the company's activities, and can be subdivided into three elements, namely intangible assets, tangible assets and investments.

Intangible assets covers such items as patents, brands and goodwill. This form of asset has been the subject of considerable debate in the UK concerning whether brands (an intangible asset) should be valued and placed on the balance sheet. In 1991, UB showed intangibles worth £146.7 m on the balance sheet.

Tangible assets includes assets with an expected long life, held not for resale but for the purposes of the company's ordinary activities. Chief amongst the assets falling under this heading are plant and machinery and buildings. UB's tangible assets were valued at £780.9 m at the end of 1991.

Finally, *investments* include shares in associated companies. The relevant note to UB's accounts reveals that it has a range of investments valued at £12.3 m. As at 28 December 1991, UB had fixed assets worth £939.9 m:

	£m
Fixed assets:	
Intangible assets	146.7
Tangible assets	780.9
Investments	12.3
	939.9

Current assets describe the assets required to maintain the short-term operation of the company. For manufacturing companies such as UB, *stocks* include the stock of raw materials, of semi-completed goods (work in progress) and of finished goods. A note to the account – note 14 – indicates the relative holdings of stock under each of these headings:

	£m
Stocks:	
Raw materials and consumables	87.3
Work in progress	17.5
Finished goods	109.4
	214.2

In addition to stocks, *debtors* of the company are included as part of the company's current assets. Debtors are individuals or companies owing amounts to the business. UB's balance sheet shows that debtors to the company owed £394.2 m.

Taxation as it appears under current assets relates to deferred taxation. The figure appearing on the balance sheet is the consequence of differences in timing which arise primarily between the payment of advance corporation tax (ACT) – see Illustration 5.3 – and the impact of capital allowances.

Illustration 5.3

ADVANCE CORPORATION TAX (ACT)
Since 1972 the UK has operated with a system of ACT alongside mainstream corporation tax. ACT is paid by a company as tax on the dividends the company pays to its shareholders, under what is termed the imputation system. A company is allowed to offset the amount of ACT it pays against its UK earnings in order to prevent profits being taxed twice. However, ACT can only be offset against UK earnings, resulting in companies with insufficient earnings generated from their UK operations incurring an additional tax charge. For example, unrelieved ACT in the case of Trafalgar House raised the company's tax charge to 33%, as some £23 m of unused ACT was written off – lost. The management of the company have indicated that as a result they are seeking acquisitions in order to increase UK profits.   Unrelieved ACT is primarily a problem for UK multinationals who earn a significant proportion of their profits overseas. It can also be a problem for companies deciding to maintain their dividend during a period of difficult trading conditions when profits are depressed.   Source: Based on a report appearing in the *Financial Times*

Short-term deposits and loans, as the name suggests, includes all short-term deposits (e.g. time deposits) held by banks and loans. At the end of 1991, UB had deposits and loans totalling £35.3 m. Finally, *cash in hand* includes all cash items, including cash at the bank and in hand, and was worth £43.2 m The company's current assets in total were as follows:

	£m
Current assets:	
Stocks	214.2
Debtors	394.2
Taxation	17.3
Short-term deposits and loans	35.2
Cash at bank and in hand	43.2
	704.2

Adding together UB's fixed and current assets provides the value of the company's total assets on 28 December 1991:

	£m
Fixed assets	939.9
Current assets	704.2
Total assets	**1,644.1**

The liabilities of the company start with *creditors – amounts falling due within one year.* This heading includes all creditors of the company who will be expected to be paid within a twelve-month period. *Trade and other creditors* include trade creditors, accruals and deferred income. Trade creditors are individuals or organizations owed money for goods supplied; accruals refer to expenses which have yet to be met, but on which the company has some liability at the time the balance sheet is determined, e.g. rent and rates. Deferred income is money the company has received, but has yet to earn. For 1991 the total for trade and other creditors amounted to £376.4 m.

Loans and overdrafts include all borrowings with up to one year to maturity, and this category will indicate the extent of the short-term funding of the company and longer term loans to be repaid shortly. The company's short-term loans at the end of 1991 totalled £71.5 m. *Taxation* indicates the amount of liability the company has to pay tax within one year. For UB the sum was £44.3 m. *Dividends* indicate the company's liability in respect of its shareholders, which in 1991 amounted to £73.3 m:

	£m
Creditors: amounts falling due within one year:	
Trade and other creditors	376.4
Loans, overdrafts and finance lease obligations	71.5
Taxation	44.3
Dividends	73.3
	565.5

The next group of liabilities relate to *creditors – amounts falling due after more than one year*. Under this heading appears medium- and long-term loans and financial lease obligations the company has entered into (£255.5 m), other creditors (£13.9 m), and taxation (£6.8 m). For each of these items the company is not required to repay creditors in less than a year. Borrowings by the company listed in this section of the balance sheet, for example, have a life of at least one more year before they become due for renewal:

	£m
Creditors! amounts falling due after more than one year:	
Loans and finance lease obligations	255.5
Other creditors	13.9
Taxation	6.8
	276.2

The next item on the balance sheet is *provisions for liabilities and charges* (£68.9 m). Provisions relate to liabilities likely or certain to occur, including those which relate to pensions and/or any amount written off by way of the reduction in the value of assets below the value previously attributed in the balance sheet. For example, in the case of UB the previous set of accounts (1990) showed the company had made provisions for deferred liabilities for pensions and for liabilities arising from the management's decision to rationalize the Ross Young business, involving the closure of three factories:

'Provision has been made by way of an extraordinary charge for the withdrawal from a number of business segments within Ross Young's. The charge covers the costs related to the sale of three factories and withdrawal from the retail store distribution business. The total cost, after tax relief of £2.1 m, is £10.4 m. A further charge of £0.7 m arose from the disposal of businesses.'

Source: Group Financial Review, *UB Annual Report 1990*, March 1991, p.27.

A further item grouped under the heading of provisions for liabilities and charges is *contingent liabilities*. Data on contingent liabilities, where it exists, will be found in a note to the accounts. Contingent liabilities refer to a potential liability that the company has, but to date has not materialized (see Illustration 5.4 for an example). UB's provisions for liabilities and charges amounted to £68.9 m in 1991.

Illustration 5.4

COLOROLL PLC

The potential importance of contingent liabilities can be illustrated with reference to Coloroll plc. The company grew rapidly during the 1980s, and was well known for employing techniques of creative accounting. It included under the heading of contingent liabilities guarantees given to banks in respect of a former subsidiary which it had disposed of through a management buy-out (MBO). The use of these guarantees relating to the buy-out was partly responsible for the demise of Coloroll plc.

In 1988, Coloroll's management decided to sell the cloth and clothing interests it had acquired when it previously purchased the John Crowther group. The method chosen by Coloroll's management to dispose of these interests was by MBO for over £90 m. To facilitate the financing of the buy-out Coloroll accepted securities worth some £19 m, which it then sold to a third party to raise cash. Written into the sale agreement was that in the event of the MBO getting into difficulties Coloroll were liable for any default on the securities. As a result of this recourse clause Coloroll's sale of the securities was shown in its 1989 accounts as a contingent liability. When subsequently the MBO did run into difficulties the recourse condition came into effect, and Coloroll was required to assume the liability. As a result this was one of the causes of the insolvency of the Coloroll group as a whole.

Source: Based on Philips and Drew (1991).

The final group of liabilities is *capital and reserves*. This heading includes the called-up share capital of the company and the reserves the company has accumulated over time. *Called-up share capital* is the sum of shares the company has issued valued at their nominal price. For UB the amount shown is £120.5 m. The *share premium account* thus records the excess or premium that shares have been issued at over and above their nominal value. The UB share premium account stood at £144.3 m.

The *revaluation reserve* is the separate repository of any surplus or shortfall arising from the revaluation of assets. During periods of rising property prices, companies with substantial real estate are likely periodically to revise upwards the value of their property assets. Such action increases total liabilities, as well as adding to the value of the company's tangible assets. The revaluation reserve shown for UB in 1991 was £141.1 m.

The *goodwill reserve* for UB arises from the company's policy on acquisitions. If a company is purchased for a sum in excess of its net asset value the difference is known as goodwill. It is the price the acquirer has had to pay in excess of the asset value to gain control. In its statement of accounting policies UB states the following:

> 'On the acquisition of a subsidiary business or associated undertaking, fair values are attributed to the net tangible assets and significant brands acquired. Where the fair value of the consideration exceeds the aggregate value of these assets the difference is treated as goodwill and charged directly to reserves.'
>
> Source: *UB Annual Report 1991*, March 1992, p.39.

Writing-off the excess of the purchase price over assets against reserves has left UB with a negative goodwill reserve of £295.3 m. The final category of reserve is the *profit and loss account*. This refers to the accumulated funds the company has been able to transfer from the P&L account after all outgoings which go through the P&L account have been met, and the balance transferred to reserves. The manner in which the P&L account and balance sheet are linked in this way was illustrated earlier using Figure 5.4. Over time UB has accumulated £579.8 m in the profit and loss account reserve.

The remaining items on the balance sheet include *called-up preference share capital issued by a subsidiary* of the group and *minority interests*. The first of these two items relates to a further form of share capital issued by a subsidiary to the value of £35.1 m, whilst minority interests are liabilities the company has in partly owned subsidiaries.

Putting all these items together gives the total amount for capital and reserves:

	£m
Capital and reserves	
Called-up share capital	120.5
Share premium account	144.3
Revaluation and other reserves	141.1
Goodwill reserve	(295.3)
Profit and loss	579.0
	690.4
Called-up preference share capital issued	
by a subsidiary	35.1
Minority interests	8.0
	733.5

The company's total liabilities can be calculated by aggregating all the individual types of liabilities identified:

	£m
Creditors: amounts falling due within one year	565.5
Creditors: amounts falling due after more than one year	276.2
Provisions for liabilities and charges	68.9
Capital and reserves	733.5
Total liabilities	**1,644.1**

Comparing the figure above with the earlier number for total assets shows that total liabilities equal total assets. The full balance sheet for UB is presented in Table 5.3.

Table 5.3 *United Biscuits consolidated balance sheet as at 28 December 1991*

	£m
Total assets	
Fixed assets	
Intangible assets	146.7
Tangible assets	780.9
Investments	12.3
	939.9
Current assets	
Stocks	214.2
Debtors	394.2
Taxation	17.3
Short-term deposits and loans	35.3
Cash at bank and in hand	43.2
	704.2
Total assets	**1,644.1**
Total liabilities	
Creditors: amounts falling due within one year	
Trade and other creditors	376.4
Loans, overdrafts and finance lease obligations	71.5
Taxation	44.3
Dividends	73.3
	565.5
Creditors: amounts falling due after more than one year	
Loans and finance lease obligations	255.5
Other creditors	13.9
Taxation	6.8
	276.2
Provisions for liabilities and charges	68.9
Capital and reserves	
Called-up share capital	120.5
Share premium account	144.3
Revaluation and other reserves	141.1
Goodwill reserve	(295.3)
Profit and loss account	579.8
	690.4
Called-up preference share capital issued by a subsidiary	35.1
Minority interests	8.0
	733.5
Total liabilities	**1644.1**

Source: *United Biscuits Annual Report 1991*, March 1992.

Enhancing profits at the expense of the balance sheet

Most company analysts focus on the P&L account and are primarily interested in the level of reported profits. This provides a strong incentive for companies to try and enhance their reported profitability and show continuous growth in EPS. In the previous sections stress has been given to how the creative – though entirely legal – treatment of extraordinary and exceptional items could enhance profit attributable to shareholders, and thereby inflate EPS. In this section attention is focused on selective creative accounting techniques capable of increasing reported profits at the expense of the balance sheet while retaining a clean audit report.

Exhaustive treatment of the complex numbers game used by companies to enhance reported profits at the expense of the balance sheet have been raised by Holmes and Sugden (1990), Smith and Hannah (1991) and Smith (1992). The four items considered in this section are selective in nature, but indicative of how numbers can mislead investors. They are:

- changes to depreciation policies
- capitalization of interest
- writing off of goodwill
- brand accounting.

The contentious treatment of these and other items (notably off-balance sheet financing and currency matching) has caused considerable concern that there has been non-compliance with the spirit, if not the letter, of accounting standards. Analysts are particularly interested in any changes in accounting policies with regard to the areas cited above, since this may indicate a creative approach to the presentation of profit at the expense of the balance sheet. If accounting policies are revised, as in the case of Lasmo plc (see Illustration 5.5), the outcome can be dramatic.

Illustration 5.5

LASMO PLC

LASMO, the independent oil and gas exploration company, which acquired fellow oil company Ultramar for £1.2 bn at the end of 1991, disappointed analysts when it announced its 1991 pre-tax profits had fallen from £48.8 m in 1990 to £28.8 m.

The company's restatement of its results going back to 1983 followed sweeping changes in its accounting practices, dramatically reducing previously reported profit levels. Post-tax profits in 1991 were £59 m lower than they would have been under the company's old accounting policies.

Source: Based on a report in the *Financial Times.*

Changes to depreciation policies

Depreciation is the expense companies charge themselves to reflect the amount of fixed assets consumed in a year. The cost of depreciation is charged to the P&L account as part of the cost of sales. UB, for example, charged itself £75.3 m for depreciation in 1991. The company's notes to the accounts reveal the basis on which this figure is calculated:

> 'Depreciation is calculated to write off the cost or valuation of the assets (net of government grants) over their expected useful lives by equal annual instalments principally at the following rates:
> Land and building (except as noted below) – 1.5% unless short leasehold
> Short leaseholds – over the life of the asset
> Plant – 3–15%
> Vehicles – 20–30%
> Fixture and fittings – 10–33%
> Revalued buildings are depreciated over their remaining useful lives as estimated at revaluation date.'
> Source: Note 1, *UB Annual Report 1991*, March 1992, p.40.

A company's reported profit is influenced by the depreciation period adopted. A simple numerical example can be used to illustrate this point. Consider again the reported profits of Company A as described in Table 5.1. The company has a turnover of some £150 m and the cost of sales amounted to £80 m, including £25 m to cover depreciation. Assume the company's output is generated from new machinery which cost £100 m. Currently, Company A writes the cost off in equal instalments over four years. Assume now that the company changes its accounting policies and writes the machinery off in equal instalments over ten years, at a cost of £10 m per annum. With this change in accounting policy reported profits for the company are dramatically altered:

	Company A (current depreciation policy)	Company A (change in depreciation policy)
	£m	£m
Turnover	150.0	150.0
Less cost of sales	55.0	55.0
Less depreciation	25.0	10.0
Gross profit	70.0	85.0

As a result of the company changing its depreciation policy, reported gross profit for the year rises from £70 m to £85 m. This example serves to make the general point that if a company lengthens the expected lives of its assets the depreciation charge to the P&L account is correspondingly reduced and profits enhanced. Changes of depreciation policy without good reason are likely to be a device adopted by management to enhance their reported profits. The consequent risk of this policy is that insufficient funds are set aside to maintain the asset base of the company.

If a company's depreciation charge is insufficient the balance sheet will overstate the value of the company's assets and liabilities. With a low depreciation charge, the risk is that the company's fixed assets will be shown on the balance sheet to be worth more than is actually the case. Each year fixed assets will be written down by the depreciation charge. In the example above the value of the fixed assets at the end of year one will be £75 m for Company A with its existing depreciation policy, and £90 m after the change in policy:

	Cost of asset £m	Depreciation £m	Value at end of year £m
Company A (current policy)	100	25	75
Company A (revised policy)	100	10	90

On the basis of the illustration above, the risk is that with the revised policy Company A's balance sheet provides an overstated view of the company's assets, the price paid for enhancing corporate earnings.

Reported profits will also be affected by a company's decision of whether or not to depreciate certain assets. For some assets, notably property, it may be acceptable to have no depreciation charge. If the company subsequently introduces a depreciation charge on an asset which previously has not been depreciated then this will reduce reported profits, as in Illustration 5.6.

Illustration 5.6

W. M. MORRISON PLC

W. M. Morrison, the West Yorkshire based food retailing group, announced on 21 May 1992 that it was making a significant change to the way in which it chose to depreciate its land assets. Prior to the company's statement land values had not been depreciated. The company's move recognized both the high values of land assets recently acquired and the significant lower valuation of sites if they were transferred to an alternative use. The effect of the company's decision is to increase the level of depreciation and to reduce declared profits below the level they would otherwise have been.

Source: Based on press reports.

Capitalization of interest

Capitalization of interest commonly occurs in relation to the development of new property assets in their non-revenue providing phase when interest costs are rolled into the cost of the asset rather than charged as an expense to the P&L account. The result of capitalizing interest is to defer the impact on the P&L account until the new property development – which might be, for example, a hotel or retail store – is open. The rationale for this is based on providing a better match between the revenue associated with the development and its expenses. Only once the development is complete and the project begins to generate a revenue stream to offset expenses do the capitalized interest charges begin to be depreciated through the P&L account.

Regardless of the justification, the effects of capitalizing interest costs leads to important timing differences in reported profit. Reported profit whilst, say, a new store or hotel is being built is not affected by the interest charges associated with the new development. It is only when the project has been completed does the balance sheet cost of the project begin to be depreciated and the P&L account bear an expense through the depreciation charge. As the beginning of the 1990s has proved, many property companies with apparently robust profits appear less impressive when capitalized interest is brought back into the P&L account, revealing an inability to service debt.

Writing off of goodwill

If, when acquiring a company, the bidder pays a price which is in excess of the net assets acquired, the difference is known as goodwill. There are two principal options when accounting for goodwill.

- The goodwill arising from the acquisition can be charged directly to the company's reserves, and the total amount of accumulated reserves correspondingly reduced. This is the policy adopted by UB. Since 1990 the company has incorporated a goodwill reserve in its accounts, resulting in a negative reserve of some £295.7 m in 1991, thereby reducing the company's total accumulated reserves by the same amount.
- Alternatively, goodwill can be capitalized as an asset and written off over a number of years. Supporters of this option argue that it allows the company to spread the expenses of the acquisition to match revenues.

Once again the importance of the choice adopted lies in understanding the effect on the two financial statements. Writing off goodwill directly to reserves has no effect on profitability, but does have a significant influence on the company's capital base. Reported profits are maintained, and indeed enhanced from the new acquisition, but at the expense of the balance sheet.

The alternative of including goodwill as an asset and depreciating or amortizing the asset over a number of years is to reduce reported profits. Not surprisingly most British companies choose the first option and report higher profits, even though the price paid for an acquisition can result in a large hole in the balance sheet. Interestingly, US practice is the exact opposite, with goodwill capitalized and subsequently amortized. This is one reason why US companies often report lower levels of profitability than their UK counterparts.

Brand accounting

By placing brands acquired through acquisition on the balance sheet as intangible assets, companies are able to reduce the amount of goodwill they are required to write off against reserves. Since 1988 UB has adopted the policy of valuing brands on acquisition and placing them on the balance sheet. As at 28 December 1991, UB has intangible assets of £146.7 m, reflecting the value the company has placed on acquired brands:

> 'A fair value is attributed to brands at the date of acquisition by the group and this is treated as an intangible asset. The value is calculated by multiplying the earnings of the brand by a factor determined by the brand's strength.
>
> 'No depreciation is provided on these assets but the directors review their value each year and the cost will be written down if, in their opinion, there has been a permanent diminution in value.'
>
> Source: Note 1, *Annual Report 1991*, March 1992, p.39.

Notice that the brands appearing on UB's balance sheet are carried at historical cost and no depreciation is charged. UB's policy of not depreciating its intangible assets means that the P&L account does not bear a charge. The argument for not using a depreciation charge is that the marketing and associated expenses required to maintain the value of the brand are already charged as separate items to the P&L account. Such an approach is a relatively common policy amongst food manufacturers who have paid prices in excess of the asset value when acquiring a business. (See Illustration 5.7.)

Illustration 5.7

INTANGIBLE ASSETS – VALUING HUMAN RESOURCES

Comparison of team players and their results is not confined to the sporting arena. Manchester United and Tottenham Hotspur are also stock exchange quoted premier league rivals, and comparison of their financial performance is hindered by how they value their most important asset, the players.

Manchester United does not place its players on the balance sheet, while Tottenham Hotspur does. If Manchester United were to adopt the same policy as its rivals, this would strengthen the company's asset base and thereby its balance sheet. The need to depreciate annually the value of its playing staff would depress reported profits by the amount of depreciation charged.

Source: Based on a report in *The Independent.*

Summary

To summarize, the casual reader of a company's accounts can easily fail to realize that a profit figure presented in the P&L account is anything but definitive. This may be due to attempts to ensure reported earnings are flattered at the expense of the balance sheet through complex adjustments to depreciation, capitalization of interest, goodwill and brand accounting. As a company's accounting policies must be disclosed in the notes to the accounts, analysts must always closely scrutinize the information they contain, and subject the reported figures to careful analysis and interpretation.

New accounting standards for profit

In an attempt to dramatically improve the quality of accounts and the clarity of their presentation, a new regulatory framework for developing and reviewing accounting standards came into existence on 1 August 1990. The Accounting Standards Board (ASB) is more independent of the accountancy profession than its predecessor, more adequately funded, and through its Financial Reporting Review Panel (FRRP) has more effective mechanisms for enforcing compliance with its standards. Where the FRRP finds significant departure from accounting standards it has the option of taking the offending company to court. The courts have the power to force companies to amend their published results (see Illustration 5.8) and to surcharge the directors of the company for the cost of the legal action.

Illustration 5.8

TRAFALGAR HOUSE PLC
Trafalgar House plc operates businesses in a range of sectors including property, engineering and shipping. The FRRP reviewed the annual report and accounts of Trafaglar House plc for the company's financial year to the end of September 1991. The FRRP ruled that property write-down, arising from a fall in property prices, should be taken through the P&L account rather than charged directly to balance sheet reserves. Consequently, Trafalgar House had to restate its 1991 profit on ordinary activities before tax (pre-tax profits) of £122.4 m as a loss of £38.5 m. Source: Based on a report appearing in the *Financial Times*.

The ASB has set a new accounting standard for profit, and in October 1992 issued a new Financial Reporting Standard (FRS3) concerned with reporting financial performance. From 23 June 1993, the P&L account presented earlier in this chapter has been remodelled and two new statements added: 'Note of historical cost profits and losses', and 'Statement of total recognized gains and losses'. Two major changes to the face of the P&L account and reported profits are as follows:

- The requirement for companies to distinguish between continuing and discontinuing operations. Continuing operations include acquisitions made during the year. For each group of activities companies are required to disclose separately turnover, cost of sales, net operating expenses and operating profit. As a result the immediate financial implications of a company's key strategic decision to acquire or dispose of a business, or to engage in a significant restructuring, will be examined more easily.
- The virtual abolition of extraordinary items, and the classification of almost all transactions previously so identified as exceptional. Extraordinary items are redefined as:

  'Material items possessing a high degree of abnormality which arise from events or transactions that fall outside the ordinary activities of the reporting entity and which are not expected to recur.'
  Source: ASB, *FRS3*, 1992, p.9.

Reflecting a move to the all-inclusive concept of profit these changes curtail the opportunity of companies to adopt creative accounting techniques in the way which was highlighted earlier in Illustration 5.1 on Albert Fisher plc.

The changes in the financial reporting of the P&L account under FRS3 will ease the interpretation of company accounts in three key areas:

- Companies are no longer able to smooth EPS by taking unusual items below the line or by exercising judgement on what constitutes an exceptional and an extraordinary item.
- More background information is available concerning the operating performance of ongoing core business activities in a company where acquisition and disposals are significant.
- Information is generally more visible than previously, with provisions in particular now appearing on the face of the P&L account.

The impact of FRS3 is further shown in Illustration 5.9.

UB, in common with a number of companies, adopted the new financial reporting standard for the publication of the company's 1992 accounts. The new format required by FRS3, in common with the P&L format discussed earlier in the chapter, begins with turnover (£2,800.5 m) from which the costs of sales (£1,620.9 m) are deducted to reveal gross profits (£1,179.6 m).

Illustration 5.9

BOC PLC
On 16 November 1992, British Oxygen Company (BOC) plc, a manufacturer and distributor of industrial gases and health care products, became one of the first companies to issue their P&L account using the new accounting standard FRS3. The company's previously declared profit before tax in the year to 30 September 1991 was £310.1 m. For the year to 30 September 1992 reported profits were recorded at £215.0 m, after some £142.5 m of exceptional items had been identified – £117.1 m of goodwill write-off on the disposal of operations, and £25.4 m for reorganising the health care division of the company. In the past the £117.1 m write-off of goodwill would have been treated as an extraordinary item and not affected profits before tax. Without the application of the new accounting rules the company would have reported a profit before tax of £341.9 m, up on the previous year, rather than a reduction of some 30%. Source: Based on company's preliminary statement.

UB Consolidated profit and loss account
(For the 52 weeks ended 2 January 1993)

		£m
Turnover		
Continuing operations	2,641.2	
Acquisitions	0.0	
		2,641.2
Discontinued operations	159.3	
		2,800.5
Cost of sales		1,620.9
Gross profit		1,179.6

Source: *UB Annual Report 1992*, April 1993, p.43.

For an activity to be classified as discontinued, the following criteria must be met:

- the sale or closure of the activity should be completed in the accounting period being reported, or before three months of the next period have been completed and the date by which the financial statements have been approved;
- if the activity is to be closed down, this must be permanent;
- the sale or closure must have a material influence on the nature and focus of the reporting entity's operations, and operating facilities – in other words the sale or closure should reflect a clear strategic decision by the organization to withdraw from an activity, or to significantly reduce its presence in a market;
- the assets and liabilities, and activities can be distinguished physically and operationally for the purposes of financial reporting.

For UB, turnover worth some £2,641.2 m was generated from continuing operations, whilst £159.3 m came from discounted operations. Further, if the company had made any acquisitions during the year these would have been shown as a separate item under continuing operations.

The Directors' report gives details of the discontinued operations whose classification is determined according to the first point in the list above.

> 'On 3rd March 1993, the sale of Terry's Group to Kraft General Foods International, part of Philip Morris Companies Inc., was announced. The profits on disposal will be accounted for in 1993 although Terry's Group results have been disclosed in the profit and loss account as discontinued operations, in accordance with FRS3.
>
> Source: Directors' Report, *UB Annual Report 1992*, April 1993, p.33.

A breakdown of the cost of sales and net operating expenses, where not shown on the face of the P&L account, is presented as a note to the accounts as below:

	Continuing £m	Discontinuing £m	Total £m
Cost of sales	<u>1,525.0</u>	<u>95.9</u>	<u>1,620.9</u>
Net operating expenses			
Distribution costs	799.0	37.0	836.0
Administrative expenses	132.3	13.0	145.3
Other operating income	<u>(5.2)</u>	<u>0.0</u>	<u>(5.2)</u>
Operating profit	190.1	13.4	203.5

Source: Note 2, *UB Annual Report 1992*, April 1993, p.43.

On the face of the P&L account, a summary of operating profit is provided. Total operating profit for UB amounted to £203.5 m in 1992, which is determined after adjusting gross profit for indirect expenses – distribution, selling and marketing costs (—£836.0 m) and administrative expenses (—£145.3 m) – and other income (+£5.2 m).

		£m
Gross profit		1,179.6
Distribution, selling and marketing costs	836.0	
Administrative expenses	145.3	
Other income	(5.2)	
Operating profit		
Continuing operations	190.1	
Acquisitions	0.0	
Discontinued operations	<u>13.4</u>	
Total operating profit		203.5
Loss on disposal of discontinued operations	(10.2)	
Less previous year's (1991) provision	14.1	
Profit/(loss) on disposal of fixed assets	<u>7.2</u>	
Profit before interest and profit sharing		200.2

Once total operating profits have been calculated a further innovation introduced with FRS3 is the requirement to show certain exceptional items as separate entries on the face of the P&L account. FRS3 prescribes three categories of exceptional items, including provisions to be shown on the face of the profit and loss account, for both continuing and discontinued operations, namely:

- profit or loss on the sale or closure of a business operation. For 1992, UB incurred a net loss of £10.2 m on discontinued operations (for details see UB's Note 2 reproduced below). Set against this loss the company has used the £14.1 m worth of *provisions* it set aside in its 1991 accounts to accommodate the loss on the sale of Ross Young's Depot Catering business. Using these provisions in the 1992 accounts reduced the impact of business closure on reported profits for the current year;
- the costs incurred from a fundamental reorganisation and restructuring, which is deemed to be significant in terms of the nature and focus of the organisation's activities; and
- the profits or losses arising from the disposal of fixed assets. In UB's case the company lost £7.2 m on the fixed assets it sold when it closed a factory.

All exceptional items other than those listed above 'should be attributed to continuing or discontinued operations as appropriate' (FRS3 p.12). As a consequence of the application of this requirement, UB includes some £5.6 m of exceptional items in its calculation of operating profits, which the company calls operating exceptional items (see below), leaving the remainder to be shown as separate items on the face of the P&L account. Note 2 to UB's accounts provides a full list of the company's exceptional items for 1992, classifying them as either operating (included in the calculation of operating profits) or non-operating exceptional items, which are shown separately on the face of the P&L account.

UB – Exceptional items, 1992

	£m
Operating exceptional items:	
Costs incurred on factory closures	3.8
Cost of Keebler reorganisation	4.3
Gain on foreign currency hedging	(2.5)
	5.6
Non-operating exceptional items:	
Profit on sale of business segment	(3.9)
Loss on sale of Ross Young's Depot Catering	14.1
Use of provision for loss on Ross Young's Depot Catering	(14.1)
Loss on sale of fixed assets on factory closure	7.2
	3.3
Total exceptional items	8.9

Source: Note 2, *UB Annual Report 1992*, April 1993, p.43.

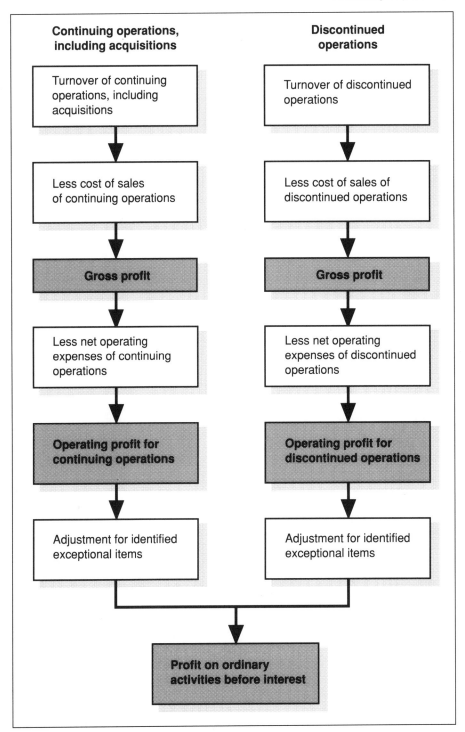

Figure 5.5 FRS3 – the new profit and loss account

Figure 5.5 provides a summary of the new face of the P&L account as introduced by FRS3, and illustrates the different steps required before profit on ordinary activities before interest, is calculated. The separate calculation of two levels of profit – *gross profit* and *operating profit* – for continuing operations and discontinued operations is emphasized in Figure 5.5, as is the position of exceptional items. Profit on ordinary activities is calculated by amalgamating operating profit for both continuing and discontinuing operations, and after adjusting for exceptional items.

Once profit on ordinary activities before interest and profit sharing has been calculated, all subsequent adjustments – interest, taxation, profit sharing, minority interests and extraordinary items – are applied to the P&L account on a corporate basis with no distinction being made between different types of activities. These adjustments follow the pattern previously described in relation to UB, although in practice extraordinary items have been virtually abolished. For completeness, the final part of UB's 1992 profit and loss account is reproduced below.

		£m
Profit before interest		200.2
Interest	36.4	
Employee profit sharing	1.5	
Profit on ordinary activities before tax		162.3
Tax on profit on ordinary activities	50.4	
Profit on ordinary activities after tax		111.9
Minority interests	1.4	
Profits attributable to shareholders		110.5
Dividends	75.7	
Balance to reserves	34.8	

Source: *UB Annual Report 1992*, April 1993, p.36.

Finally, FRS3 requires companies to reconcile profit for the financial year with the movement in shareholders' funds. As a result it will be much easier to see how movements in the P&L account are linked to the balance sheet. Beginning with profit for the financial year, companies will need to show the dividend payout they have announced, together with any actions which have directly led to changes in the amount of shareholders' funds shown on the face of the balance sheet. For UB, in addition to the £34.8 m transferred from the profit and loss account to the balance sheet, three further items had an effect on shareholders' funds – translation differences, the issue of new shares and goodwill written off. As a result total shareholders' funds increased by £168.7 m during the year.

UB – Reconciliation of movements in shareholders' funds

	£m
Profits attributable to shareholders	110.5
Dividends	(75.7)
Balance to reserves	34.8
Translation differences on foreign currency net investments	26.1
New share capital subscribed	118.6
Goodwill written off	(10.8)
Net addition to shareholders' funds	168.7

Source: Note 20, *UB Annual Report 1992*, April 1993, p.54.

Business unit profitability

Analysis of the P&L account has to this point focused on the total contributions of all the businesses contained within the organization. There has been no attempt to describe which parts of the group differ substantially in performance, or whether significant contributions in operating profits can be attributed to different geographical markets. Stock exchange listed companies normally supply (i) the turnover, (ii) operating profit, and (iii) capital employed for each substantive business segment and for each geographical area served for both current and previous years. This is the only information provided by companies on how different parts of the business perform, so that segmental reporting merits careful analysis.

Segmenting UB's turnover and operating profit by *business activity* and *geographical area* for 1990 and 1991 is undertaken in Tables 5.4 and 5.5 respectively. Information relating to capital employed has not been reproduced. In each table the segmental reporting of absolute levels of turnover and operating profit is recorded in column (a), the respective percentage totals in column (b), and the net profit margin in column (c). Net profit margin is calculated using the following expression:

$$\text{Net profit margin (NPM)} = (\text{Operating profit/Turnover}) \times 100$$

The separate information on turnover and operating profit in Tables 5.4 and 5.5 can be related in an important way by calculating the profit margin. The profit margin – strictly speaking the net profit margin – calibrates the amount of operating profit the company gains from every £1 of turnover. Operating profit is used because of the difficulty of allocating corporate payments – interest and taxation – across segments. The balancing item in Table 5.5 arises primarily because of the need to make adjustments for discontinued operations. It is interesting to note that where the percentage of total turnover is exceeded by the percentage of operating profit for either a business activity or geographical area, net profit margin is above the corporate average (and vice versa).

Table 5.4 *UB Segmental reporting by business activity, 1990 and 1991*

Business activity	1990 (a) £m	1990 (b) % of total	1990 (c) Net margin	1991 (a) £m	1991 (b) % of total	1991 (c) Net margin
UK sourced biscuits (McVitie's Group):						
Turnover	652.5	24.2		803.9	26.9	
			13.9			13.3
Operating profit	90.8	39.3		106.7	41.4	
USA sourced biscuits (Keebler):						
Turnover	900.8	33.4		983.0	32.9	
			6.1			6.7
Operating profit	54.7	23.7		65.6	25.5	
Confectionery (Terry's Group):						
Turnover	138.9	5.1		153.4	5.1	
			10.1			9.3
Operating profit	14.0	6.0		14.3	5.5	
Savoury snacks (KP Foods):						
Turnover	442.3	16.4		504.3	16.9	
			9.4			8.6
Operating profit	41.5	18.0		43.5	16.9	
Frozen & chilled foods (Ross Young):						
Turnover	564.4	20.9		542.9	18.2	
			5.3			5.1
Operating profit	<u>30.1</u>	<u>13.0</u>		<u>27.5</u>	<u>10.7</u>	
Total:						
Turnover	2,698.9	100.0		2,987.5	100.0	
			8.6			8.6
Operating profit	231.1	100.0		257.6	100.0	

*Continuing activities only, turnover/operating profit by division (£m), excluding discontinued operations, development operations and inter-company sales.

Source: *UB Annual Report 1991*, March 1992, p.37.

By taking one example of business activity (Table 5.4) and geographical area (Table 5.5), it is possible to show the links between the different aspects of segmental analysis. While UK sourced biscuits in 1991 achieved a profit margin of 13.3% (= (£106.7 m/£803.9 m) × 100), in the same year, the geographical area of the UK and Ireland recorded a lower NPM of 9.7% (= (£157.6 m/ £1,627.4 m) × 100). Both figures indicate that after meeting the cost of sales and all net overhead expenses, the company was able to make respective segmental returns above the average NPM of 8.6%, or 8.6 pence operating profit on every £ of its turnover.

Table 5.5 *Segmental reporting by geographical area*, 1990 and 1991*

Geographical area	1990 (a) £m	(b) % of total	(c) Net margin	1991 (a) £m	(b) % of total	(c) Net margin
United Kingdom & Ireland:						
Turnover	1,607.6	59.6		1,627.4	54.5	
			9.5			9.7
Operating profit	153.4	66.4		157.6	61.2	
Continental Europe:						
Turnover	186.8	6.9		336.1	11.2	
			5.0			6.0
Operating profit	9.4	4.1		20.0	7.8	
USA:						
Turnover	923.2	34.2		1,006.7	33.7	
			6.0			6.6
Operating profit	55.6	24.0		66.6	25.9	
Rest of the world:						
Turnover	6.0	0.2		8.9	0.3	
			(5.0)			7.9
Operating profit	(0.3)	(0.1)		0.7	0.2	
Balancing items:						
Turnover	(24.7)	(0.9)		8.4	0.3	
Operating profit	13.0	5.6		12.7	4.9	
Total:						
Turnover	2,698.9	100.0		2,987.5	100.0	
			8.6			8.6
Operating profit	231.1	100.0		257.6	100.0	

*Continuing activities only, turnover/operating profit by division (£m), excluding discontinued operations, development operations and inter-company sales.
Source: *UB Annual Report 1991*, March 1992, p.37.

It is important to be able to explain differences between business activity and geographical area NPM. The NPM of 9.7% for the geographical area of the UK and Ireland is understandably lower than 13.3% for UK sourced biscuits, as the geographical area figure also includes substantial turnover from both savoury snacks and frozen and chilled foods. The NPM on these two business activities in 1991 was 8.6% and 5.1% respectively (Table 5.4), thereby helping to depress the strong performance recorded by UK sourced biscuits. Given that frozen and chilled foods accounts for one-fifth of turnover and only one-tenth of operating profit, it is not surprising that UB has as a stated priority to 'improve returns on the investment in our frozen and chilled food operations' (*UB Annual Report 1991*, March 1992, p.7).

Not only does the NPM differ for the various business activities in the UK and Ireland, but substantial variations exist between UK sourced biscuits (McVitie's) and US sourced biscuits (Keebler). Since biscuits collectively account for approximately 60% of total turnover and operating profit it is a matter of concern that in 1991 and 1992 net margin in the UK (McVitie's) was double that for the US (Keebler). The function of the analyst is to provide a clear explanation of these differences. For example, whilst in the UK McVitie's is the market leader for biscuits, has efficient production facilities and manages a number of strong brands, the company's position in the US is weaker. Keebler based in the US operates in a market with very strong competitive rivalry, and one in which the actions of competitors, which include Proctor & Gamble, have depressed profitability. To the extent that margins may have been depressed in the short term by competitors' actions and/or conditions in the business environment it is important to review the trend in the profit margin.

Analysis on the basis of geographical area suggests that UB is highly dependent on the UK and US economies, but is seeking to develop its European operations. Turnover in Continental Europe almost doubled between 1990 and 1991, from 6.9% to 11.2% of the total. Newspaper comment on the publication of the company's interim results for 1990 makes this point very clearly, and suggests the reason for a number of acquisitions the company had recently made:

> 'United Biscuit's long march into the Continent is finally gaining momentum. Yesterday's announcement of the purchase of four snack companies in Spain and Portugal continues a year of activity which has already seen the group buy Dutch group Verkade, Chocometz in France and double its stake in the Italian ICA group.
>
> 'The acquisitions mean continental sales will double this year to about £200 m, rising to £300 m in a full year.
>
> 'But this is still only around 12 per cent of total turnover, although UB's target is 25 per cent within five years. The UK and US biscuit and snack markets are mature so growth will become harder to find. More than ever, therefore, UB needs new markets.
>
> 'To be fair, the delay is not necessarily for want of trying, nor is UB alone. The average continental exposure of the UK food sector, excluding Unilever, is only 13 per cent. Continental food businesses tend to be small, private companies and, hitherto, had no good reason for selling out to a predator. This is changing as they feel the heat of competition from aggressive groups such as BSN of France. UB thinks its decentralized management style will make it attractive to the few which do decide to sell.'
>
> Source: 'View from City Road', *The Independent*, 14 September 1990.

Moving attention from the specific issues of geographical segmentation, four general issues relate to the reporting of operating profits and turnover by business activity and geographic area, namely:

- transfer prices
- exchange rates
- scope of business segment
- seasonality.

Transfer prices describe the prices at which products are traded between businesses within a group. Where there is considerable inter-divisional trading, the NPM can be distorted by artificially set transfer prices. By setting a low transfer price the profitability of the sourcing division will be depressed (and that of the recipient division artificially inflated), while a high transfer price will artificially inflate the profit margin of the sourcing division at the expense of the recipient division. With inter-divisional trading accounting for 0.1% of UB's 1991 turnover, this difficulty can be seen to be of little relevance to interpreting UB's accounts in Table 5.4. Where there is significant inter-divisional trading considerable care is required to avoid misinterpretation of the NPM associated with particular business activities.

Companies which have a sizeable proportion of their operations located overseas are vulnerable to fluctuations in the *exchange rate*. Currency movements increase or decrease profitability when earnings are translated into the company's home currency. For example, if the pound sterling (£) appreciates against the dollar ($) profits generated in the US are worth less in sterling (and vice versa). This is illustrated below:

US profits ($m):	10.0	10.0	10.0
Exchange rate ($ – £):	2.00	1.80	1.40
Profits in sterling (£m):	5.00	5.55	7.14

This also illustrates why in 1990 Keebler's profits, when translated into sterling, fell. The company's report and accounts show that in dollar terms the sales of Keebler rose by 10% and profits by some 22%. In sterling terms, however, Keebler's sales fell by almost 1% and profits advanced by only 8%. The chairman's statement indicates the impact on the company's earnings of changes in exchange rates:

> 'Our other continuing businesses produced trading profits 11% ahead of 1989 and, with an unchanged average sterling/dollar exchange rate, would have shown an improvement of 16%.'
> Source: *UB Annual Report 1990*, Chairman's Statement, March 1991.

Although not relevant in the case of UB, analysts should be watchful of companies changing the basis on which overseas earnings are translated into a domestic currency.

Companies have considerable discretion in determining the *scope of the business segment* for which they report. Often this results in information being provided for large geographical areas, or a combination of different business activities. Since reporting procedures require information for broad geographical areas, this prevents the figures revealing the company's performance in any one national market. If the company is principally operating in four major European national markets, say France, Germany, Italy and Spain, the reported figures do not assist the analyst in understanding the company's performance in each country. Moreover, companies may combine different business activities together to hide from the analyst's eyes the differing performances on the individual activities. For example, if a company reports its retailing and property profits as one, it is difficult to determine whether it is the property activities or retail activities which have been the main generator of any reported profit. Finally, some companies change business activity boundaries thereby making comparisons with previous periods unreliable.

The final item is *seasonality*. Some companies are highly dependent on a short period of the year to achieve their results. Firework manufacturers, manufacturers of diaries, jewellery retailers and wine merchants all provide examples of this phenomenon. Comparison of the NPM as reported in a company's interim report can provide an indication of when seasonality is present. If the company consistently over a number of years reports a higher NPM in one half of its year, this is a strong indicator that for trading purposes its sales in one period are more critical than for the year as a whole.

Concluding remarks

It is easy to blame the misinterpretation of publicly issued accounts on the inadequacies of the accounting standards. Whilst certainly in the past there have been weaknesses to the accounting standards, fault must also be placed at the door of the reader. All too frequently only a careful reading of the annual report will reveal the extent to which the company's reported profits are robust and the extent to which they are being 'manufactured'. Notwithstanding changes in the financial reporting requirements, at all times readers of financial reports must be more vigilant.

This chapter has focused on profits and how, with careful interpretation, much can be revealed about a company and its performance. Despite the improving information base upon which analysts are able to operate, the subjective nature of accounts will always require judgement to be used when evaluating company performance. It is hoped that this chapter as summarized in the checklist below has revealed to the reader how that judgement may be improved.

An even more fundamental question is whether analysts should be focusing on levels of profit and the balance sheet, or whether their energies would be better employed in reviewing the cash flow position of the company. This question is the subject of the next chapter.

Checklist

- Read carefully the company's P&L account and balance sheet, and the accompanying notes to the accounts.
- When reviewing the P&L account, take notice of the extent to which turnover and profits/losses have been generated from businesses acquired or disposed of during the period covered by the accounts.
- Analyse the size and incidence of exceptional items.
- Has the company made any provisions for future losses?
- Identify the company's accounting policies, including how it deals with:
  (a) depreciation
  (b) capitalizing interest
  (c) goodwill
  (d) brand accounting.
  What is the effect of these policies on reported profits and the strength of the balance sheet?
- Has the company recently changed its accounting policies in any aspect of its business? If so, how have the changes affected reported profit?
- Evaluate performance at the level of the business unit.
- Identify from the organization's activities which are the key profit drivers, and those parts of the business which are underperforming.
- Is management taking action to improve the areas of underperformance? If so, how might this improve financial performance?
- Assess the company's pattern of geographical exposure and the extent to which this is changing.

CHAPTER 6

Accounting for cash

With the onset of recession in the late 1980s and early 1990s numerous companies which had adopted creative accounting techniques to report ever increasing profits – BCCI, Coloroll, Mirror Group Newspapers and Polly Peck – suddenly found themselves with insufficient cash to meet their expenses. Without cash a business cannot survive. While it is relatively easy for companies to adjust profits to suit their own purposes by enhancing profits at the expense of the balance sheet, creating cash is virtually impossible. It is our view that a cash flow statement showing movements of cash within a company over a period of time normally provides a more accurate assessment of the state of a company's affairs than declared profits. The following topics are discussed in this chapter:

- the importance of cash flow
- why profit and cash are different
- the cash flow statement
- how to use the cash flow statement
- why having a cash generator is so important.

The chapter begins by examining why cash is so important, and what determines whether a company is a cash generator or cash sink. How cash and profits differ is then discussed in detail, before exploring the key components of a cash flow statement. Issues of detail are amplified by examining the case of UB, and how the cash flow statement can be reconciled with movements in the P&L account and the balance sheet. The opportunity is taken to illustrate how the cash flow statement may be used to investigate key business decisions through a series of generic questions. The cash flow characteristics of companies within a consolidated group are then discussed and the need for a cash generator highlighted. Finally, the chapter concludes with a checklist on accounting for cash.

The importance of cash flow

Focusing on the cash flow statement brings to the fore the question of which is more important – cash or profits? Whilst in periods of economic growth some companies have been able to create ever increasing profits and earnings per share, with the onset of recession the same organizations have found the generation of cash more difficult. Paying more attention to the cash flow statement enables the analyst to gain insights into the business which are simply not possible by reviewing the P&L account.

The importance of cash to the survival and growth of a business lay behind the Accounting Standard Board's (ASB) decision to issue their first Financial Reporting Standard (FRS1) on cash flow. Commenting at the time of its publication, Professor David Tweedie, Chairman of the ASB, argued that the new statement was necessary on the following grounds:

> 'A cash flow statement gives a guide to the quality of a company's profits.'
>
> 'Profits are not necessarily a reliable measure of a company's performance. Companies can adjust profits to suit their own purposes by using provisions.'
>
> Source: *Financial Times*, 26 September 1991.

The cash flow statement offers the analyst the opportunity to consider:

- whether the company is a cash generator or cash sink;
- whether cash is being produced/absorbed from operating or non-operating activities;
- how the company is financing any cash shortfall or using any cash surplus;
- the quality of a company's profits.

Is the company a cash generator or cash sink?

The first important question for the analyst is to consider the overall balance between how much cash the company is generating and how much it is absorbing over the accounting period. As Figure 6.1 illustrates, if a company is able to produce cash in excess of its needs, it is known as a *cash generator*. Conversely, a *cash sink* is a business whose cash needs are in excess of its ability to generate cash. In either instance the reason for the cash characteristics of the business need to be clearly understood. A company is said to be *cash neutral* when its cash inflows and outflows broadly balance.

As Figure 6.2 illustrates, a company may be placed on a continuum comprising cash generators at one extreme and cash sinks at the other. The position that a company occupies on this continuum summarizes its cash position for the current accounting period. By looking at previous years' figures it is possible to ascertain changes, namely whether the trend is towards the business becoming

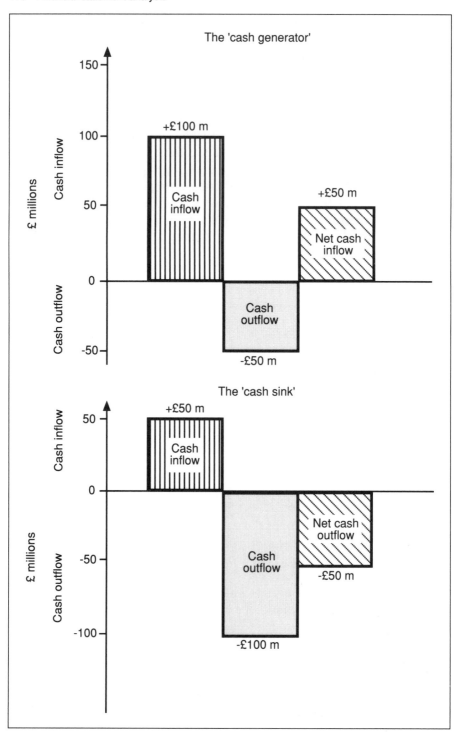

Figure 6.1 *'Cash generators' and 'cash sinks'*

increasingly a cash sink or cash generator. This information offers important evidence on the financial position of the company.

Is cash being produced/absorbed from operating or non-operating activities?

The cash a company is generating or absorbing can result from either its operating or non-operating activities. The cash position in respect of operating activities may be exacerbated or improved according to the company's non-operating activities. Acquisitions are likely to worsen the company's cash position, whilst asset disposals will result in a cash inflow.

With the exception of those corporate traders who buy and sell businesses on a regular basis, the cash generating capacity of a company's operating activities is of vital consideration. It is a proxy for management's ability to creatively craft and implement the strategic direction necessary to take advantage of the organization's competitive environments. Where operations are absorbing cash it is important to assess for how long and to what extent the business will remain a cash sink. Equally, even where ordinary activities are generating an operational profit, it is necessary to establish the underlying trends in operating effectiveness.

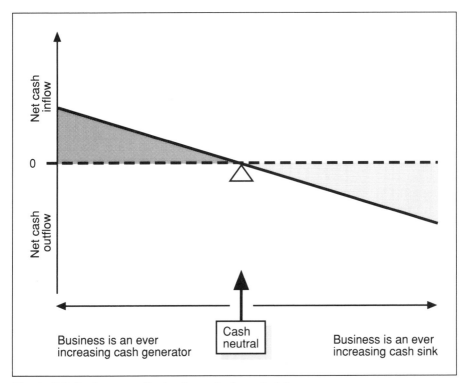

Figure 6.2 Business positioning by cash characteristics

How is the company financing a cash shortfall, or absorbing a cash surplus

Once the company's overall cash position has been established the next question is how the company is financing any cash shortfall or using any cash surplus. Should a company be a cash generator then it has the option of using the surplus cash created either to repay borrowings, to increase its cash reserves or even to repurchase issued shares. Alternatively, if the company has a cash deficit, it may either seek to borrow funds, ask its shareholders for additional sums or run down its cash reserves (if it has any). This is summarized below.

The cash generator	The cash sink
How is the money used:	How is the money found:
• borrowings repaid?	• additional funds borrowed (debt)?
• shares repurchased?	• new shares issued (equity)?
• cash reserves increased?	• cash reserves run down?

A guide to the quality of a company's profits

A healthy profit from operations, when matched with a net cash inflow, will tend to indicate a favourable state of affairs. Conversely, if reported operating profit is healthy but the business has a net cash outflow, there is the possibility that profits have been inflated by creative accounting and the company's position is less robust. Whilst over time cash and profits will converge, in the short term the ability of a business to generate cash is a better guide to its financial position.

The difference between profit and cash

Differences between profit and cash arise from the following four aspects of accounting:

- timing differences between when cash is paid or received and when transactions appear in the P&L statement;
- the effect of depreciation;
- accounting transactions which are recorded on the balance sheet but do not go through the P&L account;
- changes in working capital requirements.

The effects of timing differences

A fundamental reason for the difference between reported profit and cash relates to the concept of *accruals*. Accounts are prepared on the basis of accruals and not cash. Preparing accounts on the basis of accruals means that revenue and costs are shown in the P&L account as they are earned or incurred, and not when cash is received or paid out. Profits may be reported before cash has been received. This can be illustrated by taking a simple example and comparing what would happen if accounts were prepared on the basis of accruals or on the basis of cash. Assume Company A gains an order for £10 m of product on 1 December 1993 and in making the order incurs expenses of £8 m. The order is completed on 31 December 1993. If this is the only work the company has done in Company A's December accounting period, then the P&L account for the month on the basis of accruals accounting shows a reported operating profit of £2 m. This suggests the company's trading performance is satisfactory.

If the company supplies the goods on 31 December 1993 to Company B, this does not mean that Company A is paid on the same day in full. The contract between the two companies may give Company B, say, one month to pay in full. If Company B does not pay until the end of January 1994, no cash is received in Company A's December accounting period. If the £8 m expenses have been paid in this month on the basis of cash accounting Company A has a cash deficit of £8 m. Such a cash outflow from the business needs to be financed whilst Company A is awaiting payment from Company B.

The table below summarizes the differences which arise from basing the accounts either on accruals or cash:

Profit and loss account of Company A
(4 weeks to the end of 31 December 1993)

	Accounts 1 Accruals based £m	Accounts 2 Cash based £m
Revenue	10.0	0.0
Expenses	8.0	8.0
Operating profit	2.0	(8.0)

In practice in most countries, as accounts are based on the accruals concept, Company A would report profits of £2.0 m, and the second method of preparing the accounts would be developed into a cash flow statement. What this simple example illustrates is that important *timing differences* arise between when a transaction is recorded in the P&L account, and cash is received or paid. Taking the example of one time period and assuming Company A earns no revenues and incurs no expenses for the month of January 1994, the profits recorded are again significantly different according to how the accounts are prepared:

Profit and loss account of Company A
(4 weeks to the end of 31 January 1994)

	Accounts 1 Accruals based £m	Accounts 2 Cash based £m
Revenue	0.0	10.0
Expenses	0.0	0.0
Operating profit	0.0	10.0

In the second accounting period under the accruals concept the company has made neither a profit or loss. On a cash basis, the company has received £10 m. This is offset by an £8 m loss from the previous period, so that under both methods ultimately a £2 m operating profit is recorded.

In practice companies generally use a twelve-month accounting period, and the time difference between transactions being recorded on the P&L account and cash movements taking place are often much longer than the simple example outlined above. Examples of transactions where timing differences frequently occur include dividends, taxation and interest payments. For both dividends and taxation the figures arising on the face of the P&L account reflect levels of payouts relating to the accounting period. The actual payment of dividends and tax generally will not correspond, with both payments in full or part being made after the end of the accounting period to which they are related on the P&L account. Comparing the figures for both of these items on the P&L account and cash flow statements emphasizes the extent to which they diverge in any one period:

UB plc
(for the 52 weeks ended 28 December 1992)

	Recorded on the P&L account £m	Recorded in the cash flow statement £m
Taxation	65.5	59.4
Dividends	71.7	63.7

Source: Tables 5.2 and 6.1.

Whilst differences in timing related to taxation and dividends tend to be for relatively short periods, the same cannot necessarily be said for the effect of capitalizing interest. If interest is capitalized during the development of a new property development which takes, say, two years to build, then a significant difference in cash transactions and reported profit arises. Even though interest is capitalized so that during the development phase an expense is not charged to the P&L account, the company is still required to make *cash* payments on any borrowed funds. In such cases, during the project's development phase the level of interest paid will be recorded as a much higher figure in the cash flow statement than the corresponding entry in the P&L account. Most analysts are not fooled by the manipulation of profit, and always take interest capitalized into consideration when judging the ability of the lender to service any level of borrowings.

Depreciation

Depreciation is a measure of the consumption of a fixed asset. Although charged against the P&L account it does not involve a movement in cash. It is simply an artificial means of accounting for the degree to which a fixed asset is consumed in the accounting period. Hence, the notional funds set aside for depreciation are available to meet cash outgoings. The effect of depreciation is thus to deflate reported profits, but to leave cash flow unaffected.

Accounting transactions which appear on the balance sheet but do not go through the P&L account

Whilst all cash transactions are registered in the cash flow statement, some of the transactions do not pass through the P&L account. Some business decisions will be taken directly to the balance sheet leaving the P&L account unchanged. Acquisitions are a good example of this process. The discussion in Chapter 5 on enhancing profits at the expense of the balance sheet highlighted the fact that most British companies write off goodwill against reserves when paying a premium over asset value to obtain control of a business. Despite the writing off of goodwill, the monies to pay for the acquisition have to come from somewhere, and whilst the transaction will not go through the P&L account, it does go through the cash flow statement. Large acquisitions can be a serious drain on a company's resources and the cash flow statement provides a much clearer picture of the financing effect of acquisitions.

Changes in working capital requirements

Changes in working capital requirements reflect the net changes to stocks, debtors and creditors. Transactions in each of these areas will have cash implications, although the extent to which reported profits are influenced will differ. If a company is gaining increasing credit from its suppliers, then it will be receiving a cash benefit to the extent that it does not have to pay immediately for goods received. Effectively, a timing difference arises to the extent that the company gains a cash inflow, which does not immediately affect profits. Similar differences arise in respect of stock changes where valuation methods also influence reported profits, and debtors.

Summary

Collectively, timing differences, depreciation, items not going through the P&L

account and changes to working capital serve to emphasize the divergence between cash and profits in any accounting period. Over the longer term, with regard to a particular transaction, timing differences are removed and profit and cash converge. Even so, on a period-by-period basis it is necessary to reconcile cash with profit, and to appreciate the fact that despite making a profit, a firm may not generate any cash from its operations. Moreover, where large acquisitions or investments in capital expenditure occur, the divergence between profit and cash can be greater.

The cash flow statement

The level of cash generation is a signal of the strategic strength of a business organization. Consequently, any assessment of strategic direction should focus attention on movement of cash. By looking at UB's full cash statement (see also Illustration 6.1), an operational assessment can be made of the extent to which the company is either generating or consuming cash. It is also possible to examine major strategic changes, since investing activities focus on the movements of cash associated with capital expenditure, acquisitions and other investments and disposals.

Illustration 6.1

THE CASH FLOW STATEMENT – FRS1
The first Financial Reporting Standard (FRS1) prescribed the general layout large companies were required to use in providing information on their cash flow position. FRS1, which became mandatory for accounting years ending after 23 March 1992, categorized cash inflows and outflows under five main headings: • *operating cash flow* – cash generated or absorbed by a company's operating activities. A note to the accounts was required to reconcile operating profit to operating cash flow; • *returns on investment and servicing of finance* – indicating dividend payouts, and the amounts of interest received and paid; • *taxation* – showing tax paid; • *investing activities* – listing the amounts the company had spent on acquisitions, investments and capital expenditure, and any cash received from disposals; • *financing* – detailing how the overall cash inflow or outflow has been absorbed or financed by describing movements in debt, equity and cash.

In looking at UB's cash flow statement it is important to remind ourselves that it sets out the movements in cash during the year rather than reconciling opening and closing balance sheets. The cash flow statement begins with the identification of the *net cash inflow to the business from operating activities*. In 1991 UB had a net cash inflow from its operations of some £281 m. This figure is some £36.1 m in excess of the £244.9 m operating profit reported in Table 5.2. Reconciling operating profit with cash flow requires adjustments to be made for (a) timing differences, (b) the amount of depreciation, (c) changes in working capital requirements, and (d) the use of provisions. The detailed nature of these adjustments is discussed later in the chapter (Table 6.2).

In 1991 UB had a net cash inflow from its operations of some £281m:

	£m
Net cash inflow from operating activities	**281.0**

The next part of the cash flow statement deals with the monies the company has generated from investments, together with the cost of servicing the company's capital base – share capital (dividends) and debt (interest payments). In 1991 the company paid out dividends, including the monies in respect of the preference dividend of one of its subsidiaries, totaling £68.3 m. Net interest payments were £25.7 m, with £31.8 m paid out and £6.1 m received. Overall the *net cash outflow from returns on investments and servicing of finance* was £94.0 m:

	£m	£m
Returns on investments and servicing of finance:		
Dividends paid	(63.7)	
Preference dividend paid by subsidiary	(4.6)	
Interest paid	(31.8)	
Interest received	6.1	
Net cash outflow from returns on investments and servicing of finance		**(94.0)**

The next adjustment is for *taxation*. During the year the company paid some £59 m in taxation to the UK and overseas governments. Interestingly, when compared to the previous year, the company had reduced significantly its UK tax bill from £57.2 m to £35 m (see Table 6.1 later). An immediate question for the analyst to investigate is whether this lower tax bill is likely to apply to one year only, or whether the company has found some way of lowering its tax rate for subsequent years. A note to the accounts reveals that UB's lower tax charges reflects a reduction in the general rate of corporation tax for the UK.

	£m	£m
Taxation:		
UK corporation tax	(35.0)	
Overseas tax paid	(24.4)	
		(59.4)

As well as the cash flows associated with the company's operating activities, a company is likely to invest in a range of strategic directional activities. Companies may, for example, decide to acquire or dispose of businesses, undertake capital expenditure or purchase investments. All of these *investing activities* have cash flow implications. UB spent £38 m on purchasing new companies during 1991:

Investing activities:	£m	£m
Purchase of subsidiaries	(38.4)	
Proceeds in respect of joint venture	7.6	
Purchase of investments	(11.7)	
Purchase of fixed assets	(156.4)	
Sale of fixed assets	12.4	
Net cash outflow from investing activities		**(186.5)**

Totalling the four items – net cash inflow from operating activities (+£281.0 m), net cash outflow from returns on investments and servicing of finance (−£94.0 m), taxation (−£59.4 m) and net cash flow from investing activities (−£186.5 m) – gives the company *net cash outflow before financing*. For 1991 UB had a net cash outflow of almost £59 m, although this was markedly down on the outflow of £150 m recorded in the previous year:

	£m
Net cash outflow before financing	**(58.9)**

This net cash outflow of £58.9 m needs to be financed in some way. The final section of the cash flow statement details how this is achieved. During the year the company borrowed an additional £107.6 m, repaid borrowings of less than £1 m and received almost £54 m from the proceeds of issuing new shares, giving a total net cash inflow from financing of £160.6 m. As the cash outflow of £58.9 m needed to be financed, this left £101.7 m, which resulted in an increase in cash and cash equivalents. Cash and cash equivalents are essentially funds in cash (or near cash) which the company has at its disposal. They are a form of balancing item, which ensures any net cash outflow or inflow not financed or absorbed by financing is met by adjusting the company's cash position. In as much as this definition of cash does not relate to any specific balance sheet items (which show cash at bank and in hand), companies are required to supply an additional note showing how opening and closing balances of cash and cash equivalents are compared, and how they relate to corresponding balance sheet items (Table 6.3 on p. 181):

Financing:	£m	£m
Proceeds from new borrowings	107.6	
Repayments of borrowings	(0.8)	
Proceeds of issue of shares for cash	53.8	
Net cash flow from financing		**160.6**
Increase/(decrease) in cash and equivalents		**101.7**

Table 6.1 draws together all the components of UB's cash flow statement discussed above and presents the company's consolidated cash flow statement for the 52 weeks ending 28 December 1991. Figures for the previous year are also reproduced for the purposes of comparison.

Table 6.1   *UB Consolidated cash flow statement (for the 52 weeks ended 28 December 1991, and for the previous year)*

	1990 £m	1991 £m
Net cash flows from operating activities	**278.5**	**281.0**
Net cash outflow from returns on investment and servicing of finance		
Dividends paid	(59.4)	(63.7)
Preference dividend paid by subsidiary	(4.7)	(4.6)
Interest paid	(25.6)	(31.8)
Interest received	2.1	6.1
Net cash outflow from returns on investments and servicing of finance	**(87.6)**	**(94.0)**
Taxation		
UK corporation tax	(57.2)	(35.0)
Overseas tax paid	(15.9)	(24.4)
Tax paid	**(73.1)**	**(59.4)**
Investing activities		
Purchase of subsidiaries (net of cash and cash equivalents)	(149.6)	(38.4)
Sale of business	9.9	—
Proceeds in respect of joint venture	—	7.6
Purchase of investments	(0.9)	(11.7)
Purchase of fixed assets	(135.3)	(156.4)
Sale of fixed assets	8.1	12.4
Net cash outflow from investing activities	**(267.8)**	**(186.5)**
Net cash outflow before financing	**(150.0)**	**(58.9)**
Net cash inflow from financing		
Proceeds from new borrowings	61.0	107.6
Repayments of borrowings	(3.3)	(0.8)
Proceeds of issue of shares for cash	3.3	53.8
Net cash flow from financing	**61.0**	**160.6**
Increase in cash and cash equivalents	**(89.0)**	**101.7**

Source: *UB Annual Report 1991*, March 1992, p.36.

Companies are required to provide two additional pieces of information which reconcile elements of the cash flow statement with:

● operating profit
● balance sheet figures.

FRS1 thus requires companies to show in a note to the accounts how net cash flows from operating activities are reconciled with the operating profit shown on the face of the P&L account. This allows the analyst to understand how the first line of the cash flow statement is derived from the reported profit figure, and provides an important link between the two statements. As noted earlier in the chapter, for UB the difference between operating profit and the net cash inflow from operating activities amounted to £36.1 m (= £281.0 m – £244.9 m). The reconciliation is shown in Table 6.2.

Table 6.2 Reconciliation of operating profit to net cash inflow from operating activities

	1990 £m	1991 £m
Operating profit	218.1	244.9
Depreciation	63.1	75.3
Profit on sale of former head office	—	(1.5)
Excess of post-retirement benefits cost charged over payments	0.9	1.6
Share of profits of associates	(0.3)	(0.6)
Decrease in stocks	13.5	12.2
(Increase)/decrease in operating debtors	3.8	(24.6)
Increase/(decrease) in operating creditors	2.8	2.7
Expenditure against provisions	12.4	(22.9)
Settlement of legal action – instalment payment and related cost	(5.4)	(6.1)
Net cash inflow from operating activities	**278.5**	**281.0**

Source: Note 22, *UB Annual Report 1991*, March 1992, p.49.

Reconciliation of the operating profit and cash inflow from operations, requires the company to provide information on, for example, the amount of depreciation it has charged, changes in its working capital requirements, and the use of provisions. As discussed earlier depreciation needs to be added back to the operating profit for, whilst it is a charge against profits, no cash is actually paid out by the company. The company charged itself £75.3 m depreciation in 1991, reducing operating profits in the process, but leaving cash flow unaffected.

Turning to changes in the company's working capital requirements, Table 6.2 also explains what has happened in respect to stocks, debtors and creditors over the year. In 1991 the company successfully ran down its stock by some £12.2 m, thereby releasing this sum of money for the business to use.

Correspondingly, the company became indebted to its creditors – individuals or companies who have supplied UB with goods and services for which it has yet to pay – to an additional £2.7 m. As the company has yet to make payment, but has effectively had use of this money, this sum needs to be added to the cash flow. Alternatively, the company debtors – individuals or companies who owe UB money – rose by £24.6 m. UB has had to fund this increase in debtors, thereby reducing cash available by the same amount. Putting these last three items together – stocks, creditors and debtors – allows the analyst to judge the extent to which the company's working capital requirements changed over the accounting period. During 1991 the company required an additional £9.7 m to fund its working capital requirements:

	£m
Decrease in stocks	12.2
(Increase)/decrease in operating debtors	(24.6)
Increase/(decrease) in operating creditors	2.7
Changes in working capital requirements	**(9.7)**

Source: Adapted from Note 22, *UB Annual Report 1991*, March 1992, p.49.

The remaining major item is expenditure against provisions. This item relates to the extent to which provisions previously made in the P&L account have been utilized in the current accounting period. Where this occurs cash flow is affected, whilst the reported profit for the accounting period is unchanged. As earlier witnessed in Illustration 5.2 on Hanson plc, the use of provisions can be a significant item, influencing the reported profit of some companies. For 1991, UB spent £22.9 m against provisions, a cash outflow.

A further requirement of FRS1 allows the analyst to see how changes in the company's financing and cash position are translated into movements on the balance sheet. The relevant note to UB accounts, reproduced as Table 6.3, enables the company net borrowings at the beginning of the 1991 accounting period as described on the face of the balance sheet of 30 December 1990 to be reconciled with net borrowing for its next balance sheet as published on 28 December 1991. Between these two dates the company's net borrowings increased by £6.6 m:

Beginning with new borrowings and repayment of borrowings these can be read directly from the cash flow statement presented in Table 6.1. Further additional items, including borrowings by acquisitions and foreign exchange effects show that net borrowings have increased since the start of the accounting period by £6.6 m, with net borrowings rising to £248.5 m at the end of 1991. This figure can be compared with the level of net borrowings shown on the face of the balance sheet. Net borrowings as shown on the balance sheet are calculated by taking the following items:

Outstanding loans:	£m
Creditors: amounts falling due within one year	
Loans, overdrafts and finance lease obligations	71.5
Creditors: amounts falling due after more than one year	
Loans and finance lease obligations	<u>255.5</u>
Total	327.0
Less **Cash and short-term deposits and loans:**	
Current assets	
Short-term deposits and loans	35.3
Cash at bank and in hand	<u>43.2</u>
Total	78.5
Net borrowings as at 28 December 1991	248.5

Source: *UB Annual Report 1991, March 1992.*

To conclude, the new cash flow statement introduced by FRS1 attempts to measure cash generation in five principal areas, namely operating cash flow, returns on investment and servicing of finance, taxation, investing activities and financing. Two additional notes to the cash flow statement assist the analyst: firstly, a note reconciling operating profit on the P&L account to operating cash flow; secondly, an important linkage between the balance sheet and cash flow is made by showing how movements in cash and cash equivalents are equated to related items in the opening and closing balance sheet.

Table 6.3 *Effect on net borrowings*

	1990 £m	1991 £m
New borrowings	61.0	107.6
Repayment of borrowings	(3.3)	(0.8)
Borrowings of acquisitions	—	3.1
(Increase in cash)/decrease in cash and cash equivalents	89.0	(101.7)
Foreign exchange effect – cash and cash equivalents	(2.6)	1.6
borrowings	<u>(19.4)</u>	<u>(3.2)</u>
Increase in net borrowings	124.7	6.6
Net borrowings at 30 December 1990	<u>117.2</u>	<u>241.9</u>
Net borrowings at 28 December 1991	241.9	248.5

Source: *UB Annual Report* 1991, March 1992, p.36.

How to use the cash flow statement

The first point to restate is that an evaluation of the cash flow statement is invaluable to the analyst attempting to understand the company's underlying cash position and the financial implications of its strategy. It is somewhat surprising that many texts on interpreting company accounts treated its predecessor, the source and application of funds statement, as the poor relation of the other two principal statements issued by companies. It is our belief that analysts should pay more attention to the cash movements of an organization than reported profits, and that cash provides the most important guide to the quality of any reported profit.

The cash flow statement allows the analyst to identify the company's overall funding requirements, and whether the company's businesses are cash positive (cash generator) or negative (cash sink). Understanding of this analysis can be linked to the nature of the businesses and the quality of management. Drawing these elements together may also provide an insight into the solvency of the business. Increasing reported profits may not be associated with positive cash flow as a number of the major business failures over the last few years has clearly highlighted. Assembling the overall view of the company's cash flow position is necessary but not sufficient for the purposes of the analyst. It is also necessary to examine the individual elements of the cash flow statement. Key components of any company's cash flow statement may be examined by considering the ten generic questions detailed below.

Ten questions designed to enable the analyst to assess a company's cash flow statement

1. *Is the company managing to increase the net cash inflow from its operating activities?*
2. *Is the company able to fund comfortably its level of dividend payment?*
3. *How much cash is being used to service borrowings?*
4. *What has happened to the company's spending on fixed assets?*
5. *How important has the disposal of fixed assets and/or businesses been in terms of generating funds?*
6. *Is the company making acquisitions?*
7. *What is the funding need?*
8. *Has the company raised new share capital?*
9. *To what extent has the company increased borrowings?*
10. *How has the company cash position changed?*

---

1. Is the company managing to increase the net cash inflow from its operating activities?

The first question to review is whether the company has shown itself able to increase the cash it is generating from its operating activities and, if so, by how much. In UB's case, Table 6.1 shows that net cash from operating activities only rose by £2.5 m between 1990 and 1991, from £278.5 m to £281.0 m. In nominal terms the company's cash generation from operating activities increased by less than 1%, far lower than the rate of inflation. In real terms cash generation fell.

Once the overall variation in net cash inflow has been established the next step is to seek an explanation for any change. Is it, for example, the result of increases in the company's operating profit, changes in depreciation, or because of better control of the company's working capital requirements? Referring to Table 6.2 allows these questions to be answered. Comparing 1991 with 1990 shows that UB not only increased operating profits by £26.8 m, but also had at its disposal an extra £12.2 m available from depreciation (£75.3 m – £63.1 m). Additionally, a further £12.2 m is recorded from a decrease in stock. There were also cash gains from an increase in creditors and an adjustment to a previous overpayment of retirement benefits. These last two items amounted to £4.3 m, making a total cash inflow of £28.7 m to be added to operating profit. Against this sum, the increase in debtors absorbed £24.6 m of cash and expenditure against provisions of £22.9 m. These two expenditures, amounting to £47.5 m, help to restrict the increase in net cash inflow from operations. The increase in the sum devoted to debtors illustrates the need to manage working capital requirements with care, in order to prevent this being a major area of cash absorption.

2. Is the company able to fund comfortably its level of dividend payments?

British companies traditionally distribute a high proportion of their profits for the financial year to shareholders. In a period of recession organizations may find their cash flow declining to such an extent that management needs to revise the company's policy on dividend distribution. In the United Kingdom in the 1990s, much discussion took place as to the whether organizations had sufficient cash to maintain dividend payments at the levels built up during the periods of high growth and declared profits.

For a company whose cash flow is under pressure dividend payments may represent a further and unacceptable drain on a company's resources. The extent to which a company can afford to make dividend payments in relation to the overall cash flow should be reviewed. If the company is paying out too high a proportion of its earnings it may be preventing reinvestment in the business and run the risk of becoming under-capitalized. This is particularly true when dividend payments are made out of reserves, since the asset base of the company is being contracted, as in Illustration 6.2.

3. How much cash is being used to service borrowings?

Any borrowings a company has undertaken will require servicing in respect of interest payments. Companies which operate with high levels of debt, or have not structured their borrowings to achieve the most advantageous interest rate terms, may find a significant proportion of their cash generating ability being used to service debt. Hence both the level and cost of debt are important

Illustration 6.2

PILKINGTON PLC
Pilkington plc, a well-known UK-based glass manufacturer, has found trading conditions very difficult in the 1990s. As a glass manufacturer the company is heavily dependent for orders from the motor vehicle and construction industries, both of which have been in recession. The company's pre-tax profits have fallen from in excess of £300 m in 1989. First half results, for the six months to 30 September 1992, revealed pre-tax profits of £15.1 m, significantly down from the £50.6 m recorded for the comparative period in 1991.

Despite the lack of profitability, and little prospect of improvement for the second half of the year, the company announced that it was maintaining its interim dividend at 2.93p per share, costing the company £22.9 m. Financing the dividend payment required the company to use its reserves, a situation which cannot be sustained longer term.

Source: Based on *Financial Times*, 11 December 1992.

considerations in assessing the extent to which servicing of finance may represent a disproportionate drain on a company's cash resources. Where companies have significant sums of variable rate debt – the interest payable on borrowings is tied to the general level of interest rates – periods of high interest rates, coupled with high levels of borrowing, can present major financing problems.

For UB, Table 6.1 illustrates that net interest payments rose marginally from £23.5 m in 1990 to £25.7 m in 1991. Set against the company's net cash inflow from operating activities in both years, these sums are modest, suggesting that interest payments do not represent an overly large burden on the company's cash flow.

Some companies, including Associated British Foods (ABF) plc and General Electric Company (GEC) plc, have operated for periods of their history with no net debt and substantial reserves of cash. For these companies periods of high interest rates can result in net interest received contributing a significant component of the organization's overall cash flow, and can on occasion exceed the net cash inflow generated from operating activities.

4. What has happened to the company's spending on fixed assets?

The level of capital spending can be ascertained from the cash flow statement. Looking at the figures over a number of years enables the analyst to consider whether capital spending is rising or falling, and at what rate. Table 6.1 shows that UB's purchases of fixed assets rose from £135.3 m in 1990 to £156.4 m in 1991, a rise of over 15%. To gauge the level of this spending it is helpful to compare it with the amount the company is setting aside for depreciation. As depreciation amounted to £75.3 m (Table 6.2) in 1991, capital spending by the company is approximately twice the level at which the value of its assets are being reduced, or as it is more commonly known, written down. This is suggestive of a company continuing to be a net investor in capital assets.

If a company has cash flow problems capital spending may be curtailed. As companies can survive in the short term without replacing equipment there may be a temptation to mortgage the future for the present if cash is in short supply. This is not a strategy which can be sustained indefinitely without undermining the company's competitive position. The case of Lucas plc (see Illustration 6.3) offers a good example of some of the problems a company can encounter.

Illustration 6.3

LUCAS INDUSTRIES PLC

Lucas Industries plc, who operate in three major markets – aerospace, automotive and applied technology – was faced with a number of difficult choices at the time of the company's interim statement in 1992. The nature of its businesses requires the company to undertake heavy research and development spending and capital investment to retain longer-term competitive advantage. Unfortunately, the depth of the recession in its major markets and the need to rationalize its cost base put the company's cash flow under severe strain. This was at a time when the company was seeking to maintain its R&D spending and continue to pay dividends to its shareholders. In trying to square the equation the company had already seen its level of debt rise, and having made three major share issues in the last six years, its financing options were limited, especially as the end of recession in its major markets was difficult to forecast. Sooner or later if the situation continued the company would be faced with some very difficult choices in order to adjust to its reduced cash flow. Should it cut dividends and continue to invest for the future? Alternatively, if it continued to reward shareholders for their past support, the company's investment plans would need to be cut, placing at risk the company's competitive advantage.

Source: Based on the *Financial Times*, 31 March 1992.

Regardless of the level of capital spending, the cash flow statement says nothing about where the funds are channelled and whether any such investments will earn net cash flow returns in excess of the cost capital. The company may, for example, increase spending to expand capacity, in which case will demand be sufficient to take up the additional supply? Alternatively, is the company's pattern of investment focused on a cost-reduction strategy allowing capital to be substituted for labour and levels of productivity increased? The function of the analyst is to answer these questions, emphasizing once again the link between assessing the company's strategic direction and its financial strategies.

5. How important has the disposal of fixed assets and/or businesses been in terms of generating funds?

Reviewing net cash flows from operating activities allows an understanding of the extent to which a company's trading position is generating cash. In addition to cash from trading activities, companies may raise cash from disposing of businesses. Such disposals may be managed in a planned way, or result from distressed sales to ease cash difficulties. In the first instance, disposals may reflect the assessment of management following the framework developed in Chapter 3, suggesting there exists a mismatch between the needs of the individual business and the group. Where this is the case, it should be possible to manage the disposal to the advantage of the group in respect of the timing and price obtained.

Where a company is facing severe financial difficulties this is unlikely to be the case. Companies with acute cash flow difficulties may be forced to make distressed sales. This may result in the company obtaining a poor price for the business it is selling as prospective purchasers recognize the financial difficulties of the parent group and its weak negotiating position. If the survival of the group is threatened by the cash flow position, it may be necessary to sell some of the best performing assets within the group in order to survive, but at the cost of severely weakening its long-term future. In all cases it is important to recognize that once assets/businesses are sold they cannot again be used to generate cash, and their disposal only buys a limited time envelope for the company to correct any fundamental cash flow difficulty. Unless the company is a corporate trader, continuously buying and selling assets, cash generation from disposals can only be used for short-term expediency.

6. Is the company making acquisitions?

Acquisitions can be a major drain on a company's resources. If companies are wishing to expand quickly this inevitably means purchasing existing companies. As companies are generally expected to pay a premium to gain control of the assets of an established business this strategy can be expensive. If acquisitions have been made, or are expected to be made, it is important to ascertain the size of the purchase in relation to the overall cash flow. The case of UB illustrates very clearly how the purchase of a number of companies during 1990 significantly affected its cash flow position. The purchase of subsidiaries – companies which UB did not wholly own – cost £149.6 m in 1990, accounting for virtually the total net cash outflow before financing for the year (Table 6.1). In other words, if UB had not made these acquisitions, overall it would have been cash neutral in 1990. Not surprisingly, with the cost of acquisitions falling to £38.4 m in 1991, and other cash items remaining substantially unchanged, UB's cash outflow before financing fell to £58.9 m.

'The lower level of acquisition activity in 1991 reduced the overall cash outflow from investing activities from £267.8 m in 1990 to £186.5 m in 1991 ...'

Source: Group Financial Director, Financial Review, *UB Annual Report 1991*, March 1992, p.28.

Where significant acquisitions or disposals are taking place, the funding implications need to be linked to the organization's corporate and business strategies. In the case of UB, spending on acquisitions represents a major element of its declared strategy of becoming a more strongly orientated European company. Attempting to realize this ambition led to a significant number of European purchases in the early 1990s:

'During 1990, we also made substantial progress towards realizing our ambition to become a more broadly based European operation, with three of our core businesses expanding their presence in continental Europe. McVitie's Group acquired the Netherlands' foremost biscuit and chocolate manufacturer; KP Foods Group acquired a further snack company in Belgium, moved to a joint control of its partner in Italy, obtained majority shareholdings in two key Spanish snack companies and an option regarding a third; and Terry's acquired a French speciality chocolate company.'

Source: Chairman's Statement, *UB Annual Report 1990*, March 1991.

Between the publication dates of a company's annual report the analyst should monitor acquisition and disposal activity to estimate the effect on the company's cash flow. For example, UB's acquisition of CCA Snack Foods, announced in November 1992, was for approximately £195.5 m, including the existing debt of the company. Without considering any other acquisitions which might occur in the company's 1992 accounting period, this one strategic move tells the analyst that the company's cash outflow resulting from investing activities will be at least £195.5 m. At this level, spending on acquisitions is in excess of the sums spent in 1990 and 1991, clearly raising the question of how this is to be financed.

For all investing activities, the cost of acquisitions gives no indication about the wisdom of the purchase, but simply indicates the cash flow implication. The paramount need is to link the financial cost to the overall strategy of the organization and rationale for the purchase. Two key questions should always be borne in mind:

- What are the strategic reasons for the acquisition?
- Do you believe the reasons advanced provide an adequate justification for the acquisition, and the price paid?

7. What is the funding need?

If the company has a negative cash flow overall the question is then raised: how is this to be financed? Assessing the ease of financing a net outflow requires consideration of (a) the level of funds sought, and (b) the context to the company. Generally speaking the larger the funding requirement the more problematic raising finance will be. Secondly, the ease with which a company gains access to additional finance will reflect its particular context. Obtaining additional funds for a respected company the management of which is highly rated may be a comparatively easy task if the company is wishing to invest for the future and needs additional funds to enable it to do so. A rather different proposition is where a company's past performance has been indifferent, its management perceived as only just adequate, and the funding need arises from an inability to generate sufficient funds from its operations. In this latter scenario raising additional finance may prove difficult.

Unless adequate cash reserves exist, in seeking additional funds a company has two choices: it can either issue new shares or borrow funds. By issuing shares, shareholders are funding the deficit, whilst in the case of borrowed funds it is likely to be either a range of national or international institutions who are providing the finance. Where companies are net cash generators the process is reversed and capital can be repaid.

8. Has the company raised new share capital?

Companies may wish to raise additional funds from their shareholders to overcome any cash shortfall. Whether this option is available to the company, in practice as well as in theory, is dependent on a number of questions. First, how often has the company recently issued new shares, and what sums has it raised? If the company has recently raised significant sums of money through a new share issue, the stock market may be unwilling to absorb further amounts of the company's 'paper'. Secondly, stock market conditions generally may or may not be conducive to raising new funds. If the company does decide to issue new shares it may opt for a rights issue, as considered in Illustration 6.4.

For a small number of companies their share structure may place severe limitations on management's ability to raise additional funds from the stock market. This applies where, for example, a company has issued both voting and non-voting shares and has a two-tier share structure. The voting shares generally are held by a small number of investors, who may well be members of the founding family, whilst the non-voting shares are held by a much wider group of investors. There are both benefits and costs to such an arrangement. The concentration of voting shares in the hands of a small number of investors provides protection from takeover, but is also likely to reduce the pressures on management to perform. The reduced accountability of management to investors is one reason why investors generally dislike two-tier share structures with some shares having limited voting rights. Consequently, investors may be reluctant to provide additional finance to fund a company's expansion if they are not at the same time enfranchized, as demonstrated in Illustration 6.5.

Illustration 6.4

RIGHTS ISSUES

A rights issue takes place when existing shareholders are offered the opportunity to purchase additional shares in the company, proportionate to their current holdings. The new shares generally will be offered at a discount in order to tempt investors to 'take up their rights' and to maintain the relative size of their investment in the company. The extent of the discount is likely to vary according to the business situation the company finds itself in and its future prospects. Poorly performing companies will need to 'deeply discount' the rights issue if investors are to be pursuaded of the wisdom of taking up their rights. The effect of a rights issue is to boost the company's reserves and correspondingly strengthen the company's balance sheet.

During the first half of 1991 many companies took the opportunity of favourable stock market conditions in the UK to launch rights issues as a means of repairing their balance sheets which had become stretched as a consequence of over-borrowing during the expansion of the economy in the late 1980s. Favourable stock market conditions were brought about by, amongst other factors, the expectation of economic recovery. The subsequent disappointment arising from the lack of clear evidence of an upturn has meant that conditions for the launch of rights issues have been much less favourable during the second half of 1991 and 1992. Consequently, companies need to consider carefully the timing of any rights issue if they are to ensure that additional equity funds can be raised successfully without having to offer very high levels of discount, and even then risk that the majority of rights are not taken up, and the new shares left with the underwriters. Should this happen the position of the company's management can be weakened severely as was illustrated in the case of British Aerospace, where the poor handling of a rights issue in the autumn of 1991 led to the resignation of the company's chairman, Sir Roland Smith.

The case of British Aerospace also provides an example of a company having to make a rights offer out of necessity due to the company's underlying financial conditions. Other companies may have alternative sources of funding, but decide to take advantage of favourable market conditions in order to secure additional equity finance. This latter situation was certainly true of a number of major food retailers – Sainsbury and Tesco – which launched successful rights issues in the early part of 1991.

Source: Authors.

Together with rights issues a company may decide to 'place' its shares as a means of raising additional finance. The *placing* of shares is a selective method of selling shares, generally to institutional investors, for example pension funds and insurance companies. The advantages to placing shares are the cost and flexibility afforded. As it is not a general sale the marketing costs when compared to a rights issue are normally significantly less. Companies may, up to a specified level, place additional shares without requiring the endorsement of existing shareholders. To prevent the abuse of this power the stock exchange's

Illustration 6.5

> ## GREENALLS PLC
>
> Greenalls plc, a North West of England based company, changed its strategic direction in the 1990s following its decision to cease brewing and to focus on becoming a national drinks retailer and hotel operator. In January 1992 Greenalls announced that they were to abolish the two-tier voting share structure which had allowed the Greenalls family to maintain control of the publicly listed company. Prior to this announcement the company's 'A' shares, held by the family, had superior voting rights when compared to the company's ordinary shares. Previously holders of its LV (limited voting) shares were entitled to only one vote per share. By comparison holders of the 'A' shares – mainly in the hands of the Greenalls family – were entitled to four votes per share.
>
> The company's motive in changing its share structure was to provide for the possibility of undertaking a rights issue. The company had ambitions to expand its market presence in public house retailing and the hotel trade, but would be unable to do this with its existing two-tier share structure without raising borrowings to a relatively high level. At a time of high interest rates this would have been an expensive and risky option. Having prepared the way to raise additional equity, the company duly announced an £86 m rights issue in October 1992.
>
> Source: Based on press reports and company annual report.

continuing obligations for listed companies normally ensure the amount of equity which can be raised by placings to be constrained in order to protect the interests of shareholders generally.

The acquisition of CCA Snacks by UB in November 1992 was partly financed by an additional placing of the company's shares. Out of the purchase consideration of £195.5 m, some £80 m was raised by a placing of new UB ordinary shares, with the balance being funded by UB existing resources:

> '24.1 million new ordinary UB shares are being placed with institutional investors at a price of 332 pence per share.'

> 'The new UB ordinary shares represent just under 5 per cent of the existing issued ordinary share capital of UB.'
>
> Source: Press release, Morgan Grenfell, 10 November 1992.

At 332 pence the new shares UB issued were placed at some 14 pence below the opening price for the company's shares on the day of the announced acquisition. The difference in share price represents the discount the company felt was required to ensure the 'take up' of the placement offer.

As Table 6.2 illustrates, according to UB's cash flow statement the company raised some £53.8 m from issuing additional shares in 1991, almost in itself sufficient to match the net cash outflow before financing. Details of the nature of the shares issued are provided in a note to the accounts. The relevant note 20 shows that the shares issued for cash consideration during 1991 comprised an additional 20.3 million shares issued by way of warrants and 1.5 million shares issued under the company's share option scheme.

A *warrant* is an example of a share option. The option is generally open to be exercised within a given period of time, during which the holder can purchase new shares in the company at a set price. As Table 6.4 shows the exercise of warrants raised £50.3 m in 1991. UB also operate *share option schemes* for its eligible employees and executives. During 1991 these schemes raised some £3.5 m in cash. The amount of additional cash raised by issuing new shares, as was discussed in the previous chapter, is allocated to two balance sheet reserves. Cash raised at the nominal or issued value of UB's shares – 25p – is allocated to the share capital reserve. Thus 21.8 m × 25p raised £5.5 m. The remaining monies raised by the shares, reflecting the premium over nominal value at which they were issued, is allocated to the share premium reserve. The total cash raised is thus the sum of the two reserves – £53.8 m – the figure appearing on the face of the cash flow statement.

Table 6.4 *Share capital and share premium account*

	Share capital £m	Share premium £m	Total sum raised £m
Shares issued for cash consideration			
20.3m through warrants	5.1	45.2	50.3
1.5m under company share option scheme	0.4	3.1	3.5
	5.5	48.3	53.8

Source: Note 20, *UB Annual Report 1991*, March 1992, p.48.

9. To what extent has the company increased borrowings?

If the company is unable or unwilling to raise new equity finance then it must rely on borrowings. For this route to be open to the company, lenders must be convinced about both the company's solvency and ability to repay the funds. The cost of borrowing funds to the company will not only reflect the general level of interest rates, but also the credit rating of the company. The higher the degree of risk in lending to a company, the greater the premium the lender will demand by way of interest rates in providing funds. Eventually if the company's creditworthiness is so poor, it will be unable to obtain additional debt.

Where a company has increased its borrowings, the analyst should consider the repayment period of new debt – is it long term or short term? In the latter case the company will need to refinance the borrowings within a short period of time. Depending on the context to the company and its ability to improve cash generation this could be difficult. Borrowing incurs a servicing cost, which particularly in times of high interest rates can be a major drain on the company's cash resources.

Companies generating cash will be in the opposite position of being able to decide whether they wish to repay debt. A further point to note is that if existing debt is costly the company may have scope for rationalizing its borrowings and replacing outstanding loans with cheaper forms of finance. Financial engineering and its implications for increasing shareholder value have been discussed in Chapter 3.

10. How has the company's cash position changed?

Where sufficient finance is not raised or repaid to offset a net outflow or inflow before financing the difference is accounted for by movements in cash and cash equivalents. If a company has a large enough cash position to meet any cash outflow, additional share issues or borrowings would not be necessary when faced with a net cash outflow to finance. In practice this is very rare.

Table 6.3 shows that in both 1990 and 1991 UB raised additional funds from borrowings. For 1990 net borrowings (after taking into account the company's cash reserves and funds placed on short-term deposit) rose by £124.7 m. Reference to Table 6.3 also indicates that, whilst the company raised a large sum – £107.6 m – in the year to 28 December 1991, almost all of this amount was used to increase the company's cash and cash equivalents. This increase in cash and cash equivalents of £101.7 m could be to increase company liquidity, or to provide a reserve for the company to spend on, say, future acquisitions. Acquisition-driven industrial conglomerates in particular may maintain large cash reserves to be used for opportunistic purchases of businesses.

Interestingly, UB's acquisition of CCA is being funded partly from its existing resource base. This suggests that a significant part of the company's cash reserves might be liquidated for the purposes of this purchase. Notice, with reference to Table 6.1, that UB's improved cash position in 1991 led to interest received rising from £2.1 m in the previous year to £6.1 m. Clearly, if cash reserves are run down to finance the acquisition of CCA in 1992, the cash inflow from interest received will be reduced.

Summary

In conclusion, whilst the cash flow statement allows the analyst to identify the cash flows over different accounting periods and how these change from one year to the next, the statement in itself does not indicate whether the company's action in, for example, buying a new business was justified or not. As with all financial information, the cash flow statement only becomes really useful if its interpretation is aided by an understanding and evaluation of the company's strategy, the quality of its management and the likely business prospects. In respect of these comments it is now helpful to link the cash flow characteristics of different businesses with their product market position.

The importance of a cash generator

Large public limited companies are inevitably multi-business organizations comprising a number of different businesses. Each of these business activities will have different cash flow needs, reflecting their corporate history, current business position and chosen strategy. Some may be young thrusting businesses attempting to grow market share, others more mature businesses, focusing on maintaining a competitive advantage. Regardless of the nature of the business, the link between the strategy and cash flow characteristics of the business is crucial.

Further, the cash flow characteristics of each individual business activity need to be aggregated into a corporate total. A business requiring additional cash in the context of a cash generative group is likely to obtain the funds providing it can show the investments it wishes to make provide satisfactory economic returns. The same business in the context of a group which is overall cash negative, may not receive any additional funds even though there are good investment opportunities. If this situation is temporary then it may not lead to difficulties, but if it is a permanent feature of the group the result will be missed investment opportunities and an under-capitalized business. The cash flow characteristics of each business activity need to be viewed from an overall focus on movements of cash within the organization. This will show whether the overall balance of activities in the group results in 'cash generation' or 'cash absorption'.

If the group does not have a cash generator or its size is insufficient, management needs to instigate a major strategic review of its portfolio of businesses using the framework developed in Figure 3.5, where attention focused primarily on internal and external strategies to create value. This might mean, for example, reducing the size of the group by disposing of those businesses which have the greatest cash needs, or running part of the group for cash in order to fund elements of the group which offer the possibility of good future returns (see Illustration 6.6 for an example). Unless this is done a company will eventually exhaust its ability to borrow funds or raise more cash from shareholders.

Being dependent on shareholders or financial intermediaries for cash is not a sustainable long-term position, and may not even be feasible in the short term. Both sources will only provide funds if they judge that the prospects of gaining an acceptable return relative to the level of risk involved is appropriate. As highlighted in Figure 3.1, unless net cash flow returns exceed the cost of capital it will not be possible to meet financing costs and provide satisfactory returns to shareholders through dividend payments. Without satisfactory dividend payments shareholders will eventually become unwilling to fund the company's strategy, and may well be pursuaded to sell their shareholdings to a management team which offers to restructure the company in such a way as to ensure added value for shareholders.

Illustration 6.6

LETTS DIARIES
Reviewing the Letts Diaries group of companies in 1992 revealed three principal businesses: worldwide marketing of diaries, manufacturing of diaries and general publishing. The company was privately owned and controlled by members of the founding family. The major problem highlighted in a television programme on the company was that none of the company's three core businesses were cash generators. They were all *cash sinks*, whose weak trading performance was underpinned by an outstanding loan from Hambros Bank, due for repayment in two years' time.

Although the three businesses had different characteristics they all had one common need: cash. The Letts Diary brand name was capable of international expansion, but needed resources to fund the development. The company's manufacturing business, located in Scotland, was under-capitalized and in urgent need of modernization. Technology in the printing industry was changing quickly, and much of the company's existing stock of equipment was old and in need of renewal. The third business within the group was general publishing. This was an embryonic business established in the last few years, which was seeking to establish itself in an already competitive market-place. Again it needed capital to develop critical mass.

Faced with the unlikelihood of the company being able to generate sufficient cash from trading on the basis of how the group was currently constituted, Sir John Harvey-Jones, acting as a management consultant, recommended to management that they needed to dramatically reduce the size of the business to achieve acceptable levels of profitability and cash generation. This might entail selling two of the three current core businesses, to enable sufficient resources to be channelled into producing one substantive cash generator.

Source: BBC 2, *Troubleshooter 2* – 'Diary Firm Letts', 8 December 1992.

Illustration 6.7 on Woolworth Holdings (now Kingfisher plc) provides an example of how, if a business has a strong cash generator or the potential to develop one, a competent management team can turn even some of the most difficult of positions around.

Reviewing the position of UB offers a further illustration of the balance of cash needs within a group. UB's strength is derived from McVitie's. McVitie's is the market leader in the UK biscuit market with strong brand names and efficient production facilities. It is the UB group's cash generator. UB have been using the surplus funds generated by McVitie's (together with additional shares issued) to pursue its vision of becoming a world leader in snack foods. This has led to significant acquisitions in Continental Europe, and more recently in the Asia-Pacific region. Clearly, this serves to illustrate the link between an organization's overall strategic direction and its financial strategies.

Unless a company can fund its strategy, then the strategy cannot be implemented. It is therefore essential to consider each of the principal

Illustration 6.7

WOOLWORTH HOLDINGS (NOW KINGFISHER) PLC

In 1982 the Paternoster Corporation, a new management team funded by City Investors, succeeded in taking over Woolworth plc. The company at the time of the takeover was seemingly in a terminal decline the existing management were unable to do anything about. At the centre of the company was the high street chain store of Woolworth, which had become increasingly 'dated' as customers demanded more specialist retail outlets and better quality products. Within the Woolworth Group the company owned a number of other businesses including the B&Q chain of DIY stores, which at the time was the second largest DIY retailer in the country. A major asset of the company, which was to provide the funds to allow the company to develop, was the substantial portfolio of freehold and long leasehold properties the company held.

The new management set about trying to turn the company around, mindful that the takeover had pushed debt to a high level and recognizing the need to reduce borrowings. The immediate actions taken by management were:

- to reduce costs and improve the operational efficiency of the Woolworth stores;
- to dispose of a number of businesses which were deemed as peripheral – generally having weak product market positions and poor future prospects;
- to fund the development of the B&Q chain, given the business's strong position in the market and prospects for an overall growth in the out-of-town DIY business;
- to sell property assets to generate funds to reduce borrowings and invest in the businesses management wished to retain.

In the context of the company's cash flow needs, the management recognized that cash could be generated from the property assets to fund the development of the B&Q chain to a point that it became cash generative. Businesses with weak business positions were sold or liquidated, minimizing their drain on cash flow. The Woolworth chain was run for cash, initially, by only making minimum levels of investment with rapid paybacks, and through 'taking out' a high proportion of the organization's cost base.

Having secured the survival of the group, management has succeeded in repositioning the Woolworth high street chain by focusing on a number of key product areas (e.g. confectionery and recorded music), acquiring a number of new businesses (e.g. Superdrug and Comet) and turning Woolworth plc into a successful retail conglomerate with a number of strong core businesses. The key to being able to undertake this process, however, was that the company had a cash generator in the form of its property assets which management could use to finance the company's corporate and business strategies until new cash generators could be developed.

Source: CORTCO Case study group.

businesses within the group and ask two key questions about each, namely:

- How much cash can they generate and contribute to the group?
- How much cash do they need?

These two questions go to the heart of running businesses. Unless there is a balance between cash generators and cash users in the group, management needs to rethink its strategy. Figure 6.3 illustrates three possible scenarios where a corporate group operates with three divisions – A, B and C. In the first scenario (Figure 6.3 (a)) the group overall is cash neutral, with the cash generated by division A financing the cash needs of division C. In the second scenario (Figure 6.3 (b)) the group has two cash generators – A and C – with the third division being cash neutral. Overall the group is generating cash, so that the company in this position has a number of options available as to how this cash is used, including making acquisitions and increasing returns to shareholders by means of higher dividend payments. In the third scenario (Figure 6.3 (c)) the company is faced with a major problem. The group has two cash sinks and no cash generator. Its sources of finance – debt, shareholders and cash – will be severely limited, so that a turnaround strategy will need to be implemented unless the problem is exceptionally short-lived.

For a company faced with a similar situation to the last scenario, an important consideration is the *time* frame. For how long is the group likely to have to fund a cash deficit? Is the cash outflow a function of a particular phase of the business cycle and how it affects the group, or is it a more fundamental problem going to the heart of the group and its management? The cyclical nature of some industries means that periods of recession may lead to temporary cash outflows which can be managed in a planned way. Fundamental cash deficits are a different issue. This distinction highlights the need to examine cash flow over a number of years to understand the financial characteristics of the group and its constituent businesses.

To be able to identify individual business's cash characteristics requires the analyst to examine the following three factors:

- nature of demand
- working capital requirements
- investment in fixed assets.

These three characteristics are the key drivers which describe the cash characteristics of a business. Figure 6.4 illustrates how the three key drivers – nature of demand, working capital requirements and investment in fixed assets – enable the overall cash needs of a business to be obtained by looking at two companies operating in very different sectors of the economy. BSkyB, the satellite television company, is continuing to invest heavily in a rapidly growing but still youthful sector of the broadcast industry. Since its inception, BSkyB has been a cash sink, and is only now at the point of becoming cash neutral. The company does, however, have the potential of becoming a major cash generator

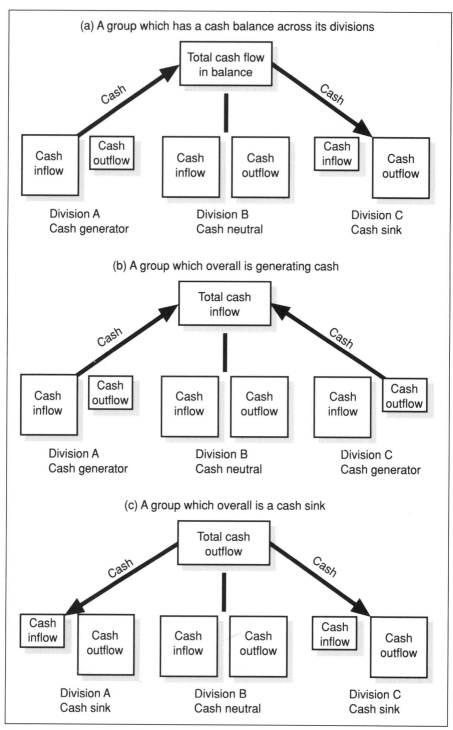

Figure 6.3 *The cash position of a corporate group*

in the future, illustrating why a corporate group may be prepared to fund a cash sink in the short term.

With high initial infrastructure investment in fixed assets, at the outset both cash and operating profit for BSkyB were negative. Having made the significant investment in fixed assets, which by their very nature cannot be depreciated as a single lump sum, it is expected that positive operating profits will precede a cash surplus.

By comparison, Imperial Tobacco, now part of Hanson plc, is a healthy cash generator. Although the tobacco market is declining, the rate of decline is slow and demand durable. With marketing expenditure being relatively modest, tightly controlled working capital needs and limited spending on fixed assets, the company is a strong cash generator.

Whilst the analyst should examine the three key cash drivers, nature of demand, working capital requirements and investments in fixed assets, by their very nature they are influenced by how management run the company. It is management who in managing the business help shape its cash characteristics. Inappropriate management decisions can result in a potential cash generator operating as cash neutral, or worse a cash sink. Similarly, a company needing a modest amount of cash, if managed poorly, can rapidly become a very large cash sink. Alternatively, if management refuses to invest, or is unable to do so because of a lack of funds, a business may be cash neutral, but only at the expense of mortgaging the future by under-investing in the replacement of fixed assets. Linking the cash characteristics of the business with the overall context of the group and quality of management is thus an important task for the analyst.

Concluding remarks

To summarize, it should now be clear that the overall cash position of a corporate group and the cash characteristics of the constituent businesses are a primary concern of the analyst. This recognizes the fact that business groups cannot survive for long if they are not generating cash. The failure to recognize this first principle of business has led to numerous corporate failures. Equally, the cash needs of individual businesses differ, as does the extent to which these requirements can be met within a single corporate group. All of these issues highlight the importance of cash. Managers who are unable to distinguish between cash and profits are unlikely to be able to manage effectively and to ensure the long-term survival and prosperity of their company.

The following checklist is designed to assist both managers and analysts to assess the cash characteristics of a company and its constituent businesses.

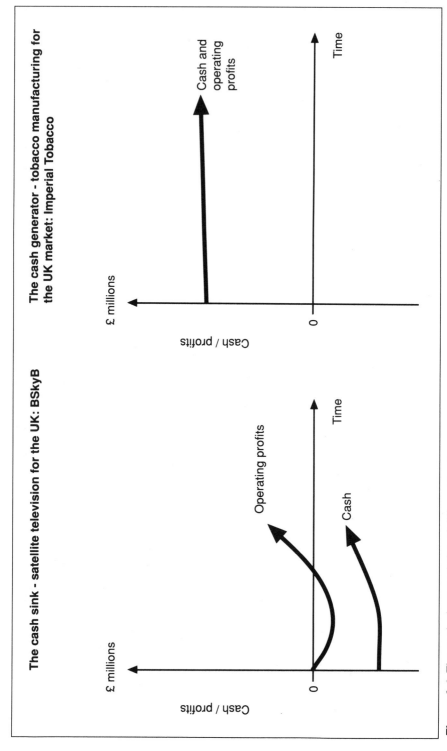

Figure 6.4 *The cash characteristics of different businesses*

What makes a business a cash generator or a cash sink?

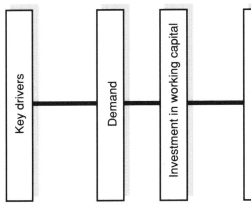
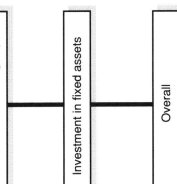

Satellite television

- Demand is growing but from a relatively small base

- Significant promotional expenditure required to grow customer base

- Company keeps working capital requirement to a minimum and where possible runs its own programmes

- Major investments required both for broadcasting infrastructure and purchase of broadcasting rights

- Whilst the level of demand is growing, heavy initial investments required; company moving to a position where it is cash neutral

Key drivers

Demand

Investment in working capital

Investment in fixed assets

Overall

Tobacco

- Although demand is declining long-term in the UK, a significant demand for the product remains

- Some promotional expenditure necessary

- Company has significant share of the market and established brands

- Working capital needs are not increasing and can be tightly controlled

- Only limited investment required - primarily to replace existing machines when due for renewal and to increase efficiency

- Whilst the tobacco market is shrinking, companies in the industry are strong cash generators and likely to remain so for the future

Figure 6.4 Cont.

Checklist

- *Assess the company's cash flow statement to see whether the organization is generating or using funds.*
- *If the company is generating funds, have these been generated from the company's operating activities, or do they result from disposals?*
- *How has the company used the funds it has generated?*
- *If the company is using cash, do you consider this a temporary difficulty?*
- *What are the funding implications of any cash deficit, and how has the company managed these in the last year?*
- *Has the company issued additional shares or borrowed funds?*
- *If the company's cash deficit arises out of acquisitions, what is the nature of the businesses purchased, and what is their fit with the organization's existing activities?*
- *Will any newly acquired companies generate or use cash for the foreseeable future?*
- *Looking at the organization's businesses identify those which are cash generators, and those who are cash users.*
- *Does the mix of cash generators and cash users in the group suggest management needs to reassess its current strategies?*

CHAPTER 7

Comparative financial analysis

Financial ratios are a convenient way to summarize large quantities of financial information, and to undertake a comparative analysis of the financial position and performance of a company. Whilst it is possible to calculate large numbers of ratios, the approach adopted in this chapter is to select only those ratios which are likely to be essential to the understanding of an organization's operating profitability and *financial base. Operating and financial ratios allow comparisons to be made, first with the company's past performance by taking a historical perspective (known as* time series comparisons*), and secondly with competitors and industry averages at a point in time (known as* cross-sectional analysis*). The structure of the chapter is as follows:*

- *choosing benchmarks for assessing corporate performance*
- *net profit margin and common size financial statements*
- *time series comparisons of financial ratios*
- *cross-sectional analysis and financial ratios*
- *future developments.*

   This chapter begins by examining the benchmarking process as a tool for understanding a company's performance over time and to enable comparisons with competitors to be made. In the context of UB, particular attention is paid as to how to select an appropriate sample of food manufacturers for the purposes of comparison. The concept of the net profit margin, introduced in an earlier chapter, is examined by considering common size statements. A detailed review of operating or activity ratios and those ratios dealing with the financing aspects of a company is then undertaken using both time series and cross-sectional comparisons. Recent proposals for introducing an operating and financial review as part of a company's annual report are discussed before concluding the chapter with a checklist on comparative financial analysis.

Choosing benchmarks for assessing corporate performance

Financial statement analysis provides analysts with the opportunity to examine how a company is performing when compared with previous years (horizontal analysis or time series comparisons) and with the performance of competitors in the industry (vertical analysis or cross-sectional comparisons). Time series analysis has already been introduced in an earlier chapter, when the net profit margin (NPM) – the ratio of operating profit expressed as a percentage of sales turnover – was calculated for each substantive business segment and for each geographical area served for both current and previous years.

Figure 7.1 illustrates the two dimensions to comparative analysis. Horizontal analysis requires information to be collected for different points of time and then compared. For example, data can be collected for successive accounting years, say 1991 and 1992. This allows the analyst to assess whether the figures have changed, and whether performance has improved or deteriorated. By contrast, cross-sectional analysis disaggregates a line of financial information or ratio into its constituent parts. This technique can be used to yield important insights into how a line of accounting information or ratio is formed, thereby

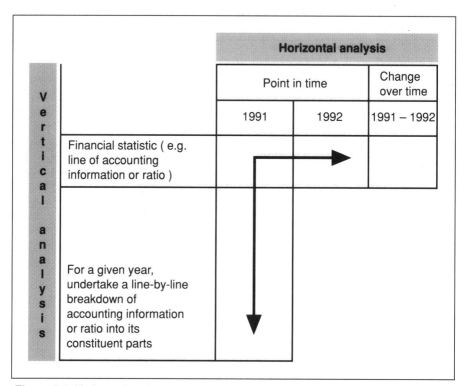

Figure 7.1 *Horizontal and vertical analysis*

assisting an understanding of what factors are important in determining a particular level of performance.

Applying vertical analysis the analyst is interested in the quantitative relationships between accounting data at a particular point in time. For example, the review of segmental reporting in Chapter 5 served to highlight the differing NPM between business activity and geographical area. As previously noted, this is the only business unit information available to the analyst which facilitates an analysis of which parts of an organization differ substantially in performance, or whether significant contributions in operating profits can be attributed to differing geographical markets.

A second type of vertical analysis associated with the profit and loss account is to indicate how turnover is distributed among its constituent components, including the relationships of cost of sales, distribution costs and administrative expenses to sales. By undertaking this analysis from year to year, the analyst is able to investigate trends, and review the intensity of the growth or decline. Finally, attempts can be made to discern why any changes have taken place.

Focusing on an individual company, using both horizontal and vertical analysis, facilitates the measurement of how an organization is performing when compared with its past achievements. This is necessary but not sufficient to enable a company's relative performance against its competitors in the industry to be assessed. The need for such comparisons is self-evident. While a company's ratio may be improving, is this improvement at the same rate as its rivals? Conversely, if performance is deteriorating is the relative achievement of the company when compared to its rivals improving, remaining unchanged, or getting worse? Comparing one company's performance with another is known as undertaking *inter-company comparisons* or benchmarking.

When making comparisons with organizations in the same industry, the financial information for ratio computation should meet the criteria of data *compatibility* and *business context*. Major differences in either the character or composition of the data being assessed will give rise to misleading comparisons. This then raises the issue of finding companies which offer an appropriate basis to enable inter-company assessments to be meaningful. The growth of large multinational conglomerates has made this task particularly onerous. Not only do such organizations operate in a large number of industries, but they also adopt national financial reporting practices that do not readily cross national frontiers.

Given the many and varied business activities undertaken by the leading biscuit manufacturers worldwide together with major international differences in their financial reporting, how do we generate a list of companies comparable with UB in terms of their business context and data compatibility? The flow diagram presented in Figure 7.2 identifies the four principal steps to resolving this complex issue.

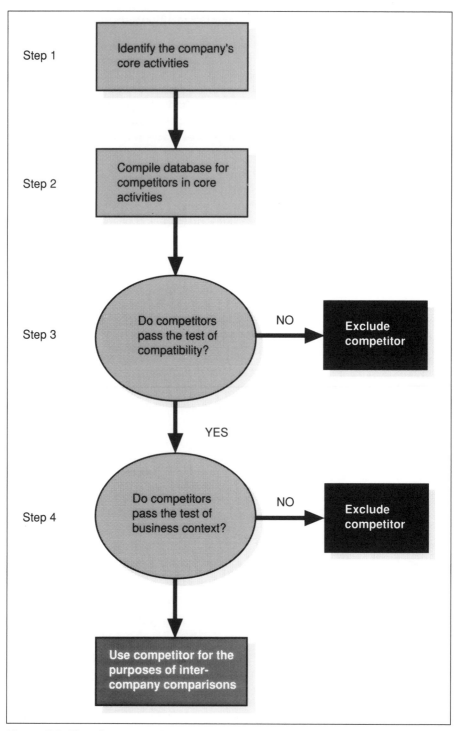

Figure 7.2 *Choosing companies for the purposes of inter-company comparisons*

Step 1 involves determining the boundaries of the industry/sector in which the company under scrutiny is operating. By identifying the core activity undertaken by UB to be food manufacturing, an industry definition which allows comparison with a group of firms offering broadly similar products from a user's perspective is adopted.

Step 2 involves compiling a database of competitors in the core activity. As virtually two-thirds of UB's turnover in 1991 was destined for the UK and Continental Europe, a comparison might be sought with the major European food producers. Table 7.1 reproduces information collated from the Financial Times European Top 500, identifying the ten largest food producers in Europe. The database excludes non-European companies together with major unquoted European companies, and is subject to change from one year to another.

Table 7.1 Top 10 European food manufacturers ranked by turnover ($m), 1991

Rank	Company	Country	Turnover $m	Market capitalization $m
1	Unilever	Netherlands/UK	38,409.0	22,655.9
2	Nestlé	Switzerland	31,311.4	19,954.2
3	BSN Group	France	9,172.7	9,332.6
4	Cadbury Schweppes	UK	5,429.0	5,094.0
5	Associated British Foods	UK	4,788.1	3,775.8
6	**United Biscuits**	**UK**	**4,699.9**	**3,101.2**
7	Hillsdown Holdings	UK	7,273.9	2,515.9
8	Northern Foods	UK	2,048.3	2,051.6
9	Danisco	Denmark	1,904.8	1,701.9
10	Dalgety	UK	7,996.9	1,611.2

Source: FT European Top 500, 1991.

Step 3 involves editing the database according to the *data compatibility* criteria. The data compatibility test requires the accounting framework of the competitor to be broadly similar to the company under review. This is necessitated by major international differences in financial reporting. The application of the data compatibility test necessitates the exclusion of the Swiss, French and Danish companies. This leaves seven out of the ten entries remaining.

Step 4 involves asking whether the remaining entries pass the *business context* criteria. The business context test is undertaken to ascertain whether the companies operate predominantly in similar product markets. On careful consideration Unilever fails to pass this criterion, with only one half of its activities devoted to food. The company is a significant producer of a range of non-food products including detergents and personal toiletries. On reflection the company is more appropriately defined as a producer of branded consumer goods. Despite owning Golden Wonder, the second largest potato crisp producer in the UK, the majority of Dalgety's turnover is generated from its North American food distribution business and its predominantly European-based agribusiness, which includes sales of animal feed compounds, seeds, fertilizers and genetically improved pigs. As a result Dalgety's is also deemed to fail the test of data compatibility.

Of the remaining companies, none provide a perfect comparison for UB, but all operate in a number of similar product markets within the food manufacturing sector. The fact that differences exist between the selected companies – Cadbury Schweppes, Associated British Foods (ABF), Hillsdown Holdings and Northern Foods – serves to emphasize both the difficulty of seeking out companies which can provide a helpful basis from which to assess a large multiproduct company's relative performance, and the level of judgement which needs to be applied to the selection process.

Table 7.2 *Food manufacturers selected for inter-company comparisons*

Rank	Company	Principal activities	Accounting year to
4	Cadbury Schweppes plc	Confectionery and beverage producer	28 December 1991
5	Associated British Foods plc	Milling and baking, sugar refining	14 September 1992
6	United Biscuits plc	Manufacturer of biscuits, salty snacks, frozen foods and confectionery	28 December 1991
7	Hillsdown Holdings plc	Food processing, fresh foods, furniture and property	31 December 1991
8	Northern Foods plc	Producer of dairy, convenience foods, meat and grocery products, including biscuits	31 March 1992

Source: Company reports.

This step by step approach to inter-firm comparisons is undoubtedly judgemental, but it is an important exercise if meaningful comparative analysis is to be undertaken. To the extent that all the five companies depicted in Table 7.2 operate in the food manufacturing sector, and are influenced by the same broad environment trends there is merit in considering UB's performance against their levels of achievement. Where differences occur the question is to what extent does this reflect one or more of the following:

- differences of accounting policies
- differences in reporting period
- different product markets
- the quality of management.

When making comparisons between companies *differences in accounting policies* make it necessary to ensure that the composition of reported data is directly comparable. As Chapter 5 highlighted, reported profit is a relative rather than an absolute concept. Creative accounting can reduce the transparency of a company's reported performance, and in extreme circumstance invalidate inter-firm ratio comparisons.

Differences in the annual closing date of the reporting period introduces the risk that changing economic conditions may explain part of any inter-firm ratio variance. As Table 7.2 shows, only Cadbury Schweppes and Hillsdown Holdings had a similar reporting period to UB. Where there are major differences in the accounting periods of companies some of the difficulties may be overcome by using a company's interim results. Unfortunately, whilst this method surmounts the problem of time differences, interim reports do not contain the same depth or breadth of information published in a company's annual report. Hence the use of interim reports is only a partial solution, although nonetheless helpful. Comparisons also are made difficult by companies occasionally changing their reporting year as ABF did in 1992, or by companies being taken over, as was Rank Hovis McDougall, previously an entry in the European Top 10 food producers, in the autumn of 1992.

Once allowances have been made for the effect of different accounting policies and reporting periods any remaining differences of performance can be traced to *different product market* exposure and the *quality of management*. The individual nature of different product markets means that each is likely to be influenced by specific factors in addition to any broad environmental factors – political, economic, social and technological (PEST) – which universally have an effect on the food manufacturing industry. Segment-specific factors may explain a significant proportion of the different levels of performance when comparing, say, UB with Northern Foods or Cadbury Schweppes. Nevertheless, it is important to remember that other than in the short term a company's exposure to different product markets is a function of its strategic direction and the decisions reached by its management team. Few companies remain in the same business for ever, and those which do so often fail or get taken over. The names of many companies reflect their original business activities from which they have radically departed in order to survive and prosper. For example, the industrial conglomerate British Electric Traction (BET) plc is no longer concerned with operating in its original core activities trams and buses. The company is now an industrial services group (see Illustration 7.1).

Over time management teams determine which product markets the company will commit resources to and how it will compete. Effective management

Illustration 7.1

BET PLC
British Electric Traction (BET) plc is today a large and diversified company predominantly focused on providing industrial services. The company's focus in the last decade of the twentieth century is a far cry from its original industrial interests. Founded at the end of the nineteenth century the company was a pioneer operator of trams as these became a popular means of transporting workers in the growing towns of Edwardian Britain. When the operation of trams was taken into municipal ownership in the 1920s the company refocused its interests on the operation of buses, until these were nationalized at the end of the 1960s. In the early 1980s the company management decided to concentrate on service industries believing these offered good growth prospects, moving into contract cleaning, textile rental, replacement windows, and crane and plant hire. Recession at the beginning of the 1990s meant the company had again to adjust its strategy and to decide which were the businesses on which it would focus.
Source: Based on press reports and the company's annual report.

teams are able to demonstrate an ability to achieve above-average performance even though external conditions are difficult. Poor companies continuously seek to blame external forces and are unable to accept their role in shaping a company's financial outcomes. Recognition of this fact emphasizes that, whilst performance differences may be explained with reference to broader environmental and industrial factors, ultimately the need is to focus on the management resource and its ability to fashion competitive advantage.

In summary, two benchmarks have been identified against which the analyst may assess a company's performance. Horizontal comparisons can be made by looking at the dynamics of the company performance over time, seeking to identify discernible trends and to assess whether performance is improving. Conversely, a vertical analysis may be conducted, decomposing key financial statistics into their component parts. Both types of analysis may be used in reviewing a single company, or from a cross-sectional perspective using competitors' performance or industry averages. Since industry groups tend to cover a wide range of products, international markets and organizational sizes, a straightforward comparison between one company and an industry average may be misleading. In an attempt to overcome this difficulty, a comparative database of competitors in food manufacturing on the basis of data compatibility and business context has been compiled.

Net profit margin and common size statements

Common size statements are a simple but highly effective technique for emphasizing the relative magnitude of accounting numbers as they appear in any one of the three principal financial statements. By translating the actual figures appearing on the face of one of the main financial statements into a percentage, the technique allows the analyst to make judgements about the relative size of individual lines of accounting information.

The technique is applied most commonly to the P&L account and can be illustrated by deriving a common size financial statement for UB. Table 7.3 provides a full statement of UB's 1991 P&L account. Deriving a common size statement of UB's P&L account simply requires the analyst to begin with the first line of accounting information, turnover. Taking UB's turnover of £2,660.5 m as 100%, a common size statement can be derived by calculating what percentage of turnover each of the items of the P&L account constitute. For example, the cost of sales is £1,490.8 m. To calculate the cost of sales as a percentage of turnover, the following expression is used:

Cost of sales (£1,490.8 m)/Turnover (£2,660.5 m) × 100 = 56.0%

The expression indicates that in 1991 UB's cost of sales were 56.0% of its turnover. By the same reasoning its gross profit was 44.0% (£1,490.8 m/ £2,660.5 m × 100), and operating profit 9.2% (£244.9 m/£2,660.5 m × 100).

Table 7.3 Common size financial statement – Consolidated profit and loss account, United Biscuits plc, 1991 (for the 52 weeks ended 28 December 1991)

		£m	%
Turnover		2,660.5	100.0
Cost of sales		1,490.8	56.0
Gross profit	1,169.7		44.0
Distribution, selling and marketing costs	786.1		29.6
Administrative expenses	141.4		5.3
Other income	(2.7)		(0.1)
Operating profit		244.9	9.2
Exceptional items		0.0	0.0
Profit on ordinary activities before interest		244.9	9.2
Interest payable		31.7	1.2
Profit before profit sharing		213.2	8.0
Profit sharing		1.9	0.1
Profit on ordinary activities before tax		211.3	7.9
Tax on profit on ordinary activities		65.5	2.5
Profit on ordinary activities after tax		145.8	5.5
Minority interests		2.3	0.1
Profit attributable to shareholders		143.5	5.4
Extraordinary charges (credits)		13.4	0.5
Profit for the financial year		130.1	4.9
Dividends		71.7	2.7
Balance to reserves		58.4	2.2

Source: *United Biscuits plc Annual Report 1991*, March 1992.

Developing a common size statement for any one year is useful, but the technique is arguably more powerful when it is used in making comparisons both with a company's past levels of performance and with competitors. To undertake these tasks it is necessary to develop a database on the company which contains information on the main financial statements over a number of years, and to collect similar data on those companies which the analyst wishes to use as a basis of comparison.

Beginning with a historical year-on-year comparison, Table 7.4 considers the principal operating components of UB's P&L account for the last three years, namely turnover, cost of sales, gross profit, distribution costs, administrative expenses and operating profit.

Table 7.4 Using common size financial statements to make vertical and horizontal comparisons of UB's performance

	Vertical analysis						Horizontal analysis			
	Point in time						Year-on-year change			
	1989		1990		1991		1990/89		1991/90	
	£m	% sales	£m	% sales	£m	% sales	£m	%	£m	%
Turnover	2,442.4	100.0	2,428.3	100.0	2,660.5	100.0	(14.1)	(5.9)	232.2	9.6
Cost of sales	1,463.4	59.9	1,434.1	59.1	1,490.8	56.0	(29.3)	(2.0)	56.7	4.0
Gross profit	979.0	40.0	994.2	40.9	1,169.7	44.0	15.2	1.6	175.5	17.6
Distribution costs	645.6	26.4	655.9	27.0	786.1	29.6	10.3	1.6	130.2	19.9
Administrative expenses	127.2	5.2	119.6	4.9	141.4	5.3	(7.6)	(6.0)	0.4	8.2
Operating profit	212.1	8.7	220.7	9.1	244.9	9.2	8.6	4.1	24.2	11.0

Source: *UB Annual Reports, 1989–91.*

Table 7.4 illustrates the techniques of vertical and horizontal analysis. Vertical analysis is the focus of the first six columns of numbers, since consideration is given to the absolute and relative size of items appearing on the face of a single year's P&L account. Horizontal analysis, the focus of the last four columns of figures, considers the year-on-year changes for each of the principal items.

Beginning with the vertical analysis, Table 7.4 reveals a number of interesting trends. These include the observation that the company has been able to reduce the relative size of its cost of sales – the *cost to sales ratio* – over the period from 59.9% in 1989 to 56.0% in 1991, with a consequent improvement in its percentage of gross profit, or *gross profit margin*, to 44.0%, an increase of four percentage points (40.0% to 44.0%) over the three years. An improvement in a company's gross profit margin will result from one or both of the following:

- an increase in prices; and/or
- improving efficiency restricting increases in the cost of sales.

If a company raises prices, and the cost of sales do not correspondingly increase, turnover will rise relative to expenses. Similarly, if a company's costs of sales are reduced relative to turnover, through, say, substituting machinery for labour, then direct expenses fall relative to turnover. Once again it is for the analyst to determine what is the correct explanation. For UB the annual report indicates a strategy of increasing efficiencies through investment. Analysis of the cash flow statement confirms that the company's capital expenditure is twice the rate of depreciation. These factors suggest at least part of the improvement in the gross profit margin is by way of increasing levels of efficiency. The company's annual report also reveals that in a number of areas the company has a strategy of developing 'added-value' products for which it can charge the customer a premium price. Hence some of the improvement in the gross margin might be the result of achieving higher prices for its products. Counterbalancing this point, however, has been the effect of recession and the tendency of consumers to buy less or trade down, that is to switch to cheaper brands. On balance, this probably suggests that improvement in efficiency is the primary reason for the company being able to increase its gross profit margin.

The increase in gross profit has not been matched by the growth of the operating profit percentage. Although the percentage of operating profit – the *net profit margin* – has grown from 8.7% to 9.2%, growth has been constrained by a rise in overhead expenses. Distribution costs – the *distribution to sales ratio* – have grown to almost 30% of turnover, whilst administrative expenses – *administrative expenses to sales ratio* – have marginally increased at the end of three years. An important task for the analyst is therefore to question why distribution costs in particular have increased, and whether such an increase is justified. One possible explanation could be that the company has been 'buying' sales at the expense of profits. In order to increase market share, companies may incur increased distribution expenses in order to 'push' additional sales to customers through marketing and promotional campaigns, and the use of incentives for distributors. Where this is a short-term tactic designed to establish a longer-term position in the market this policy can be defended. If, however, a company is pursuing additional sales which will not enable a profitable market position to be established this is a different matter. As a general point, if a company cannot turn sales growth into profits this is a worrying sign.

Returning to Table 7.4, the horizontal analysis reveals different aspects of the company's performance. Analysing the entries on turnover reveals that the company's sales fell by some £14 m in 1990 on the previous year, but rose £232 m in the following year. This at first sight appears puzzling, particularly given the business markets into which the company was selling were depressed. The answer, however, has already been flagged in Chapter 6. During 1990 UB spent some £150 m on acquisitions. The results of these acquisitions did not appear fully in the company's P&L account until 1991.

This example illustrates one of the difficulties in using horizontal analysis. Analysts should be alert as to whether any change in, say, turnover or operating profit results from a change in the composition of the company by way of acquisitions or disposals. If acquisitions or disposals have taken place it is important to focus on whether the performance of the company's continuing operations has improved. Such comparisons will in the future be facilitated by the implementation of FRS3 on financial reporting (see Chapter 5).

The problem of companies changing their shape is not the only difficulty inherent in using horizontal analysis. As the financial information published by companies is prepared on the basis of historical information no account is taken of changing prices. If the real increase – after adjusting for movements in price levels – is to be determined, a company's published figures should be compared with the movements in the rate of inflation (see Illustration 7.2). Whilst adjusting for inflation is technically complex, it is relatively easy to gain a broad understanding of how much of the improvement in a company's performance is due to price changes by comparing the inflation rate with, say, the company's turnover and operating profit.

Comparing UB's performance with the rate of price change shown in Illustration 7.2 suggests that the fall in turnover in 1990 was even more pronounced in real terms, and that once inflation is included operating profit was broadly unchanged on the previous year. Similarly, a significant proportion of the increase in operating profit in 1991 can be attributed to inflation.

The horizontal analysis illustrated above has been conducted by comparing changes across three years. In practice it is often helpful to construct a time series for a longer period, say five years, to try and discern developing trends, and to avoid any distortions arising from a single year's performance. Using a longer time period means that taking inflation into account becomes even more important, given the cumulative effect of annual changes in price levels. The technique of horizontal analysis applied to a longer time period is illustrated below with reference to UB's turnover. In more than half of the years shown, the increase in price levels was greater than the year-on-year change in turnover.

	1986	1987	1988	1989	1990	1991
Turnover (£m)	1,818.4	1,832.4	2,165.2	2,442.4	2,428.3	2,660.5
Turnover, year-on-year change (%)	0.7	0.8	18.2	12.8	(0.6)	9.6
Price change (%)*	2.8	2.6	3.8	4.9	4.3	4.5

*Source: CSO, Monthly Digest of Statistics, April 1992.

Illustration 7.2

WHAT INFLATION RATE TO USE?

For consumer goods and services the most common index used is the *retail price index (RPI)*, which reflects the retail price of a basket of goods and services purchased by consumers. For manufacturing industry *producer price indices* published by the Business Statistics Office show how output prices for individual industries have moved over time. It is important to try and find an index which as closely as possible reflects price changes for the industries to which a company belongs. Using an inappropriate price index leads to distortions to the extent that different industries experience varying rates of inflation.

As UB is predominantly a food manufacturer, selling biscuits, confectionery, snacks and frozen food, an index which reflects movements in the price of food is required. The index chosen is the producer price index for the output of food manufacturing industries – Groups 411–423 of the Standard Industrial Classification. The index for producer prices can be found in the *Monthly Digest of Statistics* published by the CSO. The values of the index between 1989 and 1991 are given below:

Producer prices, Food Manufacturing – Output home sales

Year	Index	Year-on-year change %
1989	114.9	
1990	119.8	4.3
1991	125.2	4.5

Source: Central Statistical Office (CSO), *Monthly Digest of Statistics*, April 1992.

For companies with significant overseas interests it is assumed that movements in the exchange rate reflect differential rates of inflation between countries. Price differences in national markets are therefore accounted for by the translation of overseas earnings in the domstic currency of the country in which the company is domiciled.

Source: Authors.

Table 7.5 below makes cross-sectional comparisons between UB's performance in 1991 and the four selected food manufacturing companies: Associated British Foods (ABF), Cadbury Schweppes, Northern Foods (NF), and Hillsdown Holdings. As no adjustments have been made for differences in accounting policies all figures should be interpreted with care.

Reviewing the comparative figures presented in Table 7.5 reveals a wide divergence of performance. Cost of sales as a percentage of sales ranges from 83% in the case of Hillsdown Holdings to less than 54% for Cadbury Schweppes. UB's ratio at 56% is the second lowest of the five selected companies. Correspondingly, UB also enjoys the second highest gross profit margin at 44%. Distribution costs form a relative large proportion of sales for both UB and Cadbury Schweppes. The latter company justified this in its 1991 Annual Report by stating:

Table 7.5 *Using common size financial statements to undertake a cross-sectional comparison for 1991/92.*

	Cadbury	ABF	UB	Hillsdown	Northern
Turnover	100.0	100.0	**100.0**	100.0	100.0
Cost of sales	53.7	74.2	**56.0**	83.3	73.1
Gross profit	46.2	25.7	**44.0**	16.7	26.8
Distribution costs	25.7	14.4	**29.5**	6.1	12.5
Administrative expenses	9.2	4.5	**5.3**	6.0	5.0
Operating profit	11.2	6.8*	**9.2**	5.0	9.5

*Operating profit for ABF does not include investment income, which if included would increase the ratio of operating profit to sales to 8.5%.

Source: Company annual reports.

> 'Marketing expenditure, key to the future strength and earning potential of our brands, increased both in absolute terms and as a percentage of sales.'
>
> Source: Chairman's Statement, Cadbury Schweppes, *Annual Report 1991*, March 1992, p.4.

Administrative costs range from 9.2% (Cadbury Schweppes) to 4.5% (ABF). Collating these figures allows the operating profit to sales, the net profit margin (NPM), to be calculated. This is the profit a company has left after it has met all its direct and indirect expenses. Cadbury Schweppes recorded the highest NPM at 11.2%, followed by Northern Foods (9.5%) and UB (9.2%).

Examining the figures presented in Table 7.5 suggests that Hillsdown Holdings' performance is at variance with some of the other companies selected. Reviewing the company's portfolio of businesses provides some explanation for the differences in performance. A significant proportion of Hillsdown's sales involve products – fresh meat and bacon, poultry and eggs – where product differentiation is difficult to achieve, and the power of large retail chains in influencing price is strong. To be competitive in such sectors the emphasis is on being a low cost producer. Lower distribution costs reflect the fact that in the case of own-label sales, responsibility for marketing is passed to the retailer. Despite the lower distribution costs to sales ratio, the NPM achieved by Hillsdown Holdings compares badly with the other food companies selected. The example of Hillsdown serves to emphasize that whilst all the companies selected can be classified as food manufacturers, their product market mix and business strategies differ markedly. It is also a timely reminder of the need to construct any comparable database from the 'bottom-up', so that judgements relating to its composition can be made and erroneous comparisons avoided.

Time series analysis and financial ratios

In this part of the chapter, an analysis of UB's financial performance over time is undertaken by selecting a small number of key financial ratios. The common size statement analysis discussed above has already yielded a number of examples of financial ratios, with accounting transactions appearing on the face of the P&L account being presented as a percentage of turnover. In general terms a financial ratio is calculated by comparing two items of accounting information. Thus comparing operating profit to turnover – the net profit margin – is an example of a financial ratio.

Analysts have the opportunity of calculating a large number of ratios, many of which are interrelated. Ratios which may be calculated with reference to a company's financial statements can be grouped into two main categories as listed in Table 7.6, namely:

- operating or activity ratios
- financial ratios.

Operating or activity ratios provide information to the analyst about how a company has been trading. Operating ratios can in turn be clustered into *overall performance* and *working capital ratios* (see Table 7.6). By contrast *financial ratios* are primarily concerned with the financial structure of the company, its ability to service debt and liquidity. *Debt ratios* are concerned with the financial structure of the business, the extent to which the company is financed by loan capital or equity and its ability to service its debt. *Liquidity ratios* focus on the company's ability to meet any short-term cash requirements.

Table 7.6

Operating ratios	Financial ratios
Overall performance:	*Debt ratios:*
• return on capital employed	• gearing ratio
• net profit margin	• debt-equity ratio
• asset turnover.	• interest cover.
Working capital or control ratios:	*Liquidity ratios:*
• stock turnover	• current ratio
• debtor turnover	• acid (or quick) ratio.
• working capital to turnover ratio.	

Overall performance ratios

The first cluster of operating ratios relates to the overall performance of the company, by focusing on *return on capital employed*. ROCE is commonly taken as an overall measure of corporate performance, and is itself determined by two ratios – *net profit margin* and *asset turnover*. NPM, based on operating profit, measures the income received by the company, whilst capital employed reflects the assets used by the business to generate the profit. Since the asset base of a company is likely to change during the year, it is appropriate to measure capital employed by taking the average of total assets at the beginning and end of the year. The relationship between NPM, asset turnover and ROCE is illustrated in Figure 7.3.

Figure 7.3 shows that ROCE is calculated by multiplying a company's NPM by its asset turnover. During 1991 UB's NPM – the operating profit to turnover ratio – was 9.2%, indicating that for every one pound (£) of sales, the company made just over 9p in the £ after meeting its direct and overhead expenses. Further, Table 7.4 shows that the company had succeeded in raising its NPM over the last three years:

	1989	1990	1991
Net profit margin (%)	8.7	9.1	9.2

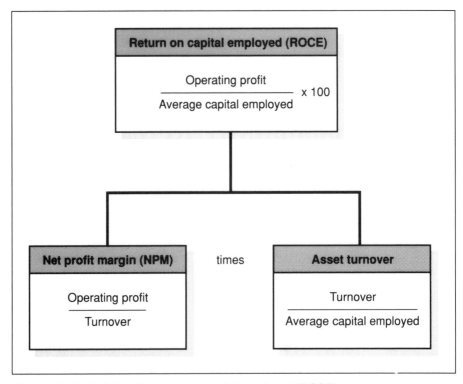

Figure 7.3 Calculating the return on capital employed (ROCE)

The *asset turnover ratio* indicates how many times a company's capital base – its total assets – have been 'turned over' in sales. A high asset turnover suggests that the company is generating a high level of sales from its available capital. Too high a level of asset turnover can be associated with overtrading, a position describing a company whose sales are too large to be sustained comfortably from its existing resource base. Conversely, a low asset turnover may suggest a company is proving itself incapable of achieving a satisfactory level of sales from the assets it has at its disposal.

Table 7. 7 UB – Selected balance sheet items for the period 1988-1991 (£m)

	1988	1989	1990	1991
Total fixed assets	748.5	757.5	863.4	939.9
Stocks	191.8	218.2	220.5	214.2
Trade debtors	249.1	281.9	302.6	331.3
Total current assets	534.0	635.1	658.9	704.2
Total assets	**1,282.5**	**1,392.6**	**1,522.3**	**1,644.1**
Trade creditors	127.2	88.0	113.6	113.4
Creditors: amounts falling due within one year	574.0	517.6	618.6	565.5
Creditors: amounts falling due after more than one year	185.1	188.8	272.2	345.1
Capital and reserves	523.4	686.2	631.5	733.5
Total liabilities	**1,282.5**	**1,392.6**	**1,522.3**	**1,644.1**

Source: UB, *Annual Reports, 1988–91.*

Information relating to capital employed by a company may be obtained with reference to the balance sheet. Selected items from UB's balance sheet for the last three years are reproduced in Table 7.7. A company's capital employed is shown by taking the figure for total assets from the balance sheet. As the balance sheet shows the company's assets and liabilities at a single date, by using the opening and closing balance sheet for an accounting period an average figure for the company's capital employed can be obtained, as demonstrated in Table 7.8.

Table 7.4 shows that UB's sales in 1991 were £2,660.5 m so that the *asset turnover ratio* is as follows:

$$\frac{\text{Turnover}}{\text{Average capital employed}} = \frac{£2,660.5 \text{ m}}{£1,583.2 \text{ m}} = 1.68 \text{ times}$$

The asset turnover ratio calculated above tells the analyst that UB generates sales worth 1.68 times the capital it employed during 1991. Once again comparisons can be made with UB's past performance, and the company's asset

Table 7.8 Calculating the average capital employed by UB for the period 1989–91

	1989	1990	1991
Capital employed at the beginning of the year	1,282.5	1,392.6	1,522.3
Capital employed at the end of the year	1,392.6	1,522.3	1,644.1
Average capital employed for the year	1,337.5	1,457.4	1,583.2

Note: As Table 7.7 illustrates, the company had total assets of £1,522.3 m at the beginning of its 1991 accounting period, and £1,644.1 m at the end. Hence the average capital employed is equal to £1,522.3 m plus £1,644.1 m, divided by two. The average capital employed for 1991 was thus £1,583.2 m. Similar calculations are shown for 1989 and 1990.

turnover ratio is shown below for the last three years. These figures reveal that UB's asset turnover ratio declined between 1989 and 1990, and broadly remained unchanged in 1991:

	1989	1990	1991
Asset turnover ratio	1.83	1.67	1.68

As Figure 7.3 demonstrated, putting the NPM and asset turnover ratio together allows the analyst to calculate a company's ROCE. The ROCE relates the profitability of the business to the amount of capital employed, which as previously noted is often used as an overall indicator of corporate performance:

Year	**NPM x Asset Turnover = ROCE**		
1989	8.7	1.83	15.9
1990	9.1	1.67	15.2
1991	9.2	1.68	15.5

Whilst UB's ROCE shows a marginal decline since 1989, the figures suggest a broadly consistent level of performance by the company. When reviewing changes in ROCE it is worth while remembering that an increase in the ratio can result from one or more of the following changes:

- increase in NPM arising from:
  - reduction in expenses (direct and/or indirect)
  - increase in prices;
- increase in asset turnover arising from:
  - increase in level of sales
  - fall in capital employed.

Illustration 7.3, describing the relative performances of Kwik Save and J. Sainsbury, indicates that the level of both NPM and asset turnover in determining ROCE should always be interpreted in relation to the company's business strategies. Sainsbury seeks to appeal to a broad spectrum of customers, including above-average income groups, offering a wide product range and combining elements of differentiation and low-cost in its business strategy. By contrast Kwik Save offers a predominantly low-cost strategy focused on a limited product range. Only by reviewing what a company is trying to achieve can it be decided whether the level of a particular ratio is appropriate.

Illustration 7.3

KWIK SAVE PLC AND J. SAINSBURY PLC

Kwik Save and J. Sainsbury are major companies operating in the UK food retailing sector. The two companies have very different business strategies, which as a consequence lead to differences in their recorded financial performance.

J. Sainsbury operates predominantly out-of-town food superstores costing sometimes in excess of £25 m per store to develop. Each store is expensively fitted out, and the store environment considered an important aspect of the company's differentiated retail strategy. The company sells both leading manufacturers' products, and a high proportion of own-brand products of good quality. As a result of its perceived quality and good operating efficiencies the company is able to achieve a high net profit margin.

By contrast Kwik Save is a food discounter, selling predominantly manufacturers' brands on the basis of highly competitive prices. Its stores are smaller than those operated by J. Sainsbury, are rented and only contain basic fixtures and fittings. Whereas Sainsbury spends upwards of £25 m on developing a new store, Kwik Save's investment in a new store is likely to be in the region of £1 m, with property being rented and not owned by the company. Whilst net profit margins are below those of Sainsbury, the lower level of capital employed means that Kwik Save's asset turnover is higher. Indeed the company's ROCE is the highest of all companies operating in the UK food retailing sector:

	NPM	Asset turnover	ROCE
J. Sainsbury (1991)	7.63	2.03	15.5
Kwik Save (1991)	5.51	4.11	22.6

Source: Company reports

Working capital or control ratios

The second cluster of ratios – *working capital ratios* – is concerned with how well a company controls its working capital requirements. For this reason the financial ratios concerned with working capital needs are also sometimes referred to as control ratios. As working capital requirements influence a company's current asset base, this second cluster of ratios help to influence the amount of capital employed by the business. Consequently these ratios have a direct bearing on the company's asset turnover. Figure 7.4 illustrates this relationship.

As Figure 7.4 demonstrates if the company's current assets are excessive, capital employed will be too large in relation to turnover, and the asset turnover ratio correspondingly depressed. This point emphasizes the need for the company to exercise careful control of its working capital ratios.

The first of the working capital ratios selected for examination is *stock turnover.* This ratio seeks to identify whether a company's management of its stock is efficient. Unnecessary money tied up in stock is a drain on the company's resources, and can result in serious cash flow implications. A company should aim to hold the lowest level of stock commensurate with its marketing strategies.

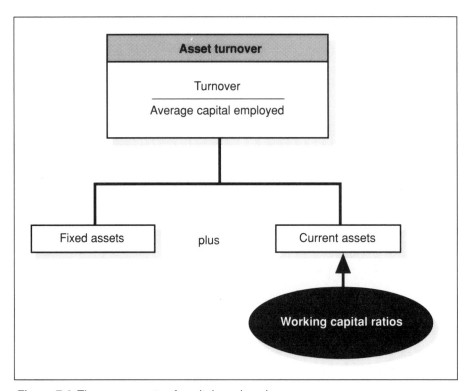

Figure 7.4 *The components of capital employed*

When calculating stock turnover the convention is to take the figure for the cost of sales and relate the company's holding of stocks to this figure, given that stocks are usually valued at cost. A company's stock turnover may be expressed as a multiple of the cost of sales, or in terms of the number of days it takes to turn the stock holding over. Table 7.9 shows how stock turnover is calculated by using UB's figures for the last three years.

Table 7.9 *UB stock turnover, 1989-91*

	1989	1990	1991
Cost of sales	1,463.4	1,434.1	1,490.8
Stocks	218.2	220.5	214.2
Stock turnover (times)	**6.7**	**6.5**	**7.0**

Within limits, the higher the stock turnover the better. A low stock turnover ratio indicates that stock is only drawn down slowly, and brings the possibility that the company has excessive stocks of raw materials or finished goods that cannot be sold. Table 7.9 shows that UB improved its stock turnover ratio in 1991, following a deterioration in the previous year. Closer inspection of the figures presented in Table 7.9 shows that stock turnover rose in 1991, reflecting a fall in the level of stocks despite a small rise in the cost of sales.

The stock turnover ratio can alternatively be expressed as the number of days its takes to 'turn over' the company's stock holding. This *stock turnover (days) ratio* is calculated by:

$$\frac{\text{Stock}}{\text{Cost of sales}} \times 365 = \frac{£214.2 \text{ m}}{£1,490.8 \text{ m}} = 52.4 \text{ days}$$

	1989	1990	1991
Stock turnover (days)	54.4	56.1	52.4

The faster the company can turn its stock over the better, as this indicates smaller amounts of money are being tied up in stock holding. Expressed as a number of days, the stock turnover not surprisingly shows the same trend as described in Table 7.9, with stock turnover deteriorating in 1990 but then improving.

The second working capital ratio selected for review is *debtor turnover*. This ratio captures the relationship between the trade debtors of the company (people who owe the company money for goods received) and sales. Again, a company should seek to reduce the monies it has tied up with debtors to the minimum level commensurate with its marketing policies. As with stock turnover, the debtor ratio can be expressed as (a) a multiple, or (b) in terms of days:

$$\text{(a) Debtor turnover} = \text{Turnover/Trade debtors}$$

From UB's 1991 accounts the debtor turnover may be calculated as follows:

$$\text{£2,660.5 m/£331.3 m} = 8.0 \text{ times}$$

Alternatively, (b) in terms of the number of days:

$$\text{(Debtors/Turnover)} \times 365 = \text{(£331.3m/£2660.5m)} \times 365 = 45 \text{ days (1991)}$$

Table 7.10 summarizes UB's debtor ratios for the last three years.

Table 7.10 UB debtor ratios, 1989–91

	1989	1990	1991
Sales	2,442.4	2,428.3	2,660.5
Trade debtors	281.9	302.6	331.3
Debtor turnover (times)	**8.7**	**8.0**	**8.0**
Debtor turnover (days)	**42.1**	**45.4**	**45.4**

Reviewing Table 7.10 UB's debtor turnover deteriorated in 1990 when compared to the previous year, but remained unchanged in 1991. One challenge for food manufacturers is the increasing power of the major retailers and the terms on which they do business. In order to gain additional business, food retailers may expect generous credit terms from suppliers.

The third ratio concerned with how a company is managing its working capital requirements is the *working capital to turnover ratio*. This ratio is designed to show how much working capital is required to support turnover, and provides an indication of overall working capital needs. It is calculated by taking the monies the company has tied up in stock and debtors, subtracting trade credit the company has been given, and expressing this figure – its working capital needs – as a percentage of its turnover. Formally, the working capital (%) ratio is calculated according to the following expression:

$$\text{((Stocks + Trade debtors)} - \text{Trade creditors)/Turnover} \times 100$$

Table 7.11 *UB working capital to turnover ratio, 1989–91*

	1989	1990	1991
Stocks	218.2	220.5	214.2
Trade debtors	281.9	302.6	331.3
Trade creditors	88.0	113.4	113.6
Working capital requirements	**412.1**	**409.5**	**432.1**
Turnover	2,442.4	2,428.3	2,660.5
Working capital to sales ratio (%)	**16.8**	**16.8**	**16.2**

If the working capital to sales ratio is increasing it suggests that the company's working capital needs in relation to its sales are growing. Table 7.11 indicates UB's ratio fell between 1990 and 1991. The working capital to sales ratio as defined above is the average figure for the organization, but it also gives an indication of the *incremental* value of the ratio. The incremental working capital to turnover ratio shows how much working capital requirements will vary as turnover changes. If we make the assumption that UB's average and incremental ratios are the same, then using the 1991 figure above, the analyst is able to calculate how much additional working capital the company will require if, say, turnover rises by £100 m:

Increase in sales × working capital to turnover ratio = Increase in working capital required

£100 m × 0.162 = £16.2 m

Increasing sales by £100 m will require the company to fund additional working capital needs of £16.2 m. Figure 7.5 plots the company's working capital requirements in relation to increases in turnover, assuming that the working capital to turnover ratio remains constant throughout. The increasing working capital needs illustrated in Figure 7.5 provides one of the main reasons why, as a company expands, its financing requirements grow. It also reminds the analyst of why it is important to reflect on the company's cash position, the focus of Chapter 6.

Financial ratios

Financial ratios represent the second principal grouping of ratios, which in turn can be clustered under the headings shown in Table 7.12.

Debt ratios

The *gearing ratio* relates a company's total borrowings to capital employed. Although definitions of the gearing ratio vary, the analysis which follows defines

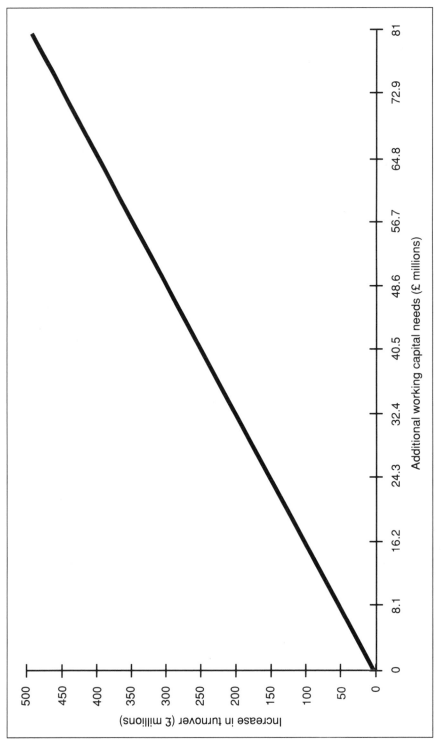

Figure 7.5 Additional working capital requirements arising from an increase in turnover

Table 7.12

Operating ratios	**Financial ratios**
Operating ratios:	*Debt ratios:*
● return on capital employed	● gearing ratio
● net profit margin	● debt-equity ratio
● asset turnover.	● interest cover.
Working capital or control ratios:	*Liquidity ratios:*
● stock turnover	● current ratio
● debtor turnover	● acid (or quick) ratio.
● working capital to turnover ratio.	

the ratio to include all the borrowings of a company, including short-term loans (up to one year), divided by the total capital employed. The rationale for this definition is that it measures the extent to which borrowed funds have been utilized to finance the company's capital base. The *gearing ratio* may be expressed as:

$$\frac{\text{Total borrowings}}{\text{Capital employed}} = \frac{£327.0 \text{ m}}{£1,644.1\text{m}} \times 100 = 19.9\% \ (1991)$$

If a company has a high gearing ratio is can be said to be financing its assets predominantly by debt. Conversely, a low gearing ratio suggests that the company is primarily financed by shareholders' funds (equity). Details of UB's debt are to be found in Note 18 to the 1991 accounts, which provides a more detailed breakdown of the borrowings of the company than is shown on the face of the balance sheet. The details contained in Note 18 are summarized below.

Table 7.13

Loans, overdrafts and finance lease obligations:	
	£m
Bank loans and overdrafts	
Bank loans	54.0
Overdrafts	30.1
Debenture and other loans	235.8
Financial lease obligations	7.1
Total borrowings*	327.0
*of which £71.5 m was repayable in under one year	

Source: Note 18, *UB Annual Report 1991*, p.47.

Having identified the company's total borrowings the gearing ratio can be calculated by taking the corresponding figure for capital employed on the balance sheet date. Note that in contrast to the calculation of asset turnover and

ROCE, the capital employed at the balance sheet date is used in the calculation of the gearing ratio to ensure consistency with the figure for borrowings, which also relate to the same date. Table 7.14 shows how the UB gearing ratio for the last three years is arrived at, as well as its final value.

Table 7.14 UB's gearing ratio, 1989–91

	1989	1990	1991
Total borrowings	193.2	313.0	327.0
Capital employed	1,392.6	1,522.3	1,643.2
Gearing ratio (%)	**13.9**	**20.6**	**19.9**

UB's gearing ratio as depicted in Table 7.14 rose sharply between 1989 and 1990, but remained virtually unchanged in 1991. The evaluation of these changes should be linked to key strategic decisions the company has taken and the analysis of the company cash flow statement in Chapter 6. In 1990 the company undertook a number of important strategic acquisitions partly financed by increased levels of borrowings.

It is important to remember that the balance sheet values that determined the denominator for the gearing ratio, and the debt–equity ratio which is to follow, is open to considerable manipulation. The discussion in Chapter 5 highlighted some of the opportunities available to companies wishing to enhance performance at the expense of the balance sheet. Common techniques which in the past have been used by companies include the revaluation of property assets, thereby increasing capital employed and reducing gearing and associated ratios at the stroke of a pen. An example is provided in Illustration 7.4. It was also noted that the use of off-balance sheet financing instruments has reduced the transparency of a company's balance sheet, thereby rendering the information on many ratios with a balance sheet component somewhat opaque.

As well as looking at a company's gearing level it is often rewarding to review the extent to which the company's borrowings are repayable in the short term (up to a year) or over longer periods. This information is again provided in a note to the accounts, thereby emphasizing the importance of analysing financial statements as opposed to relying on published summaries and database material.

Illustration 7.4

HOW REVALUING PROPERTY ASSETS CAN REDUCE STATED GEARING

Assume a company has the following balance sheet:

	£m
Fixed assets	
Property	1,000
Other	1,000
Current assets	1,000
Total assets	3,000
Total borrowings	2,000

On the basis of the figures above, the company has a gearing ratio (£2,000m/ £3,000 m) of 66.7%. If property values are rising, and the company's directors decide to revalue the company's property assets so that they are now worth £2,000 m, gearing (£2,000 m/£4,000 m) falls to 50%. Conversely, if property values fall and the directors of the company reduce the value of the company's property by halving its value, gearing (£2,000 m/£2,500 m) becomes 80%.

This very simple example highlights the need to treat the value of the company's capital employed as shown on the balance sheet with care.

Table 7.15   Term structure of UB's debt, 1990–91

Repayment periods	1990 £m	1990 %	1991 £m	1991 %
Over five years	131.5	42.0	157.9	48.2
Over two years but under five	42.2	13.5	97.6	29.8
Under one year	139.3	44.5	71.5	21.9
Total	313.0	100.0	327.0	100.0

Source: Note 18, *UB Annual Report 1991*, March 1992, p.47.

The term structure of UB's debt as detailed in Table 7.15 shows that at the end of 1991 the majority of the company's borrowings did not have to be repaid in less than two years. The more short term the repayment period the more vulnerable a company may be to cash flow difficulties if the renegotiation of borrowings proves difficult or expensive. Table 7.15 further illustrates that UB reduced its short-term borrowings and increased medium- and long-term debt in 1991 when compared to the previous year. This serves to emphasize that analysts should attempt to compare changes to the term structure of the company borrowings between years in order to gain a better appreciation of the company's financing policies. UB's policies between 1990 and 1991 were highlighted by the Group Finance Director:

'In March, we refinanced certain of the short-term borrowings arising from our 1990 and 1991 acquisition programme onto a long-term basis through the private placement in the USA of $125 m of 10-year bonds carrying a coupon of 9%. These funds have since been swapped onto a floating rate basis and into the appropriate European currencies. Mainly as a result of this refinancing, only 22% of gross borrowings at year end were repayable within one year and 48% has a maturity of greater than five years.'

Source: Financial Review, *UB Annual Report 1991*, March 1992, p.28.

The *debt–equity ratio* is related closely to the gearing ratio. As a general rule this ratio is a more sensitive measure of a company's gearing. The ratio is calculated by taking the total borrowing of a company and expressing it as a percentage of shareholders' funds. Shareholders' funds (capital and reserves) may be obtained from the summary balance sheet presented in Table 7.7 earlier in the chapter. Table 7.16 presents UB's debt–equity ratio for the last three years.

Table 7.16 UB's debt–equity ratio, 1989–91

	1989	1990	1991
Total borrowings	193.2	313.0	327.0
Shareholders' funds	686.2	631.5	733.5
Debt–equity ratio (%)	**28.1**	**49.5**	**44.5**

As the denominator for the debt–equity ratio is made up of shareholders' funds rather than capital employed (shareholders' funds plus borrowings), the value for the debt–equity ratio is inevitably greater than for the gearing ratio. Table 7.16 again indicates a marked rise in the company's borrowing between 1989 and 1990, followed by a small reduction in the ratio in 1991. As in the case of the gearing ratio, these changes in level should be related to the company's cash flow position. Between balance sheet dates it is important to monitor the company's activities, particularly acquisitions and disposals, to gain an appreciation of how the company's level of borrowings may change.

Taken together the debt–equity and gearing ratios allow the analyst to determine the extent to which the business is predominantly funded by debt or equity. Using borrowed funds to part finance the business up to a certain level of debt generally reduces the cost of capital, not least because of the fact that interest payments on such borrowings can be offset against tax. A critical issue is the level at which a company becomes over-geared and finds the servicing (i.e. interest payments) of the debt difficult to meet.

The *interest cover ratio* is designed to assist in answering this question. This ratio calculates how many times interest payments are covered by profit before interest and tax (operating profits):

Interest cover (×) = Profits before interest and tax/Interest paid

Table 7.17 *UB's interest cover, 1989–91*

	1989	1990	1991
Profit on ordinary activities before interest	212.1	220.7	244.9
Interest paid	21.4	21.3	31.7
Interest cover (times)	**9.9**	**10.3**	**7.7**

UB's interest cover for the last three years is calculated in Table 7.17. It shows that in 1991 UB's interest payments were covered over seven times by profits before interest indicating that profits would have to fall to one-seventh of their 1991 level before the company found it difficult to service its debt. At the current level of interest cover lenders to UB would appear to be fairly certain of receiving their due interest. Nevertheless, the company's interest cover fell markedly in 1991 when compared to the previous year, as interest payments rose by almost 50% to £31.7 m.

Whilst UB does not capitalize interest it is important to remember that where companies do adopt this practice the interest paid on the face of the P&L account can be misleading as to the true level of interest payments the company is making in cash terms. Analysts should always check the relevant note to the accounts to see what, if any, interest payments have been capitalized.

As the level of interest payments is at least partially linked to the level of debt, the risk of a company not being able to service its borrowings increases as the level of gearing rises. The ability of a company to service a high level of debt over time is also linked to the industry(ies) in which the company operates. As a major food manufacturer with a number of strong consumer brands, UB's earnings can be regarded as fairly stable. By contrast cyclical companies do not enjoy the same stability of earnings. Correspondingly, some companies, which with hindsight over-borrowed in the 1980s, have found it difficult to meet interest payments at the start of the 1990s when sales were falling, and interest rates high.

Summarizing these different factors suggests that the interest cover of companies is likely to increase during periods of economic expansion, when sales are generally rising and interest rates relatively low, but to decrease when economic conditions become more difficult. Hence the analyst needs to judge the level of borrowing, and the level of interest cover *relative* to the business cycle and the characteristics of the industry in which the company operates. It is also important, of course, for the analyst to be concerned with what the company is doing with any additional borrowings, and whether the uses to which the company is putting such funds can be justified on the basis of future earnings.

Operational gearing

An important concept to consider in relation to highly financially geared companies, is the extent to which a company is also highly geared operationally. *Operational gearing* describes the relationship between a change in a company's sales turnover and profitability. A company is said to be highly geared operationally when it has a high proportion of fixed, and therefore in the short term inescapable, costs which results in any change in turnover having a disproportionate effect on profitability. Companies which have high operational gearing may well be driven into a loss-making situation if sales begin to fall. Equally, an increase in sales may bring forth a large increase in profitability. Companies with both high operational and financial gearing are likely to experience considerable variations in profits attributable to shareholders if sales fluctuate markedly. This is demonstrated in Illustration 7.5.

Rising interest rates potentially increase the cost of debt servicing to the extent that borrowings have been made at *floating* (market) rates of interest. Companies which borrowed at fixed rates of interest, or whose cost of borrowing is capped (i.e. there is a maximum level to which rates can rise) are less exposed to an upward movement in interest rates. Similarly, the same companies may not receive such a large benefit from a fall in interest rates when compared to a company the borrowings of which predominantly reflect current rates of interest. It is only by careful examination of notes to accounts that the analyst can gain a full understanding of a company's term structure for interest payments.

Liquidity ratios

The final two ratios to be computed relate to a company's liquidity position. The *current ratio* describes the relationship between the company's current assets and its current liabilities, and provides an indication of whether the company could meet its short-term liabilities by liquidating its current assets if the need arose. It is calculated by dividing current assets by current liabilities. Current liabilities are described on the face of the balance sheet as creditors: amounts falling due within one year. The calculation of the ratio is illustrated in Table 7.18.

Table 7.18 UB *current ratio, 1989–91*

	1989	1990	1991
Current assets	635.1	658.9	704.2
Current liabilities	517.6	618.6	565.5
Current ratio (times)	**1.22**	**1.01**	**1.24**

Illustration 7.5

MFI

MFI, a furniture retailer, was subject to a management buy-out in November 1987. A high proportion of the finance for the buy-out was in the form of debt: the company was highly financially geared. The initial intention following the buy-out was that the company would be floated on the stock market within two years and the company's borrowings largely replaced by equity finance.

Unfortunately, the movement of the UK economy into recession and the general problems facing the housing market led the company to begin to experience falling sales during 1989. As the company was highly operationally geared – space costs, labour, etc. – falling sales resulted in the company failing to reach profit targets and being forced to refinance borrowings with its bankers. For the next few years the company struggled to survive, but managed to do so through strong management and a policy of reducing costs.

By the middle of 1992 the company was in a strong enough business situation to consider again a flotation on the stock market, which if successful, would reduce debt from some £500 m to £100 m and improve profitability. Further, given the company's high operational gearing, any small improvement in sales would bring forth a substantial increase in profitability.

The case of MFI illustrates the intrinsic dangers of high operational and financial gearing being present in one company. Given the fall in sales experienced during the recession the company only just survived. Many others in a similar position did not.

Source: Based on press reports at the time of the company's flotation.

A current ratio in excess of 1.0 shows a company's current liabilities are more than covered by current assets. Table 7.18 shows that UB's current ratio fell in 1990, but more than recovered to its previous level in 1991. Given the overall strength of the company, the current ratio does not suggest that the company has a liquidity problem.

A second ratio concerned with a company's liquidity is the *acid test* (or *quick*) *ratio*. This ratio is similar to the current ratio, but excludes the value of stocks from the figure for current assets on the basis that they may be difficult to liquidate in an emergency. As a consequence it is a more severe examination of a company's short-term liquidity than the current ratio. Table 7.19 shows that for UB there has been no major change in stock values, since the acid test ratio mirrors the trend shown by the current ratio.

Given the ability of most large companies to raise quickly additional funds to meet any short-term liquidity problems, companies tend to work on lower acid ratios than was formerly the case. As a consequence it is difficult to suggest absolute values for the ratios against which to measure a company's performance. Most textbooks indicate a current ratio of between 1.0 and 1.5, and an acid test of around 1.0 is acceptable. Many companies work below these levels and

Table 7.19 *UB acid test or quick ratio, 1989–91*

	1989	1990	1991
Current assets less stocks	416.9	658.9	704.2
Current liabilities	517.6	618.6	565.5
Acid test or quick ratio (times)	**0.8**	**0.7**	**0.9**

the analyst should assess the relative changes to a company's liquidity ratios against the context of the needs and position of the business.

Summary

In summary, attention throughout this section has focused on the need to conscientiously abstract the raw data from published financial statements and to calculate pertinent operating and financial ratios over time. Such comparative analysis assists in probing the links between financial ratios and strategic imperatives. As such, ratios are a means to an end, not an end in themselves. Table 7.20 provides a summary of the key operating and financial ratios used, how they are calculated, and what they mean.

Cross-sectional analysis and financial ratios

Comparative analysis may be approached either through a time series comparison of a company's previous results, or from a cross-sectional perspective using competitors' performance or industry averages. Given that industry groups vary widely in product range and firm size, analysts should be extremely cautious in using proprietary databases as the basis for their inter-company comparisons. Not only can little or no insight be gained into various accounting policies adopted by relevant companies, but the defined ratios used by external agencies may not match the user's requirements. Our approach is to compare UB's performance with food manufacturers who pass the compatibility and business context tests outlined in Figure 7.2 and listed in Table 7.2. The key clusters of ratios examined relate to (a) overall performance, (b) working capital, (c) debt and (d) liquidity.

The different ratios are considered in the same order as previously presented, beginning with those operating ratios – ROCE, NPM and asset turnover – which provide an indication of overall trading performance. Comparisons of overall performance between the selected companies are set out in Table 7.21. Unless otherwise stated companies are ranked in order of turnover, as shown in Table 7.1.

Table 7.20 *Summary of operating and financial ratios*

	Ratio	How calculated	Interpretation
Operating ratios	**Overall performance**		
	Return on capital employed (%)	Operating profit/Average capital employed x 100	Provides an overall measure of corporate performance
	Net profit margin (%)	Operating profit/Turnover x 100	Describes the percentage profit for each £ of turnover after direct and indirect expenses have been deducted
	Asset turnover (x)	Turnover/Average capital employed	Shows how many times sales generated from the capital employed
	Working capital		
	Stock turnover (x)	Cost of sales/Stocks	Indicates how many times stocks are being turned over in a year
	Debtor turnover (x)	Turnover/Trade debtors	The number of times trade debtors are rotated in a year
	Working capital to turnover ratio (%)	(Stocks + Trade debtors - Trade creditors)/Turnover x 100	Proides a measure of the overall working capital needs of the company. High ratios suggest working capital needs are greater
Financial ratios	**Debt ratios**		
	Gearing ratio (%)	Total borrowings/Capital employed x 100	Measures the extent of borrowings to capital employed
	Debt – equity ratio (%)	Total borrowings/Shareholders' funds x 100	Relates total debt to shareholders' funds to indicate how company is financed
	Interest cover (x)	Profit on ordinary activities before interest/Interest paid	How many times profits cover interest payments. A measure of the ability to service debt
	Liquidity ratios		
	Current ratio (x)	Current assets/Current liabilities	How many times current assets cover current liabilities
	Acid test (x)	Current assets less stocks/Current liabilities	Current ratio less stocks. A more stringent test of liquidity

Table 7.21 *Inter-company comparisons of overall financial performance**

Company	NPM	Asset turnover	ROCE
Cadbury Schweppes	11.2	1.22	13.6
ABF	6.8	1.43	9.7
United Biscuits	**9.2**	**1.68**	**15.5**
Hillsdown Holdings	5.0	2.06	10.3
Northern Foods	9.5	1.59	15.1

*Figures relate to the following accounting periods: ABF 9/92, Cadbury Schweppes 12/91, Hillsdown 12/91, Northern 3/92 and UB 12/91.

Source: Company reports.

Of the five companies selected UB recorded the highest ROCE at 15.5%, and ABF and Hillsdown Holdings the lowest. Interestingly the company with the highest NPM – Cadbury Schweppes – had the lowest asset turnover. Conversely, Hillsdown Holdings with the lowest NPM, had the highest asset turnover.

A company's asset turnover should be examined with care. A high asset turnover may either reflect a healthy level of sales generation, or the use of capital in the business which is largely worn out and in need of replacement. Old capital equipment which has been largely depreciated will have a low balance sheet value, inflating the asset turnover ratio through the presence of a small denominator. In such circumstances a high asset turnover ratio reflects an under-capitalized business. Consequently, when companies invest in replacing assets they correspondingly increase the level of capital employed and this can reduce asset turnover if sufficient additional sales are not forthcoming. For example, Cadbury Schweppes' continuing programme of modernizing its fixed asset base during a period of slow growth of sales in 1991 resulted in the asset turnover falling (Financial Review, *Annual Report 1991*, p.28). The company's asset ratio fell from 1.33 in 1990 to 1.22.

The age profile, and hence value, of a company's assets is only one reason why the asset turnover and ROCE figures should be treated with care. Further difficulties arise in respect of both ratios as the amount of capital employed by a company is influenced strongly by a range of accounting policies. To illustrate the difficulties two examples are considered below, namely:

- revaluation of property assets
- brand accounting.

Notwithstanding the depressed nature of the commercial and residential property markets in the UK during the early 1990s, for much of the post-war period property prices have risen. Rises in property prices have offered the opportunity for companies to revalue their property assets upwards. This action results in the capital employed by the company increasing and asset turnover correspondingly being reduced. Companies may also be motivated to adopt a policy of asset revaluation by the opportunity it affords to reduce the company's gearing.

A second problematic area is that of brand accounting, which is particularly relevant for food manufacturers. Companies which place brands on the balance sheet raise the level of their recorded intangible assets and correspondingly increase the level of capital employed. Companies may value internally developed brands and/or brands purchased on acquisition. Table 7.22 summarizes the policies adopted by different food manufacturers.

Table 7.22 *Valuing and placing brands on the balance sheet*

Food company	Brands valued on acquisition?	Internally developed brands valued?
ABF	No	No
Northern Foods	No	No
Hillsdown Holdings	No	No
Cadbury Schweppes	Yes	No
UB	Yes	No
RHM	Yes	Yes

Source: Company reports.

Table 7.22 reveals the extent to which the five companies differ in their policies on valuing brands and placing them on the balance sheet. The potential effect of the different treatments of brands may be illustrated by taking the case of Rank Hovis McDougall (RHM) prior to its acquisition by Tomkins plc in the autumn of 1992. Table 7.23 illustrates the effect of brands on the calculation of RHM's ROCE and debt–equity ratios.

Table 7.23 *Calculation of ROCE and debt–equity ratios for RHM, 1991*

	ROCE (%)	Debt/equity ratio (%)
Including intangible assets	8.80	14.4
Excluding intangible assets	13.91	34.3

Source: *RHM Annual Report 1991*, November 1991.

The effect of including intangible assets in the calculation of ROCE is to reduce the ratio from almost 14% to less than 9%, representing a reduction of in excess of 35%. Equally, the inclusion of intangible assets has a dramatic effect on the debt–equity ratio. If intangible assets are included the debt–equity ratio stands at 14.4%, but if they are excluded the ratio rises to 34.3%.

The second set of ratios to review for the purposes of inter-company comparisons are the working capital ratios. These are summarized in Table 7.24. Leaving aside trade creditors, the higher the stock and debtor turnover ratios, the lower the working capital to turnover ratio.

Table 7.24   *Inter-company comparisons – working capital ratios*

Company	Stock turnover (×)	Debtor turnover (×)	Working capital to sales (%)
Cadbury Schweppes	5.2	7.5	15.4
ABF	7.9	16.6	8.8
United Biscuits	6.9	8.0	16.2
Hillsdown Holdings	7.0	15.0	11.8
Northern Foods	14.4	8.6	5.7

Source: Company reports.

Analysis of the working capital ratios reveals ABF has the highest debtor turnover, the second highest stock turnover and the lowest working capital to sales ratio. Northern Foods shows the highest stock turnover and the lowest working capital to sales ratio. UB's stock turnover and debtor's ratio are marginally, but importantly, ahead of Cadbury Schweppes whose stock turnover is the lowest of the selected companies. UB's total working capital requirements, as reflected in the working capital to sales ratio, is the highest of the selected companies.

Table 7.25   *Inter-company comparisons – financing ratios*

Company	Gearing ratio (%)	Debt–equity ratio (%)	Interest cover (x)
Cadbury Schweppes	25.6	68.8	6.3
ABF	11.0	17.3	8.2
United Biscuits	19.9	44.5	7.7
Hillsdown Holdings	21.2	47.1	5.2
Northern Foods	27.0	88.4	14.2

Source: Company reports.

Careful consideration of Table 7.25 reveals a number of interesting points. Northern Foods appears to have both a very high debt–equity ratio and very high interest cover. The company has almost no medium- or long-term debt, and virtually all its debt is of less than one year's duration. If short-term debt were excluded its debt–equity ratio would be less than 2%. The majority of the short-term debt is held in the form of bills payable.

On closer inspection of Northern Foods' accounts short-term borrowings increased from £68.2 m in 1991 to £239.3 m in 1992. The company spent some £382.1 m on acquisitions, principally Express Diary Ltd and Eden Vale Ltd, of which £233.9 m was financed by the issue of additional shares, with the remainder being met, for the present, by using short-term borrowings. Further, the writing off of goodwill arising from the acquisitions amounted to £282 m, thereby reducing shareholders' funds from £305.4 m in 1991, when the debt–equity ratio was at a more comfortable level of 24%. Why then does the company's interest cover appear to be so high? As the major acquisitions were not completed until 3 February 1992, and the company's reporting period ended on 31 March 1992, the interest paid in the year has yet to fully reflect the rise in borrowings. Unless the company is able to significantly reduce borrowings during 1992/93, at the next balance sheet date interest cover would be much lower. Again this example illustrates the need to read the notes to the accounts with care and consistently monitor the actions of the company between the publication dates of its annual reports.

ABF has the lowest gearing ratios of the sample companies, and the second highest interest cover. Cadbury Schweppes and UB have similar financing ratios, but the former has a higher level of gearing and lower interest cover.

Table 7.26 *Inter-company comparisons – liquidity ratios*

Company	Current ratio (%)	Acid test ratio (%)
Cadbury Schweppes	1.22	0.89
ABF	2.36	1.75
United Biscuits	1.24	0.87
Hillsdown Holdings	1.91	1.16
Northern Foods	0.61	0.49

Source: Company reports.

A number of interesting points can be made when evaluating Table 7.26. ABF's liquidity ratios are high due to the presence of a significant amount of short-term investment, totalling some £663 m for the year in question. Northern Foods' ratios look low because of the presence of sizeable short-term debt discussed above. Similarly, the ratios for Hillsdown Holdings are partly explained by the presence of some £354.0 m of cash at bank and in hand, thereby increasing the level of the company's current assets. The ratios for Cadbury Schweppes and UB are virtually identical.

The caveats introduced earlier in respect of comparative analysis, together with some of the difficulties highlighted at each stage in the text, suggest that the technique of inter-company comparisons should be applied with great care. The technique clearly necessitates careful judgements to be made at each stage of the process. Certainly of the companies examined, perhaps Cadbury Schweppes, whilst operating in different product markets, comes closest to offering an appropriate basis for assessing UB's performance.

Concluding remarks

This chapter has introduced a range of financial techniques which are designed to help the analyst evaluate the financial performance of a company both in the context of its historical performance and in relation to competitors. Although focusing primarily on financial information the text contains many examples of how the financial understanding of a company needs to be linked with non-financial analysis to enable the full implications of the financial data to become clear.

In this context it is interesting to reflect on the discussion paper issued in April 1992 by the Accounting Standards Board (ASB) on the need for companies to issue an *Operating and Financial Review (OFR)* as part of their annual report. It is proposed that the OFR would provide management with an opportunity to discuss in a structured way some of the main factors underlying the performance and financial position portrayed in the financial statements. By such means users of the annual report would be given a fuller understanding of the business and the environment in which it operates. (ASB, 1992, p.1):

> 'What we're after is management going behind the numbers and helping people understand their business. I suspect many private shareholders will read this rather than the accounts.'
> Source: David Tweedie, Chairman of the ASB, quoted in the *Financial Times*, 30 April 1992, p.22.

The ASB proposes that the OFR would give management the opportunity to comment on three main areas:

- *The operating results*. This part of the OFR would explain 'to the user of financial statements the main influences and uncertainties affecting the enterprises' results and operating cash flow, by major segment, ... thus assisting the user in making his own assessment of likely further results' (p.4). The review would also include a discussion of the main risks and uncertainties facing consumers, including the sensitivity to the economic and business environment.

- *A review of the financial needs and resources.* This part of the OFR would focus on the organization's liquidity and solvency, and include the management's approach to managing interest and exchange rates.
- *Commentary on shareholders' return and value.* This part of the report would discuss the 'relationship between the company's operating results and shareholders' earnings and dividend payments; and the relationship between financial statements and the overall value of the enterprise' (p.6).

The proposed development of an OFR mirrors North American practice where similar requirements are already in existence, although the ASB is at this stage proposing a voluntary rather than regulatory approach to the adoption of the new statement. The potential lack of an enforcing mechanism in the UK could prove to be problematic as to whether the OFR is indeed of value to the analyst.

The proposed introduction of the OFR together with the continuing work of the ASB offers the prospect of external users of financial information having a much improved base from which to undertake the analysis of companies. This does not, however, mean that vigilance in assessing corporate performance will need to be any less. Whilst it is hoped that the worst excesses of creative accounting exposed in the 1980s are no longer employed, some companies and their auditors are likely to continue to test the boundaries of the new accounting framework being developed. Evidence that some companies are not being guided by the spirit of the new framework brought forth a strong response from the Chairman of the ASB, Mr David Tweedie. He was reported as having threatened to introduce a 'monumental rule-book' itemizing every conceivable accounting practice if companies did not desist from attempting to circumvent the reasoning behind the new reporting frameworks being introduced by the ASB (*Financial Times*, 12 December 1992, p.6). Companies operating against the spirit of the new standards were liable to find themselves subject to detailed investigation by the Financial Reporting Review Panel. This only serves to emphasize that external users of accounts must be on their guard.

The following checklist and accompanying figures are designed to enable both managers and analysts to be able to make comparisons between the relative performance of companies operating in similar markets.

Checklist

- *Identify the company's core activities and consider which competitors can be used for the purposes of inter-company comparisons.*
- *Undertake a common size analysis of the company's P&L account.*
- *Review the vertical analysis of the P&L account and assess movements in the key ratios.*

- *Using a horizontal analysis of the company P&L account identify key trends. Make sure due account has been taken of changes in the composition of the company and the effect of inflation.*

- *Calculate the overall performance ratios for the company and evaluate. (Figure 7.6 provides a pro-forma for this task.)*

- *Review the company working capital ratios. Do you believe the company is controlling its working capital needs effectively?*

- *Assess the company's levels of debt and its ability to service interest payments. Do these areas give cause for concern?*

- *Check the company's liquidity levels. Are they acceptable?*

- *Repeat the ratio analysis using inter-company comparisons. Is the company's relative performance satisfactory? (Figure 7.7 provides a pro-forma for this task.)*

Ratio	Year		Change	Interpretation
Overall performance	1991	1992	1992/91	
Return on capital employed (%)				
Net profit margin (%)				
Asset turnover (x)				
Working capital				
Stock turnover (x)				
Debtor turnover (x)				
Working capital to turnover ratio (%)				
Debt ratios				
Gearing ratio (%)				
Debt – equity ratio (%)				
Interest cover (x)				
Liquidity ratios				
Current ratio (x)				
Acid test (x)				

Operating ratios / Financial ratios

Time series analysis may be extended adding further columns to accommodate additional years.

Figure 7.6 Time series comparison checklist: operating and financial ratios

	Ratio	Focus company	Competitors			Interpretation
			A	B	C	
O p e r a t i n g r a t i o s	**Overall performance**					
	Return on capital employed (%)					
	Net profit margin (%)					
	Asset turnover (x)					
	Working capital					
	Stock turnover (x)					
	Debtor turnover (x)					
	Working capital to turnover ratio (%)					
F i n a n c i a l r a t i o s	**Debt ratios**					
	Gearing ratio (%)					
	Debt – equity ratio (%)					
	Interest cover (x)					
	Liquidity ratios					
	Current ratio (x)					
	Acid test (x)					

Cross-sectional analysis may be extended adding further columns to accommodate additional companies.

Figure 7.7 *Cross-sectional comparison checklist: operating and financial ratios*

PART FOUR

Stock Market Assessment

As illustrated below, this part:

- illustrates **how to produce an analyst's report** from the information sources included in the text;
- introduces unique insights into **forecasting** future corporate performance by using **short-term** and **long-term** time horizons;
- explores how to assess whether the company's current share price is an **over- or underestimate** of the company's worth;
- considers how strategic choices lead to changes in the value of companies by **linking financial outcomes and strategy.**

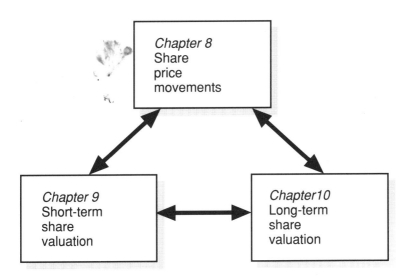

Chapter 8
Share price movements

Chapter 9
Short-term share valuation

Chapter 10
Long-term share valuation

CHAPTER 8

Share price movements

Individual share prices respond in varying proportions to three separate but interrelated factors, namely: (a) the broad context *to current and anticipated stock market movements; (b) the* industry/sector *to which the company belongs; and (c) the* company's *future strategic and financial performance as perceived by investors. The focus of this chapter is how an amalgam and synthesis of these factors determine a company's share price. A detailed assessment of the valuation of shares from a short- and long-term perspective is left to Chapters 9 and 10 respectively, while the current chapter provides a general overview to share price movements under the following topics:*

- *measuring the total return from alternative investments*
- *a general framework for assessing movements in share prices*
- *broad context to the likely movement in share prices*
- *industry/sector divergence*
- *the market's assessment of the company's future strategic and financial performance*
- *making an overall assessment and how this can change.*

The chapter begins by considering the total return from alternative forms of investment, namely cash deposits, government bonds and equities. The assessment of alternative investments is then incorporated into a general framework of share price movements focusing on explanatory factors at three levels: the broad context, the industry and the company. Each of these factors is explained in detail before consideration is given as to how an overall market assessment is reached. Following a discussion of share price dynamics, brokers' recommendations are reviewed. The chapter is concluded with a checklist.

Measuring the total return from alternative investments

In valuing investment opportunities, including cash deposits, gilt-edged securities (government bonds) and company shares (equities), investors are interested in the value of the anticipated returns over time relative to the sum they have invested. Anticipated returns consist of interest payments or dividends, together with any change in the value of the sum of money invested at the end of the investment period, known as the holding period. If the investor initially invested £100 and is able to sell the investment for £120, then a capital gain of £20 has been made in addition to any interest or dividend payments received. Conversely, should the same investment be sold for £80, then the capital loss is £20. The total *return* an investor receives from holding a security – cash, government bond or shares – will comprise the interest or dividend payment, plus (for a capital gain) or minus (for a capital loss) the change in the capital value of the initial investment.

The extent to which the investor is offered a return which is a reflection of the level of interest or dividend payments received as opposed to the likely capital gain will vary according to the nature of the investment. For example, compare the returns from cash deposits and shares. If an investor invests £100 as cash deposits with a bank or building society then the total return will be wholly made of interest payments. Alternatively, the total returns to equities will be formed both from the dividends received and any capital gain or loss recorded during the holding period.

Table 8.1 shows how the total returns from cash returns and shares may differ. Taking a twelve-month holding period, it is assumed that interest rates on cash, ignoring tax, are 6%. Company A pays a dividend of £2 and sees its share price rise by 10%, whilst Company B pays a dividend of £6, but its share price falls by 5%. A company's dividend payment expressed as a percentage of its share price is known as the d*ividend yield*. Thus if a share is priced at £100 and dividend payments are £2, the dividend yield is 2%. *Total return* comprises the interest or dividend yield, together with the capital gain or loss. The figure is frequently expressed as a proportion of the initial investment, thereby giving the total return as a percentage. Of the three investments which offers the greatest return?

Comparing the three investments listed in Table 8.1, Company A has provided the investor with the highest return at 12%, and Company B the lowest. In both cases the total return received has been strongly influenced by the capital gain or loss component of the total return. Cash deposits have provided the investor with a return of 6% which is wholly in the form of interest payments, as cash deposits offer the investor no prospect of a capital gain.

Turning to gilt-edged securities these also offer the investor a fixed interest payment. As shown in Illustration 8.1, the price of government bonds will fluctuate so that the interest or running yield – interest rate expressed as a percentage of the bond price – is in line with the return an investor is able to

Table 8.1 *The total return from alternative investments*

	Investment	Interest or dividend	Capital gain or loss	Total return	Total return*
Cash deposits	£100	£6	£0	£6	6%
Company A	£100	£2	£10	£12	12%
Company B	£100	£6	−£5	£1	1%

* Strictly speaking these figures relate to the gross total return as any tax payment due is ignored.

obtain on alternative investments of similar risk. Due to the fact that gilts do not offer the same prospect of a capital gain as equities which, if a company is successful, tend to rise over time, they traditionally attract a higher yield than the dividend yield on shares.

Illustration 8.1

INTEREST RATES AND GILT-EDGED SECURITIES

To illustrate how the price of government bonds fluctuates with interest rates, take the example of a non-redeemable bond issued with a face value of £100, paying a coupon or nominal rate of interest of 4% (£4) per annum. If the price of the bond remains at £100 then the interest yield (£4/£100 × 100) is also 4%. An investor, however, is unlikely to be satisfied if the interest yield on investments with a similar level of risk is, say, 8%. Investors will certainly sell gilts and buy the alternative investment. If sufficient investors sell gilts the price will fall to £50, when the yield on government bonds is in line with investments of similar risk (£4/£50 × 100 = 8%). Conversely, if yields on an investment are above those on alternative investments of similar risk the price of gilts will rise. By such mechanisms the price of gilts will adjust over time.

Issued value	Coupon	Price of gilt	Interest yield
£100	£4	£100	4.0%
£100	£4	£50	8.0%
£100	£4	£200	2.0%

This simple example illustrates that if interest rates are expected to fall, then the prices of gilts are likely to rise, and fall when interest rates rise.

In practice the pricing of gilt is made more complex by the government issuing gilts that it will buy back at some date in the future which may or may not be fixed. For such gilts there is also the need to calculate the redemption yield, reflecting the total return to the investor from holding the gilts to the date of redemption. Governments also issue index-linked bonds the prices of which are adjusted with inflation.

Source: Authors.

In making the decision to invest in shares, as opposed to government bonds or cash deposits, the investor will form expectations about their future performance, which in part will be influenced by the current levels of performance. A shareholder may adopt two very different investment positions. They may invest in shares where the market value of the share is considered to be a fair value, being prepared to pay a full price for the anticipated income (dividend growth) or capital gain (share price growth) the company is expected to deliver. Alternatively, the investor may be interested in attempting to identify mispriced shares where the market rating is at variance with the company's prospects. If the market rating is below the level sustainable by the company's prospects a buying opportunity exists. Providing the company is able to improve on the level of performance the market anticipates the share price is likely to rise.

When selecting an individual share for investment shareholders may wish to consider whether they are interested predominantly in an income or capital gain from holding a share. (There are other factors to consider in addition – see Illustration 8.2.) Companies vary as to whether they are likely to offer the prospect of the majority of the total return from holding their shares being primarily in the form of dividends or share price appreciation. Where the total return from holding a share is predominantly in the form of dividends this is known as holding the share for its *yield*. Companies offering high yielding shares fall into two categories:

- Companies considered to be in mature industries with limited prospects of future growth, and whose investment needs are relatively small. Such companies can afford to pay out a high proportion of their earnings to shareholders as dividends, given the relatively small reinvestment needs. Indeed, in Chapter 3 it was suggested that such a policy frequently adds far greater shareholder value than diversified growth into faster, but to the company, unknown markets. Companies which are past their main phase of growth are sometimes referred to as *ex-growth*.
- Those companies the prospects of which are uncertain and whose investors demand a higher than average dividend payment compared to the price of the share to compensate for the risk of the company being forced to cut or pass a dividend payment.

By contrast, initial shareholders in recently floated new technology companies, or rapidly growing companies with substantial investment needs, may expect little or no dividend payments in the early years of holding the company's shares. The attraction to holding shares in these companies is the prospect of a substantial share price appreciation, allied to declared dividends at some future date. By preserving funds and reinvesting in the business the shareholders' long-term return from their share holdings in such companies should be enhanced, and the share price should rise even though the prospect of increased dividend payments may be a number of years away.

Illustration 8.2

TAX CONSIDERATIONS
For the investor, tax considerations may have a significant influence on the decision to invest in a *high-yield* or *high-growth* company. Prior to April 1988 capital gains were taxed at a lower rate than dividend income, and this made high-growth shares more attractive than those with high yields to shareholders in the higher tax bands. With capital gains and dividends (income) taxed at the same rate, the tax advantage of capital gains has been reduced significantly. It has not been completely eliminated to the extent that tax on capital gains can be deferred until shares are sold, whereas tax on dividends must be paid each year. Whilst tax efficiency is an important element in making choices between alternative investments, rarely, if ever, are tax considerations able to turn a fundamentally poor investment into a good one. Source: Authors.

Regardless of whether a share is purchased for income or capital growth, a judgement still needs to be made as to whether the current share price represents a full valuation of the company's prospects or not. Investors and analysts continuously update their views on a company and calculate the intrinsic value of the company's shares. The comparison of these valuations with the current market price of the share results in buy, hold or sell decisions based on whether a share's intrinsic value is greater than or less than its market value. Should the majority of investors believe that the current market value of a share exceeds it intrinsic value the share price will fall to a point where its market value equals its perceived intrinsic value. The converse applies if shares are undervalued when compared to their perceived intrinsic value. It is only when market value and perceived intrinsic value correspond with one another that the share price will be relatively stable.

A general framework for assessing movements in share prices

Markets thrive on rumours, partial rumours and sheer make-believe, so that share prices are always in a state of flux. There is, however, an important distinction to be made between short-term fluctuations and major discontinuities. The former results from the vagaries of random buy or sell orders, while the latter is occasioned by events which cause a substantive imbalance and reappraisal of share prices. In proposing a general framework to explain share price movements outside of a narrow trading range, three sets of factors relating to the *broad context*, the *industry/sector* and the *company* are dominant.

These factors, incorporated in Figure 8.1, do not necessarily have equal weight in driving share price movements at any one point in time. In one time

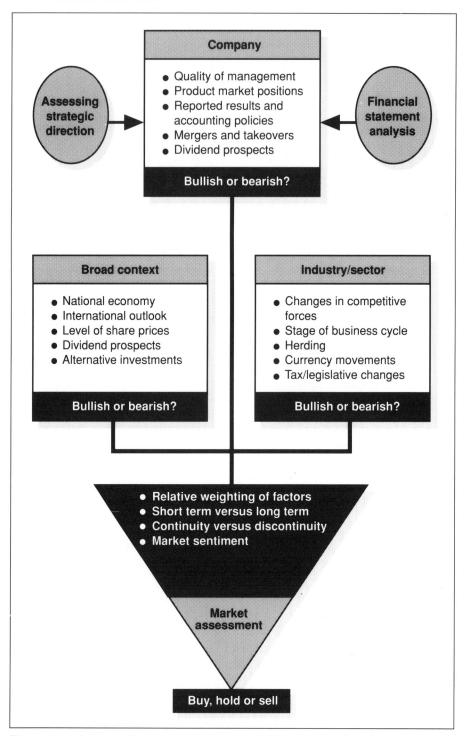

Figure 8.1 *A general framework for assessing movements in share prices*

period, it may be broad contextual factors which are dominating share price movements in general. Conversely, company-specific factors relating to strategic positioning and financial performance may be all pervasive and swamp any factors operating at the level of the industry/sector or broad context. Moreover, the relative weight of each of the three factors in driving share prices will change over time. Since the timing and relative weightings are difficult to discern, it is even more problematic to ascertain whether the effect on share prices will be measured in days, weeks or months.

Mindful of the judgemental differences in making market assessments of a company's share price, each of the three constituent components – broad, industry/sector and company – are examined below individually. Furthermore, an assessment is made as to whether each of the three share price drivers is 'bullish' or 'bearish' in outlook for the company. A bullish sentiment for any one of the three factors reflects the judgement that on balance the effect of that component of the model is positive for the company's share price. Conversely, a bearish view suggests that sentiment is negative, and the factor will undermine current share prices.

Broad context to the likely movement in share prices

Five key drivers influencing the broad context to share price movements have been identified, namely:

- the national economy
- the international outlook
- the level of share prices
- dividend prospects
- alternative investments.

The prospects for the *national economy* exert a powerful influence on share prices. Analysts will be constantly assessing the latest economic information and adjusting their forecasts of likely future events. Some of the important concerns of the stock market will be the likely pattern of growth in the economy and how this might influence corporate earnings and hence dividend payments. Similarly, the future pattern of exchange rates and interest rates will be key concerns of the market.

Both of these factors will require a view on the *international outlook* to be overlaid on the prospects for the national economy. The increasing integration of economies results in the prospects for a single national economy becoming ever more closely dependent on the major locomotive economies of the world – USA, Japan and Germany – all of which have an important influence on the world trading environment. Similarly, both at the national and international levels political events which have significant implications for economic performance will influence the stock market. In all cases the stock market will judge the importance of the event for share prices and trading levels in the stock market will adjust accordingly. Favourable news will send stock market levels higher, whilst unwelcome news will drive share prices down.

Whilst the links between economies of different countries become greater, the influence of country-specific factors on national stock markets remains important. This is illustrated in Table 8.2 where the performance of selected national stock markets in 1992 is reviewed.

Table 8.2 *International stock market performance, 1992*

National stock market	% change in local currency	% change in sterling	% change in US $
France	+4.29	+20.90	−2.17
Germany	−5.33	+9.58	−11.33
UK	+14.93	+14.93	−7.00
Europe	**+6.29**	**+13.81**	**−7.91**
Australia	−8.35	+2.50	−17.06
Hong Kong	+25.02	+55.25	+25.03
Japan	−22.74	−4.44	−22.67
USA	+4.84	+29.55	+4.84
World Index	**−3.67**	**+14.06**	**−7.71**

Source: *Financial Times*, 9 January 1993.

Considering performance measured in terms of the local currency the influence of country-specific factors can be seen clearly. The Hong Kong and UK stock markets were the best performers in 1992, with Japan and Australia the worst. If stock market performance is translated into sterling, the effect of the UK leaving the European exchange rate mechanism (ERM), when sterling was effectively devalued, is dramatic. With the exception of Japan, investment in overseas markets would have brought a positive return. As the dollar appreciated during 1992 the exact opposite is true for the US investor.

Table 8.2 emphasizes two points. First is the importance of national political and economic factors influencing stock market performance. For example, the weak German performance reflects deteriorating prospects for its national economy and German companies. Secondly, investing overseas adds a further complication and risk. Movements in the exchange rate can radically alter the returns investors will receive from investing overseas. For the UK the overall performance masks the fact that it was a year of mixed fortunes, with the devaluation of sterling and the lowering of interest rates in the fourth quarter of the year resulting in the year's strong performance.

Illustration 8.3

AMERICAN DEPOSITORY RECEIPTS
A number of British companies have their shares quoted on the New York (Wall Street) stock exchange. The mechanism to enable securities of a non-US company to be traded in the US is through what is known as American Depository Receipts (ADRs). ADRs offer international companies the opportunity to broaden their shareholder base by being quoted in the US. ADR prices are quoted in US dollars.
Where a company has sponsored the issue of ADRs, and as a consequence there is a sizeable holding of the company's shares in the US, movements in the company's share price in New York can have a strong influence on the company's share price in London. If prices in the two markets diverge, if for example the exchange rate changes, an arbitrage opportunity may arise. Since brokers will seek to exploit such an opportunity, respective share prices will quickly adjust to remove inter-market differences.
Source: Authors.

Fundamental changes in international stock market performance together with currency movements can have a significant effect on internationally traded stocks. Traders can seek to exploit any differential price gap, so that shares will be traded until prices are aligned in the various markets. The interrelatedness of stock markets can also affect confidence, so that changes in one market influence trading levels in other markets (see Illustration 8.3).

Table 8.2 also raises the question of how stock market movements are measured. In practice investors will consult a market index which provides a performance indicator of movements in the market. Each major national stock market will have at least one market index and the discussion below focuses on examples of the indices used to measure the performance of the London stock market. Table 8.3 provides a brief resume of the main indices and their coverage.

When reviewing prospects in respect of the national and international economy a critical question to ask is whether share prices *relative* to future prospects offer good value for money and the chance of the investor achieving a healthy total return. The emphasis should always be on the word relative. If the stock market is trading at record levels but the future prospects are insufficiently 'in the price' of shares, then equities may offer a good investment opportunity. Alternatively, if trading levels are unsustainable as future prospects are discouraging then the expectation is that share prices will fall and equities may well be best avoided.

One of the methods used by the market to gain a view as to the level of share prices is the price–earnings (p/e) ratio. The historic p/e ratio represents the relationship between earnings per share and the market price for shares, thereby indicating how much the investor is having to pay for access to a company's

Table 8.3 *Principal indices of the London stock market*

Market index	Coverage and use as performance indicator
FT Ordinary Share Index (also known as the 30 share index)	Covers the shares of some thirty companies, designed to provide a representative sample of the industrial and commercial companies quoted on the stock market. The index provides a reasonable indicator of short-term market movements.
FT-SE 100 (also known as the 'Footsie')	Includes the 100 largest quoted companies. These companies by their very size tend to trade internationally, often having significant overseas operations. Amongst the constituents of the FT-SE 100 are the food manufacturers ABF, Cadbury Schweppes, Hillsdown Holdings, Northern Foods and United Biscuits featured in Chapters 7 and 9. The Footsie is the principal real-time index for the market whilst it is trading.
FT-SE Mid 250	Offers a representation of the second tier of companies quoted on the stock market whose share prices do not necessarily move in line with the companies included in the FT-SE 100. In general, companies in the FT-SE 250 tend to be more focused on the UK economy.
FT-A All Share	An index offering comprehensive coverage of quoted companies, including those companies included in the two previous indices listed. The FT-A index is also subdivided into a number of sectors enabling the performance of different industries to be examined. The FT-A provides the principal indicator at the end of the day as to how share prices have moved.

earnings. For example, a market p/e ratio of 11 indicates that share prices in the market are eleven times the level of earnings companies have declared when making their latest annual or interim announcement. Over time p/e ratios fluctuate, as investors become more bullish or bearish about future prospects. If investors are becoming more positive then they will buy shares pushing the market p/e ratio higher. Conversely, if investors become bullish they may switch out of shares into other forms of investment depressing share prices and the p/e ratio.

Analysts examine the current market p/e ratio to see how it relates to previous levels, and attempt to forecast the *prospective* p/e ratio for the market. Table 8.4 provides a comparison between the market's p/e ratio at the start of 1993, the forecast level for the end of 1993, and the average for the period 1976–93.

Table 8.4 *Market price–earnings ratios – FT 500 share index (actual and prospective*)*

	Average 1976–93	January 1993	December 1993
P/E ratio	11.2	17.3	13.7*

Source: P. Coggan, 'The fundamental approach to shares', *Financial Times*, 23 January 1993, Section II, p.2, and *Financial Times*, 25 January 1993.

On the basis of the figures presented in Table 8.4, at the start of 1993 equities would not appear to be cheap, with the historical p/e ratio in January 1993 being well in excess of the average for the period 1976–93. Of course, taking the average for the period 1976–93 masks the fact that during that period the p/e ratio showed marked fluctuation reaching a peak of 21 in the summer of 1987. The higher the ratio, the more expensive are shares relative to declared earnings.

A more critical issue is that historical p/e ratios do not fully reflect the future, and may be irrelevant. If future earnings are likely to be considerably ahead of those declared in the past, then the prospective p/e ratio taking into account these higher earnings will be lower than the historical p/e ratio. Hence, stockbrokers spend considerable time on attempting to forecast future corporate earnings to judge whether share prices are expensive or cheap. Table 8.4 shows that prospective earnings result in a p/e ratio of 13.7 for the end of 1993, somewhat below the historical p/e ratio on which shares were trading at the start of the year. The prospective p/e ratio is nevertheless still above the average for 1976–93, which further suggests that equities are not particularly cheap. Should, however, sufficient investors decide that equities do offer a worthwhile investment opportunity, their purchase decisions will tend to drive up share prices and consequently increase the current p/e ratio at which the market is trading.

Earnings forecasts are also important in enabling judgements about *dividend prospects* to be made. As earnings rise companies will be able to enhance dividend payments and thereby reward shareholders of the company. If, however, corporate earnings are weak dividend prospects are likely to be poor. Poor dividend payments in such circumstances will reduce the attractiveness of shares by shrinking their total return. If this should happen investors may well attempt to switch their funds to *alternative investments*.

Previous discussion highlighted that cash deposits and government bonds are two of the alternative investments available if the prospects for equities are perceived to be poor. Both these alternatives have accompanying risks. Cash deposits are likely to be attractive when interest rates are high and inflation low, but become less attractive as interest rates fall. As cash deposits offer investors no prospect of a capital gain, interest payments have to compensate for a fall in the value of money (inflation) before enabling investors to achieve a real return on their investment.

Government bonds are highly sensitive to interest rate changes and to inflation. Bond prices are also influenced by the level of borrowing the government needs to fund in a period, and the extent to which the market will have to absorb large amounts of newly issued gilts. Where a government's funding requirement is large, this may not only restrain gilt prices, but also equities to the extent that funds which would have been invested in the equity market are diverted to the bond market. Clearly the more funds being invested in shares the higher prices are likely to go on the basis of supply and demand.

Falling interest rates tend to boost bond prices, and investors may be attracted to gilts when interest rates are high. Inflation is a major problem for gilts, as once again the prospects for achieving a capital gain from holding gilts is less than for equities. For these reasons gilts have historically paid a higher interest yield than the dividend yield paid by equities. Comparing the two yields results in the calculation of the *gilt–equity yield ratio* which, although its validity continues to be actively discussed by supporters and critics, has in the past provided an indicative guide as to when to switch between equities and gilts.

According to proponents of the gilt–equity yield ratio, if the value of the ratio is high, with gilt returns considerably ahead of equities reflecting high share prices relative to dividends, shares should be avoided. Alternatively, if the ratio is low, there may exist a buying opportunity for equities. The average for the period 1976–93 was 2.3, with the peak of 3.5 being reached prior to the major adjustment in share prices that took place in October 1987. Conversely, the gilt-equity yield ratio reached a sixteen-year low of 1.73 in July 1992 (*Financial Times*, 23 January 1993). The conventional wisdom, based on past trends, is that when the yield ratio falls below the average equities offer an attractive form of investment.

Drawing together the five factors operating at the level of the broad context, but also feeding in information as it relates to industries and companies, the strategists of the investment houses will attempt to forecast future levels of the stock market. Taking an overall view of the likely movements in the market equity strategists will be taking a top-down approach, rather than starting at the level of the company and building from the bottom–up. On occasions the two different approaches may yield different views of likely future stock market movements.

Using the top-down approach the forecaster will use one of the main stock market indices previously discussed as a performance indicator. The FT-SE 100, an index of the 100 largest UK quoted companies, is commonly the subject of brokers' forecasts. At the end of the third full trading week in January 1993 the index stood at almost 2800. Table 8.5 provides a range of illustrative estimates as to possible levels the market might be trading at by the end of the year. The forecasts can be described as bullish, broadly neutral and bearish with respect to the prospects for the UK stock market in 1993.

Table 8.5 provides a range of outcomes, which, depending on what is the actual out-turn, will determine whether equities in general will have proved a worthwhile investment over the year. The process of forecasting movements in the general level of share prices requires that judgements about each of the five

Table 8.5 *Illustrative forecasts of the FT-SE 100 share index at the end of 1993*

Forecast	Current trading level	Forecast at end of 1993	% change	Reasons
Bullish	2800	3360	20.0	Confidence about speed of recovery in UK and the US. Expectation that German interest rates will fall steeply, allowing UK rates to follow, thereby boosting consumer spending.
Broadly neutral	2800	2940	5.0	Belief that share prices already fully reflect likely extent of recovery in economy and corporate earnings.
Bearish	2800	2744	−2.0	World and national economic conditions in 1993 will continue to prove a difficult backdrop to company performance.

factors operating at the level of the broad context previously discussed are analysed carefully and a decision made as to whether they have a bullish, bearish or broadly neutral influence. Table 8.6 offers an illustration of the reasons why an assessment of each factor might be described as bullish or bearish.

In the final analysis the assessment of the broad context requires the five factors to be combined and an overall judgement as to whether conditions are bullish or bearish to be made. It is impossible to be prescriptive as to the relative weighting of the five factors in the overall assessment, as over time their importance will change. At any one point in time one factor may be of overriding importance in driving the overall assessment of the broad context.

Industry/sector divergence

Although the broad context to share prices may be bullish or bearish the extent to which an individual industry or sector will mirror overall trends in the market will vary. The shares of companies traded on the London stock market are allocated to an FT-A sector, allowing movements in each sector to be compared with trends in the market overall. By reviewing the performance of each sector against the main stock market indices the analyst can gain an appreciation of whether a stock market sector has out-performed, mirrored or under-performed the market in general. The weekend *Financial Times* also publishes a table of leaders and laggards to help distinguish which sectors have performed well or

Table 8.6   *The broad context: bullish or bearish?*

Bullish	Key drivers	Bearish
Prospects for the economy are much better than the stock market is anticipating.	National economy	Increasing lack of confidence in the likely future performance of the national economy.
Outlook for world economy and major overseas economies is improving.	International outlook	Too many uncertainties exist to be confident about the prospects for the world economy. Forecasts of growth in the major economies are being reduced.
Current level of share prices do not fully reflect improving economic environment.	Current level of share prices	Share prices are likely to fall as the market becomes more realistic about likely trading conditions.
Prospects for improved company earnings and dividend payments have not been appreciated fully by the market. When this happens share prices can be expected to rise.	Dividend prospects	Deteriorating conditions for corporate earnings are not reflected in share prices, and prices can be expected to fall.
Alternative investments do not offer encouraging returns, especially when the prospects for share prices are improving.	Alternative investments	With an expected fall in share prices, alternative investments offer the prospect of a superior return.

indifferently. Table 8.7 offers a list of selected leading and laggard sectors for 1992, and their respective percentage change.

Table 8.7 shows that not all sectors performed equally well in 1992. At the top is the water sector containing recently privatized companies and banks where the takeover of one of the 'big four' clearing banks – Midland Bank plc – helped the overall performance of the sector. Food manufacturing under-performed the index, rising by just over 7%. At the bottom of Table 8.7 are a number of sectors which have suffered disproportionately during the recession of the early 1990s and whose prospects at the end of 1992 were considered to remain poor. It is interesting to note that the sector which performed best in 1991 – Health & Household – is one of the worst performing sectors of 1992, as confirmed in Illustration 8.4.

Table 8.7 *Stock market performance by selected sector: percentage changes since 2 January 1992 based on Thursday, 31 December 1992*

Stock market sector	Change in sector level %
Water	+49.83
Banks	+39.94
Electronics	+38.53
FT-A All Share Index	**+14.76**
Food Manufacturing	+7.63
Health & Household	−3.17
Engineering-Aerospace	−8.88
Contracting, Construction	−14.24
Property	−18.21
Insurance Brokers	−19.46
Gold Mines index	−53.66

Source: *Financial Times*, 2 January 1993.

Illustration 8.4

TR CITY OF LONDON TRUST PLC

The City of London Trust is a well-known investment trust, managed from London. Investment trusts exist to channel the monies of investors into the shares of other companies, government bonds and cash. Trusts vary as to their scope and investment objectives. The objective of the City of London Trust is to 'provide a higher than average yield together with long-term growth of capital and income in excess of the FT Actuaries All-Share Index'. Consequently, the company's 1992 Annual Report, reflecting on its investment strategy in 1991, states that in respect of the Consumer Group sector (including Health & Household) of the FT-A the company had been forced to be underweight: 'Given the Company's objective of providing shareholders with an above average yield it is impossible for us to have a full weighting in this low yielding sector.' In other words, in order to achieve a satisfactory level of income for its investors, and reflecting its objectives, the trust was under-invested in that part of the stock market which did not offer sufficient dividend income when compared to the level of share prices. As Health & Household (Pharmaceuticals) was the best performing sector in 1991, the prices of the shares in the sector had been pushed too high, and dividend yield was consequently too low for the Trust to be a strong investor in the sector. Indeed the company's investment in the Health & Household sector was only 69% of the relative weight of the sector in the FT-A All Share Index.

Source: *Annual Report*, TR City of London plc, 1992.

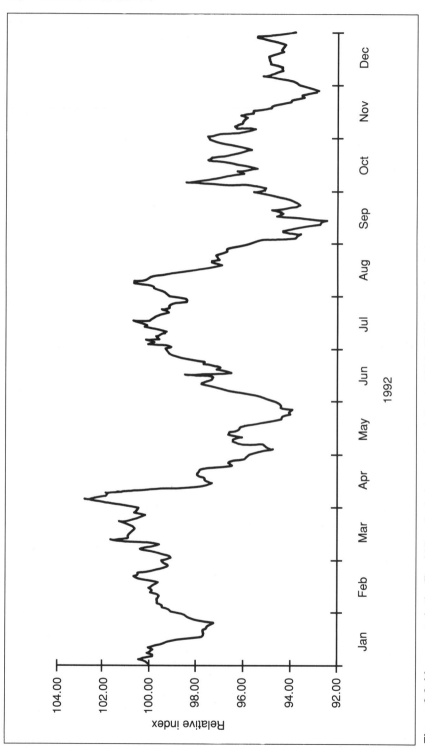

Figure 8.2 *Movements in the Food Manufacturing sector relative to FT-A All Share Index during 1992*

Source: Micro, Extel Financial.

Whilst Table 8.7 shows that the food manufacturing sector fell relative to the FT-A All Share Index for the year to the end of 1992, the end-of-year figure masks important fluctuations during the year. Figure 8.2 plots the movement of the FT-A Food Manufacturing sector relative to the FT-A All Share Index for 1992. If the value of the index is in excess of 100, the food manufacturing index has risen relative to the FT-A All Share Index. Below 100, share prices in general have risen relative to the food manufacturing sector.

Movements in the relative index, illustrated by Figure 8.2, suggest that the investor would have seen the food sector rise relative to the market during the first four months of 1992. The re-election of the Conservative government in April 1992 improved confidence in the market and the prospect of faster economic recovery led to an initial switch out of defensive sectors, including food, and investment in sectors likely to gain disproportionately during the recovery phase of the business cycle. After a period when the sector recovered in the summer, increasing fears that customers were trading down from manufacturers' brands to cheaper, lower margin, own-label products, together with concerns about over-capacity in the industry, led the sector's relative performance to decline dramatically in the third quarter of the year, from which it has yet to fully recover.

Figure 8.2 also illustrates how volatile the stock market was during 1992. The relative performance of individual stock market sectors can be explained by examining the following five factors, namely:

- changing competitive forces
- currency movements
- stage of the business cycle
- herding
- tax and legislative changes.

The intensity of competition operating at the level of the industry will be influenced by *changing competitive forces*. Such forces operating at the level of the industry are constantly changing and these may well change in a way which makes it more difficult for companies in the industry to earn above-average returns. For example, increasing market concentration in the food retailing sector has led to a rise in the buying power of the major food retailers, thereby intensifying the competitive pressures affecting food manufacturing companies. Conversely, for the food retailing sector, periodic concerns about superstore saturation in the UK and the possibility of companies becoming ex-growth has led to falls in the share price of major food retailers from time to time.

Similarly, *currency movements* may improve or undermine prospects for a sector. For those sectors of the economy producing internationally tradeable goods and services the relative prices of home-produced and overseas products will have an important influence on demand and hence corporate earnings. If the value of the home currency falls (devaluation) then the price of exported goods becomes cheaper, but imported products or raw materials are made more expensive. Devaluation should therefore make it easier for a company to sell its products overseas, and to be more competitive within its home market. (The effects of devaluation are considered further in Illustration 8.5.) If a high proportion of its raw materials are imported, however, it will experience a rise in the cost of its inputs which may reduce, or in some cases remove, the benefits of devaluation. Where a country's currency appreciates in value exporting overseas is made more difficult, and companies face the threat of greater import penetration.

Illustration 8.5

DEVALUATION – HOW IT CHANGES COMPETITIVENESS

The effect of devaluation can be illustrated by taking movements in the sterling (£) – dollar ($) exchange rate. Assume the exchange rate is £1 = $2:

- Goods produced in the UK for £1,000 will be sold in the US for $2,000.
- Goods produced in the US for $2,000 will be sold in the UK for £1,000.

If the exchange rate falls to £1 = $1.50, what happens to the prices of the same goods?

Goods produced in the UK for £1,000 will be sold in the US for $1,500. As British exports are cheaper, the industry should sell more goods to the US.

Goods produced in the US for $2,000 will be sold in the UK for £1,333. As US imports are now more expensive, home producers should be more competitive.

Source: Authors.

A third factor influencing the prospects for a sector is the *stage of the business cycle*. Some industries are inherently more cyclical than others, experiencing violent swings in the demand for their products as the economy moves through its business cycle. Many cyclical industries also operate with high levels of operational gearing so that if demand does fall, the predominantly fixed nature of the industry's costs, which in the short term are inescapable, leads to a disproportionate fall in profits. Hence the cyclical industries experience a greater volatility of earnings than do those industries whose demand is less affected by the vagaries of the business cycle. Depending on the position of the business cycle various industries will offer the investor very different prospects. If the economy is moving into recession this may not be the best time to buy shares in a cyclical industry, whilst once share prices have fallen ahead of recovery there may be good opportunities to buy for the economic upturn. Getting the timing to such investment decisions right is, however, difficult, and investors can make expensive mistakes.

Very often the stock market can demonstrate the characteristics of *herding* in respect to different sectors. If a sector becomes generally favoured by investors, it can become 'over-bought', only for an adverse reaction to set in

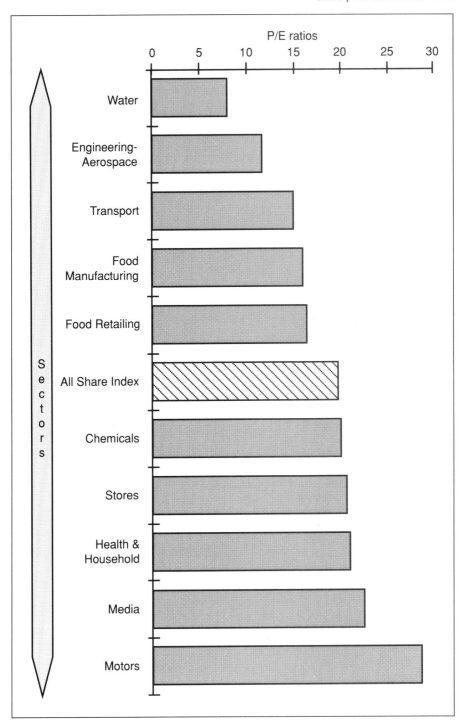

Figure 8.3 *Industry p/e ratios*
Source: *Financial Times,* 26 January 1993.

some time afterwards. Once this characteristic becomes apparent it is likely to be too late for the investor buy into the sector, and the sector may be better avoided until a genuine buying opportunity re-emerges at some date in the future.

Finally, tax and legislative changes may target specific industries in ways which can either be helpful or destructive to their performance. If an industry succeeds in persuading a government to reduce specific taxes, this may be helpful, whilst the application of a new or existing tax to the sector is likely to adversely affect demand and the future performance of companies in the industry.

Drawing the five factors operating at the level of the industry/sector together, Table 8.8 suggests why at any one point in time they may exert a bullish or bearish influence.

Table 8.8 The industry/sector: bullish or bearish?

Bullish	Key drivers	Bearish
A view is emerging that competitive forces operating at the level of the industry are becoming easier for companies to manage.	Changing competitive forces	The market has yet to appreciate that a significant increase in one or more of the competitive forces will depress average returns of companies in the industry.
Movements in the exchange rate have improved the prospects of overseas sales, and reduced the threat of increased import penetration and loss of sales in the home market.	Currency movements	Currency movements are unhelpful to the industry's ability to be competitive.
Increased economic activity will benefit the earnings of companies within the industry.	Stage of the business cycle	Movements in the overall level of activity are likely to depress industry returns.
Investors are generally 'bullish' towards the sector.	Herding	Market in general is strongly disinclined to invest within the sector.
Anticipated tax and legislative changes are likely to assist the industry's further performance.	Tax and legislative changes	Tax changes had not been anticipated and will adversely affect prospects for the sector.

Recognizing that industries differ as to their future prospects leads the stock market to vary the p/e rating it affords sectors. If the market expects a sector to achieve above-average growth, then it will be placed on a higher p/e ratio. Sectors where growth prospects are below the average, so that companies are held primarily for their dividend yield, will be traded on lower p/e ratios. A selected range of industry p/e ratios for 26 January 1993 is illustrated in Figure 8.3.

Amongst the sectors selected, motors has the highest p/e ratio and water the lowest. Utility companies, including those in the water sector, are primarily held for their dividend yield given that they have limited prospects for growth. The dividend yield for water companies at 5.6% is above the FT-A All Share Index of 4.4%. Food Manufacturing has a below-average p/e rating indicating that the market expects the sector to grow more slowly than the market overall.

The market's assessment of the company's strategic and future financial performance

Any assessment of share price movement must move beyond the broad context to share prices and prospects for the sector, and incorporate an assessment of the company's strategic direction and future financial performance. The general framework outlined in Figure 8.1 suggests that based on Parts Two (Chapters 2, 3 and 4) and Three (Chapters 5, 6 and 7) of the text – assessing strategic direction and financial statement analysis – the analyst should focus again on a number of key factors, namely:

- quality of management
- product market position
- reported performance and accounting policies
- mergers and takeovers
- dividend prospects.

Throughout the text stress has been placed on the *quality of management* as the key differentiator of corporate performance. A company's destiny is to a large extent shaped by its management and its ability to design and implement appropriate strategies to deliver superior financial performance. The stock market will focus strongly on the quality of the management team and its past record when making judgements about a company. Companies with unconvincing strategies which have in the past failed to deliver are unlikely to be accorded a high stock market rating.

The ability of management to add value both at the level of corporate and business strategies is critical. At the business unit level companies need to be able to develop competitive advantage by fashioning strong *product–market positions*. For many companies the importance of customer goodwill and brand strength will be a key factor when assessing competitive position. Where companies have weak product-market positions they are likely to be faced with significant challenges in order to build competitive advantage, a reality recognized by the stock market when valuing the company.

Discussion on financial statement analysis has highlighted the need to examine a company's *reported performance and accounting policies* with care. In particular, a company's announced results should be examined to ensure they are not the outcome of clever applications of accounting policies, but do reflect the underlying strength and performance of the company. If the quality of a company's financial results are questionable, then the market is likely to adjust its view of the company and its performance accordingly. Alternatively, if the quality of a company's performance is impressive, its shares are likely to be marked up.

The influence of actual or rumoured mergers and takeovers can operate in a number of ways. The detailed analysis of Chapter 3 emphasized that inappropriate mergers or takeovers are likely to destroy rather than create value. Stock markets soon become unimpressed about the acquisitions a company has made if management is unable to deliver the promised performance. Conversely, companies which use acquisitions to strengthen their existing core businesses and which have a successful record of acquisitions may well find support for a policy of external growth from the stock market. A further complication is the extent to which a company may need to issue additional shares in order to finance acquisitions, by, say, a rights issue. Unless there exists an unsatisfied demand for the company's shares, the issue of additional shares on the market is likely, at least in the short term, to depress share price. Similar considerations apply if a company is needing to issue additional equity in order to finance corporate restructuring or strengthen the balance sheet. Correspondingly if the stock market expects a company to be shortly 'coming to the market' to raise additional funds, its shares prices are likely to be marked down by traders.

As well as seeking to make acquisitions companies may also become the subject of a takeover. In such circumstances the buyer of a company may be expected to pay a premium over existing market price in order to gain corporate control. This inevitably means that companies which are the subject of an actual or rumoured takeover will find their share prices rising notwithstanding their current trading position. In such circumstances there may well be a substantial increase in the day's volume of shares traded.

With the exception of a company which is the subject of a takeover, the previous factors can be related to the company's expected future financial performance and its *dividend prospects*. Company-specific factors mean that the dividend prospects of an individual company may be at variance with the likely payout rates current in the market or in the sector. A company able to achieve strong earnings growth, with funds available to reinvest in the business and/or increase dividend payments, will be afforded a premium rating by the market. Depending on how the funds are used, dividend prospects either now or in the future will be enhanced.

Table 8.9 *The company: bullish or bearish?*

Bullish	Key drivers	Bearish
Shrewd, good track record of consistently delivering sound corporate performance. Believes share price does not fully reflect strength of management team.	Quality of management	Questionable strategic direction; ability to meet future strategic objectives is in doubt.
Strong portfolio of brands, reflecting good product market positions. Improving opportunities to exploit market positions.	Product market position	Product portfolio is weak, and market positions are increasingly coming under pressure from competitors.
View that market has not appreciated fully the real quality of the underlying financial performance. Company has consistently adopted conservative accounting policies, and does not 'hide' problems.	Reported performance and accounting policies	Emerging concern that the company's reported earnings indicate major deficiencies of performance. Management are manipulating company's results by use of changes in accounting policies.
Management is on the point of making a strategic acquisition which will strengthen its current market position.	Mergers and takeovers	Company has a weak track record on acquisitions and may be tempted to enter into further purchases. Market fears further rights issues.
The competitive positioning of the company in its chosen markets, allied with good operational management, is likely to deliver an improving dividend stream.	Dividend prospects	Company's trading prospects are deteriorating and the share price is currently an over-valuation of expected future performance and dividend payments.

Table 8.9 summarizes the five company-specific factors influencing a company's share price, and illustrates each with reasons why the analyst might be bullish or bearish.

Making an overall assessment and how this can change

Following the detailed discussion of the three components of the general framework illustrated in Figure 8.1, the task facing the analyst is how to bring the different elements together to make an overall market assessment. Figure 8.1 shows that there are four key elements to this process, namely:

- relative weighting of factors
- short term versus long term
- continuity versus discontinuity
- market sentiment.

The first issue needing resolution is the *relative weighting of factors* illustrated in Figure 8.1, namely the broad context, the industry/sector and the company. If all three are indicating that prospects are bullish then this is not a problem; clearly there are strong grounds for buying the company's shares. Conversely, if at the three interrelated levels of broad context, industry/sector and company prospects are bearish, there is a strong basis for selling the company's shares. If an assessment of the three levels offers conflicting signals, then the analyst needs to make a judgement about the relative importance of each and which factor on balance is the most critical.

As a general rule company-specific factors are likely to be the most important. For example, if the assessment of the company-specific factors leads to a bearish view then, notwithstanding a positive assessment in relation to the broad context and the industry/sector, the investor is likely to be better advised to seek alternative companies in which to invest. Similarly, a highly bullish view of a company may overcome a generally bearish stance on the industry/sector and broad context. It is our view that primacy should be afforded to the importance of the individual company and its prospects, since this reflects the fact that good companies are able to deliver above-average performance even when external conditions are adverse.

The second factor to be considered in reaching an overall judgement is the time frame. Share price performance in the *short term* may be very different from the *long term*. Investors looking for short-term gains rather than long-term performance are likely to seek out companies whose share price in the short term is likely to be strong. Conversely, investors whose holding period for the shares is intended to be much longer, say three years, will be more concerned with the longer-term performance of the company and its shares and less worried if in the short term the company's shares under-perform the market.

Analysts are continuously updating and revising their views on companies. At any one time there will be a broad consensus amongst analysts as to the company's future performance. If the new information received generally reinforces the accepted view of the company's prospects, and the revision to anticipated performance small, the process of change can be described as one of *continuity*. Nevertheless, share prices will not be constant, as random buy and sell orders come from people who have cash to invest or who need to raise cash. However, unless a fundamental reappraisal of a company's prospects takes place, shares will tend to be traded within a relatively narrow price range. (See also Illustration 8.6.)

Many different events can and do occur which lead to a fundamental reassessment of a company's share price. If new information results in the company's prospects being downgraded, the shares will be re-rated downwards. Alternatively, if the new information leads to analysts revising upwards their expectations of the company's future performance, the company's shares will be re-rated upwards to trade at a higher price. Where a fundamental reappraisal of a company's prospects, of the industry/sector or of the broad context takes place, the degree of change can be described as *discontinuous*.

Translation from continuity to discontinuity can be almost instantaneous, or can take place over several months. In practice it is particularly difficult to discern whether any share price fluctuation will be constrained within antici-pated limits, or whether the trend will continue with great amplitude for hours, days or weeks to follow. On reaching the limit of perceived continuity, uncertainty will increase until a consensus emerges as to which direction the market will move.

Illustration 8.6

OPTIONS
Investors not only trade shares at the prevailing market price, but may also be interested in buying and selling options. An option is simply the right to buy or sell a contract related to the level of the FT-SE 100 or to purchase or sell an individual share. Whilst different types of options exist, a number of general principles apply.
By using options investors are able to take a view as to the level of the FT-SE 100 or an individual company's share price at some date in the future and purchase an option to buy or sell at a set level or price. Options can be categorized according to whether they are a 'call' (a right to buy), a 'put' (the right to sell, or a double (involving both).
When the market is predominantly bullish, call options are more expensive than put options as the prevailing expectation is of rising share prices. Conversely, in a bear market the reverse applies.
Although private investors can purchase options, this part of the stock market is predominantly the preserve of the professional investor.
Source: Authors.

The recognition that the information base upon which market assessments are based is continuously changing results in the framework illustrated in Figure 8.1 becoming dynamic. If new information causes only minor adjustments to the views of analysts and other important opinion formers, for example financial journalists, the change is incremental and the process described as continuous. Where a fundamental reappraisal of the current market assessment takes place the change can be described as discontinuous. Figure 8.4 illustrates this distinction.

Information changes which drive either an incremental or fundamental revision of the analyst's view of a company's share price can be related to one of the three components of the general framework shown in Figure 8.1. A discontinuous change in the broad context is likely to have a generally pervasive influence on share prices. The UK's decision to leave the exchange rate mechanism (ERM) in the autumn of 1992, causing a reappraisal of the prospects for equities in general, is one illustration of a broad contextual change which was discontinuous. At the industry level the imposition of a new tax, to the extent that it had not been foreseen and discounted by the market, would again be discontinuous.

In relation to the individual company discontinuous change may occur when the company's interim or preliminary results are announced, to the extent that these are not in line with market expectations. Conversely, if announcements are broadly in line with market expectations any change is likely to be incremental and share price movements on the day, leaving aside any general factors affecting share prices, will be relatively small.

Discontinuous changes may also result if a company issues a profits warning. Under the London Stock Exchange's Continuing Obligations, a listed company is required to notify the market of any events likely to have a significant bearing on the share price:

> 'The Company must notify any major new developments in its sphere of activity which are not public knowledge and which:
>
> (a) in the event of a company having listed shares may, by virtue of their effect on assets and liabilities or financial position or on the general course of its business, lead to substantial movements in its share price; or
>
> (b) in the case of a company having listed debt securities in issue may significantly affect its ability to meet its commitments.'
>
> London Stock Exchange, Continuing Obligations, Chapter 2, Section 5, as set out in the Stock Exchange, *Official Yearbook, 1991-92*, p.26.

As a consequence of the stock exchange's listing requirements, companies will from time to time issue statements about different aspects of their activities. Statements containing a profits warning, indicating that due to a particular set of circumstances profits for the current period are likely to be below the levels anticipated by the market, are likely to have a dramatic effect on the company's share price as in Illustration 8.7. Following a profits warning

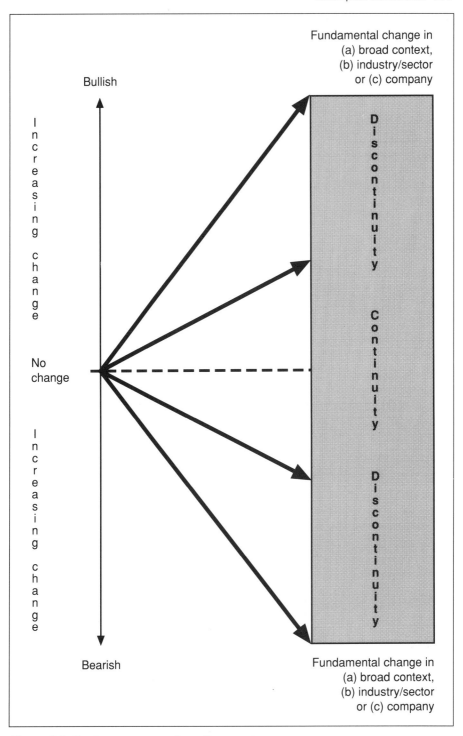

Figure 8.4 *Continuous versus discontinuous change*

Illustration 8.7

ALBERT FISHER PLC

Albert Fisher plc is a major food distribution and processing company. On Thursday, 9 July 1992 the company issued a profits warning with less than two months to go to the company's accounting year end. The company's chairman, Mr Tony Miller, indicated that high crop yields for many of the fruit and vegetable products in which the company traded had resulted in an excess of supply and as a consequence downward pressure on product prices. As a result the company's profitability would be reduced. *The Financial Times* reported (10/7/92) that analysts reacted by cutting pre-tax profit forecasts for the company from £77 m to £63 m for the company's reporting year to 31 August 1992.

The stock market was not only concerned about the fall in profits but also about the likely non-payment or cut in the dividend. The company issued a press statement saying, 'Whilst the board considers it inappropriate to make a dividend forecast at this stage of the year, it remains conscious of the importance of dividends to shareholders.' The market was unconvinced by this vague promise and, consequently, the company's share price fell by 25p to 41p.

Source: Based on *Financial Times*, 10 July 1992.

analysts are likely to revise their forecasts of future earnings downwards, generally resulting in the market lowering the company's rating. Alternatively, if a company announces it has secured a major new project which has been unexpected, earnings forecasts are likely to be revised upwards.

Illustration 8.7 indicates that in some circumstances the time period for the market revising its view of a company can be very short indeed – a matter of minutes after the company makes an announcement. On other occasions the process of changing the market's view on a company can take longer. Applying the idea of Lewin's (1952) change model to the stock market, Figure 8.5 illustrates the dynamics of share price change.

The model encapsulated in Figure 8.5 has three stages – unfreezing, reconfiguring and refreezing. The first stage – unfreezing – describes the process by which the accepted view of the broad context, industry/sector or company becomes questioned and no longer universally accepted. The second stage – reconfiguration – describes the process by which a new view becomes formulated. This may happen quickly, as in the case of Albert Fisher, when there is an agreed interpretation of the new information, but relatively slowly when no single consensus view emerges. If genuine uncertainty exists then differing views may exist in parallel until further information becomes available which conclusively supports one view. Once a new view has become accepted this then becomes the accepted norm and is refrozen until such time as the process starts all over again.

The final factor influencing the overall assessment, *market sentiment*, is

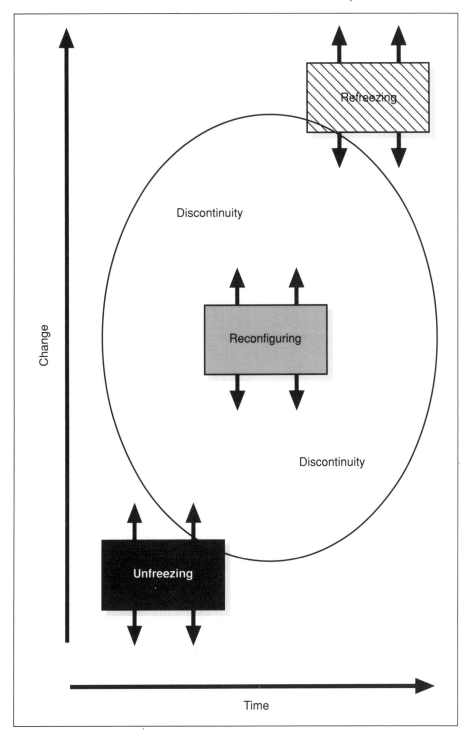

Figure 8.5 *Share price dynamics: discontinuous change*

perhaps the most difficult to define. The term market sentiment is essentially an amalgam and synthesis of all the other factors, and depending on whether sentiment is positive or negative, the consensus in the stock market towards equities in general, towards an industry/sector or towards a particular company will either be bullish or bearish.

On the basis of the judgements driving market sentiment at each of the three levels identified in Figure 8.1 brokers will make recommendations to investors. In respect of a single company brokers will advise on whether, on the basis of their judgements, the company's shares should be bought, held or sold. Table 8.10 offers examples of the nature of brokers' recommendations.

Table 8.10 *Examples of brokers' recommendations*

Advice	Comment
Buy	The investor is recommended to buy shares in the company. The broker may suggest immediate purchase, or advise waiting for a period of price weakness.
	A purchase recommendation is likely to reflect the fact that the broker is more bullish about the company than the current market price suggests. This might reflect a fundamental reappraisal of the company, suggesting a re-rating, or the fact that the company's shares have recently been over-sold. The broker may suggest a company should be bought for recovery – future improvements in performance – or income.
Hold	The broker is neither bullish or bearish about the company and its shares. It suggests that based on the broker's view the current stock value is a fair reflection of the worth of the company. The recommendation is for investors who currently hold shares in the company to neither decrease or increase their holdings.
Sell	The broker believes that the current share price is in excess of the true value of the company. Again the advice may be to sell immediately, or wait for an opportunity when the share price is relatively firm.

As brokers vary as to the prominence they give different factors it is not uncommon to find recommendations from two analysts being at variance. One broker might, for example, offer a relatively optimistic assessment of a company, whilst another places more emphasis on some of the risks inherent in the company's strategy. When evaluating brokers' recommendations the key focus should be in deciding whether the market's rating, as reflected in the company's share price, accurately reflects the company's prospects.

An excellent company on a high market rating may, for example, be a poor buy as its shares are already fully valued on the basis of its expected future profits. Alternatively, a company currently on a low market rating may have much better prospects than its market rating, and therefore offers a buying opportunity. This, of course, returns to the question of for what purpose – income, capital gain or a combination of the two – is the investor seeking to invest when purchasing the share, and what is the investor's attitude to risk. In all events the investor must exercise judgement as to the extent to which the intrinsic value of the share is 'already in the price'. Having calculated the intrinsic value of the share, investors must then compare the calculated value for each stock with its current market price. The decision whether to buy or sell is dependent on the extent to which a share's intrinsic value is greater or less than its market value.

Concluding remarks

The factors generating continuity or discontinuity in share price movements have been seen to be an amalgam and synthesis of broad context, industry/sector and company factors. Key drivers have been identified at each level, together with the need to assess whether the respective tension is towards a bearish or bullish outlook. When reaching an overall assessment as to whether to buy, hold or sell, consideration needs to be given to four factors: the relative weighting of factors; short term versus long term; continuity and discontinuity; and market sentiment. All these issues are captured in Figure 8.6 which provides a checklist for assessing share price movements.

Checklist

For the chosen company complete the three interrelated boxes, as in Figure 8.6, to arrive at an overall market assessment. Conclude by making a recommendation to buy, hold or sell shares in the company.

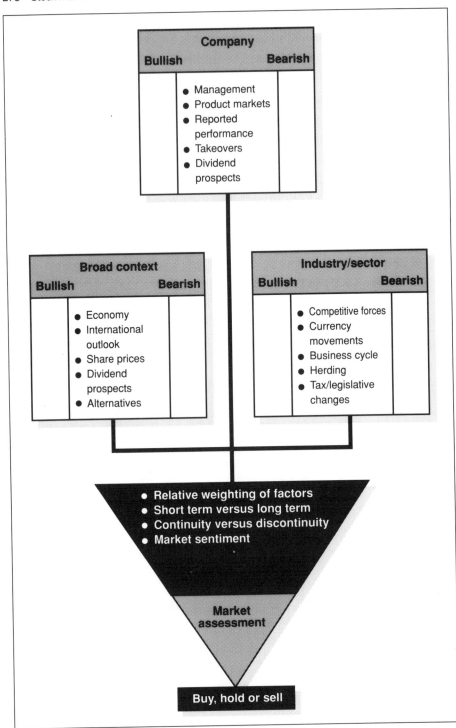

Figure 8.6 *Assessing share price movements*

CHAPTER 9

Short-term share valuation

All share price valuation techniques seek to discount future earnings in order to determine the anticipated total return – dividends plus change in share price – from holding a share. Short-term estimates of future earnings are produced on a regular basis by market analysts, who typically forecast company profits for the next two financial years. This chapter provides practical insights into what analysts report about a company, how such information is compiled, and why the information produced should be interpreted with care under the following topics:

- *the content of an analyst's report*
- *interpreting an analyst's report*
- *time series analysis of performance indicators*
- *cross-sectional analysis of performance indicators*
- *developing a forecast of future earnings*
- *share price movements.*

The chapter begins by presenting an example of an analyst's report based on UB. This example contains the main components found in a typical analyst's report on a major company. The individual elements of an analyst's report are reviewed in depth, beginning with a time series analysis of key performance indicators. Time series analysis enables the analyst to investigate how the company's performance has changed over time when compared to its previous levels of attainment. This analysis is extended by making inter-company comparisons using cross-sectional analysis. Having assessed the current position of the company, discussion is then focused on how future earnings and share prices can be forecast. This leads on to a consideration of where to obtain new information for the purposes of forecasting, and the corresponding movements to a company's share price. Once again the chapter is concluded with a checklist.

The role of the analyst and the content of an analyst's report

Company analysts exist to provide in-depth comment on a company's past and to forecast future performance in order to advise investors whether a company's shares should be bought, held or sold. In order to fulfil this function a company analyst will generally focus on a single stock market sector and undertake detailed research into the companies allocated to that sector. Analysts will constantly update their views on the sector and the companies within the sector. Periodically, the analyst will issue circulars or reports on a company, detailing their research findings and advising clients as to what action, if any, they should take in respect of the company's shares.

Generally circulars will be issued when a company reports its preliminary and interim results and at such times as the company makes a major public announcement with respect to, say, an acquisition. As well as reacting to a company's public announcements, analysts will, at irregular intervals, publish detailed studies of the company, offering the latest conclusions to their research.

Whilst the individual investment institutions for whom the analysts work have their own house styles, a typical analyst's assessment of a company is likely to contain information on some or all of the following elements:

- segmental information, discussing the performance and prospects of the different divisions;
- discussion of any recently announced or anticipated takeovers or disposals;
- stock market statistics, showing recent trends in the company's share price;
- major shareholders;
- announcements;
- investment ratios and future profit forecast;
- overall assessment and recommendation as to what the investor should do.

The inclusion of a recommendation in respect of share purchases and disposals recognizes that, whilst the role of the analyst is to advise clients, the investment house, for which the analysts works, will wish to assist customers in buying and selling shares and thereby earn commission through its sales staff, whose job is to trade shares on the stock market.

To illustrate the nature of an analyst's report, the example given looks at United Biscuits plc (UB) and shows what a typical assessment of a company might focus on.

Analyst's report

FOOD MANUFACTURING UPDATE – UNITED BISCUITS PLC
Recommendation: Buy long-term   **Share price 362p**
                                             February 1993

Summary
Company offers good long-term value from developing its European operations and its recent purchase of CCA snacks in Australia. Whilst Keebler has recently under-performed and affected the overall profits of the Group, we believe appropriate action to correct this has been taken. Although profits this year may be unexciting, beyond this year profits should start to recover strongly as both the USA and UK economies pick up. Our recommendation is for the investor to add to their shareholdings in the company.

Company strategy and quality of management
The company has a clear strategy to become a world leader in the snack market and continues to make acquisitions to strengthen its product market scope. The company's strategy of building a strong base in Europe is beginning to deliver improved profitability.

The management team is youthful, but has shown itself prepared to take difficult decisions when the need arises.

Business divisions

McVitie's Group
Market leader in the UK, which has shown itself able to maintain profits during the recession, despite trading volumes in the industry falling. Company continues to invest in new plant and machinery in order to reduce costs and to sustain competitive advantage.

European operations are expanding and integration with the UK business is beginning to deliver improved profitability. Further links between continental businesses and UK operations should enhance performance in the future.

Keebler
Disappointing performance in the first half of 1992, leading to a sharp fall in profits. We believe the company has taken action to correct the problem, and expect future profits to recover. The new chief executive has a good track record, and rationalization of production facilities will significantly reduce the company's cost base.

KP Foods
Very difficult trading conditions in the UK resulted in no change to division's profits in the first half despite sales up by 2%. Company has maintained its market leadership position in the UK, and is expanding its European sales network.

FOOD MANUFACTURING UPDATE – UNITED BISCUITS PLC

Ross Young
The previously announced rationalization programme is continuing, reflecting the company's objective to raise the division's profitability. Whilst rationalization will result in some reduction in sales volumes, profit margins should be improved.

Terry's
Division achieved a very creditable sales performance in the first half of the year despite the UK market declining in overall terms. Sales rose by almost 11%, and trading profits were up by over 3%.

Overall reported performance
Whilst sales in the first half of 1992 were flat, profits fell due to the difficulties experienced by Keebler in the US.

Summary of UB interim results *(half year to September 1992)*		
	First six months 1992	(%) change on first half 1991
Sales (£m)	1,525.5	–0.2
Trading profit (£m)	87.2	–15.6
Profit margin (%)	5.7	–15.7
Interest (£m)	17.2	–9.0
Pre-tax profits (£m)	70.0	–17.1
Tax (£m)	21.7	–22.5
Minority interests (£m)	1.1	–42.1
Profits to shareholders (£m)	47.2	–13.3

Acquisitions
The company announced it was purchasing Bake-Line on 5 January 1993 for £50 m. Acquisition of Bake-Line will complement the company's Keebler business, and strengthen the Group's presence in the North American market.

This latest purchase follows the earlier acquisition (November 1992) of Coca-Cola Amatil (CCA) for some £180 m. The financing effect of both acquisitions will be cash negative, and raise borrowing levels.

Market statistics
As the accompanying table and graph illustrate, the company share price performance in the last quarter of the year has shown a marked improvement on trends in the previous quarter:

FOOD MANUFACTURING UPDATE – UNITED BISCUITS PLC

| Company | Share price (p) | Market capitalization (£m) | Change relative to FT-A | | |
			1 month (%)	3 months (%)	6 months (%)
UB	362	1,771.6	–2.3	+2.7	–16.1

UB share price relative to the FT-A, 1992/93

Source: MicroView, Extel.

Recent weakness of share price, we believe, offers a good opportunity for long-term investors to buy into the company.

Announcements
| Final results: | March | Report and accounts: | April |
| Final dividend: | March | Interim results: | September |

Major shareholders
The company's annual report shows that the company had three shareholders who owned more than 3% of the company's ordinary shares:

FOOD MANUFACTURING UPDATE – UNITED BISCUITS PLC

Shareholder	Percentage of issued share capital held
Schroder Investment Management	3.3
Prudential Corporation	3.2
Robert Fleming Holdings and subsidiaries	3.1

Performance indicators

For the latest financial year the company's earnings per share (eps) were 30.8p, and dividend per share (dps) 15.3p. Dividend cover has been maintained at 2.00, and earnings yield is currently at 5.6%. The company's yield is significantly above the average for the sector or the FT-A, offering the investor an above-average income. The company's p/e ratio is 11.7. Forecast earnings for year to the end of 1992 will be down on last year, reflecting difficulties in the US, but profits are expected to recover during 1993.

Profits before tax are forecast to be £169.0 m in 1993, giving an eps of 22.9p. We are assuming the dividend payment will remain unchanged this year at 15.3p despite the reduction of earnings.

UB performance indicators

Company	Pre-tax profits (£m)	Earnings per share (p)	Net dividend per share (p)	Dividend cover (times)	Yield (%)	P/E ratio	Future profits before tax (£m)	Prospective p/e ratio
UB	211.3	30.8	15.3	2.00	5.63	11.7	169.0	15.8

Overall assessment

In reaching our overall assessment we have set out the positive and negative factors in the accompanying table:

FOOD MANUFACTURING UPDATE – UNITED BISCUITS PLC

Bullish	Bearish
Young, dynamic management team who have a strong desire to succeed.	Management team is relatively unproven.
Company will benefit from recovery in the UK and US.	Recovery in the UK is unlikely to be rapid.
Continental European operations have significant profit potential.	Europe is still a relatively small part of the company.
Recent acquisition of CCA will strengthen the company in the one significant market – Asia- Pacific – where they currently have little presence.	Unsure how much value the company can add to a business which is already well run, and for which the company paid a full price.
Prompt action in US, plus recent acquisition, will lead to profits rebound.	Keebler's position remains weak in the US, and acceptable levels of profitability may be difficult to achieve.
Gearing, whilst high, is not threatening and will be reduced.	Company's level of gearing is high, and management might be tempted to make a rights issue.
Corporate earnings are expected to improve beyond the current year.	Earnings growth is still uncertain.

On balance we are considerably more bullish about the company, believing the company has been over-sold. Short-term attractions are the relatively high level of yield offered by shares compared to other similar food manufacturers, and the comfortable dividend cover. Long term the company offers the investor good value for money.

Interpreting the analyst's report

Whilst the scope and detail of individual reports will vary, all circulars issued by analysts will seek to identify the critical issues driving a company's share price. As a consequence, an individual report will focus on one or more of the key areas highlighted in the report, namely:

- company's strategy and quality of its management
- segmental information
- reported performance
- acquisitions and disposals
- stock market statistics
- announcements
- major shareholders
- investment ratios and future profits forecast
- overall assessment and recommendations.

A *company's strategy and quality of its management* is the first key factor often highlighted in an analyst's report. The discussion in Chapter 2 emphasized the importance of companies crafting an effective and efficient strategy, an outcome shaped by the quality of a company's management. Management is recognized as a key differentiator of corporate performance. The stock market's assessment of a company's management, and in particular its 'track record', is thereby an important factor influencing sentiment towards a company.

The varied product market nature of companies is recognized by emphasizing the importance of *segmental information*. Often accompanied by a table showing the results of the trading divisions, analysts will assess the likely performance of a company's major divisions and forecast the contribution they are expected to make to group profits. This task will require the analyst to review the business context and industry against which each division is trading, and to evaluate the business's competitive position. The previous assessment of UB's business divisions' reported performance undertaken in Chapter 5 offers the analyst one of the key elements of developing this area of analysis.

When a company announces its interim or preliminary results analysts will focus on *reported performance*. They will be concerned to see if the company's results are in line with the market's forecasts, in respect of both the overall performance of the company and its principal trading divisions. Analysts will also use the figures released by the company to inform their estimates of the future, and will in the light of the new information revise their forecasts of pre-tax profits for the next trading period.

The announcement of *acquisitions or disposals* by a company are also important events on which analysts will wish to comment. Where acquisitions or disposals have taken place, or are anticipated, the analyst is likely to focus on two potential concerns: (a) how will future earnings be affected; and (b) what are the funding implications of the changes. Analysts will comment on whether the changes announced will enhance or restrain future earnings and hence the company's ability to pay dividends. Equally, the funding implications of the acquisition or disposal will be important. If the company has made a major purchase, the question will be how this is to be financed. Alternatively, if the company is making a disposal how will the proceeds of the sale be used?

Stock market statistics are generally included in the analyst's report showing the company's share price and market capitalization. Market capitalization is an indication of the company's size. The figure for market capitalization is determined by taking the price of the company's shares and multiplying by the number of shares issued. As UB's share price is 362p per share, and taking the latest estimate of the number of issued shares as 489.4 million, market capitalization is 362p × 489.4 m = £1,771.6 m.

As part of the stock market statistics presented, an analyst's report may well provide data on the relative price movements of the company's shares over different periods of time. The company's share price movements will be generally matched against the FT-All Share Index to indicate how the share price has performed when compared to the market as a whole. This enables the prospective investor to gain an appreciation of recent trends in the share price. Very often these movements are emphasized by the inclusion of a relative price graph in the report.

Alongside any discussion of recent share price trends, an analyst's report may provide information on the company's *announcements*. All companies have an annual reporting cycle, with the publication of the interim and final results being two of the key dates in the company's calendar. It is on these occasions, in particular, that analysts will revise their forecasts of the company's performance for the next reporting period. Together with the announcement of the company's reports, the dates when a shareholder becomes eligible for receiving the company's dividend may also be highlighted.

The analyst's report may also report who the *major shareholders* are in the company and whether there have been any recent significant changes. Most UK companies are largely owned by the major institutional investors, so these would typically be identified amongst the largest shareholders. There are still, however, a few large companies where family holdings are important. For smaller companies the presence of one or two large shareholders can be highly significant in the event of an offer to buy the company being received.

Linking with the company's share price will be the presentation of *investment ratios and future profits forecast*. Together investment ratios and the future profits forecast may be termed performance indicators as they summarize past financial results and forecasted future performance. As a group, performance indicators are concerned with helping the analyst to assess the company for the purposes of investment. Whilst the indicators highlighted by individual analysts may differ, the analyst's report on UB focused on the following ratios:

Company	Pre-tax profits (£m)	Earnings per share (p)	Net dividend per share (p)	Dividend cover (times)	Yield (%)	P/E ratio	Future profits before tax (£m)	Prospective p/e ratio
UB	211.3	30.8	15.3	2.00	5.63	11.7	169.0	15.8

What do these performance indicators mean?

- *Pre-tax profits (£m)*: states how much profit on ordinary activities, before tax, the company generated in its last financial year.
- *Earnings per share (p)*: shows how much profit per share the company made in its last financial year.
- *Net dividend per share (p)*: tells you how much the company paid out in dividends to its shareholders.
- *Dividend cover (times)*: indicates how many times profits generated by the company cover the amount which has been paid out in dividends.
- *Price–earnings ratio (p/e)*: the p/e ratio shows the relationship between the company's share price and its earnings per share. It shows how many years' worth of earnings the company share price represents.
- *Yield (%)*: strictly speaking, the gross dividend yield – indicates what percentage the gross dividend per share is of a company's share price. The yield is used to show how much income as a percentage of the share price the shares offer the investor.
- *Future profits before tax*: this figure represents the analyst's forecasted profits for the company.
- *Prospective p/e ratio*: based on the forecast profits, this ratio embodies the analyst's estimate of future eps, and on the basis of the current share price what the prospective p/e ratio is on which the company is trading.

Finally, the analyst's report will make an *overall assessment and recommendation* in respect of the company's shares. This may well include a balancing of the bullish and bearish factors identified in the body of the report before the analyst reaches an overall judgement on the company and its current share price. A synopsis of the analyst's overall assessment and recommendation often appears as a summary at the start of the report.

Time series analysis of performance indicators

Analysts will be interested to see how the range of performance indicators have changed over time, and to what extent they provide evidence of trends in a company's performance. A company's performance indicators will be carefully scrutinized in order to assess the likely total return from holding the company's shares. The total return from holding a share is dependent upon the change in the value of the share (the capital component) and the dividend received (the income component). The potential change in the capital value of the share, and hence the capital component, is indicated by a company's p/e ratio. As Figure 9.1 shows the p/e ratio is dependent on a company's earnings per share and the share price. It also shows that the income component is measured by reference to the company's gross dividend yield and the share price.

As Figure 9.1 demonstrates, in order to calculate a company's p/e ratio and yield the analyst needs to identify the company's earnings per share and dividends per share. How these measures are calculated and related back to a company's current market rating will be considered in the following sequence:

- earnings per share (eps)
- dividends per share (dps)
- current market rating.

Earnings per share (eps)

The *earnings per share (eps)* figure shows how much per share the company is earning in profits. Formally, eps is calculated by taking the profit attributable to ordinary shareholders and dividing the figure by the number of shareholders in the company:

$$\text{eps} = \frac{\text{Profits attributable to ordinary shareholders}}{\text{Number of ordinary shares}}$$

'Earnings per share should be calculated on the profit attributable to equity shareholders of the reporting entity, after accounting for minority interests, extraordinary items, preference dividends and other appropriations in respect of preference shares.'
Source: ASB, *FRS3 Reporting Financial Performance*, 1992, p.4.

The number of ordinary shares issued may, however, be calculated on an *undiluted* or *diluted* basis. Calculating eps on an undiluted basis means only including the number of shares the company has issued to date. Alternatively, on a fully diluted basis, the number of shares also includes any additional shares which are likely to be issued when, for example, investors exercise 'conversion rights' on convertible loan stock. Illustration 9.1 explains the nature of this process.

The number of shares a company has issued on both an undiluted and diluted basis can be determined by reference to the company's annual report, or by consulting the Extel Card Service described in Chapter 4. For UB details of the shares issued by the company at its last balance sheet date are reproduced as follows (on p.291):

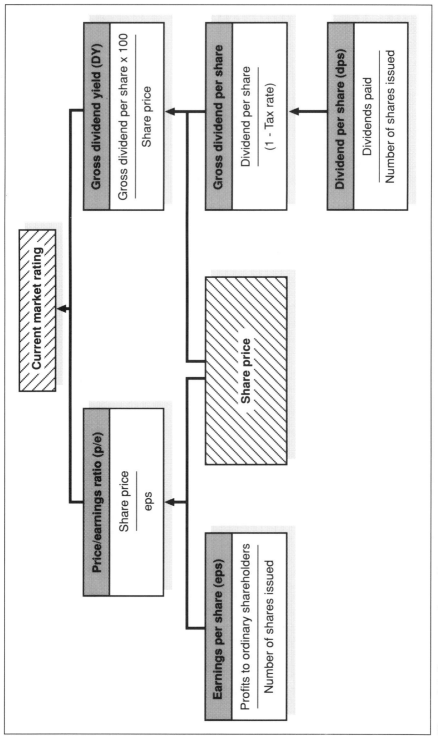

Figure 9.1 Current market rating

Illustration 9.1

CONVERTIBLES
Whilst some kinds of capital instruments are classified as debt, they are often considered as 'hybrids' to the extent that they have characteristics of both debt and equity. One such example is *convertible loan stock*. This form of capital instrument pays a fixed rate of interest (the coupon) until a determined date when the debt is redeemed by the company. The stock is described as 'convertible' as the investor has the option of converting the stock into ordinary shares in the company (equity) at a set price. The following illustration provides an example of a convertible bond issue. On 2 February 1993, Northern Foods raised £91 m in an issue of convertible bonds. The issue was designed to reduce short-term borrowings and to give the company a more balanced debt profile. The bonds have a 6.75% semi-annual coupon, with 15 years to maturity. The conversion price was set at 326p, a premium of almost 20% above the company's closing share price (272p) on the day the bonds were issued. Source: Authors and *The Independent*, 3 February 1993, p.23.

'The calculation of the undiluted earnings per share is based on the profit attributable to shareholders of £143.5 m (1990 £128.1m) and on the weighted average number of shares in issue during the year of 465.3 m (1990 443.1 m).

'The fully diluted earnings per share is based on the adjusted profit attributable to shareholders of £149.5 m (1990 £136.2 m) and 506.2 m shares (1990 502.7 m) allowing for the full conversion of the convertible preference shares issued by a subsidiary and full exercise of outstanding share options.'

Source: Note 9, *UB Annual Report 1991*, March 1992, p.42.

If eps is calculated on a fully diluted basis the number of shares issued is increased if the company has issued, for example, convertible loan stock, hence the figure for eps is below the corresponding calculation for undiluted eps – see Table 9.1.

Table 9.1 *UB – earnings per share, 1991*

	Pence per share
Undiluted eps	30.8
Diluted eps	29.5

Source: *UB Annual Report 1991*, March 1992, p.34.

The calculation of both undiluted and diluted eps in the past has been based on profits attributable to shareholders, which excludes extraordinary items. Until the introduction of FRS3 (see Chapter 5) companies had some flexibility in classifying non-recurring items as either exceptional or extraordinary. Almost without exception, where non-recurring items led to losses being incurred, they were classified as extraordinary and removed from the calculation of eps. UB, for example, incurred an extraordinary charge of £13.4 m in 1991. If this sum had been included in the calculation of undiluted eps, UB would have reported a figure of 28.0p, a reduction of some 9% on the published figure.

The rationale for excluding extraordinary items is to identify the level of earnings – the maintainable or core earnings of the company – the company is capable of generating over a number of years. The rejection of this view as the basis for the calculation of eps by the Accounting Standards Board (ASB) by including extraordinary items in the calculation of eps is expected to mean that a company's published figure for eps is likely to be much more volatile than in the past. Previously, the categorization of non-recurring items as extraordinary items and their exclusion from the calculation of eps tended to smooth changes to reported earnings. This is further considered in Illustration 9.2.

Illustration 9.2

HOW ANALYSTS ADJUST EPS FIGURES
Concern that the implementation of FRS3 will make the published eps figure a less reliable guide to maintainable or core earnings has prompted a number of different investment houses to indicate that they will be adjusting a company's published eps figure. BZW will issue its own eps figure which excludes profits or losses on business disposals, asset sales and fundamental restructuring. BZW will report its own eps figure alongside reported earnings in its published circulars. Similarly, James Capel have announced their own formulae for calculating a continuing earnings figure. The company will take the reported figure and exclude costs of closure or withdrawal from a business segment, gains or losses on disposals and some other specific unusual items. Source: Based on *Financial Times*, 1 and 4 February 1993.

The seriousness of the changes now being introduced relates to the fact that the eps figure is often taken by analysts to be the most important indicator of a company's performance. The ASB stance on eps is an attempt to make analysts and investors understand that there is no one single indicator that can encapsulate a company's performance, and that there is no substitute for a thorough assessment of a company's strategy and its published financial statements:

'The Board believes that the performance of complex organizations cannot be summarized in a single number and has therefore adopted an "information set" approach that highlights a range of important components of performance... It is widely accepted that certain totals in the profit and loss account, such as profit before tax and earnings per share, have been used too simplistically and have obscured the significance of relevant underlying components of financial performance.'

Source: ASB, *FRS3 Reporting Financial Performance*, 1992, p.51.

The reason why eps has often been seen as the most important indicator of a company's performance is that it allows the analyst to assess how much a company has available to pay out in dividends or to reinvest in the business, as illustrated in Figure 9.2. If monies are reinvested in the business, providing these funds create shareholders' value, the investor's future dividend stream will be enhanced. Reinvesting money in this way provides the investor with deferred income. As either allocation of the company's earnings influences dividend growth – often the principal driver of share price performance – a company's eps figure is always carefully examined by analysts.

Before leaving the question of eps it is important to understand what factors can lead to a change in the figure a company reports. Remember, eps is calculated according to the following expression:

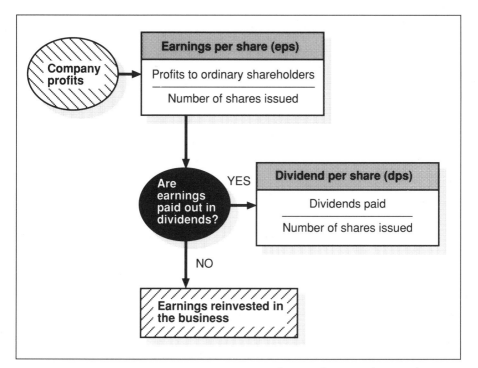

Figure 9.2 *The relationship between company profits, earnings per share and dividends per share*

$$\frac{\text{Profits attributable to ordinary shareholders}}{\text{Number of ordinary shares issued}}$$

The eps figure may change if there is an *above-the-line* change in profits attributable to ordinary shareholders, and/or if there is a *below-the-line* change to the number of shares issued. Above-the-line changes include:

- Changes to how a company reports its profits. Chapter 5 highlighted how changes in accounting policies may influence the reported profit figure. Equally, a number of the changes introduced by the ASB, including the virtual abolition of extraordinary items, will significantly influence the eps figure companies report in the future.
- The trading performance of the company's continuing operations. Improving performance from a company's continuing operations, other things remaining equal, will raise eps, whilst declining performance will, other things remaining equal, lead to a falling eps figure.
- The trading performance of newly acquired acquisitions. To what extent will the acquisition of a new business enhance corporate earnings? To determine the overall influence of an acquisition on eps it is necessary to consider how the new purchase is to be financed.

Below-the line changes to eps include:

- Issuing new shares to finance acquisitions. Purchasing a company will give the acquirer the right to an additional profit stream. This additional profit stream is not, however, costless. The acquisition has to be financed. If the company chooses to finance the purchase by debt this will affect the reported profits (an above-the line change) by increasing the cost of servicing debt, but will leave the number of issued shares unchanged. Alternatively, the acquisition might be financed in full or in part by issuing new shares. Choosing this method of funding the acquisition will clearly increase the number of issued shares.

  If the number of new shares issued increases more quickly than the reported profits of the enlarged company, the acquisition is said to result in a *dilution* of earnings. In other words, the company's reported eps is lower than it would otherwise have been. Given the emphasis placed on eps, this may be of some concern to analysts, especially if they are unsure of the long-term benefit from acquiring the company. If dilution of earnings does occur the company may be unable to increase dividends at the rate it hitherto achieved.
- Periodically a company may decide to make a *scrip* or *bonus* issue. Should a company believe its share price is rising to a level which might make its shares less marketable then it may decide to reduce its share prices by issuing new shares in proportion to existing shareholders' holdings. For example, a company might decide to issue one new bonus share for two existing shares.

A bonus issue will increase the number of shares in issue and correspondingly reduce a company's eps. In these circumstances the analyst will need to restate the eps figure in order to make an assessment of the company's performance.

To conclude, it is important not only to identify the extent to which a company's eps figure has changed, but what factors are responsible for the change.

Dividend per share (dps)

Analysts consider the dividends a company pays in relation to:

- dividend per share (dps)
- gross dividend per share
- dividend risk.

The amount the company chooses to pay in dividends is indicated by the *dividend payment per share (dps)*. This information may be found with reference to the company's annual report or the Extel Card Service. Companies tend to pay two dividends a year, the interim and the final. The interim dividend is based on the company's half-yearly profits, and the final dividend on the year's profits. UB's dividend payments for 1991 are detailed in Table 9.2.

Table 9.2   UB – dividends per share, 1991

Dividend	Payment (p)
Interim dividend	5.5
Final dividend	9.8
Total dividend	15.3

Source: Note 8, *UB Annual Report 1991*, March 1992, p.42.

Investors are not only interested in the current year's dividend but also in understanding the past trend and prospects for future dividend payments. Figure 9.3 compares UB's eps and dps for the period 1985–91. Unsurprisingly, the company's dps has generally increased in line with eps. UB's pattern of dividend payments is fairly typical of most companies and reflects the fact that generally dividends can be expected to increase in line with earnings. The relationship between the two raises the question of the company's *dividend policy*.

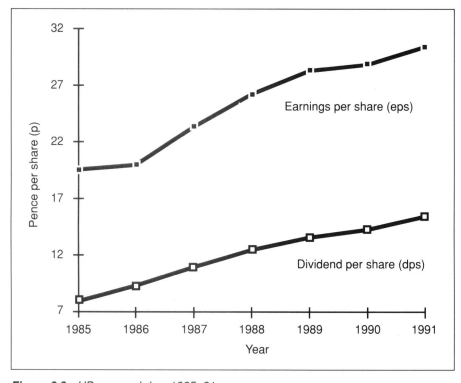

Figure 9.3   *UB: eps and dps, 1985–91*

A company's dividend policy is a key area to analyse when reviewing the financial management of a company. Companies are often very reluctant to cut or even hold their dividend constant unless forced to do so by difficult trading conditions, as in Illustration 9.3. Management often fears the threat of takeover, and may be persuaded to increase dividend payments even though there is a strong argument for retaining resources within the company. As a general rule, management prefers to engineer smooth increases in the company's dividend, and often uses the announcement of a rise in dividends as the basis of declaring their confidence in the company's future prospects.

During periods of poor trading companies may be faced with the difficult option of:

● cutting their dividend; or
● maintaining the dividend, partly financed out of reserves.

The question of the whether or not to pay a dividend when a company is experiencing difficulties is complex and very much influenced by company-specific factors. Some of the key points that managers and shareholders need to consider include:

- If sufficient profits are not available should the company fund dividends out of distributable reserves, providing these are sufficient?
- Does the company have sufficient cash to meet a dividend payment? If so, should the dividend have the first call on the resources the company has available? For a growing company, or one which needs to sustain R&D spending to maintain its competitive position, dividend payments may be at the cost of undermining the company's future position. These questions link back to Chapter 6 and the company's overall cash flow position.
- For how long are the company's difficulties likely to persist?
- Are shareholders expecting to be rewarded for a recent rights issue? Shareholders may have been persuaded to subscribe for additional shares on the basis of the rising dividend payments the company was forecasting at the time.
- Is the cost of cutting or passing the dividend really worth the adverse reaction that could result from investor sentiment towards the company changing adversely?

Companies facing difficult trading conditions need to weigh these arguments carefully before announcing their dividends.

Illustration 9.3

ELECTROLUX

Electrolux, one of Sweden's leading manufacturing companies, is a well known multinational producer of white goods, including washing machines, tumble dryers, refrigerators and freezers. At the beginning of February 1993 the company announced it was cutting its dividend from SKr 6.25 per share, following two years in which the company's dividend had been uncovered and met out of reserves. In response, the company's shares fell by 6%.

   The company's action reflected a continuing weakness of consumer demand in its major European markets, despite encouraging signs in North America. Management concluded that there was too much uncertainty about future levels of consumer confidence and when sales might recover to maintain dividends at their previous level.

Source: Based on the *Financial Times*, 4 February 1992.

Gross dividend per share

Investors receive their dividend per share net of tax. To be able to compare the income return from holding the company's shares with alternative investments, the tax paid by the company on behalf of the investor has to be added back to calculate the *gross dividend per share* the investor receives.

Figure 9.1 illustrates that a company's declared dps can be converted into a gross figure by dividing dps by 1 minus the tax rate. As at the time of writing the basic rate of taxation is 25%, and UB's net dividend is 15.3p, this process can be illustrated as follows:

$$\text{Net dividend (p)}/(1 - \text{Tax rate}) = \text{Gross dividend (p)}$$
$$15.3\text{p}/(1 - 0.25) = 20.4\text{p}$$

In 1991 UB paid its shareholders 15.3p per share, equivalent to a gross payment of 20.4p, the difference (20.4p – 15.3p) being accounted for by the tax the company paid on behalf of its shareholders to the tax authorities.

Dividend cover

The extent to which a company can afford to pay dividends is suggested by its *dividend cover*. This ratio measures the extent to which the declared dividend is covered by the company's profits. As dividends are paid after interest charges, tax payments and other items have been met, profit attributable to shareholders is used in the calculation. The dividend cover ratio is an important measure of the safety of the shareholders' dividend.

The calculation of dividend cover is illustrated with reference to UB in 1991:

$$\text{Dividend cover }(\times) = \text{Profits attributable to ordinary shareholders/Dividends}$$
$$= \pounds143.5 \text{ m}/\pounds71.7 \text{ m}$$
$$= 2.00 \text{ times}$$

At the current level of dividend cover of 2, the profits attributable to shareholders would have to halve before dividends would need to be financed from reserves. The higher the level of cover the more secure is the investor's dividend. A dividend cover of less than one would indicate that dividends exceeded earnings and the company was meeting all or part of its dividend payments out of reserves. As any company's reserves are limited this can only be used as a short-term measure.

The likely volatility of a company's earnings is a key factor when examining the level of dividend cover. Food manufacturers and retailers are often considered to be *defensive* stocks, to the extent that their earnings are relatively unaffected by a downturn in the economy. Given that food is a basic human need, a significant proportion of food spending is relatively insensitive to changes in consumers' income (i.e. it has a low income elasticity of demand), although balanced against this is the fact that increasingly consumers have a choice between basic foodstuffs and processed products. The ability of consumers to trade down to own-label products in times of economic difficulty means that food manufacturers are not completely insulated from economic downturns. Nevertheless, when compared to cyclical sectors of the economy, food manufacturers are unlikely to experience large fluctuations in earnings.

Together with current dividend cover, the analyst may wish to review the ratio's trend over time. Table 9.3 gives information on UB's dividend cover since 1984, and reveals that the ratio has been at its current level since 1990.

An alternative way of looking at dividend cover is to think of the percentage that dps is of eps. Calculating dps as a percentage of eps provides a figure for a company's payout rate. In 1991 UB's undiluted eps was 30.8p of which it paid out some 15.3p as dps, giving a pay-out rate of 49.7%. This indicates that the

Table 9.3 *UB – dividend cover, 1984–91*

	1984	1985	1986	1987	1988	1989	1990	1991
Dividend cover (×)	2.59	2.18	2.13	2.13	2.14	2.06	2.00	2.00

Source: *UB Annual Reports*, 1984–91

company paid out almost half of its earnings in the form of dividend payments. A major concern to analysts is that if a company's payout rate is raised to too high a level, dividend cover will become unacceptably low. In such circumstances the company may well need to rebuild the level of cover before it is in a position of recommencing or increasing dividend payments.

Current market rating

A company's current market rating is summarized by its yield and p/e ratio. The calculation of these ratios and how they are related is illustrated by Figure 9.4. This shows that the relationship between the dividend paid by the company to the ordinary share price is described by the *gross dividend yield*. An important point to remember is that the gross dividend yield is historical, based on the latest annual dividend the company has paid. The ratio looks to the past and not to the future. As the gross dividend yield is related to the share price, every time the share price changes so does the yield.

Taking UB's share price as at the beginning of February 1993, which was 362p, the gross dividend yield can be calculated as follows:

$$\text{Gross dividend yield} = (\text{Gross dividend/Ordinary share price}) \times 100$$
$$= (20.4p/362p) \times 100$$
$$= 5.63\%$$

A company's dividend yield is linked both to its p/e ratio and the extent of risk the market believes exists of the company reducing or failing to pay a dividend. When the market perceives the risk is considerable, and the company has generally poor prospects, the share price will adjust until the dividend yield is sufficient to compensate the investor for the risk involved. Table 9.4 illustrates how UB's share price might be adjusted to provide different levels of dividend yield.

If the prevailing view in the market is that it requires an 8% dividend yield to compensate for the company's expected future earnings and the risk of holding UB shares, the company's share price would fall to 255p on the basis of the current gross dividend. Conversely, if the market view became more positive towards the company, and a dividend yield of 4% was acceptable, the share price would rise to 510p. Examples of high yielding stocks are given in Illustration 9.4.

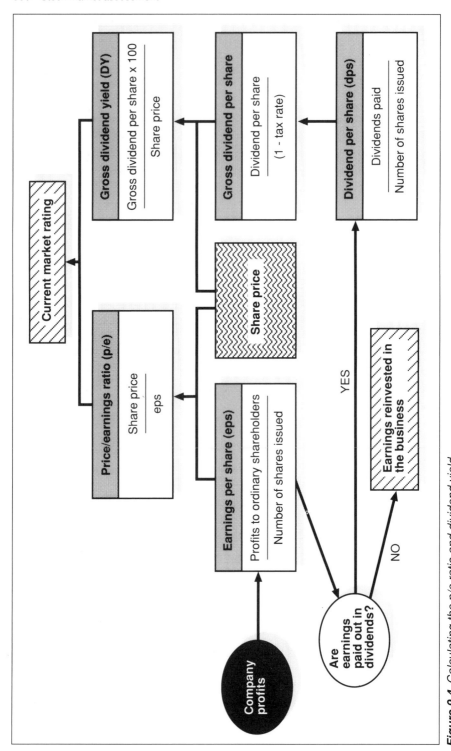

Figure 9.4 *Calculating the p/e ratio and dividend yield*

Table 9.4 *Examples of share price movements to adjust the dividend yield*

Gross dividend (p)	Dividend yield required by market (%)	Share price (p)
20.4	8.0	255
20.4	6.0	340
20.4	4.0	510

Illustration 9.4

HIGH YIELDING STOCKS
The stock market places companies on a high yield when there is an expectation that the company will have problems in maintaining dividend payouts at their previous level. For the investor high yielding stocks carry a significant risk, but may also turn out to be a profitable investment. The risk is that the company's problems will intensify and the dividend will either be cut or passed. The hope is that the market has overestimated the dangers faced by the company, and that the company's performance will improve and with it the share price. At the same time the investor will benefit from the high dividend income. In the latter scenario high yielding stocks can prove to be highly profitable to the investor. For example, on 18 October 1991 Asda plc the food retailer's shares were yielding 15.2% and were priced at 42p. By the start of 1993 the market believed the company was on the way to recovery with a new management team installed. At the end of January 1993 the company's shares were priced at 67p and yielding 3.3%. Clearly investors had done very well. By contrast over the same period shareholders in Ratners plc, the jewellery retailer, saw their shares move from 72p to 15p, and the dividend yield increase from 18.5% to 21.3%. Source: Authors.

Together with the yield ratio, analysts focus on a company's p/e ratio. The company p/e ratio is similar in concept to the market and industry p/e ratios introduced in the previous chapter, but relates only to one company. The company's historical p/e ratio relates the company's earnings per share to the price at which the company's shares can be bought or sold. As Figure 9.2 illustrates, the p/e ratio indicates how many years the company's shares have to be held on the basis of current earnings for the share price to be recovered. Once again, as in the case of the dividend yield, the inclusion of the share price in the calculation means that every time the share price changes so does the value of the p/e ratio. On the basis of UB's shares being priced at 362p in the market and using the figure for undiluted eps of 30.8p, the company's historical p/e ratio is:

$$362p/30.8p = 11.7$$

If a company's share price rises the p/e ratio will correspondingly rise, and fall when the share price falls. It is important to understand that as share price changes, the p/e ratio and yield move in opposite directions. Table 9.5 illustrates this process by extending the illustrative numbers set out in Table 9.4.

Table 9.5 *Movements in the dividend yield and p/e ratio*

Gross dividend (p)	Dividend yield required by market (%)	Share price (p)	Earnings per share (p)	P/E ratio
20.4	8.0	255	30.8	8.3
20.4	6.0	340	30.8	11.0
20.4	4.0	510	30.8	16.6

Table 9.5 shows that at a share price of 255p UB would be trading on a yield of 8.0% and a p/e ratio of 8.3. If the company's share price then rises to 340p, the yield on the shares falls to 6.0% and the p/e ratio rises to 11.0. A further rise in the share price to 510p would place the company on a yield of 4.0% and a p/e of almost 17. The inverse relationship between a company's yield and p/e ratio is linked to the total return the investor anticipates gaining from holding the shares and will be discussed in detail later in the chapter.

As a general rule the bigger a company's p/e ratio the more highly the stock market rates the company. A growth company, where the market expects a strong growth in future earnings and dividends, is likely to be placed on a high p/e ratio. By contrast, a company with poor growth prospects, often described as ex-growth, is likely to be given a low p/e. Given poorer prospects the company will, however, be on a higher yield. Rating a company on the basis of its p/e ratio indicates that the market is valuing the shares according to expected future earnings.

Although a relatively high p/e ratio may be suggestive of a company with higher than average growth prospects, this is not always the case. Companies where a substantial profit recovery is expected may trade for short periods on a relatively high p/e ratio. Further, a relatively high p/e ratio may not be justified by the company's underlying trading position, indicating that the shares are over-valued on the basis of anticipated earnings.

The expectation of a future takeover bid can have a significant influence on the stock market's rating of a company. For instance, the prospect of a contested takeover bid is likely to lead to the company's share price being marked up, and the p/e ratio increasing above the level justified on the basis of the company's trading performance. The market recognizes that to be successful, a bidder is likely to have to pay a premium over current market price in order to gain control of the company. In these circumstances, valuing the company on the basis of its current and prospective earnings becomes less material than judging how much the bidder is likely to have to pay in order to gain control.

Discussion surrounding the introduction of FRS3 referred to earlier has led to some questions as to the future importance of the p/e ratio. The future absence of extraordinary items and the corresponding greater volatility of the eps figure has raised doubts in some people's minds as to whether the p/e ratio will retain such a central role in the work of analysts. Work undertaken by the Institute of Investment Management and Research (1993) has suggested using different earnings figures according to the purpose for undertaking the calculation. Further, as noted earlier, a number of investment houses have already indicated that they will adjust the eps published by a company to exclude a number of non-recurring items in an attempt to calculate maintainable earnings.

On the basis of the comments above it seems likely that a modified eps figure to the one published by a company in fulfilling the requirements laid down in FRS3 will be employed by analysts as the basis of making their estimates of future earnings. It may also be the case that, notwithstanding the previous comments, analysts, as the ASB intended in publishing FRS3, will look at a wider range of indicators of a company's performance than they have in the past. Many analysts would, however, argue that this already happens with a range of indicators – company's cash flow, balance sheet, quality of management, products, etc. – being employed, and that they do not exclusively focus on a company's p/e ratio.

Cross-sectional analysis of performance indicators

A company's price–earnings ratios are also influenced by the overall level of the stock market, and the market's view of the sector in which the company is operating. In periods when the stock market is rising strongly the overall market p/e ratio tends to rise and with it the p/e ratios of companies. Rising p/e ratios may be reversed if investors become more pessimistic about the prospects for companies generally, leading to a fall in the market p/e ratio.

When considering the relative rating of a company it is often instructive to compare its yield and p/e ratio with the averages for its sector and the FT-A All Share Index, by way of cross-sectional analysis. This technique is illustrated in Table 9.6 where UB's market rating is compared to the average for food manufacturers and the FT-A.

Examining Table 9.6 reveals that UB dividend yield is in excess of both the average for the sector and the FT-A Industrial Group. Conversely, illustrating the link between the dividend yield and p/e ratio, the company p/e rating is below the average for the food sector and Industrial Group. On the basis of these figures the market is indicating that UB prospects are below the average for companies in its sector or quoted in the market in general.

Table 9.6 *UB's relative market rating*

Ratio	UB	Food manufacturing sector	FT-A*	UB relative to sector (%)	UB relative to FT-A*(%)
Yield	5.6	3.9	4.1	144	137
P/E ratio**	12.7	16.0	17.1	79	74

* FT-A Industrial Group which excludes Oil and Gas sector and financial companies from FT-A All Share Index.
** Adjusted p/e ratios as published in the FT.
Source: *Financial Times*, 30 January 1993.

The market rating of a single company can also be compared to similar companies in the same sector. A framework for choosing companies for inter-company comparisons was discussed in Chapter 7, and four companies – Associated British Foods (ABF), Cadbury Schweppes, Hillsdown Holdings and Northern Foods — were selected for comparison with UB. Market ratings for these four companies and UB are presented in Table 9.7.

Table 9.7 *Inter-company comparisons – companies ranked by p/e ratio**

Company	Share price (p)	Earnings per share (p)	Dividend per share (p)	Dividend cover	Earnings yield	P/E ratio
Cadbury Schweppes	464	27.7	12.5	2.21	3.6	16.7
Northern Foods	272	19.1	7.9	2.24	3.9	14.2
UB	**362**	**30.8**	**15.3**	**2.00**	**5.6**	**11.7**
ABF	475	43.7	14.0	2.63	3.9	10.9
Hillsdown Holdings	148	21.0	8.8	1.75	7.9	7.0

*(a) Eps is shown on an undiluted basis; (b) p/e ratios are based on company's latest annual report, and do not include interim figures; (c) eps and dps figures for Northern Foods have been adjusted to reflect the company's scrip issue.
Source: Share prices are based on those quoted in the *Financial Times*, 3 February 1993. All other figures based on information contained in the companies' annual reports or press releases.

Comparing the five food manufacturers shown in Table 9.7 indicates how differently the stock market values individual companies (see also Illustration 9.5). On the basis of their historical p/e ratio and level of yield, Cadbury Schweppes and Northern Foods are rated by the market most highly, followed by UB. At the other end of the spectrum, Hillsdown Holdings has been given a much lower p/e rating and consequently a higher yield. The yield on the shares of Hillsdown Holdings is twice as large as for the company with the highest p/e ratio and lowest yield, Cadbury Schweppes.

Illustration 9.5

UNIGATE & NORTHERN FOODS – MARKET PERCEPTIONS
Unigate (9 June 1992) and Northern Foods (10 June 1992) announced their results for 1991/92 within one day of each other. The contrasting levels of performance provide an explanation as to why the stock market values their shares differently. Currently (3 February 1993) Unigate is trading with a p/e of 11.5 and a yield of 6.5%. By contrast, Northern Foods is trading with a p/e of 14.2 and a yield of 3.9%.

Unigate (9 June 1992) and Northern Foods (10 June 1992) announced their results for 1991/92 within one day of each other. The contrasting levels of performance provide an explanation as to why the stock market values their shares differently. Currently (3 February 1993) Unigate is trading with a p/e of 11.5 and a yield of 6.5%. By contrast, Northern Foods is trading with a p/e of 14.2 and a yield of 3.9%.

Unigate's reported performance for 1991/92 showed some encouraging signs after a number of years of indifferent results. Since the appointment of a new chief executive in 1990, the company had announced that it was withdrawing from a number of business sectors, and the group's overall level of efficiency had been improved. Nevertheless, the future direction of the company remained unclear, and profit margins for a number of the company's businesses were still low. Dividend payments for the year were unchanged at 15.3p.

By contrast Northern Foods was able to announce a strong improvement in its underlying profitability, helped by recent acquisitions but primarily reflecting the company's continuing heavy investment programme and clear strategic direction. The company's results reinforced the view that continued earnings growth could be expected, not least from improving the cost base of the company's recent acquisitions. A final dividend of 9.27p was proposed to give a total payment for the year up by almost 15% on the previous year.

Source: Company reports and press comment.

The link between a company's p/e ratio and yield can be related to the total return the investor anticipates from holding a share. The total return from holding a share is dependent upon the dividend received (the income component) and the change in the value of the share (the capital component). Different shares, even though the investor may seek the same total return, will offer alternative combinations of income and capital growth. As Table 9.8 illustrates, a total return of 15% over, say, a year can be arrived at in at least three ways.

Table 9.8 *Different combinations of total return for holding alternative shares*

Company	Capital gain	Income return	Total return
Company A	14%	1%	15%
Company B	10%	5%	15%
Company C	5%	10%	15%

Of the three companies illustrated in Table 9.8, Company A offers virtually all its total return in the form of anticipated share price appreciation (capital gain), whilst Company B's return is largely in the form of dividends (income).

What Table 9.8 emphasizes is that, if a company has poor growth prospects, then the investor will expect to be compensated by way of a higher level of income, in order to make the company's shares as attractive as those of a company which is expected to grow quickly and whose shares are likely to enjoy a significant increase in value. The fact that a company's yield and p/e ratio move in opposite directions, as illustrated in Table 9.5, explains how share price movements automatically bring about a change in the balance between expected capital and income gain from holding a company's shares.

In practice the relationship between the p/e ratio and yield is complicated by two further factors, namely (a) different levels of risk, and (b) tax. First, investors adjust the total return they expected from a share to reflect their estimation of risk. Secondly, the individual investor's tax position is one of the factors likely to influence whether they are primarily interested in capital or income growth.

Developing a forecast of future earnings

When seeking to arrive at a 'buy, sell or hold' recommendation, the analyst's forecast of prospective earnings and expected p/e ratio from which to compute a future share price are the key variables. The growth in earnings and the choice of future p/e ratio on which a company might be trading are inherently judgemental, with the forecaster adopting a combination of intuition and analysis in reaching a view.

It is the quality of the analyst's prediction as to a company's future earnings, dividends and p/e ratio that is critical to the determination of the expected total return from holding a share. Consequently, this section focuses on how the company's potential growth in earnings can be assessed and the relationship between earnings and share prices.

Whilst it is difficult to discern the precise relationship between future earnings and share prices, four general observations can be made, namely:

- Share prices and forecast earnings contain substantially similar information concerning future changes in the value (profit) of the company. It can be expected that there will be a strong correlation between expected future earnings and share prices; as expected future earnings rise (and the p/e falls), share price rises; as expected future earnings fall (and p/e rises), share price falls.
- While share prices and earnings are related the time delay inherent in the preparation and publication of a company's accounts implies that the share price is able to act as a lead indicator, pre-empting the disclosure of accounting information. As noted in the previous chapter, share prices act as a barometer for market expectations concerning forthcoming earnings disclosures.
- Notwithstanding the two previous points, share prices do react to reported performance when disclosure takes place, implying that accounting disclo-

sures – the interim announcement, preliminary announcement of final results, followed by the publication of the annual report and accounts – do offer new information to the market.

- Unforeseen company announcements, including profits warnings, announcements of takeovers or disposals, and the resignation of key managers, can have a profound effect on market sentiment and share prices. To the extent that these announcements provide discontinuous information they may be related to the dynamic model of share prices introduced in Chapter 8.

From the foregoing analysis it would appear that share prices recognize earnings as they become foreseeable. It is widely accepted that the forecasts of earnings produced by market analysts are a sound description of market expectations. This information is now available to the private investor through the monthly publication of both the *Earnings Guide* and *The Estimate Directory* (see Chapter 4). These publications contain analysts' forecasts of profits, earnings and dividends for quoted companies over the next two years. As shown in Figure 9.5, the average estimate for UB's profits before tax for 1992 is £169.0 m.

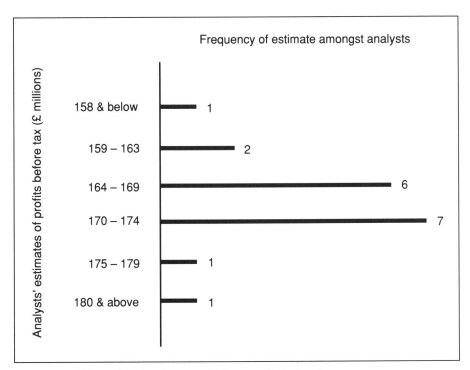

Figure 9.5 UB: analysts' estimates of future profits before tax
Source: *Earnings Guide* and *The Earnings Directory*, January 1993.

The process by which earnings forecasts and prospective p/e ratios are generated is not widely discussed. From a synthesis of our discussion with numerous analysts, it is possible to discern three separate but interrelated foci of attention, namely: financial forecasting, company communications and expert judgement. Naturally, the emphasis will vary from analyst to analyst, as will the iterative process undertaken. As Figure 9.6 shows there are many points of entry to the forecasting model, but to complete the process attention needs to be successively and repeatedly focused on the three key overlapping inputs listed above. Providing no major discontinuities arise, then a point will be reached at which further information merely reinforces and at best marginally revises future earnings estimates.

Each of the three factors identified in Figure 9.6 will now be examined in detail:

- financial forecasts
- company communications
- expert judgement.

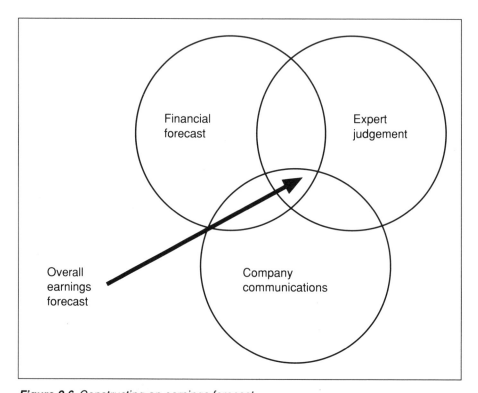

Figure 9.6 *Constructing an earnings forecast*

Financial forecasts

Most analysts follow a 'break down' and 'build up' approach to *financial forecasts*. To assist the reader's understanding the process is broken into four distinct stages:

- review of segmental information;
- assessment of broad and industry/sector contexts and company-specific factors;
- development of profits forecast;
- estimate of earnings per share.

The first stage of the process relates to the *review of segmental information*. Segmental information relating to turnover, operating profit and capital employed for each substantive business activity and each geographical area is published in a company's annual report. It is the only information publicly provided by a company on how the different parts of the business have performed, and provides the basis for qualitative judgement concerning future divisional operating profitability. By aggregating the various segmental forecasts, the analyst is able to provide an estimate of future operating profits.

The second stage of the forecasting process will be for the analyst to make judgements about the *broad and industry/sector contexts,* together with an assessment of *company-specific factors*. Since analysts focus on specific sectors of industry they will have a detailed knowledge of each of these areas and be able to judge their likely effect on business performance. Rarely do analysts use highly sophisticated and technically demanding computer models, but rather rely on establishing simple heuristic, or rules of thumb, between previously reported performance and future profit estimates. Particular attention is generally paid to any trading statements the company's chief executive has made with the publication of the company's interim or final results.

Having gained a view of likely operating profits, the analyst will need to make a number of adjustments in order to arrive at profits before tax, and subsequently profits to ordinary shareholders. Figure 9.7 outlines the detailed adjustments which need to be undertaken ignoring the question of exceptional items, on the basis that most analysts are likely to 'normalize' earnings by adding back any exceptional items identified by the company. The analyst is generally faced with making two major adjustments – interest received/paid and tax – in order to arrive at a figure for profits for ordinary shareholders.

Calculation of a company's interest paid/received requires the analyst to take the latest debt position of the company as published in the annual report and to adjust this figure for changes in the company's borrowings for the year. On the basis of this and a knowledge of prevailing interest rates and the extent to which the company has debt at floating rates of interest, the analyst will arrive at a figure for interest paid/received. Similarly, the company's past tax charge (tax as a percentage of earnings), together with knowledge of changes in the

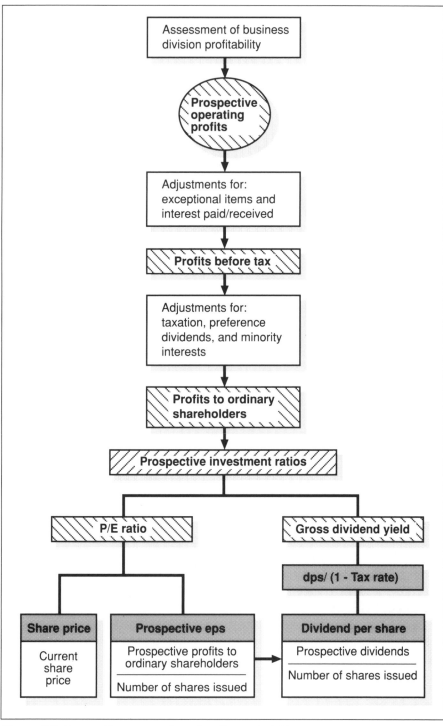

Figure 9.7 *Forecasting prospective p/e ratios and yields*

general tax regime or any company-specific factors, will enable the analyst to estimate the company's tax bill. As Figure 9.7 demonstrates additional adjustments may need to be made for preference dividends and/or minority interests. For most companies these are small items.

To arrive at an *estimate of earnings per share* the analyst will need to calculate whether the company has made any changes to the number of shares issued. For example, if the company has announced a rights issue or undertaken a share placing, then the number of shares issued by the company can be accordingly adjusted. Figure 9.7 shows that by dividing the revised figure for issued shares into the analyst's estimate of profits attributable to shareholders an estimate for earnings per share is gained. Once this figure has been calculated the analyst's knowledge of the company's dividend policy will enable a judgement to be made as to any potential change to dividend payments, and hence an estimate of future dividends per share. This base forecast produced by an analyst will be reviewed and revised as part of an ongoing updating process, but unless there is a major discontinuity any additional financial information will only result in minor revisions to the earnings forecast.

Company communications

Company communications play an important role in constructing an analyst's earnings and share price forecast. A distinction may be made between formal and informal company communications. Formal communications refer to the following information sources: company annual and interim reports, press releases, other company publications and updated material filed at Companies House. Informal disclosure of information takes place when leading sector analysts meet with a company's management to probe for reasons why the share price might change. These meetings take place several times a year, with significant share price changes accompanying such meetings if major discontinuities are anticipated or announced. Companies may equally choose to use the media to inform the investment community by, for example, giving a journalist material to write a feature on the company.

Analysts' briefings, in particular, can have an important role in affecting the way analysts forecast future earnings and estimate the appropriate p/e ratio for a company. Both of these estimates are critical to the assessment of the potential return from holding shares in a company. In order to make estimates about the quality of earnings as measured by the p/e ratio, informal briefings act as a sounding board for making informed judgements as to the underlying prospects of a company. The interaction of analysts and the company at these meetings is thereby an important vehicle for shaping sentiment about the company.

The forecasts made by analysts are highly visible, being published monthly in the *Earnings Guide* and *The Estimate Directory*. With the exception of times when sentiment towards a company is highly polarized, such estimates tend to regress towards the mean and collectively are a good description of market expectations. This may be the result of the informal briefings referred to above, providing the company with the opportunity to communicate in a planned and controlled manner any anticipated gap between market expectations and actual outcomes. In this way the analysts' forecasts are adjusted in line with new market realities, so that when interim and annual reports are published it is common to find that the information released matches market sentiment.

In short, there is a shared dependency between market analysts and companies. It is most probable that the consensus earnings estimates of analysts are a good description of market sentiment, and that this is partly attributable to the role the analyst plays as an information intermediary between the company and the market as a whole. By making incremental adjustments in a well planned way, companies hope to avoid negative sentiment and uncertainty about future prospects. In turn, by using analysts as an information intermediary companies do not need to communicate with institutional shareholders directly. When rumours about a company emerge, institutions go to their analyst for their informed opinion.

Expert judgement

Expert judgement is an important consideration in the generation of financial forecasts, as well as in determining the *expected* total returns to be gained from holding shares in the company. The expected total return will be determined by (a) *expected* future dividend payments, and (b) the *expected* change in the price of the share. Both of these will be driven by forecasts of the company's future earnings and likely dividend policy. Such analysis is undertaken in an attempt to identify which shares seem to be over- or under-valued.

In order to calculate a value with which to compare the current market value, a company's earnings for the subsequent year are estimated and compared with the current share price. The analyst's report on UB at the beginning of the chapter suggested that profits before tax were forecast to be £169 m for 1992, leading to an eps of 22.9p. The expectation was that dps would remain unchanged at 15.3p despite a fall in eps. On the basis of these estimates UB's *prospective* p/e ratio can be calculated as follows:

$$\text{Current share price}/\textit{prospective eps} = 362p/22.9p$$
$$= 15.8p$$

Reference to the analyst's report at the beginning of the chapter shows that a forecast fall in eps (from 30.8p to 22.9p) results in a rise in the p/e ratio (from 11.7 to 15.8). The inverse relationship between changes in eps and p/e ratio is entirely to be expected. Circular referencing ensures that the product of the prospective p/e ratio and the eps is the current share price (15.8 × 22.9p). To the first time reader it may seem somewhat perplexing as to how the prospective p/e ratio as calculated above, and similarly calculated in the *Earnings Guide* and

The Estimate Directory, can be an indicator as to whether a share is under- or over-valued.

The simple answer is that an 'appropriate' p/e ratio, based on the analyst's experience and intuition, is applied to estimated earnings to obtain a view as to future market value. As outlined in the previous chapter, the p/e ratio will depend on the analyst's interpretation of three interrelated factors: (a) predicted trends in the overall stock market p/e ratio (Table 8.4); (b) industry/sector comparisons (Table 8.3); and (c) company-specific factors (Table 8.9). Consequently, the methodology as to how analysts arrive at the appropriate p/e ratio is largely problematic.

Assuming that the analyst considers an appropriate p/e ratio is 17 for UB at the end of a holding period for the company's shares, then by multiplying the eps for the current year by this p/e ratio, a prediction of the future share price will be obtained. This predicted market price is then compared to the current market price to see if the share is currently under- or over-valued:

$$\text{Future share price} = \text{eps} \times \text{p/e ratio}$$
$$= 22.9 \times 17$$
$$= 389.3\text{p}$$

The change in the share price is an increase of 27.3p (389.3p − 362p). If the p/e ratio on which the company was trading at the end of the period was expected to be below the prospective p/e of 15.8, the investor would expect the share price to fall and a capital loss to be made.

It is the combination of an evaluation of the future earnings relevant to a share with an assessment of an appropriate p/e ratio that facilitates the computation of a future share price. Expected changes in the price of a share and its associated future dividend payment will yield the return on the investment in shares in a company. Assuming UB maintains its dividend at 15.3p as forecast, the total return from holding the shares can be calculated as follows:

a) Capital return (%) = (Share price change/Price at the beginning of the holding period)
$$= (27.3\text{p}/362\text{p}) \times 100$$
$$= 7.54\%$$

(b) Gross dividend yield (%) = (Net dividend per share/(1 − Tax rate)) × 100/ Share price
$$= (15.3\text{p}/(1 − 0.25)) \times 100/362\text{p}$$
$$= (20.4 \times 100)/362$$
$$= 5.63\%$$

(c) Expected total return (%) = Capital return + Gross dividend yield
$$= 7.54 + 5.63$$
$$= 13.62\%$$

Thus the expected total return from holding UB's shares will be 13.62% (7.54% + 5.63%). This may be compared with alternative shares and investments and, after adjusting for any differences of risk, the analyst should be able to make a buy, sell or hold recommendation to clients.

Share price movements

In looking at the relationship between information disclosure and share price over time it is important to make a distinction between (a) the 'search' for information concerning the quality and quantity of future earnings, and (b) the 'evaluation' of accounting disclosures in the form of annual and interim results and dividend payments. Such accounting disclosures are heavily discounted by the search process, so that share price movements will largely precede accounting announcements. Nevertheless, accounting disclosures do contain valuable information as is shown by the share price reaction to a company's public disclosure of its results.

Since the timing of annual and interim results is known in advance, it is important to be aware of a company's financial reporting calendar. Table 9.9 shows UB's key accounting announcements for the financial year. Not surprisingly the annual general meeting has little effect on share prices, since the main information release with respect to the company's annual results occurs with the announcement of preliminary results. The precise dates for the forthcoming year are not defined in the annual accounts, but unless a company changes its financial year, it is normal for companies to retain the same monthly dates for key announcements.

Table 9.9 UB – financial reporting calendar

Results	
Interim results	Announced 12 September 1991
Final year results	Announced 12 March 1992
Report and accounts	Posted 14 April 1992
Annual general meeting	Edinburgh, 12 May 1992
Dividend payments	
(a) Interim	Announced 12 September 1991
	Ex-dividend date 14 October 1991
	Paid 3 January 1992
(b) Final	Proposed 12 March 1992
	Ex-dividend date 23 March 1992
	Payable 1 July 1992

Source: *UB Annual Report 1991*, March 1992, p.54.

Accounting disclosures in the form of annual and interim accounts and dividend payments are only a few examples of the types of information which can affect share price. The following four discontinuities typically prompt significant price movements in a company's shares:

- management changes, for example share price falls on the basis of a highly respected chief executive resigning;
- formal trading announcement or informal briefing of analysts, leading either to the analysts revising upwards or downwards their forecasts of the company's expected future profits;
- actual or rumoured major acquisition and takeover activity; and
- announced, or fears of, fund raising by the company – for example, fears that the company is likely to make a rights issue will normally depress the share price.

All four categories of change have a significant effect on forecast eps and market sentiment towards the company. Major changes in market sentiment often have an amplified effect on share price movements. If the market views a share favourably, the concerted demand may force share prices up to a level where the share is over-priced. Likewise, if a share is hit by adverse market sentiment, a lemming-like reaction to sell that can afflict investors may well force share prices below their intrinsic value. In both cases, these amplified movements to share prices will take some time to work themselves out, and for the shares price to readjust to a trading band which reflects the company's underlying value.

How share prices adjust to new information over a number of months can be illustrated with reference to movements in UB's share price over the fourteen-month period illustrated in Figure 9.8. Some of the general features of share price movements which can be highlighted include the following:

- Whether the share price trend is upwards or downwards, remembering that market trading ensures oscillation around the trend.
- Ex-dividend adjustment to a company's share price. On two dates in the year a company's share will go ex-dividend (xd). This means that a purchaser of the shares is no longer entitled to the previously announced dividend. As a result on the day a share goes xd its price will drop by the amount of the dividend, a process known as the xd adjustment. Figure 9.8 provides an illustration of this process by indicating that UB's shares fell on 23 March by the amount of the company's final dividend payment.
- The search for information regarding the company's current earnings. Between May 1992 and September 1992 the share price fell from a peak of 432p to a low of 222p, as the market became concerned about the company's trading in the US.
- The company's poor interim results, largely the result of problems in the US, had been fully discounted by the market when they were published on 12 September 1992. Confirmation that the first half performance in 1992 was no worse than expected, and that the company was taking appropriate action to improve performance in the US, led to the share price rising by 2p on the date the interim results were announced.

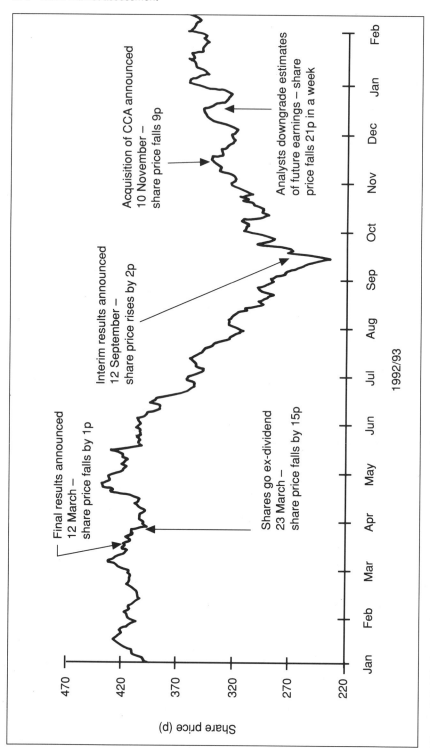

Figure 9.8 *UB share price 1992/93, and major company announcements*
Source: Microview, Extel Financial and press releases.

- The announcement of major acquisitions, unless they have been anticipated by the market, prompt significant price changes. As Figure 9.8 shows, the acquisition of CCA resulted in a 19p fall in share price, primarily due to the fact that the company undertook a placing of shares worth some £80 m. The share price change occurred notwithstanding the fact that the market generally felt the decision to make the acquisition was correct.
- The effect of an analysts' meeting resulting in a lowering of forecasted profits for the year. UB's share price fell almost 6% in one week in December, with shares being marked down by 21p.

One further approach to predicting share price movements is examined in Illustration 9.6.

Illustration 9.6

CHARTISTS
Chartists look for recognized patterns to previous share price movements in order to predict future movements of share prices. No attempt is made to look at the process by which share prices move up or down, since chartists, models are solely concerned with prediction.

Chartists look for recognized patterns to previous share price movements in order to predict future movements of share prices. No attempt is made to look at the process by which share prices move up or down, since chartists, models are solely concerned with prediction.

Simple chartist analysis looks for either 'continuation' patterns suggesting that prices will continue in the same direction, or 'reversal' patterns indicating a change of direction. While with hindsight it is easy to discern a continuous pattern analysis to UB's share price movements for much of 1992/93, looking to the future the pattern is much less clear.

More sophisticated approaches by chartists attempt to identify when a share is 'over-bought' or over-sold', and thereby when to sell or buy. As with all approaches to share prices chartists are still required to make judgements when interpreting their charts of share price movements, particularly when seeking to identify turning points to an existing trend to a company's share price.

Whilst some analysts may refer to charts of share prices, few rely solely on their predictive power, believing that understanding the process of what drives share prices is important to assist in predicting future share price levels

Source: Authors.

Concluding remarks

This chapter has focused on short-term movements in share prices and the role of the analyst in influencing market sentiment. A range of performance indicators has been introduced, and their use in assessing a company discussed. The estimation of future earnings, a key driver of share prices, has been considered and the reader made aware of how they can gain access to analysts' forecasts through either the *Earnings Guide* or *The Earnings Directory*. Finally, movements in UB's share prices over 1992/93 have been used to illustrate how different events influence the value of a company's shares.

To enable the reader to carry out a similar exercise for a company of their choice, a checklist for short-term share valuation follows.

Checklist

To undertake a short-term share valuation for a company:

- *Calculate performance indicators for the company and other firms in its sector.*
- *Evaluate the company's performance by comparing the current level of its indicators with (a) its past performance; and (b) other companies in the same sector.*
- *Assess the extent that the market is suggesting that future returns from holding the company's shares are likely to come from dividends or changes in the share price.*
- *What do analysts estimate future earnings to be?*
- *What effect is earnings growth likely to have on future dividend payments?*
- *Is there a risk to the dividend?*
- *Might the company become a takeover target? If so, on what basis might the company be valued, and how much might it be worth?*
- *How has the company's share price moved over, say, the last twelve months, and why?*
- *Compare the company's share price performance with its sector and FT-A.*
- *What is the current share price telling you about the company? What future events has the market already discounted and are in the share price?*
- *Do you believe the share price is an accurate reflection of the company's underlying value? If not, what would you advise an investor to do?*

CHAPTER 10

Long-term share valuation

In this chapter consideration is given as to how 'shareholder value approach' (SVA), which concentrates on the long-term valuation of cash flows, provides a more sophisticated and robust view of a company's value than the accounting approach featured in the previous chapter. The obsessive fixation with eps growth rates and prospective p/e ratios gives rise to the popular belief that share prices are strongly influenced, if not totally determined, by forecasted earnings. Long-term share valuation gives more credence to sustainable cash flows than to short-term earnings forecasts, since shareholder value is created when a company generates positive net cash flows discounted by the appropriate cost of capital. This is discussed under the following headings:

- *limitations of short-term share valuation techniques*
- *short term versus long term*
- *determining an appropriate discount rate*
- *the shareholder value approach*
- *calculating the business value of an actual company*
- *investor and managerial perspectives on shareholder value.*

In the first section attention is focused on why earnings do not reliably measure the present value of a business. The leads to a discussion of the reasons why short-term share valuation techniques have been popular, but why on closer inspection it is found that the stock market often takes a longer-term view of a company's value. A critical component of the long-term approach to share prices is the cost of capital and this is the subject of a separate section. The shareholder value approach is developed by first considering a simple illustration to emphasize the general principles, before assessing the business value of a major FT-SE 100 company. This prompts consideration of how both investors and managers can employ shareholder value analysis to both inform their judgements about the value of a company's shares, and to appraise alternative strategic options. The chapter is concluded with a checklist.

Limitations of short-term share valuation techniques

While the accounting approach that values a company on this year's or next year's earnings times an 'appropriate' p/e ratio continues to enjoy considerable popularity, there are a number of serious limitations as to why earnings fail to measure changes in business value. Eps does not take into account the following important considerations, namely:

- risk
- investment requirements
- time value of money
- cost of capital
- inflation.

Risk

Overall business risk is determined by two factors: (a) the nature of a firm's operations and its associated business context, and (b) the relative proportion of debt and equity – its 'gearing' – used to finance its strategy. The former is commonly referred to as 'business risk', the latter as 'financial risk'. Both business and financial risk are excluded from eps considerations.

By ignoring the variability of possible outcomes when comparing two alternative business strategies, eps is indifferent between two prospective outcomes which offer the same average growth in earnings. Once risk is introduced into the analysis, consideration needs to be given to the distribution of outcomes around the mean: the narrower the range of outcomes, the less risky the strategy; the wider the range of outcomes, the higher the degree of risk. Notwithstanding identical average earnings growth, the investor will not be indifferent to the different degrees of risk associated with the two sets of outcomes, and will prefer the company which offers the lower degree of risk.

With regard to financial risk the relative proportion of debt and equity financing are important considerations. Due to its prior claim on a company's assets and because of the deductibility of interest payments for tax purposes, the cost of debt is lower than the cost of equity. Consequently, a company can improve its eps by funding its strategy by debt rather than equity. Such an improvement in eps does not necessarily improve business value on two accounts. First, increases in the level of debt prompt a corresponding increase in financial risk on account of the greater danger of insolvency. In turn, this ensures that as the relative proportion of debt increases so does the cost of equity. This arises because shareholders demand higher rates of return as compensation for the increase in financial risk.

Secondly, increased variability of earnings associated with higher gearing also increases financial risk. In a totally equity funded company any increase or decrease in reported earnings and eps is necessarily identical. Given that interest payments have a first call on a company's assets, in a geared company the relationship between earnings and eps is not identical:

- Faced with poor sales and rising interest rates, the eps generated by a highly geared company will fall well below that of its totally equity funded counterpart.
- With rising sales and falling interest rates the opposite scenario will occur with the eps generated by a highly geared company greatly exceeding its totally equity funded counterpart.

In short, with gearing, any changes in eps will be greater than the corresponding change in company earnings. Both the increased variability and greater chance of insolvency associated with gearing introduce a financial risk to shareholders, so that increases in debt financing raise the cost of equity.

Investment requirements

The eps does not take into account the incremental fixed capital and working capital requirements needed to sustain any anticipated sales increase. As witnessed in earlier discussions concerning incremental fixed (Chapter 6) and working capital (Chapter 7) requirements, it is possible for a company to achieve high earnings even though the associated cash flow is much lower. This is particularly the case where the company is growing quickly and needs to make significant cash transfers to meet fixed investment and working capital needs. In such circumstances the relationship between change in business value and eps is obscured by the exclusion of the necessary incremental fixed and working capital requirements from the earnings calculation.

For ease of exposition, consider the hypothetical company illustrated in Table 10.1 that expects to double both its turnover (from £200 m to £400 m) and earnings (from £60 m to £120 m) over the twelve-month forecast period. If total shares issued is expected to remain at 240 million over the forecast period, the eps can be expected to double over the next 12 months. The current eps of 25p per share (£60 m/240 m) in year 1 is anticipated to rise to a prospective eps of 50p per share (£120 m/240 m) at the end of year 2. This increase in earnings may not necessarily lead to an increase in business value, since no consideration has been given to the impact of investment requirements.

Table 10.1 shows that the improvement in eps is the result of a projected growth in sales and earnings, which in turn will require significant cash outflows for incremental fixed and working capital outlays. As a result, the forecasted £120 m earnings is expected to generate only £6 m cash – a fall of £6 m from the £12 m cash currently generated. On the basis of these illustrative figures, cash flow per share will move in the opposite direction to the projected eps. While eps is expected to rise, cash per share is anticipated to fall from 5p (£12 m/240 m) to 2.5p (£6 m/240 m). The recognition that eps and cash can diverge in the way illustrated by this example has prompted a number of

Table 10.1 *Eps growth and business value*

Year	Actual/ forecast	No of shares (m)	Turnover (£m)	Earnings (£m)	Cash (£m)	Eps (p)	Cash per share (p)
1	Current	240	200	60	12	25	5.0
2	Forecast	240	400	120	6	50	2.5

investment analysts to publish figures of the cash per share for companies they report on (see Illustration 10.1).

Illustration 10.1

UB – COMPARISON OF EPS AND CASH PER SHARE

Using UB for illustrative purposes, the methods used by analysts to compare eps and cash per share will be discussed. Most analysts tend to define cash for the purposes of calculating cash per share to be net cash inflow from operations adjusted for returns on investments and servicing of finance and taxation. This information can be obtained from a company's cash flow statement published in the annual accounts (for UB's see Chapter 6). On this definition cash flow ignores investing activities, which can be significantly affected by acquisitions and disposals.

Comparing eps and cash per share over the last two years for UB reveals a close relationship between the figures:

	1990 (p)	1991 (p)
Earnings per share (undiluted)	28.9	30.8
Cash flow per share	27.4	26.6

If, however, capital investment is included in the cash flow calculation, cash flow per share becomes *negative* in both years:

Cash flow per share (after funding fixed investment)	−2.0	−3.5

Clearly this example shows how eps and cash per share can diverge in practice. It also indicates to the investor that whilst the company is making reported profits, it is not generating cash.

Source: Authors and company report.

Time value of money

A further drawback of eps as a measure of business value is its failure to specify a time preference rate for the earnings stream. Consider the illustrative example in Table 10.2 where two companies are identical in all respects other than the timing of their earnings flow.

Table 10.2 *Comparing earnings streams*

	Earnings (current) £m	Earnings (next year) £m	Total earnings £m
Company A	60	120	180
Company B	120	60	180

Under the eps criteria investors are supposed to be indifferent between the two companies since total earnings over the two years are identical. Most investors, however, would prefer to have higher earnings flows sooner rather than later. As a result, investors would prefer Company B. This is because £1 received today is worth more than £1 received twelve months from now, because today's £1 can be invested to earn interest over the next year.

How much more £1 today is worth compared to in a year's time is explained by the principle of *compounding*. If interest rates are at 6%, then an individual who invests £1 for a year will receive the following interest:

$$\text{Interest received} = \text{Sum invested} \times \text{Rate of interest}$$
$$= £1 \times 0.06$$
$$= 6p$$

The total sum the investor will receive at the end of one year is thus:

$$\text{Sum invested} + \text{Interest earned} = £1 + 6p$$
$$= £1.06$$

As a general rule, to determine the value investors will receive in the future, the formula for compounding is:

$$\text{Sum to be received} = (1 + \text{Rate of interest})^n \times \text{Sum invested}$$

where n = the number of years the money is invested.

For the example above, this gives:

$$(1.06)^1 \times £1 = 1.06 \times £1$$
$$= £1.06$$

This example shows that £1 today is actually worth £1.06 in a year's time, and £1 today is not the same as £1 next year.

The converse to the process of compounding is *discounting*. This process discounts values in the future to give their current, or present, value on the basis of what the future sums would be if they were received today. In other words, how much is £1 to be received next year worth today? To answer this question the sum to be received in the future must be divided by the discount rate. The discount rate is the reciprocal of the formula used for compounding derived above.

Present value = Sum received in the future *divided by* the Discount factor

How much is £1.06 to be received in a year's time worth today?

$$\text{Present value} = £1.06 / (1 + 0.06)^1$$
$$= £1.06/1.06$$
$$= £1$$

This tells us what we already knew, that £1.06 to be received in twelve months is worth £1 today. Notice that the discount factor $1/(1 + 1.06) = 0.943$. This is how much £1 in a year's time is worth today: 94.3p. Reworking the example set out in Table 10.2 gives Table 10.3 which suggests that the investor will prefer the earnings stream of Company B, given that most earnings are available at the present time and the investor is not required to wait a year. The present value of the earnings next year for Company A are £113.2 m (£120 m × 0.943) and £56.6 m (£60 m × 0.943) for Company B. When added to the present value of current earnings, the present value of total earnings for Company B (£176.60 m) is greater than for Company A (£173.20 m).

Table 10.3 *Comparing the present value of earnings streams*

	Present value of current earnings £m	Present value of earnings next year £m	Present value of total earnings £m
Company A	60.0	113.2	173.20
Company B	120.0	56.6	176.60

To be able to compare future income streams with income received today, all future values should be discounted to their present value to offer a consistent basis for comparison. To be able to discount future income streams an appropriate discount rate needs to be determined and it is to this issue that we now turn.

Cost of capital

In order for business value to increase it is necessary for a company to earn a rate of return on its business activities that exceeds the cost of capital. The cost of capital reflects the cost of employing the capital in the business, which might otherwise be used for alternative purposes, in order to generate a future income stream. The cost of capital thus reflects the opportunity cost of employing capital in the business: the opportunities forgone by investors not being able to fund alternative strategies or businesses once they have committed their capital. If the business value created is less than the cost of capital then the investment should not be undertaken. The capital should be used for alternative purposes where the business value is in excess of the cost of capital.

Not only does the eps ignore the cost of capital, but earnings growth does not necessarily lead to the creation of business value. A business is worth the anticipated future cash flows discounted by the cost of capital in order to calculate the business's present value. The cost of capital thus determines the discount rate introduced earlier. Unless there is recognition of the importance of the cost of capital a decrease in business value can occur despite earnings growth, if a firm chooses not to include an appropriate cost of capital in assessing whether its strategies create value.

How the cost of capital can be incorporated in the assessment of business value can be illustrated by extending the previous numerical example. Given that the £6 m anticipated cash flow in Table 10.1 is worth less in twelve months' time than today on account of lost interest earning opportunities, it is important to scale down future cash flows. The present value of a delayed cash flow can be found by multiplying the cash flow by a discount factor which is the reciprocal of 1 plus the rate of interest. Given a 6% rate of interest, £6 m cash in 1 year's time is worth £5.66 m (£6 m × 0.943 (or 1/1.06)). At the end of year 2, the present value is reduced further to £5.34 m (£6 m × 0.890 (or 1/(1.06)^2). The present value of an annual cash flow of £6 m over a five-year period discounted by a 6% interest rate is shown in Table 10.4.

Table 10.4   *The present value of £6 m cash flow for five years, discounted by a 6% cost of capital (the discount rate)*

Period (years)	Discount rate (6%)	Discount factor (A)	Cash flow (£) (B)	Present value of cash flow (C) = (A) × (B)
1	1/(1.06)^1	0.943	6.00	5.66
2	1/(1.06)^2	0.890	6.00	5.34
3	1/(1.06)^3	0.840	6.00	5.04
4	1/(1.06)^4	0.792	6.00	4.75
5	1/(1.06)^5	0.747	6.00	4.48
Total				25.27

The discounting process is critically dependent on the selected compound discount rate. The lower the anticipated rate of interest (the cost of capital), the less severely future cash flows will be scaled down. Conversely, with higher anticipated interest rates associated with an increase in the cost of capital, the greater the reduction in future cash flows. This can be illustrated by looking at the present value of the same £6 m cash flow over five years, but with a 12% discount factor instead of the initial 6%, as shown in Table 10.5. The present value of the cumulative cash flow falls by 14.4%, from £25.27 m to £21.63 m.

Table 10.5 *The present value of £6 m cash flow for five years, discounted by a 12% cost of capital (the discount rate)*

Period	Discount rate (12%)	Discount factor (A)	Cash flow (£) (B)	Present value of cash flow (C) = (A) × (B)
1	$1/(1.12)^1$	0.893	6.00	5.36
2	$1/(1.12)^2$	0.797	6.00	4.78
3	$1/(1.12)^3$	0.712	6.00	4.27
4	$1/(1.12)^4$	0.636	6.00	3.82
5	$1/(1.12)^5$	0.567	6.00	3.40
Total				21.63

Inflation

The final element ignored by the eps approach is the problem of inflation. Changes in the level of prices distort the yardstick by which performance is measured, namely money. By using a cost of capital based on, say, five years as in Tables 10.4 and 10.5, the discount rate will also reflect investors' views as to the anticipated inflation which is incorporated in the rate of interest they demand in order to provide capital for the business. Hence discounting by the cost of capital will also scale down future cash flows by an amount reflecting anticipated inflation. The eps makes no adjustment for any such changes in prices, implying the value of money over time remains unchanged.

Summary

In summary, all too frequently earnings and business value move in conflicting directions on account of eps and p/e ratios failing to take account of *business and financial risk*; the level of *investment*, the *time value of money*, the *cost of capital*, and *inflation*. Moreover, the unreliable linkage between earnings progression and business value can be demonstrated empirically. Harvey and Smith (1991), for example, found from a sample of the 250 largest UK commercial and industrial companies in 1991 that over a five-year period there was no correlation between eps and share value.

Short term versus long term

Notwithstanding compelling theoretical and empirical evidence of the failings of eps progression as a measure of share value, there still persists a strong belief that share prices are influenced greatly by short-term earnings fluctuations. It is not sufficient to show that long-term discounted cash flows, where value creation results from corporate investments at rates in excess of the cost of capital is conceptually superior, it is also necessary to show that the stock market judges business less by reference to accounting profits than by reference to sustainable cash flows.

Many investors continue to believe that the market naively responds only to short-term earnings. There are three intuitively appealing reasons which support this belief:

- simplicity
- visibility
- plausibility.

The *simplicity* of the eps calculation is a major attraction, together with the fact that it answers many business valuation questions quite well (see Illustration 10.2). This is particularly true where earnings reflect cash flow, so that short-term earnings growth provides a good proxy for anticipated long-term cash flows. Not all companies generate the same cash flow for each £ of earnings, so at the very best an accounting approach is only useful for approximate value estimates. Where reported earnings flows diverge significantly from one another, eps provides an unreliable indicator of underlying business value.

The *visibility* of eps and p/e indicators is such that they are difficult to ignore. Eps figures are routinely reported in the business press, analysts' reports feature current and prospective eps and p/e ratios, while some acquisition specialists continue to argue that market valuation can be achieved simply by assigning the appropriate p/e ratio to an annual earnings flow. Equally difficult to ignore is the arbitrary and somewhat subjective accounting conventions that govern eps calculations (see Chapter 5), together with the increased volatility that will result from the introduction of the FRS3 accounting standard. These changes to UK accounting standards will devalue p/e ratios to some degree and hopefully force analysis beyond the use of this simple, single and somewhat misleading indicator.

There is also a *plausibility* concerning the link between short-term earnings and business valuation. Any major reworking of a company's short-term earnings forecast, providing there is an overall consensus, will affect market valuation. The strong association between short-term earnings; fluctuations and share price does not necessarily imply causation. The market is not reacting myopically to forecast changes in prospective earnings; it is the present value of a company's cash flows, not earnings, that determines share prices. As such, the market uses unexpected changes in earnings as a lead indicator for reassessing a company's long-term cash flow prospects.

It is a mistaken belief that market valuation depends on the short-term progression of earnings instead of a long-term valuation of cash flows. None of the three intrinsic grounds – namely *simplicity, visibility* and *plausibility* – can be sustained; only earnings increases that are associated with strong sustainable cash flow generation will increase share prices. Furthermore, the discounted

Illustration 10.2

VALUING COMPANIES ON THE BASIS OF THEIR P/E RATIO

Valuing a company on the basis on its earnings may be undertaken using p/e ratios. For example, if a food manufacturer is generating profits attributable to shareholders of £50 m, and operates on a p/e ratio of 16.0, then the company valuation would be £800 m (£50 m × 16). If the company had 200 million shares issued, then ignoring all other complications (e.g. debt, tax, etc.), a bidder might be prepared to pay 400p (£800 m/£200 m) per share for the company. In this case the bidder would be paying 16 times the historical earnings of the company, sometimes described as the exit p/e ratio.

Buying the company on the basis just described, however, assumes that the past earnings stream is a reliable guide to the level of earnings the purchaser might be able to achieve in the future. Future earnings may be very different from past performance. If this is likely to be the case it is necessary to estimate how much the business might be worth when linked with the buyer's existing business to gain synergies, and/or following the installation of new management, if, for example, the quality of the existing management is perceived to be poor. Under another company's control, a business's earnings potential may be very different than what is currently being achieved. Where future earnings are expected to be in advance of past performance, the company is in effect buying future earnings on a multiple of less than 16. Clearly, these factors require the exercise of judgement.

Regardless of whether past earnings or future earnings are used as the basis of the valuation, an approach basis on some form of the p/e ratio suffers from the generic weakness identified in the text in respect of using eps measures. Correspondingly, unless the business value rather than the earnings stream is reviewed in valuing a company, corporate value can easily end up being destroyed.

Source: Authors.

cash flow perspective is strongly supported by research into how stock markets actively value companies. This evidence can be grouped into three categories:

- evidence demonstrating that residual value often accounts for a large proportion of a share's value;
- evidence showing that cosmetic earnings increases do not improve share prices; and
- evidence analysing the translation of competitive advantage into sustainable cash flows.

Evidence demonstrating that residual value often accounts for a large proportion of a share's value

Table 10.6 shows the percentage of UB's share price determined by expected dividends over the next five years. If dividends are expected to grow at 10% per year, and the discount rate for the cost of capital is 9%, the present value of dividends over the next five years would be 77.92p. This simple calculation shows that the present value of dividends over the next five years accounts for slightly more than one-fifth of the current share price (19 February 1993). To summarize, no less than 78% of the share price can be attributed to expected dividends beyond the five-year forecast period.

Table 10. 6 Percentage of UB's share price determined by expected dividends over the next five years (1993–98)

Year	Dividends	Discount rate	PV dividends
0	15.30	1.00	15.30
1	16.83	0.92	15.48
2	18.51	0.84	15.55
3	20.36	0.77	15.67
4	22.40	0.71	15.90
		Total	77.90
		Share price (p)	354.00
		Dividends %	22.51%

Rappaport (1983; 1992) shows that for most American industries an average of about 80% of the price of any share can be attributed to its long-term or *residual value.* This research into share prices suggests that the market looks well into the future, with residual value accounting for a large proportion of a share's value. In pricing a company's shares, the relative size of the proportion explained by residual value may be looked upon as an index of the market's confidence in a company's ability to create business value through long-term competitive advantage.

Evidence showing that cosmetic earnings increases do not improve share prices

The market is not deceived by changes in accounting procedures that improve reported eps but not expected cash flows. It is easy to see why this is the case, since by simply comparing trends in earnings and cash flows, it is readily apparent the extent to which earnings and cash flow diverge. A number of studies show that in instances where earnings and cash flow are divergent, the market chooses to base its market valuation on cash flows.

Take, for example, stock valuation for the purposes of reported earnings. In instances where companies switch from 'First In First Out' (FIFO) to 'Last In Last Out' (LILO) accounting procedures for stock valuation, share prices tend to rise. This effect is due to the cost of goods sold incorporating higher and more recent stock costs in periods of rising prices, leading to lower reported earnings, but an improvement in cash flow when tax is taken into consideration. Conversely, a change in depreciation policy can have the opposite effect. If a company lengthens its depreciation period (see Chapter 5) it earnings will be enhanced through a lower depreciation charge, but its cash flow will be lower to the extent that a higher tax charge will be incurred from its reported earnings which have been increased. On the same basis the action of valuing and placing its brands on the balance sheet by Rank Hovis McDougall had no discernible influence on its share price, as press comment at the time reported that the market realized that the company's cash flows remained unchanged.

In a similar vein, an announcement of a major downgrading in earnings can result in an increase in share price if it relates to a management decision to abandon an unprofitable business. In such circumstances the market is revealing its preferences concerning the long-term consequences of redeploying corporate resources in a way which enhances the value creating potential of the organization, rather than taking note of the immediate reduction in earnings.

Evidence analysing the translation of competitive advantage into sustainable cash flows

Any company that is concerned with creating and sustaining a competitive advantage may need to sacrifice short-term earnings for long-term cash flow. Companies seeking to build a strong competitive position may need to invest in a way which is a drain on their short-term earnings and cash flow needs, recognizing the imperative of building a strong and secure financial future. Contrary to the view that the market will penalize companies that make long-term investments, Woolridge (1988) found that there was no conflict between sustainable long-term strategic investments and short-term increases in share values providing the market has confidence in the ability of management to sustain competitive advantage. Where the market has little or no faith in management and its strategic direction the market's time horizon will neither be as long or as positive as the company would like. In short, if the market is knowledgeable about the company's competitive position and confident of management's ability to sustain competitive advantage it will give credit for long-term investments.

Summary

To conclude, throughout this section its has been argued that less emphasis should be placed on reported progression of earnings per share and more attention paid to long-term cash generation. As a result the value creating potential of any strategic action will depend upon (a) estimated cash flows generated over the planning period and (b) the estimated longer-term or residual value of the business which acts as a barometer of market confidence in management's ability to implement sustainable competitive advantage.

Determining an appropriate discount rate

The relevant discount rate for scaling down a company's cash flow stream is the weighted average of the costs of debt and equity capital. The respective costs of debt and equity to a company will be reflected in the market rates providers of debt and equity finance will require the company to pay in order to gain access to new sources of funding. The price a company will need to offer an investor will be equal to the rate of return an investor could expect to receive on other investments of equivalent risk.

It is one thing to argue that the weighted average cost of debt and equity – the cost of capital – is the appropriate discount rate, but quite a different matter to determine the appropriate cost of capital. This section provides technical insights into the practical task of the determination of a company's cost of capital. The weighted average cost of capital (WACC) can be determined in a sequential manner by following three steps:

Step 1   Determine the respective costs of debt and equity the company will need to pay an investor.

Step 2   Establish the target proportions of debt and equity in the company's capital structure.

Step 3   Weight the costs of debt and equity finance by their relative contribution to the overall future capital base of the company.

It is important to stress that the process is forward looking. Calculating the WACC should be based on the relative weights that a company targets for its capital structure over its future planning period, and not on the current capital structure. Similarly, any tax implications must be recognized, and in particular adjustments made to the cost of debt given the deductibility of interest payments for tax purposes.

Table 10.7 shows a simple illustrative WACC calculation for a company showing that the after-tax cost of debt is 5.6% and the estimated cost of equity 12%. Over its planning period the company expects to raise capital in the following proportions: debt 30% and equity 70%, so that the WACC is 10.08%.

A forward-looking estimate of the WACC for UB over the next five years needs to follow the process outlined above, but with figures grounded as firmly as possible in the reality of market expectations concerning the actual cost of capital for the company. In order to generate a broad estimate for UB, each of the three steps to determining the WACC are examined in turn.

Table 10.7 Calculating the weighted average cost of capital

Source of capital	Market cost %	Tax benefit (%)	After-tax cost (A)	Weight (B)	Weighted cost (C) = (A) × (B)
Debt	8	(1–0.30)	5.60	0.30	1.68
Equity	12	–	12.0	0.70	8.40
WACC					10.08

Determining the costs of debt and equity

Cost of debt capital

The approximate cost of UB's debt is relatively straightforward to calculate once it is recognized that future borrowings rather than outstanding debt is the central issue. Prospective investment during the planning period depends upon future costs and not past, sunk costs. The future cost of debt to the company equals the market rate required by investors, less any tax benefit to the company.

Assuming a planning period of five years, the relevant rate for the cost of debt should be equal to the current market rate on debt of similar risk, issued for the same period. The FT-Actuaries Fixed Interest Indices, printed daily in the *Financial Times*, show the market cost of debt over five, 15 and 25 year time periods. On the assumption that the five-year figure approximates to UB's cost of debt over the same period, the company's cost of debt capital is 6.01% after tax, if a tax rate of 30% is assumed (see Table 10.8).

Table 10.8 UB's five-year cost of debt (1993–98)

	%
Gross interest yield*	8.59
Tax benefit	(1–0.30)
After-tax cost	6.01

* FT-A Fixed interest index

Whilst the FT-A Fixed interest index provides a good indicator of the average cost of new debt fund raising, it is possible for analysts to adjust the average figure according to whether they perceive the company to have a higher or lower risk profile, which will be reflected in the specific cost of new debt finance the company would be expected to pay. To this end a company's credit rating is an important factor to bear in mind when assessing the likely cost of raising new capital by issuing debt. Credit rating agencies, of which Standard and Poor and

Moody's are the best known, constantly adjust their ratings of companies to provide an important aid to the market's assessment of the credit risk of providing new funds to a corporate borrower.

Cost of equity capital

Estimating the cost of equity capital is a particularly difficult task. In contrast to debt capital, where the company is obliged to pay a particular rate for the use of capital, there is no formal agreement to make dividend payments to shareholders. Even so, there is an implicit minimum rate of return – the cost of equity capital – to induce investors to accept the risk of holding shares. To calculate the cost of equity capital, it is important to estimate the return on *risk-free government securities* plus an additional *equity risk premium* to adjust for the risk of holding UB's shares. The equation for the cost of holding equity is as follows:

$$\text{Cost of equity} = \text{Risk-free rate} + \text{Equity risk premium}$$

The time horizon for estimating the risk-free rate should be consistent with the long-term planning horizon of the cash flow forecast. The use of British government long-term Treasury bonds facilitates such a comparison, as well as capturing the premium for expected inflation. Given an assumed five-year planning period, a five-year Treasury bond best estimates the expected risk-free rate over the planning period. The redemption yield for British government Treasury bonds (1993–1998) approximates to 6.50% as at 1 March 1993.

The second component of the cost of equity is the *equity risk premium*, which is equal to the *market risk premium* multiplied by the *systematic risk of the equity*. The market risk premium is the difference between the expected risk-free rate and the average expected return provided to the holders of equity. The premium represents the additional compensation that investors demand for holding shares as opposed to risk-free Treasury bonds. Over a 20-year period, equities provided a 12.7% return, compared to 7.5% by fixed-interest government securities. Thus the forward looking market risk premium for UK equity may approximate to something approaching 5.2%.

The additional factor required to estimate the equity risk premium is the beta coefficient. The beta for the entire stock market is 1.00. This means that on average a company's equity will also approximate to 1.00. Stocks with betas greater than 1.00 are more volatile than the market on average, so that they attract a risk premium greater than for the overall market. The London Business School provides a comprehensive range of industry and company betas through its Risk Measurement Service. It shows the beta for UB to be 1.04 (LBS Risk Measurement Service, January–March 1993).

In summary, assuming a risk-free rate of 6.50% and a market risk premium of 5.20% and a company beta of 1.04, UB's cost of equity is estimated as follows:

$$\text{Cost of equity} = \text{Risk-free rate} + (\text{beta} \times \text{Market risk premium})$$
$$= 6.50 + (1.04 \times 5.20)$$
$$= 6.50\% + 5.41$$
$$= 11.91\%$$

Establishing the target proportions of debt and equity

The second step in the process of estimating the WACC is to identify the company's target proportions of debt and equity. In judging the company's target capital structure, consideration needs to be given to, for example, the nature of the industry in which the company operates and the attitude of management to alternative forms of finance. For the purposes of developing an estimate of UB's cost of capital we will assume that the company's target capital structure over the five-year planning period will be 45% debt and 55% equity.

Computing the WACC

Having established the company's target capital structure the company's WACC can be readily computed, as shown in Table 10.9.

Table 10.9 *UB's weighted average cost of capital*

	Net cost % (A)	Proportion of capital base (B)	Weighted cost (C) = (A) × (B)
Debt	6.01	0.45	2.70
Equity	11.91	0.55	6.55
WACC			9.25

The shareholder value approach

Having explored many of the key components of the two contrasting methods of valuation, it is now appropriate to develop fully the alternative, longer-term cash flow approach to share prices based on calculating the shareholder value. The shareholder value approach (SVA) is based on the proposition that what is important is the cash generating ability of a business. By generating cash, an organization is able to pay dividends and reinvest in the business for the future. Reinvesting for the future, if wisely done, will enable the production of an enhanced future dividend stream, and is thus deferred income for the shareholder. On this basis the shareholder is interested in the ability of a business to generate cash over time.

The shareholder value approach begins with the organization's business strategy as shown in Figure 10.1. To understand how much value any given strategy will create it is necessary to focus on three key areas of management decision, namely *operations, financing* and *investment*. Operations covers a range of business functions including marketing, production and distribution. Important variables to forecast, known as key drivers, include the expected growth of sales the strategy is forecast to deliver, together with the operating profit margin on the additional sales generated. The operating profit margin describes the difference between the income derived from the sales generated and the cost of producing and marketing the product or service. Management will need to decide what trade-off they wish to pursue in respect of sales growth (volume) and profit margin. Do they, for example, wish to go for a high volume sales strategy, but at the price of accepting a lower margin in order to maximize sales? Alternatively, is their strategy to be a niche player, offering a highly specialized product with a low sales potential but a high profit margin? Whatever strategy management decide upon they must also remember that any cash inflows the strategy will generate will be taxed. The tax rate is the third key driver relating to the area of operations as described in Figure 10.1.

The importance of the key drivers can be illustrated by taking a simple numerical example which assumes the forecast period is one year. Further, it is assumed that sales growth in the year is £200 m, the operating profit margin 25% and the tax rate is 10%. How much cash does the strategy generate? Pre-tax cash inflows can be calculated by multiplying the sales growth by the operating margin:

$$\text{Pre-tax cash inflow} = \text{Sales growth} \times \text{Operating profit margin}$$
$$= \text{£200 m} \times 0.25$$
$$= \text{£50 m}$$

If the tax rate is 10%, then the after-tax cash inflow is calculated as follows:

$$\text{After-tax cash inflows} = \text{Pre-tax cash inflows} \times (1 - \text{Tax rate})$$
$$= \text{£50 m} \times (1 - 0.10)$$
$$= \text{£50 m} \times 0.90$$
$$= \text{£45 m}$$

At the end of the year the strategy will have generated an after-tax cash inflow of £45 m. Some of this amount, however, will be required to cover cash invested in working capital or fixed assets. These are key management decisions, and require managers to ask how much in the way of additional stock does the strategy require and how much additional fixed investment is necessary in order to allow goods or services to be produced and sold. The two value drivers in respect of investment are:

• incremental working capital needs
• incremental fixed capital needs.

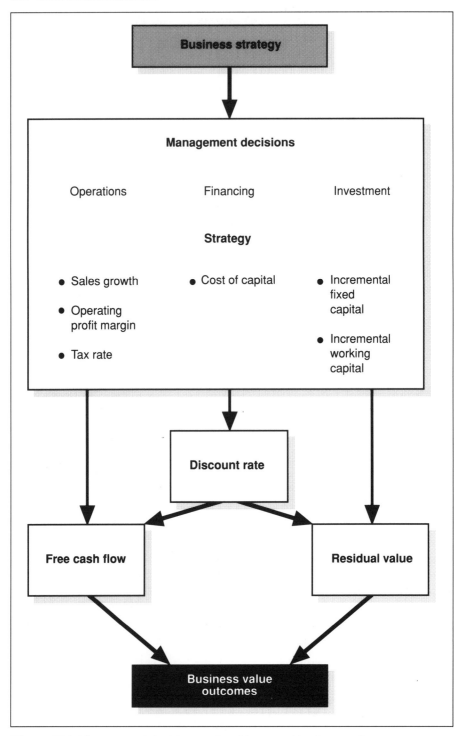

Figure 10.1 *Management decisions, value drivers and business value*

Incremental working capital needs will cover the additional amounts the company will need to invest in stock and debtors, less any additional credit the company can gain from its trade creditors. These three elements are included in the working capital to sales ratio, which was described in detail in Chapter 7. If the incremental working capital to sales ratio is 10%, it means that if sales rise by £200 m, working capital needs will rise by £20 m.

$$\text{Incremental working capital needs} = \text{Sales growth} \times \text{Incremental working} \\ \text{capital to sales ratio} \\ = £200 \text{ m} \times 0.10 \\ = £20 \text{ m}$$

Similarly, if the company incremental fixed investment ratio is 10%, indicating that for every £1 worth of sales the company invests 10p, then the additional fixed capital required is as follows:

$$\text{Incremental fixed capital} = \text{Sales growth} \times \text{Incremental fixed capital ratio} \\ = £200 \text{ m} \times 0.10 \\ = £20 \text{ m}$$

Hence the total investment needs of the strategy are the incremental working capital needs (£20 m) plus the incremental fixed capital needs (£20 m) which come to £40 m. Subtracting this figure from the after-tax cash inflow allows the free cash inflow to be calculated:

$$\text{Free cash inflow} = \text{After-tax cash inflow} - \text{Incremental working capital and} \\ \text{fixed investment needs} \\ = £45 \text{ m} - £40 \text{ m} \\ = £5 \text{ m}$$

The free cash inflow generated from the strategy at the end of the year is £5 m. To gain this £5 m cash inflow at the end of year 1, the investments in working capital and fixed capital need to be financed. Management must therefore decide how they are going to finance the strategy, and in particular the relative balance between debt and equity funding. Determining the relative proportions of debt and equity used to finance the strategy will be one of the key factors in determining a further key driver, the *cost of capital*. As this topic has been examined in detail earlier, for the purposes of this illustrative example a cost of capital of 9.25% is assumed. This figure can then be used to discount the free cash inflow at the end of year 1 in order to calculate its present value. The discount rate is calculated using the following expression:

$$\text{Discount rate} = 1/(1 + \text{Cost of capital}/100)^n$$

where n = number of years.

For one year the discount rate is: $1/(1 + 9.25/100)^n$
$$= 1/(1.0925) \\ = 0.915$$

Hence the present value of the free cash flow at the end of the year can be calculated using the following expression:

$$\text{Present value of free cash flow} = \text{Free cash flow} \times \text{Discount rate}$$
$$= \text{£5 m} \times 0.915$$
$$= \text{£4.6 m}$$

After discounting the value of the free cash flow generated by the business strategy is thus £4.6 m. The free cash flow does not represent the total business value as is shown on Figure 10.1. In addition to the free cash flow, the business is assumed to have a value at the end of the forecast period and this is known as the *residual value*. This emphasizes that at the end of the forecast period the business is a going concern and could be sold as such. As Figure 10.1 shows, the residual value is determined by the same value drivers as the free cash flow, and also needs to be adjusted by the cost of capital. One of the simplest ways of calculating the residual value is to take the after-tax cash inflows and to capitalize them, by dividing by the cost of capital:

$$\text{Residual value} = \frac{\text{Annual cash flow}}{\text{Cost of capital}}$$
$$= \text{£45 m} / 0.0925$$
$$= \text{£486.5 m}$$

As with the free cash flow the residual value could be discounted by the cost of capital:

$$\text{Present value of residual value} = \text{Residual value} \times \text{Discount rate}$$
$$= \text{£486.5 m} \times 0.915$$
$$= \text{£445.1 m}$$

To calculate the total business value the present value free cash flow (£4.6 m) needs to be added to the residual value (£445.1 m). In this example the business value amounts to £449.7 m. The reader will see at once that most of the value of the strategy is based on the residual value. This is not uncommon, although by only taking a single year as the basis of forecasting the free cash flow this simple example exaggerates the norm, as will be observed with the example based on UB.

The steps required to calculate the business value of any strategy are summarized in Figure 10.2. This shows that the key steps are as follows:

Preliminary steps:
Step 1   Calculate the increase in sales for a given year.
Step 2   Multiply the increase in sales by the operating margin and one minus the tax rate in order to determine the after-tax cash inflow.

To calculate the free cash flow (Figure 10.2 left-hand side):
Step 3   Subtract from the after-tax cash inflow the incremental working capital and fixed capital needs in order to arrive at the free cash flow.

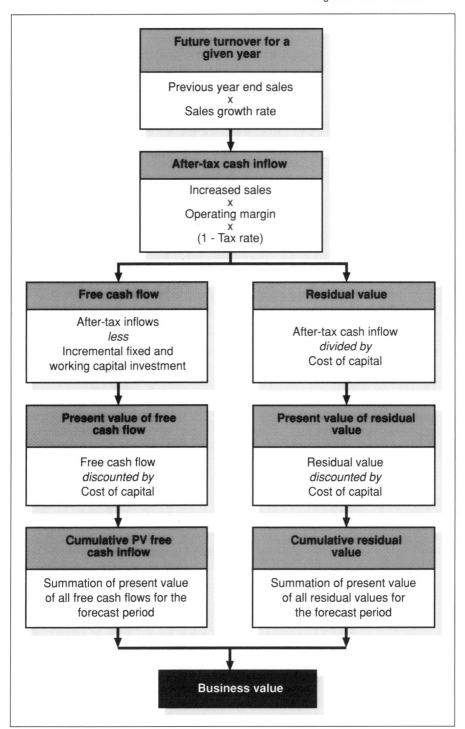

Figure 10.2 *Calculating business value*

Step 4   Discount the free cash flow by the discount rate in order to calculate the present value of the free cash flow.

Step 5   Repeat steps 1 to 4 every year for the forecast period and determine the cumulative present value of the free cash flow for the period.

To calculate the residual value (Figure 10.2 right-hand side):

Step 6   Capitalize the after-tax cash value for the year by dividing by the cost of capital to determine the residual value for the year.

Step 7   Multiply the residual value by the discount rate in order to arrive at the present value.

Step 8   Repeat steps 6 and 7 for all years of the forecast period and determine the cumulative present value of all the residual values.

To calculate business value:

Step 9   Sum the cumulative present values of the free cash flow and the residual value for the forecast period.

Once the calculation of the business value has been achieved, progression to determine corporate value and shareholder value is relatively easy. Corporate value requires any marketable securities into which the company has invested spare resources not required for the trading operations of the business to be added to the business value. For example, if we assume for the purposes of illustration the company has trade investments of £10 m then this may be added to the business value as below:

	£m
Business value	449.7
Marketable securities	10.0
Corporate value	459.7

The corporate value in the above example is £459.7 m. This, however, is not the value of the company to shareholders as no adjustment has been made for the extent to which the company is financed by debt. If the company has outstanding net debt of £200 m, then this should be subtracted from the figure for corporate value in order to determine shareholder value – the net value of the business to shareholders:

	£m
Corporate value	459.70
Debt	200.0
Shareholder value	259.70

By dividing shareholder value by the number of issued shares, shareholder value per share can be calculated. Assuming the company has issued some 400 million shares, then the shareholder value per share is:

Shareholder value per share = Shareholder value *divided by* the number of
issued shares
= £259.7 m/400 m
= 0.65p

On the basis of the simple example above, the SVA indicates that the intrinsic value of the company's shares is 65p.

Calculating the business value of an actual company

The preceding section indicated in broad terms how a company's strategies and the key drivers of business value may be valued. This section develops the approach by applying the technique of SVA to a public listed company on the basis of the information available to somebody outside of the company who does not have the benefit of detailed management information. Once again the company chosen to illustrate how to value a business is United Biscuits plc.

Key drivers

The starting point in making a business valuation is to determine the values of the key drivers, namely:

• forecast period
• sales growth
• operating profit margin
• tax rate
• incremental fixed investment
• incremental working capital
• cost of capital.

Each of these key drivers has been estimated using publicly available information to which judgement has been applied. At the start of the process of estimating a company's business value a decision has to be made as to the *forecast period* to be employed. The central forecast of the value of the business is based on five years to illustrate the techniques of arriving at a business value, although a longer forecast of six years is also developed to indicate how lengthening the forecast period can affect business value.

Developing a view of a company's *sales growth* requires a thorough under-standing and assessment of the company's broad context, industry and relative position within its product markets. These elements have been dealt with earlier, and Chapter 4 has indicated where information can be gained to make the necessary assessments. Based on UB's past performance and assessment of its management and current strategies the assumption made for the purposes of the model is that during the period 1993–98 the company will achieve sales growth of 8.00%. This takes into account the expected slow growth of key product markets for the first part of the period, but also the company's recent acquisitions and likely disposals.

Together with the assessment of the anticipated growth of sales, a judgement needs to be made as to the likely *operating profit margin* the company will achieve. Again this will require a comprehensive assessment of the company drawing on all the relevant data sources. Deciding on a prospective operating profit margin of 9.5% recognizes some of the scope the company has to improve its current and past levels of performance. Improved performance is anticipated given the commitment of the management team, and the potential benefits arising out of recent acquisitions made to strengthen the company.

The *tax rate* chosen reflects the prevailing level of taxation in the UK, and the fact that over the last few years mainstream corporation tax has been falling. Whilst many technicalities, not least issues of timing, make tax a complicated area, putting the tax rate at 30% is, if anything, a full estimate of the likely future level of tax payments.

Incremental fixed investment needs to recognize that to generate cash flows the company will need to spend money on capital equipment. The likely level of capital spending, based on unchanging strategies, can be gained by reviewing the company's past pattern of capital investment and any statements management has made as to its capital investment policies. Based on UB's 1991 figures, capital spending is estimated to account for 29.5% of sales. This is arrived at by taking the company's net investment in fixed assets (£144 m) less depreciation (£75.3 m) in 1991 as a proportion of the sales increase (£232.5 m). To smooth annual changes in the proportion of sales to fixed investment it is possible to average the level of capital spending over a number of years. In UB's case, fluctuations in its performance and changes in the scope of its activities render it inappropriate to take an average figure for the company's capital spend over a number of years. This again emphasizes the degree of judgement required when determining the magnitude of a company's key drivers.

The working capital to sales ratio introduced in Chapter 7 is helpful in estimating likely working capital needs arising from sales growth. For simplicity it is assumed that the *incremental working capital* needs occur in the same proportion as suggested by the company's average working capital to sales ratio calculated earlier. This gives a working capital to sales ratio of 16.5%.

Earlier discussion of how to estimate the *cost of capital* reveals that at the beginning of 1993, UB might be expected to pay 9.25% based on achieving a gearing ratio of 45% (i.e. debt 45%; equity 55%). On this basis the cost of capital is estimated to be 9.25% for the purposes of the illustrative example.

The values of the key drivers are summarized in Table 10.10.

Calculating the business value

The starting point for estimating a company's business value is the current level

Table 10.10 *UB – key drivers*

	%		£m
Sales growth rate	8.0	Sales for the last period	2,720.0
Operating profit margin	9.5	Marketable securities	0.0
Incremental fixed investment	29.5	Debt	474.0
Incremental working capital	16.5	Shares issued (number millions)	489.4
Cash tax rate	30.0		Years
Cost of capital	9.25	Forecast period	5

of sales. Based on UB's 1992 interim figures and press comment, sales are assumed to be £2,720 m at the start of 1993. At this level, sales are assumed to have increased by just over 2% in 1992, reflecting the company's difficulties in North America. Levels of future turnover can be calculated by multiplying sales at the end of the previous year by the sales growth rate (8%). For the first year, the calculation is as follows:

$$\text{Increase in sales} = \text{Sales in previous year} \times \text{Sales growth rate}$$
$$= £2,720.00 \text{ m} \times 0.08$$
$$= £217.60 \text{ m}$$

Total sales at the end of the year 1 are as follows:

$$\text{Total sales} = \text{Sales at the beginning of the period} + \text{Increase in sales}$$
$$= £2,720.00 \text{ m} + £217.60 \text{ m}$$
$$= £2,937.60 \text{ m}$$

Table 10.11 calculates the total sales up to the final year of the forecast period.

Table 10. 11 *Calculating future turnover*

Year	Sales in the previous year (£m) (A)	Sales growth rate (%) (B)	Increase in sales (£m) (C) = (A) × (B)	Total sales for the year (£m) (A) + (C)
1	2,720.00	0.08	217.60	2,937.60
2	2,937.60	0.08	235.01	3,172.61
3	3,172.61	0.08	253.81	3,426.42
4	3,426.42	0.08	274.11	3,700.53
5	3,700.53	0.08	296.04	3,996.57

Once the sales for each period have been calculated it is possible to compute operating profit and tax paid in order to arrive at after-tax cash inflow. This may be illustrated by taking the figures for year 1:

$$\text{Operating profit} = \text{Sales} \times \text{Profit margin}$$
$$= \pounds2,937.60 \text{ m} \times 0.095$$
$$= \pounds279.07 \text{ m}$$

$$\text{Tax paid} = \text{Operating profit} \times \text{Tax rate}$$
$$= \pounds279.07 \text{ m} \times 0.3$$
$$= \pounds83.72 \text{ m}$$

$$\text{After-tax cash inflow} = \text{Operating profit} - \text{Tax paid}$$
$$= \pounds279.07 \text{ m} - \pounds83.72 \text{ m}$$
$$= \pounds195.35 \text{ m}$$

Table 10.12 provides complete figures for all years of the forecast period.

Table 10. 12 Calculating after-tax cash inflow (ATCI)

Year	Sales (A)	Profit margin (B)	Operating profit (C) = (A) × (B)	Tax rate (D)	Tax paid (E) = (B) × (1− (D))	After-tax cash inflow (F) = (C) − (E)
1	2,937.60	0.095	279.07	0.30	83.72	195.35
2	3,172.61	0.095	301.40	0.30	90.42	210.98
3	3,426.42	0.095	325.51	0.30	97.65	227.86
4	3,700.53	0.095	351.55	0.30	105.47	246.09
5	3,996.57	0.095	379.67	0.30	113.90	265.77

Before the free cash flow can be calculated the incremental fixed and working capital needs must be calculated. Incremental fixed investment is computed by multiplying the sales growth by the incremental fixed investment rate. For year 1 this yields an incremental fixed investment need of £64.19 m (£217.60 m × 29.5%). Similarly, incremental working capital needs are obtained by multiplying the sales growth by the incremental working capital to sales ratio. In year 1 incremental working capital needs are £35.90 m (£217.60 m × 0.165). Table 10.13 provides details of the incremental investment needs for all years covered by the forecast period.

Subtracting the incremental fixed and working capital needs from the after-tax cash inflow gives the free cash flow. For year 1 this process yields a free cash flow of £95.25 m (£195.35 m – (£64.19 m + £35.90 m)). Table 10.14 provides the detailed figures for all years in the forecast.

Table 10.13 Incremental investment needs

Year	Sales growth (£m)	Incremental fixed investment (%)	Increase in fixed investment (£m)	Incremental working capital to sales ratio (%)	Increase in working capital (£m)
	(A)	(B)	(C) = (A)/(B)	(D)	(E) = (A) × (D)
1	217.60	0.295	64.19	0.165	35.90
2	235.01	0.295	69.33	0.165	38.78
3	253.81	0.295	74.87	0.165	41.88
4	274.11	0.295	80.86	0.165	45.23
5	296.04	0.295	87.33	0.165	48.85

Table 10.14 Calculating the free cash flow

Year	After-tax cash inflow	Incremental fixed investment	Incremental working capital	Free cash flow
1	195.35	64.19	35.90	95.25
2	210.98	69.33	38.78	102.87
3	227.86	74.87	41.88	111.10
4	246.09	80.86	45.23	119.99
5	265.77	87.33	48.85	129.59

The free cash flows shown in Table 10.14 need to be discounted by the appropriate discount rate in order to calculate the present values of the cash flow stream. The discount rate is dependent on the cost of capital which was previously shown to be 9.25% for UB. As previously discussed the discount rate is determined according to the following formula:

$$1/(1 + 0.0925)^n$$

where n = number of years.

The present value of the free cash flow in year 1

$$= £95.25 \text{ m} \times 1/(1 + 0.0925)^1$$
$$= £95.25 \text{ m} \times 0.915$$
$$= £87.19 \text{ m}$$

Once again the present values for all years are set out in Table 10.15.

Table 10.15 *Calculating the present value of free cash flows*

Year	Free cash flow (A)	Discount rate (B)	Present value of free cash flow (C) = (A) × (B)	Cumulative present value of free cash flow
1	95.25	0.915	87.19	87.19
2	102.87	0.838	86.19	173.38
3	111.10	0.767	85.21	258.59
4	119.99	0.702	84.23	342.82
5	129.59	0.643	83.27	426.08

Turning to the question of calculating residual value, the starting point is the after-tax cash flows derived in Table 10.12. The residual value for each year is computed by dividing the after-tax cash flow by the cost of capital and discounting the resulting sum by the discount rate. For example in year 1 the residual value is:

$$\frac{£195.35 \text{ m}}{0.0925} = £2,111.9 \text{ m}$$

The present value of the year 1 residual value can be found by:

$$£2,111.90 \text{ m} \times 1/(1 + 0.0925)^1$$
$$= £2,111.90 \times 0.915$$
$$= £1,933.09 \text{ m}$$

The full set of residual values and their corresponding present values is set out in Table 10.16.

Table 10.16 *Calculating the residual value*

Year	After-tax cash inflow £m (A)	Cost of capital (B)	Residual value £m (C) = (A)/(B)	Discount rate (D)	Present value of residual value (E) = (C) × (D)
1	195.35	0.0925	2,111.90	0.915	1,933.09
2	210.98	0.0925	2,280.85	0.838	1,910.97
3	227.86	0.0925	2,463.32	0.767	1,889.10
4	246.09	0.0925	2,660.38	0.702	1,867.49
5	265.77	0.0925	2,873.21	0.643	1,846.12

Calculating the business value for UB requires adding the present value of the free cash flows and residual values for all the years of the forecast period as shown in Table 10.17.

Table 10. 17 Calculating business value

Year	Present value of free cash flows (A)	Present value of residual value (B)	Business value (C) = (A) × (B)
1	87.19	1,933.09	2,020.28
2	173.38	1,910.97	2,084.35
3	258.59	1,889.10	2,147.69
4	342.82	1,867.49	2,210.31
5	426.08	1,846.12	2,272.21

For the five-year forecast period UB's total business value amounts to £2,272.21 m. In excess of 80% of this figure is represented by the residual value. Calculating shareholder value requires that the figure for business value be adjusted by marketable securities and debt, as shown in Table 10.18. In UB's case the last annual report suggests that there are no marketable securities to be accounted for, leaving debt of £474.0 m to be subtracted from the business value, to leave shareholder value of £1,798.21 m. Dividing this figure by the weighted average of the number of shares on issue as reported in the company's last annual report gives a share price value of 367p. This figure may be compared with the current trading range of the company's share price to determine whether the company is currently under-valued, about right or over-valued.

Table 10.18 Calculating shareholder value

	£m
Business value	2,272.21
plus Marketable securities	0.00
Corporate value	2,272.21
minus Debt	474.00
Shareholder value	1,798.21
Number of issued shares	489.40
Share price value	3.67

The SVA described above represents the base case, using the 'best' estimates of the individual key drivers. By varying each of the values of the key drivers, it is possible to observe how sensitive the company's value is to changes to the principal variables. This is known as undertaking sensitivity analysis and the results of changing six of the key drivers plus or minus one percentage point and the forecast period by one year are set out in Table 10.19.

Table 10.19 Sensitivity analysis for share price value (p) – effect of changing key drivers by +1 percentage point, and forecast period by 1 year

Variable	−1	Base case	+1	Range	Sensitivity
Sales growth	358	367	377	19	Low
Operating profit margin	309	367	426	117	High
Incremental fixed investment	369	367	365	4	Low
Incremental working capital	369	367	365	4	Low
Cash tax rate	375	367	359	16	Low
Cost of capital	435	367	313	122	High
Years in forecast	355	367	380	25	Low/medium

The results presented in Table 10.19 indicate that shareholder value is most sensitive to changes in the operating profit margin and the cost of capital. Changes in both variables by one percentage point have a significant effect on the intrinsic value of the company. To explore further how combinations of changes to the operating profit margin and the cost of capital influence SVA, Table 10.20 offers a range of permutations around the base forecast for these variables.

Recognition of the sensitivity of the share price outcome to the cost of capital emphasizes the importance of the cost of capital in determining appropriate share price values. Falling market interest rates according to the model should result in higher share prices, higher interest rates in lower prices. This indeed is the general pattern of events, with the prospect of lower interest rates generally leading to higher share prices.

Comment

The preceding analysis has concentrated on calculating UB's business value on the basis of applying SVA to the overall group as a single entity. Two further enhancements to the SVA model are possible which are likely to improve its predictive power. First, the key drivers can be changed across the forecast period,

Table 10.20 Changing the operating profit margin and/or the cost of capital

		COST OF CAPITAL						
		8.25%	8.75%	9.00%	9.25%	9.50%	9.75%	10.25%
M	8.50%	370	337	323	309	296	283	261
A	9.00%	403	368	353	338	324	311	287
R	9.25%	419	384	368	353	339	325	300
G								
I	9.50%	435	399	383	367	353	339	313
N	9.75%	452	415	398	382	367	353	326
	10.0%	468	430	413	397	381	367	339
	10.5%	501	461	443	426	410	394	366

in recognition that unchanging single value estimates are unlikely to be appropriate for the whole of the forecast period. Secondly, the corporate group can be dissaggregated into its constituent businesses. This enables the business value for each principal business unit or division to be calculated, and the overall value of the group to be developed using a 'bottom-up' approach. This has the merit of being able to identify within the corporate group which business divisions are creating or destroying value. Whilst this may be readily undertaken by the company's management using internal management information, for the external investor or analyst undertaking SVA on a disaggregated basis it is difficult.

As we have previously drawn the reader's attention to, the amount of segmental information UK-based companies are required to report is highly limited. Companies have considerable scope in determining the boundaries to their business divisions for which they choose to make accounting disclosures, and this together with the lack of segmental information on investment needs by division makes a disaggregated SVA difficult to achieve. It is perhaps the case that the ASB could profitably look at this area and prevent many companies being able to hide under-performance by individual businesses or divisions. Until such time as the situation changes in the UK – and indeed most other reporting countries – the lack of information will continue to be a hindrance to developing SVA analysis based on divisional performance.

Finally, before leaving discussion of the technical aspects of SVA analysis it is perhaps advisable to draw attention to some of the other difficulties of using the approach. First, as implicitly suggested earlier, determining the values of the key drivers can be a difficult task. Certainly, the cost of equity capital which has a major influence on the overall cost of capital is a particularly difficult area, but clearly on the basis of the sensitivity analysis it is a critical area. Secondly, whilst the model seeks to forecast future cash flows it is dependent upon non-cash measures, including the forecast operating profit margin, to do this.

Investor and managerial perspectives on shareholder value

This section considers in detail *who* should use the shareholder value approach, and *how* they should seek to use the technique. Broadly those individuals who might use the technique fall into two categories: external users and internal users. Each of these categories may be subdivided as follows:

- External:
  - stock market investors
  - corporate raiders;
- Internal:
  - corporate management
  - business unit management.

External users are defined as individuals or groups who are outside of the company, but are nevertheless seeking to value the organization either for the purposes of investment or takeover. *Internal* users are defined as those individuals or groups inside the company who have some interest in, or responsibility for, the determination or management of the organization's strategy.

Stock market investors will be interested in using shareholder value analysis to evaluate whether, on the basis of the company's current share price, what action, if any, they should take in respect of any investment they have, or might wish to make, in the company. If, for example, the analysis values the company's shares at 400p, and the shares are only trading at 300p, then clearly a buying opportunity exists for the investor. In this case the SVA is clearly stating that on the basis of its long-term value the company is currently undervalued. Conversely, if the SVA indicated that the company's long-term value was only 250p an investor would be advised to avoid purchasing the shares on a long-term basis, given that the current share price was in excess of the company's intrinsic value.

A second group of external users likely to wish to employ shareholder value analysis are those companies potentially interested in unbundling poorly performing conglomerates. Should a corporate raider seek to gain control of another company, the raider will be required to value the company on the basis of its break-up value. Calculating a company's break-up value requires a view to be taken as to how much the takeover target is worth to the bidder. Arriving at a value for a company in these circumstances was considered in Chapter 3, where the prospective bid for ICI plc by Hanson plc, and the contested bids for Rank Hovis McDougall (RHM) plc were discussed in detail. Essentially by employing shareholder value analysis the potential bidder will be able to value a target company and calculate whether it is worthwhile bidding for the company on the basis of what the business is worth and how much will have to be paid in order to gain control of the target.

Internal users of shareholder value analysis include both *corporate management* and *management at the business unit level*. One of the principal concerns of corporate management will be the shape and scope of the portfolio of businesses within the corporate group. As such corporate management will wish to examine their portfolio and determine whether individual businesses add or destroy value. Given their access to internally generated management information there is no excuse for corporate management not undertaking this task. Once again discussion in this chapter has highlighted that unless a business is able to generate more than its cost of capital then continuing to operate that business destroys corporate and shareholder value. Consequently, the message is that corporate management should decide when it is appropriate to action acquisitions or disposals to ensure shareholder value is maximized.

Similarly, management at the level of the business unit have the opportunity of using the shareholder value approach to determine which business strategies create shareholder value and, amongst the options available, which creates the greatest value. In seeking to undertake such an appraisal, management should always measure the strategic alternatives against the base case of 'do nothing'. For example, take the three strategic options in Table 10.21.

Table 10.21 *Alternative strategic options*

Strategic option	Product market strategy
A	Maintain market share; continue with current product market strategy of following competition; currently no competitive advantage.
B	Aggressively expand market share by increasing penetration from market; based on aggressive sales techniques; competitors likely to retaliate.
C	Move up market by developing new products in order to craft a sustainable competitive advantage.

Strategic option A is based on the business unit continuing to pursue its current strategies. Figure 10.3 shows that this strategy neither creates or destroys value. By contrast Figure 10.3 shows that option B destroys value and places the business in a worse position than doing nothing. Finally, option C creates value in excess of the cost of capital and is clearly the option management should be pursuing in this particular case.

Figure 10.3 emphasizes the importance of the cost of capital and why it is sometimes referred to as the *hurdle rate*. Unless a strategy or project can create value in excess of the cost of capital it should not be undertaken. The comparison of the different business strategies highlighted above illustrates the great strength of the SVA approach. When compared to other approaches it offers two positive benefits:

- It enables management to link the process of formulating and valuing strategies. All too often the formulation of a strategy is decoupled from its valuation, resulting in management failing to understand that their actions are actually destroying value.
- Having linked the formulation and valuation of a strategy, management can see how the adoption of a particular policy will be reflected in stock market performance. If value enhancing strategies are adopted, stock market performance will be improved. Conversely, if value destroying strategies are chosen stock market performance will deteriorate.

It is the linkage between strategic direction, financial performance and stock market value which renders SVA such a powerful tool when used effectively. This is not to say management should immediately adopt the technique.

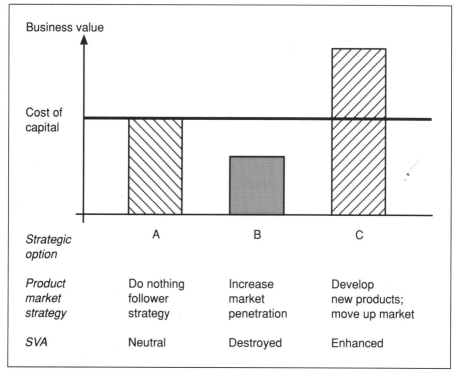

Figure 10.3 *Appraising alternative strategic options*

Clearly to move a company away from its previous methods of strategic appraisal is not always easy. As with virtually any major strategic change the introduction of SVA within a company requires very careful consideration. Whilst discussion about the management of change is outside of the present text, the literature on change management emphasizes that changing corporate behaviour can be a difficult process. Nevertheless some companies have successfully introduced SVA and the underlying strength of the approach suggests that many more would be well advised to consider it carefully.

Concluding remarks

This chapter has introduced the reader to the principles of SVA and emphasized its superior conceptual basis over an approach based on eps. A practical demonstration of the shareholder value approach using a major FT-SE 100 listed company has been undertaken, and suggestions as to how the model in its simplest form may be extended and refined. The shareholder value approach offers practically useful outcomes both to internal management and the external investor, and enables the formulation and valuation of strategy to be linked in a manner not previously possible. This offers management the opportunity of carefully assessing whether they are adopting value creating strategies, and as a consequence to be confident of the stock market's favourable reaction to the actions they take. For these reasons we believe that those companies and investors who are not currently using the shareholder value approach would be well advised to investigate the benefits of using the technique in the strategic management of their organizations.

Checklist

- *Calculate the business value for each of the principal divisions by identifying the values assigned to each of the following key drivers:*
  - *forecast period*
  - *sales growth*
  - *operating profit margin*
  - *tax rate*
  - *incremental working capital needs*
  - *incremental fixed capital needs*
  - *cost of capital.*
- *Sum the individual business values of each of the main business divisions in order to arrive at a total value for the group.*
- *If a divisional breakdown cannot be undertaken identify the key drivers for the group as a whole and calculate overall business value.*

- *Check the sensitivity of your calculation to changes in the key drivers and recheck critical assumptions.*
- *Develop a range of estimates for business value based on changes to key drivers.*
- *Add any marketable securities to the calculated business value and derive a figure for corporate value.*
- *Subtract the company's debt from the calculated corporate value in order to arrive at shareholder value.*
- *Divide shareholder value by the number of shares issued to calculate the long-term value of the company per share.*
- *Compare the SVA valuation of the company with the current share price and take action accordingly.*

PART FIVE

The General Framework Revisited

The final chapter which makes up this part seeks to draw together some of the key conceptual elements of the text, by indicating ten critical areas on which the researcher, either internal or external to the company, should focus. Beginning by a review of the general framework which has provided the central spine to the text, each of the ten topics listed below is discussed to highlight issues for careful consideration:

- the general framework
- multiple points of entry
- top-down or bottom-up?
- the quality of management
- benchmarking
- forecasting
- time horizons
- over-priced or under-priced?
- linking financial outcomes and strategy
- a way forward.

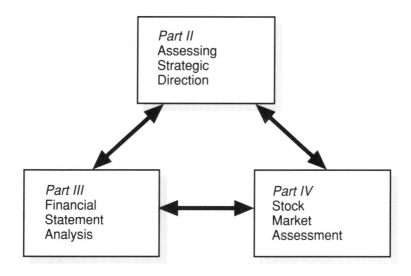

Part I	The General Framework
Part II	Assessing Strategic Direction
Part III	Financial Statement Analysis
Part IV	Stock Market Assessment
Part V	**The General Framework Revisited**

Part II
Assessing Strategic Direction

Part III
Financial Statement Analysis

Part IV
Stock Market Assessment

CHAPTER 11

Some concluding thoughts

The general framework

The text has been developed around the general framework illustrated on p.355 which emphasizes the links between the three earlier parts of the book: assessing strategic direction, financial analysis and stock market assessment. These elements, whilst they been discussed separately, collectively provide the three interlocking elements to assessing managerial, accounting and stock market perspectives. Without an appreciation of all of these areas and how they are related, the overall assessment of a company will be deficient. Consequently, focusing exclusively on one of the three areas, or even two, militates against the power of the general framework in assessing the corporate and business imperatives that a company is facing. For this reason the emphasis of many traditional texts on strategic management offers a distorted view of corporate performance and does the reader a disservice in only offering a partial analysis.

Multiple points of entry

Given the three building blocks to the generic framework, internal or external analysts of a company are faced with multiple entry points in undertaking their analysis. Do they start, for example, with the predominantly non-financial analysis of Part One – assessing strategic direction – or focus on analysis of financial factors as discussed in Part Two, or Part Three stock market assessment? In practice the starting point is less material than the need to cover all three areas, given that an understanding of each helps to inform judgements about the other two areas and the company overall.

Top-down or bottom-up?

Regardless of the starting point, as Chapter 4 emphasized, the need is to examine the three components of the general framework in terms of the broad context, the industry(s) and the company. Once again the analyst is offered a choice as to the starting point with some preferring to begin by exploring issues at the level of the company, before reflecting on the industry and broad context, using a 'bottom-up' approach. Alternatively, the analyst may prefer to begin with the broad context, before turning to analysing the industry and the company. Again, however, the three areas are not mutually exclusive and there are strong linkages between each.

Data deficiencies and the need to verify the information set from which the analyst is working will inevitably require the triangulation of data. This enables a cross referencing of data sources, identifying any areas of weakness in the information set and prompting future searches for information in order to complete the analysis. In practice, the process of information gathering and synthesis is likely to require a series of iterations as key conclusions are confirmed and additional data needs are identified. The essential point is that the analyst or strategic manager is seeking to ensure that assessment in one area is confirmed by the evaluation of data from alternative sources, thereby ensuring that the data base is validated.

Table 11.1 emphasizes once more, in respect of multiple points of entry and the choice of a bottom-up or top-down approach, that both the vertical dimension of analysis – broad context, industry and company – and the horizontal dimension – assessing strategic direction, financial analysis and stock market assessment – must be undertaken and synthesized in order to achieve a full evaluation of the company's position and prospects.

The quality of management

Throughout the text a strong emphasis has been placed on the role of management. All too frequently there is a tendency to assess a company's external context and to view the organization as a passive agent unable to determine its own destiny. The reality is that management is a critical ingredient to corporate performance. Equally, past performance brings no guarantees of future success. All too often companies become too complacent or set in their ways, finding themselves unable to change. It is for good reason that many analysts focus on the quality of a company's management and their proven ability to be proactive in the face of ever changing competitive challenges.

A new management team may bring in far-reaching changes which result in the need for both competitors and investors to reappraise the company. If the new management team have the vision and drive which was previously lacking, the company's prospects for the future may quickly change. Consequently, a change in the management team should be a strong signal to review carefully the organization's prospects and monitor the company's reported performance carefully. If the company's financial performance appears to be moving in a new direction this will often provide the early proof of the effect the new management team is having on the company.

Table 11.1 Linking the vertical and horizontal dimensions

	Assessing strategic direction	Financial statement analysis	Stock market assessment
Company	1. Identify and assess corporate and business unit strategies, management resource, product market positions, etc.	2. Assessment of current and future outcomes to company's strategies – sales, profitability, cash flow, etc.	3. Understand market assessment and rating of the company
Industry /sector	4. Evaluate competitive forces, and relative strength of competitors. Review key industry drivers and likely future pattern of industry development	5. Make comparisons with other companies operating in the same or similar product markets	6. Compare company's rating to other companies in the same sector. Review performance of sector against overall market
Broad context	7. Assess key PEST change agents, i.e. P – political, E – economic, S – social, T – technological factors, etc.	8. Evaluate opportunities for funding raising (debt and equity), likely tax and interest rate changes, etc.	9. Identify movements in the overall stock market, and likely future pattern of share prices

Benchmarking

The assessment of the outcomes to a company's strategy and the business environment in which it is operating will inevitably be in terms of a range of financial performance indicators. Judgement on the adequacy or otherwise of the levels of the relevant performance indicators requires the use of benchmarks. Discussion in Chapter 7 emphasized both the need to use benchmarks which assist the assessment of a company's performance over time and against a compatible peer group. Choice of an appropriate peer group, whilst often difficult, is crucial if a company's performance is to be assessed relative to other companies in its industry. Only by such comparisons can it be determined whether the company is gaining upon the competition or falling further behind.

Forecasting

Assessing a company's strategic direction, its likely financial performance and stock market performance requires not just an appreciation of the past and current outcomes, but the need to forecast the future. This is difficult given the uncertainties and dynamics of the business environment. Indeed the recognition of this fact explains why it is easy to spot with hindsight past solutions, but so difficult to be as confident about future predictions. Living with uncertainty is a necessity of assessing future performance both for managers and analysts alike. The primary need to forecast future performance means that the past and current levels of performance are only useful to the extent that they provide the basis of reaching informed judgements about the future.

Nowhere is this more true than for the relationship between reported performance and the company's share price. Frequently, the share price falls before the bad news has been confirmed by reported performance. Remember that financial performance is the past not the future. Unfortunately a company may have lost its competitive edge some time ago, only for this to be belatedly confirmed by its reported results. Recognizing this fact, the stock market often pays more attention to the chairman's statement, or a company's trading announcements.

Time horizons

Looking to the future requires assessments of different time periods, according to the factors which drive financial and stock market performance. The short-term share valuation model, employing earnings as the key forecast variable, essentially looks to a maximum of two years. This is the time horizon for which analysts' forecasts are published in *The Earnings Guide* and *The Estimate Directory*, key documents for anyone interpreting the role of earnings in determining share prices. The alternative approach based on the shareholder value analysis (SVA) looks to a minimum of five years in most instances and sometimes longer, and is based on prospective cash flows.

Over-priced or under-priced?

Irrespective of whether a short-term or long-term view of share price determination is favoured, a judgement will need to be made as to what action, if any, an investor should take in relation to a company's shares. If the investor believes the intrinsic value of the company is inadequately reflected in the share price then either the investor is privy to information that the market is not, or the market has interpreted the same information in a different way. In either case the investor needs to decide whether he or she wishes to back their judgement against the current market view of the company as embodied in the share price, by either purchasing or selling stock.

Linking financial outcomes and strategy

One of the major advances of the SVA model is its ability to link financial outcomes to strategy. All too frequently the non-financial aspects of strategic formulation are decoupled from the financial assessment. As a result too many companies take strategic choices that destroy rather than create value for their shareholders, or indeed other stakeholders of the company including suppliers and employees. A company which ultimately fails certainly will have helped few, if any, of its stakeholders.

The SVA model stresses the role of cash and the need for strategic actions to create value. As an approach, although not without its difficulties, it does offer the prospect of linking strategic decisions with financial outcomes and ultimately stock market performance. To this end it offers both managers and investors a practically useful tool from which to assess strategic options. It also stresses once again the lessons emphasized in Chapter 6 that cash is the key to understanding much about a company's performance.

A way forward

Over the last few years much has changed in seeking to evaluate company strategies and assess financial performance. Not least the work of the Accounting Standards Board (ASB) has made real progress in helping the external users of accounts to have a much improved information set on which to base their judgements. Whilst weaknesses remain, most notably as we have indicated in the area of segmental reporting, the work of the ASB is to be commended. This is not, however, to ignore the fact that just as in the past some companies have tested the boundaries of new accounting standards, or others are likely to do so in the future (and indeed some have already have), but rather to suggest that this time around the new financial reporting structure for company reporting is more robust than hitherto.

With so many changes taking place it is an exciting time to study companies and to identify what their key success factors are. Equally, unless managers understand the linkage between strategic direction, financial outcomes and stock market performance they are unlikely to appreciate fully the general context against which they are required to manage. For in the final analysis companies do not take action automatically. It is for management to make things happen and it is all too easy to blame the failings of the company on external factors rather than managers taking the responsibility for their own actions. Companies with good management teams will continue to outperform and displace other companies who were once considered strong. Managers who understand the relationship between strategy, financial performance and share price valuation are the ones who will survive and grow. Those who fail to understand the relationship between these areas run the risk of delivering weak performance and/or of being taken over. Never has it been more important for managers to take a strategic approach to managing but also to understand the linkage to financial and stock market performance. If this book has assisted in this aim by helping such an understanding it will have achieved its purpose.

BIBLIOGRAPHY

Accounting and Investment Analysis Committee (1993), Exposure Draft: The definition of Earnings, *Institute of Investment Management and Research*.

Accounting Standards Board (1991), *Cash Flow Statements*, Financial Reporting Standard Number 1, Accounting Standards Board Limited.

Accounting Standards Board (1992), *Reporting Financial Performance*, Financial Reporting Standard Number 3, Accounting Standards Board Limited.

Accounting Standards Board (1992), *Operating Financial Statement*, Accounting Standards Board Limited.

Andrews P W S and Brunner E (1975), *Studies in Pricing*, Macmillan.

Baden-Fuller C and Stopford J M (1992), *Rejuvenating the Mature Business*, Routledge.

Bell (1989), *Directory of International Sources of Business Information*, Pitman Publishing.

Cadbury Committee (1992), *The Financial Aspects of Corporate Governance*, Gee.

Copeland T, Koller T and Murran J (1990), *Valuation: measuring and managing the value of companies*, Wiley.

Cronshaw M, Davis E and Kay J (1990), 'On being stuck in the middle or good food costs less at Sainsburys', *London Business School Working Paper Series*, Number 83, August.

Dent J (1990), 'Strategy, Organisation and Control: some possibilities for accounting research', *Accounting , Organisation and Society*, Vol 15 (1/2), pp 3-25.

Goold M and Campbell A (1987a), *Strategies and Styles: the role of the centre in managing diversified corporations*, Blackwell.

Goold M and Campbell A (1987b), 'Many best ways to make strategy', *Harvard Business Review*, Vol 65 (3) pp 70-76.

Goold M and Campbell A (1989), 'Good "Corporate parents" can see off "Unbundlers" ', *Financial Times* letters, 6 November.

Gilbert X and Strebel P (1988), 'Developing Competitive Advantage' in Quinn J B, Mintzberg H and James M J (1988), *'The Strategy Process'*, pp 70-79, Prentice- Hall.

Hamel G (1992), 'Competing for industry futures', presentation to the annual conference of the international Strategic Management Society; quoted in C Lorenz (1992), 'Into the great wide open', *Financial Times*, 2 November.

Hax A C and Majluf N S (1984), *Strategic management: an integrative perspective*, Prentice-Hall.

Holmes and Sugden (1990), *Interpreting Company Reports and Accounts*, Woodhead-Faulker, 4th Edition.

Johnson G (1987), *Strategic Change and the Management Process*, Blackwell.

Johnson G and Scholes K (1993), *Exploring Corporate Strategy*, Prentice-Hall.

Levitt T, (1983), 'The globalisation of markets', *Harvard Business Review*, Vol 61 (3), May-June, pp 92-102.

Lorenz C (1986), 'How Japan is dumping a dated dogma', *Financial Times*, 27 October.

Mort D (1992), *European Market Information: a handbook for managers*, Financial Times/Pitman Publishing.

Porter M E (1990), *Competitive Strategy: Techniques for Analysing Industries and Competitors*, Free Press.

Porter (1986), 'Competition in Global Industries: a conceptual framework' in M Porter, ed. (1986), *Competition in Global Industries,* Harvard Business School Press.

Prahalad C K and Hamel G (1990), 'The core competence of the corporation', *Harvard Business Review*, Vol 68 (3), May-June, pp 79-93.

Pugh P (1991), *A Clear and Simple Vision*, Cambridge Business Publishing.

Philips and Drew (1991), *Accounting for Growth*, Global Research Group.

Rappaport A (1983), *Creating Shareholder Value: the new standard for business performance*, Free Press.

Rappaport A (1992), 'CEO and Strategists: Forging a Common Framework', *Harvard Business Review*, Vol 70 (3), May-June, pp 84-91.

Slater J (1992), *The Zulu Principle: making extraordinary profits from ordinary shares*, Orion.

Stalk G and Hout T (1990), *Competing against time: how time based competition is reshaping global markets*, Free Press.

Smith T (1992), *Accounting for Growth*, Century Business.

United Biscuits plc (1989-1992), Annual and Interim Reports.

Woolridge (1988), 'Competitive decline and corporate restructuring: Is a myopic stock market to blame?' *Continental Bank Journal of Applied Corporate Finance*, Spring, pp 26-36.

SUBJECT INDEX

INDEX OF COMPANIES